THE WILL
TO
POWER

THE WILL TO POWER

FRIEDRICH NIETZSCHE

A New Translation

by

WALTER KAUFMANN

and

R. J. HOLLINGDALE

Edited, with Commentary,

by

WALTER KAUFMANN

with Facsimilies of the Original Manuscript

Vintage Books NEW YORK

A DIVISION OF RANDOM HOUSE

for

MARTHA LINDE

1881-1966

VINTAGE BOOKS EDITION, September, 1968

Acknowledgment is made to the Nationale Forschungs- und Gedenkstätten der Klassischen Deutschen Literatur in Weimar for permission to reproduce eight facsimile pages from the original manuscript.

Manufactured in the United States of America
13579F8642

CONTENTS

Neither the table of contents nor the headings in the text are Nietzsche's; both were introduced by the German editors to create the impression of a major systematic work. They are retained here with minor modifications to assist those who want to locate notes discussing particular problems.

See also the comprehensive index, made especially for this edition.

EDITOR'S INTRODUCTION xiii

ON THE EDITIONS OF *The Will to Power* xxvii

CHRONOLOGY OF NIETZSCHE'S WORKS xxxi

FACSIMILES *from Nietzsche's manuscript*

NIETZSCHE'S PREFACE 3

BOOK ONE. EUROPEAN NIHILISM

I. Nihilism 9

II. History of European Nihilism 40

BOOK TWO. CRITIQUE OF THE HIGHEST VALUES HITHERTO

I. Critique of Religion

1. *Genesis of Religions* 85
2. *History of Christianity* 98
3. *Christian Ideals* 127

II. Critique of Morality

1. *Origin of Moral Valuations* 146
2. *The Herd* 156
3. *General Remarks on Morality* 162
4. *How Virtue is Made to Dominate* 170
5. *The Moral Ideal* 180

A. Critique of Ideals 180

B. Critique of the "Good Man," the Saint, etc. 191

C. Disparagement of the So-Called Evil Qualities 197
D. Critique of the Words:
Improvement, Perfecting, Elevation 210
6. *Further Considerations for a Critique of Morality* 215

III. Critique of Philosophy
1. *General Observations* 220
2. *Critique of Greek Philosophy* 231
3. *Truth and Error of Philosophers* 247
4. *Further Considerations for a Critique of Philosophy* 253

BOOK THREE. PRINCIPLES OF A NEW EVALUATION

I. The Will to Power as Knowledge
1. *Method of Inquiry* 261
2. *The Epistemological Starting Point* 262
3. *Belief in the "Ego." The Subject* 267
4. *Biology of the Drive to Knowledge. Perspectivism* 272
5. *Origin of Reason and Logic* 276
6. *Consciousness* 283
7. *Judgment. True—False* 286
8. *Against Causalism* 293
9. *Thing-in-Itself and Appearance* 300
10. *Metaphysical Need* 307
11. *Biological Value of Knowledge* 322
12. *Science* 324

II. The Will to Power in Nature
1. *The Mechanistic Interpretation of the World* 332
2. *The Will to Power as Life* 341
A. The Organic Process 341
B. Man 347
3. *Theory of the Will to Power and of Values* 366

III. The Will to Power as Society and Individual
1. *Society and State* 382
2. *The Individual* 403

IV. The Will to Power as Art 419

BOOK FOUR. DISCIPLINE AND BREEDING

I. Order of Rank

1. *The Doctrine of Order of Rank* 457
2. *The Strong and the Weak* 459
3. *The Noble Man* 493
4. *The Masters of the Earth* 500
5. *The Great Human Being* 504
6. *The Highest Man as Legislator of the Future* 509

II. Dionysus 520

III. The Eternal Recurrence 544

APPENDIX: Commentary on the FACSIMILES 551

INDEX 558

A Note on This Edition

For the present volume I enlisted as a collaborator R. J. Hollingdale, author of *Nietzsche: The Man and His Philosophy* (University of Louisiana Press, 1965). I made a new translation of Book I, and he furnished new translations of Books II, III, and IV, which I subsequently corrected and revised very extensively, after comparing them with the original German, sentence for sentence. I am also responsible for the notes and the editorial apparatus—indeed, for the volume as a whole.

W. K.

Editor's Introduction

1

THE WILL TO POWER is a very famous and interesting book, but its stature and its reputation are two very different things. Indeed, the nature and contents of the book are as little known as its title is familiar. In a way this is odd because the book has been so widely cited and discussed; but in the history of ideas one finds perpetually that Hegel was right when he said in the preface to his first book: "What is well-known is not necessarily known merely because it is well-known."

Two false views of *The Will to Power* have had their day, in turn. The first was propagated by Elisabeth Förster-Nietzsche, the philosopher's sister, when she first published the book after his death: for a long time, it was widely held to represent Nietzsche's crowning systematic achievement, to which one had to turn for his final views. Alfred Bäumler began his postscript to the handy one-volume edition of the work (Kröner's *Taschenausgabe,*[1] vol. 78, 1930): *"The Will to Power* is Nietzsche's philosophical *magnum opus.* All the fundamental results of his thinking are brought together in this book. The aversion of its author against systematizers must not deter us from calling this work a system." Philosophically, Bäumler was a nobody, but the editions of Nietzsche's works for which he wrote his postscripts were the most convenient and least expensive and read very widely. Being a Nazi, Bäumler was called to Berlin as professor of philosophy after Hitler came to power. His ideas about Nietzsche were accepted not only by large numbers of Germans but also by many of Nietzsche's detractors outside Germany. Ernest Newman, for example, admits in the fourth volume of his *Life of Richard Wagner* (1946) that his account of Nietzsche relies heavily on Bäumler's "masterly epitome of Nietzsche's thinking, *Nietzsche, Der Philosoph und Politiker*"[2] (p. 335).

After World War II this view of *The Will to Power* was dis-

---

[1] Literally, Kröner's pocket edition: an inexpensive hard-cover series of books of scholarly interest.

[2] "The Philosopher and Politician [*sic*]," published in 1931.

credited along with the Nazis; and in the process the book itself was discredited, too. The gist of the new view was that *The Will to Power* is not worth reading at all. The man who has done more for this new myth than anyone else is Karl Schlechta, whose edition of Nietzsche's works in three thin-paper volumes (*Werke in drei Bänden,* 1954-1956) created something of an international sensation—particularly the third volume with its odd handling of *The Will to Power* and its lengthy "Philological Postscript." A passage from the postscript makes clear what is at stake: "*The Will to Power* contains nothing new, nothing that could surprise anyone who knows everything N published or intended to publish" (p. 1,403).

This is as untenable as Bäumler's view: the book contains a good deal that has no close parallel in the works Nietzsche finished; for example, but by no means only, much of the material on nihilism in Book I, some of the epistemological reflections in Book III, and the attempts at proofs of the doctrine of the eternal recurrence of the same events—and scores of brilliant formulations. But Schlechta's express view matters much less than what he *did* to *The Will to Power;* and matters are further complicated by the fact that what he did and what he said he did are two different things.

He did away with the systematic arrangement of the older editions and with the title *The Will to Power* and offered the material in his third volume under the heading "*Aus dem Nachlass der Achtzigerjahre,*" that is, "From the unpublished manuscript material of the eighties." And he claimed that his arrangement was faithful to the manuscripts and chronological (*manuskriptgetreu-chronologisch,* p. 1,393), although in fact it is neither.

This question cannot be avoided here because it would be unscholarly and perverse to reproduce the old systematic arrangement in this translation if a far superior arrangement of the material had been made available in 1956. But Schlechta's arrangement is utterly pointless, and indeed explicable only as an over-reaction against the Bäumler view: it represents an attempt to render *The Will to Power* all but unreadable.

Suppose, first of all, Schlechta's arrangement did follow the manuscripts faithfully; even then it could not claim to be chronological. For as Schlechta himself notes in passing in his postscript (p. 1,396), Nietzsche had the habit of using over and over old notebooks that had not yet been completely filled, and of writing in them now from the front toward the back, now from the back toward the front; and sometimes he filled right-hand pages only, at other times left-hand pages only. And Erich Podach claims in *Ein Blick in Notizbücher Nietzsche's* ("A Glance into Nietzsche's Notebooks," 1963) that "Nietzsche as a rule used his notebooks from back to front" (p. 8). Plainly, an arrangement that was really faithful to the manuscripts would not be an arrangement at all, but simply chaotic—and almost literally unreadable.

Moreover, Podach shows in the same book (pp. 202-206) that Schlechta did not always follow the manuscripts (see my notes on sections 2 and 124 below). Nor did Schlechta merely fail to consult the manuscripts, using the printed text of the standard edition instead; he did not even make a point of consulting the twenty-odd pages of notes at the end of the 1911 edition where scores of departures from the manuscripts are registered.

Even if it is granted that by taking these departures into account the present translation is philologically preferable to Schlechta's edition, it may seem odd that the old systematic arrangement has been followed here once again. There are two reasons for this. *First,* for all its faults, this arrangement has the virtue of making it easy for the reader to locate passages and to read straight through a lot of notes dealing with art or religion or the theory of knowledge. Provided one realizes that one is perusing notes and not a carefully wrought systematic work, the advantages of such an arrangement outweigh the disadvantages. But would it not have been possible to improve the systematic arrangement? This brings us to the *second* reason for following the old editions: there is something drastically wrong with scholarly translations that are not based on, do not correspond to, and cannot be easily checked against any original. This translation should be useful to scholars and critics, philosophers and historians, professors and students; it should be possible to cite it and also to find in it passages cited by others; and it should be easy to compare the text with readily available German editions.

2

The question still remains to be answered: what *is* the nature of this strange work? The answer is plain: it offers a selection from Nietzsche's notebooks of the years 1883 through 1888. These notes were not intended for publication in this form, and the arrangement and the numbering are not Nietzsche's. Altogether, this book is not comparable to the works Nietzsche finished and polished, and we do him a disservice if we fudge the distinction between these hasty notes and his often gemlike aphorisms. Superficially they may look alike, and the numbering contributes to this appearance, but in both style and content the difference is considerable.

To remind the reader of the difference, the approximate date of composition is furnished in brackets after the number of each note, and every attempt has been made to preserve the stylistic character of the original. The temptation to complete sentences, spruce up the punctuation, and turn jottings into attractive epigrams has been resisted with a will.[3] And in my notes I have called attention to passages in Nietzsche's late books in which some of these notes have been put to use—sometimes almost literally, but often with an interesting and perhaps unexpected twist. And in some notes I offer cross references to other passages in which Nietzsche takes a different tack.

A generation ago, many readers might have felt that if this book did not offer Nietzsche's final system, it could surely be ignored. But now that people have become used to reading the notebooks of Gide, Kafka, and Camus, for example, without taking them for anything but what they are, there is no need to downgrade Nietzsche's notes because they are mere notes. Of course, the reason he did not use some of them in his later works, although he could have included a lot of them quite easily in a chapter of aphorisms in *Twilight of the Idols,* was that many of them did not altogether satisfy him. Whether he used or did not use them, these notes obviously do not represent his final views: in his last active year, 1888, he completed five books; during the immediately preceding two years, another two. So we clearly need not turn to his notes to find what he really thought in the end. But it is fascinating to look, as it were, into the workshop of a great thinker; and Nietzsche's notes need not fear comparison with the notes of other great writers. On the contrary.

---

[3] Nietzsche often employs three or four periods as a punctuation mark to indicate that a train of thought is not concluded. Since this device is so regularly employed in English to indicate omissions, dashes (two if there are a lot of periods) have been substituted in this translation to avoid misunderstanding. And not all of Nietzsche's eccentricities have been retained; e.g., his frequent use of dashes before other punctuation marks. Also, I have sometimes started new paragraphs where the German editors run on.

3

The history of the text can be given briefly. Nietzsche himself had contemplated a book under the title *The Will to Power.* His notebooks contain a great many drafts for title pages for this and other projected works, and some of the drafts for this book suggest as a subtitle: *Attempt at a Revaluation of All Values.* Later on Nietzsche considered writing a book of a somewhat different nature (less aphoristic, more continuous) under the title *Revaluation of all Values,* and for a time he conceived of *The Antichrist,* written in the fall of 1888, as the first of the four books comprising the *Revaluation of All Values.*

In 1901, the year after Nietzsche's death, his sister published her first version of *The Will to Power* in volume 15 of her edition of his collected works, arranging 483 notes under topical headings. In 1904 she included 200 pages of additional notes "from *The Will to Power*" in the last volume of her biography of Nietzsche, to help its sales. And in 1906 another edition of the collected works offered a new version of *The Will to Power* in two volumes: the new material was mixed in with the old, and the total number of notes now came to 1,067. In the so-called Grossoktav edition of Nietzsche's *Werke* the same 1,067 notes appear in volumes 15 and 16, and volume 16 (1911) also features an appendix which contains "uncertain aphorisms and variants," numbered 1,068 through 1,079; "plans, dispositions, drafts" (pp. 413-67); a postscript (pp. 471-80); a list furnishing the numbers of the notebooks in which each of the notes and drafts was found; and notes indicating small departures from the manuscripts. I have made abundant use of these notes in the pages that follow, sometimes citing the volume in which they are found as "1911."[4] For these notes were not reprinted in the otherwise superior Musarion edition of Nietzsche's *Werke,* in which *The Will to Power* comprises volumes 18 and 19. The other material found in 1911 is offered in that edition, too, except that the list of the notebooks is superseded by a list giving the approximate date of composition of each of the 1,067 notes. The dates given in the following pages in brackets, immediately after the number of each note, are taken from that list.

---

[4] Where departures from the MSS are indicated in the editorial notes in the following pages and no authority is cited, the information is derived from 1911.

The handiest edition of the work is probably the one-volume edition in Kröner's *Taschen* edition, volume 78, published in 1930 with Alfred Bäumler's postscript (discussed above). Kröner has seen fit to reprint these Nietzsche editions, complete with Bäumler's postscripts. On close examination, however, it appears that some changes have been made in Bäumler's remarks about *The Will to Power,* although this is not indicated anywhere. This edition contains none of the scholarly apparatus.

In 1940 Friedrich Würzbach published his own rearrangement of the notes of *The Will to Power,* under the title "The Legacy of Friedrich Nietzsche: Attempt at a new interpretation of all that happens and a revaluation of all values, from the unpublished manuscript material and arranged in accordance with Nietzsche's intentions."[5] The claim that these notes rather than the books Nietzsche finished represent his legacy is as untenable as the boast that this—or any—arrangement can claim the sanction of Nietzsche's own intentions. The bulk of Würzbach's material was taken from *The Will to Power,* but he also included some other notes (all of them previously published in the Grossoktav edition and the Musarion edition), and he amalgamated notes of all periods, from 1870 to 1888. On pages 683-97 he furnished the dates, but he nowhere indicated the numbers of the notes in the standard edition of *The Will to Power.* This edition was translated into French but has won no acceptance in Germany or among scholars elsewhere.

What needs to be said about the standard arrangement followed in the present translation I said in my *Nietzsche* in 1950: "To arrange the material, Frau Förster-Nietzsche chose a four-line draft left by her brother, and distributed the notes under its four headings. Nietzsche himself had discarded this draft, and there are a dozen later ones, about twenty-five in all; but none of these were briefer than this one which listed only the titles of the four projected parts and thus gave the editor the greatest possible freedom. (It was also the only draft which suggested "Zucht und Züchtung" as the title of Part IV, and Frau Förster-Nietzsche may have been charmed by these words, although her brother, as we shall see, did not consider 'breeding' a function of race.) His

[5] *Das Vermächtnis Friedrich Nietzsches: Versuch einer neuen Auslegung alles Geschehens und einer Umwertung aller Werte, aus dem Nachlass und nach den Intentionen Nietzsche's geordnet,* Verlag Anton Pustet, Salzburg and Leipzig 1940.

own attempt to distribute some of his notes among the four parts of a later and more detailed plan was ignored, as was the fact that Nietzsche had abandoned the entire project of *The Will to Power* in 1888. . . . Moreover, the *Antichrist,* however provocative, represents a more single-minded and sustained inquiry than any of Nietzsche's other books and thus suggests that the major work of which it constitutes Part I [or at least was for a while intended to form Part I] was not meant to consist of that maze of incoherent, if extremely interesting, observations which have since been represented as his crowning achievement. While he intended to use some of this material, he evidently meant to mold it into a coherent and continuous whole; and the manner in which he utilized his notes in his other finished books makes it clear that many notes would have been given an entirely new and unexpected meaning.

"The publication of *The Will to Power* as Nietzsche's final and systematic work blurred the distinction between his works and his notes and created the false impression that the aphorisms in his books are of a kind with these disjointed jottings. Ever since, *The Will to Power,* rather than the *Götzen-Dämmerung* [*Twilight of the Idols*], *Antichrist,* and *Ecce Homo,* has been searched for Nietzsche's final position; and those who find it strangely incoherent are led to conclude that the same must be true *a fortiori* of his *parva opera.*

"The two most common forms of the Nietzsche legend can thus be traced back to his sister. In the manner just indicated, she unwittingly laid the foundation for the myth that Nietzsche's thought is hopelessly incoherent, ambiguous, and self-contradictory; and by bringing to her interpretation of her brother's work the heritage of her late husband [a prominent anti-Semite whose ideology Nietzsche had excoriated on many occasions], she prepared the way for the belief that Nietzsche was a proto-Nazi" (Prologue, section I).

Four years later, in 1954, when I published *The Portable Nietzsche* and presented four complete works as well as selections from Nietzsche's other books, notes, and letters, all arranged in chronological order, I included a few notes from *The Will to Power* under such headings as "NOTES (1887)" with footnotes reading: "Published as part of *The Will to Power* by Nietzsche's executors."

Schlechta's edition of 1956 thus did not require me to change my mind about *The Will to Power*. But it may seem odd that in the light of my own estimate of *The Will to Power* I should have decided to publish a translation. The explanation is simple.

Nietzsche's late works had to be made available first of all. Toward that end I made entirely new translations of *Thus Spoke Zarathustra, Twilight of the Idols, The Antichrist,* and *Nietzsche contra Wagner* (all included in *The Portable Nietzsche*), and more recently of *Beyond Good and Evil* (with commentary, 1966), *The Birth of Tragedy* and *The Case of Wagner* (with commentary, 1967), and *Ecce Homo* (1967). And I collaborated on a new translation of the *Genealogy of Morals* (1967). Beginning with *Zarathustra,* then, all of Nietzsche's later works will be available in new translations. At that point *The Will to Power* should be made accessible, too, for those who cannot read these notes in the original German.

To be sure, there is an old translation, done by Anthony M. Ludovici for *The Complete Works of Friedrich Nietzsche,* edited by Dr. Oscar Levy. Originally published in 1914, the two volumes of *The Will to Power* were "revised afresh by their translator" for the edition of 1924, and reprinted without further revision in 1964. Dr. Levy was probably quite right when in a prefatory note he called Ludovici "the most gifted and conscientious of my collaborators," but unfortunately this does not mean that Ludovici's translations are roughly reliable. Even in the revised version, the heading of section 12, for example, refers to "Cosmopolitan Values" instead of "Cosmological Values." Let us say that Ludovici was not a philosopher, and let it go at that. It would be pointless to multiply editorial notes in order to catalogue his mistranslations. But as long as we shall never mention him in the notes, one other example may be permissible. Section 86 begins: "Your Henrik Ibsen has become very clear to me." Evidently confusing *deutlich* (clear) and *deutsch,* Ludovici renders this: "In my opinion, Henrik Ibsen has become very German."

4

On the surface, Nietzsche seems easy to read, at least by comparison with other philosophers. In fact, however, his style poses unusual difficulties, and anyone who has taken the trouble to compare most of the existing translations with the originals must realize how easy it is to miss Nietzsche's meaning, not merely occasionally but in section upon section. The reasons are not difficult to find.

Nietzsche loved brevity to the point of ellipsis and often attached exceptional weight to the nuances of the words he did put down. Without an ear for the subtlest connotations of his brilliant, sparkling German, one is bound to misunderstand him. Nietzsche is Germany's greatest prose stylist, and his language is a delight at every turn like a poet's—more than that of all but the very greatest poets.

At the same time Nietzsche deals with intricate philosophical questions, especially but not only in *The Will to Power,* and whoever lacks either a feeling for poetry or some knowledge of these problems and their terminology is sure to come to grief in trying to fathom Nietzsche, sentence for sentence, as a translator must.

Yet Nietzsche's writings have an appeal that those of most other philosophers—and of *all* other German philosophers—lack. People turn to him for striking epigrams and brilliant formulations; they remember phrases out of context; indeed, he is more often than not read out of context—casually, carelessly, as if the details did not matter. If one turns to translations—whether the old ones of *The Complete Works* or the more recent paperback versions that flaunt their modernity—one usually falls victim to translators who have read him that way.

In addition to all this, Nietzsche writes as a "good European" (his coinage), alluding freely to Greek and Roman, French, Italian, and German literature and history, and he uses foreign phrases when they have nuances that might easily be lost in German. If we simply rendered all such phrases into English, not only subtle shades of meaning would be lost but—infinitely more important—something of this European flavor. If we simply left them all in the original, most students would be stumped by them; hence I have offered English translations in footnotes, with apologies to those who do not need them. Occasionally, no English equivalents are offered because the meaning seems so obvious, usually because the words are almost the same in English.

Similarly, some of the men referred to are identified in notes. In all such matters compromises seem unavoidable: to identify all would be insufferable, to identify none would leave even some scholars baffled, and no mean could answer every student's needs without at the same time striking some others as superfluous.

Precisely the same consideration applies to all other notes.

Listing all parallel passages at every point would swell the editorial notes beyond all reason: after all, there are many indices to Nietzsche's collected works (three different ones by Richard Oehler—for the Grossoktav edition, the Musarion edition, and Kröner's *Taschen* edition—and one by Karl Schlechta for his edition, as well as one in English for *The Collected Works*[6]), and my recent translations furnish indices for individual works. Moreover, cross references and indices always do harm as well as good, especially in Nietzsche's case: there is no substitute for reading his main works straight through, giving attention to the movement of his thought and to the context in which various things are said. But if no passages were cited in which Nietzsche put to use the notes his sister published posthumously in *The Will to Power,* the following pages would be as misleading as all previous editions, English and German.

As it is, this translation offers a great deal of information not to be found in any German edition, though it owes a great deal to the editorial apparatus of the Grossoktav edition and a little to that of the Musarion edition. It should facilitate a better understanding of Nietzsche, of the nineteenth century, and perhaps also of some of the problems with which he dealt—and therefore of the twentieth century, too.

5

Even in this introduction Nietzsche should have the last word. So I shall conclude by citing one of his drafts for a preface —*not* included in any previous edition of *The Will to Power,* but found in the Musarion edition of the works (volume XIV, pp. 373 *f.*):

Fall of 1885

THE WILL TO POWER

A book for *thinking,* nothing else: it belongs to those for whom thinking is a *delight,* nothing else—

That it is written in German is untimely, to say the least: I wish I had written it in French so that it might not appear to be a confirmation of the aspirations of the German *Reich.*

---

[6] All five are incomplete even as far as names are concerned and omit some of the most crucial passages in which terms that *are* listed appear.

The Germans of today are no thinkers any longer: something else delights and impresses them.

The will to power as a principle might be intelligible to them.

It is precisely among the Germans today that people think less than anywhere else. But who knows? In two generations one will no longer require the sacrifice involved in any nationalistic squandering of power and in becoming stupid.

(Formerly I wished I had not written my *Zarathustra* in German.)

ACKNOWLEDGMENTS

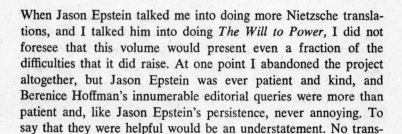

When Jason Epstein talked me into doing more Nietzsche translations, and I talked him into doing *The Will to Power,* I did not foresee that this volume would present even a fraction of the difficulties that it did raise. At one point I abandoned the project altogether, but Jason Epstein was ever patient and kind, and Berenice Hoffman's innumerable editorial queries were more than patient and, like Jason Epstein's persistence, never annoying. To say that they were helpful would be an understatement. No translator or author could ask for more cooperation from his editors.

Further, I am indebted to Professor Dr. Hahn at the Goethe- and Schiller-Archiv, Nationale Forschungs- und Gedenkstätten der klassischen deutschen Literatur in Weimar, East Germany, for sending me the reproductions of Nietzsche manuscripts that appear at the front of this volume, and for granting me permission to publish them. These pictures have not been published previously and contain passages that have never before appeared in print in any language.

W. K.

On the Editions of THE WILL TO POWER

THE FIRST EDITION appeared in 1901 in volume XV of Nietzsche's *Werke* (in the so-called Grossoktav edition). The title page read

NACHGELASSENE WERKE.

Der Wille zur Macht.
Versuch einer Umwerthung aller Werthe.
(*Studien und Fragmente.*)

VON
Friedrich Nietzsche.

LEIPZIG
Druck und Verlag von C. G. Naumann
1901.

In English: "Works Not Published by Nietzsche. The Will to Power. Attempt at a Revaluation of All Values. (Studies and Fragments.) By Friedrich Nietzsche." The facing left page was headed "Nietzsche's Werke" and subtitled "Zweite Abtheilung. Band XV. (Siebenter Band der zweiten Abtheilung.)" The first eight volumes, comprising the first section of the works, contained Nietzsche's books; the second section, of which this was the seventh volume, offered his *Nachlass.*

The editors were Peter Gast, Ernst Horneffer, and August Horneffer. On the last page of her preface, Nietzsche's sister wrote: "But I emphasize expressly that I myself am not the editor of this volume but at most a collaborator in the most modest sense of that word. The only circumstance that permits me to write this preface is that the collected edition of my brother's works is published at my behest, and hence the heaviest part of the responsibility, with all its cares and fights, has been resting on my shoulders for many years now. This 15th volume is to be considered as the culmination of the perennial, troublesome, conscientious labors of the editors: Peter Gast, Ernst and August Horneffer . . ." 483 sections (490 pages) plus 23 pages of Nietzsche's plans, and another 23 pages of editorial notes. The editors did not have time to do the job as they themselves felt it ought to be done, because Elisabeth Förster-Nietzsche, as head of the Nietzsche-Archive, insisted that the volume be published in a hurry. There were recriminations between her and the brothers Horneffer, and they left the Archive.

The second edition of 1906, in the so-called Taschen edition of the *Werke* (for the different editions of the works in German see the bibliography at the end of my translation of *The Birth of Tragedy* and *The Case of Wagner* in one volume, Vintage Books, New York 1967), followed roughly the same plan as the first edition but comprised 1,067 sections. Peter Gast checked all the material against Nietzsche's manuscripts, which he is said to have been able to decipher better than anyone else, and he seems to have had a fairly free hand in Books I and III.

The reprint of 1911 (in vols. XV and XVI of the revised edition of the Grossoktav edition) follows the text of 1906, but Dr. Otto Weiss contributed an appendix of invaluable scholarly notes on the manuscripts.

In the so-called Musarion edition (23 vols., 1920-29), published by the Musarion Verlag in Munich, the text of 1906 and 1911, which had been published by Kröner in Leipzig, is reprinted in vols. XVIII and XIX, but the apparatus differs in two important respects from the edition of 1911: on the basis of the information given by Dr. Weiss on p. 480 *ff*, a table is included that furnishes the approximate date of composition for every one of the 1,067 sections; and the editorial notes listing departures from the manuscripts are omitted. Indeed, these notes are found only in the edition of 1911, and the list of dates appears only in the Musarion edition. These two editions are therefore the most scholarly and helpful, that of 1911 being by far the best.

No subsequent edition has made any important scholarly contribution. The editions of Bäumler, Würzbach, and Schlechta are discussed in the Editor's Introduction to the present edition, and the editorial notes contain many examples showing how Schlechta's edition is *less* faithful to the manuscripts than the edition of 1911, notwithstanding his explicit claims which have been widely taken on credit on both sides of the Atlantic.

Finally, it may be noted that Bäumler's first edition of *Der Wille zur Macht,* in volume 78 of Króners Taschen edition (1930) presented the work as one of Nietzsche's books: the title page mentions no editors. In the reprint in *Sämtliche Werke in zwölf Bänden,* 12 vols., Kröner, Stuttgart 1964-65, the text follows volume 78 with the same pagination, but the title page adds "Ausgewählt und geordnet von Peter Gast unter Mitwirkung von Elisabeth Förster-Nietzsche" (selected and arranged by Peter Gast with the aid of Elisabeth Förster-Nietzsche); and in a postscript (pp. 711-15) to his editorial afterword (pp. 699-711—a slightly revised version of the earlier afterword, though neither the publisher nor Bäumler calls attention to the fact that some changes have been made) Alfred Bäumler deals briefly with Karl Schlechta's and Erich Podach's criticisms of the editing of Nietzsche's *Nachlass.*

Chronology of Nietzsche's Works

A much more comprehensive bibliography is included in my translation of *The Birth of Tragedy* and *The Case of Wagner,* New York, Vintage Books, 1967.

Selections from the aphoristic books (1878-82) are included in *The Portable Nietzsche,* New York, The Viking Press, 1954, and in my edition of *The Genealogy of Morals* and *Ecce Homo,* New York, Vintage Books, 1967.

THE BIRTH OF TRAGEDY 1872

Slightly revised 2nd edition, 1878; in 1886 a new preface was added to the remaining copies of both editions. Translation with commentary by Walter Kaufmann, 1967.

UNTIMELY MEDITATIONS

David Strauss 1873

On the Use and Disadvantage of History 1873

Schopenhauer as Educator 1874

Richard Wagner in Bayreuth 1876

HUMAN, ALL-TOO-HUMAN 1878

Mixed Opinions and Maxims (1st sequel) 1879

The Wanderer and His Shadow (2nd sequel) 1880

Second editions, with new prefaces, 1886.

THE DAWN 1881

Second edition, with a new preface, 1887.

THE GAY SCIENCE 1882

Second edition, with substantial additions, 1887.

THUS SPOKE ZARATHUSTRA 1883-1892

Parts I and II published separately in 1883, Part III in 1884, forty copies of Part IV printed in 1885 (but only seven distributed among friends); first public ed. of Part IV, dated 1891 and published in 1892. Translation with commentary by Walter Kaufmann, 1954 (originally in *The Portable Nietzsche*).

BEYOND GOOD AND EVIL 1886
Translation with commentary by Walter Kaufmann, 1966.

ON THE GENEALOGY OF MORALS 1887
Translation with commentary by Walter Kaufmann and R. J. Hollingdale, 1967.

THE CASE OF WAGNER
Translation with commentary by Walter Kaufmann, 1967.

THE TWILIGHT OF THE IDOLS (*written 1888*) 1889
Translation with preface and notes by Walter Kaufmann, 1954 (in *The Portable Nietzsche*).

THE ANTICHRIST (*written 1888*) 1895
Translation with preface and notes by Walter Kaufmann, 1954 (in *The Portable Nietzsche*).

ECCE HOMO (*written 1888*) 1908
Translation with commentary by Walter Kaufmann, 1967.

NIETZSCHE CONTRA WAGNER (*written 1888*) 1895
Translation with notes by Walter Kaufmann, 1954.
(in *The Portable Nietzsche*).

THE WILL TO POWER (*Notes written 1883-1888*) 1901
Revised edition, containing twice as much material, 1906, reprinted with considerable scholarly apparatus in 1911. Translated by Walter Kaufmann and R. J. Hollingdale, edited with notes by Walter Kaufmann, 1967.

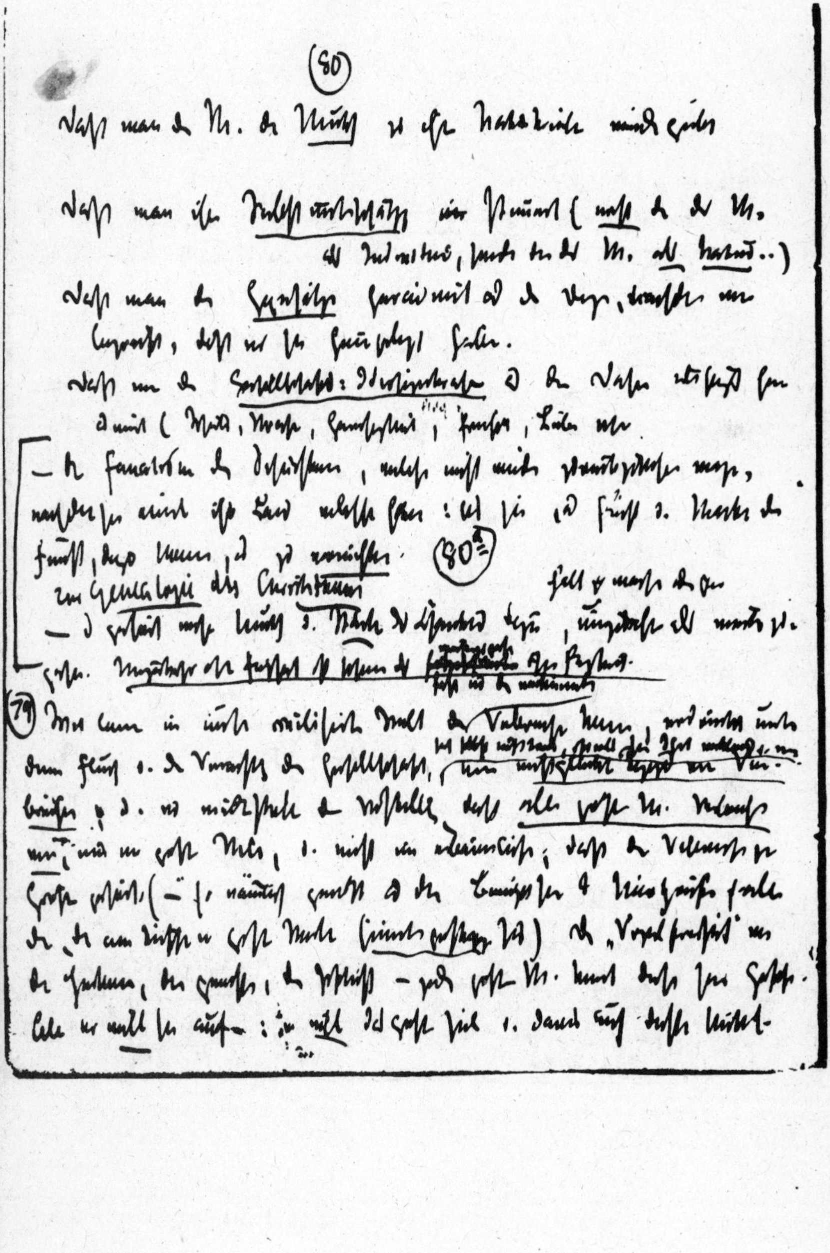

Das Problem der civilisirten [illegible].

(79)

Fortschritt zur „Natürlichkeit“: in allen politischen Fragen, auch im Verhältniß von Parteien, selbst von merkantilen oder Arbeiter- o. Unternehmer-Parteien handelt es sich um Machtfragen — „was man kann“ u. erst darauf hin, was man soll?

Daß dabei, mitten in der Mechanik der großen Politik, noch der christliche Gesang erschallt (z. B. in Siegesbülletins oder in Ansprachen des Kaisers an das Volk) gehört immer mehr zu dem, was unmöglich wird: weil es wider den Geschmack geht. [illegible]

---

(80) Fortschritt des neunzehnten Jhs. gegen das 18te.

— im Grunde führen wir guten Europäer einen Krieg gegen das 18te Jahrh. —

[illegible] 1. „Rückkehr zur Natur“ immer entschiedener im umgekehrten Sinne verstanden als sie Rousseau verstand. Weg vom Idyll u. der Oper!

2. immer entschiedener antiidealistisch, gegenständlicher, furchtloser, arbeitsamer, maßvoller, mißtrauischer gegen plötzliche Veränderungen, antirevolutionärer,

3. immer entschiedener die Frage der Gesundheit des Leibes der der „Seele“ voran. [illegible]

[illegible]

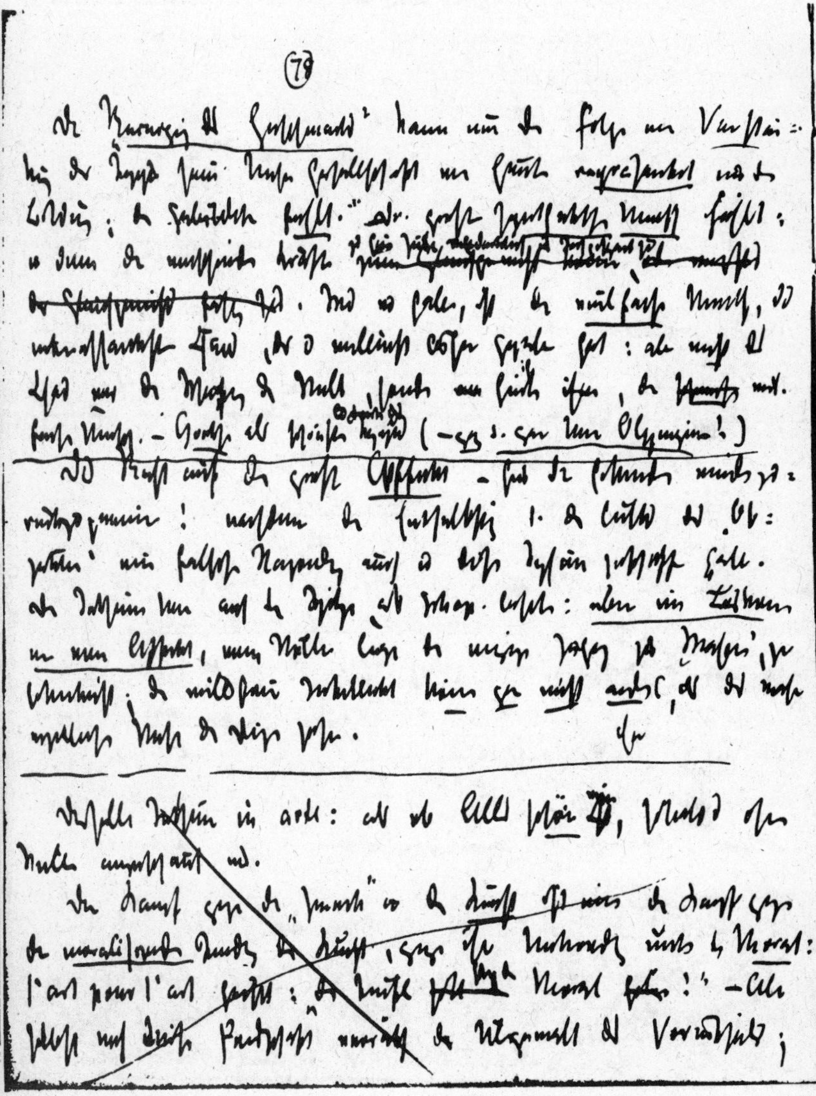

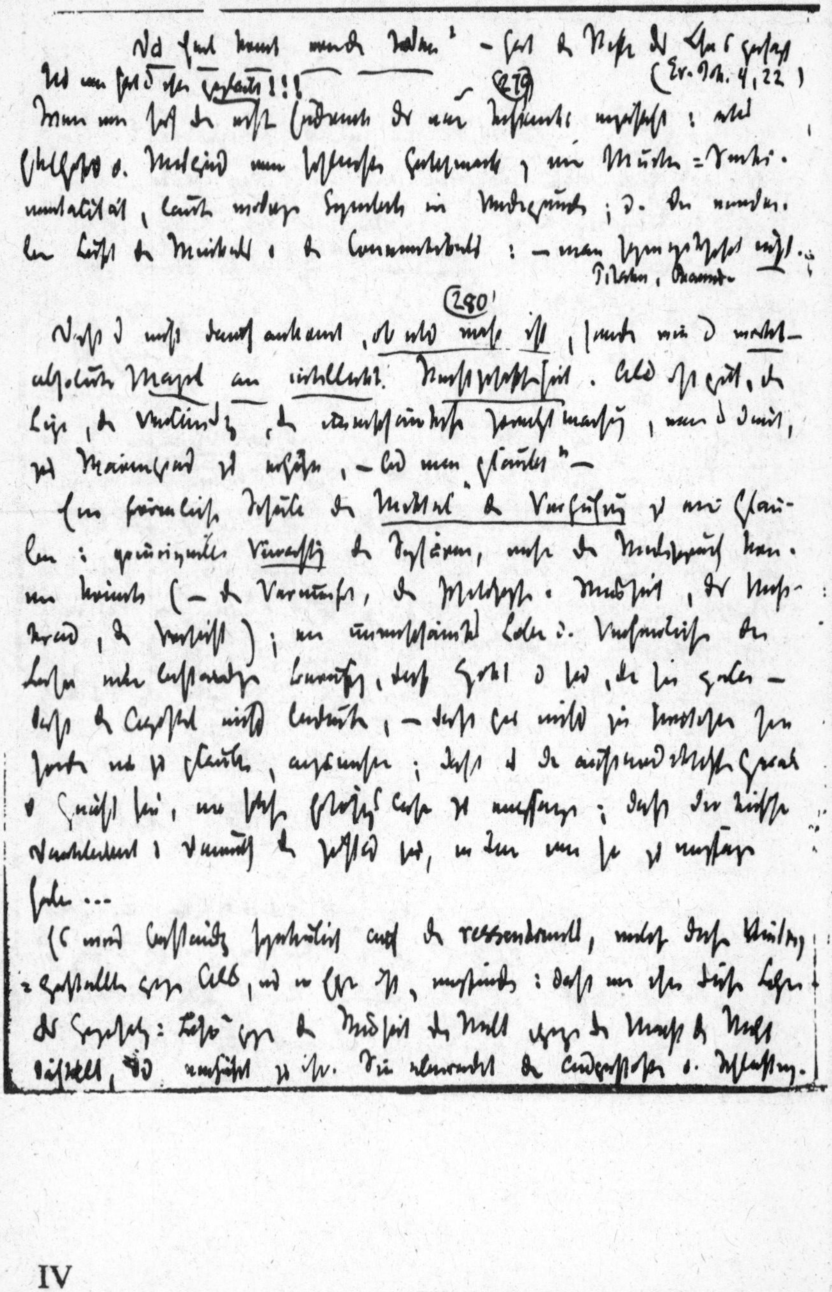

IV

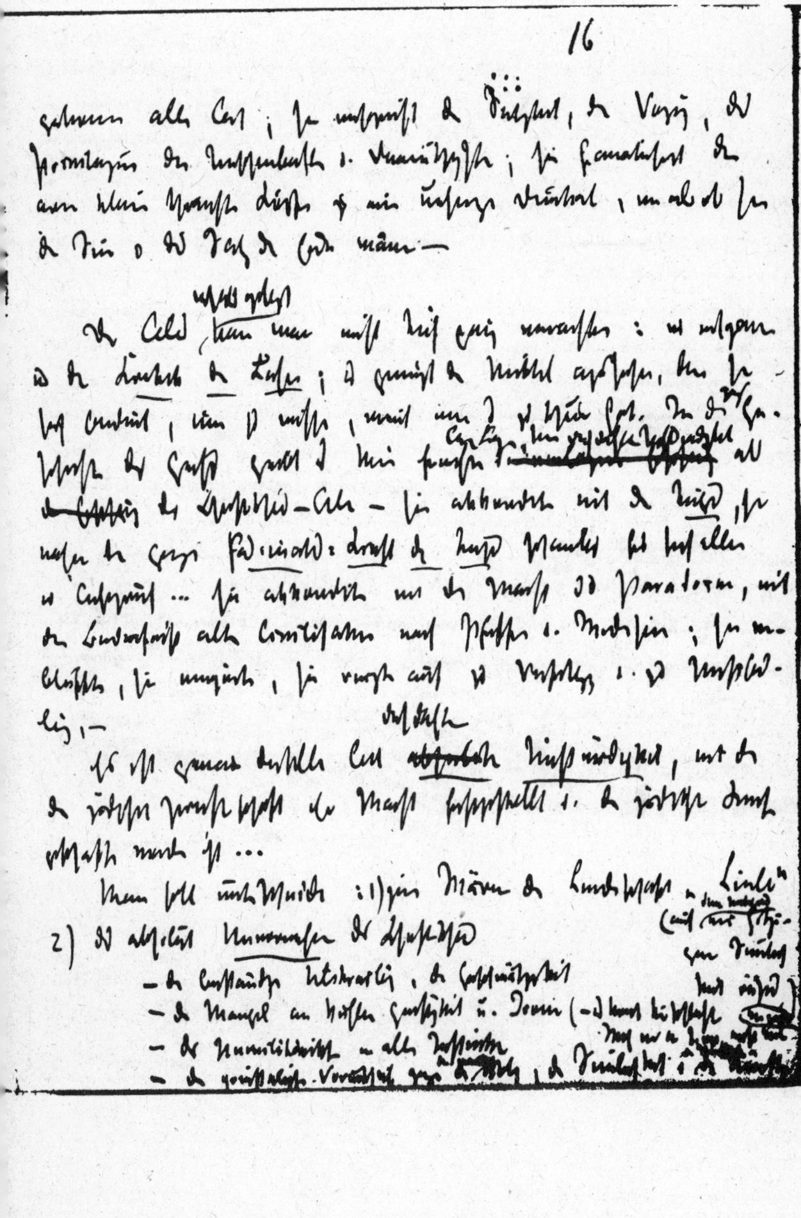

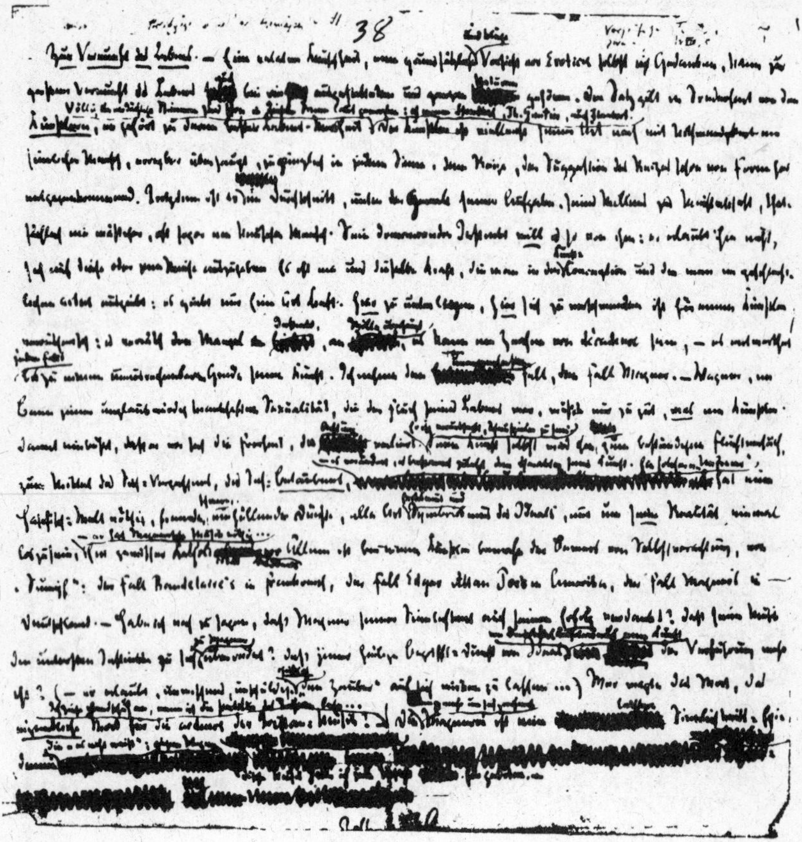

Wagner, im Bann jener [illegible] krankhaften Sexualität, die der Fluch seines Lebens war, wusste nur zu gut, was ein Künstler damit einbüßt, daß er vor sich die Freiheit, die Achtung verliert. Seine Kunst selbst wird ihm zum beständigen Flucht-versuch, zum Mittel des Sich-Vergessens, des Sich-Betäubens [illegible]

[illegible]

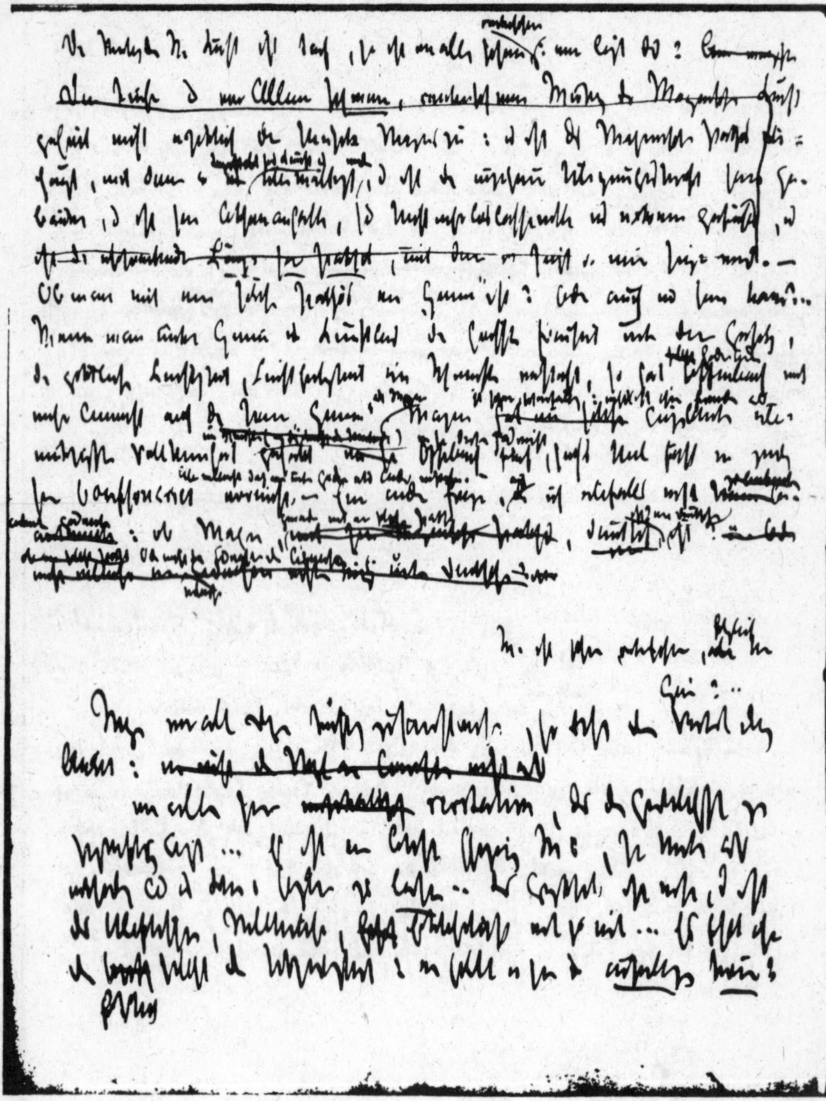

PREFACE
(Nov. 1887-March 1888)

1

Of what is great one must either be silent or speak with greatness. With greatness—that means cynically and with innocence.

2

What I relate is the history of the next two centuries. I describe what is coming, what can no longer come differently: *the advent of nihilism.* This history can be related even now; for necessity itself is at work here. This future speaks even now in a hundred signs, this destiny announces itself everywhere; for this music of the future all ears are cocked even now. For some time now, our whole European culture has been moving as toward a catastrophe, with a tortured tension that is growing from decade to decade: restlessly, violently, headlong, like a river that wants to reach the end, that no longer reflects, that is afraid to reflect.

3

He that speaks here, conversely, has done nothing so far but reflect: a philosopher and solitary by instinct, who has found his advantage in standing aside and outside, in patience, in procrastination, in staying behind; as a spirit of daring and experiment that has already lost its way once in every labyrinth of the future; as a soothsayer-bird spirit who *looks back* when relating what will come; as the first perfect nihilist of Europe who, however, has even now lived through the whole of nihilism, to the end, leaving it behind, outside himself.

4

For one should make no mistake about the meaning of the title that this gospel of the future wants to bear. "*The Will to Power*: Attempt at a Revaluation of All Values"—in this formulation a countermovement finds expression, regarding both principle and task; a movement that in some future will take the place of this perfect nihilism—but presupposes it, logically and psychologically, and certainly can come only after and out of it. For why has the advent of nihilism become *necessary*? Because the values we have had hitherto thus draw their final consequence; because nihilism represents the ultimate logical conclusion of our great values and ideals—because we must experience nihilism before we can find out what value these "values" really had.— We require, sometime, *new values.*

BOOK ONE

EUROPEAN NIHILISM

1 (*1885-1886*)
Toward an Outline

1. Nihilism stands at the door: whence comes this uncanniest of all guests? Point of departure: it is an error to consider "social distress" or "physiological degeneration" or, worse, corruption, as the *cause* of nihilism. Ours is the most decent and compassionate age. Distress, whether of the soul, body, or intellect, cannot of itself give birth to nihilism (i.e., the radical repudiation of value, meaning, and desirability). Such distress always permits a variety of interpretations. Rather: it is in one particular interpretation, the Christian-moral one, that nihilism is rooted.

2. The end of Christianity—at the hands of its own morality (which cannot be replaced), which turns against the Christian God (the sense of truthfulness, developed highly by Christianity, is nauseated by the falseness and mendaciousness of all Christian interpretations of the world and of history; rebound from "God is truth" to the fanatical faith "All is false"; Buddhism of *action*—).

3. Skepticism regarding morality is what is decisive. The end of the moral interpretation of the world, which no longer has any sanction after it has tried to escape into some beyond, leads to nihilism. "Everything lacks meaning" (the untenability of one interpretation of the world, upon which a tremendous amount of energy has been lavished, awakens the suspicion that *all* interpretations of the world are false). Buddhistic tendency, yearning for Nothing. (Indian Buddhism is *not* the culmination of a thoroughly moralistic development; its nihilism is therefore full of morality that is not overcome: existence as punishment, existence construed as error, error thus as a punishment—a moral valuation.) Philosophical attempts to overcome the "moral God" (Hegel, pantheism). Overcoming popular ideals: the sage; the saint; the poet. The antagonism of "true" and "beautiful" and "good"—

4. Against "meaninglessness" on the one hand, against moral value judgments on the other: to what extent has all science and philosophy so far been influenced by moral judgments? and won't this net us the hostility of science? Or an antiscientific mentality? Critique of Spinozism. Residues of Christian value judgments are found everywhere in socialistic and positivistic systems. A *critique of Christian morality* is still lacking.

5. The nihilistic consequences of contemporary natural science (together with its attempts to escape into some beyond). The industry of its pursuit eventually leads to self-disintegration, opposition, an antiscientific mentality. Since Copernicus man has been rolling from the center toward *X*.*

6. The nihilistic consequences of the ways of thinking in politics and economics, where all "principles" are practically histrionic: the air of mediocrity, wretchedness, dishonesty, etc. Nationalism. Anarchism, etc. Punishment. The *redeeming* class and human being are lacking—the justifiers—

7. The nihilistic consequences of historiography and of the "*practical* historians," i.e., the romantics. The position of art: its position in the modern world absolutely lacking in originality. Its decline into gloom. Goethe's allegedly Olympian stance.

8. Art and the preparation of nihilism: romanticism (the conclusion of Wagner's *Nibelungen*).

* Cf. *Genealogy of Morals,* third essay, section 25.

I. NIHILISM

2 (*Spring-Fall 1887*)[1]

What does nihilism mean? *That the highest values devaluate themselves.* The aim is lacking; "why?" finds no answer.

3 (*Spring-Fall 1887*)[2]

Radical nihilism is the conviction of an absolute untenability of existence when it comes to the highest values one recognizes; plus the realization that we lack the least right to posit a beyond or an in-itself of things that might be "divine" or morality incarnate.

This realization is a consequence of the cultivation of "truthfulness"—thus itself a consequence of the faith in morality.

4 (*June 10, 1887*)[3]

What were the advantages of the Christian moral hypothesis?

1. It granted man an absolute value, as opposed to his smallness and accidental occurrence in the flux of becoming and passing away.

---

[1] According to Erich Podach, notes 2, 13, 22, and 23 form a single note in Nietzsche's notebooks—not in that order. The note begins:

"*Nihilism as a normal condition.* Nihilism: the aim is lacking; 'why?' finds no answer. What does nihilism mean? *That the highest values devaluate themselves.*

"It is *ambiguous*:

"A. Nihilism as a sign of increased power of the spirit: active nihilism.

"It can be a sign of strength: . . ."

(See Podach *Ein Blick in Notizbücher Nietzsches,* Heidelberg, Wolfgang Rothe, 1963, pp. 205 *f.* In Schlechta's edition the note appears in four parts, in the same sequence as in the standard editions: 2, 13, 22, and 23. For further discussion of Podach and Schlechta see Kaufmann, "Nietzsche in the Light of his Suppressed Manuscripts," in *Journal of the History of Philosophy,* October 1964 (II.2), pp. 205-225.

[2] In Nietzsche's manuscript this note is marked "For the Plan" (*Zum Plane*). See *Werke,* Grossoktav edition, XVI (1911), p. 497. In subsequent references this volume is cited as "1911."

[3] In the manuscript this note is number 1 under the heading *"European Nihilism.* Lenzer Heide [Heath of Lenz], June 10, 1887"; and it is followed by note 5, which Nietzsche superscribed 2; note 114, which he numbered 3; and note 55, whose thirteen sections Nietzsche numbered 4 through 16. See 1911, p. 497.

2. It served the advocates of God insofar as it conceded to the world, in spite of suffering and evil, the character of perfection—including "freedom": evil appeared full of meaning.

3. It posited that man had a *knowledge* of absolute values and thus *adequate knowledge* precisely regarding what is most important.

4. It prevented man from despising himself as man, from taking sides against life; from despairing of knowledge: it was a *means of preservation.*

In sum: morality was the great *antidote* against practical and theoretical *nihilism.*

5 (*June 10, 1887*)[4]

But among the forces cultivated by morality was *truthfulness*: this eventually turned against morality, discovered its teleology, its partial perspective—and now the recognition of this inveterate mendaciousness that one despairs of shedding becomes a stimulant. Now we discover in ourselves needs implanted by centuries of moral interpretation—needs that now appear to us as needs for untruth; on the other hand, the value for which we endure life seems to hinge on these needs. This antagonism—*not* to esteem what we know, and not to be *allowed* any longer to esteem the lies we should like to tell ourselves—results in a process of dissolution.

6 (*Spring-Fall 1887*)

This is the *antinomy*:

Insofar as we believe in morality we pass sentence on existence.

7 (*Nov. 1887-March 1888*)

The supreme values in whose service man *should* live, especially when they were very hard on him and exacted a high price—these *social values* were erected over man to strengthen their voice, as if they were commands of God, as "reality," as the "true" world, as a hope and *future* world. Now that the shabby origin of these values is becoming clear, the universe seems to

---

[4] See footnote to section 4 above.

have lost value, seems "meaningless"—but that is only a *transitional stage.*

8 (*1883-1888*)

The nihilistic consequence (the belief in valuelessness) as a consequence of moral valuation: *everything egoistic has come to disgust us* (even though we realize the impossibility of the unegoistic); *what is necessary has come to disgust us* (even though we realize the impossibility of any *liberum arbitrium*[5] or "intelligible freedom"). We see that we cannot reach the sphere in which we have placed our values; but this does not by any means confer any value on that other sphere in which we live: on the contrary, we are *weary* because we have lost the main stimulus. "In vain so far!"

9 (*Spring-Fall 1887*)

Pessimism as a preliminary form of nihilism.

10 (*Spring-Fall 1887*)

Pessimism as strength—in what? in the energy of its logic, as anarchism and nihilism, as analytic.

Pessimism as decline—in what? as growing effeteness, as a sort of cosmopolitan fingering, as *"tout comprendre"*[6] and historicism.

The critical tension: the extremes appear and become predominant.

11 (*Spring-Fall 1887, rev. Spring-Fall 1888*)

The logic of pessimism down to ultimate nihilism: what is at work in it? The idea of valuelessness, meaninglessness: to what extent moral valuations hide behind all other high values.

Conclusion: *Moral value judgments are ways of passing sentence, negations; morality is a way of turning one's back on the will to existence.*

Problem: *But what is morality*?

---

[5] Free will.

[6] Understanding everything.

12 (*Nov. 1887-March 1888*)
Decline of Cosmological Values

(A)

Nihilism as a psychological state will have to be reached, *first,* when we have sought a "meaning" in all events that is not there: so the seeker eventually becomes discouraged. Nihilism, then, is the recognition of the long *waste* of strength, the agony of the "in vain," insecurity, the lack of any opportunity to recover and to regain composure—being ashamed in front of oneself, as if one had *deceived* oneself all too long.— This meaning could have been: the "fulfillment" of some highest ethical canon in all events, the moral world order; or the growth of love and harmony in the intercourse of beings; or the gradual approximation of a state of universal happiness; or even the development toward a state of universal annihilation—any goal at least constitutes some meaning. What all these notions have in common is that something is to be *achieved* through the process—and now one realizes that becoming aims at *nothing* and achieves *nothing.*— Thus, disappointment regarding an alleged aim of becoming as a cause of nihilism: whether regarding a specific aim or, universalized, the realization that all previous hypotheses about aims that concern the whole "evolution" are inadequate (man no longer the collaborator, let alone the center, of becoming).

Nihilism as a psychological state is reached, *secondly,* when one has posited a totality, a systematization, indeed any organization in all events, and underneath all events, and a soul that longs to admire and revere has wallowed in the idea of some supreme form of domination and administration (—if the soul be that of a logician, complete consistency and real dialectic are quite sufficient to reconcile it to everything). Some sort of unity, some form of "monism": this faith suffices to give man a deep feeling of standing in the context of, and being dependent on, some whole that is infinitely superior to him, and he sees himself as a mode of the deity.— "The well-being of the universal demands the devotion of the individual"—but behold, there is no such universal! At bottom, man has lost the faith in his own value when no infinitely valuable whole works through him; i.e., he conceived such a whole in order *to be able to believe in his own value.*

Nihilism as psychological state has yet a *third* and *last* form.

Given these two insights, that becoming has no goal and that underneath all becoming there is no grand unity in which the individual could immerse himself completely as in an element of supreme value, an escape remains: to pass sentence on this whole world of becoming as a deception and to invent a world beyond it, a *true* world. But as soon as man finds out how that world is fabricated solely from psychological needs, and how he has absolutely no right to it, the last form of nihilism comes into being: it includes disbelief in any metaphysical world and forbids itself any belief in a *true* world.[7] Having reached this standpoint, one grants the reality of becoming as the *only* reality, forbids oneself every kind of clandestine access to afterworlds and false divinities —but *cannot endure this world though one does not want to deny it.*

What has happened, at bottom? The feeling of valuelessness was reached with the realization that the overall character of existence may not be interpreted by means of the concept of "aim," the concept of "unity," or the concept of "truth." Existence has no goal or end; any comprehensive unity in the plurality of events is lacking: the character of existence is not "true," is *false.* One simply lacks any reason for convincing oneself that there is a *true* world. Briefly: the categories "aim," "unity," "being" which we used to project some value into the world—we *pull out* again; so the world looks *valueless.*

(B)

Suppose we realize how the world may no longer be interpreted in terms of these three categories, and that the world begins to become valueless for us after this insight: then we have to ask about the sources of our faith in these three categories. Let us try if it is not possible to give up our faith in them. Once we have devaluated these three categories, the demonstration that they cannot be applied to the universe is no longer any reason for devaluating the universe.

Conclusion: The faith in the categories of reason is the cause of nihilism. We have measured the value of the world according to categories *that refer to a purely fictitious world.*

Final conclusion: All the values by means of which we have

---

[7] Cf. *Twilight of the Idols,* Chapters III and IV (*Portable Nietzsche,* pp. 482-86).

tried so far to render the world estimable for ourselves and which then proved inapplicable and therefore devaluated the world—all these values are, psychologically considered, the results of certain perspectives of utility, designed to maintain and increase human constructs of domination—and they have been falsely *projected* into the essence of things. What we find here is still the *hyperbolic naiveté* of man: positing himself as the meaning and measure of the value of things.

13 (*Spring-Fall 1887*)[8]

Nihilism represents a pathological transitional stage (what is pathological is the tremendous generalization, the inference that there is no meaning at all): whether the productive forces are not yet strong enough, or whether decadence still hesitates and has not yet invented its remedies.

Presupposition of this hypothesis: that there is no truth, that there is no absolute nature of things nor a "thing-in-itself." This, too, is merely nihilism—even the most extreme nihilism. It places the value of things precisely in the lack of any reality corresponding to these values and in their being merely a symptom of strength on the part of the value-positers, a simplification for the sake of life.

14 (*Spring-Fall 1887*)

Values and their changes are related to increases in the power of those positing the values.

The measure of *unbelief*, of permitted "freedom of the spirit" as *an expression of an increase in power.*

"Nihilism" an ideal of the highest degree of powerfulness of the spirit, the over-richest life—partly destructive, partly ironic.

15 (*Spring-Fall 1887*)

What is a *belief*? How does it originate? Every belief is a considering-something-true.

The most extreme form of nihilism would be the view that *every* belief, every considering-something-true, is necessarily false because there simply is no *true world*. Thus: a *perspectival ap-*

[8] See the footnote for section 2 above.

pearance whose origin lies in us (in so far as we continually *need* a narrower, abbreviated, simplified world).

—That it is the measure of strength to what extent we can admit to ourselves, without perishing, the merely *apparent* character, the necessity of lies.

To this extent, nihilism, as the denial of a truthful world, of being, might be *a divine way of thinking.*

16 (*Nov. 1887-March 1888*)

If we are "disappointed," it is at least not regarding life: rather we are now facing up to all kinds of "desiderata." With scornful wrath we contemplate what are called "ideals"; we despise ourselves only because there are moments when we cannot subdue that absurd impulse that is called "idealism." The influence of too much coddling is stronger than the wrath of the disappointed.

17 (*Spring-Fall 1887; rev. 1888*)

To what extent Schopenhauer's nihilism still follows from the same ideal that created Christian theism.— One felt so certain about the highest desiderata, the highest values, the highest perfection that the philosophers assumed this as an absolute certainty, as if it were a priori: "God" at the apex as a *given truth.* "To become as God," "to be absorbed into God"—for thousands of years these were the most naive and convincing desiderata (but what convinces is not necessarily true—it is merely convincing: a note for asses).

One has unlearned the habit of conceding to this posited ideal the reality of a person; one has become atheistic. But has the ideal itself been renounced?— At bottom, the last metaphysicians still seek in it true "reality," the "thing-in-itself" compared to which everything else is merely apparent. It is their dogma that our apparent world, being so plainly *not* the expression of this ideal, cannot be "true"—and that, at bottom, it does not even lead us back to that metaphysical world as its cause. The unconditional, representing that highest perfection, cannot possibly be the ground of all that is conditional. Schopenhauer wanted it otherwise and therefore had to conceive of this metaphysical ground as the opposite of the ideal—as "evil, blind will": that way it could be that "which appears," that which reveals itself in the world of appearances. But even so he did not renounce the absoluteness of the ideal—he sneaked by.—

(Kant considered the hypothesis of "intelligible freedom" necessary in order to acquit the *ens perfectum*[9] of responsibility for the world's being such-and-such—in short, to account for evil and ills: a scandalous bit of logic for a philosopher.—)

18 (*1883-1888*)

The most universal sign of the modern age: man has lost *dignity* in his own eyes to an incredible extent. For a long time the center and tragic hero of existence in general; then at least intent on proving himself closely related to the decisive and essentially valuable side of existence—like all metaphysicians who wish to cling to the *dignity of man,* with their faith that moral values are cardinal values. Those who have abandoned God cling that much more firmly to the faith in morality.[10]

19 (*1883-1888*)

Every purely moral value system (that of Buddhism, for example) ends in nihilism: this to be expected in Europe. One still hopes to get along with a moralism without religious background: but that necessarily leads to nihilism.— In religion the constraint is lacking to consider *ourselves* as value-positing.

20 (*Spring-Fall 1887*)

The nihilistic question "for what?" is rooted in the old habit of supposing that the goal must be put up, given, demanded *from outside*—by some *superhuman authority.* Having unlearned faith in that, one still follows the old habit and seeks *another* authority that can *speak unconditionally* and *command* goals and tasks. The authority of *conscience* now steps up front (the more emancipated one is from theology, the more imperativistic morality becomes)

---

[9] Perfect being.

[10] Cf. *Twilight,* Chapter IX, section 5 (*Portable Nietzsche,* p. 515): "*G. Eliot.* They are rid of the Christian God and now believe all the more firmly that they must cling to Christian morality. That is an English consistency; we do not wish to hold it against little moralistic females à la Eliot. . . ."

to compensate for the loss of a *personal* authority. Or the authority of *reason*. Or the *social instinct* (the herd). Or *history* with an immanent spirit and a goal within, so one can entrust oneself to it. One wants to get around the will, the willing of a goal, the risk of positing a goal *for oneself*; one wants to rid oneself of the responsibility (one would accept fatalism). Finally, *happiness*—and, with a touch of Tartuffe, the *happiness of the greatest number*.

One says to oneself:

1. a definite goal is not necessary at all,
2. cannot possibly be anticipated.

Just now when the greatest strength of will would be necessary, it is weakest and least confident. Absolute mistrust regarding the organizing strength of the will for the whole.[11]

21 (*Spring-Fall 1887; rev. 1888*)

The perfect nihilist.— The nihilist's eye idealizes in the direction of ugliness and is unfaithful to his memories: it allows them to drop, lose their leaves; it does not guard them against the corpselike pallor that weakness pours out over what is distant and gone. And what he does not do for himself, he also does not do for the whole past of mankind: he lets it drop.

22 (*Spring-Fall 1887*)[12]

Nihilism. It is *ambiguous*:

A. Nihilism as a sign of increased power of the spirit: as *active* nihilism.

B. Nihilism as decline and recession of the power of the spirit: as *passive* nihilism.

23 (*Spring-Fall 1887*)[13]

Nihilism as a *normal* condition.

It can be a sign of strength: the spirit may have grown so strong that previous goals ("convictions," articles of faith) have

---

[11] In the margin: "Individual goals and their conflict; collective goals versus individual ones. *Everybody merely a partisan,* including the philosophers." See 1911, p. 497.

[12] See footnote to section 2, above.

[13] See footnote to section 2, above.

become incommensurate (for a faith generally expresses the constraint of conditions of existence, submission to the authority of circumstances under which one flourishes, grows, gains power). Or a sign of the lack of strength to posit for oneself, productively, a goal, a why, a faith.

It reaches its maximum of relative strength as a violent force of destruction—as active nihilism.

Its opposite: the weary nihilism that no longer attacks; its most famous form, Buddhism; a passive nihilism, a sign of weakness. The strength of the spirit may be worn out, exhausted, so that previous goals and values have become incommensurate and no longer are believed; so that the synthesis of values and goals (on which every strong culture rests) dissolves and the individual values war against each other: disintegration—and whatever refreshes, heals, calms, numbs emerges into the foreground in various disguises, religious or moral, or political, or aesthetic, etc.

24 (*Nov. 1887-March 1888*)

Nihilism does not only contemplate the "in vain!" nor is it merely the belief that everything deserves to perish: one helps to destroy.— This is, if you will, illogical; but the nihilist does not believe that one needs to be logical.— It is the condition of strong spirits and wills, and these do not find it possible to stop with the No of "judgment": their nature demands the No of the deed. The reduction to nothing by judgment is seconded by the reduction to nothing by hand.

25 (*Spring-Fall 1887*)

On the genesis of the nihilist.— It is only late that one musters the courage for what one really knows.[14] That I have hitherto been a thorough-going nihilist, I have admitted to myself only recently: the energy and radicalism with which I advanced as a nihilist deceived me about this basic fact. When one moves toward a goal it seems impossible that "goal-lessness as such" is the principle of our faith.

[14] This note was used in the second aphorism of *Twilight of the Idols*: "Even the most courageous among us only rarely has the courage for that which he really knows."

26 (*Spring-Fall 1887*)

The pessimism of active energy: the question "for what?" after a terrible struggle, even victory. That something is a hundred times more important than the question of whether we feel well or not: basic instinct of all strong natures—and consequently also whether others feel well or not. In sum, that we have a goal for which one does not hesitate to offer human sacrifices, to risk every danger, to take upon oneself whatever is bad and worst: the *great passion.*

27 (*Spring-Fall 1887*)

Causes of nihilism: 1. The higher species is lacking, i.e., those whose inexhaustible fertility and power keep up the faith in man. (One should recall what one owes to Napoleon: almost all of the higher hopes of this century.)

2. The lower species ("herd," "mass," "society") unlearns modesty and blows up its needs into cosmic and metaphysical values. In this way the whole of existence is vulgarized: in so far as the mass is dominant it bullies the exceptions, so they lose their faith in themselves and become nihilists.

All attempts to think up higher types failed ("romanticism"; the artist, the philosopher; against Carlyle's attempt to ascribe to them the highest moral values).

The resistance to higher types as a result.

Decline and insecurity of all higher types. The fight against the genius ("folk poetry," etc.). Pity for the lowly and suffering as a measure for the height of a soul.

The philosopher is lacking who interprets the deed and does not merely transpose it.

28 (*Spring-Fall 1887*)

Main proposition. How *complete nihilism* is the necessary consequence of the ideals entertained hitherto.[15]

Incomplete nihilism; its forms: we live in the midst of it.

Attempts to escape nihilism without revaluating our values so far: they produce the opposite, make the problem more acute.

---

[15] See 1911, p. 498. This paragraph has been omitted in all editions.

29 (*1883-1888*)

The ways of self-narcotization.—[16] Deep down: not knowing whither. *Emptiness.* Attempt to get over it by intoxication: intoxication as music; intoxication as cruelty in the tragic enjoyment of the destruction of the noblest; intoxication as blind enthusiasm for single human beings or ages (as hatred, etc.).— Attempt to work blindly as an instrument of science: opening one's eyes to the many small enjoyments; e.g., also in the quest of knowledge (modesty toward oneself); resignation to generalizing about oneself, a pathos; mysticism, the voluptuous enjoyment of eternal emptiness; art "for its own sake" (*"le fait"*) and "pure knowledge" as narcotic states of disgust with oneself; some kind or other of continual work, or of some stupid little fanaticism; a medley of all means, sickness owing to general immoderation (debauchery kills enjoyment).

1. Weakness of the will as a result.
2. Extreme pride and the humiliation of petty weakness *felt* in contrast.

30 (*Nov. 1887-March 1888; rev. 1888*)

The time has come when we have to pay for having been Christians for two thousand years: we are losing the center of gravity by virtue of which we lived; we are lost for a while. Abruptly we plunge into the opposite valuations, with all the energy that such an extreme overvaluation of man has generated in man.

Now everything is false through and through, mere "words" chaotic, weak, or extravagant:

a. one attempts a kind of this-worldly solution, but in th same sense—that of the eventual triumph of truth, love, and justice (socialism: "equality of the person");

b. one also tries to hold on to the moral ideal (with the pre-eminence of what is un-egoistic, self-denial, negation of the will);

c. one tries to hold on even to the "beyond"—even if only as some antilogical *"x"*—but one immediately interprets it in such

---

[16] This heading was supplied by Peter Gast. (See my note "On the Editions of *The Will to Power*.")

a way that some sort of old-fashioned metaphysical comfort can be derived from it;

d. one tries to find in events an old-fashioned divine governance—an order of things that rewards, punishes, educates, and betters;

e. one still believes in good and evil and experiences the triumph of the good and the annihilation of evil as a task (that is English; typical case: the flathead John Stuart Mill);

f. contempt for what is "natural," for desire, for the ego: attempt to understand even the highest spirituality and art as the consequence of depersonalization and as *désintéressement*;

g. the church is still permitted to obtrude into all important experiences and main points of individual life to hallow them and give them a higher meaning: we still have the "Christian state," "Christian marriage"—[17]

31 (*1884*)

There have been more thoughtful and thought-addicted ages than ours: ages, e.g., like that in which the Buddha appeared, when after centuries of quarrels among sects the people themselves were as deeply lost in the ravines of philosophic doctrines as European nations were at times in the subtleties of religious dogmas. Surely, one should not let "literature" and the press seduce us to think well of the "spirit" of our time: the existence of millions of spiritists and a Christianity that goes in for gymnastics of that gruesome ugliness that characterizes all English inventions are more instructive.

European pessimism is still in its early stages—bears witness against itself: it still lacks that tremendous, yearning rigidity of expression in which the Nothing is reflected, once found in India; it is still far too contrived and too little "organic"—too much a pessimism of scholars and poets: I mean, much of it is excogitated and invented, is "created" and not a "cause."

---

[17] According to 1911, p. 498, the manuscript contains an alternative draft for the end of the first paragraph, as follows:

"with the same amount of energy with which we used to be Christians —with which the absurd exaggeration of the Christian. . . ."

This sentence breaks off, but a few other phrases follow:

"(1) the 'immortal soul'; the eternal value of the 'person'— (2) the solution, the judgment the evaluation in the 'beyond'— (3) moral values as the supreme values, the 'salvation of the soul' as one's cardinal interest— (4) 'sin,' 'earthly,' 'flesh,' 'appetites' stigmatized as 'world.' "

32 (*Summer-Fall 1888*)

Critique of pessimism to date.— Resistance to eudaemonistic considerations as the last reduction to the question: what does it *mean*? The reduction of growing gloom.—

Our pessimism: the world does not have the value we thought it had. Our faith itself has so increased our desire for knowledge that today we have to say this. Initial result: it seems worth less; that is how it is experienced initially. It is only in this sense that we are pessimists; i.e., in our determination to admit this revaluation to ourselves without any reservation, and to stop telling ourselves tales—lies—the old way.

That is precisely how we find the pathos that impels us to seek *new values*. In sum: the world might be far more valuable than we used to believe; we must see through the naiveté of our ideals, and while we thought that we accorded it the highest interpretation, we may not even have given our human existence a moderately fair value.

What has been *deified*? The value instincts in the community (that which made possible its continued existence).

What has been *slandered*? That which *set apart* the higher men from the lower, the desires that create clefts.

33 (*Spring-Fall 1887*)

Causes of the advent of pessimism:

1. that the most powerful desires of life that have the most future have hitherto been slandered, so a curse weighs on life;

2. that the growing courage and integrity and the bolder mistrust that now characterize man comprehend that these instincts are inseparable from life, and one therefore turns against life;

3. that only the most mediocre, who have no feeling at all for this conflict, flourish while the higher kind miscarries and, as a product of degeneration, invites antipathy—that the mediocre, on the other hand, when they pose as the goal and meaning, arouse indignation (that nobody is able any more to answer any "for what?");

4. that diminution, sensitivity to pain, restlessness, haste, and hustling grow continually—that it becomes easier and easier to recognize this whole commotion, this so-called "civilization,"

and that the individual, faced with this tremendous machinery, loses courage and submits.

34 (*1885-1886*)

Modern pessimism is an expression of the uselessness of the *modern* world—not of the world of existence.

35 (*Spring-Fall 1887*)

The "predominance of suffering over pleasure" or the opposite (*hedonism*): these two doctrines are already signposts to nihilism.

For in both of these cases no ultimate meaning is posited except the appearance of pleasure or displeasure.

But that is how a kind of man speaks that no longer dares to posit a will, a purpose, a meaning: for any healthier kind of man the value of life is certainly not measured by the standard of these trifles. And suffering might predominate, and in spite of that a powerful will might exist, a Yes to life, a need for this predominance.

"Life is not worthwhile"; "resignation"; "why the tears?"—a weakly and sentimental way of thinking. *"Un monstre gai vaut mieux qu'un sentimental ennuyeux."*[18]

36 (*Nov. 1887-March 1888*)

The philosophical nihilist is convinced that all that happens is meaningless and in vain; and that there ought not to be anything meaningless and in vain. But whence this: there ought not to be? From where does one get *this* "meaning," *this* standard?—At bottom, the nihilist thinks that the sight of such a bleak, useless existence makes a philosopher feel *dissatisfied,* bleak, desperate. Such an insight goes against our finer sensibility as philosophers. It amounts to the absurd valuation: to have any right to be, the character of existence *would have to give the philosopher pleasure.*—

Now it is easy to see that pleasure and displeasure can only be *means* in the course of events: the question remains whether

[18] "A gay monster is worth more than a sentimental bore." Cf. section 91 below.

we are at all able to see the "meaning," the "aim," whether the question of meaninglessness or its opposite is not insoluble for us.—

37 (*Spring-Fall 1887*)

The development of pessimism into nihilism.— Denaturalization of values. Scholasticism of values. Detached and idealistic, values, instead of dominating and guiding action, turn against action and condemn it.

Opposites replace natural degrees and ranks. Hatred against the order of rank. Opposites suit a plebeian age because easier to comprehend.

The repudiated world versus an artificially built "true, valuable" one.— Finally: one discovers of what material one has built the "true world": and now all one has left is the repudiated world, and one adds this supreme disappointment to the reasons why it deserves to be repudiated.

At this point nihilism is reached: all one has left are the values that pass judgment—nothing else.

Here the problem of strength and weakness originates:

1. The weak perish of it;
2. those who are stronger destroy what does not perish;
3. those who are strongest overcome the values that pass judgment.

In sum this constitutes the tragic age.

38 (*1883-1888*)

Recently much mischief has been done with an accidental and in every way unsuitable word: everywhere "pessimism" is discussed, and the question is debated whether pessmism or optimism is right, as if there must be answers to that.

One fails to see, although it could hardly be more obvious, that pessimism is not a problem but a symptom, that the name should be replaced by "nihilism," that the question whether not-to-be is better than to be is itself a disease, a sign of decline, an idiosyncrasy.

The nihilistic movement is merely the expression of physiological decadence.

39 (*Nov. 1887-March 1888*)

To be comprehended: That every kind of decay and sickness has continually helped to form overall value judgments; that decadence has actually gained predominance in the value judgments that have become accepted; that we not only have to fight against the consequences of all present misery of degeneration, but that all *previous* decadence is still residual, i.e., survives. Such a total aberration of mankind from its basic instincts, such a total decadence of value judgments—that is the question mark par excellence, the real riddle that the animal "man" poses for the philosopher.

40 (*March-June 1888*)

The concept of decadence.— Waste, decay, elimination need not be condemned: they are necessary consequences of life, of the growth of life. The phenomenon of decadence is as necessary as any increase and advance of life: one is in no position to abolish it. Reason demands, on the contrary, that we do justice to it.

It is a disgrace for all socialist systematizers that they suppose there could be circumstances—social combinations—in which vice, disease, prostitution, distress would no longer grow.— But that means condemning life.— A society is not free to remain young. And even at the height of its strength it has to form refuse and waste materials. The more energetically and boldly it advances, the richer it will be in failures and deformities, the closer to decline.— Age is not abolished by means of institutions. Neither is disease. Nor vice.

41 (*Jan.-Fall 1888*)

Basic insight regarding the nature of decadence: *its supposed causes are its consequences.*

This changes the whole perspective of *moral problems.*

The whole moral struggle against vice, luxury, crime, even disease, appears a naiveté and superfluous: there is no "improvement" (against repentance).

Decadence itself is nothing *to be fought*: it is absolutely necessary and belongs to every age and every people. What should be fought vigorously is the contagion of the healthy parts of the organism.

Is this being done? The *opposite* is done. Precisely that is attempted in the name of *humanity.*

—How are the supreme values held so far, related to this basic biological question? Philosophy, religion, morality, art, etc.

(The cure: e.g., *militarism,* beginning with Napoleon who considered civilization his natural enemy.)[19]

42 (*March-June 1888*)

First principle:

The supposed causes of degeneration are its consequences.

But the supposed remedies of degeneration are also mere palliatives against some of its effects: the "cured" are merely one type of the degenerates.

Consequences of decadence: vice—the addiction to vice; sickness—sickliness; crime—criminality; celibacy—sterility; hystericism—weakness of the will; alcoholism; pessimism; anarchism; libertinism (also of the spirit). The slanderers, underminers, doubters, destroyers.

43 (*March-June 1888*)

On the concept of decadence.

1. Skepticism is a consequence of decadence, as is libertinism of the spirit.

2. The corruption of morals is a consequence of decadence (weakness of the will, need for strong stimuli).

3. Attempted cures, psychological and moral, do not change the course of decadence, do not arrest it, are physiologically *naught*:

Insight into the great nullity of these presumptuous "reactions"; they are forms of narcotization against certain terrible consequences; they do not eliminate the morbid element; often they are heroic attempts to annul the man of decadence and to realize the minimum of his harmfulness.

[19] With sections 41-44 cf. *Twilight of the Idols,* "Morality as Anti-Nature" and "The Four Great Errors," the first being "The error of confusing cause and effect"; also sections 334 and 380 below.

4. Nihilism is no cause but merely the logical result of decadence.

5. The "good" and "bad" man are merely two types of decadence: in all basic phenomena they agree.

6. The social question is a consequence of decadence.

7. Sicknesses, especially those affecting nerves and head, are signs that the defensive strength of the strong natures is lacking; precisely this is suggested by irritability, so pleasure and displeasure become foreground problems.

44 (*Spring-Summer 1888*)[20]

Most general types of decadence:

1. Believing one chooses remedies, one chooses in fact that which hastens exhaustion; Christianity is an example (to name the greatest example of such an aberration of the instincts); "progress" is another instance.—

2. One loses one's power of resistance against stimuli—and comes to be at the mercy of accidents: one coarsens and enlarges one's experiences tremendously—"depersonalization," disintegration of the will; example: one whole type of morality, the altruistic one which talks much of pity—and is distinguished by the weakness of the personality, so that it is sounded, too, [21] and like an overstimulated string vibrates continually—an extreme irritability.—

3. One confuses cause and effect: one fails to understand decadence as a physiological condition and mistakes its consequences for the real cause of the indisposition; example: all of religious morality.—

4. One longs for a condition in which one no longer suffers: life is actually experienced as the ground of ills; one esteems unconscious states, without feeling, (sleep, fainting) as incomparably more valuable than conscious ones;[22] from this a method—

---

[20] In the margin: "On the History of Nihilism."

[21] "*Sodass sie mitklingt*": Cf. Rilke's famous "*Liebes-Lied*" (1907), reprinted with translation in Walter Kaufmann, *Twenty German Poets;* also, *Thus Spoke Zarathustra IV* (pity as Zarathustra's great temptation), in *Portable Nietzsche.*

[22] Cf. Wagner's *Tristan und Isolde* and Novalis' *Hymnen an die Nacht* (also in *Twenty German Poets*).

45 (*March-June 1888*)

On the hygiene of the "weak."— Everything done in weakness fails. Moral: do nothing. Only there is the hitch that precisely the strength to suspend activity, *not* to react, is sickest of all under the influence of weakness: one never reacts more quickly and blindly than when one should not react at all.—

A strong nature manifests itself by waiting and postponing any reaction:[23] it is as much characterized by a certain *adiaphoria*[24] as weakness is by an involuntary countermovement and the suddenness and inevitability of "action."— The will is weak—and the prescription to avoid stupidities would be to have a strong will and to do *nothing.*— *Contradictio.*— A kind of self-destruction; the instinct of preservation is compromised.— The weak harm themselves.— That is the type of decadence.—

In fact, we find a tremendous amount of reflection about practices that would lead to impassability. The instinct is on the right track insofar as doing nothing is more expedient than doing something.—

All the practices of the orders, the solitary philosophers, the fakirs are inspired by the right value standard that a certain kind of man cannot benefit himself more than by preventing himself as much as possible from acting.—

Means of relief: absolute obedience, machinelike activity, avoidance of people and things that would demand instant decisions and actions.

46 (*March-June 1888*)

Weakness of the will: that is a metaphor that can prove misleading. For there is no will, and consequently neither a strong nor a weak will.[25] The multitude and disgregation of impulses and the lack of any systematic order among them result in a "weak will"; their coordination under a single predominant impulse results in a "strong will": in the first case it is the oscillation and

---

[23] Cf. *Twilight* (*Portable Nietzsche*), "Morality as Anti-Nature," section 2 (p. 487), "What the Germans Lack," section 6 (p. 511), and also "Skirmishes," section 10 (p. 519).

[24] Indifference.

[25] Contrast section 84.

the lack of gravity; in the latter, the precision and clarity of the direction.

47 (*March-June 1888*)

What is inherited is not the sickness but *sickliness*: the lack of strength to resist the danger of infections, etc., the broken resistance; *morally* speaking, resignation and meekness in face of the enemy.

I have asked myself if all the supreme values of previous philosophy, morality, and religion could not be compared to the values of the weakened, the *mentally ill,* and *neurasthenics*: in a milder form, they represent the same ills.—

It is the value of all morbid states that they show us under a magnifying glass certain states that are normal—but not easily visible when normal.—

Health and sickness are not essentially different, as the ancient physicians and some practitioners even today suppose. One must not make of them distinct principles or entities that fight over the living organism and turn it into their arena. That is silly nonsense and chatter that is no good any longer. In fact, there are only differences in degree between these two kinds of existence: the exaggeration, the disproportion, the nonharmony of the normal phenomena constitute the pathological state (Claude Bernard).

Just as *"evil"* can be considered as exaggeration, disharmony, disproportion, "*the good*" may be a *protective diet* against the danger of exaggeration, disharmony, and disproportion.

Hereditary weakness as the *dominant* feeling: cause of the supreme values.

N.B. One *wants* weakness: why? Usually because one is *necessarily* weak.

—*Weakness* as a *task*: weakening the desires, the feelings of pleasure and displeasure, the will to power, to a sense of pride, to want to have and have more; weakening as meekness; weakening as faith; weakening as aversion and shame in the face of everything natural, as negation of life, as sickness and habitual weakness—weakening as the renunciation of revenge, of resistance, of enmity and wrath.

The error in treatment: one does not want to fight weakness

with a *système fortifiant,*[26] but rather with a kind of justification and *moralization*; i.e., with an *interpretation.*—

—Two totally different states confounded: e.g., the *calm of strength,* which is essentially forbearance from reaction (type of the gods whom nothing moves)—and the *calm of exhaustion,* rigidity to the point of anesthesia. All philosophic-ascetic procedures aim at the second, but really intend the former—for they attribute predicates to the attained state as if a divine state had been attained.

48 (*March-June 1888*)

The most dangerous misunderstanding.— One concept apparently permits no confusion or ambiguity: that of *exhaustion.* Exhaustion can be acquired or inherited—in any case it changes the aspect of things, the *value of things.*—

As opposed to those who, from the fullness they represent and feel, involuntarily *give* to things and see them fuller, more powerful, and pregnant with future—who at least are able to bestow something—the exhausted diminish and botch all they see—they impoverish the value: they are harmful.—

About this no mistake seems possible: yet history contains the gruesome fact that the exhausted have always been mistaken for the fullest—and the fullest for the most harmful.

Those poor in life, the weak, impoverish life; those rich in life, the strong, enrich it. The first are parasites of life; the second give presents to it.— How is it possible to confound these two?

When the exhausted appeared with the gesture of the highest activity and energy (when degeneration effected an excess of spiritual and nervous discharge), they were mistaken for the rich. They excited fear.— The cult of the *fool* is always the cult of those rich in life, the powerful. The fanatic, the possessed, the religious epileptic, all eccentrics have been experienced as the highest types of power: as divine.

This kind of strength that excites *fear* was considered preeminently divine: here was the origin of authority; here one interpreted, heard, sought wisdom.— This led to the development, almost everywhere, of a *will* to "deify," i.e., a will to the typical degeneration of spirit, body, and nerves: an attempt to find the way to this higher level of being. To make oneself sick, mad, to

[26] A method that strengthens.

provoke the symptoms of derangement and ruin—that was taken for becoming stronger, more superhuman, more terrible, wiser.[27] One thought that in this way one became so rich in power that one could give from one's fullness. Wherever one adored one sought one who could give.

Here the experience of intoxication proved misleading. This increases the feeling of power in the highest degree—therefore, naively judged, power itself. On the highest rung of power one placed the most intoxicated, the ecstatic. (—There are two sources of intoxication: the over-great fullness of life and a state of pathological nourishment of the brain.)[28]

49 (*Jan.-Fall 1888*)

Acquired, not inherited, exhaustion: (1) Inadequate nourishment, often from ignorance about norishment; e.g., among scholars. (2) Erotic precociousness: the curse in particular of French youth, above all in Paris, who emerge into the world from their *lycées* botched and soiled and never free themselves again from the chain of contemptible inclinations, ironical and disdainful toward themselves—galley slaves with all refinements (incidentally, in most cases already a symptom of the decadence of race and family, like all hypersensitivity; also the contagion of the milieu—to let oneself be determined by one's environment is decadent). (3) Alcoholism—not the instinct but the habit, the stupid imitation, the cowardly or vain assimilation to a dominant regime:

What a blessing a Jew is among Germans! How much dullness, how blond the head, how blue the eye; the lack of *esprit* in face, word, posture; the lazy stretching-oneself, the German need for a good rest—not prompted by overwork but by the disgusting stimulation and overstimulation through alcoholica.—

50 (*1888*)

Theory of exhaustion.— Vice, the mentally ill (resp., the artists—), the criminals, the anarchists—these are not the oppressed classes but the scum of previous society of all classes.—

Realizing that all our classes are permeated by these elements, we understand that modern society is no "society," no "body,"

[27] Cf. *The Dawn,* section 14.

[28] Cf. *ibid.,* section 188.

but a sick conglomerate of chandalas—a society that no longer has the strength to *excrete.*

To what extent sickliness, owing to the symbiosis of centuries, goes much deeper:

modern virtue,
modern spirituality, } as forms of sickness.
our science

51 (*March-June 1888*)

The state of corruption.— To understand how all forms of corruption belong together, without forgetting the Christian corruption (Pascal as type) as well as the socialist-communist corruption (a consequence of the Christian—from the point of view of the natural sciences, the socialists' conception of the highest society is the lowest in the order of rank); also the "beyond" corruption: as if outside the actual world, that of becoming, there were another world of being.

Here no terms are permissible: here one has to eradicate, annihilate, wage war; everywhere the Christian-nihilistic value standard still has to be pulled up and fought under every mask; e.g., in present-day sociology, in present-day music, in present-day pessimism (all of them forms of the Christian value ideal).

Either the one is true or the other: true here means elevating the type of man.

The priest, the shepherd of souls, as objectionable forms of existence. All of education to date, helpless, untenable, without center of gravity, stained by the contradiction of values.

52 (*Jan.-Fall 1888*)

Nature is not immoral when it has no pity for the degenerate: on the contrary, the growth of physiological and moral ills among mankind is the consequence of a pathological and unnatural morality. The sensibility of the majority of men is pathological and unnatural.

Why is it that mankind is corrupt morally and physiologically?— The body perishes when an organ is altered. The right of altruism cannot be derived from physiology; nor can the right to help and to an equality of lots: these are prizes for the degenerate and underprivileged.

There is no solidarity in a society in which there are sterile, unproductive, and destructive elements—which, incidentally, will have descendants even more degenerate than they are themselves.

53 (*March-June 1888*)

Even the ideals of science can be deeply, yet completely unconsciously influenced by decadence: our entire sociology is proof of that. The objection to it is that from experience it knows only the form of the decay of society, and inevitably it takes its own instincts of decay for the norms of sociological judgment.

In these norms the life that is declining in present-day Europe formulates its social ideals: one cannot tell them from the ideals of old races that have outlived themselves.—

The *herd instinct,* then—a power that has now become sovereign—is something totally different from the instinct of an *aristocratic society*: and the value of the *units* determines the significance of the sum.— Our entire sociology simply does not know any other instinct than that of the herd, i.e., that of the *sum of zeroes*—where every zero has "equal rights," where it is virtuous to be zero.—

The valuation that is today applied to the different forms of society is entirely identical with that which assigns a higher value to peace than to war: but this judgment is antibiological, is itself a fruit of the decadence of life.— Life is a consequence of war, society itself a means to war.— As a biologist, Mr. Herbert Spencer is a decadent; as a moralist, too (he considers the triumph of altruism a desideratum! ! !).[29]

54 (*Jan.-Fall 1888*)

It is my good fortune that after whole millennia of error and confusion I have rediscovered the way that leads to a Yes and a No.

I teach the No to all that makes weak—that exhausts.

I teach the Yes to all that strengthens, that stores up strength, that justifies the feeling of strength.

So far one has taught neither the one nor the other: virtue

[29] Cf. *Twilight* (*Portable Nietzsche*), section 37 (p. 541): "Mr. Herbert Spencer is a decadent too: he considers the triumph of altruism a desideratum!"

has been taught, mortification of the self, pity, even the negation of life. All these are the values of the exhausted.

Prolonged reflection on the physiology of exhaustion forced me to ask to what extent the judgments of the exhausted had penetrated the world of values.

My result was as surprising as possible, even for me who was at home in many a strange world: I found that all of the supreme value judgments—all that have come to dominate mankind, at least that part that has become tame—can be derived from the judgments of the exhausted.

Under the holiest names I pulled up destructive tendencies; one has called God what weakens, teaches weakness, infects with weakness.— I found that the "good man" is one of the forms in which decadence affirms itself.

That virtue of which Schopenhauer still taught that it is the supreme, the only virtue, and the basis of all virtues—precisely pity I recognized as more dangerous than any vice. To cross as a matter of principle selection in the species and its purification of refuse—that has so far been called virtue *par excellence*.—

One should respect fatality—that fatality that says to the weak: perish!—

One has called it God—that one resisted fatality, that one corrupted mankind and made it rot.— One should not use the name of God in vain.—

The race is corrupted—not by its vices but by its ignorance; it is corrupted because it did not recognize exhaustion as exhaustion: mistakes about physiological states are the source of all ills.—

Virtue is our greatest misunderstanding.

Problem: How did the exhausted come to make the laws about values? Put differently: How did those come to power who are the last?— How did the instinct of the human animal come to stand on its head?—[30]

---

[30] Cf. the beginning of *The Antichrist*, which was written a little later.

According to 1911, pp. 498 *f*, this note is superscribed "A Preface" and has the appearance of a quick draft—and "a few paragraphs that did not fit well into the context had to be omitted." The original version of the second paragraph read: "Vice is whatever weakens—whatever exhausts." And the next paragraph: "Conversely, I call good whatever makes strong, whatever stores. . . ." And the following passages were omitted by the original editor:

"I have to teach first of all that crime, celibacy, and sickness are consequences of exhaustion. [Nietzsche himself, of course, was celibate and far from well.]

55 (*June 10, 1887*)[31]

Extreme positions are not succeeded by moderate ones but by extreme positions of the opposite kind. Thus the belief in the absolute immorality of nature, in aim- and meaninglessness, is the psychologically necessary affect once the belief in God and an essentially moral order becomes untenable. Nihilism appears at that point, not that the displeasure at existence has become greater than before but because one has come to mistrust any "meaning" in suffering, indeed in existence. One interpretation has collapsed; but because it was considered *the* interpretation it now seems as if there were no meaning at all in existence, as if everything were in vain.

*

That this "in vain" constitutes the character of present-day nihilism remains to be shown. The mistrust of our previous valuations grows until it becomes the question: "Are not all 'values' lures that draw out the comedy without bringing it closer to a solution?" Duration "in vain," without end or aim, is the most paralyzing idea, particularly when one understands that one is being fooled and yet lacks the power not to be fooled.

*

Let us think this thought in its most terrible form: existence as it is, without meaning or aim, yet recurring inevitably without any finale of nothingness: *"the eternal recurrence."*[32]

"Plunging down—negating life—that, too, was supposed to be experienced as a kind of sunrise transfiguration, deification.

"I want to make the concept of 'progress' more precise and am afraid that toward that end I have to fly in the face of modern ideas (but I am comforted by the fact that they really have no faces but only *masks*).

"Diseased limbs should be amputated: the first moral of society.

"A correction of the instincts: their detachment from ignorance—

"I despise those who demand of society that it ought to protect itself from those who would harm it. That is not enough by a long shot. Society is a body in which no member may be diseased without endangering the whole. A diseased member that corrupts [the reading of this word is not certain] has to be amputated: I shall name the amputable types of society."

[31] See the footnote to section 4 above.

[32] For a detailed discusion of this idea, see Kaufmann's *Nietzsche,* Chapter 11. Cf. also sections 1,053 *ff* below.

This is the most extreme form of nihilism: the nothing (the "meaningless"), eternally!

The European form of Buddhism: the energy of knowledge and strength compels this belief. It is the most *scientific* of all possible hypotheses. We deny end goals: if existence had one it would have to have been reached.

*

So one understands that an antithesis to pantheism is attempted here: for "everything perfect, divine, eternal" also compels a faith in the "eternal recurrence." Question: does morality make impossible this pantheistic affirmation of all things, too? At bottom, it is only the moral god that has been overcome. Does it make sense to conceive a god "beyond good and evil"? Would a pantheism in this sense be possible? Can we remove the idea of a goal from the process and then affirm the process in spite of this?— This would be the case if something were attained at every moment within this process—and always the same. Spinoza reached such an affirmative position in so far as every moment has a logical necessity, and with his basic instinct, which was logical, he felt a sense of triumph that the world should be constituted that way.

*

But his case is only a single case. Every basic character trait that is encountered at the bottom of every event, that finds expression in every event, would have to lead every individual who experienced it as his own basic character trait to welcome every moment of universal existence with a sense of triumph. The crucial point would be that one experienced this basic character trait in oneself as good, valuable—with pleasure.

*

It was morality that protected life against despair and the leap into nothing, among men and classes who were violated and oppressed by *men*: for it is the experience of being powerless against men, not against nature, that generates the most desperate embitterment against existence. Morality treated the violent despots, the doers of violence, the "masters" in general as the enemies against whom the common man must be protected, which means first of all encouraged and strengthened. Morality consequently taught men to hate and despise most profoundly what is the basic character trait of those who rule: their will to power. To abolish, deny, and dissolve this morality—that would mean looking at the best-hated drive with an opposite feeling and valuation. If the suffering and oppressed lost the faith that they have the right to despise the will to power, they would enter the phase of hopeless despair. This would be the case if this trait were essential to life and it could be shown that even in this will to morality this very "will to power" were hidden, and even this hatred and contempt were still a will to power. The oppressed would come to see that they were on the same plain with the oppressors, without prerogative, without higher rank.

*

Rather the opposite! There is nothing to life that has value, except the degree of power—assuming that life itself is the will to power. Morality guarded the underprivileged against nihilism by assigning to each an infinite value, a metaphysical value, and by placing each in an order that did not agree with the worldly order of rank and power: it taught resignation, meekness, etc. Supposing that the faith in this morality would perish, then the underprivileged would no longer have their comfort—and they would perish.

*

This perishing takes the form of self-destruction—the instinctive selection of that which must destroy. Symptoms of this self-destruction of the underprivileged: self-vivisection, poisoning, intoxication, romanticism, above all the instinctive need for actions that turn the powerful into mortal enemies (as it were, one breeds one's own hangmen); the will to destruction as the will of a still deeper instinct, the instinct of self-destruction, the will for nothingness.

*

Nihilism as a symptom that the underprivileged have no comfort left; that they destroy in order to be destroyed; that without morality they no longer have any reason to "resign themselves" —that they place themselves on the plain of the opposite principle and also want power by *compelling* the powerful to become their hangmen. This is the European form of Buddhism—*doing* No after all existence has lost its "meaning."

*

It is not that "distress" has grown: on the contrary. "God, morality, resignation," were remedies on terribly low rungs of misery: active nihilism appears in relatively much more favorable conditions. The feeling that morality has been overcome presupposes a fair degree of spiritual culture, and this in turn that one is relatively well off. A certain spiritual weariness that, owing to the long fight of philosophical opinions, has reached the most hopeless skepticism regarding all philosophy, is another sign of the by no means low position of these nihilists. Consider the situation in which the Buddha appeared. The doctrine of the eternal recurrence would have scholarly presuppositions (as did the Buddha's doctrine; e.g., the concept of causality, etc.).

*

What does "underprivileged" mean? Above all, physiologically—no longer politically. The unhealthiest kind of man in Europe (in all classes) furnishes the soil for this nihilism: they will experience the belief in the eternal recurrence as a curse, struck by which one no longer shrinks from any action; not to be extinguished passively but to extinguish everything that is so aim- and meaningless, although this is a mere convulsion, a blind rage at the insight that everything has been for eternities—even this moment of nihilism and lust for destruction.— It is the value of such a crisis that it purifies, that it pushes together related elements to perish of each other, that it assigns common tasks to men who have opposite ways of thinking—and it also brings to light the weaker and less secure among them and thus promotes an order of rank according to strength, from the point of view of health: those who command are recognized as those who command, those who obey as those who obey. Of course, outside every existing social order.

*

Who will prove to be the strongest in the course of this? The most moderate; those who do not require any extreme articles of faith; those who not only concede but love a fair amount of accidents and nonsense; those who can think of man with a considerable reduction of his value without becoming small and weak on that account: those richest in health who are equal to most misfortunes and therefore not so afraid of misfortunes—human beings who are sure of their power and represent the attained strength of humanity with conscious pride.

*

How would such a human being even think of the eternal recurrence?

56 (*Nov. 1887-March 1888*)
Periods of European Nihilism

The period of unclarity, of all kinds of tentative men who would conserve the old without letting go of the new.

The period of clarity: one understands that the old and the new are basically opposite, the old values born of declining and the new ones of ascending life—that all the old ideals are hostile to life (born of decadence and agents of decadence, even if in the magnificent Sunday clothes of morality). We understand the old and are far from strong enough for something new.

The period of the three great affects: contempt, pity, destruction.

The period of catastrophe: the advent of a doctrine that sifts men—driving the weak to decisions, and the strong as well—

II. HISTORY OF EUROPEAN NIHILISM

57 (*1884*)

My friends, it was hard for us when we were young: we suffered youth itself like a serious sickness. That is due to the time into which we have been thrown[33]—a time of extensive inner decay and disintegration, a time that with all its weaknesses, and even with its best strength, opposes the spirit of youth. Disintegration characterizes this time, and thus uncertainty: nothing stands firmly on its feet or on a hard faith in itself; one lives for tomorrow, as the day after tomorrow is dubious.[34] Everything on our way is slippery and dangerous, and the ice that still supports us has become thin: all of us feel the warm, uncanny breath of the thawing wind;[35] where we still walk, soon no one will be able to walk.

58 (*1885-1888*)

If this is not an age of decay and declining vitality, it is at least one of headlong and arbitrary *experimentation*:—and it is probable that a superabundance of bungled experiments should create an overall impression as of decay—and perhaps even decay itself.

59 (*1885-1886*)

Toward a History of the Modern Eclipse[36]

The state nomads (civil servants, etc.): without home.
The decline of the family.
The "good man" as a symptom of exhaustion.
Justice as will to power (breeding).

---

[33] *Geworfen.* In Heidegger's *Sein und Zeit* (1927; *Being and Time,* 1962), *Geworfenheit* (thrownness) becomes an important category (sections 29, 31, 38, 58, 68b).

[34] This is not how most of Nietzsche's contemporaries felt in 1884.

[35] Cf. *Zarathustra* III, "On Old and New Tablets," section 8 (*Portable Nietzsche,* p. 313).

[36] *Verdüsterung.*

Lasciviousness and neurosis.

Black music: whither refreshing music?

The anarchist.

Contempt for man, nausea.

Deepest difference: whether hunger or overabundance becomes creative? The former generates the ideals of romanticism.[37]

Nordic unnaturalness.

The need for alcoholica: the "distress" of the workers.

Philosophical nihilism.

60 (*1885*)

The slow emergence and rise of the middle and lower classes (including the lower kind of spirit and body), of which one finds many preludes before the French Revolution—and it would have taken place without the Revolution, too—on the whole, then, the predominance of the herd over all shepherds and bellwethers—involves

1. eclipse of the spirit (the fusion of a Stoic and a frivolous appearance of happiness, characteristic of noble cultures, decreases; one lets much suffering be seen and heard that one formerly bore and hid);

2. *moral* hypocrisy (a way of wishing to distinguish oneself not by means of morality, but by means of the herd virtues: pity, consideration, moderation, which are not recognized and honored outside the herd ability);

3. a *really* great amount of shared suffering (pity) and joy (the pleasure in large-scale associations found in all herd animals —"community spirit," "Fatherland," everything in which the individual does not count).

61 (*Summer-Fall 1883*)

Our time, with its aspiration to remedy and prevent accidental distresses and to wage preventive war against disagreeable possibilities, is a time of the *poor*. Our "rich"—are poorest of all. The true purpose of all riches is forgotten.

---

[37] Cf. *The Gay Science*, section 370 (in Book V, which was added only to the 2nd ed., 1887), and section 1,009 below.

62 (*Spring-Fall 1887*)

Critique of modern man (his moralistic mendaciousness):[38] —the "good man" corrupted and seduced by bad institutions (tyrants and priests); —reason as authority; —history as overcoming of errors; —the future as progress; —the Christian state ("the Lord of hosts"); —the Christian sex impulse (or marriage); —the kingdom of "justice" (the cult of "humanity"); —"freedom."

The romantic pose of modern man: —the noble man (Byron, Victor Hugo, George Sand); —noble indignation; —consecration through passion (as true "nature"); —siding with the oppressed and underprivileged: motto of the historians and novelists; —the Stoics of duty;—selflessness as art and knowledge;—altruism as the most mendacious form of egoism (utilitarianism), most sentimental egoism.

All this is eighteenth century. What, on the other hand, has *not* been inherited from it: insouciance, cheerfulness, elegance, brightness of the spirit. The tempo of the spirit has changed; the enjoyment of refinement and clarity of the spirit has given place to the enjoyment of color, harmony, mass, reality, etc. Sensualism in matters of the spirit. In short, it is the eighteenth century of *Rousseau.*

63 (*Jan.-Fall 1888*)

On the whole, a tremendous quantum of *humaneness* has been attained in present-day mankind. That this is not felt generally is itself a proof: we have become so sensitive concerning small states of distress that we unjustly ignore what has been attained.

Here one must make allowance for the existence of much decadence, and seen with such eyes our world has to look wretched and miserable. But such eyes have at all times seen the same things:

1. a certain overirritation even of the moral feelings;
2. the quantum of embitterment and eclipse that pessimism

[38] The parenthesis is printed in 1911, p. 499, but omitted in subsequent editions.

carries into judgments: these two together account for the predominance of the opposite notion, that our morality is in a bad way.

The fact of credit, of worldwide trade, of the means of transportation—here a tremendous mild trust in man finds expression.— Another contributing factor is

3. the emancipation of science from moral and religious purposes: a very good sign that, however, is usually misunderstood.

In my own way I attempt a justification of history.

64 (*Spring-Fall 1887*)

The second Buddhism. The nihilistic catastrophe that finishes Indian culture.— Early signs of it: The immense increase of pity. Spiritual weariness. The reduction of problems to questions of pleasure and displeasure. The war glory that provokes a counterstroke. Just as national demarcation provokes a countermovement, the most cordial "fraternity." The impossibility for religion to go on working with dogmas and fables.

65 (*Nov. 1887-March 1888*)

What is attacked deep down today is the instinct and the will of tradition: all institutions that owe their origins to this instinct violate the taste of the modern spirit.— At bottom, nothing is thought and done without the purpose of eradicating this sense for tradition. One considers tradition a fatality; one studies it, recognizes it (as "heredity"), but one does not *want* it. The tensing of a will over long temporal distances, the selection of the states and valuations that allow one to dispose of future centuries —precisely this is antimodern in the highest degree. Which goes to show that it is the disorganizing principles that give our age its character.

66 (*Spring-Fall 1887*)

"Be simple!"—for us complicated and elusive triers of the reins a demand that is a simple stupidity.— Be natural! But how if one happens to be "unnatural"?

67 (*1884*)

The former means for obtaining homogeneous, enduring characters for long generations: unalienable landed property, honoring the old (origin of the belief in gods and heroes as ancestors).

Now the breaking up of landed property belongs to the opposite tendency: newspapers (in place of daily prayers), railway, telegraph. Centralization of a tremendous number of different interests in a single soul, which for that reason must be very strong and protean.

68 (*March-June 1888*)

Why everything turns into *histrionics*.— Modern man lacks: the sure instinct (consequence of a long homogeneous form of activity of one kind of man); the inability to achieve anything perfect is merely a consequence of this: as an individual one can never make up for lost schooling.

That which creates a morality, a code of laws: the profound instinct that only automatism makes possible perfection in life and creation.

But now we have reached the opposite point; indeed, we wanted to reach it: the most extreme consciousness, man's ability to see through himself and history. With this we are practically as far as possible from perfection in being, doing, and willing: our desire, even our will for knowledge is a symptom of a tremendous decadence. We strive for the opposite of that which strong races, strong natures want—understanding is an ending.—

That science is possible in this sense that is cultivated today is proof that all elementary instincts, life's instincts of self-defense and protection, no longer function. We no longer collect, we squander the capital of our ancestors, even in the way in which we seek knowledge.—

69 (*1885-1886*)[39]

Nihilistic Trait

a. In the natural sciences ("meaninglessness"); causalism, mechanism. "Lawfulness" an *entr'acte*, a residue.

---

[39] According to 1911, p. 499, a through e were taken by the editor from one of Nietzsche's plans for a book, and there they comprised items 5

b. Ditto in politics: one lacks the faith in one's right, innocence; mendaciousness rules and serving the moment.

c. Ditto in economics: the abolition of slavery. The lack of a redeeming class, one that justifies—advent of anarchism. "Education"?

---

through 9. The whole plan is printed in 1911, p. 416 *ff*, and it seems appropriate to translate it here in full—mainly on account of its intrinsic interest, but also to show how the editor of the standard edition obtained some of his "aphorisms":

The Will to Power
Attempt at a Revaluation of all Values.
(In four books)

FIRST BOOK: *The danger of dangers* (presentation of nihilism as the *necessary consequence* of our valuations so far). Tremendous forces have been unleashed; but they conflict with each other; they *annihilate* each other. In a democratic commonwealth, where everybody is a specialist, the what-for? and for-whom? are lacking. The class [*Stand*] in which the thousandfold atrophy of all individuals (into mere functions) acquires *meaning*.

SECOND BOOK: *Critique of values* (logic, etc.). Everywhere the disharmony between the ideal and its individual conditions (e.g., honesty among Christians who are continually forced to lie).

THIRD BOOK: *The problem of the legislator* (including the history of solitude). The forces that have been unleashed must be harnessed again lest they annihilate each other; eyes have to be opened for the actual *increase* of strength.

FOURTH BOOK: *The hammer*. What would men have to be like whose valuations are the opposite? Men who have *all* the traits of the modern soul but are strong enough to transform them into so much health—their means for their task.

SILS MARIA. *Summer 1886.*

Plan of the first book

What is dawning is the opposition of the world we revere and the world we live and are. So we can abolish either our reverence or ourselves. The latter constitutes nihilism.

1. The advent of nihilism, theoretical and practical. Its faulty derivation (pessimism, its kinds: preludes of nihilism, although not necessary).

2. Christianity perishing of its morality. "God is truth"; "God is love"; "the just God."— The greatest event—"God is dead"—perceived dimly.

3. Morality, now without any sanction, no longer knows how to maintain itself. Eventually one *drops* the moral interpretation (echoes of the Christian value judgments still fill men's feelings).

4. But it was upon moral judgments that *value* was based so far; above all, the value of philosophy ("of the will to truth"). (The popular ideals—"the sage," "the prophet," "the saint"—have collapsed.)

5. *Nihilistic* trait in the natural sciences. . . .

[(5) through (9) appear above as (a) through (e).]

10. The whole European system of human aspirations has the feeling it is partly meaningless, partly even now "immoral." Probability of a new

d. Ditto in history: fatalism, Darwinism; the final attempts to read reason and divinity into it fail. Sentimentality in face of the past; one could not endure a biography!— (Here, too, phenomenalism: character as a mask; there are no facts.)

e. Ditto in art: romanticism and its counterstroke (aversion against romantic ideals and lies). The latter, moral as a sense of greater truthfulness, but pessimistic. Pure "artists" (indifferent toward content). (Father-confessor psychology and puritan psychology, two forms of psychological romanticism: but even its counterproposal, the attempt to adopt a purely artistic

---

Buddhism. The greatest danger.— "How are truthfulness, love, and justice related to the *actual* world?" Not at all!—

For the second book

Origin and critique of moral valuations. These two things don't coincide, as is often supposed (this belief itself is the result of a moral judgment to the effect that "something that has come to be in such and such a way is worth little because its origin is immoral"). Standard for determining the value of moral valuations: critique of the words, "Improvement, perfecting, enhancement."

The basic fact that has been overlooked: the contradiction between "becoming more moral" and the enhancement and strengthening of the type of man.

Homo natura. The "will to power."

For the third book

The will to power.

How those men would have to be constituted who would accomplish this revaluation in themselves.

The order of rank as an order of power: war and danger as presuppositions that a rank maintains its conditions. The grandiose model: man in nature—the weakest, cleverest being making itself master and subjugating the more stupid elements.

For the fourth book

The *greatest* struggle: for that a new *weapon* is needed. The hammer: to conjure up a terrible decision, to confront Europe with the final choice whether its will "wills" its own destruction [*Untergang*]. Prevention of the decline into mediocrity [*Vermittelmässigung*]. Rather even destruction [*Lieber noch Untergang*]!

In the preface to *Twilight of the Idols,* written in 1888 and published in January 1889, the image of the hammer is sublimated: "For once to pose questions here with a *hammer,* and, perhaps, to hear as a reply that famous hollow sound which speaks of bloated entrails—what a delight for one who has ears even behind his ears, for me, an old psychologist . . ."

For the dictum, "God is dead," see *The Gay Science,* section 125 (*Portable Nietzsche,* pp. 95 *f*) and *Zarathustra,* Prologue (*ibid.*, p. 124); also Kaufmann's *Nietzsche,* Chapter 3.

attitude toward man—even there the opposite valuation is not yet ventured!)

70 (*1885-1886*)

Against the doctrine of the influence of the milieu and external causes: the force within is infinitely superior; much that looks like external influence is merely its adaptation from within. The very same milieus can be interpreted and exploited in opposite ways: there are no facts.— A genius is not explained in terms of such conditions of his origin.[40]

71 (*Spring-Fall 1887; rev. Spring-Fall 1888*)

"Modernity" in the perspective of the metaphor of nourishment and digestion.—

Sensibility immensely more irritable (—dressed up moralistically: the increase in *pity*—); the abundance of disparate impressions greater than ever: cosmopolitanism in foods, literatures, newspapers, forms, tastes, even landscapes. The tempo of this influx *prestissimo;* the impressions erase each other; one instinctively resists taking in anything, taking anything deeply, to "digest" anything; a weakening of the power to digest results from this. A kind of adaptation to this flood of impressions takes place: men unlearn spontaneous action, they merely react to stimuli from outside. They spend their strength partly in assimilating things, partly in defense, partly in opposition. *Profound weakening of spontaneity:* the historian, critic, analyst, the interpreter, the observer, the collector, the reader—all of them *reactive* talents —all science!

Artificial change of one's nature into a "mirror"; interested but, as it were, merely epidermically interested; a coolness on principle, a balance, a fixed low temperature closely underneath the thin surface on which warmth, movement, "tempest," and the play of waves are encountered.

Opposition of external mobility and a certain deep heaviness and weariness.

---

[40] Cf. section 109.

72 (*Jan.-Fall 1888*)

Where does our modern world belong—to exhaustion or ascent?— Its manifoldness and unrest conditioned by the attainment of the highest level of consciousness.

73 (*Spring-Fall 1887*)

Overwork, curiosity and sympathy—our *modern vices.*

74 (*Spring-Fall 1887*)

Toward a characterization of *"modernity."*— Overabundant development of intermediary forms; atrophy of types; traditions break off, schools; the overlordship of the instincts (prepared philosophically: the unconscious *worth more*) after the will power, the willing of end *and* means, has been weakened.

75 (*1885*)

An able craftsman or scholar cuts a fine figure when he takes pride in his art and looks on life content and satisfied. But nothing looks more wretched than when a shoemaker or schoolmaster gives us to understand with a suffering mien that he was really born for something better. There is nothing better than what is good—and good is having some ability and using that to create, *Tüchtigkeit* or *virtù* in the Italian Renaissance sense.

Today, in our time when the state has an absurdly fat stomach, there are in all fields and departments, in addition to the real workers, also "representatives"; e.g., besides the scholars also scribblers, besides the suffering classes also garrulous, boastful ne'er-do-wells who "represent" this suffering, not to speak of the professional politicians who are well off while "representing" distress with powerful lungs before a parliament. Our modern life is extremely expensive owing to the large number of intermediaries; in an ancient city, on the other hand, and, echoing that, also in many cities in Spain and Italy, one appeared oneself and would have given a hoot to such modern representatives and intermediaries—or a kick!

76 (*Spring-Fall 1887*)

The predominance of dealers and intermediaries in spiritual matters, too: the scribbler, the "representative," the historian (who fuses past and present), the exotician and cosmopolitan, the intermediaries between science and philosophy, the semitheologians.

77 (*1883-1888*)

Nothing to date has nauseated me more than the parasites of the spirit: in our unhealthy Europe one already finds them everywhere—and they have the best conscience in the world. Perhaps a little dim, a little *air pessimiste,* but in the main voracious, dirty, dirtying, creeping in, nestling, thievish, scurvy—and as innocent as all little sinners and microbes. They live off the fact that other people have spirit and squander it: they know that it is of the very essence of the rich spirit to squander itself carelessly, without petty caution, from day to day.— For the spirit is a bad householder and pays no heed to how everybody lives and feeds on it.

78 (*1885-1886*)
Histrionics

The colorfulness of modern man and its charm. Essentially concealment and satiety.

The scribbler.

The politician (in "the nationalist swindle").

Histrionics in the arts:

lack of probity in prior training and schooling (Fromentin);[41]

the romantics (lack of philosophy and science and superabundance of literature);

the novelists (Walter Scott, but also the Nibelungen monsters along with the most nervous music);

the lyric poets.

Being "scientific."

Virtuosos (Jews).

Popular ideals overcome, but not yet in the eyes of the people: the saint, the sage, the prophet.

---

[41] Eugène Fromentin (1820-1876), French painter.

79 (*Spring-Fall 1887*)

The modern spirit's lack of discipline, dressed up in all sorts of moral fashions.— The showy words are: tolerance (for "the incapacity for Yes and No"); *la largeur de sympathie*[42] (= one-third indifference, one-third curiosity, one-third pathological irritability); "objectivity" (lack of personality, lack of will, incapacity for "love"); "freedom" versus rules (romanticism); "truth" versus forgery and lies (naturalism); being "scientific" (the *"document humain"*: in other words, the novel of colportage and addition in place of composition); "passion" meaning disorder and immoderation; "depth" meaning confusion, the profuse chaos of symbols.

80 (*Nov. 1887-March 1888*)

Toward a critique of the big words.— I am full of suspicion and malice against what they call "ideals": this is *my* pessimism, to have recognized how the "higher feelings" are a source of misfortune and man's loss of value.

One is deceived every time one expects "progress" from an ideal; every time so far the victory of the ideal has meant a retrograde movement.

Christianity, the revolution, the abolition of slavery, equal rights, philanthropy, love of peace, justice, truth: all these big words have value only in a fight, as flags: *not* as realities but as *showy words* for something quite different (indeed, opposite!).[43]

81 (*1883-1888*)

One knows the kind of human being who has fallen in love with the motto, *tout comprendre c'est tout pardonner.*[44] It is the weak, it is above all the disappointed: if there is something to be forgiven in all, perhaps there is also something to be despised in all. It is the philosophy of disappointment that wraps itself so humanely in pity and looks sweet.

These are romantics whose faith flew the coop: now they

---

[42] The breadth of sympathy.

[43] Cf. *Twilight*, section 38 (*Portable Nietzsche*, p. 541).

[44] To understand all is to forgive all.

at least want to watch how everything passes and goes. They call it *l'art pour l'art,* "objectivity," etc.

82 (*Spring-Fall 1887*)

Chief symptoms of pessimism: the *dîners chez* Magny;[45] Russian pessimism (Tolstoy, Dostoevsky); aesthetic pessimism, *l'art pour l'art,* "description" (romantic and antiromantic pessimism); epistemological pessimism (Schopenhauer, phenomenalism); anarchistic pessimism; the "religion of pity," Buddhistic premovement; cultural pessimism (exoticism, cosmopolitanism); moralistic pessimism: I myself.

83 (*Spring-Fall 1887*)

"Without the Christian faith," Pascal thought, "you, no less than nature and history, will become for yourselves *un monstre et*

---

[45] Cf. Nietzsche's Letters to Gast (*Gesammelte Briefe,* vol. IV), November 10, 1887: "The second volume of the *Journal des Goncourts* has appeared: the most interesting new publication. It covers the years 1862-1865; here the famous *dîners chez* Magny are described most vividly, those *dîners* at which the cleverest [*geistreichste*] and most skeptical band of Parisian spirits of that time assembled twice a month (Sainte-Beuve, Flaubert, Théophile Gautier, Taine, Renan, the Goncourts, Schérer, Gavani, occasionally Turgenev, etc.). Exasperated pessimism, cynicism, and nihilism alternating with much exuberance [*Ausgelassenheit*] and good humor; I myself shouldn't fit in badly at all. I know these gentlemen by heart, *so well* that I am really weary of them [*sie satt habe*]. One must be more radical: at bottom they all lack the same thing—*'la force.'* " See also section 915 below.

Of the men enumerated in the parenthesis, all but the last three are mentioned in *The Will to Power* (see the Index), and of these all but Gautier are also mentioned in the books Nietzsche himself published. In *Twilight,* "Skirmishes," whole sections are devoted to Renan (#2) and Sainte Beuve (#3), the brothers Goncourt are characterized in sections 1 and 7; and Flaubert is mentioned often, also in Nietzsche's other books. Practically all of these references are hostile. (For Renan see also my note on *Genealogy* III, section 26.) Hippolyte Taine, on the other hand, is mentioned favorably in *Beyond Good and Evil* and in the *Genealogy,* and Nietzsche corresponded with him.

Edmond Henri Adolphe Schérer (1815-89), ordained and appointed to a professorship in the Ecole Evangélique at Geneva in 1843, resigned six years later and gradually abandoned Protestant doctrine. He became a Hegelian, settled in Paris, and made his reputation as a literary critic.

Gavarni was the pen name of Sulpice Guillaume Chevalier (1801-66), an outstanding Parisian caricaturist. He is said to have initiated the *dîners chez* Magny, mentioned in the text.

Ivan Sergeyevich Turgenev (1818-83), the great Russian novelist, is never mentioned in Nietzsche's books.

un chaos." This prophecy we have fulfilled, after the feeble-optimistic eighteenth century had prettified and rationalized man.

Schopenhauer and Pascal.— In an important sense, Schopenhauer is the first to take up again the movement of Pascal: *un monstre et un chaos,* consequently something to be negated.— History, nature, man himself.

"Our inability to know the truth is the consequence of our corruption, our moral decay"; thus Pascal. And thus, at bottom, Schopenhauer. "The deeper the corruption of reason, the more necessary the doctrine of salvation"—or, in Schopenhauer's terms, negation.

84 (*Spring-Fall 1887*)

Schopenhauer as throwback (state before the revolution): Pity, sensuality, art, weakness of the will, catholicism of spiritual cravings—that is good eighteenth century *au fond.*[46]

Schopenhauer's basic misunderstanding of the *will* (as if craving, instinct, drive were the *essence* of will) is typical: lowering the value of the will to the point of making a real mistake. Also hatred against willing; attempt to see something higher, indeed that which is higher and valuable, in willing no more, in "being a subject *without* aim and purpose" (in the "pure subject free of will"). Great symptom of the *exhaustion* or the *weakness* of the *will*: for the will is precisely that which treats cravings as their master and appoints to them their way and measure.[47]

85 (*Jan.-Fall 1888*)

The unworthy attempt has been made to see Wagner and Schopenhauer as types of mental illness: one would gain an incomparably more essential insight by making more precise scientifically the type of decadence both represent.

86 (*1888*)

Your[48] Henrik Ibsen has become very clear to me. For all

---

[46] At bottom.

[47] But see section 46.

[48] The beginning of this note was prompted by Georg Brandes' letters to Nietzsche, January 11 and March 7, 1888, as is pointed out correctly in

his robust idealism and "will to truth" he did not dare to liberate himself from the illusionism of morality that speaks of "freedom" without wishing to admit to itself what freedom is: the second stage in the metamorphosis of the "will to power"—for those who lack freedom. On the first stage one demands justice from those who are in power. On the second, one speaks of "freedom"—that is, one wants to get away from those in power. On the third, one speaks of *"equal rights"*—that is, as long as one has not yet gained

---

1911, p. 499. The dating in the Musarion edition reads: "Spring-Fall 1887; revised 1888." The attempt of the editors of the standard edition to turn this kind of a hasty note into an "aphorism" by omitting "Your" in the text (the word is duly mentioned in the note on p. 499) is as unfortunate as it is in keeping with their procedure throughout much of the book. All subsequent editions, including Schlechta's, also omit "Your."

On January 11, 1888, Brandes had written Nietzsche that he was sending him the proofs of a collection of his essays: ". . . The essay on Ibsen is relatively the best. . . . There is a Nordic writer whose works would interest you. *Søren Kierkegaard;* he lived 1813-1855 and is in my view one of the most profound psychologists of all time. . . ."

Nietzsche replied February 19: ". . . I have decided that during my next trip to Germany I want to study the psychological problem of Kierkegaard. . . ." Ibsen he did not mention—and he never got around to reading Kierkegaard.

On March 7, Brandes wrote Nietzsche: "Ibsen must interest you as a personality. Unfortunately he does not have the same stature as a human being that he has as a poet. As a mind he has been very dependent on Kierkegaard and is still rather full of theology. Bjornson actually became a common lay preacher during his last phase. . . ."

And November 23, 1888, Brandes wrote Nietzsche: "Believe me, I make propaganda for you wherever I can. Only last week I seriously urged Henrik Ibsen to study your works. There is a way in which you are related to him, too, although very distantly. This oddball is great and strong and unfriendly but nevertheless *deserving* of love. Strindberg will be pleased that you esteem him. . . ."

Nietzsche refers to Ibsen in two other places: in section 747 in *The Will to Power* and in *Ecce Homo,* Chapter III, section 5, where he says: "A whole species of malignant 'idealism'—which, incidentally, is encountered among men, too; for example in Henrik Ibsen, this typical old maid—has the aim of *poisoning* the good conscience, that which is natural in sexual love."

What Nietzsche had actually read of Ibsen's works is uncertain. His friend Franz Overbeck wrote him on October 14, 1888: "In Munich I have also had a few strange impressions in the theater, and have scarcely ever seen a more skillful German play than *The Pillars of Society* by Ibsen, by whom I had not known anything before this. . . ."

Michael Meyer, the Ibsen scholar and translator, informs me that the only record he has found of any comment on Nietzsche by Ibsen is in an interview printed in the newspaper *Ørebladet,* November 26, 1900, when Ibsen was 72: "A great thinker has died since we last spoke, Herr Ibsen—Nietzsche. 'Yes. I wasn't well acquainted with his work. It wasn't until a few years ago that he really became well known. He had a remarkable

superiority one wants to prevent one's competitors from growing in power.

87 (*Spring-Fall 1887*)

Decline of *Protestantism:* understood as a halfway house both theoretically and historically. Actual superiority of Catholicism; the feeling of Protestantism extinguished to such an extent that the strongest *anti-Protestant* movements are no longer experienced as such (for example, Wagner's *Parsifal*). All of the higher regions of the spirit in France are *Catholic* in their instincts; Bismarck realizes that Protestantism simply doesn't exist any more.

88 (*Spring-Fall 1887*)

Protestantism, that spiritually unclean and boring form of decadence in which Christianity has been able so far to preserve itself in the mediocre north: valuable for knowledge as something complex and a halfway house, in so far as it brought together in the same heads experiences of different orders and origins.

89 (*March-June 1888*)

How did the German spirit transform Christianity!— And to stick to Protestantism: how much beer there is in Protestant Christianity! Can one even imagine a spiritually staler, lazier, more comfortably relaxed form of the Christian faith than that of the average Protestant in Germany?[49]

---

talent, but his philosophy prevented him from becoming popular in our democratic age.' Some say that Nietzsche was a spirit who emerged from the dark—a Satan— 'Satan—no. No, Nietzsche wasn't that.' " Which isn't much. And according to Meyer, Ibsen often said he had "read little of Kierkegaard and understood less."

Nevertheless it is widely taken for granted—and perhaps rightly—that Ibsen's *Brand* was profoundly influenced by Kierkegaard and Ibsen's *An Enemy of the People* brings to mind Kierkegaard's paean on "That Individual," with its refrain "The crowd is untruth" (found, e.g., in my *Existentialism from Dostoevsky to Sartre,* 1956, pp. 92-99). And *Beyond Good and Evil* (1886) contains some very striking parallels to *An Enemy of the People* (written in 1882), which evidently are not due to any influence of the play on Nietzsche's book: see my note on section 213 of *Beyond Good and Evil,* as well as section 4 of my "Translator's Preface."

[49] *"Ist eine geistig verdumpftere, faulere, gliederstreckendere Form des Christen-Glaubens noch denkbar, als die eines deutschen Durchschnitts-Protestanten?" Faul* can mean "rotten" as well as "lazy"; *gliederstreckend* means literally "limb-stretching."

That's what I call a modest version of Christianity! A homoeopathy of Christianity is what I call it.

One reminds me that today we also encounter an *immodest* Protestantism—that of the court chaplains[50] and anti-Semitic speculators: but nobody has claimed yet that any "spirit" whatever "moved" on the faces of these waters.— That is merely a more indecent form of Christianity, by no means more sensible.

90 (*Jan.-Fall 1888*)

Progress.— Let us not be deceived! Time marches forward; we'd like to believe that everything that is in it also marches forward—that the development is one that moves forward.

The most level-headed are led astray by this illusion. But the nineteenth century does not represent progress over the sixteenth; and the German spirit of 1888 represents a regress from the German spirit of 1788.

"Mankind" does not advance, it does not even exist. The overall aspect is that of a tremendous experimental laboratory in which a few successes are scored, scattered throughout all ages, while there are untold failures, and all order, logic, union, and obligingness are lacking. How can we fail to recognize that the ascent of Christianity is a movement of decadence?— That the German Reformation is a recrudescence of Christian barbarism?— That the Revolution[51] destroyed the instinct for a grand organization of society?

Man represents no progress over the animal: the civilized tenderfoot is an abortion compared to the Arab and Corsican; the Chinese is a more successful type, namely more durable, than the European.

91 (*1885*)
On German Pessimism[52]

The eclipse, the pessimistic coloring, comes necessarily in the

[50] An illusion to the anti-Semitic Hofprediger Adolf Stöcker (1835-1909), who was then court chaplain in Berlin and the founder of the Christian Socialist Workers' Party. As a member of the Prussian diet, he sat and voted with the Conservatives.

[51] French Revolution.

[52] This title was omitted in the standard editions but is mentioned in 1911, p. 499.

wake of the Enlightenment. Around 1770 the decline of cheerfulness began to be noticed; women, with that feminine instinct which always sides with virtue, supposed that immorality was the cause. Galiani hit the nail on the head: he cites Voltaire's verse:

Un monstre gai vaut mieux
Qu'un sentimental ennuyeux.[53]

When I believe now that I am a few centuries ahead in Enlightenment not only of Voltaire but even of Galiani, who was far profounder—how far must I have got in the increase of darkness![54] And this is really the case, and I bewared in time, with some sort of regret, of the German and Christian narrowness and inconsequence of pessimism à la Schopenhauer or, worse, Leopardi, and sought out the most quintessential forms (Asia).[55] But in order to endure this type of extreme pessimism (it can be perceived here and there in my *Birth of Tragedy*) and to live alone "without God and morality" I had to invent a counterpart for myself. Perhaps I know best why man alone laughs: he alone suffers so deeply that he *had* to invent laughter. The unhappiest and most melancholy animal is, as fitting, the most cheerful.

92 (*1883-1888*)

Regarding German culture, I have always had the feeling of *decline*. This fact, that I first became acquainted with a type in decline, has often made me unfair to the *whole* phenomenon of European culture. The Germans always come after the others, much later: they are carrying something in the depths; e.g.,—

Dependence on other countries; e.g., *Kant*—Rousseau, Sensualists, Hume, Swedenborg.

Schopenhauer—Indians and romanticism, Voltaire.

---

[53] *A gay monster is worth more*
Than a sentimental bore.
Nietzsche omitted the text of this verse, which was inserted in the book by Peter Gast; cf. section 35 above.

[54] *In der Verdüsterung.*

[55] According to 1911, p. 499, the MS continued at this point: "Among those thinkers who developed pessimism further I do not include Eduard von Hartmann whom I'd far sooner lump with 'agreeable literature'. . . ." This was presumably omitted in the 1906 edition because Hartmann, born in 1842 (two years before Nietzsche), did not die until 1906; but although the passage was printed in the notes at the end of the 1911 volume, it was omitted in all subsequent editions.

Wagner—French cult of the gruesome and of grand opera, Paris and the flight into primeval states (marriage with the sister). —The law of the latecomers (province to Paris, Germany to France). Why the Germans of all people discovered the Greek spirit (the more one develops a drive, the more attractive does it become to plunge for once into its opposite).

Music is swan song.[56]

93 (*Jan.-Fall 1888*)

Renaissance and Reformation.— What does the Renaissance prove? That the reign of the individual has to be brief. The squandering is too great; the very possibility of collecting and capitalizing is lacking; and exhaustion follows immediately. These are times when everything is *spent,* when the very strength is spent with which one collects, capitalizes, and piles riches upon riches.— Even the opponents of such movements are forced into an absurd waste of energy; they, too, soon become exhausted, spent, desolate.

In the Reformation we possess a wild and vulgar counterpart to the Italian Renaissance, born of related impulses; only in the retarded north, which had remained coarse, they had to don a religious disguise; for there the concept of the higher life had not yet detached itself from that of the religious life.

Through the Reformation, too, the individual sought freedom; "everybody his own priest" is also a mere formula of libertinage. In truth, one word was enough—"evangelical freedom"—and all instincts that had reason to remain hidden broke out like wild dogs, the most brutal requirements suddenly acquired the courage to face themselves, and everything seemed justified.— One was careful not to understand what liberty one had really meant at bottom; one shut one's eyes before oneself.— But shutting one's eyes and moistening one's lips with enthusiastic orations did not prevent one's hands from grasping whatever could be grabbed, and the belly became the god of the "free evangel," and all the cravings of revenge and envy satisfied themselves with insatiable rage.—

This took a while; then exhaustion set in, just as it had in the south of Europe—and here, too, a *vulgar* kind of exhaustion, a general *ruere in servitium.*[57]— The *indecent* century of Germany arrived.—

---

[56] *"Musik ist Ausklingen."*

[57] "Plunging into servitude."

94 (*1884*)

Chivalry as the conquered position of power: its gradual breaking up (and in part transition into what is more spread out, bourgeois). In La Rochefoucauld we find a consciousness of the true motive springs of noblesse of the mind—and a view of these motive springs that is darkened by Christianity.

The French Revolution as the continuation of Christianity. Rousseau is the seducer: he again unfetters woman who is henceforth represented in an ever more interesting manner—as suffering. Then the slaves and Mrs. Beecher-Stowe. Then the poor and the workers. Then the vice addicts and the sick—all this is moved into the foreground (even to develop sympathy for the genius one no longer knows any other way for the past five hundred years than to represent him as the bearer of great suffering!). Next come the curse on voluptuousness (Baudelaire and Schopenhauer); the most decided conviction that the lust to rule is the greatest vice;[58] the perfect certainty that morality and disinterestedness are identical concepts and that the "happiness of all" is a goal worth striving for (i.e., the kingdom of heaven of Christ). We are well along on the way: the kingdom of heaven of the poor in spirit has begun.— Intermediary stages: the bourgeois (a parvenu on account of money) and the worker (on account of the machine).

Comparison of Greek culture and that of the French in the age of Louis XIV. Decided faith in oneself. A leisure class whose members make things difficult for themselves and exercise much self-overcoming. The power of form, the will to give form to oneself. "Happiness" admitted as a goal. Much strength and energy behind the emphasis on forms. The delight in looking at a life that seems so easy.— To the French, the Greeks looked like children.

95 (*Spring-Fall 1887*)
The Three Centuries

Their different sensibilities are best expressed thus:

Aristocratism: Descartes, rule of reason, testimony of the sovereignty of the will;

---

[58] Cf. the chapter "On the Three Great Evils" in *Zarathustra* III (*Portable Nietzsche*, p. 298).

Feminism: Rousseau, rule of feeling, testimony of the sovereignty of the senses, mendacious;

Animalism: Schopenhauer, rule of craving, testimony of the sovereignty of animality, more honest but gloomy.

The seventeenth century is aristocratic, imposes order, looks down haughtily upon the animalic, is severe against the heart, not cozy, without sentiment, "un-German," averse to what is burlesque and what is natural, inclined to generalizations and sovereign confronted with the past—for it believes in itself. Much beast of prey *au fond,* much ascetic habit to remain master. The century of strong will; also of strong passion.

The eighteenth century is dominated by woman, given to enthusiasm, full of *esprit,* shallow, but with a spirit in the service of what is desirable, of the heart, libertine in the enjoyment of what is most spiritual, and undermines all authorities; intoxicated, cheerful, clear, humane, false before itself, much canaille *au fond,* sociable.—

The nineteenth century is more animalic and subterranean, uglier, more realistic and vulgar, and precisely for that reason "better," "more honest," more submissive before every kind of "reality," truer; but weak in will, but sad and full of dark cravings, but fatalistic. Not full of awe and reverence for either "reason" or "heart"; deeply convinced of the rule of cravings (Schopenhauer spoke of "will"; but nothing is more characteristic of his philosophy than the absence of all genuine willing). Even morality reduced to one instinct ("pity").

Auguste Comte is a continuation of the eighteenth century (domination of *coeur* over *la tête,* sensualism in the theory of knowledge, altruistic enthusiasm).

That science has become sovereign to such a degree proves how the nineteenth century has rid itself of the domination of ideals. A certain frugality of desire makes possible our scientific curiosity and severity—which is *our* kind of virtue.—

Romanticism is an echo of the eighteenth century; a kind of piled-high desire for its enthusiasm in the grand style (as a matter of fact, a good deal of histrionics and self-deception: one wanted to represent strong natures and grand passions).

The nineteenth century looks instinctively for theories that seem to justify its fatalistic submission to matters of fact. Already *Hegel's* success against "sentimentality" and romantic idealism was due to his fatalistic way of thinking, to his faith in the greater reason on the side of the victorious, to his justification of the actual "state" (in place of "mankind," etc.).—

Schopenhauer: we are something stupid and, at best, even something that cancels itself.[59] Success of determinism, of the genealogical derivation of obligations that had formerly been considered absolute, the doctrine of milieu and adaptation, the reduction of will to reflexes, the denial of the will as an "efficient cause"; finally—a real rechristening: one sees so little will that the word becomes free to designate something else. Further theories: the doctrine of objectivity—"will-less" contemplation—as the only road to truth; also to beauty (—also the faith in the "genius" to justify a right to submission); mechanism, the calculable rigidity of the mechanical process; the alleged "naturalism," elimination of the choosing, judging, interpreting subject as a principle—

Kant, with his "practical reason" and his moral fanaticism is wholly eighteenth century; still entirely outside the historical movement; without any eye for the actuality of his time, e.g., Revolution; untouched by Greek philosophy; fanciful visionary of the concept of duty; sensualist with the backdrop of the pampering of dogmatism.—

The movement back to Kant in our century is a movement back to the eighteenth century: one wants to regain a right to the old ideals and the old enthusiasm—for that reason an epistemology that "sets boundaries," which means that it permits one to posit as one may see fit a beyond of reason.—

Hegel's way of thinking is not far different from *Goethe's*: one needs only to listen to Goethe about *Spinoza*. Will to deify the universe and life in order to find *repose* and *happiness* in contemplation and in getting to the bottom of things; Hegel seeks reason everywhere—before reason one may submit and acquiesce. In Goethe a kind of almost *joyous* and *trusting fatalism* that does not revolt, that does not flag, that seeks to form a totality out of himself, in the faith that only in the totality everything redeems itself and appears good and justified.[60]

---

[59] *Etwas Sich-selbst-Aufhebendes. Aufheben,* one of Hegel's favorite terms, is an ordinary German word that can mean cancel, preserve, and lift up. For a detailed discussion of this term see Walter Kaufmann, *Hegel,* Doubleday, Garden City, 1965, sections 37 and 42.

[60] Cf. *Twilight,* "Skirmishes," section 49 (*Portable Nietzsche,* p. 553). Indeed, long after adding this note I found in 1911, p. 500, that "in the manuscript this aph[orism—*sic!*] is followed by a preliminary version" of that section. The above is surely a mere note; section 49 *is* an "aphorism."

96 (*Spring-Fall 1887*)

Period of the *Enlightenment*—followed by the period of *sentimentality*. To what extent Schopenhauer belongs to "sentimentality" (Hegel to spirituality).[61]

97 (*Spring-Fall 1887*)

The seventeenth century suffers of man as of a sum of contradictions (*"l'amas de contradictions"* that we are); it seeks to discover, order, excavate man—while the eighteenth century seeks to forget what is known of man's nature in order to assimilate him to its utopia. "Superficial, tender, humane"—enthusiastic about "man"—

The seventeenth century seeks to erase the tracks of the individual to make the work look as similar to life as possible. The eighteenth uses the work in an attempt to arouse interest in the author. The seventeenth century seeks in art—art, a piece of culture; the eighteenth uses art to make propaganda for reforms of a social and political nature.

"Utopia," the "ideal man," the deification of nature, the vanity of posing, the subordination to propaganda for social goals, charlatanism—these are our gifts from the eighteenth century.

The style of the seventeenth century: *propre, exact et libre.*

The strong individual, self-sufficient or zealously occupied before God—and this modern obtrusiveness of authors who all but leap out at you—these furnish some contrast. "To perform" —compare that with the scholars of Port-Royal.

Alfieri[62] had a sense for grand style.

Hatred of the burlesque (undignified), lack of a sense for nature belong to the seventeenth century.

98 (*Spring-Fall 1887*)

Against Rousseau.— *Unfortunately,* man is no longer evil enough; Rousseau's opponents who say "man is a beast of prey" are unfortunately wrong. Not the corruption of man but the extent to which he has become tender and moralized is his curse.[63]

---

[61] The two German terms here are *Empfindsamkeit* and *Geistigkeit.*

[62] Count Vittorio Alfieri (1749-1803), Italian dramatist.

[63] Cf. *Twilight,* "Skirmishes," section 37 (*Portable Nietzsche,* p. 538).

Precisely in the sphere that Rousseau fought most violently one could find the *relatively* still strong and well-turned-out type of man (those in whom the grand affects were still unbroken: will to power, will to enjoyment, will and capacity to command). The man of the eighteenth century has to be compared with the man of the Renaissance (also with the man of the seventeenth century in France), so that one feels what is at stake: Rousseau is a symptom of self self-contempt and heated vanity—both signs that the domineering will is lacking: he moralizes and, as a man of rancor, seeks the cause of his wretchedness in the ruling classes.

99 (*Spring-Fall 1887*)

Against Rousseau.[64]— The state of nature is terrible, man is a beast of prey; our civilization represents a tremendous triumph over this beast-of-prey nature: thus argued Voltaire. He felt the mitigation, the subtleties, the spiritual joys of the civilized state; he despised narrowmindedness, also in the form of virtue, and the lack of delicatesse, also among ascetics and monks.

The moral reprehensibility of man seemed to preoccupy Rousseau; with the words "unjust" and "cruel" one can best stir up the instincts of the oppressed who otherwise smart under the ban of the *vetitum* and disfavor, so their conscience advises them against rebellious cravings. Such emancipators seek one thing above all: to give their party the grand accents and poses of the higher nature.

100 (*Spring-Fall 1887*)

Rousseau: the rule based on feeling; nature as the source of justice; man perfects himself to the extent to which he approaches nature (according to Voltaire, to the extent to which he moves away from nature). The very same epochs are for one ages of the progress of humanity; for the other, times when injustice and inequality grow worse.

Voltaire still comprehended *umanità* in the Renaissance sense; also *virtù* (as "high culture"); he fights for the cause of the *"honnêtes gens"* and *"de la bonne compagnie,"*[65] the cause of

---

[64] This heading was changed by the editors to read *"Voltaire—Rousseau."*

[65] These terms might be translated as humanity, virtue, honorable people,

taste, of science, of the arts, of progress itself and civilization.

The fight began around 1760: the citizen of Geneva and *le seigneur de Ferney*.[66] Only from that moment on Voltaire becomes the man of his century, the philosopher, the representative of tolerance and unbelief (till then merely *un bel esprit*).[67] Envy and hatred of Rousseau's success impelled him forward, "to the heights."

Pour "la canaille" un dieu remunerateur et vengeur[68]—Voltaire.

Critique of both points of view in regard to the *value of civilization*. The social invention is for Voltaire the most beautiful there is: there is no higher goal than to maintain and perfect it; precisely this is *honnêteté*,[69] to respect social conventions; virtue as obedience to certain necessary "prejudices" in favor of the preservation of "society." *Missionary of culture*, aristocrat, representative of the victorious, ruling classes and their valuations. But Rousseau remained a *plebeian*, also as *homme de lettres*;[70] that was *unheard of*; his impudent contempt of all that was not he himself.

What was *sick* in Rousseau was admired and *imitated* most. (Lord Byron related to him; also worked himself up into sublime poses and into vindictive rancor; sign of "meanness"; later attained balance through Venice and comprehended what produces more ease and well-being—*l'insouciance*.)[71]

Rousseau is proud in regard to what he is, in spite of his origins; but he is beside himself when one reminds him of it.—

Rousseau, beyond a doubt, mentally disturbed; in Voltaire an uncommon health and light touch. *The rancor of the sick;* the periods of his insanity also those of his contempt of man and his mistrust.

The defense of *providence* by Rousseau (against the pessimism of Voltaire): he *needed* God in order to be able to cast a curse upon society and civilization; everything had to be good in itself

---

and good society, but each of them has a distinctive flavor in the original language, which accounts for Nietzsche's use of foreign words.

[66] The squire of Ferney. In the MS erroneously: Tourney.

[67] A wit.

[68] For the rabble, a rewarding and avenging god.

[69] Decency.

[70] Man of letters.

[71] Nonchalance.

because God had created it; *only man has corrupted men.* The "good man" as the natural man was pure fantasy; but with the dogma of God's authorship it seemed probable and well-founded.

Romanticism à la Rousseau: passion ("the sovereign right of passion"); "naturalness"; the fascination of madness (folly included in greatness); the absurd vanity of the weak man; the rancor of the mob as judge ("for a hundred years now, a sick man has been accepted as a leader in politics").[72]

101 (*Spring-Fall 1887*)

Kant: makes the epistemological skepticism of the English possible for Germans:

1. by enlisting for it the sympathy of the moral and religious needs of the Germans; just as the later philosophers of the Academy used skepticism for the same reason, as a preparation for Platonism (*vide* Augustin); and as Pascal used even moralistic skepticism in order to excite the need for faith ("to justify it");

2. by scholastically involuting and curlicueing it and thus making it acceptable for the German taste regarding scientific form (for Locke and Hume in themselves were too bright, too clear, i.e., judged according to German value instincts, "too superficial"—)

Kant: inferior in his psychology and knowledge of human nature; way off when it comes to great historical values (French Revolution); a moral fanatic à la Rousseau; a subterranean Christianity in his values; a dogmatist through and through, but ponderously sick of this inclination, to such an extent that he wished to tyrannize it, but also weary right away of skepticism; not yet touched by the slightest breath of cosmopolitan taste and the beauty of antiquity—a *delayer* and *mediator,* nothing original (just as *Leibniz mediated* and built a *bridge* between mechanism and spiritualism, as *Goethe* did between the taste of the eighteenth century and that of the "historical sense" (which is essentially a sense for the exotic), as *German music* did between French and Italian music, as *Charlemagne* did between *imperium Romanum* and nationalism—*delayers par excellence.*)[73]

---

[72] The final paragraph was composed by the German editors from different drafts (1911, p. 500).

[73] Cf. *The Antichrist,* section 61 (*Portable Nietzsche,* p. 653).

102 (*Spring-Fall 1887*)

In how far the *Christian* centuries with their pessimism were *stronger* centuries than the eighteenth century—like the *tragic* era of the Greeks.

The nineteenth century vis-à-vis the eighteenth century. In what respects heir—in what respects a regression (poorer in "spirit" and taste)—in what respects progress (darker,[74] more realistic, stronger).

103 (*1883-1888*)[75]

What does it mean that we have such a feeling for the *campagna Romana?* And for high mountain ranges? What is the *meaning* of our nationalism?[76]

Chateaubriand in 1803, in a letter to M. de Fontanes, gives the first impression of the *campagna Romana.*

President de Brosses says of the *campagna Romana: "il fallait que Romulus fût ivre, quand il songea à bâtir une ville dans un terrain aussi laid."*[77]

Delacroix, too, did not like Rome, it frightened him. He was enthusiastic about Venice, like Shakespeare, like Byron, like George Sand. This aversion to Rome also in Theoph. Gautier—and in Rich. Wagner.

Lamartine has found language for Sorrent and Posilipp.

Victor Hugo was enthusiastic about Spain, *"parce que aucune autre nation n'a moins emprunté à l'antiquité, parce qu'elle n'a subi aucune influence classique."*[78]

104 (*Jan.-Fall 1888*)

The *two great tentative* ones, made to overcome the eighteenth century:

---

[74] *Düsterer*. Above, *Verdüsterung* has been rendered sometimes as "eclipse."

[75] Composed by the editor of the standard edition from various drafts.

[76] This sentence is found only in 1911, p. 500.

[77] Romulus must have been drunk when he thought of building a city in such an ugly place.

[78] Because no other nation borrowed less from antiquity, because she underwent no classical influence.

Napoleon, by awakening again the man, the soldier, and the great fight for power—conceiving Europe as a political unit;

Goethe, by imagining a European culture that would harvest the full inheritance of *attained* humanity.

German culture of this century arouses mistrust—in music this full, redeeming and binding element of Goethe is lacking—The Austrians have remained German only by virtue of their music.[79]

105 (*1883-1888*)

The preponderance of *music* in the romantics of 1839 and 1840. Delacroix. Ingres, a passionate musician (cult of Gluck, Haydn, Beethoven, Mozart), said to his students in Rome, *"si je pouvais vous rendre tous musiciens, vous y gagneriez comme peintres"*;[80] also Horace Vernet, with a special passion for *Don Giovanni* (as Mendelssohn testifies, 1831); also Stendhal, who said of himself: *Combien de lieues ne ferais-je pas à pied, et à combien de jours de prison ne me soumetterais-je pas pour entendre Don Juan ou le Matromonio segreto: et je ne sais pour quelle autre chose je ferais cet effort.*[81] At that time he was 56.

Borrowed forms; e.g., Brahms as typical "epigone"; Mendelssohn's educated Protestantism, ditto (an earlier "soul" is *re*captured poetically—)

—moral and poetical substitutions in Wagner, *one* art as stopgap for deficiencies in the others

—the "historical sense," inspiration from poetry and ancient sagas

—that typical transformation of which G. Flaubert offers the clearest example among the French and Richard Wagner among the Germans, in which the romantic faith in love and the future is transformed into the desire for the nothing, 1830 into 1850.

106 (*Nov. 1887-March 1888*)

Why does German music culminate in the period of German

[79] The last sentence is found only in 1911, p. 500.

[80] If I could make you all musicians you'd become better painters.

[81] How many leagues would I not walk and how many days in prison would I not endure to hear *Don Giovanni* or *Le Matrimonio Segreto;* and I don't know for what else I should make such an effort.

romanticism? Why is Goethe missing in German music? How much Schiller—more precisely, how much "Thekla"[82]—there is in Beethoven!

Schumann has in himself Eichendorff, Uhland, Heine, Hoffmann, Tieck. Richard Wagner has *Freischütz,*[83] Hoffmann, Grimm, the romantic saga, the mystical catholicism of instinct, symbolism, the "libertinism of passion" (Rousseau's intent). *The Flying Dutchman* tastes of France, where *le ténébreux*[84] was the type of the seducer in 1830.

Cult of music, of the revolutionary romanticism of form. Wagner sums up romanticism, German as well as French—

107 (*1888*)

Estimated merely for his value for Germany and German culture, Richard Wagner remains a great question mark, perhaps a German misfortune, in any case a destiny: but what does it matter? Isn't he very much more than merely a German event? It even seems to me that there is no place where he belongs less than Germany: nothing was prepared for him there; his whole type remains simply strange among Germans, odd, uncomprehended, incomprehensible. But one is careful not to admit this to oneself: for that one is too kindly, too square,[85] too German. *"Credo quia absurdus est"*:[86] that is what the German spirit wants and also wanted in this case—and so it believes for the present whatever Wagner wanted people to believe about him. The German spirit has at all times lacked subtlety and divination *in psychologicis*. Today, under the high pressure of fatherlandism and self-admiration, it is visibly thickening and becoming coarser: how should it be capable of coping with the problem of Wagner!—

---

[82] Woman in the cast of Schiller's *Wallenstein*.

[83] Opera by Lortzing.

[84] The dark (or devilish) man.

[85] *Viereckig*. Nietzsche's use of this word, which literally means quadrangular or square, is somewhat eccentric. He means, angular, solid, unsubtle—and the overtones of the American "square" seem entirely appropriate.

[86] "I believe because he is absurd." Variation of the famous, "I believe because it is absurd," usually ascribed to Tertullian.

108 (*1885*)

So far, the Germans are nothing, but they will become something; thus they have no culture yet—thus they cannot have any culture yet. That is my proposition: let those who cannot help it take offense.— So far they are nothing: that means, they are all sorts of things. They will become something: that means, they will stop some day being all sorts of things. The latter is at bottom a mere wish, scarcely a hope; fortunately, a wish on which one can live, a matter of will, of work, of discipline, of breeding, as well as a matter of annoyance,[87] of desire, of missing something, of discomfort, even of embitterment—in brief, we Germans desire something from ourselves that has not yet been desired from us—we desire something more!

That this "German as he is not yet" deserves something better than today's German *"Bildung"*;[88] that all who are "in the process of becoming" must be furious when they perceive some satisfaction in this area, an impertinent "retiring on one's laurels" or "self-congratulation": that is my second proposition on which I also have not yet changed my mind.

109 (*1885*)

Principle: There is an element of decay in everything that characterizes modern man: but close beside this sickness stand signs of an untested force and powerfulness of the soul. *The same reasons that produce the increasing smallness of man* drive the *stronger and rarer individuals up to greatness.*[89]

---

[87] *Unwillen,* literally: un-will. A play on words.

[88] The word means both culture and education—that which is taken to distinguish those who are "educated."

The early editors' intent in placing this note of 1885 after the preceding note of 1888, by way of concluding a subsection (the subheads have been dropped above), is palpable: one did not wish to conclude with a sharp criticism of Germany and dredged up an older note in which Nietzsche had identified himself with the Germans, at least to some extent. The published statements of his last year speak for themselves: see *The Case of Wagner* and the chapter on the Germans (p. 505 in *Portable Nietzsche*) in *Twilight of the Idols;* also the chapter on *The Case of Wagner* in *Ecce Homo.*

[89] Compare section 70 above.

110 (*Spring-Fall 1887*)

Overall insight: the ambiguous character of our *modern world* —the very same symptoms could point to *decline* and to *strength.* And the signs of strength, of the attainment of majority, could be misconstrued as weakness on the basis of traditional (residual) negative emotional valuations. In brief, our feelings, as feelings about values, are not up to date.

To generalize: feelings about values are always behind the times; they express conditions of preservation and growth that belong to times long gone by; they resist new conditions of existence with which they cannot cope and which they necessarily misunderstand: thus they inhibit and arouse suspicion against what is new.—

111 (*Spring-Fall 1887*)

The problem of the nineteenth century. Whether its strong and weak sides belong together? Whether it is all of one piece? Whether the diverseness of its ideals and their mutual inconsistency are due to a higher aim: *as* something higher?— For it could be the precondition of greatness to grow to such an extent in violent tension. Dissatisfaction, nihilism *could* be a good sign.

112 (*Spring-Fall 1887*)

Overall insight.— Actually, every major growth is accompanied by a tremendous crumbling and passing away: suffering, the symptoms of decline *belong* in the times of tremendous advances; every fruitful and powerful movement of humanity has also created at the same time a nihilistic movement. It could be the sign of a crucial and most essential growth, of the transition to new conditions of existence, that the most extreme form of pessimism, genuine *nihilism,* would come into the world. *This I have comprehended.*

113 (*1883-1888*)

(A)

To begin with a full and cordial tribute to contemporary humanity: not to be deceived by appearances—this type of humanity is less striking but gives far better warranties of duration; its tempo is slower, but the beat is much richer. Health is increasing, the actual conditions for a strong body get recognized and are slowly created, "asceticism" *ironice.*[90] One shrinks from extremes; a certain confidence in the "right road";[91] no enthusing; temporary acclimatization to narrower values (like "fatherland," like "scholarship," etc.).

Still, this whole picture would remain *ambiguous:* it could be an ascending but also a descending movement of life.

(B)

Faith in *"progress"*—in the lower spheres of intelligence it appears as ascending life; but this is self-deception; in the higher spheres of intelligence as decending life.

Description of the symptoms.

Unity of point of view: uncertainty about standards of value.

Fear of a general "in vain."

Nihilism.

114 (*June 10, 1887*)[92]

Actually, we have no longer such need of an antidote to the *first* nihilism: life in our Europe is no longer that uncertain, capricious, absurd. Such a tremendous increase in the value of man, the value of trouble, etc., is not so needful now; we can take a significant decrease of this value, we may concede much absurdity and caprice: the power man has attained now permits a demotion of the means of breeding of which the moral interpretation was the strongest. "God'" is far too extreme a hypothesis.

115 (*Jan.-Fall 1888*)

If anything signifies our *humanization*—a genuine and actual *progress*—it is the fact that we no longer require excessive oppositions, indeed no opposites at all—

we may love the senses, we have spiritualized and made them artistic in every degree;

---

[90] Ironically.

[91] Allusion to Goethe's *Faust,* line 329.

[92] See footnote to section 4 above.

we have a right to all those things which were most *maligned* until now.[93]

116 (*Jan.-Fall 1888*)

The inversion of the order of rank.— The pious counterfeiters, the priests, among us become chandalas—they replace the charlatans, quacks, counterfeiters, and wizards; we consider them corrupters of the will, great slanderers of life on which they wish to revenge themselves, *rebels* among the underprivileged. We have turned the caste of servants, the Sudras, into our middle class, our "*Volk*" ["people"], those who make political decisions.[94]

On the other hand, the chandala of former times is at the top: foremost, those who *blaspheme God, the immoralists,* the nomads of every type, the artists, Jews, musicians—at bottom, all disreputable classes of men—

We have raised ourselves to the level of *honorable* thoughts; even more, we *determine* honor on earth, "nobility"— All of us are today *advocates of life.*— *We immoralists* are today the *strongest power*: the other great powers need us—we construe the world in our image—

We have transferred the concept of the "chandala" to the *priests, teachers of a beyond,* and the *Christian society* that is grown together with them, as well as all who are of the same origin, the pessimists, nihilists, romantics of pity, criminals, vice addicts—the whole sphere in which the concept of "God" is imagined as a *savior*—

We are proud of no longer having to be liars, slanderers, men who cast suspicion on life—[95]

---

[93] An exceptionally interesting note, though of course no more than a note. *Vermenschlichung,* our becoming more humane, is the only thing worthy of being considered genuine progress, and it consists in spiritualizing (*vergeistigen*) the senses instead of condemning them as evil. The naiveté of postulating opposites where in fact there are only differences in degree is also condemned in Nietzsche's books, e.g., in *Beyond Good and Evil,* section 24 (New York: Vintage, 1966). For the final remark, see the chapter "On the Three Evils" in *Zarathustra,* Part III, p. 300 *ff* in *Portable Nietzsche.*

[94] At this point the MS continued, according to 1911, p. 500, although the standard editions omit the following words: "business and land owners—the military—the scholarly classes."

[95] In the ancient Hindu Law of Manu the priestly caste (Brahmins) is the highest, the Sudras form the lowest caste, and the chandalas are outcasts. For Nietzsche's critique of the Law of Manu see the chapter on "The 'Improvers' of Mankind" in *Twilight* (*Portable Nietzsche,* pp. 503-505). In

117 (*Spring-Fall 1887*)[96]

Progress of the nineteenth century against the eighteenth (—at bottom we *good Europeans* wage a war against the eighteenth century—):

1. "Return to nature" understood more and more decisively in the opposite sense from Rousseau's. *Away from idyl and opera!*
2. more and more decisively anti-idealistic, more concrete, more fearless, industrious, moderate, suspicious against sudden changes, *antirevolutionary*;
3. more and more decisively the question concerning the *health of the body* is put ahead of that of "the soul": the latter being understood as a state consequent upon the former, and the former at the very least as a precondition of the health of the soul.

118 (*1883-1888*)

If anything at all has been achieved, it is a more innocuous relation to the senses, a more joyous, benevolent, Goethean attitude toward sensuality; also a prouder feeling regarding the search for knowledge, so that the "pure fool"[97] is not given much credit.

119 (*Spring-Fall 1887; rev. 1888*)

We who are *"objective."*— It is not "pity" that opens the gates to the most distant and strange types of being and culture to *us*, but rather our accessibility and lack of partiality that does *not* empathize with or share suffering[98] but on the contrary takes delight in a hundred things that formerly led people to suffer (feel outraged or deeply moved, or prompted hostile and cold looks—). Suffering in all its nuances has become interesting for us: in this respect

---

this note two terms Gide used in book titles occur together: *The Immoralist* and *The Counterfeiters*. The former was published before this note, but influenced by Nietzsche's use of the same term elsewhere.

[96] See the footnote to section 124 below; also the Appendix.

[97] Glorified by Wagner in *Parsifal*.

[98] *"Nicht das 'Mitleid'"* and *"welche gerade* nicht *'mitleidet'"*: the German word for pity (*Mitleid*) means literally "suffering with"—like "compassion" and "sympathy."

we are certainly *not* fuller of pity, even when we are shaken by the sight of suffering and moved to tears: we do not by any means for that reason feel like helping.

In this *voluntary* desire to contemplate all sorts of distress and transgressions [99] we have become stronger and more vigorous than the eighteenth century was; it is a proof of our increase in vigor (we have come closer to the seventeenth and sixteenth centuries—). But it is a profound misunderstanding to construe our "romanticism" as a proof that our "souls" have become "more beautiful"—

We desire *strong* sensations as all *coarser* ages and social strata do.— This should be distinguished from the needs of those with weak nerves and the decadents: they have a need for pepper, even for cruelty—

All of us seek states in which bourgeois morality *no longer has any say*, and priestly morality even less (—every book to which some of the air of pastors and theologians still clings gives us the impression of a pitiable *niaiserie*[100] and poverty.— "Good society" consists of those whom at bottom nothing interests except what is *forbidden* in bourgeois society and gives a bad reputation: the same applies to books, music, politics, and the estimation of woman.

120 (*Spring-Fall 1887*)

How man has become more natural in the nineteenth century (the eighteenth century is that of elegance, refinement, and *sentiments généreux*).— *Not* "return to nature"—for there has never yet been a natural humanity. The scholasticism of un- and *anti*-natural values is the rule, is the beginning; man reaches nature only after a long struggle—he never "returns"— Nature: i.e., daring to be immoral like nature.

We are coarser, more direct, full of irony against generous feelings even when we succumb to them.

More natural is our first society, that of the rich, the leisure class: they hunt each other, love between the sexes is a kind of sport in which marriage furnishes an obstacle and a provocation; they amuse themselves and live for pleasure; they esteem physical advantages above all, are curious and bold.

---

[99] *Vergehen* could also mean "passing away" instead of "transgressions."

[100] Silliness.

More natural is our attitude to the search for knowledge: we possess libertinage of the spirit in all innocence, we hate pompous and hieratical manners, we delight in what is most forbidden, we should hardly know any longer of any interest of knowledge if the way to it were paved with boredom.

More natural is our attitude toward morality. Principles have become ridiculous; nobody permits himself any longer to speak without irony of his "duty." But a helpful, benevolent disposition is esteemed (morality is found in an *instinct*, and the rest is spurned.[101] In addition a few concepts of points of honor—).

More natural is our position in *politicis*: we see problems of power, of one quantum of power against another. We do not believe in any right that is not supported by the power of enforcement: we feel all rights to be conquests.

More natural is our estimation of great human beings and great things: we consider passion a privilege, we consider nothing great unless it includes a great crime; we conceive all being-great as a placing-oneself-outside as far as morality is concerned.

More natural is our attitude toward nature: we no longer love it on account of its "innocence," "reason," or "beauty"; we have made it nicely "devilish" and "dumb." But instead of despising it on that account, we have felt more closely related to it ever since, more at home in it. It does *not* aspire to virtue, and for that we respect nature.

More natural is our attitude toward art: we do not demand beautiful illusory lies from it, etc.; brutal positivism reigns, recognizing facts without becoming excited.

In summa: there are signs that the European of the nineteenth century is less ashamed of his instincts; he has taken a goodly step toward admitting to himself his unconditional naturalness, i.e., his immorality, *without becoming embittered*—on the contrary, strong enough to endure only this sight.

This sounds to some ears as if corruption had progressed—and it is certain that man has not come close to that *"nature"* of which *Rousseau* speaks but has progressed another step in civilization, which Rousseau *abhorred*. We have become *stronger*: we have again come closer to the seventeenth century, especially to the taste of its end (Dancourt, Lesage, Regnard).[102]

---

[101] *"Dédaignirt."*

[102] Florent Carton Dancourt (1661-1725), French dramatist; Alain René

121 (*1888*)

Culture contra civilization.[103]— The high points of culture and civilization do not coincide: one should not be deceived about the abysmal antagonism of culture and civilization. The great moments of culture were always, morally speaking, times of corruption; and conversely, the periods when the taming of the human animal ("civilization") was desired and enforced were times of intolerance against the boldest and most spiritual natures. Civilization has aims different from those of culture—perhaps they are even opposite—

122 (*January-Fall 1888*)

What I warn against: the instincts of decadence should not be confused with *humaneness;*[104]

the means of civilization, which lead to disintegration and necessarily to decadence, should not be confused with culture;

the libertinage, the principle of *"laisser aller,"* should not be confused with the will to power (—which is the counterprinciple).

123 (*Spring-Fall 1887*)

The unfinished problems I pose anew: the problem of civilization, the fight between Rousseau and Voltaire around 1760. Man becomes more profound, mistrustful, "immoral," stronger, more confident of himself—and to this extent "more natural": this is "progress."— At the same time, in accordance with a kind of division of labor, the strata that have become more evil are separated from those that have become milder and tamer—so that the overall fact is not noticed immediately.— It is characteristic of strength, of the self-control and fascination of strength, that these stronger strata possess the art of making others experience their progress in

---

Lesage (1668-1747), French novelist and dramatist; and Jean François Regnard (1655-1709), French comic dramatist.

[103] This title was added by the German editors.

[104] *Humanität.*

evil as something higher. It is characteristic of every "progress" that the strengthened elements are reinterpreted as "good."

124 (*Spring-Fall 1887*)

To give men back the courage to their natural drives—

To check their self-underestimation (not that of man as an individual but that of man as nature—)—

To remove antitheses from things after comprehending that we have projected them there—

To remove the idiosyncrasies of society from existence (guilt, punishment, justice, honesty, freedom, love, etc.)—

Progress toward "naturalness": in all political questions, also in the relations of parties, even of commercial, workers', and employers' parties, questions of power are at stake—"what one *can* do," and only after that what one ought to do.[105]

---

[105] Podach, *op. cit.*, pp. 203 *ff*, says of Schlechta's edition that "some most important points have eluded him. Only two examples:

I. In the one-volume edition of *The Will to Power* [1901], the aphorism to which Nietzsche assigned number 80 in W. II 1, 47/48 [the reference is to pp. 47/48 of one of his notebooks], was reproduced as aphorism 36. Weiss [in the two-volume edition of 1911, which—except for the important editorial apparatus at the end of the second volume—is merely a reprint of the second edition of 1906] made two [aphorisms] out of it (117 and 124), although Nietzsche had also listed this aphorism in W II 4 as '80: Progress of the growing naturalness of the nineteenth century.' A juxtaposition of the two versions shows that in 124 in Weiss's version the paragraph is missing that in the one-volume edition concludes the aphorism:

'that meanwhile, in the midst of the mechanics of grand politics, the Christian trumpet is still sounded (for example, in bulletins about victories or in the Kaiser's addresses to the nation), belongs more and more with the things that are becoming impossible; for it offends good taste.'

"Schlechta knows nothing of this, although it would have been useful to him in his reprint. It is equally unknown to him that the editors of *The Will to Power* of 1901 recorded in their notes (p. 131 [actually, 531]): 'A short sentence has been omitted here.' Otto Weiss did not mention this.

"The unpublished sentence reads: 'The throat of the crown prince is not one of God's affairs.'"

This is scarcely an earth-shaking revelation. Indeed, it is of interest mainly as negative evidence: this is offered as one of the two "most important points"—*Wichtigstes* might also be rendered as "most significant"—that have eluded Podach's predecessors down to Schlechta. Podach's second example has already been considered in the footnote to section 2. (See also my article, cited at the end of that note.)

The "unpublished sentence" was evidently written in 1887, when the crown prince of Germany was suffering from a throat ailment that killed him a hundred days after he succeeded to the imperial throne in 1888. In his correspondence Nietzsche then expressed his respect for him and his

125 (*1885*)[106]

Socialism—as the logical conclusion of the *tyranny* of the least and the dumbest, i.e., those who are superficial, envious, and three-quarters actors—is indeed entailed by "modern ideas" and their latent anarchism; but in the tepid air of democratic well-being the capacity to reach conclusions, or to finish, weakens. One follows —but one no longer sees what follows. Therefore socialism is on the whole a hopeless and sour affair; and nothing offers a more amusing spectacle than the contrast between the poisonous and desperate faces cut by today's socialists—and to what wretched and pinched feelings their *style* bears witness!—and the harmless lambs' happiness of their hopes and desiderata. Nevertheless, in many places in Europe they may yet bring off occasional coups and attacks: there will be deep "rumblings" in the stomach of the next century, and the Paris commune, which has its apologists and advocates in Germany, too, was perhaps no more than a minor indigestion compared to what is coming. But there will always be too many who have possessions for socialism to signify more than an attack of sickness—and those who have possessions are of one mind on one article of faith: "one must possess something in order to *be* something." But this is the oldest and healthiest of all instincts: I should add, "one must want to have more than one has in order to *become* more." For this is the doctrine preached by life itself to all that has life: the morality of development. To have and to want to have more—*growth,* in one word—that is life itself. In the doctrine of socialism there is hidden, rather badly, a "will to negate life"; the human beings or races that think up such a doctrine must be bungled. Indeed, I should wish that a few great experiments might prove that in a socialist society life negates itself, cuts off its own roots. The earth is large enough and man still sufficiently unexhausted; hence such a practical instruction and

---

disappointment—Friedrich III was a more likable emperor than his son and successor, Wilhelm II. The "unpublished sentence" clearly was not closely related to the contents of either section 117 or section 124 but merely a note Nietzsche had jotted down for himself, and posterity was not cheated by its suppression. It was evidently no more than a reaction to someone who had dragged in God in a way that had irritated Nietzsche.

For facsimiles and further discussion see front of book and Appendix.

[106] The manuscript is not in Nietzsche's handwriting but was evidently dictated by him—and then corrected and amplified in his hand. See 1911, p. 500.

demonstratio ad absurdum would not strike me as undesirable, even if it were gained and paid for with a tremendous expenditure of human lives. In any case, even as a restless mole under the soil of a society that wallows in stupidity, socialism will be able to be something useful and therapeutic: it delays "peace on earth" and the total mollification of the democratic herd animal; it forces the Europeans to retain spirit, namely cunning and cautious care, not to abjure manly and warlike virtues altogether, and to retain some remnant of spirit, of clarity, sobriety, and coldness of the spirit—it protects Europe for the time being from the *marasmus*[107] *femininus* that threatens it.

126 (*Spring-Fall 1887*)

The *most favorable inhibitions and remedies of modernity:*

1. universal military service with real wars in which the time for joking is past;
2. national bigotry (simplifies, concentrates);
3. improved nutrition (meat);
4. increasing cleanliness and healthfulness of domiciles;
5. hegemony of physiology over theology, moralism, economics, and politics;
6. military severity in the demand for and handling of one's "obligations" (one does not praise any more—).

127 (*1884*)

I am *glad* about the military development of Europe; also of the internal states of anarchy: the time of repose and Chinese ossification, which Galiani predicted for this century, is over. Personal *manly virtù,*[108] *virtù* of the body,[109] is regaining value, estimation becomes more physical, nutrition meatier. Beautiful men are again becoming possible. Pallid hypocrisy (with mandarins at the top, as Comte dreamed) is over. The barbarian in each of us is affirmed; also the wild beast. Precisely for that reason philosophers have a future.— Kant is a scarecrow, some day![110]

---

[107] Withering: a Greek medical term found in Galen, the second-century (A.D.) physician.

[108] *Tüchtigkeit.*

[109] *Leibes-Tüchtigkeit.*

[110] Gerade deshalb *wird es mehr werden mit den Philosophen.—Kant ist eine Vogelscheuche, irgend wann einmal!* A very rough note, quite unpolished.

128 (*1884*)

I have as yet found *no* reason for discouragement. Whoever has preserved, and bred in himself, a strong will, together with an ample spirit, has more favorable opportunities than ever. For the trainability of men has become very great in this democratic Europe; men who learn easily and adapt themselves easily are the rule: the herd animal, even highly intelligent, has been prepared. Whoever can command finds those who *must* obey: I am thinking, e.g., of Napoleon and Bismarck. The rivalry with strong and *un*-intelligent wills, which is the greatest obstacle, is small. Who doesn't topple these "objective" gentlemen with weak wills, like Ranke or Renan!

129 (*1885*)

Spiritual enlightenment is an infallible means for making men unsure, weaker in will, so they are more in need of company and support—in short, for developing the *herd animal* in man. Therefore all great artists of government so far (Confucius in China, the *imperium Romanum,* Napoleon, the papacy at the time when it took an interest in power and not merely in the world), in the places where the dominant instincts have culminated so far, also employed spiritual enlightenment—at least let it have its way (like the popes of the Renaissance). The self-deception of the mass concerning this point, e.g., in every democracy, is extremely valuable: making men smaller and more governable is desired as "progress"!

130 (*1883-1888*)

The highest equity and mildness as a state of *weakening* (the New Testament and the original Christian community—apparent as complete *bêtise*[111] in the Englishmen, Darwin and Wallace[112]). Your equity, you higher natures, impels you toward *suffrage universel,* etc.; your "humanity," toward mildness confronted with crime and stupidity. In the *long run* you thus make stupidity and the unscrupulous victorious: comfort and stupidity—*the mean.*

Externally: age of tremendous wars, upheavals, explosions.

---

[111] Stupidity.

[112] Alfred Russell Wallace (1823-1913).

Internally: ever greater weakness of man, *events* as *excitants.* The Parisian as the European extreme.

Consequences: (1) *barbarians* (at first, of course, below the form of culture so far [e.g., Dühring[113]]); (2) *sovereign individuals* (where masses of barbarian force are crossed with a lack of all restraint regarding whatever has been). Age of the greatest stupidity, brutality, and the *masses,* and of the *highest individuals.*

131 (*1884*)

Innumerable individuals of a higher type now perish: but whoever *gets away* is strong as the devil. Similar to the situation at the time of the Renaissance.

132 (*1885*)

Good Europeans that we are—what distinguishes us above the men of fatherlands?— First, we are atheists and immoralists, but for the present we support the religions and moralities of the herd instinct: for these prepare a type of man that must one day fall into our hands, that must *desire* our hands.

Beyond good and evil—but we demand that herd morality should be held sacred unconditionally.

We hold in reserve many types of philosophy which need to be taught: possibly, the pessimistic type, as a hammer; a European Buddhism might perhaps be indispensable.

We probably support the development and maturing of democratic institutions: they enhance weakness of the will: in socialism we see a thorn that protects against comfortableness.

Position toward peoples. Our preferences; we pay attention to the results of interbreeding.

Apart, wealthy, strong: irony at the expense of the "press" and its culture. Worry lest scholars become journalistic. We feel contemptuous of every kind of culture that is compatible with reading, not to speak of writing for, newspapers.

We take our accidental positions (like Goethe, Stendhal), our experiences, as foreground and stress them to deceive about our depths. We ourselves are *waiting* and beware of staking our hearts on them. They serve us as hostels for a night, which a wanderer needs and accepts—we beware of settling down.

---

[113] "E.g., Dühring" is found only in 1911, p. 500.

We are ahead of our fellow men in possessing a *disciplina voluntatis.* All strength applied to development of *strength of the will,* an art that permits us to wear masks, an art of understanding *beyond* the affects (also to think in a "supra-European" way, at times).

Preparation for becoming the legislators of the future, the masters of the earth, at least our children. Basic concern with marriages.

133 (*1885*)

The twentieth century.— Abbé Galiani once said: *La prévoyance est la cause des guerres actuelles de l'Europe. Si l'on voulait se donner la peine de ne rien prévoir, tout le monde serait tranquille, et je ne crois pas qu'on serait plus malheureux parce qu'on ne ferait pas la guerre.*[114] Since I do not by any means share the unwarlike views of my friend Galiani, I am not afraid of predicting a few things and thus, possibly, of conjuring up the cause of wars.

A tremendous *stock-taking*[115] after the most terrible earthquake: with new questions.

134 (*1885-1886*)

This is the time of the *great noon, of the most terrible* clearing up: my type of pessimism—great point of departure.

I. Basic contradiction in civilization and the enhancement of man.

II. Moral valuations as a history of lies and the art of slander in the service of a will to power (the *herd* will that rebels against the human beings who are stronger).

III. The conditions of every enhancement of culture (making possible a *selection*[116] at the expense of a mass) are the conditions

[114] "Foresight is the cause of Europe's present wars. If one would take pains to foresee nothing, the whole world would be tranquil, and I do not believe that one would be worse off for not waging war." The quotation was inserted by Peter Gast.

[115] *Besinnung* has no exact English equivalent. *Sinn* is sense (in most of the meanings of "sense"); *sich besinnen* is to reflect; *sich auf etwas besinnen,* to remember something; *zur Besinnung kommen,* to regain consciousness or come to one's senses again; and *besonnen,* sober, prudent, deliberate.

[116] *Auswahl.* Here it is well to think not only of Darwin and natural

of all growth.

IV. The *multiple ambiguity*[117] of the world as a question of *strength* that sees all things in the *perspective of its growth.* Moral-Christian value judgments as slaves' rebellion and slaves' mendaciousness (against the aristocratic values of the *ancient* world). How far does art reach down into the essence of strength?[118]

---

selection but also of the Bible, the concept of the chosen people (*auserwähltes Volk*), and above all the prophetic idea of the remnant.

[117] *Vieldeutigkeit.*

[118] For the final question, omitted in most editions, see 1911, p. 500.

BOOK TWO

CRITIQUE OF THE HIGHEST VALUES HITHERTO

I. CRITIQUE OF RELIGION[1]

All the beauty and sublimity we have bestowed upon real and imaginary things I will reclaim as the property and product of man: as his fairest apology. Man as poet, as thinker, as God, as love, as power: with what regal liberality he has lavished gifts upon things so as to impoverish himself and make himself feel wretched! His most unselfish act hitherto has been to admire and worship and to know how to conceal from himself that it was he who created what he admired.—[2]

1. Genesis of Religions

135 (*March-June 1888*)

On the *origin of religion.*— In the same way as today the uneducated man believes that anger is the cause of his being angry, spirit the cause of his thinking, soul the cause of his feeling—in short, just as there is still thoughtlessly posited a mass of psychological entities that are supposed to be causes—so, at a yet more naive stage, man explained precisely the same phenomena with the aid of psychological personal entities. Those conditions that seemed to him strange, thrilling, overwhelming, he interpreted as obsession and enchantment by the power of a person. (Thus the Christian, the most naive and backward species of man today, traces hope, repose, the feeling of "redemption," back to psychological inspiration by God: to him, as an essentially suffering and disturbed type, the feeling of happiness, resignation and repose naturally seems strange and in need of explanation.) Among intelligent, strong, and vigorous races it is mainly the epileptic who inspires the conviction that a strange power is here at work; but every related condition of subjection, e.g., that of the inspired man, of the poet, of the great criminal, of passions such as love and revenge, also leads to the invention of extra-

---

[1] Much of the material brought together in this first part of Book Two might have been given the title "Journal of *The Antichrist*" (after André Gide's "Journal of *The Counterfeiters*"), but some of these notes were also utilized in *Twilight of the Idols*. With a very few exceptions, the corresponding passages in these two books have not been indicated specifically in the following pages, lest the number of editorial notes become excessive.

[2] The German editors furnish no MS source, date, or number for this note.

human powers. A condition is made concrete in a person, and when it overtakes us is thought to be effected by that person. In other words: In the psychological concept of God, a condition, in order to appear as effect, is personified as cause.

The psychological logic is this: When a man is suddenly and overwhelmingly suffused with the *feeling of power*—and this is what happens with all great affects—it raises in him a doubt about his own person: he does not dare to think himself the cause of this astonishing feeling—and so he posits a stronger person, a divinity, to account for it.

In summa: the origin of religion lies in extreme feelings of power which, because they are strange, take men by surprise: and like a sick man who, feeling one of his limbs uncommonly heavy, comes to the conclusion another man is lying on top of him, the naive *homo religiosus*[3] divides himself into several persons. Religion is a case of *"altération de la personalité."* A sort of feeling of fear and terror at oneself— But also a feeling of extraordinary happiness and exaltation— Among the sick the feeling of health is sufficient to inspire belief in God, in the nearness of God.

136 (*March-June 1888*)

Rudimentary psychology of the religious man:— All changes are effects; all effects are effects of will (—the concept "nature," "law of nature" is lacking); all effects suppose an agent. Rudimentary psychology: one is a cause oneself only when one knows that one has performed an act of will.

Result: when man experiences the conditions of power, the imputation is that he is not their cause, that he is not responsible for them: they come without being willed, consequently we are not their author: the will that is not free (i.e., the consciousness that we have been changed without having willed it) needs an external will.

Consequence: man has not dared to credit himself with all his strong and surprising impulses—he has conceived them as "passive," as "suffered," as things imposed upon him: religion is the product of a doubt concerning the unity of the person, an *altération* of the personality: in so far as everything great and

---

[3] Religious man.

strong in man has been conceived as superhuman and external, man has belittled himself—he has separated the two sides of himself, one very paltry and weak, one very strong and astonishing, into two spheres, and called the former "man," the latter "God."

He has continued to think in this way; in the period of the moral idiosyncrasy he did not interpret his exalted and sublime moral states as "willed," as "work" of the person. The Christian too divides his person into a mean and weak fiction which he calls man, and another which he calls God (redeemer, savior)—

Religion has debased the concept "man"; its ultimate consequence is that everything good, great, true is superhuman and bestowed only through an act of grace—

137 (*March-June 1888*)

One way of raising man from the abasement produced by the subtraction of exalted and strong states as foreign conditions was the family theory. These exalted and strong states could at least be interpreted as the influence of our ancestors; we belonged together, in solidarity; we grow greater in our own eyes when we act according to a norm known to us.

Attempt by noble families to square religion with the feeling of their own worth. Poets and seers do the same: they feel proud, honored, and *chosen* for such an association—they attach great importance to not being considered at all as individuals, but merely as mouthpieces (Homer).

Step by step man takes possession of his exalted and proud states, he takes possession of his acts and works. Formerly one believed one was doing oneself an honor by denying responsibility for one's highest acts and attributing them to—God. Absence of free will counted as that which imparted a higher value to an action: a god was conceived as its author.[4]

138 (*1883-1888*)

Priests are the actors of something superhuman which they have to make easily perceptible, whether it be in the nature of

[4] In the MS this section is entitled "A form of religion for establishing human pride." And the MS version also contains the following sentence, crossed out by Nietzsche: "Another form of religion. The god elects, the god becomes man, and god dwells among men and leaves behind great benefactions. The local legend, eternally represented as 'drama.'"

ideals, gods, or saviors: in this they find their calling, for this their instincts serve them; to make everything as believable as possible they have to go as far as possible in posturing and posing; the shrewdness of their actor's art must above all aim at giving them a good conscience, by means of which alone is it possible to carry true conviction.

139 (*March-June 1888*)

The priest wants to have it understood that he counts as the highest type of man, that he rules—even over those who wield power—that he is indispensable, unassailable—that he is the strongest power in the community, absolutely not to be replaced or undervalued.

Means:[5] he alone possesses knowledge; he alone possesses virtue; he alone has sovereign lordship over himself; he alone is in a certain sense God and goes back to the divinity; he alone is the intermediary between God and other people; the divinity punishes every opposition to, every thought directed against a priest.

Means: truth exists. There is only one way of attaining it: to become a priest. Everything good in society, in nature, in tradition, is to be traced back to the wisdom of the priests. The holy book is their work. The whole of nature is only a fulfillment of the dogmas contained in it. There is no other source of the good than the priests. Every other kind of excellence is of a different *order* from that of the priest; e.g., that of the warrior.

Consequence: if the priest is to be the highest type, then the degrees which lead to his virtues must constitute the degrees of value among men. Study, emancipation from the senses, the non-active, the impassible, absence of affects, the solemn; antithesis: the *lowest* order of man.

The priest has taught one kind of morality: in order that he shall be considered the highest type of man. He conceives an antithetical type: the chandala. To make these contemptible by every means provides a foil to the order of castes.— The priest's extreme fear of sensuality is also conditioned by the insight that this is the most serious threat to the order of castes (that is, to order in general)— Every "more liberal tendency" *in puncto puncti* throws the marriage laws overboard—

[5] *Mittel*, i.e., means in the sense of instrument.

140 (*March-June 1888*)

The *philosopher* as a further development of the priestly type:—has the heritage of the priest in his blood; is compelled, even as rival, to struggle for the same ends with the same means as the priest of his time; he aspires to supreme authority.

What gives authority when one does not have physical power in one's hands (no army, no weapons of any kind—)? How, in fact, does one gain authority over those who possess physical strength and authority? (They compete with the awe inspired by princes, by the victorious conqueror, by the wise statesman).

Only by arousing the belief that they have in their hands a higher, mightier strength—*God.* Nothing is sufficiently strong: the mediation and service of the priests is *needed.* They establish themselves as indispensable intermediaries: they need as conditions of their existence: (1) belief in the absolute superiority of their God, belief in *their* God; (2) that there is no other, no direct access to God. The second demand alone creates the concept "heterodoxy," the first the concept "unbeliever" (i.e., one who believes in *another* God—).

141[6] (*Jan.-Fall 1888*)

Critique of the holy lie.— That the lie is permitted as a means to pious ends is part of the theory of every priesthood—to what extent it is part of their practice is the object of this inquiry.

But philosophers too, as soon as, with priestly ulterior motives, they form the intention of taking in hand the direction of mankind, at once also arrogate to themselves the right to tell lies: Plato before all. The most imposing is the twofold lie developed by the typically Aryan philosophers of the Vedanta: two systems contradictory in all their main features but for educational reasons alternating, supplementary and complementary. The lie of the one is intended to create a condition in which alone the truth of the other can become audible—

How far does the pious lie of priests and philosophers go?— One must ask what presuppositions they require for the purpose

[6] Sections 141-43 were utilized in the chapter on "The 'Improvers' of Mankind" in *Twilight* (*Portable Nietzsche*).

of education, what dogmas they have to invent to satisfy these presuppositions.

First: they must have power, authority, unconditional credibility on their side.

Secondly: they must have the whole course of nature in their hands, so that everything that affects the individual seems to be conditioned by their laws.

Thirdly: they must also possess a more extensive domain of power whose control eludes the eyes of its subjects: power of punishment in the beyond, in the "after death"—and of course the means of discovering the way to bliss.

—They have to set aside the concept of a natural course of events: but since they are clever and thoughtful people they are able to *promise* a host of effects, conditioned, of course, by prayers or the strict observance of their laws.— They can, moreover, *prescribe* a host of things that are absolutely reasonable—provided only that they do not point to experience or empiricism as the source of this wisdom, but to revelation or the consequence of "the sternest penances."

The holy lie therefore applies principally: to the *purpose* of an action (—natural purpose, reason are made to vanish: a moral purpose, the fulfillment of a law, a service to God appears as purpose—): to the *consequence* of an action (—natural consequence is interpreted as supernatural and, to produce a surer effect, the prospect of other, uncontrollable consequences is held out).

In this way a concept of good and evil is created that seems to be altogether divorced from the natural concept "useful," "harmful," "life-promoting," "life-retarding"—in so far as *another* life is imagined, it can even be directly inimical to the natural concept of good and evil.

In this way the famous "conscience" is at last created: an inner voice which does *not* measure the value of every action with regard to its consequences, but with regard to its intention and the degree to which this intention conforms with the "laws."

The holy lie therefore invented (1)[7] a *God* who punishes and rewards, who strictly observes the law-book of the priests and is strict about sending them into the world as his mouthpieces and plenipotentiaries; (2) an *afterlife* in which the great punishment

---

[7] These numbers are not found in the MS.

machine is first thought to become effective—to this end the *immortality of the soul*; (3) *conscience* in man as the consciousness that good and evil are permanent—that God himself speaks through it when it advises conformity with priestly precepts; (4) *morality* as denial of all natural processes, as reduction of all events to a morally conditioned event, moral effects (i.e., the idea of punishment and reward) as effects permeating all things, as the sole power, as the creator of all transformation; (5) *truth* as given, as revealed, as identical with the teaching of the priests: as the condition for all salvation and happiness in this life and the next.

In summa: what is the price of moral improvement?— Unhinging of reason, reduction of all motives to fear and hope (punishment and reward); dependence upon a priestly guardianship, upon pedantic formalities which claim to express a divine will; the implanting of a "conscience" which sets a false knowing in place of testing and experiment: as if what should be done and what left undone had already been determined—a kind of castration of the seeking and forward-striving spirit; *in summa*: the worst mutilation of man that can be imagined presented as the "good man."

In practice, all the reason, the whole heritage of prudence, subtlety, caution which is the presupposition of the priestly canon, is afterwards arbitrarily reduced to a mere mechanism: conformity with the law itself counts as an end, as the highest end, life no longer has any problems; the whole conception of the world is polluted by the idea of punishment; with the object of representing the priestly life as the *non plus ultra* of perfection, life itself is transformed into a defamation and pollution of life; the concept "God" represents a turning away from life, a critique of life, even a contempt for it; truth is transformed into the priestly lie, the striving for truth into study of the scriptures, into a means of becoming a theologian—

142 (*Jan.-Fall 1888*)

Toward a critique of the law-book of Manu.— The whole book is founded on the holy lie. Was the well-being of mankind the inspiration of this system? Was this species of man, who believes in the interestedness of every action, interested or not in imposing this system? To improve mankind—how is this intention inspired? Where is the concept of improvement derived from?

We find a species of man, the priestly, which feels itself to be the norm, the high point and the supreme expression of the type man: this species derives the concept "improvement" from itself. It believes in its own superiority, it wills itself to be superior in fact: the origin of the holy lie is the *will to power*—

Establishment of rule: to this end, the rule of those concepts that place a *non plus ultra* of power with the priesthood. Power through the lie—in the knowledge that one does not possess it physically, militarily—the lie as a supplement to power, a new concept of "truth."

It is a mistake to suppose an *unconscious and naive* development here, a kind of self-deception— Fanatics do not invent such carefully thought-out systems of oppression— The most cold-blooded reflection was at work here; the same kind of reflection as a Plato applied when he imagined his "Republic." "He who wills the end must will the means"—all lawgivers have been clear in their minds regarding this politician's insight.

We possess the classic model in specifically *Aryan* forms: we may therefore hold the best-endowed and most reflective species of man responsible for the most fundamental lie that has ever been told— That lie has been copied almost everywhere: *Aryan influence* has corrupted all the world—[8]

143 (*March-June 1888*)

A lot is said today about the *Semitic* spirit of the New Testament: but what is called Semitic is merely priestly—and in the racially purest Aryan law-book, in Manu, this kind of "Semitism," i.e., the *spirit of the priest,* is worse than anywhere else.

The development of the Jewish priestly state is *not* original: they learned the pattern in Babylon: the pattern is Aryan. When, later on, the same thing became dominant in a Europe with a preponderance of Germanic blood, this was in accordance with the spirit of the *ruling* race: a great atavism. The Germanic Middle Ages aimed at a revival of the Aryan order of castes.

Mohammedanism in turn learned from Christianity: the employment of the "beyond" as an instrument of punishment.

The pattern of an unchanging community with priests at its head—this oldest of the great cultural products of Asia in the

---

[8] See footnote 6, especially section 4f. of the chapter cited there.

realm of organization—was bound to invite reflection and imitation in every respect. Again Plato: but above all the Egyptians.

144 (*1885*)

Moralities and religions are the principal means by which one can make whatever one wishes out of man, provided one possesses a superfluity of creative forces and can assert one's will over long periods of time—in the form of legislation, religions, and customs.[9]

145 (*1884-1888*)

What an *affirmative* Aryan religion, the product of the *ruling* class, looks like: the law-book of Manu. (The deification of the feeling of power in Brahma: interesting that it arose among the warrior caste and was only transferred to the priests.)

What an *affirmative* Semitic religion, the product of a *ruling* class, looks like: the law-book of Mohammed, the older parts of the Old Testament. (Mohammedanism, as a religion for men, is deeply contemptuous of the sentimentality and mendaciousness of Christianity—which it feels to be a woman's religion.)

What a *negative* Semitic religion, the product of an *oppressed* class, looks like: the New Testament (—in Indian-Aryan terms: a chandala religion).

What a *negative* Aryan religion looks like, grown up among the *ruling* orders: Buddhism.

It is quite in order that we possess no religion of oppressed Aryan races, for that is a contradiction: a master race is either on top or it is destroyed.[10]

146 (*1885-1886*)

In itself, religion has nothing to do with morality: but both descendants of the Jewish religion are essentially moralistic re-

---

[9] The final clause is found only in 1911, p. 501.

[10] Yet it was above all the "Aryans" who accepted Christianity, while most of the Jews did not.

This section must be taken in the context of the immediately preceding sections and should be compared with the chapters on "The 'Improvers' of Mankind" in *Twilight* (p. 501, *Portable Nietzsche*), and with *The Antichrist* (p. 565, *Portable Nietzsche*), both of which were written later.

See also my preface to *The Antichrist* in *The Portable Nietzsche* and Chapter 10, "The Master-Race," and Chapter 7, section III, in my *Nietzsche*.

ligions—such as offer precepts about how one ought to live, and create a hearing for their demands by rewards and punishments.

147 (*Spring-Fall 1887*)

Pagan-Christian. The affirmation of the natural, the sense of innocence in the natural, "naturalness," is pagan. The denial of the natural, the sense of degradation in the natural, unnaturalness, is Christian.

Petronius, e.g., was "innocent": compared with this happy man, a Christian is absolutely without innocence. But since ultimately the Christian status must be merely a natural condition —which, however, dares not conceive itself to be such—"Christian" signifies raising to a principle the counterfeiting of psychological interpretations—

148 (*1883-1886*)

The Christian priest is from the first a mortal enemy of sensuality: no greather antithesis can be imagined than the innocently awed and solemn attitude adopted by, e.g., the most honorable women's cults of Athens in the presence of the symbols of sex. The act of procreation is the mystery as such in all nonascetic religions: a sort of symbol of perfection and of the mysterious design of the future: rebirth, immortality.

149 (*1880-1881*)

Belief in ourselves is the strongest fetter and the supreme whipping-on—and the strongest wing. Christianity should have made the innocence of man an article of faith—men would have become gods: belief was still possible in those days.[11]

150 (*Spring-Fall 1887*)

The great lie in history: as if it was the *corruption* of paganism which opened the road to Christianity! It was, on the con-

[11] Karl Schlechta omits this section in his edition because he considers the source (*Werke*, XI, 310) "problematical": unlike almost all of the other sections in *The Will to Power*, this section is not supported by a reference to Nietzsche's notebooks. And the date is much earlier.

trary, the weakening and *moralization* of the man of antiquity! Natural drives had already been reinterpreted as vices![12]

151 (*1885-1886*)

Religions are destroyed by belief in morality. The Christian moral God is not tenable: hence "atheism"—as if there could be no other kinds of god.

Similarly, culture is destroyed by belief in morality. For when one discovers the necessary conditions out of which alone it can grow, one no longer wants it (Buddhism).

152 (*March-June 1888*)

Physiology of the nihilistic religions. Each and every nihilistic religion: a systematized case history of sickness employing religious-moralistic nomenclature.

With pagan cults, it is around the interpretations of the great annual cycles that the cult revolves. With the Christian cult, it is around a cycle of paralytic phenomena that the cult revolves—

153 (*Nov. 1887-March 1888*)

This nihilistic religion gathers together those decadence elements and the like that it finds in antiquity; namely:

a. the party of the weak and ill-constituted (the refuse of the antique world: that which it thrust out most forcefully);

b. the party of the morally-obsessed and antipagan;

c. the party of the politically weary and the indifferent (*blasé* Romans), those without a country for whom life was emptiness;

d. the party of those who were tired of themselves—who were glad to participate in a subterranean conspiracy—

154 (*March-June 1888*)

Buddha against the "Crucified." Among the nihilistic religions, one may always clearly distinguish the Christian from the Buddhist. The Buddhist religion is the expression of a fine evening, a perfect

---

[12] In the MS this section is followed immediately by section 381, and both together are entitled "Great lies in history."

sweetness and mildness—it is gratitude toward all that lies behind, and also for what is lacking: bitterness, disillusionment, rancor; finally, a lofty spiritual love; the subtleties of philosophical contradiction are behind it, even from these it is resting: but from these it still derives its spiritual glory and sunset glow. (—Origin in the highest castes—)

The Christian movement is a degeneracy movement composed of reject and refuse elements of every kind: it is not the expression of the decline of a race, it is from the first an agglomeration of forms of morbidity crowding together and seeking one another out— It is therefore not national, not racially conditioned; it appeals to the disinherited everywhere; it is founded on a rancor against everything well-constituted and dominant: it needs a symbol that represents a curse on the well-constituted and dominant— It also stands in opposition to every spiritual movement, to all philosophy: it takes the side of idiots[13] and utters a curse on the spirit. Rancor against the gifted, learned, spiritually independent: it detects in them the well-constituted, the masterful.

155 (*Spring-Fall 1887*)

In Buddhism this thought predominates: "All desires, all that produces affects and blood, draw one toward actions"—only to this extent is one warned against evil. For action—has no meaning, action binds one to existence: but all existence has no meaning. They see in evil a drive toward something illogical: to the affirmation of means to an end one denies. They seek a way of nonexistence and therefore they regard with horror all affective drives. E.g., take no revenge! be no one's enemy!— The hedonism of the weary is here the supreme measure of value. Nothing is further from Buddhism than the Jewish fanaticism of a Paul: nothing would be more repellent to its instincts than this tension, fire, unrest of the religious man, above all that form of sensuality that Christianity has sanctified with the name "love." Moreover, it is the cultured and even the overspirited orders that find satisfaction in Buddhism: a race satiated and wearied by centuries of philosophical contentions, not, however, beneath all culture, like the classes from which Christianity arose— Emancipation even from good and evil appears to be of the essence of the Buddhist ideal:

[13] Cf. my footnote to section 29 of *The Antichrist* (*Portable Nietzsche*, p. 601).

a refined state beyond morality is conceived that is identical with the state of perfection, in the presupposition that one needs to perform even good actions only for the time being, merely as a means—namely, as a means to emancipation from *all* actions.

156 (*Nov. 1887-March 1888*)

A nihilistic religion [like Christianity],[14] sprung from and appropriate to a people grown old and tame, having outlived all strong instincts—transferred step by step to another milieu, at length entering into youthful peoples which have not yet lived at all—very curious! The bliss of the close, the fold, the evening preached to barbarians and Germans! How thoroughly all that I first had to be barbarized, Germanized! To those who had dreamed a Valhalla: who found happiness only in war!—A supramational religion preached in a chaos where no nations even existed yet—

157 (*Jan.-Fall 1888*)

The only way to refute priests and religions is this: to show that their errors have ceased to be beneficial—that they rather do harm; in short, that their own "proof of power" no longer holds good—

2. History of Christianity[15]

158 (*1888*)

One should not confuse Christianity as a historical reality with that one root that its name calls to mind: the other roots from which it has grown up have been far more powerful. It is an

---

[14] The words I have placed in brackets are not found in the MS and were added by the German editors in 1906. Although this was expressly admitted in 1911, p. 501, Schlechta, who boasts of being faithful to the MSS, follows the standard editions, as usual. The editorial emendation could be improved by omitting the bracketed words and placing at the beginning of the section: "Christianity:. . . ."

[15] Most of the sections that follow were utilized in *The Antichrist* (*Portable Nietzsche*).

unexampled misuse of words when such manifestations of decay and abortions as "Christian church," "Christian faith" and "Christian life" label themselves with that holy name. What did Christ *deny?* Everything that is today called Christian.

159 (*Nov. 1887-March 1888*)

The entire Christian teaching as to what shall be believed, the entire Christian "truth," is idle falsehood and deception: and precisely the opposite of what inspired the Christian movement in the beginning.

Precisely that which is Christian in the ecclesiastical sense is anti-Christian in essence: things and people instead of symbols; history instead of eternal facts; forms, rites, dogmas instead of a way of life. Utter indifference to dogmas, cults, priests, church, theology is Christian.

The Christian way of life is no more a fantasy than the Buddhist way of life: it is a means to being happy.

160 (*Nov. 1887-March 1888*)

Jesus starts directly with the condition the "Kingdom of Heaven" in the heart, and he does not find the means to it in the observances of the Jewish church; the reality of Judaism itself (its need to preserve itself) he regards as nothing; he is purely inward.—

He likewise ignores the entire system of crude formalities governing intercourse with God: he opposes the whole teaching of repentance and atonement; he demonstrates how one must live in order to feel "deified"—and how one will not achieve it through repentance and contrition for one's sins: "Sin is of no account" is his central judgment.

Sin, repentance, forgiveness—none of this belongs here—it is acquired from Judaism, or it is pagan.

161 (*Nov. 1887-March 1888*)[16]

The Kingdom of Heaven is a condition of the heart (—it is said of children "for theirs is the Kingdom of Heaven"): Not some-

[16] In the MS under a general heading: "Christian misunderstandings."

thing "above the earth." The Kingdom of God does not "come" chronologically-historically, on a certain day in the calendar, something that might be here one day but not the day before: it is an "inward change in the individual," something that comes at every moment and at every moment has not yet arrived—

162 (*Nov. 1887-March 1888*)

The thief on the Cross:— When even the criminal undergoing a painful death declares: "the way this Jesus suffers and dies, without rebelling, without enmity, graciously, resignedly, is the only right way," he has affirmed the gospel: and with that he is in Paradise—

163 (*Nov. 1887-March 1888*)

Neither by deeds nor in your heart should you resist him who harms you.

You should admit of no ground for divorcing your wife.

You should make no distinction between strangers and neighbors, foreigners and fellow countrymen.

You should be angry with no one, you should show contempt to no one. Give alms in secret. You should not want to become rich. You should not swear. You should not judge. You should be reconciled with foes; you should forgive. Do not pray publicly.

"Bliss" is not something promised: it is there if you live and act in such and such a way.[17]

164 (*Nov. 1887-March 1888*)

The entire prophet and miracle-worker attitude, the anger, the calling down of judgment is a dreadful corruption (e.g., Mark 6, 11. And whosoever shall not receive you . . . verily I say unto you, it shall be more tolerable for Sodom and Gomorrha, etc.). The "fig tree" (Matt. 21, 18): Now in the morning as he re-

---

[17] The German editors added "Jesus commands" at the beginning of this section. They also omitted the third paragraph in the MS: "Perhaps also: one should castrate oneself." And the penultimate paragraph: "Let only good men be seen, let your light shine: who will enter heaven? whoever does the will of my father in heaven."

Schlechta, of course, reproduces the text of the standard editions, ignoring 1911, p. 501.

turned into the city, he hungered. And when he saw a fig tree in the way, he came to it, and found nothing thereon, but leaves only, and said unto it, "Let no fruit grow on thee henceforward forever." And presently the fig tree withered away.[18]

165 (*Nov. 1887-March 1888*)

In a quite absurd way, the doctrine of reward and punishment has been crowded in: everything has thereby been ruined.

In the same way, the practice of the first *ecclesia militans*,[19] of the apostle [Paul][20] and his attitude, has been represented in a quite falsifying way as commanded, as predetermined——.

The subsequent glorification of the actual life and teaching of the first Christians: as if it had all been prescribed and the prescription merely followed—

And as for the fulfillment of prophesies: what a mass of falsification and forgery!

166 (*Nov. 1887-March 1888*)

Jesus opposed the commonplace life with a real life, a life in truth: nothing was further from him than the stupid nonsense of an "eternalized Peter," an eternal personal survival. What he fights against is this exaggerated inflation of the "person": how can he desire to eternize precisely *that*?

In the same way he fights against hierarchy within the community: he does not promise that reward shall be proportionate to performance: how can he have meant punishment and reward in the beyond!

167 (*Nov. 1887-March 1888*)

Christianity: a naive beginning to a Buddhistic peace movement in the very seat of *ressentiment*—but reversed by Paul into a pagan mystery doctrine, which finally learns to treat with the entire state organization—and wages war, condemns, tortures, swears, hates.

---

[18] The MS continues: "And when the disciples saw this they were astonished and said: How did the fig tree wither so soon?" 1911, p. 502.

[19] Militant church.

[20] The name I have placed in brackets was added by the German editors, perhaps mistakenly: Peter may have been meant.

Paul starts from the need for a mystery felt by the broad, religiously excited masses: he seeks a sacrifice, a bloody phantasmagoria which will stand up in competition with the images of the mystery cults: God on the cross, blood-drinking, the *unio mystica* with the "sacrifice."

He seeks to bring the afterlife (the blissful, atoned afterlife of the individual soul) as resurrection into a causal relationship with that sacrifice (after the type of Dionysus, Mithras, Osiris).

He needs to bring the concept guilt and atonement into the foreground, not a new way of life (as Jesus himself had demonstrated and lived) but a new cult, a new faith, a faith in a miraculous transformation ("redemption" through faith).

He understood what the pagan world had the greatest need of, and from the facts of Christ's life and death made a quite arbitrary selection, giving everything a new accentuation, shifting the emphasis everywhere—he *annulled* primitive Christianity as a matter or principle—

The attempt to destroy priests and theologians culminated, thanks to Paul, in a new priesthood and theology—in a new ruling order and a church.

The attempt to destroy the exaggerated inflation of the "person" culminated in faith in the "eternal person" (in concern for "eternal salvation"—), in the most paradoxical excess of personal egoism.

This is the humor of the situation, a tragic humor: Paul re-erected on a grand scale precisely that which Christ had annulled through his way of living. At last, when the church was complete, it sanctioned even the existence of the state.

168 (*Nov. 1887-March 1888*)

—The church is precisely that against which Jesus preached—and against which he taught his disciples to fight—

169 (*Nov. 1887-March 1888*)

A god who died for our sins: redemption through faith; resurrection after death—all these are counterfeits of true Christianity for which that disastrous wrong-headed fellow [Paul][21] must be held responsible.

---

[21] German editors' emendation.

The exemplary life consists of love and humility; in a fullness of heart that does not exclude even the lowliest; in a formal repudiation of maintaining one's rights, of self-defense, of victory in the sense of personal triumph; in faith in blessedness here on earth, in spite of distress, opposition and death; in reconciliation; in the absence of anger; not wanting to be rewarded; not being obliged to anyone; the completest spiritual-intellectual independence; a very proud life beneath the will to a life of poverty and service.

After the church had let itself be deprived of the entire Christian way of life and had quite specifically sanctioned life under the state, that form of life that Jesus had combatted and condemned, it had to find the meaning of Christianity in something else: in faith in unbelievable things, in the ceremonial of prayers, worship, feasts, etc. The concept "sin," "forgiveness," "reward" —all quite unimportant and virtually excluded from primitive Christianity—now comes into the foreground.

An appalling mishmash of Greek philosophy and Judaism; asceticism; continual judging and condemning; order of rank, etc.

170 (*Nov. 1887-March 1888*)

Christianity has from the outset transformed the symbolic into crudities:

1. the antithesis "real life" and "false" life: misunderstood as "this life" and "the life to come";

2. the concept "eternal life," the antithesis to transient personal life, as "personal immortality";

3. brotherhood on the basis of sharing food and drink together after the Hebrew-Arabic custom, as "the miracle of transubstantiation";

4. "resurrection—" understood as entry into "real life," as a state of "rebirth"; this is made into an historical eventuality which takes place some time or other after death;

5. the teaching that the son of man is the "Son of God," the living relationship between God and man; this is made into the "second person of the divinity"—the filial relationship to God of every man, even the lowliest, is abolished;

6. salvation through faith (namely, that there is no means of becoming a son of God except by following the way of life taught by Christ) reversed into the faith that one is to believe in some sort of miraculous subtraction of sins, accomplished not

through man but through Christ's deed:

With that, "Christ on the cross" had to be interpreted anew. This death in itself was not at all the main thing—it had been only one more sign of how one ought to behave in relation to the authorities and laws of this world: *not to defend oneself*— That had been the lesson.

171 (*March-June 1888*)

Toward a psychology of *Paul*.— The given fact is the death of Jesus. This has to be explained— That an explanation may be true or false has never entered the minds of such people as these: one day a sublime possibility comes into their heads: "this death *could* mean such and such"—and at once it *does* mean such and such! A hypothesis is proved true by the sublime impetus it imparts to its originator—

"The proof of power": i.e., an idea is proved true by its effect—("by their fruits" as the Bible naively says); what inspires must be true—that for which one sheds one's blood must be true—

Here, the sudden feeling of power that an idea arouses in its originator is everywhere accounted proof of its value:—and since one knows no way of honoring an idea other than by calling it true, the first predicate with which it is honored is the predicate "true"— How otherwise could it be so effective? It was imagined by some power: if that power were not real, it could not be effective— The idea is understood to have been inspired: the effect that it exercises possesses something of the violence of a demonic influence—

An idea that such a decadent is unable to resist, to which he completely succumbs, is thus "proved" true! ! !

None of these holy epileptics and seers of visions possessed a thousandth part of that integrity in self-criticism with which a philologist today reads a text or proves the truth of an historical event— Compared with us, they are moral cretins—[22]

172 (*Spring-Fall 1887*)

That it does not matter whether a thing is true, but only what

[22] Some of the formulations in this section seem better than any of the parallel passages in Nietzsche's works.

effect it produces—absolute lack of intellectual integrity. Everything is justified, lies, slander, the most shameless forgery, if it serves to raise the temperature—until one "believes"—

A systematic school of the means to seduction to a faith: contempt, on principle, for the spheres from which contradiction might come (—the spheres of reason, philosophy and wisdom, mistrust, caution); a shameless praising and glorification of the doctrine, with constant reference to the fact that it was God who gave it—that the apostle signifies nothing—that nothing here is to be criticized, but only believed, accepted; that it is the most extraordinary grace and favor to receive such a doctrine of redemption; that the deepest gratitude and humility is the condition in which to receive it—

The *ressentiment* which these lowly-placed persons feel toward everything held in honor is constantly gambled upon: that one represents this doctrine as a counterdoctrine in opposition to the wisdom of the world, to the power of the world, seduces them to it. It convinces the outcast and underprivileged of all kinds; it promises blessedness, advantage, privilege to the most insignificant and humble; it fills poor little foolish heads with an insane conceit, as if *they* were the meaning and the salt of the earth—

All this, I repeat, one cannot sufficiently despise. We shall spare ourselves a critique of the doctrine; it suffices to observe the means it uses to know what it is one is dealing with. It identified with virtue, it shamelessly claimed for itself alone the whole fascinating force of virtue—it identified with the power of paradox and with the need felt by old civilizations for spice and absurdity; it amazed, it enraged, it provoked persecution and mistreatment—

It is precisely the same well-pondered baseness with which the Jewish priesthood established its power and the Jewish church was created—

One should distinguish: (1) that warmth of the passion "love" (resting on the subterranean basis of a heated sensuality); (2) the absolute ignobility of Christianity: —the continual exaggeration, the verbosity; —the lack of cool spirituality and irony; —the unmilitary nature of all its instincts; —the priestly prejudice against manly pride, against sensuality, the sciences, the arts.[23]

---

[23] In this section the German editors omitted one sentence—and Schlechta, as usual, followed them.

See the Appendix, below.

173 (*Summer-Fall 1888*)

Paul: he seeks power in opposition to ruling Judaism—his movement is too weak— Revaluation of the concept "Jew": the "race" is set aside—: but that means negating what is fundamental. The "martyr," the "fanatic," the value of all strong faith—

Christianity is the decadent form of the old world sunk into deepest impotence, so that the sickest and unhealthiest elements and desires come to the top.

Consequently, in order to create a unity, a resisting power, *other* instincts had to step into the foreground—in short, a kind of calamity was needed such as that from which the Jews had acquired their instinct for self-preservation—

In this regard, the persecutions of the Christians were invaluable—a sense of community in danger, mass-conversion as the only means of putting an end to individual persecution (—consequently he takes as lightly as possible the concept "conversion"—).

174 (*Spring-Fall 1887; rev. Spring-Fall 1888*)

The Christian-Jewish life: here *ressentiment* did *not* predominate. Only the great persecutions could have developed this passion to this extent—the ardor of love as well as that of hatred.

When one sees one's dearest sacrificed for one's faith, one becomes aggressive; we owe the triumph of Christianity to its persecutors.

The asceticism in Christianity is not specifically Christian: this is what Schopenhauer misunderstood: it only makes inroads into Christianity wherever asceticism also exists apart from Christianity.

Hypochondriac Christianity, the torturing and vivisection of the conscience, is in the same way only characteristic of a certain soil in which Christian values have taken root: it is not Christianity itself. Christianity has absorbed diseases of all kinds from morbid soil: one can only reproach it for its inability to guard against any infection. But that precisely is its essence: Christianity is a type of decadence.

175 (*Spring-Fall 1887; rev. Spring-Fall 1888*)

The reality upon which Christianity could be raised was the little Jewish family of the Diaspora, with its warmth and affection, with its readiness to help and sustain one another—unheard-of and perhaps not understood in the whole Roman Empire—with its concealed pride of the "chosen" disguised as humility, with its innermost denial, untouched by envy, of all that is on top and possesses power and splendor. To have recognized in this a form of power, to have recognized that this blissful condition was communicable, seductive, infectious to pagans also—that was Paul's genius: to employ this store of latent energy, of prudent happiness for a "Jewish church of freer confession"—the entire Jewish experience and mastery of communal self-preservation under foreign rule, also Jewish propaganda—he divined that as his task. What he lit upon was just this absolutely unpolitical and withdrawn species of *little people*: their art of asserting themselves and prevailing, cultivated through a number of virtues which constituted virtue in its entirety ("means by which a particular species of man preserves and enhances himself").

The principle of *love* derives from the little Jewish communities: it is a soul of the more passionate kind that glows here under the ashes of humility and wretchedness: this was neither Greek, nor Indian, nor Germanic. The song in praise of love that Paul composed[24] is nothing Christian, but a Jewish outburst of the eternal flame that is Semitic. If Christianity has done anything essential psychologically, it is that it *raised the temperature of the soul* among those cooler and nobler races that were then on top; it was the discovery that the most wretched life can become rich and inestimable through a rise in temperature—

It goes without saying that such a transference could not take place in respect to the ruling orders: the Jews and Christians had their bad manners against them—and when allied to bad manners, strength and passion of soul are repellent and almost disgusting (—I *see* these bad manners whenever I read the New Testament).

---

[24] I Corinthians 13. The point Nietzsche makes here was utterly revolutionary at that time and constitutes a major contribution to our understanding of Judaism and Christianity, even if the form of expression here is deliberately hyperbolical and paradoxical. For further discussion, see my *Nietzsche*, Chapter 12, section II.

One had to be related through lowliness and want to the type of lowly people who spoke here to feel their attraction—

How one reacts to the New Testament is a test of whether one has any *classical taste* in one's bones (cf. Tacitus); whoever is not revolted by it, whoever does not honestly and profoundly sense something of *foeda superstitio*[25] in it, something from which one withdraws one's hand as if to avoid being soiled, does not know what is classical. One must feel about the "cross" as Goethe did[26]—

176 (*March-June 1888*)

Reaction of the little people:— Love gives the greatest feeling of power. To grasp to what extent not man in general but a certain species of man speaks here. This is to be exhumed more precisely.[27]

"We are divine through love, we become 'children of God'; God loves us and wants nothing whatever from us save love"; this means: no morality, obedience, or activity produces that feeling of power that love produces; one does nothing bad from love, one does much more than one would do from obedience and virtue.

Here is the happiness of the herd, the feeling of community in great and small things, the living feeling of unity experienced as the sum of the feeling of life. Being helpful and useful and caring for others continually arouses the feeling of power; visible success, the expression of pleasure underlines the feeling of power; pride is not lacking, in the form of community, the abode of God, the "chosen."

What has in fact happened is that man has again experienced an *altération* of personality: this time he calls his feeling of love God. One must picture to oneself what the awakening of such a feeling is like: a kind of ecstasy, a strange language, a "gospel"—it was this novelty that forbade him to ascribe love to himself—: he thought God was walking before him and coming alive within him.— "God descends to man," one's "neighbor" is transfigured into a god (in so far as he arouses the feeling of love). Jesus is

---

[25] "Abominable superstition."

[26] An allusion to Goethe's *Venetian Epigrams* (1790): the original text and a verse translation will be found in *Twenty German Poets*, ed. and tr. Walter Kaufmann (New York: Modern Library, 1963), pp. 32 *f*.

[27] This sentence is omitted in the standard editions.

one's neighbor as soon as he is conceived as godhead, as a cause of the feeling of power.

177 (*Jan.-Fall 1888*)

The faithful are conscious that they are endlessly indebted to Christianity, and therefore conclude that its originator is a personage of the first rank— This conclusion is false, but it is typical of conclusions drawn by worshipers. Objectively considered, it is possible, first, that they are in error about the value of that for which they are indebted to Christianity: convictions prove nothing in favor of that of which one is convinced; in the case of religions they establish rather a suspicion against it— It is possible, secondly, that the debt to Christianity ought not to be ascribed to its founder but to the finished structure, to the whole thing, the church, etc. The concept "originator" is so ambiguous it can even mean the accidental cause of a movement: the figure of the founder has been enlarged in proportion as the church has grown; but precisely this perspective of worship permits the conclusion that at some time or other this founder was something very uncertain and insecure, in the beginning— Consider with what degree of freedom Paul treats, indeed almost juggles with, the problem of the person of Jesus: someone who died, who was seen again after his death, who was delivered over to death by the Jews— A mere "motif": *he* then wrote the music to it— A zero in the beginning.[28]

178 (*1884*)

The founder of a religion *can* be insignificant—a match, no more!

179 (*Nov. 1887-March 1888*)

On the psychological problem of Christianity.— The driving force is: *ressentiment*, the popular uprising, the revolt of the underprivileged. (It is otherwise with Buddhism: this is not *born* out of a *ressentiment* movement but fights *ressentiment* because it leads to action.)

This peace party grasps that the renunciation of enmity in thought and deed is a condition of distinction and preservation.

[28] The final phrase is omitted in the standard editions.

Herein lies the psychological difficulty that has hampered the understanding of Christianity: the drive that created it forces one to fight against it as a matter of principle.

Only as a peace and innocence party has this insurrectionary movement any possibility of success: it must conquer through extreme mildness, sweetness, softness; it grasps this by instinct— Masterstroke: to deny and condemn the drive whose expression one is, continually to display, by word and deed, the antithesis of this drive—

180 (*Nov. 1887-March 1888*)

Pretended youth. One is deceiving oneself if one imagines here a naive and youthful people rising up against an ancient culture; superstition has it that the deeper springs of life gushed forth anew in those classes of the lowliest people where Christianity grew and took root: one understands nothing of the psychology of Christianity if one takes it to be the expression of a newly arisen national youthfulness and racial invigoration. On the contrary: it is a typical form of decadence, the moral hypersensitivity and hysteria of a sick mishmash populace grown weary and aimless. The extraordinary company that here gathered around this master-seducer really belongs wholly in a Russian novel: all the neuroses keep a rendezvous in them—the absence of duties, the instinct that everything is really coming to an end, that nothing is worth while any more, contentment in a *dolce far niente.*[29]

The power and certainty of the future in the Jewish instinct, its tremendously tough will to exist and to power, lies in its ruling classes: those orders which primitive Christianity raised up are most clearly distinguished by the exhaustion of their instincts. On one hand, one has had enough: on the other, one is content with oneself, in oneself, for oneself.

181 (*Spring-Fall 1887*)

Christianity as emancipated Judaism (in the same way as a local and racially conditioned nobility at length emancipates itself from these conditions and goes in search of related elements—)

---

[29] Sweet doing-nothing. The sentence was utilized and elaborated in *The Antichrist,* section 31 (*Portable Nietzsche,* pp. 602-604).

1. As church (community) within the state, as an unpolitical structure;

2. As life, discipline, practice, art of living;

3. As religion of sin (of transgression against God as the only kind of transgression, as the sole cause of suffering in general), with a universal cure for it. There are only sins against God; men shall not judge acts done against men, nor demand a reckoning, except in the name of God. Ditto, all commands (love): everything is associated with God and done to man for God's sake. A higher prudence lies in this (—a very narrow life, as with the Eskimos, is endurable only by the most peaceable and cautious disposition: Jewish-Christian dogma turns against sin in favor of the "sinner"—).

182 (*Spring-Fall 1887*)

The Jewish priesthood had understood how to present everything which it claimed as a divine precept, as obedience to a command of God—also how to introduce whatever served to preserve Israel and make possible its existence (e.g., a number of works: circumcision, sacrificial cult as the center of national consciousness) not as nature, but as "God."— This process continued; within Judaism, where the necessity for "works" was not felt (that is to say, as a means of segregation from the outside world), a priestly species of man could be conceived that behaved as the "noble nature" behaves toward the aristocracy; a classless and at the same time spontaneous priestliness of soul, which now, in order to contrast itself sharply with its opposite, attached value not to "works," but to the "disposition"—

Fundamentally it was again the question of making a certain species of soul prevail: as it were, a popular uprising within a priestly people—a pietistic movement from below (sinners, publicans, women, the sick). Jesus of Nazareth was the sign by which they recognized themselves. And again, in order to believe in themselves they need a theological transfiguration: they require nothing less than "the Son of God" to create a faith for themselves— And just as the priesthood had falsified the entire history of Israel, so again the attempt was here made to forge the history of mankind in general, so that Christianity might appear to be its most cardinal event. This movement could have arisen only on the soil of Judaism, whose principal deed was to associate guilt with misfortune and to reduce all guilt to guilt against God: Christianity raised all this to the second power.

183 (*Nov. 1887-March 1888*)

The symbolism of Christianity is based on the Jewish, which had already resolved all reality (history, nature) into a holy unnaturalness and unreality—which no longer recognized real history, which was no longer interested in natural consequences—

184 (*March-June 1888*)

The Jews tried to prevail after they had lost two of their castes, that of the warrior and that of the peasant; in this sense they are the "castrated": they have the priests—and then immediately the chandala—

As is only fair, a break develops among them, a revolt of the chandala: the origin of Christianity.

Because they knew the warrior only as their master, they brought into their religion enmity toward the noble, toward the exalted and proud, toward power, toward the ruling orders—: they are pessimists from indignation—

Thus they created an important new posture: the priest at the head of the chandala—against the noble orders—

Christianity drew the ultimate conclusion of this movement: even in the Jewish priesthood it still sensed caste, the privileged, the noble—it abolished the priest—

The Christian is the chandala who repudiates the priest—the chandala who redeems himself—

That is why the French Revolution is the daughter and continuation of Christianity—its instincts are against caste, against the noble, against the last privileges——

185 (*Spring-Fall 1887*)

The *"Christian ideal":* staged with Jewish subtlety. The basic psychological drives, its "nature":

the revolt against the ruling spiritual power;

attempt to make the virtues through which happiness is possible for the lowliest into the standard ideal of all values—to call it God: the instinct for preservation in the least vital classes;

to justify absolute abstention from war and resistance through this ideal—including obedience;

love of one another as consequence of love of God.

Artifice: to deny all natural *mobilia* and to transfer them to the spiritual realm beyond—to exploit virtue and its veneration entirely for one's own ends, step by step to deny virtue to everything non-Christian.

186 (*Spring-Fall 1887*)

The profound contempt with which the Christian was treated in the noble areas of classical antiquity is of a kind with the present instinctive aversion to Jews: it is the hatred of the free and self-respecting orders for those who are pushing and who combine timid and awkward gestures with an absurd opinion of their worth.

The New Testament is the gospel of a wholly ignoble species of man; their claim to possess more value, indeed to possess *all* value, actually has something revolting about it—even today.

187 (*Spring-Fall 1887*)

How little the subject matters! It is the spirit that gives life! What stuffy and sickroom air arises from all that excited chatter about "redemption," love, blessedness, faith, truth, "eternal life"! Take, on the other hand, a really pagan book, e.g., Petronius, where fundamentally nothing is done, said, desired and valued but what by peevish Christian standards is sin, mortal sin even. And yet how pleasant is the purer air, the superior spirituality of its quicker pace, the liberated and overflowing strength that feels sure of the future! In the entire New Testament there is not one single *bouffonnerie*: but that fact refutes a book—

188 (*Spring-Fall 1887*)

The profound unworthiness with which all life outside the Christian life is condemned: they are not content with thinking meanly of their real opponents, they require nothing less than a collective defamation of everything which is not themselves— Arrogance of holiness gets along famously with a base and crafty soul: witness the first Christians.

The future: they see they are well paid— Theirs is the most

uncleanly kind of spirit there is. The entire life of Christ is so presented as to help to justify the prophecies: he acts in this way *in order* that they may be justified—

189 (*Spring-Fall 1887*)

The lying interpretation of the words, gestures and conditions of the dying: fear of death, for example, is systematically confused with fear of the "after death"—[30]

190 (*Spring-Fall 1887*)

The Christians did as the Jews did and put into the mouth of their master and encrusted his life with what they conceived to be a condition of their existence and an innovation. At the same time they restored to him all proverbial wisdom—: in short, they represented their actual life and activity as *obedience* and thus, as sanctified for their propaganda.

What it all depends upon can be gathered from Paul: it is not much. What remains is the elaboration of a type of saint on the basis of what they considered holy.

The entire "miraculous doctrine," including the resurrection, is a consequence of self-glorification by the community, which ascribed to its master in a higher degree whatever it thought itself capable of (it derived its strength *from* him—).

191 (*Nov. 1887-March 1888*)

Christians have never put into practice the acts Jesus prescribed for them, and the impudent chatter about "justification by faith" and its unique and supreme significance is only the consequence of the church's lack of courage and will to confess the *works* which Jesus demanded.

The Buddhist acts differently from the non-Buddhist; *the Christian acts as all the world does* and possesses a Christianity of ceremonies and *moods.*

The profound and contemptible mendaciousness of Christianity in Europe—: we really are becoming the contempt of the Arabs, Hindus, Chinese— Listen to the speeches of Germany's

[30] This confusion is still rampant, even among philosophers and psychologists.

first statesman on what has really occupied Europe for forty years now—listen to the language, the court-chaplain Tartuffery.

192 (*Spring-Fall 1887; rev. Spring-Fall 1888*)

"Faith" or *"works"?*— But that "works," the habit of certain works, should engender a certain evaluation and finally a certain *disposition* is as natural as it is unnatural that mere evaluation should produce "works." One must practice deeds, not the strengthening of one's value-feelings; one must first have some *ability*— The Christian *dilettantism* of Luther. Faith is a *pons asinorum.*[31] The background is a profound conviction on the part of Luther and his kind of their incapacity for Christian works, a personal fact disguised beneath an extreme doubt as to whether activity of all kinds is not sin and the work of the Devil: so that the value of existence resides in single highly tensed conditions of *inactivity* (prayer, effusion, etc.).— In the last resort he was right: the instincts expressed in all the actions of the Reformers are the most brutal that exist. Only by an absolute turning away from themselves, by absorption in their opposite, only as an illusion ("faith") was existence endurable to them.

193 (*Nov. 1887-March 1888*)

"What to do in order to believe?"—an absurd question. What is wrong with Christianity is that it refrains from doing all those things that Christ commanded should be done.

It is the mean life, but interpreted through the eye of contempt.

194 (*Nov. 1887-March 1888*)

Entry into *real* life—one rescues one's personal life from death by living a common life—

195 (*Nov. 1887-March 1888*)

"Christianity" has become something fundamentally different from what its founder did and desired. It is the great antipagan

---

[31] Bridge for asses: a help for the inept.

movement of antiquity, formulated through the employment of the life, teaching and "words" of the founder of Christianity but interpreted in an absolutely arbitrary way after the pattern of fundamentally different needs: translated into the language of every already existing subterranean religion—

It is the rise of pessimism (—while Jesus wanted to bring peace and the happiness of lambs): and moreover the pessimism of the weak, the inferior, the suffering, the oppressed.

Its mortal enemy is (1) power in character, spirit and taste; "worldliness"; (2) classical "happiness," the noble levity and skepticism, the hard pride, the eccentric intemperance and the cool self-sufficiency of the sage, Greek refinement in gesture, word, and form. Its mortal enemy is the Roman just as much as the Greek.

Attempt by antipaganism to found and make itself possible philosophically: predilection for the ambiguous figures of the old culture, above all for Plato, that instinctive Semite and anti-Hellene —also for Stoicism, which is essentially the work of Semites (—"dignity" as strictness, law, virtue as greatness, self-responsibility, authority, as supreme sovereignty over one's own person— this is Semitic. The Stoic is an Arabian sheik wrapped in Greek togas and concepts).[32]

196 (*Nov. 1887-March 1888*)

Christianity only takes up the fight that had already begun against the *classical* ideal and the *noble* religion.

In fact, this entire transformation is an adaption to the needs and the level of understanding of the religious masses of that time: those masses which believed in Isis, Mithras, Dionysus, the "Great Mother," and which desired of a religion: (1) hope of a beyond, (2) the bloody phantasmagoria of the sacrificial animal (the mystery), (3) the redemptive deed, the holy legend, (4) asceticism, world-denial, superstitious "purification," (5) a hierarchy, a form of community. In short: Christianity accommodated itself to already existing and established antipaganism, to the cults that had been combatted by Epicurus—more precisely, to the religions of the lower masses, the women, the slaves, the non-noble classes.

We therefore have the following misunderstandings:

---

[32] Zeno of Citium, on Cyprus, the founder of the Stoic school, was probably a Semite.

1. the immortality of the person;

2. the presumed *other* world;

3. the absurdity of the concept of punishment and the concept of sin at the heart of the interpretation of existence;

4. instead of the deification of man his un-deification, the digging of the deepest chasm, which only a miracle, only prostration in deepest self-contempt can bridge;

5. the whole world of corrupt imagination and morbid affects instead of a kindly and simple way of life, instead of a Buddhistic happiness attainable on earth;

6. an ecclesiastical order with priesthood, theology, cult, sacrament; in short, everything that Jesus of Nazareth had *combatted;*

7. miracles all over, superstition: while the distinguishing mark of Judaism and earliest Christianity is its repugnance to miracles, its relative rationality.

197 (*Spring-Fall 1887*)

The *psychological presupposition:* lack of *knowledge* and culture, ignorance which has forgotten all shame: imagine these impudent saints in Athens;

the Jewish instinct of the "chosen": they claim all the virtues for themselves without further ado, and count the rest of the world their opposites; a profound sign of a vulgar soul;

a complete lack of real aims, of real tasks, for which one needs other virtues than those of the bigot—the state took this work from their shoulders: these impudent people nonetheless behaved as if they had no need of the state.

"Except ye become as little children—": oh, how far we are from this psychological naiveté!

198 (*Nov. 1887-March 1888*)

The founder of Christianity had to pay for having directed himself to the lowest class of Jewish society and intelligence. They conceived him in the spirit they understood— It is a real disgrace to have concocted a salvation story, a personal God, a personal redeemer, a personal immortality and to have retained all the meanness of the "person" and "history" in a doctrine that contests the reality of all that is personal and historical—

The salvation legend in place of the symbolic now-and-always, here and everywhere; the miracle in place of the psychological symbol.

199 (*Spring-Fall 1887*)

Nothing is less innocent than the New Testament. One knows from what soil it sprang. This people of an inflexible self-will which knew how to prevail after it had lost every natural support and had long since forfeited its right to existence, and to that end had to raise itself up by unnatural, purely imaginary presuppositions (as chosen people, as community of saints, as the people of the promise, as "church"): this people handled the *pia fraus*[33] with such perfection, such a degree of "good conscience," that one cannot be sufficiently cautious when it preaches morality. When Jews step forward as innocence itself then the danger is great: one should always have one's little fund of reason, mistrust, and malice to hand when one reads the New Testament.

People of the basest origin, in part rabble, outcasts not only from good but also from respectable society, raised away from even the *smell* of culture, without discipline, without knowledge, without the remotest suspicion that there is such a thing as conscience in spiritual matters; simply—Jews: with an instinctive ability to create an advantage, a means of seduction out of every superstitious supposition, out of ignorance itself.[34]

200 (*Spring-Fall 1887; rev. 1888*)

I regard Christianity as the most fatal seductive lie that has yet existed, as the great unholy lie: I draw out the after-growth and sprouting of its ideal from beneath every form of disguise, I reject every compromise position with respect to it—I force a war against it.

Petty people's morality as the measure of things: this is the most disgusting degeneration culture has yet exhibited. And this kind of ideal still hanging over mankind as "God"!!

---

[33] Pious fraud, or holy lie.

[34] For Nietzsche's attitude toward the Jews see my preface to *The Antichrist* (*Portable Nietzsche,* p. 565 *ff*) and my *Nietzsche,* Chapter 10.

201 (*Spring-Fall 1887*)

However modest one may be in one's demand for intellectual cleanliness, one cannot help feeling, when coming into contact with the New Testament, a kind of inexpressible discomfiture: for the unchecked impudence with which the least qualified want to raise their voice on the greatest problems, and even claim to be judges of such things, surpasses all measure. The shameless levity with which the most intractable problems (life, world, God, purpose of life) are spoken of, as if they were not problems at all but simply things that these little bigots *knew!*

202 (*Spring-Fall 1887; rev. Spring-Fall 1888*)

This was the most fatal kind of megalomania there has ever been on earth: when these lying little abortions of bigots began to lay claim to the words "God," "Last Judgment," "truth," "love," "wisdom," "Holy Spirit" and with them made a boundary between themselves and "the world"; when this species of man began to reverse values according to his own image, as if *he* were the meaning, the salt, the measure, and the standard of all the rest—one should have built madhouses for them and nothing more. That one *persecuted* them was a piece of ancient folly in the grand manner: that meant taking them too seriously, that meant making something serious out of them.

The whole fatality was made possible by the presence in the world already of a similar kind of megalomania, the Jewish (—once the chasm had opened up between the Jews and the Christian-Jews, the Christian-Jews *had* to employ once more and in an ultimate intensification for their own self-preservation the self-preservative procedures devised by the Jewish instinct—); on the other hand, Greek moral philosophy had already done everything to prepare the way for and to make palatable moral fanaticism even among Greeks and Romans—Plato, the great viaduct of corruption, who first refused to see nature in morality, who had already debased the Greek gods with his concept "good," who was already marked by Jewish bigotry (—in Egypt?)

203 (*Spring-Fall 1887; rev. Spring-Fall 1888*)

On the denaturing of morality.— These little herd-animal virtues do not by any means lead to "eternal life": to put them on show in this way, and oneself with them, may be very clever, but to him who keeps his eyes open even here, it remains in spite of all the most ludicrous of all plays. One does not by any means deserve a privileged position on earth and in heaven by attaining perfection as a little, good-natured sheep; one remains at best a little, good-natured, absurd sheep with horns—provided one does not burst with vanity—as the court chaplains do[35]—or provoke scandal by posing as a judge.

What a tremendous transfiguration of color here illumines the little virtues—as if they were the reflection of divine qualities!

The *natural* task and utility of every virtue is systematically hushed up; it is of value only with reference to a *divine* command, a divine model, only with reference to heavenly and spiritual goods. (Magnificent: as if it had to do with "salvation of the soul": but it was a means of "enduring" things here with as many beautiful feelings as possible.)

204 (*Spring-Fall 1887; rev. Spring-Fall 1888*)

The *law,* the thoroughly realistic formalization of certain conditions for the self-preservation of a community, forbids certain actions directed to certain ends, namely those that are directed against the community: it does *not* forbid the disposition that produces these actions—for it needs these actions for other ends, namely against the enemies of the community. Then the moral idealist appears and says: "God beholds the heart: the action itself is nothing; one must exterminate the aggressive disposition that produces it—" Under normal conditions one laughs at this; only in those exceptional instances when a community lives absolutely outside the necessity of waging war for its existence does one lend an ear to such things. One abandons a disposition whose *utility* is no longer apparent.

This was the case, e.g., when Buddha appeared amidst a very peaceable and even spiritually exhausted community.

[35] These words—a dig at Hofprediger Stöcker, the leading German anti-Semite of the time—are found only in 1911, p. 502. This is also true of the title of this section. For Stöcker see also 89 and 191 above.

This was also the case with the earliest Christian community (also Jewish community), whose presupposition is the absolutely unpolitical Jewish society. Christianity could grow only in the soil of Judaism, i.e., amidst a people that had already renounced politics and lived a kind of parasitic existence within the Roman order of things. Christianity is a step further on: one is even more free to "emasculate" oneself—circumstances permit it.

One drives nature out of morality when one says "Love your enemies": for then the natural "Thou shalt love thy neighbor and hate thy enemy" in the law (in instinct) has become meaningless; then this love of one's neighbor must also find a new basis (as a kind of love of God). Everywhere, God is inserted and utility withdrawn; everywhere the real origin of morality is denied: the veneration of nature, which lies precisely in the recognition of a natural morality, is destroyed at its roots—

Whence comes the seductive charm of such an emasculated ideal of man? Why are we not disgusted by it as we are perhaps disgusted by the idea of a castrato?— The answer lies precisely here: the voice of a castrato does *not* disgust us, despite the cruel mutilation that is its condition: it has grown sweeter— Just because the "male organ" has been amputated from virtue, a feminine note has been brought to the voice of virtue that it did not have before.

If we think, on the other hand, of the fearful hardship, danger, and accidents that a life of manly virtue brings with it—the life of a Corsican even today or that of the pagan Arab (which is similar even in its details to the life of the Corsican: their songs might have been written by Corsicans)—we grasp how precisely the most robust kind of man is fascinated and affected by this lustful note of "goodness," of "purity"— A shepherd's song—an idyl —the "good man": these things produce the strongest effect in ages when tragedy walks abroad.

*

But we have with this also recognized to what extent the "idealist" (—ideal-castrato) also emerges from a quite definite reality and is not merely a fantasist—he has arrived at the knowledge that for his kind of reality such a coarse injunction forbidding definite actions has no meaning (because the very instinct for these actions has been weakened through long lack of practice, of need for practice). The castrator formulates a number of new self-preservative measures for men of a quite definite species: in this he is a realist. His means of legislation are the same as those of the older legislators: the appeal to authority of all kinds, to "God," the employment of the concept "guilt and punishment"—i.e., he makes use of all the appurtenances of the older ideal, only in a new interpretation, punishment, for example, made more inward (perhaps as the pang of conscience).

In practice this species of man goes under as soon as the exceptional conditions of his existence cease—a kind of Tahiti and island happiness, as in the life of the little Jews in the provinces. Their only natural opponent is the soil from which they grew: against this they need to fight, against this they must let the offensive and defensive affects grow again: their opponents are the adherents of the old ideal (—this species of enmity is championed on a grand scale by Paul in relation to Judaism, by Luther in relation to the priestly-ascetic ideal). The mildest form of this opposition is certainly that of the early Buddhists: perhaps no greater amount of work has been expended upon anything than upon the discouragement and weakening of feelings of emnity. The fight against *ressentiment* seems to be almost the first duty of the Buddhist: only thus is peace of soul assured. To disengage oneself, but without rancor: that presupposes, to be sure, an astonishingly mild and sweet humanity—saints—

*

The prudence of moral castrationism.— How can one wage war against the manly affects and valuations? One possesses no means of physical force, one can wage only a war of cunning, sorcery, lies, in short "of the spirit."

First recipe: one claims virtue in general for one's ideal; one negates the older ideal to the point of presenting it as the antithesis of all ideals. For this one employs an art of defamation.

Second recipe: one sets up one's own type as the measure of value in general; one projects it into things, behind things, behind the fate of things—as God.

Third recipe: one sets up the opponent of one's ideal as the opponent of God; one fabricates for oneself the right to great pathos, to power, to curse and to bless.

Fourth recipe: one derives all suffering, all that is uncanny, fearful and fateful in existence from opposition to one's own ideal: —all suffering is punishment, even in the case of one's followers (—unless it accompanies a test, etc.).

Fifth recipe: one goes so far as to conceive nature as the antithesis of one's own ideal; one regards it as a great test of patience, as a sort of martyrdom to endure natural conditions for very long; one practices *dédain*[36] of mien and manners in respect to all "natural things."

Sixth recipe: the victory of unnaturalness, of the castrationist ideal, the victory of the world of the pure, good, sinless, blessed is projected into the future as conclusion, finale, great hope, as the "coming of the kingdom of God."

——I hope that at this artificial inflation of a small species into the absolute measure of things one is still permitted to *laugh?*

205 (*Spring-Fall 1887*)

I do not like at all about that Jesus of Nazareth or his apostle Paul that they put so many ideas into the heads of little people, as if their modest virtues were of any consequence. We have had to pay too dearly for it: for they have brought the more valuable qualities of virtue and man into ill repute; they have set the bad conscience of the noble soul against its self-sufficiency; they have led astray, to the point of self-destruction, the brave, magnanimous, daring, excessive inclinations of the strong soul—

206 (*Spring-Fall 1887*)

In the New Testament, and specifically in the Gospels, I hear absolutely nothing "divine" speaking: much rather an indirect form of the most abysmal rage for defamation and destruction—one of the most dishonorable forms of hatred. It lacks all knowledge of the qualities of a higher nature. Clumsy abuse of all kinds of philistinism; the entire treasury of proverbs is laid claim to and fully utilized; was it necessary for a *god* to come in order to say to these publicans etc.—

Nothing is more vulgar than this battle against the Pharisees with the aid of an absurd and impractical moral pretence; the people have always taken pleasure in such a *tour de force*. The reproach of "hypocrisy!" coming from this mouth! Nothing is more

[36] Disdain.

vulgar than this kind of treatment of an opponent—a most insidious criterion of nobility or its reverse—

207 (*Nov. 1887-March 1888*)

Primitive Christianity is abolition of the state: forbids oaths, war service, courts of justice, self-defense and the defense of any kind of community, the distinction between fellow countrymen and foreigners, and also the differentiation of classes.

Christ's example: he does not resist those who are harming him; he does not defend himself; he does more: he "turns the other cheek" (to the question: "Tell us whether thou be the Christ" he answers: "Hereafter shall ye see the Son of Man sitting on the right hand of power and coming in the clouds of heaven"). He forbids his disciples to defend him; he makes it clear that he could get help but *will* not.

Christianity is also abolition of society: it prefers all that society counts of little worth, it grows up among outcasts and the condemned, among lepers of all kinds, "sinners," "publicans," prostitutes, the most stupid folk (the "fishers"); it disdains the rich, the learned, the noble, the virtuous, the "correct"—

208 (*Nov. 1887-March 1888*)

The war against the noble and powerful as it is waged in the New Testament is a war after the manner of Reynard the Fox and with the same methods: but always with priestly unction and a decided refusal to recognize one's own cunning.

209 (*Nov. 1887-March 1888*)

The gospel: the news that a gateway to happiness stands open for the poor and lowly—that all one has to do is free oneself from the institutions, traditions, guardianship of the upper classes: to this extent the rise of Christianity is nothing more than the *typical socialist doctrine.*

Property, gain, fatherland, rank and status, tribunals, police, state, church, education, art, the army: all are so many hindrances to happiness, errors, snares, works of the devil, upon which the gospel passes judgment—all typical of socialist doctrine.

In the background is insurrection, the explosion of a stored-up antipathy towards the "masters," the instinct for how much happiness could lie, after such long oppression, simply in feeling oneself free— (Usually a sign that the lower orders have been too well treated, their tongues have already tasted a happiness forbidden them— It is not hunger that provokes revolutions, but that the people have acquired an appetite *en mangeant*[37]—).

210 (*Spring-Fall 1887*)

Read the New Testament as a book of seduction: virtue is appropriated in the instinct that with it one can capture public opinion—and indeed the most modest virtue, which recognizes the ideal sheep and nothing further (including the shepherd—): a little, sweet, well-meaning, helpful, and enthusiastically cheerful kind of virtue that expects absolutely nothing from the outside —that sets itself altogether apart from "the world." The most absurd arrogance, as if on one hand the community represented all that is right, and on the other the world all that is false, eternally reprehensible, and rejected, and as if the destiny of mankind revolved about this fact. The most absurd hatred toward everything in power: but without touching it! A kind of inner detachment that outwardly leaves everything as it was (servitude and slavery; to know how to turn *everything* into a means of serving God and virtue).

211 (*Spring-Fall 1887; rev. Spring-Fall 1888*)

Christianity is possible as the most *private* form of existence; it presupposes a narrow, remote, completely unpolitical society— it belongs in the conventicle. A "Christian state," "Christian politics," on the other hand, are a piece of impudence, a lie, like for instance a Christian leadership of an army, which finally treats the "God of Hosts" as if he were chief of staff. The papacy, too, has never been in a position to carry on Christian politics; and when reformers indulge in politics, as Luther did, one sees that they are just as much followers of Machiavelli as any immoralist or tyrant.

212 (*Nov. 1887-March 1888*)

Christianity is still possible at any time. It is not tied to any

---

[37] Through eating.

of the impudent dogmas that have adorned themselves with its name: it requires neither the doctrine of a personal God, nor that of sin, nor that of immortality, nor that of redemption, nor that of faith; it has absolutely no need of metaphysics, and even less of asceticism, even less of a Christian "natural science." Christianity is a *way of life,* not a system of beliefs. It tell us how to act, not what we ought to believe.

Whoever says today: "I will not be a soldier," "I care nothing for the courts," "I shall not claim the services of the police," "I will do nothing that may disturb the peace within me: and if I must suffer on that account, nothing will serve better to maintain my peace than suffering"—he would be a Christian.[38]

213 (*Nov. 1887-March 1888*)

Toward a history of Christianity. Continual change of milieu: Christian doctrine is therefore continually changing its emphasis— Favoring of lowly and little people— The development of *caritas*[39]— The type "Christian" reassumes step by step everything that it originally negated (in the negation of which it endured—). The Christian becomes citizen, soldier, judge, worker, merchant, scholar, theologian, priest, philosopher, farmer, artist, patriot, politician, "prince"—he takes up again all the activities he has forsworn (—self-defense, judgment, punishment, oath-taking, distinguishing between nation and nation, contempt, wrath—). The whole life of the Christian is at last exactly the life from which Christ preached deliverance—

The church is what is as much a symptom of the triumph of the anti-Christian as the modern state, modern nationalism— The church is the barbarization of Christianity.

214 (*Nov. 1887-March 1888*)

These have mastered Christianity: Judaism (Paul); Platonism (Augustine); the mystery cult (doctrine of redemption, emblem of the "cross"); asceticism (—enmity toward "nature," "reason," "the senses"—the Orient—).

---

[38] Cf. *The Antichrist,* section 39 (*Portable Nietzsche,* p. 612).

[39] Charity.

215 (*Spring-Fall 1887*)

Christianity as a denaturalization of herd-animal morality: accompanied by absolute misunderstanding and self-deception. Democratization is a more natural form of it, one less mendacious.

Datum: the oppressed, the lowly, the great masses of slaves and semi-slaves *desire power.*

First step: they make themselves free—they ransom themselves, in imagination at first, they recognize one another, they prevail.

Second step: they enter into battle, they demand recognition, equal rights, "justice."

Third step: they demand privileges (—they draw the representatives of power over to their side).

Fourth step: they demand *exclusive* power, and they get it—

In Christianity, three elements must be distinguished: (a) the oppressed of all kinds, (b) the mediocre of all kinds, (c) the discontented and sick of all kinds. With the first element Christianity fights against the political nobility and its ideal; with the second element, against the exceptional and privileged (spiritually, physically—) of all kinds; with the third element, against the natural instinct of the healthy and happy.

When a victory is won, the second element steps into the foreground; for then Christianity has persuaded the healthy and happy to its side (as warriors in its cause), likewise the powerful (as interested parties on account of the conquest of the mob)—and now it is the herd instinct, the mediocre nature which is of value from any point of view, which gets its supreme sanction through Christianity. This mediocre nature at last grows so conscious of itself (—acquires courage for itself—) that it arrogates even *political* power to itself—

Democracy is Christianity made natural: a kind of "return to nature" after, on account of its extreme antinaturalness, it could be overcome by the opposite values.— Consequence: the aristocratic ideal henceforth loses its naturalness ("the higher man," "noble," "artist," "passion," "knowledge," etc.; romanticism as cult of the exception, the genius, etc.).

216 (*Spring-Fall 1887; rev. Spring-Fall 1888*)

When the "masters" could also become Christians.— It lies in the instinct of a community (family, race, herd, tribe) to feel that the conditions and desires to which it owes its survival are valuable in themselves, e.g., obedience, reciprocity, consideration, moderation, sympathy—consequently to suppress everything that contradicts or stands in the way of them.

Likewise, it lies in the instinct of the rulers (be they individuals or classes) to patronize and applaud the virtues that make their subjects useful and submissive (—conditions and affects which may be as different as can be from their own).

The herd instinct and the instinct of the rulers agree in praising a certain number of qualities and conditions—but for differing reasons: the former from direct egoism, the latter from indirect egoism.

Submission of the master races to Christianity is essentially the consequence of the insight that Christianity is a herd religion, that it teaches obedience: in short, that Christians are easier to rule than non-Christians. With this hint, the pope recommends Christian propaganda to the emperor of China even today.

It should be added that the seductive force of the Christian ideal works most strongly perhaps upon such natures as love danger, adventure and opposition—as love all that involves risking themselves while at the same time engendering a *non plus ultra* of the feeling of power. Consider Saint Teresa, surrounded by the heroic instincts of her brothers:— Christianity here appears as a form of orgy of the will, of strength of will, as a heroic quixotism—

3. Christian Ideals

217 (*Spring-Fall 1887*)

War against the Christian ideal, against the doctrine of "blessedness" and "salvation" as the goal of life, against the supremacy of the simple, the pure in heart, the suffering and unfortunate.[40]

---

[40] In the MS the two paragraphs comprising this section are separated by a few pages, and the first paragraph contains a few more words at the end, omitted in the standard editions and also by Schlechta: "(What does

When and where has any man of consequence resembled the Christian ideal—at least in such eyes as a psychologist and student of man must have?—check all of Plutarch's heroes.

218 (*Nov. 1887-March 1888*)

Our pre-eminence: we live in the age of comparison, we can verify as has never been verified before: we are in every way the self-consciousness of history. We enjoy differently, we suffer differently: our instinctive activity is to compare an unheard-of number of things. We understand everything, we experience everything, we no longer have in us any hostile feelings. Although we may harm ourselves by it, our importunate and almost amorous inquisitiveness attacks, unabashed, the most dangerous things—

"Everything is good"—it requires an effort for us to deny anything. We suffer if we should happen to be so unintelligent as to take sides against anything— Fundamentally, it is we scholars who today best fulfill the teaching of Christ—

219 (*1885-1886*)

Irony against those who believe Christianity has been overcome by the modern natural sciences. Christian value judgments have not by any means been overcome this way. "Christ on the cross" is the most sublime symbol—even today.

220 (*Nov. 1887-March 1888*)

The two great nihilistic movements: (a) Buddhism, (b) Christianity. The latter has only now attained to approximately the state of culture in which it can fulfill its original vocation—a level to which it belongs—in which it can show itself pure.

221 (*Nov. 1887-March 1888*)

We have recovered the Christian ideal: it remains to determine its value:

God, the faith in God, matter to us any longer? 'God' today merely a faded word, not even a concept any longer!) But as Voltaire says on his deathbed: 'only don't speak of that man there!' "

1. What values are *negated* by it? What does its *counterideal* comprise?— Pride, pathos of distance, great responsibility, exuberance, splendid animality, the instincts that delight in war and conquest, the deification of passion, of revenge, of cunning, of anger, of voluptuousness, of adventure, of knowledge—; the noble ideal is negated: the beauty, wisdom, power, splendor and dangerousness of the type "man": the man who fixes goals, the "man of the future" (—here Christianity appears as a logical consequence of Judaism—).

2. Can it be *realized?*— Yes, under the right climatic conditions, as the Indian ideal was. Work is missing in both.— It detaches the individual from people, state, cultural community, jurisdiction; it rejects education, knowledge, cultivation of good manners, gain, commerce—it lets everything go that comprises the usefulness and value of man—it shuts him off by means of an idiosyncrasy of feeling. Unpolitical, antinational, neither aggressive nor defensive—possible only within the most firmly ordered political and social life, which allows these holy parasites to proliferate at public expense—

3. It is a consequence of the will to *pleasure*—and to nothing else! "Blessedness" counts as something self-evident, which no longer requires any justification—everything else (how to live and let live) is only a means to an end—

But this way of thinking is base: fear of pain, of defilement, of corruption as a sufficient motive for letting everything go— This is a *wretched* way of thinking— Sign of an *exhausted* race— One should not let oneself be deceived. ("Become as little children"—. Of related nature: Francis of Assisi, neurotic, epileptic, a visionary, like Jesus.)

222 (*Nov. 1887-March 1888*)

The higher man is distinguished from the lower by his fearlessness and his readiness to challenge misfortune: it is a sign of degeneration when eudaemonistic valuations begin to prevail (—physiological fatigue, feebleness of will—). Christianity, with its perspective of "blessedness," is a mode of thought typical of a suffering and feeble species of man. Abundant strength wants to create, suffer, go under: the Christian salvation-for-bigots is bad music to it, and its hieratic posture an annoyance.

223 (*1885-1886*)

Poverty, humility, and chastity—dangerous and slanderous ideals, but, like poisons in the case of certain illnesses, useful cures, e.g., in the Roman imperial era.

All ideals are dangerous: because they debase and brand the actual; all are poisons, but indispensable as temporary cures.

224 (*Nov. 1887-March 1888*)

God created man happy, idle, innocent, and immortal: our actual life is a false, decayed, sinful existence, an existence of punishment— Suffering, struggle, work, death are considered as objections and question marks against life, as something that ought not to last; for which one requires a cure—and *has* a cure!—

From the time of Adam until now, man has been in an abnormal state: God himself has sacrificed his son for the guilt of Adam, in order to put an end to this abnormal state: the natural character of life is a curse; Christ gives back the state of normality to him who believes in him: he makes him happy, idle and innocent.— But the earth has not begun to be fruitful without work; women do not bear children without pain; sickness has not ceased; the most devout believers have just as hard a time of it here as the least devout unbelievers. That man has been freed from death and sin (assertions which permit of no verification)—has been asserted by the church with all the more emphasis. "He is free from sin"—not through his own deed, not through a stern struggle on his part, but ransomed for freedom through the act of redemption—consequently perfect, innocent, paradisiacal—

The *true* life is only a faith (i.e., a self-deception, a madness). The whole of struggling, battling, actual existence, full of splendor and darkness, only a bad, false existence: the task is to be redeemed from it.

"Man innocent, idle, immortal, happy"—this conception of "supreme desiderata" must be criticized above all. Why are guilt, work, death, suffering (*and*, from a Christian viewpoint, *knowledge*—) contrary to the supreme desiderata?— The lazy Christian concepts "blessedness," "innocence," "immortality"—

225 (*Nov. 1887-March 1888*)

The eccentric concept of "holiness" is lacking—"God" and "man" have not been torn asunder. "Miracles" are lacking—this sphere simply isn't there: the only sphere worth consideration is the "spiritual" (i.e., the symbolic-psychological). As decadence: pendant to "epicureanism"— Paradise, as conceived by the Greeks, also only the "garden of Epicurus."

Any *task* is lacking in such a life:— it *desires* nothing; a form of the "Epicurean gods;" all reason is lacking to set up any further goals, to have children:— everything has been attained.

226 (*March-June 1888*)

They despised the body: they left it out of the account: more, they treated it as an enemy. It was their delusion to believe that one could carry a "beautiful soul" about in a cadaverous abortion— To make this conceivable to others they needed to present the concept "beautiful soul" in a different way, to revalue the natural value, until at last a pale, sickly, idiotically fanatical creature was thought to be perfection, "angelic," transfiguration, higher man.

227 (*Jan.-Fall 1888*)

Ignorance *in psychologicis*—the Christian has no nervous system—; contempt for, and a deliberate desire to disregard the demands of the body, the *discovery* of the body; the presupposition that this is in accordance with the higher nature of man, that it must necessarily be good for the soul; the systematic reduction of all bodily feelings to moral values; illness itself conceived as morally conditioned, perhaps as punishment or as testing or also as a state of salvation in which man becomes more perfect than he could be if he were healthy (—Pascal's idea); under certain circumstances, making oneself sick deliberately.

228 (*1883-1888*)

What, then, is this struggle of the Christian "against nature"? Do not let us be deceived by his words and explanations! It is nature against something that is also nature. With many it is fear, with some disgust, with others a certain spirituality, with the best, love of an ideal without flesh and desires, of an "abstraction from nature"—these try to live up to their ideal. It goes without saying that humility in place of self-reliance, anxious circumspection toward the desires, liberation from normal duties (whereby a higher feeling of rank is re-created), the incitement of a continual war over tremendous things, habituation to effusions of feeling—all this composes a type: in this type the excitability of a degenerate body predominates, but this nervousness and the inspirations it induces are interpreted otherwise. The taste of natures of this kind tends (1) to subtlety, (2) to floweriness, (3) to extreme feelings.

Natural inclinations *are* satisfied, but under a new form of interpretation, e.g., as "justification before God," "the feeling of redemption through grace" (—every undeniable pleasant feeling is interpreted thus!—), pride, voluptuousness, etc.

General problem: what will become of the man who defames the natural, and denies and degrades it in practice? In fact, the Christian proves himself to be an exaggerated form of self-control: in order to restrain his desires he seems to find it necessary to extirpate or crucify them.

229 (*March-June 1888*)

Through the long succession of millennia, man has not known himself physiologically: he does not know himself even today. To know, e.g., that one has a nervous system (—but no "soul"—) is still the privilege of the best informed. But man is not content not to know in this case. One must be very humane to say "I don't know that," to afford ignorance.

If he is suffering or in a good mood, he has no doubt that he can find the reason for it if only he looks. So he looks for the reason— In truth, he cannot find the reason, because he does not even suspect where he ought to look for it— What happens?— He takes a *consequence* of his condition for its *cause*; e.g., a work undertaken in a good mood (really undertaken because the good mood had provided the courage for it) succeeds: *ecco*, the work is the *reason* for the good mood.— In fact, the success was determined by the same thing that determined the good mood—by the happy coordination of physiological forces and systems.

He feels ill: and *consequently* he has not got over some worry, some scruple, some self-criticism.— In truth, the man believes his ill condition is a consequence of his scruple, his "sin," his "self-criticism"—

But the condition of recovery returns, often after a profound exhaustion and prostration. "How is it possible for me to feel so free, so redeemed? It is a miracle; only a god can have performed that."— Conclusion: "He has forgiven me my sin"—

From this there follows a certain practice: to excite feelings of sin, to prepare the way for contrition, one has to reduce the body to a morbid and nervous condition. The method of doing this is well known. As one might expect, there is no suspicion of the causal logic of the case: there is a religious interpretation of the mortification of the flesh, it seems an end in itself, whereas it is only a means of making possible the morbid indigestion of repentance (the *"idée fixe"* of sin, the hypnotizing of the hen by the chalk line "sin").

The maltreatment of the body prepares the ground for the sequence of "feelings of guilt," i.e., a general state of suffering that demands an explanation—

On the other hand, the method of "redemption" follows in the same way: one provokes all kinds of orgies of feeling by prayers, motions, gestures, oaths—exhaustion follows, often abruptly, often in the form of epilepsy. And—after a condition of deep somnolence comes the appearance of recovery—in religious language: "redemption."[40a]

230 (*Jan.-Fall 1888*)

Formerly one considered these conditions and consequences of physiological exhaustion more important than conditions of health and their consequences, because they are rich in the sudden, the fearful, the inexplicable and the incalculable. One was afraid: one postulated here a higher world. Sleep and dream, shadows, the night, natural terrors, have been held responsible for the creation of two worlds: above all, the symptoms of physiological exhaustion should have been considered in this regard. The ancient religions actually disciplined the pious into a condition of exhaustion in

[40a] This discussion of mistaking consequences for causes should be compared with the chapter on "The Four Great Errors" in *Twilight.*

which they *must* experience such things— One believed one had entered a higher order of things where everything ceased to be familiar.— The *appearance* of a higher power—

231 (*March-June 1888*)

Sleep as consequence of every exhaustion, exhaustion as consequence of every excessive excitement—

The necessity for sleep, the deification and adoration of the very concept "sleep" in all pessimistic religions and philosophies—

The exhaustion is in this case a racial exhaustion: sleep, regarded psychologically, is only a symbol of a much deeper and longer *compulsion to rest*— In practice it is death that works so seductively behind the image of its brother, sleep—

232 (*March-June 1888*)

The entire Christian training in repentance and redemption can be conceived as a deliberately provoked *folie circulaire*:[41] but, as one might expect, producible only in predestined, that is, morbidly inclined individuals.

233 (*March-June 1888*)

Against remorse and the purely psychological treatment of it.— To be unable to have done with an experience is already a sign of decadence. This reopening of old wounds, this wallowing in self-contempt and contrition, is one more illness, out of which no "salvation of the soul" can arise but only a new form of soul sickness—

These "states of redemption" in the Christian are mere variations of one and the same diseased state—interpretations of the epileptic crisis by a certain formula supplied, not by science, but by religious delusion.

One is *good* in a sickly manner when one is sick— We now count the greater part of the psychological apparatus with which Christianity operated as forms of hysteria and epilepsy.

The entire practice of psychological healing must be put back

[41] An earlier name for manic-depressive insanity, sometimes rendered as alternating insanity.

on to a *physiological* basis: the "bite" of conscience as such is a hindrance to recovery—one must try to counterbalance it all by new activities, in order to escape from the sickness of self-torture as quickly as possible— One should discredit the purely psychological practice of the church and the sects as harmful to health— One cannot cure an invalid by prayers and the exorcizing of evil spirits: the conditions of "repose" that supervene under the influence of such things are very far from inspiring confidence, in a psychological sense—

One is healthy when one can laugh at the earnestness and zeal with which one has been hypnotized by any single detail of our life, when one feels that the "bite" of conscience is like a dog biting on a stone—when one is ashamed of one's remorse—

Previous practice, which was purely religious and psychological, aimed only at a change in the symptoms: it held a man to be cured when he abased himself before the cross and swore to be a good man— But a criminal who with a certain sombre seriousness cleaves to his fate and does not slander his deed after it is done has more *health of soul*— The criminals among whom Dostoevsky lived in prison were one and all unbroken natures—are they not worth a hundred times more than a "broken" Christian?

(—I recommend that the "bite" of conscience be treated with Mitchell's cure[42]——)

234 (*1883-1888*)

The "bite" of conscience: sign that the character is not equal to the deed. There is such a thing as a "bite" of conscience after *good* works: the unfamiliar in them, that which raises them out of the old milieu.—[43]

---

[42] The "rest cure" of Dr. Silas Weir Mitchell (1829-1914, American), consisting primarily in isolation, confinement to bed, dieting, and massage. Cf. *Genealogy* I, section 6, where Nietzsche mentions isolation and overeating.

[43] With sections 233-35 compare section 10 of the first chapter of *Twilight* (*Portable Nietzsche*, p. 467): "Not to perpetrate cowardice against one's own acts! Not to leave them in the lurch afterward! The bite of conscience is indecent."

The influence of these passages and others on Sartre's *The Flies* is discussed in detail in my essay on "Nietzsche between Homer and Sartre: Five Treatments of the Orestes Story," in *Révue Internationale de Philosophie*, 67 (1964.1), especially pp. 65-73.

235 (*Spring-Fall 1887; rev. Spring-Fall 1888*)

Against remorse.— I do not like this kind of cowardice toward one's own deeds; one should not leave oneself in the lurch at the onset of unanticipated shame and embarrassment. An extreme[44] pride, rather, is in order. After all, what is the good of it! No deed can be undone by being regretted; no more than by being "forgiven" or "atoned for." One would have to be a theologian to believe in a power that annuls guilt: we immoralists prefer not to believe in "guilt." We hold instead that every action is of identical value at root—and that actions that turn *against* us may, economically considered, be nonetheless useful, generally desirable actions.

In any particular case we will allow that an act could easily have been spared us—but circumstances favored it. Which of us, if favored by circumstance, would not have gone through the entire gamut of crime?

One should never say on that account: "You should not have done this or that," but always: "How strange that I should not have done that a hundred times before!"

After all, very few actions are typical actions and real epitomes of a personality; and considering how little personality most men have, a man is seldom *characterized* by a single action. Acts of circumstance, merely epidermal, merely reflexes that respond to a stimulus: long before the depths of our being are touched by it, consulted about it. A rage, a reach, a knife thrust: what of personality is in that?[45]

A deed often brings with it a numbness and lack of freedom: so that the doer is as if spellbound at its recollection and feels as if he were an *accessory* of it. This spiritual disorder, a form of hypnotism, must be resisted at all cost: a single deed, whatever it may be, is, in comparison with everything one has done, a zero, and may be deducted without falsifying the account. The iniquitous interest that society may have in treating our entire existence from a single point of view, as if its meaning lay in bringing forth one single deed, should not infect the doer himself: unfortunately this

---

[44] This word is illegible in the MS and represents a conjecture by the German editors. See also the preceding footnote.

[45] Cf. Camus, *The Stranger*.

happens almost all the time. That stems from the fact that a spiritual disturbance follows every deed with unusual consequences, whether these consequences are good or ill. Observe a lover who has received a promise, or a poet applauded by an audience: so far as *torpor intellectualis* is concerned, they differ in no way from an anarchist confronted with a search warrant.

There are actions which are *unworthy* of us: actions that, if regarded as typical, would reduce us to a lower class of man. Here one has only to avoid the error of regarding them as typical. There are other kinds of actions of which *we* are unworthy: exceptions born of a particular abundance of happiness and health, our highest floodtide driven so high for once by a storm, an accident: such actions and "works" are likewise not typical. One should never measure an artist by the standard of his works.

236 (*Jan.-Fall 1888*)

a. In proportion as Christianity still seems necessary today, man is still savage and fateful—

b. From another point of view it is not necessary, but extremely harmful, although enticing and seductive because it corresponds to the morbid character of whole classes, whole types of contemporary humanity—decadents of all kinds, they follow their inclinations when they aspire to Christianity—

One must distinguish clearly between a. and b. In case a. Christianity is a cure, at least a means of taming (—under certain circumstances it serves to make sick: which can be useful in breaking savagery and brutality). In case b. it is itself a symptom of sickness, propagates decadence; here it works against a corroborating system of treatment, here it is the invalid's instinct against that which is good for him—

237 (*Jan.-Fall 1888*)

The party of the serious, dignified, reflective: and opposed to them the savage, unclean, incalculable beast—: merely a problem of animal taming—in which the animal tamer must be hard, fearsome and terror-inspiring toward his beasts.

All essential demands must be made with a brutal clarity, i.e., exaggerated a thousandfold:

even the fulfilment of the demand must be represented in a coarsened way, so it may inspire awe, e.g., emancipation from the senses on the part of the Brahmins.

*

The struggle with the canaille and the cattle. If a certain taming and order is to be achieved, the chasm between these purified and reborn people and the remainder must be made as fearful as possible—

This chasm increases in the higher castes their self-regard, their faith in that which they represent—hence the chandala. Contempt and an excess of it is perfectly correct psychologically, that is to say, exaggerated a hundredfold, so that it may at least be copied.[46]

238 (*Jan.-Fall 1888*)

The struggle against the brutal instincts is different from the struggle against the sick instincts; to make sick may even be a means of mastering brutality. Christian psychological practice often leads to the conversion of a brute into a sick and consequently tame animal.

The struggle against brutal and savage natures must be a struggle using means that affect them: superstitions are indispensable and essential—[47]

239 (*Nov. 1887-March 1888*)

Our age is in a certain sense ripe (that is to say, decadent), as the age of Buddha was— Therefore a Christianity is possible, but without the absurd dogmas (the most repellent abortions of antique hybridism).

240 (*1885-1886*)

Even granted that the Christian faith might not be disprovable, Pascal thinks, nonetheless, that, in view of a *fearful* possibility that it is true, it is in the highest degree prudent to be a Christian.

---

[46] But cf. *Twilight*, "The 'Improvers' of Mankind," sections 3-5, (*Portable Nietzsche*, pp. 503-505), which were written later.

[47] See the footnote to section 237.

Today one finds, as a sign of how much Christianity has declined in fearfulness, that other attempt to justify it by saying that even if it were an error, one might yet have during one's life the great advantage and enjoyment of this error:— it therefore seems that this faith ought to be maintained precisely for the sake of its tranquilizing effect—not, therefore, from fear of a threatening possibility, rather from fear of a life that has lost one charm. This hedonistic turn, the proof from *pleasure*, is a symptom of decline: it replaces the proof from *strength*, from that which overpowers us in the Christian idea, from *fear*. In fact, with this reinterpretation Christianity is approaching exhaustion: one is content with an *opiate* Christianity because one has the strength neither to seek, to struggle, to dare, to wish to stand alone, nor for Pascalism, for this brooding self-contempt, for faith in human unworthiness, for the anguished feeling that one is "perhaps damned." But a Christianity intended above all to soothe diseased nerves has really ***no need*** of that fearful solution of a "God on the cross": which is why Buddhism is silently gaining ground everywhere in Europe.

241 (*Nov. 1887-March 1888*)

The humor of European culture: one holds *this* to be true but does *that*. E.g., what is the point of the arts of reading and criticism as long as the ecclesiastical interpretation of the Bible, Protestant as well as Catholic, is cultivated as ever?

242 (*Nov. 1887-March 1888*)

One does not consider closely enough how barbarous the concepts are by which we Europeans still live. That men have been capable of believing that "salvation of the soul" depended on a book!— And they tell me this is still believed today.

What is the point of scientific education, criticism and hermeneutics if such a lunatic exposition of the Bible as is still cultivated by the church has not yet turned the blush of shame into a permanent skin color?

243 (*Spring-Fall 1887; rev. Spring-Fall 1888*)

To consider: to what extent the fateful belief in divine providence—the most paralyzing belief for hand and reason there has ever been—still exists; to what extent Christian presuppositions and interpretations still live on under the formulas "nature," "progress," "perfectibility," "Darwinism," under the superstitious belief in a certain relationship between happiness and virtue, unhappiness and guilt. That absurd trust in the course of things, in "life," in the "instinct of life," that comfortable resignation that comes from the faith that if everyone only does his duty *all* will be well—this kind of thing is meaningful only by supposing a direction of things *sub specie boni.* Even fatalism, the form philosophical sensibility assumes with us today, is a consequence of this long belief in divine dispensation, an unconscious consequence: as if what happens were no responsbility of ours (—as though it were permissible to let things take their course: every individual self only a mode of absolute reality—).

244 (*Nov. 1887-March 1888*)

It is the height of psychological mendaciousness in man to frame according to his own petty standard of what seems good, wise, powerful, valuable, a being that is an origin and "in-itself"—and therewith to abolish in his mind the entire causal process by means of which any kind of goodness, any kind of wisdom, any kind of power exists and possesses value. In short, to posit elements of the most recent and contingent origin as not created but "in-themselves" and perhaps even as the cause of creation in general—

Judging from experience, from every instance in which a man has raised himself significantly above the average of humanity, we see that every high degree of power involves *freedom* from good and evil and from "true" and "false," and cannot take into account the demands of goodness: we see that the same applies to every high degree of wisdom—goodness is abrogated in it as much as veracity, justice, virtue, and other popular fancies in valuation. Finally, every high degree of goodness itself: is it not patent that it presupposes a spiritual myopia and coarseness? including the inability to distinguish at a distance between true and false, between useful and harmful? not to discuss the fact that a high degree of power in the hands of the highest degree of goodness would lead to the most calamitous consequences ("the abolition of evil")?— In fact, one needs only to see what tendencies the

"God of love" inspires in his believers: they ruin mankind for the sake of the "good."— In practice, the actual constitution of the world has shown this same God to be the God of the extremest shortsightedness, devilry and impotence: which reveals how much value there is in this conception of him.

Knowledge and wisdom in themselves have no value; no more than goodness: one must first be in possession of the goal from which these qualities derive their value or nonvalue—there *could* be a goal in the light of which great knowledge might represent a great disvalue (if, for instance, a high degree of deception were one of the prerequisites of the enhancement of life; likewise if goodness were perhaps able to paralyze and discourage the springs of the great longing)—

Taking our human life as it is, all "truth," all "goodness," all "holiness," all "divinity" in the Christian style has up to now shown itself to be highly dangerous—even now mankind is in danger of perishing through an idealism inimical of life.[48]

245 (*Spring-Fall 1887*)

Consider the damage all human institutions sustain if a divine and transcendent higher sphere is postulated that must first sanction these institutions. By then growing accustomed to seeing their value in this sanction (e.g., in the case of marriage), one has reduced their natural dignity, in certain circumstances denied it— Nature has been ill-judged to the extent to which one has brought into honor the antinaturalness of a God. "Natural" has come to mean the same as "contemptible," "bad"—

The fatefulness of a belief in God as the *reality of the highest moral qualities*: all actual values were therewith denied and systematically conceived as non-values. Thus antinaturalness assumed the throne. With relentless logic one arrived at the absolute demand to deny nature.

246 (*Jan.-Fall 1888*)

In moving the doctrine of selflessness and love into the foreground, Christianity was in no way establishing the interests of

[48] In the MS this section follows a draft for *Antichrist*, section 47.

the species as of higher value than the interests of the individual. Its real *historical* effect, the fateful element in its effect, remains, on the contrary, in precisely the enhancement of egoism, of the egoism of the individual, to an extreme (—to the extreme of individual immortality). Through Christianity, the individual was made so important, so absolute, that he could no longer be sacrificed: but the species endures only through human sacrifice— All "souls" became equal before God: but this is precisely the most dangerous of all possible evaluations! If one regards individuals as equal, one calls the species into question, one encourages a way of life that leads to the ruin of the species: Christianity is the counterprinciple to the principle of *selection*. If the degenerate and sick ("the Christian") is to be accorded the same value as the healthy ("the pagan"), or even more value, as in Pascal's judgment concerning sickness and health, then unnaturalness becomes law—

This universal love of men is in practice the *preference* for the suffering, underprivileged, degenerate: it has in fact lowered and weakened the strength, the responsibility, the lofty duty to sacrifice men. All that remains, according to the Christian scheme of values, is to sacrifice oneself: but this residue of human sacrifice that Christianity concedes and even advises has, from the standpoint of general breeding, no meaning at all. The prosperity of the species is unaffected by the self-sacrifice of this or that individual (—whether it be in the monkish and ascetic manner or, with the aid of crosses, pyres, and scaffolds, as "martyrs" of error). The species requires that the ill-constituted, weak, degenerate, perish: but it was precisely to them that Christianity turned as a conserving force; it further enhanced that instinct in the weak, already so powerful, to take care of and preserve themselves and to sustain one another. What is "virtue" and "charity" in Christianity if not just this mutual preservation, this solidarity of the weak, this hampering of selection? What is Christian altruism if not the mass-egoism of the weak, which divines that if all care for one another each individual will be preserved as long as possible?—

If one does not feel such a disposition as an extreme immorality, as a crime against life, one belongs with the company of the sick and possesses its instincts oneself—

Genuine charity demands sacrifice for the good of the species —it is hard, it is full of self-overcoming, because it needs human sacrifice. And this pseudo humaneness called Christianity wants it established that no one should be sacrificed—

247 (*March-June 1888*)

Nothing would be more useful or more to be encouraged than a thoroughgoing *practical nihilism.* As I understand all the phenomena of Christianity and pessimism, they say: "We are ripe for nonexistence; for us it is reasonable not to exist." This language of "reason" is also, in this case, the language of selective nature.

What, on the other hand, is to be condemned in the sternest terms is the ambiguous and cowardly compromise of a religion such as Christianity: more precisely, such as the church: which, instead of encouraging death and self-destruction, protects everything ill-constituted and sick and makes it propagate itself—

Problem: with what means could one attain to a severe form of really contagious nihilism: such as teaches and practices voluntary death with scientific conscientiousness (—and *not* a feeble, vegetable existence in expectation of a false afterlife—)?

One cannot sufficiently condemn Christianity for having devaluated the value of such a great purifying nihilistic movement, which was perhaps already being formed, through the idea of the immortal private person: likewise through the hope of resurrection: in short, through continual deterrence from the *deed of nihilism,* which is suicide—

It substituted slow suicide: gradually a petty, poor, but durable life; gradually a quite ordinary, bourgeois, mediocre life, etc.

248 (*March-June 1888*)

Christian moral quackery.— Pity and contempt succeed one another in quick alternation, and occasionally I get enraged, as at the sight of some mean crime. Here error is made a duty—a virtue; blundering is made into an art, the instinct for destruction systematized as "redemption"; here every operation becomes an injury, an amputation even of those organs whose energy is a precondition of any return to health. And the most that is achieved is never healing, but only the substitution of one set of evil symptoms for another—

And this dangerous nonsense, this systematized disfiguring and castration of life, is counted holy, inviolable; to live in its service, to be an instrument of this healing art, to be a *priest,* makes one distinguished, venerable, makes one holy and even inviolable. Only divinity can be the author of this highest healing art: only as revelation can redemption be understood, as an art of grace, as the most undeserved gift granted to the creature.

First proposition: health of soul is regarded as sickness, as suspicious—

Second proposition: the prerequisites of a strong and flourishing life, strong desires and passions, count as objections to a strong and flourishing life.

Third proposition: all that threatens man with danger, all that might master and destroy him, is evil, is reprehensible—is to be torn from his soul by its roots.

Fourth proposition: man made harmless to himself and others, weak, prostrated in humility and modesty, conscious of his weakness, the "sinner"—this is the most desirable type, and one that can also be *produced* with a little surgery to the soul—

249 (*Spring-Fall 1887*)

What is it I protest against? That one should take this petty, peaceable mediocrity, this equilibrium of a soul that knows nothing of the mighty motivation of great accumulations of strength, for something exalted, possibly even for the *measure of man.*

Bacon of Verulam says: *Infimarum virtutum apud vulgus laus est, mediarum admiratio, supremarum sensus nullus.*[49] Christianity, however, belongs, as a religion, to the *vulgus*: it has no feeling for the highest species of *virtus.*

250 (*Spring-Fall 1887*)

Let us see what "the true Christian" does with all that which his instinct opposes:—he sullies and suspects the beautiful, the splendid, the rich, the proud, the self-reliant, the knowledgeable, the powerful—in summa, the whole of culture: his object is to deprive it of a good conscience—

251 (*Jan.-Fall 1888*)

Hitherto one has always attacked Christianity not merely in

---

[49] The ordinary ruck has praise for the lowest virtues, admiration for the mediocre, and for the highest virtues no sense at all.

a modest way but in the wrong way. As long as one has not felt Christian morality to be a capital crime against life its defenders have had it all their own way. The question of the mere "truth" of Christianity—whether in regard to the existence of its God or the historicity of the legend of its origin, not to speak of Christian astronomy and natural science—is a matter of secondary importance as long as the question of the value of Christian *morality* is not considered. Is Christian morality *worth* anything, or is it a shame and digrace despite all the holiness of its arts of seduction? The problem of truth can slip away into hiding places of all kinds; and the greatest believers may finally avail themselves of the logic of the greatest unbelievers to create for themselves a right to affirm certain things as irrefutable—namely, as *beyond* the means of all refutation—(this artifice is today called "Kantian Criticism").

252 (*Nov. 1887-March 1888*)

One should never forgive Christianity for having destroyed such men as Pascal. One should never cease from combating just this in Christianity: its will to break precisely the strongest and noblest souls. One should never rest as long as this one thing has not been utterly and completely destroyed: the ideal of man invented by Christianity, its demands upon men, its Yes and its No with regard to men. The whole absurd residue of Christian fable, conceptual cobweb-spinning and theology does not concern us; it could be a thousand times more absurd and we would not lift a finger against it. But we do combat the ideal that, with its morbid beauty and feminine seductiveness, with its furtive slanderous eloquence appeals to all the cowardices and vanities of wearied souls—and the strongest have their weary hours—as if all that might, in such states, seem most useful and desirable—trust, guilelessness, modesty, patience, love of one's fellows, resignation, submission to God, a sort of unharnessing and abdication of one's whole ego—were also the most useful and desirable as such; as if the petty, modest abortion of a soul, the virtuous average-and-herd man, did not only take precedence over the stronger, more evil, covetous, defiant, prodigal, and therefore a hundred times more imperiled kind of man, but provided nothing less than the ideal, the goal, the measure, the highest *desideratum* for mankind in general. To erect *this* ideal was the most sinister temptation ever placed before mankind: for with it, the more strongly constituted exceptions and fortunate cases among men, in whom the will to power and to the growth of the whole type "man" took a step forward, were threatened with destruction; with the values of this ideal, the growth of these higher men, who for the sake of their superior claims and tasks also freely accept a life more full of peril (expressed economically: a rise in the cost of the undertaking in proportion to the decline in the probability of its success) would be attacked at the roots. What is it we combat in Christianity? That it wants to break the strong, that it wants to discourage their courage, exploit their bad hours and their occasional weariness, convert their proud assurance into unease and distress of conscience, that it knows how to poison and sicken the noble instincts until their strength, their will to power turns backward, against itself—until the strong perish through orgies of self-contempt and self-abuse: that gruesome way of perishing of which Pascal provides the most famous example.

II. CRITIQUE OF MORALITY

1. Origin of Moral Valuations

253 (*1885-1886*)

For the Preface of The Dawn[50]

An attempt to think about morality without falling under its spell, mistrustful of the seductiveness of its beautiful gestures and glances. A world we can revere, that is adequate to our drive to worship—that continually proves itself—by providing guidance in the particular and the general—: this is the Christian viewpoint in which we have all grown up.

Through an increase in our acuteness, mistrust, scientificality (also through a more ambitious instinct for veracity, thus under anti-Christian influences), this interpretation has grown more and more impermissible to us.

Subtlest way of escape: Kantian Criticism. The intellect disputes its right to make interpretations of this sort as well as to

[50] The first edition of *The Dawn* appeared in 1881; the second, with a new preface, in 1887. This heading has always been omitted so far.

reject interpretations of this sort. One contents oneself with an increase in one's trust and faith, with a renunciation of all provability in matters of faith, with an inconceivable and superior "ideal" (God) as a stopgap.

The Hegelian way out, following Plato, a piece of romanticism and reaction, at the same time a symptom of the historical sense, of a new *strength*: the "spirit" itself is the "self-revealing and self-realizing ideal": more and more of this ideal in which we believe manifests itself in the course of its "process," in "becoming"—: thus the ideal realizes itself; faith is directed into the *future* when, in accordance with its noble requirements, it can worship. In short,

1. God is unknowable for *us* and not demonstrable by us (the hidden meaning of the epistemological movement);

2. God is demonstrable but as something in process of becoming, and we are part of it, as witness our impulse toward the ideal (the hidden meaning of the historical movement).

Observe: criticism is never directed at the ideal itself, but only at the problem, where the opposition to it originates: why it has not yet been achieved or why it is not demonstrable in small things and in great.

*

It makes all the difference whether one feels this state of distress as a state of distress from passion, from a yearning, or whether one barely reaches it as a problem after the utmost thought and with a certain force of historical imagination.

We discover the same phenomenon outside religion and philosophy: utilitarianism (socialism, democracy) criticizes the origin of moral evaluations, but it *believes* them just as much as the Christian does. (Naiveté: as if morality could survive when the *God* who sanctions it is missing! The "beyond" absolutely necessary if faith in morality is to be maintained.)

Basic problem: whence this omnipotence of *faith*? Of faith in morality? (—Which betrays itself in this, too, that even the basic conditions of life are falsely interpreted for the benefit of morality: despite our knowledge of the animal world and the world of plants. "Self-preservation": the reconciliation of altruistic and egoistic principles in the perspective of Darwinism.)

254 (*1885-1886*)

The inquiry into the *origin of our evaluations* and tables of the good is in absolutely no way identical with a critique of them, as is so often believed: even though the insight into some *pudenda origo*[51] certainly brings with it *a feeling* of a diminution in value of the thing that originated thus and prepares the way to a critical mood and attitude toward it.

What are our evaluations and moral tables really worth? What is the outcome of their rule? For whom? in relation to what?— Answer: for life. But *what is life?* Here we need a new, more definite formulation of the concept "life." My formula for it is: Life is will to power.

What is the meaning of the act of evaluation itself? Does it point back or down to another, metaphysical world? (As Kant still believed, who belongs *before* the great historical movement.) In short: where did it originate? Or did it not "originate"?— Answer: moral evaluation is an *exegesis,* a way of interpreting. The exegesis itself is a symptom of certain physiological conditions, likewise of a particular spiritual level of prevalent judgments: Who interprets?— Our affects.

255 (*1883-1888*)

All virtues physiological *conditions:* particularly the principal organic functions considered as necessary, as good. All virtues are really refined *passions* and enhanced states.

Pity and love of mankind as development of the sexual drive. Justice as development of the drive to revenge. Virtue as pleasure in resistance, will to power. Honor as recognition of the similar and equal-in-power.

256 (*1887-1888*)

I understand by "morality" a system of evaluations that partially coincides with the conditions of a creature's life.

---

[51] Shameful origin.

257 (*March-June 1888*)

Formerly one said of every morality: "By their fruits ye shall know them." I say of every morality: "It is a fruit by which I recognize the *soil* from which it sprang."

258 (*1885-1886*)

My attempt to understand moral judgments as symptoms and sign languages which betray the processes of physiological prosperity or failure, likewise the consciousness of the conditions for preservation and growth—a mode of interpretations of the same worth as astrology, prejudices prompted by the instincts (of races, communities, of the various stages of life, as youth or decay, etc.).

Applied to the specific Christian-European morality: Our moral judgments are signs of decline, of disbelief in life, a preparation for pessimism.

My chief proposition: there are no moral phenomena, there is only a moral interpretation of these phenomena. This interpretation itself is of extra-moral origin.[52]

What does it mean that our interpretation has projected a *contradiction* into existence?— Of decisive importance: behind all other other evaluations these moral evaluations stand in command. Supposing they were abolished, according to what would we measure then? And then of what value would be knowledge, etc., etc. ? ? ?

259 (*1884*)

Insight: all evaluation is made from a definite perspective: that of the preservation of the individual, a community, a race, a state, a church, a faith, a culture.— Because we forget that valuation is always from a perspective, a single individual contains within him a vast confusion of contradictory valuations and consequently of contradictory drives. This is the expression of the diseased condition in man, in contrast to the animals in which all existing instincts answer to quite definite tasks.

This contradictory creature has in his nature, however, a great method of acquiring knowledge: he feels many pros and

[52] Cf. section 266.

cons, he raises himself to justice—to comprehension beyond esteeming things good and evil.

The wisest man would be the one richest in contradictions, who has, as it were, antennae for all types of men—as well as his great moments of *grand harmony*—a rare accident even in us! A sort of planetary motion—

260 (*1883-1888*)

"Willing": means willing an end. "An end" includes an evaluation. Whence come evaluations? Is their basis a firm norm, "pleasant" and "painful"?

But in countless cases we first *make* a thing painful by investing it with an evaluation.

The extent of moral evaluations: they play a part in almost every sense impression. Our world is *colored* by them.

We have invested things with ends and values: therefore we have in us an enormous fund of latent force: but by comparing values it appears that contradictory things have been accounted valuable, that *many* tables of value have existed (thus nothing is valuable "in itself").

Analysis of individual tables of value revealed that their erection was the erection of the conditions—often erroneous—of existence of a limited group—for its preservation.

Observation of *contemporary* man reveals that we employ *very diverse* value judgments and that they no longer have any creative force—the basis, "the condition of existence," is now missing from moral judgment. It is much more superfluous, it is not nearly so painful.— It becomes *arbitrary*. Chaos.

Who creates *the goal* that stands above mankind and above the individual? Formerly one employed morality for preservation: but nobody wants to preserve any longer, there is nothing to preserve. Therefore an *experimental morality*: to *give* oneself a goal.

261 (*1883-1888*)

What is the criterion of a moral action? (1) its disinterestedness, (2) its universal validity, etc. But this is armchair moralizing. One must study peoples to see what the criterion is in every case, and what is expressed by it: a belief that "such a scheme of behavior is one of the first conditions of our existence." Immoral means "bringing destruction." Now, all the communities in which these propositions are discovered have perished: certain of these propositions have been reaffirmed again and again because every new community that arose had need of them again; e.g., "Thou shalt not steal." In ages when it was impossible to demand any feeling for the community (e.g., in the *imperium Romanum*), the drive was directed to "salvation of soul," in religious language: or "the greatest happiness," in philosophical terms. For even the Greek moral philosophers no longer had any feeling for their *polis*. [53]

262 (*1888*)

The necessity of false values.— One can refute a judgment by proving its conditionality: the need to retain it is not thereby removed. False values cannot be eradicated by reasons any more than astigmatism in the eyes of an invalid. One must grasp the need for their existence: they are a consequence of causes which have nothing to do with reasons.

263 (*1885*)

To see and to demonstrate the problem of morality—that seems to me the new principal task. I deny that it has been done in previous moral philosophy.

264 (*Nov. 1887-March 1888*)

How false, how mendacious mankind has always been about the basic facts of its inner world! To close one's eyes to this, to speak and not to speak about that—

265 (*1885-1888*)

There is lacking a knowledge and consciousness of the revolutions that have already occurred in moral judgments, and of how fundamentally "evil" has several times been renamed "good." I indicated one of these displacements with the term "morality of

[53] City-state.

custom."[54] Even conscience has changed its sphere: there used to be a pang of conscience of the herd.

266 (*1883-1886*)

A. Morality as the work of immorality.
  1. For moral values to gain dominion they must be assisted by lots of immoral forces and affects.
  2. The origin of moral values is the work of immoral affects and considerations.

B. Morality as the work of error.

C. Morality always contradicts itself.

Requital.— Veracity, doubt, *epochē,*[55] judging.— The "immorality" of *belief* in morality.

The steps:
  1. absolute dominion of morality: all biological phenomena measured and judged by moral values.
  2. attempt to identify life with morality (symptom of an awakened skepticism: morality must no longer be felt as an antithesis); several means, even a transcendental way.
  3. opposition of life and morality: morality judged and condemned from the point of view of life.

D. To what extent morality has been detrimental to life:
  a) to the enjoyment of life, to gratitude towards life, etc.,
  b) to the beautifying, ennobling of life,
  c) to knowledge of life,
  d) to the development of life, in so far as it sought to set the highest phenomena of life at variance with itself.

E. Counter-reckoning: its usefulness for life.
  1. Morality as the principle that preserves the general whole, as a limitation upon its members: "the *instrument.*"
  2. Morality as the principle that preserves man from the inner peril of his passions: "the *mediocre.*"
  3. Morality as the principle that preserves man from the

---

[54] *Sittlichkeit der Sitte*: cf. *Dawn,* sections 9, 14, 18, 33; *Gay Science,* 43, 143, 149, 296; *Genealogy*, Preface and II:2 and III:9.

[55] The suspension of judgment cultivated by the ancient skeptics.

life-destroying effects of profound misery and atrophy: "the *suffering*."

4. Morality as the principle that opposes the fearful outbursts of the powerful: "the *lowly*."

267 (*1885-1886*)

It is a good thing to take "right," "wrong," etc., in a definite, narrow, bourgeois sense, as in "Do right and fear no man": i.e., to do one's duty according to a definite rude scheme within which a community exists.

—Let us not think meanly of that which two thousand years of morality have bred in our spirit!

268 (*Jan.-Fall 1888*)

Two types of morality must not be confused: the morality with which the healthy instinct defends itself against incipient decadence—and another morality with which this very decadence defines and justifies itself and leads downwards.

The former is usually stoical, hard, tyrannical (—*Stoicism* itself was such a brake-shoe morality); the latter is enthusiastic, sentimental, full of secrets; it has the women and "beautiful feelings" on its side (—primitive *Christianity* was such a morality).

269 (*1883-1888*)

To get the whole of moralizing into focus as a phenomenon. Also as a riddle. The phenomena of morality have occupied me like riddles. Today I would know how to answer the question: What does it mean that the welfare of my neighbor *ought* to possess for me a higher value than my own? but that my neighbor himself *ought* to assess the value of his welfare differently than I, that is, that he should subordinate it to *my* welfare? What is the meaning of that "Thou shalt," which even philosophers regard as "given"?

The apparently crazy idea that a man should esteem the actions he performs for another more highly than those he performs for himself, and that this other should likewise, etc. (that one should call good only those actions that a man performs with an eye, not to himself, but to the welfare of another) has a meaning: namely, as the social instinct resting on the valuation that the single individual is of little account, but all individuals together are of very great account provided they constitute a community with a common feeling and a common conscience. Therefore a kind of training in looking in a certain definite direction, the will to a perspective that seeks to make it impossible to see oneself.

My idea: goals are lacking and these must be *individuals'!* We observe how things are everywhere: every individual is sacrificed and serves as a tool. Go into the street and you encounter lots of "'slaves." Whither? For what?

270 (*Spring-Fall 1887*)

How is it possible that a man has respect for himself with regard to moral values *alone,* that he considers everything else subordinate and of little worth compared with good, evil, improvement, salvation of soul, etc.? e.g., Henri Fréd. Amiel.[56] What is the meaning of the moral idiosyncrasy?— I mean in a psychological sense, also in a physiological sense; e.g., Pascal. That is, in cases where other great qualities were not lacking; also in the case of Schopenhauer, who obviously valued that which he did not and could not have—is it not the consequence of a merely habitual moral interpretation of actual states of pain and displeasure? is it not a definite kind of sensibility that does not understand the cause of its frequent feelings of displeasure but believes it explains them with moral hypotheses? So that even a transitory feeling of health and strength immediately appears, in the perspective of a "good conscience," to be illumined by the nearness of God, by the consciousness of redemption?—

Thus the man of moral idiosyncrasy has (1) either really acquired his worth through approximating society's model of virtue: "the good man," "the righteous"—a highly respectable condition of mediocrity: mediocre in all his abilities but decent, conscientious, solid, respected, trusty; (2) or he believes he has acquired it because he does not know how otherwise to understand all his states—he is unknown to himself, so he interpretes himself in this way.—

Morality as the only scheme of interpretation by which man can endure himself—a kind of pride?—

---

[56] Swiss philosophy professor, critic, and poet (1821-1881).

271 (*March-June 1888*)

The predominance of moral values.— Consequences of this predominance: the corruption of psychology, etc.; the universal fatality which follows from it. What does this predominance mean? What does it point to?—

To a certain greater urgency for a definite Yes and No in this field. All kinds of imperatives have been employed to make moral values appear permanent: they have been commanded for the longest time:— they *seem* instinctive, like inner commands. Moral values reveal themselves to be conditions of the existence of society, in that they are felt to be beyond discussion. The practice, which is to say the utility, of agreement about the highest values has here acquired a kind of sanction. We observe that every means is employed to paralyze reflection and criticism in this field:— look at the attitude of Kant! not to speak of those who reject as immoral all "inquiry" here—

272 (*Spring-Fall 1887*)

My purpose: to demonstrate the absolute homogeneity of all events and the application of moral distinctions as conditioned by perspective; to demonstrate how everything praised as moral is identical in essence with everything immoral and was made possible, as in every development of morality, with immoral means and for immoral ends—; how, on the other hand, everything decried as immoral is, economically considered, higher and more essential, and how a development toward a greater fullness of life necessarily also demands the advance of immorality. "Truth" the extent to which we permit ourselves to understand this fact.

273 (*1883-1888*)

But don't worry: for one needs a great deal of morality to be immoral in this subtle way; I will speak in a parable:

A physiologist interested in a disease and an invalid who claims to be cured of it do not have identical interests. Let us suppose the disease is morality—for it is a disease—and that we Europeans are the invalids: what subtle torment and difficulties would arise if we Europeans were at the same time inquisitive spectators and physiologists! Would we then really desire to be free of morality? Would we want to be? Quite apart from the question whether we *could* be. Whether we could be "cured."—

2. The Herd

274 (*Spring-Fall 1887*)

Whose will to power is morality?— The common factor in the history of Europe since Socrates is the attempt to make moral values dominate over all other values: so that they should be the guide and judge not only of life but also of (1) knowledge, (2) the arts, (3) political and social endeavors. "Improvement" the sole duty, everything else a means to it (or a disturbance, hindrance, danger: consequently to be combatted to the point of annihilation—). A similar movement in China. A similar movement in India.

What is the meaning of this will to power on the part of moral values which has developed so tremendously on earth?

Answer:— three powers are hidden behind it: (1) the instinct of the herd against the strong and independent; (2) the instinct of the suffering and underprivileged against the fortunate; (3) the instinct of the mediocre against the exceptional.— Enormous advantage possessed by this movement, however much cruelty, falseness, and narrow-mindedness have assisted it (for the history of the struggle of morality with the basic instincts of life is itself the greatest piece of immorality that has yet existed on earth—).

275 (*1883-1888*)

Very few manage to see a problem in that which makes our daily life, that to which we have long since grown accustomed—our eyes are not adjusted to it: this seems to me to be the case especially in regard to our morality.

The problem "every man as an object for others" is the occasion of the highest honors: for himself—no!

The problem "thou shalt": an inclination that cannot explain itself, similar to the sexual drive, shall not fall under the general condemnation of the drives; on the contrary, it shall be their evaluation and judge!

The problem of "equality," while we all thirst after dis-stinction: here, on the contrary, we are supposed to make exactly the same demands on ourselves as we make on others. This is so insipid, so obviously crazy: but—it is felt to be holy, of a higher rank, the conflict with reason is hardly noticed.

Sacrifice and selflessness as distinguishing, unconditional obedience to morality, and the faith that one is everyone's equal before it.

The neglect and surrender of well-being and life as distinguishing, the complete renunciation of making one's own evaluations, and the firm desire to see everyone else renounce them too. "The value of an action is determined: everyone is subject to this valuation."

We see: an authority speaks—who speaks?— One may forgive human pride if it sought to make this authority as high as possible in order to feel as little humiliated as possible under it. Therefore—God speaks!

One needed God as an unconditional sanction, with no court of appeal, as a "categorical imperator"—: or, if one believed in the authority of reason, one needed a metaphysic of unity, by virtue of which this was logical.

Now suppose that belief in God has vanished: the question presents itself anew: "who speaks?"— My answer, taken not from metaphysics but from animal physiology: *the herd instinct speaks.* It wants to be master: hence its "thou shalt!"— it will allow value to the individual only from the point of view of the whole, for the sake of the whole, it hates those who detach themselves—it turns the hatred of all individuals against them.

276 (*1886-1887*)

The whole of European morality is based upon what is useful to the herd: the affliction of all higher, rarer men lies in this, that everything that distinguishes them enters their consciousness accompanied by a feeling of diminution and discredit. The *strong points* of contemporary men are the causes of their pessimistic gloom: the mediocre are, like the herd, little troubled with questions and conscience—cheerful. (On the gloominess of the strong: Pascal, Schopenhauer.)

The more dangerous a quality seems to the herd, the more thoroughly is it proscribed.

277 (*1883-1888*)

Morality of truthfulness in the herd. "You shall be knowable, express your inner nature by clear and constant signs—otherwise you are dangerous: and if you are evil, your ability to dissimulate is the worst thing for the herd. We despise the secret and unrecognizable.— Consequently you must consider yourself knowable, you may not be concealed from yourself, you may not believe that you change." Thus: the demand for truthfulness presupposes the knowability and stability of the person. In fact, it is the object of education to create in the herd member a definite faith concerning the nature of man: it first invents this faith and then demands "truthfulness."

278 (*1885*)

Within a herd, within any community, that is to say *inter pares,*[57] the overestimation of truthfulness makes good sense. Not to be deceived—and consequently, as a personal point of morality, not to deceive! a mutual obligation between equals! In dealing with what lies outside, danger and caution demand that one should be on one's guard against deception: as a psychological preconditioning for this, also in dealing with what lies within. Mistrust as the source of truthfulness.

279 (*1883-1888*)

Toward a critique of the herd virtues.— Inertia operates (1) in trustfulness, since mistrust makes tension, observation, reflection necessary;— (2) in veneration, where the difference in power is great and submission necessary: so as not to fear, an attempt is made to love, esteem, and to interpret the disparity in power as disparity in value: so that the relationship no longer makes one rebellious;— (3) in the sense of truth. What is true? Where an explanation is given which causes us the minimum of spiritual effort (moreover, lying is very exhausting);— (4) in sympathy. It is a relief to count oneself the same as others, to try to feel as they do, to *adopt* a current feeling: it is something passive compared with the activity that maintains and constantly practices

[57] Among equals.

the individual's right to value judgments (the latter allows of no rest);— (5) in impartiality and coolness of judgment: one shuns the exertion of affects and prefers to stay detached, "objective";— (6) in integrity: one would rather obey an existing law than create a law oneself, than command oneself and others: the fear of commanding—: better to submit than to react;— (7) in toleration: the fear of exercising rights, of judging.

280 (*Spring-Fall 1887*)

The instinct of the herd considers the middle and the mean as the highest and most valuable: the place where the majority finds itself; the mode and manner in which it finds itself. It is therefore an opponent of all orders of rank, it sees an ascent from beneath to above as a descent from the majority to the minority. The herd feels the exception, whether it be below or above it, as something opposed and harmful to it. Its artifice with reference to the exceptions above it, the stronger, more powerful, wiser, and more fruitful, is to persuade them to assume the role of guardians, herdsmen, watchmen—to become its *first servants*:[58] it has therewith transformed a danger into something useful. Fear ceases in the middle: here one is never alone; here there is little room for misunderstanding; here there is equality; here one's own form of being is not felt as a reproach but as the right form of being; here contentment rules. Mistrust is felt toward the exceptions; to be an exception is experienced as guilt.

281 (*March-June 1888*)

When, following the instinct of the community, we make prescriptions and forbid ourselves certain actions, we quite reasonably do not forbid a mode of "being," a "disposition," but only a certain direction and application of this "being," this "disposition." But then the ideologist of virtue, the moralist, comes along and says: "God sees into the heart! What does it matter if you refrain from certain actions: you are no better for that!" Answer: My dear Sir Long-Ears-and-Virtuous, we have no desire whatever to be better, we are very contented with ourselves, all we desire is not to harm one another—and therefore we forbid certain actions

---

[58] Frederick the Great (King of Prussia from 1740 to 1786) called himself "the first servant of my state."

when they are directed in a certain way, namely against us, while we cannot sufficiently honor these same actions provided they are directed against enemies of the community—against you, for instance. We educate our children in them; we cultivate them— If we shared that "God-pleasing" radicalism that your holy madness recommends, if we were fools enough to condemn together with those actions the source of them, the "heart," the "disposition," that would mean condemning our own existence and with it its supreme prerequisite—a disposition, a heart, a passion we honor with the highest honors. By our decrees, we prevent this disposition from breaking out and expressing itself in an inexpedient way —we are prudent when we make such law for ourselves, we are also moral— Have you no suspicion, however faint, what sacrifice it is costing us, how much taming, self-overcoming, severity toward ourselves it requires? We are vehement in our desires, there are times when we would like to devour each other— But the "sense of community" masters us: please note that this is almost a definition of morality.

282 (*Fall 1888*)

The weakness of the herd animal produces a morality very similar to that produced by the weakness of the decadent: they understand one another, they form an alliance (—the great decadence religions always count on the support of the herd). In itself, there is nothing sick about the herd animal, it is even invaluable; but, incapable of leading itself, it needs a "shepherd"— the priests understand that— The state is not intimate, not clandestine enough; "directing the conscience" eludes it. And that is how the herd animal has been made sick by the priest?—

283 (*1883-1888*)

Hatred for the privileged in body and soul: revolt of the ugly, ill-constituted souls against the beautiful, proud, joyous. Their means: inculpation of beauty, pride, joy: "there is no merit," "the danger is tremendous: one *should* tremble and feel ill," "naturalness is evil; it is right to oppose nature." Also "reason." (The antinatural as the higher).

Again it is the priests who exploit this condition and win the "people" over. "The sinner" in whom God has more joy than in the "just man." *This* is the struggle against "paganism" (the pang of conscience as the means of destroying harmony of soul).

The hatred of the average for the exceptional, of the herd for the independent. (Custom as true "morality."[59]) Turning *against* "egoism": only the "for another" has value. "We are all equal";— against lust for dominion, against "dominion" in general;— against privilege;— against sectarians, free spirits, skeptics;— against philosophy (as opposing the tool-and-corner instinct); with philosophers themselves "the categorical imperative," the essence of morality "universal and general."

284 (*Spring-Fall 1887*)

The conditions and desires that are *praised*:— peaceable, fair, moderate, modest, reverent, considerate, brave, chaste, honest, faithful, devout, straight, trusting, devoted, sympathetic, helpful, conscientious, simple, mild, just, generous, indulgent, obedient, disinterested, unenvious, gracious, industrious—

To distinguish: to what extent such qualities are conditioned as *means* to a definite aim and end (often an "evil" end); or as natural *consequences* of a dominating affect (e.g., spirituality) or expression of a state of distress, which is to say: as condition of existence (e.g., citizen, slave, woman, etc.).

Summa: they are none of them felt to be "good" for their own sake, but from the first according to the standards of "society," "the herd," as means to the ends of society and the herd, as necessary to their preservation and advancement, at the same time as the consequence of an actual herd instinct in the individual: thus in the service of an instinct which is fundamentally different from these conditions of virtue. For the herd is, in relation to the outside world, hostile, selfish, unmerciful, full of lust for dominion, mistrust, etc.

In the "shepherd" this antagonism becomes patent: he must possess opposite qualities to the herd.

Mortal enmity of the herd toward orders of rank: its instinct favors the leveller (Christ). Toward strong individuals (*les souverains*) it is hostile, unfair, immoderate, immodest, impudent, inconsiderate, cowardly, mendacious, false, unmerciful, underhand, envious, revengeful.

[59] *Die Sitte als eigentliche "Sittlichkeit"*: *mores* as the essence of morality. Cf. section 265 above.

285 (*1884*)

I teach: the herd seeks to preserve one type and defends itself on both sides, against those who have degenerated from it (criminals, etc.) and those who tower above it. The tendency of the herd is directed toward standstill and preservation, there is nothing creative in it.

The pleasant feelings with which the good, benevolent, just man inspires us (in contrast to the tension, fear which the great, new man arouses) are our own feelings of personal security and equality: the herd animal thus glorifies the herd nature and then it feels comfortable. This judgment of comfort masks itself with fair words—thus "morality" arises.— But observe the hatred of the herd for the truthful.—

286 (*1883-1888*)

Let one not be deceived about oneself! If one hears within oneself the moral imperative as it is understood by altruism, one belongs to the herd. If one has the opposite feeling, if one feels one's danger and abberration lies in disinterested and selfless actions, one does not belong to the herd.

287 (*1883-1888*)

My philosophy aims at an ordering of rank: not at an individualistic morality.[60] The ideas of the herd should rule in the herd—but not reach out beyond it: the leaders of the herd require a fundamentally different valuation for their own actions, as do the independent, or the "beasts of prey," etc.

3. General Remarks on Morality

288 (*March-June 1888*)

Morality as an attempt to establish human pride.— The theory of "free will" is antireligious. It seeks to create the right for man to think of himself as cause of his exalted state and actions: it is a form of the growing *feeling of pride*.

---

[60] Cf. section 361.

Man feels his power, his "happiness," as they say: there must be "will" behind this state—otherwise it would not be his. Virtue is the attempt to set the fact of willing and having-willed before every exalted and strong feeling of happiness as a necessary antecedent:— if the will to certain actions is regularly present in the consciousness, a feeling of power may be interpreted as its effect.— This is merely a perspective of psychology: always based on the false presupposition that nothing belongs to us that we have not consciously willed. The entire theory of responsibility depends upon the naive psychology that the only cause is will and that one must be aware of having willed in order to believe in *oneself* as cause.

—Comes the countermovement: that of the moral philosophers, still subject to the same prejudice that one is responsible only for what one has willed. The value of man is posited as a *moral* value: consequently his morality must be a *causa prima;*[61] consequently there must be a principle in man, a "free will" as *causa prima.*— The idea behind it is: if man is not *causa prima* as will, then he is irresponsible—consequently he has no business before the moral tribunal—virtue and vice would be automatic and mechanical—

In summa: so that man may respect himself he must be capable of doing evil.

289 (*March-June 1888*)

Play-acting as a consequence of the morality of "free will."— It is a step in the development of the feeling of power itself to have caused one's own exalted states (one's perfection)—consequently, one immediately concludes, to have *willed* them—

(Critique: All perfect acts are unconscious and no longer subject to will; consciousness is the expression of an imperfect and often morbid state in a person. Personal perfection as conditioned by will, as consciousness, as reasoning with dialectics, is a caricature, a kind of self-contradiction— A degree of consciousness makes perfection impossible— Form of *play-acting.*)

290 (*Spring-Fall 1887*)

The moral hypothesis with the object of *justifying God* was:

---

[61] First cause.

evil must be voluntary (merely so that the voluntariness of goodness can be believed in), and on the other hand: the object of evil and suffering is salvation.

The concept "guilt" as *not* extending back to the ultimate ground of existence, and the concept "punishment" as an educative benefit, consequently as the act of a *good* God.

Absolute dominion of moral valuation over all others: one did not doubt that God could not be evil and could not do anything harmful, i.e., by "perfection" one meant merely a moral perfection.

291 (*March-June 1888*)

How false is the idea that the value of an action must depend upon that which preceded it in consciousness!— And morality has been judged according to this, even criminality—

The value of an action must be judged by its consequences—say the Utilitarians—: to judge it by its origins implies an impossibility, namely that of *knowing* its origins.

But does one know its consequences? For five steps ahead, perhaps. Who can say what an action will stimulate, excite, provoke? As a stimulus? Perhaps as a spark to touch off an explosion?— The Utilitarians are naive— And in any case we must first *know what* is useful: here too they look only five steps ahead— They have no conception of the grand economy, which cannot do without evil.

One does not know the origin, one does not know the consequences:— does an action then possess any value at all?

The action itself remains: its epiphenomena in consciousness, the Yes and the No that follow its performance: does the value of an action lie in its subjective epiphenomena? (—that would be like assessing the value of the music according to the pleasure or displeasure it gives us—it gives its *composer*—). Obviously value feelings accompany it, a feeling of power, compulsion, impotence; e.g., freedom, ease—put in another way: could one reduce the value of an action to physiological values: whether it is the expression of a complete or an inhibited life?[62]— It may be that

---

[62] In all editions the immediately following words in the MS have been omitted: "is it permitted to measure its value according to epiphenomena, such as pleasure and displeasure, the play of the affects, the feeling of discharges, explosion, freedom. . . ." Also the following words at the end of

its *biological* value is expressed in this—

If therefore an action can be evaluated neither by its origin, nor by its consequences, nor by its epiphenomena, then its value is *"x,"* unknown—

292 (*Spring-Fall 1887*)

On the denaturalization of morality. To *separate* the action from the man; to direct hatred or contempt against the "sin"; to believe there are actions that are good or bad in themselves.[63]

Restoration of "nature": an action in itself is perfectly devoid of value: it all depends on *who* performs it. One and the same "crime" can be in one case the greatest privilege, in another a stigma. In fact, it is the selfishness of the judges which interprets an action, or its performer, in relation to its utility or harmfulness to themselves (—or in relation to its similarity or unlikeness to them).

293 (*March-June 1888*)

The concept "reprehensible action" presents us with difficulties. Nothing that happened at all can be reprehensible in itself: for one should not want to eliminate it: for everything is so bound up with everything else, that to want to exclude something means to exclude everything. A reprehensible action means: a reprehended world—

And then further: in a reprehended world reprehending would also be reprehensible— And the consequence of a way of thinking that reprehended everything would be a way of living that affirmed everything— If becoming is a great ring, then everything is equally valuable, eternal, necessary.— In all correlations of Yes and No, of preference and rejection, love and hate, all that is expressed is a perspective, an interest of certain types of life: in itself, everything that is says Yes.

294 (*Jan.-Fall 1888*)

Critique of subjective value feelings.— The conscience. For-

---

this section: "In sum, in the language of the church hymn: 'crawl, fly, and creep upon God's ways [*Kreuch, fleuch und schleich auf Gottes Wegen*].' "

[63] Thus in the MS. In all editions: "It is a denaturalization of morality to. . . ."

merly one concluded: the conscience reprehends this action; consequently this action is reprehensible. In fact, the conscience reprehends an action because it has been reprehended for a long time. It merely repeats: it creates no values. That which in the past decided to reprehend certain actions was not conscience: but the insight into (or the prejudice against) their consequences—

The assent of the conscience, the pleasant feeling of "at peace with oneself," is of the same order as the pleasure of an artist in his work—it proves nothing at all—

Self-contentment is as little a standard for that to which it relates as its absence is an argument against the value of a thing. We do not know nearly enough to be able to measure the value of our actions: in addition, it is impossible for us to be objective about them: even when we reprehend an action, we are not judges but interested parties—

If noble agitation accompanies an action, this proves nothing about its value: an artist can go through the highest possible pathos of passion and bring forth something wretched. One should say rather that these agitations are a means of seduction: they lure our eyes, our strength away from criticism, from caution, from suspicion, so that we perpetrate a stupidity—they make us stupid—

295 (*1885-1886*)

We are the heirs of the conscience-vivisection and self-crucifixion of two millennia: in these we have had longest practice, in these lies our mastery perhaps, certainly our subtlety; we have conjoined the natural inclinations and a bad conscience.

A reverse attempt would be possible: to conjoin the unnatural inclinations, I mean the inclination for the beyond, for things contrary to sense, reason, nature, in short all previous ideals, which were all world-slandering ideals, with a bad conscience.

296 (*Spring-Fall 1887*)

The great crimes in psychology:

1. that all displeasure, all misfortune has been falsified with the idea of wrong (guilt). (Pain has been robbed of innocence);

2. that all strong feelings of pleasure (wild spirits, voluptuousness, triumph, pride, audacity, knowledge, self-assurance and

happiness as such) have been branded as sinful, as a seduction, as suspicious;

3. that feelings of weakness, inward acts of cowardice, lack of courage for oneself have been overlaid with sanctifying names and taught as being desirable in the highest degree;

4. that everything great in man has been reinterpreted as selflessness, as self-sacrifice for the sake of something else, someone else, that even in the man of knowledge, even in the artist, depersonalization has been presented as the cause of the greatest knowledge and ability;

5. that love has been falsified as surrender (and altruism), while it is an appropriation or a bestowal following from a superabundance of personality. Only the most complete persons can love; the depersonalized, the "objective," are the worst lovers (—one has only to ask the girls!) This applies also to love of God or of "fatherland"; one must be firmly rooted in oneself. (Egoism as *ego*-morphism, altruism as *alter*-ation.[64]

6. Life as punishment (happiness as temptation); the passions as devilish, confidence in oneself as godless.

This whole psychology is a psychology of prevention, a kind of immuring out of fear; on one hand the great masses (the underprivileged and mediocre) seek to defend themselves by means of it against the stronger (—and to destroy them in their development—), on the other all the drives through which they best prosper, sanctified and alone held in honor. Compare the Jewish priesthood.

297 (*Spring-Fall 1887*)

The vestiges of debasement of nature through moral transcendence: value of selflessness, cult of altruism; belief in repayment within the play of consequences; belief in "goodness," in "genius" even, as if the one and the other were consequences of selflessness; the continuance of the ecclesiastical sanction of bourgeois life; absolute desire to misunderstand history (as an educative work toward moralization) or pessimism in the face of history (—the latter as much a consequence of the debasement of nature as that pseudo justification, as that not desiring to see that which the pessimist sees—).

---

[64] Ver-*Ichlichung* . . . Ver-*Aenderung*. English "equivalents" mine.

298 (*Spring-Fall 1887*)

"Morality for morality's sake"—an important step in its denaturalization: it itself appears as the ultimate value. In this phase it has permeated religion: e.g., in Judaism. And there is likewise a phase in which it separates itself again from religion and in which no God is "moral" enough for it: it then prefers the impersonal ideal— This is the case at present.

"Art for art's sake"—this is an equally dangerous principle: therewith one introduces a false antithesis into things—it culminates in a defamation of reality ("idealization" into the ugly). If one severs an ideal from reality one debases the real, one impoverishes it, one defames it. "The beautiful for the sake of the beautiful," "the true for the sake of the true," "the good for the sake of the good"—these are three forms of evil eye for the real.

—Art, knowledge, morality are *means*: instead of recognizing in them the aim of enhancing life, one has associated them with the antithesis of life, with "God"—also as the revelation of a higher world which here and there looks down upon us through them—

"Beautiful and ugly," "true and false," "good and evil"—these distinctions and antagonisms betray certain conditions of existence and enhancement, not only of man but of any kind of firm and enduring complex which separates itself from its adversary. The war that is thus created is the essential element: as a means of separation that strengthens isolation—

299 (*Spring-Fall 1887*)

Moralistic naturalism: the tracing back of apparently emancipated, supranatural moral values to their "nature": i.e., to natural immorality, to natural "utility," etc.

I might designate the tendency of these reflections as moralistic naturalism: my task is to translate the apparently emancipated and denatured moral values back into their nature—i.e., into their natural "immorality."

—N.B. Comparison with Jewish "holiness" and its natural basis: it is the same with the moral law made sovereign, emancipated from its nature (—to the point of becoming the antithesis of nature—).

Steps in the denaturalization of morality (so-called "idealization"):

as a way to individual happiness,
as a consequence of knowledge,
as the categorical imperative,
as a way to salvation,
as denial of the will to live.

(The gradual hostility to life of morality.)

300 (*Spring-Fall 1887*)

Suppressed and effaced *heresy* in morality.— Concepts: pagan, master morality, *virtù*.

301 (*1885-1886*)

My problem: What harm has come to mankind through morals and through its morality? Harm to the spirit, etc.

302 (*Nov. 1887-March 1888*)

If only human values would be put back once and for all into the places in which alone they belong: as loafers' values. Many species of animals have already vanished; if man too should vanish nothing would be lacking in the world. One must be sufficient of a philosopher to admire *this* nothing, too (—*Nil admirari*).[65]

303 (*Spring 1888*)

Man a little, eccentric species of animal, which—fortunately —has its day; all on earth a mere moment, an incident, an exception without consequences, something of no importance to the general character of the earth; the earth itself, like every star, a hiatus between two nothingnesses, an event without plan, reason, will, self-consciousness, the worst kind of necessity, *stupid* necessity— Something in us rebels against this view; the serpent vanity says to us: "all that *must* be false, *for* it arouses indignation— Could all that not be merely appearance? And man, in spite of all, as Kant says—"

[65] Admire nothing—usually quoted in the sense of "wonder at nothing" (from Horace, *Epistles,* I.6.1.).

4. How Virtue Is Made to Dominate

304 (*Nov. 1887-March 1888*)

Of the ideal of the moralists.[66]— This treatise deals with the grand *politics* of virtue. It is intended for the use of those whose interest must lie in learning, not how one *becomes* virtuous, but how one *makes* virtuous—how virtue is made to dominate. I even intend to prove that to desire the one—the domination of virtue—one absolutely must *not* desire the other; one automatically renounces becoming virtuous oneself. This is a great sacrifice: but such a goal is perhaps sufficient reward for such a sacrifice. And for even greater sacrifices!— And some of the most famous moralists have risked as much. For they had already recognized and anticipated the truth, which is in this treatise to be taught for the first time, that one can achieve the domination of virtue only by the same means as those by which one can achieve domination of any kind, in any case not by means of virtue—

This treatise, as already stated, deals with the politics of virtue: it posits an ideal of these politics, it describes them as they would have to be, if anything on this earth could be perfect. Now, no philosopher will be in any doubt as to the type of perfection in politics; that is Machiavellianism. But Machiavellianism *pur, sans mélange, cru, vert, dans toute sa force, dans toute son âpreté*,[67] is superhuman, divine, transcendental, it will never be achieved by man, at most approximated. Even in this narrower kind of politics, in the politics of virtue, the ideal seems never to have been achieved. Even Plato barely touched it. One discovers, if one has eyes for hidden things, traces in even the most unpreju-

---

[66] In the MS this section begins: "Of great things one should not speak at all or speak with greatness: with greatness—i.e., cynically and with innocence."

In the standard editions these words are omitted, obviously to avoid duplication of the section the German editors placed at the beginning of *The Will to Power*. Schlechta ignores 1911 (p. 503) and reproduces the printed versions, not the text of the MS.

Plainly, this is a draft Nietzsche rejected. And it should be compared with *Twilight,* Chapter VII, section 5 (*Portable Nietzsche,* pp. 509-511), and, e.g., section 142 above.

[67] Pure, without admixture, crude, fresh, with all its force, with all its pungency.

diced and conscious moralists (and that is indeed the name for such politicians of morality, for every kind of founder of new moral forces) that show that they too have paid their tribute to human weakness. They all aspired, at least when they were weary, to virtue for themselves: first and capital error for a moralist—who must as such be an immoralist in practice. That he must not appear to be so is another matter. Or rather, it is *not* another matter: such a fundamental self-denial (in moral terms, dissimulation) is part of the canon of the moralist and his most specific duties: without it he will never attain to *his* kind of perfection. Freedom from morality, *also from truth*, for the sake of that goal that outweighs every sacrifice: for the sake of the domination of virtue—that is the canon. Moralists need the *gestures* of virtue, also the gestures of truth; their error begins only when they yield to virtue, when they lose domination over virtue, when they themselves become moral, become true. A great moralist is, among other things, necessarily a great actor; his danger is that his dissimulation may unintentionally become nature, while it is his ideal to keep his *esse* and his *operari*[68] in a divine way apart; everything he does must be done *sub specie boni*[69]—a high, remote, exacting ideal! A *divine* ideal! And indeed, it is said that the moralist imitates in that no less a model than God himself: God, the greatest of all immoralists in practice, who nonetheless knows how to remain what he is, the *good* God—

305 (*Nov. 1887-March 1888*)

One cannot establish the domination of virtue by means of virtue itself; with virtue itself one renounces power, loses the will to power.

306 (*1883-1886*)[70]

The victory of a moral ideal is achieved by the same "immoral" means as every victory: force, lies, slander, injustice.

---

[68] His being and his operating.

[69] With the appearance of goodness.

[70] In the MS, on the margin: *rücksichtlose Rechtschaffenheit,* which might be rendered as "unsparing honesty."

307 (*Spring-Fall 1887*)

He who knows how all fame originates will be mistrustful even of the fame virtue enjoys.

308 (*Spring-Fall 1887*)

Morality is just as "immoral" as any other thing on earth; morality is itself a form of immorality.

The great liberation this insight brings. Contradiction is removed from things, the homogeneity of all events is saved—

309 (*Nov. 1887-March 1888*)

There are those who go looking for immorality. When they judge: "This is wrong," they believe one should abolish and change it. I, on the contrary, cannot rest as long as I am not yet clear about the immorality of a thing. When I unearth it I recover my equanimity.

310 (*Spring-Fall 1887*)

a. The paths to power: to introduce a new virtue under the name of an old one—to excite "interest" in it ("happiness" as its consequence and vice versa)—the art of slandering what stands in its way—to exploit advantages and accidents for its glorification—to turn its followers into fanatics by means of sacrifice and separation;—grand symbolism.

b. Power attained: (1) virtue as force; (2) virtue as seduction; (3) virtue as (court) etiquette.

311 (*Spring-Fall 1887*)

By which means does a virtue come to power?— By exactly the same means as a political party: the slandering, inculpation, undermining of virtues that oppose it and are already in power, by rebaptizing them, by systematic persecution and mockery. Therefore: through sheer "immorality."

What does a desire do with itself to become a virtue?— Rebaptism; systematic denial of its objectives; practice in self-misunderstanding; alliance with existing and recognized virtues; ostentatious hostility against their opponents. Where possible it purchases the protection of sanctifying powers; it intoxicates, it inspires; the tartuffery of idealism; it forms a party which must either conquer with it or perish—it becomes unconscious, naive—

312 (*Spring-Fall 1887; rev. Spring-Fall 1888*)

Cruelty has been refined to tragic pity, so that it is denied the name of cruelty. In the same way sexual love has been refined to *amour-passion*; the slavish disposition to Christian obedience; wretchedness to humility; a pathological condition of the *nervus sympathicus*, e.g., to pessimism, Pascalism, or Carlylism, etc.

313 (*March-June 1888*)

It would arouse doubts in us concerning a man if we heard he needed *reasons* for remaining decent: certainly, we would avoid him. The little word "for" can be compromising in certain cases; one can even refute oneself now and then with a single "for."[71] Now, if we hear further that such an aspirant to virtue needed *bad* reasons for remaining respectable, this would be no reason for us to feel an increased respect for him. But he goes further, he comes to us and tells us to our face: "Unbeliever, you are disturbing my morality with your unbelief; as long as you do not believe in my bad reasons, which is to say in God, in a punishment in the beyond, in freedom of will, you hamper my virtue—Moral: unbelievers must be abolished: they hamper the moralization of the masses."

314 (*Nov. 1887-March 1888*)

Our most sacred convictions, the unchanging elements in our supreme values, are judgments of our muscles.

315 (*Spring-Fall 1887*)

Morality in the valuation of races and classes.— In view of the fact that the affects and fundamental drives in every race and

---

[71] Cf. *The Antichrist,* section 45.

class express something of the conditions of their existence (—at least of the conditions under which they have prevailed for the longest time), to desire that they should be "virtuous" means:

that they change their character, shed their skin and blot out their past:

means that they should cease to be distinct:

means that they should begin to resemble one another in their needs and demands—more clearly: that they should perish—

The will to a single morality is thereby proved to be a tyranny over other types by that type whom this single morality fits: it is a destruction or a leveling for the sake of the ruling type (whether to render the others no longer fearsome or to render them useful). "Abolition of slavery"—supposedly a tribute to "human dignity," in fact a destruction of a fundamentally different type (—the undermining of its values and happiness—).

The qualities in which an opposing race or class is strong are interpreted as its most evil, worst qualities: for it is with those that it can harm us (—its "virtues" are defamed and rebaptized—).

It counts as an objection against a man or people if they harm us: but from their point of view we are desirable, because we are such as one can make use of.

The demand for "humanization" (which quite naively believes itself to possess the formula for "what is human?") is a tartuffery, behind which a quite definite type of man seeks to attain domination: more exactly, a quite definite instinct, the herd instinct.— "Human equality": which is concealed behind the tendency to make men more and more alike.

"Interestedness" with reference to communal morality. (Artifice: to transform the great passions of lust for power and possessions into protectors of virtue).

To what extent all kinds of businessmen and the avaricious, all who have to give and claim credit, find it necessary to become more and more alike in character and in conception of value: world trade and exchange of every kind extorts and, as it were, buys virtue.

The same applies to the state and to every kind of rule by means of officials and soldiers; likewise science, in order to work in security and with economy of its forces.— Likewise the priesthood.

—Here, therefore, a communal morality is enforced because it procures an advantage; and to make it victorious, war and force are practiced against immorality—with what "right"? With no right whatever: but in accordance with the instinct for self-preservation. These same classes make use of immorality when it serves their purpose.

316 (*Spring-Fall 1887*)

The hypocritical show with which all civil institutions are whitewashed, as if they were products of morality—e.g., marriage; work; one's profession; the fatherland; the family; order; law. But since they are one and all founded on the most mediocre type of man, as protection against exceptions and exceptional needs, it is only to be expected that they are full of lies.

317 (*Spring-Fall 1887; rev. Spring-Fall 1888*)

One should defend virtue against the preachers of virtue: they are its worst enemies. For they teach virtue as an ideal *for everyone*; they take from virtue the charm of rareness, inimitableness, exceptionalness and unaverageness—its aristocratic magic. One should also take a stand against the obdurate idealists who eagerly knock on all vessels and are satisfied when they ring hollow: what naiveté to demand the great and rare and then to establish, with rage and misanthropy, that they are absent!— It is obvious, e.g., that a marriage is worth as much as those whom it joins together, i.e., that in general it will be something wretched and inept: no priest, no mayor can make anything else of it.

Virtue has all the instincts of the average man against it: it is unprofitable, imprudent, it isolates; it is related to passion and not very accessible to reason; it spoils the character, the head, the mind—according to the standards of mediocre men; it rouses to enmity toward order, toward the *lies* that are concealed in every order, institution, actuality—it is the worst of vices, if one judges it by its harmful effect upon others.

—I recognize virtue in that (1) it does not desire to be recognized; (2) it does not presuppose virtue everywhere, but precisely something else; (3) it does not suffer from the absence of virtue, but on the contrary regards this as the distancing relationship on the basis of which there is something to honor in virtue; it does not communicate itself; (4) it does not propagandize— (5) it permits no one to judge it, because it is always virtue for itself;

(6) it does precisely all that is generally forbidden: virtue, as I understand it, is the real *vetitum*[72] within all herd legislation; (7) in short, it is virtue in the style of the Renaissance, *virtù*, moraline-free virtue.[73]

318 (*Spring-Fall 1887*)

Above all, gentlemen of virtue, you are not our superiors: we should like you to be a little more modest: it is a miserable self-interest and prudence that suggests your virtue to you. And if you had more strength and courage in you, you would not reduce yourselves to virtuous nonentities in this way. You make what you can of yourselves: partly what you must—what your circumstances force you to—partly what gives you pleasure, partly what seems useful to you. But if you do only what is in keeping with your inclinations, or what necessity demands of you, or what is useful to you, then you should neither praise yourselves nor let others praise you!— One is a thoroughly small type of man if one is *only* virtuous: do not be misled about that! Men who have been in any way notable were never such virtuous asses: their innermost instinct, that of their quantum of power, did not find satisfaction that way: while, with your minimum of power, nothing can seem wiser to you than virtue. But you have numbers on your side; and in so far as you play the tyrant, we shall make war on you—

319 (*Spring-Fall 1887*)

A virtuous man is a lower species because he is not a "person" but acquires his value by conforming to a pattern of man that is fixed once and for all. He does not possess his value apart: he can be compared, he has his equals, he *must* not be an individual—

Reckon up the qualities of the good man: why do they give us pleasure? Because we have no need to fight against them, because they impose upon us no mistrust, no need for caution, no marshalling of forces and severity: our laziness, good nature, frivolity, have a good time. It is this pleasant feeling in us that

[72] What is forbidden.

[73] The coinage of a man who neither smoked nor drank coffee; cf. *The Antichrist,* section 2.

we project out of us and bestow upon the good man as a quality, as a value.

320 (*1888*)

Virtue is under certain circumstances merely an honorable form of stupidity: who could be ill-disposed toward it on that account? And this kind of virtue has not been outlived even today. A kind of sturdy peasant simplicity, which, however, is possible in all classes and can be encountered only with respect and a smile, believes even today that everything is in good hands, namely in the "hands of God"; and when it maintains this proposition with the same modest certainty as it would that two and two make four, we others certainly refrain from contradicting. Why disturb *this* pure foolishness? Why darken it with our worries about man, people, goal, future? And even if we wanted to do it, we could not. They project their own honorable stupidity and goodness into the heart of things (the old God, *deus myops*,[74] still lives among them!); we others—we read something else into the heart of things: our own enigmatic nature, our contradictions, our deeper, more painful, more mistrustful wisdom.

321 (*Spring-Fall 1887; rev. Spring-Fall 1888*)

He who finds virtue easy also laughs at it. It is impossible to maintain seriousness in virtue: one attains it and leaps beyond it —whither? into devilry.

In the meantime, how intelligent all our wicked tendencies and impulses have become! how much scientific inquisitiveness plagues them! So many fishhooks of knowledge!

322 (*Spring-Fall 1887*)

—To associate vice so closely with something decidedly painful that at last one flees from vice in order to be rid of that which is associated with it. This is the famous case of Tannhäuser. Driven out of patience by Wagnerian music, Tannhäuser can no longer endure it even with Frau Venus: suddenly virtue acquires a charm;

---

[74] Myopic god.

a Thuringian virgin increases in value; and, to tell the worst, he even enjoys Wolfram von Eschenbach's tune—

323 (*Spring-Fall 1887*)

The patrons of virtue.— Avarice, lust to rule, laziness, simplicity, fear: all have an interest in the cause of virtue: that is why it stands so firm.

324 (*Spring-Fall 1887*)

Virtue is no longer believed in, its power of attraction is gone; to restore it, someone would have to know how to take it to market as an unfamiliar form of adventure and excess. It demands too much extravagance and narrow-mindedness of its believers not to have the conscience against it today. To be sure, precisely that may constitute its new charm for unconscionable and totally unscrupulous people:— it is now what it never was before, a vice.

325 (*Jan.-Fall 1888*)

Virtue is still the most expensive vice: it should remain so!

326 (*1883-1888*)

Virtues are as dangerous as vices in so far as one lets them rule over one as authorities and laws from without and does not first produce them out of oneself, as one should do, as one's most personal self-defense and necessity, as conditions of precisely *our own* existence and growth, which we recognize and acknowledge independently of whether other men grow with us under similar or different conditions. This law of the dangerousness of impersonally understood, objective virtue applies also to modesty: many of the choicest spirits perish through it. The morality of modesty is the worst form of softening for those souls for which it makes sense that they should become hard in time.

327 (*Spring-Fall 1887*)

One should reduce and limit the realm of morality step by step: one should bring to light and honor the names of the instincts that are really at work here after they have been hidden for so long beneath hypocritical names of virtue; out of respect for one's "honesty," which speaks more and more imperiously, one should unlearn the shame that would like to deny and lie away one's natural instincts. It is a measure of strength how far one can divest oneself of virtue; and a height can be imagined where the concept "virtue" is so understood that it sounds like *virtù,* Renaissance virtue, moraline-free virtue.[75] But in the meantime—how distant we are from this ideal!

The reduction of the domain of morality: a sign of the progress of this ideal. Wherever one has not yet been capable of *causal* thinking, one has thought *morally.*

328 (*Spring-Fall 1887; rev. Spring-Fall 1888*)

In the end: what have I achieved? Let us not hide from ourselves this most curious result: I have imparted to virtue a new charm—the charm of something forbidden. It has our subtlest honesty against it, it is spiced *"cum grano salis"*[76] of the sting of scientific conscience; it smells old-fashioned and antique, so that at last it lures the refined and makes them inquisitive—in short, it appears as a vice. Only after we have recognized everything as lies and appearance do we regain the right to this fairest of falsehoods, virtue. There is no court of appeal left that could deny it to us: only by exhibiting virtue as a form of immorality do we again justify it—it is classified and compared with reference to its fundamental significance, it is part of the fundamental immorality of all existence—as a form of luxury of the first order, the haughtiest, dearest and rarest form of vice. We have removed its scowl and its cowl, we have rescued it from the importunity of the many, we have taken from it its absurd rigidity, its vacant expression, its stiff false hair, its hieratic muscular system.

329 (*Spring-Fall 1887; rev. 1888*)

Have I thereby harmed virtue?— As little as the anarchists harm princes: only since they have been shot at do they sit securely on their thrones again— For thus has it ever been and always will

---

[75] Cf. section 317 above.

[76] With a grain of salt.

be: one cannot serve a cause better than by persecuting it and hunting it down— This—is what I have done.[77]

5. The Moral Ideal

A. Critique of Ideals

330 (*1886-1887*)

To tackle this in such a way as to abolish the word "ideal": critique of *desiderata.*

331 (*1883-1888*)

Very few are clear as to what the standpoint of *desirability,* every "thus it should be but is not" or even "thus it should have been," comprises: a condemnation of the total course of things. For in this course nothing exists in isolation: the smallest things bear the greatest, upon your little wrongful act stands the entire structure of the future, every critique of the smallest thing also condemns the whole. Now, granted that the moral norm, even as Kant understood it, has never been completely fulfilled and remains suspended over actuality as a kind of beyond without ever falling down into it, then morality would contain a judgment concerning the whole, which, however, still permits the question: whence does it derive the right to this judgment? How does the part come to sit as judge over the whole?—

And if this moral judging and dissatisfaction with actuality were in fact, as has been suggested, an ineradicable instinct, might this instinct not be one of the ineradicable stupidities and immodesties of our species?—

But in saying this we do that which we censure; the standpoint of desirability, of unauthorized playing-the-judge, is part of the character of the course of things, as is every injustice and imperfection—it is precisely our concept of "perfection" which is never satisfied. Every drive that desires to be satisfied expresses its dissatisfaction with the present state of things: what? is the whole perhaps composed of dissatisfied parts, which all have

---

[77] Utilized in *Twilight,* Chapter I, section 36 (*Portable Nietzsche,* pp. 471-72).

desiderata in their heads? is the "course of things" perhaps precisely this "away from here? away from actuality!" eternal dissatisfaction itself? is desirability perhaps the driving force itself? is it—*deus?*[78]

*

It seems to me important that one should get rid of the all, the unity, some force, something unconditioned; otherwise one will never cease regarding it as the highest court of appeal and baptizing it "God." One must shatter the all; unlearn respect for the all; take what we have given to the unknown and the whole and give it back to what is nearest, what is ours.

When, e.g., Kant says: "Two things[79] remain forever worthy of reverence" (conclusion of the [*Critique of*] *Practical Reason*) —today we should sooner say: "Digestion is more venerable." The all would always bring the old problems with it— "How is evil possible?" etc. Therefore: there is no all, there is no great sensorium or inventarium or storehouse of force.

332 (*Nov. 1887-March 1888*)

A man as he *ought* to be: that sounds to us as insipid as "a tree as it ought to be."[80]

333 (*1883-1888*)

Ethics: or "philosophy of desirability."— "Things *ought* to be different," "things *shall* be different": dissatisfaction would thus be the germ of ethics.

One could rescue oneself from it, firstly by selecting states in which one did not have this feeling; secondly by grasping the presumption and stupidity of it: for to desire that something should be different from what it is means to desire that everything should be different—it involves a condemnatory critique of the whole.[81] But life itself is such a desire!

---

[78] God.

[79] "The starry heavens above me and the moral law within me."

[80] This section was used in *Twilight*, in section 6 of the chapter "Morality as Anti-Nature" (*Portable Nietzsche*, pp. 491-92): "Let us finally consider how naive it is altogether to say: 'Man *ought* to be such and such!' Reality shows us an enchanting wealth of types, the abundance of a lavish play and change of forms . . ."

[81] At this point the MS still has the words: "It is to that extent. . . ."

To ascertain what is, as it is, seems something unspeakably higher and more serious than any "thus it ought to be," because the latter, as a piece of human critique and presumption, appears ludicrous from the start. It expresses a need that desires that the structure of the world should correspond with our human well-being; also the will to bring this about as far as possible.

On the other hand, it is only this desire "thus it ought to be" that has called forth that other desire to know what *is*. For the knowledge of what is, is a consequence of that question: "How? is it possible? why precisely so?" Wonder at the disagreement between our desires and the course of the world has led to our learning to know the course of the world. But perhaps the case is different: perhaps that "thus it ought to be" is our desire to overcome the world—

334 (*March-June 1888*)

Today, when every "man *ought* to be thus and thus" is spoken with a grain of irony, when we are altogether convinced that, in spite of all, one will become only that which one is[82] (in spite of all: that means education, instruction, milieu, chance, and accident), we have learned to reverse cause and consequence[83] in a curious way in moral matters—nothing perhaps distinguishes us more completely from the old believers in morality. We no longer say, e.g.: "Vice is the cause that a man also goes to ruin physiologically"; and just as little: "A man prospers through virtue, it brings long life and happiness." Our view is rather that vice and virtue are not causes but only consequences. One becomes a decent man because one *is* a decent man: i.e., because one was born a capitalist of good instincts and prosperous circumstances—

If one comes into the world poor, of parents who have squandered everything and saved nothing, one is "incorrigible," which means ripe for prison or the madhouse—

Today we no longer know how to separate moral and physiological degeneration: the former is merely a symptom-complex of the latter; one is necessarily bad, just as one is necessarily ill—

Bad: here the word expresses a certain incapacity associated physiologically with the degenerating type: e.g., weakness of will,

[82] Cf. the subtitle of *Ecce Homo*: "How One Becomes What One Is."

[83] Cf. *Twilight,* Chapter VI (*Portable Nietzsche,* pp. 492 *ff*), and sections 41-44 above and 380 below.

insecure and even multiple "personality," inability to resist reacting to a stimulus and to "control" oneself, constraint before every kind of suggestion from the will of another. Vice is not a cause; vice is a consequence—

Vice is a somewhat arbitrarily limited concept designed to express in one word certain consequences of physiological degeneration. A universal proposition such as Christianity teaches—"Man is evil"—would be justified if one were justified in taking the degenerate type as the normal type of man. But perhaps this is an exaggeration. To be sure, the proposition is correct wherever Christianity prospers and stays on top: for that demonstrates a morbid soil, a field for degeneration.

335 (*Nov. 1887-March 1888*)

One cannot have too much respect for man when one sees how well he understands how to fight his way through, to endure, to turn circumstances to his own use, to overthrow his adversaries; but when one looks at his *desires* he appears the absurdest of animals—

It is as if he required a playground of cowardice, laziness, weakness, lusciousness, submissiveness for the recreation of his strong and manly virtues: observe human *desiderata,* his "ideals." *Desiring* man recovers from the eternally valuable in him, from his deeds: he employs nothingness, the absurd, the valueless, the childish for his recovery. The spiritual poverty and lack of inventiveness of this inventive and resourceful animal are terrible. The "ideal" is, as it were, the penalty man pays for the tremendous expenditure he has to meet in all actual and pressing tasks. When reality ceases, dream, weariness, weakness come along: "the ideal" is simply a form of dream, weariness, weakness—

The strongest and the most powerless natures become equal when this condition overtakes them: they deify the cessation of work, of war, of passion, of tension, of oppositions, of "reality" *in summa*—the struggle for knowledge, the *exertion* of knowledge.

"Innocence": that is their name for the ideal state of stupefaction; "blessedness": the ideal state of sloth; "love": the ideal state of the herd animal that no longer wants to have enemies. Therewith one has raised everything that debases and lowers man to an ideal.[84]

---

[84] Cf. *Twilight,* section 38 (*Portable Nietzsche,* p. 541)—and James Hilton's *Lost Horizon.*

336 (*Spring-Fall 1887; rev. Spring-Fall 1888*)

Desire magnifies that which one desires; it grows even by not being fulfilled—the greatest ideas are those that have been created by the most violent and protracted desires. The more our desire for a thing grows, the more value we ascribe to that thing:[85] if "moral values" have become the highest values, this betrays the fact that the moral ideal has been the least fulfilled[86] (—to that extent it represented a "beyond all suffering," as a means to blessedness). Mankind has embraced, with ever-increasing ardor, nothing but clouds: finally it called its despair, its impotence "God"—

337 (*1887-1888*)

Naiveté in respect of ultimate *"desiderata"*—while one does not know the "why" of mankind.

338 (*Jan.-Fall 1888*)

What is the *counterfeiting* aspect of morality?— It pretends to *know* something, namely what "good and evil" is. That means wanting to know why mankind is here, its goal, its destiny. That means wanting to know that mankind *has* a goal, a destiny—

339 (*Nov. 1887-March 1888*)

The very obscure and arbitrary idea that mankind has a single task to perform, that it is moving as a whole toward some goal, is still very young. Perhaps we shall be rid of it again before it becomes a "fixed idea"—

This mankind is not a whole: it is an inextricable multiplicity of ascending and descending life-processes—it does not have a youth followed by maturity and finally by old age; the strata are twisted and entwined together—and in a few millennia there may still be even younger types of man than we can show today. Decadence, on the other hand, belongs to all epochs of mankind:

---

[85] Cf. R. B. Perry's *General Theory of Value* (1926).

[86] Cf. Freud.

refuse and decaying matter are found everywhere; it is one of life's processes to exclude the forms of decline and decay.[87]

*

When Christian prejudice was a power, this question did not exist: meaning lay in the salvation of the individual soul; whether mankind could endure for a long or a short time did not come into consideration. The best Christians desired that it should end as soon as possible—concerning that which was needful to the individual there was no doubt—

The task of every present individual was the same as for a future individual in any kind of future: value, meaning, domain of values were fixed, unconditional, eternal, one with God— That which deviated from this eternal type was sinful, devilish, condemned—

For each soul, the gravitational center of valuation was placed within itself: salvation or damnation! The salvation of the *immortal* soul! Extremest form of personalization— For every soul there was only one perfecting; only one ideal; only one way to redemption— Extremest form of equality of rights, tied to an optical magnification of one's own importance to the point of insanity— Nothing but insanely important souls, revolving about themselves with a frightful fear—

*

No man believes now in this absurd self-inflation: and we have sifted our wisdom through a sieve of contempt. Nevertheless, the optical habit of seeking the value of man in his approach to an ideal man remains undisturbed: fundamentally, one upholds the perspective of personalization as well as equality of rights before the ideal. *In summa*: one believes one knows what the ultimate *desideratum* is with regard to the ideal man—

This belief, however, is only the consequence of a dreadful deterioration through the Christian ideal: as one at once discovers with every careful examination of the "ideal type." One believes one knows, *first* that an approach to one type is desirable; *secondly*, that one knows what this type is like; *thirdly*, that every

---

[87] For a comparison with Oswald Spengler, who said in the preface to *The Decline of the West* that he owed "everything" to Goethe and Nietzsche, see the Epilogue of my *Nietzsche,* footnote 2.

deviation from this type is a regression, an inhibition, a loss of force and power in man—

To dream of conditions in which this perfect man will be in the vast majority: even our socialists, even the Utilitarians have not gone farther than this.—

In this way a goal seems to have entered the development of mankind: at any rate, the belief in progress towards the ideal is the only form in which a goal in history is thought of today. *In summa*: one has transferred the arrival of the "kingdom of God" into the future, on earth, in human form—but fundamentally one has held fast to the belief in the *old* ideal—

340 (*Spring-Fall 1887*)

The more concealed forms of the cult of the Christian moral ideal.— The insipid and cowardly concept "nature" devised by nature enthusiasts (—without any instinct for what is fearful, implacable and cynical in even the "most beautiful" aspects), a kind of attempt to read moral Christian "humanity" into nature—Rousseau's concept of nature, as if "nature" were freedom, goodness, innocence, fairness, justice, an idyl—still a cult of Christian morality fundamentally.— Collect together passages to see what the poets really admired in, e.g., high mountains, etc.— What Goethe wanted from them—why he admired Spinoza—. Complete ignorance the presupposition for this cult—

The insipid and cowardly concept "man" à la Comte and Stuart Mill, perhaps even the object of a cult— It is still the cult of Christian morality under a new name— The freethinkers, e.g., Guyau.

The insipid and cowardly concept "art" as sympathy with all that suffers and is ill-constituted (even history, e.g., Thierry's): it is still the cult of the Christian moral ideal.

And now, as for the entire socialist ideal: nothing but a clumsy misunderstanding of that Christian moral ideal.

341 (*Nov. 1887-March 1888*)

The origin of the ideal. Investigation of the soil in which it grows.

a. Proceeding from the "aesthetic" states, in which the world is seen fuller, rounder and more perfect—: the pagan ideal: self-affirmation predominates (one bestows—). The highest type: the classical ideal—as the expression of the well-constitutedness of all the chief instincts. Therein the highest style: the grand style. Expression of the "will to power" itself. The instinct that is most feared dares to acknowledge itself.

b. Proceeding from states in which the world is seen emptier, paler, more diluted, in which "spiritualization" and nonsensuality assume the rank of perfection, in which the brutal, the animalic-direct, the proximate are most avoided (—one removes, one chooses—): the "sage," the "angel," priestly = virginal = ignorant, physiological characteristics of idealists of this sort—: the anemic ideal. Under certain circumstances it can be the ideal of those who *represent* the first ideal, the pagan (thus Goethe sees his "saint" in Spinoza).

c. Proceeding from states in which we find the world more absurd, worse, poorer, more deceptive than we suppose or desire can be consistent with embodying the ideal (—one negates, one destroys—): the projection of the ideal into the antinatural, antiactual, illogical; the state of him who thus judges (—the "impoverishment" of the world as consequence of suffering: one takes, one no longer gives—): the antinatural ideal.

(The Christian ideal is an intermediate form between the second and third, now with the former, now with the latter predominating.)

The three ideals: a. either a strengthening of life (—pagan) or b. a dilution of life (anemic) or c. a denial of life (—antinatural). The state of "deification" is felt: in the greatest abundance—in the most fastidious selectivity—in contempt for and destruction of life.

342 (*Nov. 1887-March 1888*)

a. The consistent type. Here it is grasped that one must not hate even evil, that one must not oppose it, that one must not make war even against oneself; that one should not merely acquiesce in the suffering that such a way of life entails; that one should live entirely in *positive* feelings; that one should take the side of one's opponent in word and deed; that through a superfetation of the peaceable, good-natured, conciliatory, helpful, and loving states one impoverishes the soil in which other states grow

—that one requires a perpetual way of living. What is achieved here?— The Buddhist type or the perfect cow.

This standpoint is possible only when no moral fanaticism prevails, i.e., when evil is hated, not for its own sake, but only because it opens the way to states that are harmful to us (unrest, work, care, entanglements, dependence).

This is the Buddhist standpoint: here sin is not hated, here the concept "sin" is lacking.

*

b. The inconsistent type. One wages war against evil—one believes that war for the sake of goodness does not have the moral consequences or effect on the character that war otherwise brings with it (and owing to which one detests it as evil). In fact, such a war against evil does much more fundamental harm than any kind of hostility of one person against another; and usually "the person" is reinterpolated as the opponent, at least in imagination (the devil, evil spirits, etc.). A hostile attitude of watching and spying on everything in us that is bad and might have a bad origin ends in a most tormented and anxious constitution: so that "miracles," reward, ecstasy, transcendent solutions now become *desirable*— The Christian type: or the perfect bigot.

*

c. The stoical type. Firmness, self-control, imperturbability, peace as the inflexibility of a protracted will—profound quiet, the defensive state, the fortress, a warrior's mistrustfulness—firmness of principle; the union of will and knowledge; respect for oneself. Hermit type. The perfect "ox."

343 (*1883-1888*)

An ideal that wants to prevail or assert itself seeks to support itself (a) by a spurious origin, (b) by a pretended relationship with powerful ideals already existing, (c) by the thrill of mystery, as if a power that cannot be questioned spoke through it, (d) by defamation of ideals that oppose it, (e) by a mendacious doctrine of the advantages it brings with it, e.g., happiness, repose of soul, peace or the assistance of a powerful God, etc.— Toward a psychology of the idealist: Carlyle, Schiller, Michelet.

If one discovers all the defensive and protective measures by which an ideal maintains itself, is it then refuted? It has employed the means by which all living things live and grow—they are one and all "immoral."

My insight: all the forces and drives by virtue of which life and growth exist lie under the ban of morality: morality as the instinct to deny life. One must destroy morality if one is to liberate life.

344 (*Nov. 1887-March 1888*)

Not to know oneself: prudence of the idealist. The idealist: a creature that has good reasons to be in the dark about itself and is prudent enough to be in the dark about these reasons too.

345 (*1885-1886*)

Tendency of moral development.— Everyone desires that no doctrine or valuation of things should come into favor but that through which he himself prospers. The basic tendency of the weak and mediocre of all ages is, consequently, to weaken and pull down the stronger: chief means, the moral judgment. The attitude of the stronger toward the weaker is branded; the higher states of the stronger acquire an evil name.

The struggle of the many against the few, the commonplace against the rare, the weak against the strong—one of the subtlest interruptions of this struggle occurs when the choice, subtle, more fastidious present themselves as the weak and repudiate the coarser means of power—

346 (*March-June 1888*)

1. The pretended pure drive after knowledge in all philosophers is dictated by their moral "truths"—is only apparently independent—

2. The "moral truths," "thus one *ought* to act," are merely forms of consciousness of a tired instinct "thus and thus one does act among us." The "ideal" is supposed to restore and strengthen an instinct; it flatters man to be obedient where he is only an automaton.

347 (*Spring-Fall 1887*)

Morality as a means of seduction.— "Nature is good, for a wise and good God is its cause. Who, then, is responsible for the 'corruption of mankind'? Its tyrants and seducers, the ruling orders—they must be destroyed"—: *Rousseau's* logic (compare *Pascal's* logic, which lays the responsibility on original sin).

Compare the related logic of *Luther*. In both cases a pretext is sought to introduce an insatiable thirst for revenge as a moral-religious duty. Hatred for the ruling order seeks to sanctify itself—(the "sinfulness of Israel": foundation of the power of the priest).

Compare the related logic of *Paul*. It is always God's cause in which these reactions come forth, the cause of right, of humanity, etc. In the case of *Christ*, the rejoicing of the people appears as the cause of his execution; an anti-priestly movement from the first. Even in the case of the *anti-Semites* it is still the same artifice: to visit condemnatory judgments upon one's opponent and to reserve to oneself the role of *retributive justice*.

348 (*Spring-Fall 1887*)

Course of the struggle: the fighter tries to transform his opponent into his *antithesis*—in imagination naturally. He tries to have faith in himself to such a degree that he may have courage for the "good cause" (as if he were the good cause); as if his opponent were attacking reason, taste, virtue—

The belief he needs as the strongest means of defense and attack is a belief in himself, which, however, knows how to misunderstand itself as belief in God:— never to imagine the advantages and utility of victory, but always victory for the sake of victory, as "the victory of God"—. Every little community (even an individual) that finds itself involved in struggle tries to convince itself: "We have good taste, good judgment, and virtue on our side."— The struggle compels to such an exaggeration of self-esteem—

349 (*Spring-Fall 1887; rev. Spring-Fall 1888*)

Whatever kind of bizarre ideal one may follow (e.g., as "Christian" or as "free spirit" or as "immoralist" or as *Reichs-*

deutscher[88]—), one should not demand that it be *the* ideal: for one therewith takes from it its privileged character. One should have it in order to distinguish oneself, not in order to level oneself.

How comes it, this notwithstanding, that most idealists at once propagandize for their ideal, as if they could have no right to the ideal if everyone did not recognize it?— This, e.g., is what all those brave little women do who permit themselves to learn Latin and mathematics. What compels them? The instinct of the herd, I fear, terror of the herd: they fight for the "emancipation of women" because it is under the form of a *generous activity,* under the banner of "For others," that they can most prudently forward their own little private separatism.

Prudence of idealists to be only missionaries and "representatives" of an ideal: they "transfigure" themselves in the eyes of those who believe in disinterestedness and heroism. Whereas: true heroism consists, in *not* fighting under the banner of sacrifice, devotion, disinterestedness, but in *not fighting at all*— "This is what *I* am; this is what *I* want:— *you* can go to hell!"—

350 (*Spring-Fall 1887*)

Every ideal presupposes love and hate, reverence and contempt. Either the positive feeling is the *primum mobile*[89] or the negative feeling is. Hate and contempt are, e.g., the *primum mobile* in all *ressentiment* ideals.

B. Critique of the "Good Man," the Saint, etc.

351 (*Jan.-Fall 1888*)

The "good man." Or: the hemiplegia[90] of virtue.— For every strong and natural species of man, love and hate, gratitude and revenge, good nature and anger, affirmative acts and negative acts, belong together. One is good on condition one also knows how to be evil; one is evil because otherwise one would not understand how to be good. Whence, then, comes the sickness and

[88] A member of the German *Reich*.

[89] First motive.

[90] Paralysis of one side.

ideological unnaturalness that rejects this doubleness—that teaches that it is a higher thing to be efficient on only one side? Whence comes the hemiplegia of virtue, the invention of the good man?—

The demand is that man should castrate himself of those instincts with which he can be an enemy, can cause harm, can be angry, can demand revenge—

This unnaturalness corresponds, then, to that dualistic conception of a merely good and a merely evil creature (God, spirit, man); in the former are summarized all the positive, in the latter all the negative forces, intentions, states.—

Such a manner of valuing believes itself to be "idealistic"; it does not doubt that, in the conception of "the good," it has posited a supreme *desideratum.* At its peak, it imagines a state in which all that is evil is annulled and in which only good creatures actually remain. It does not even consider it settled that this antithesis of good and evil is conditional on the existence of both; on the contrary, the latter should vanish and the former remain, the one has a right to exist, the other ought not to be there at all—

What is it really that desires this?——

Much labor has been expended in all ages, and especially in the Christian ages, to reduce mankind to this half-sided efficiency, to the "good": even today there is no lack of those deformed and weakened by the church for whom this object coincides with "humanization" in general, or with the "will of God," or with "salvation of the soul." The essential demand here is that mankind should do nothing evil, that it should under no circumstances do harm or desire to do harm. The way to achieve this is: the castration of all possibility of enmity, the unhinging of all the instincts of *ressentiment,* "peace of soul" as a chronic disease.

This mode of thought, with which a definite type of man is bred, starts from an absurd presupposition: it takes good and evil for realities that contradict one another (not as complementary value concepts, which would be the truth), it advises taking the side of the good, it desires that the good should renounce and oppose the evil down to its ultimate roots—it therewith actually denies life, which has in all its instincts both Yes and No. Not that it grasps this: it dreams, on the contrary, that it is getting back to wholeness, to unity, to strength of life: it thinks it will be a state of redemption when the inner anarchy, the unrest between those opposing value drives, is at last put an end to.— Perhaps there has never before been a more dangerous ideology, a greater mischief *in psychologicis*, than this will to good: one has reared the most repellent type, the unfree man, the bigot; one has taught that only as a bigot is one on the right path to godhood, only the bigot's way is God's way.

And even here, life is still in the right—life, which does not know how to separate Yes from No—: what good is it to hold with all one's strength that war is evil, not to do harm, not to desire to negate! one wages war nonetheless! one cannot do otherwise! The good man who has renounced evil, afflicted, as seems to him desirable, with that hemiplegia of virtue, in no way ceases to wage war, have enemies, say No and act No. The Christian, for example, hates "sin"! Precisely because of his faith in a moral antithesis of good and evil the world has become for him overfull of things that must be hated and eternally combated. "The good man" sees himself as if surrounded by evil, and under the continual onslaught of evil his eye grows keener, he discovers evil in all his dreams and desires; and so he ends, quite reasonably, by considering nature evil, mankind corrupt, goodness an act of grace (that is, as impossible for man). *In summa*: he denies life, he grasps that when good is the supreme value it condemns life—

Therewith he ought to consider his ideology of good and evil as refuted. But one cannot refute an illness. And so he conceives *another* life!—

352 (*Nov. 1887-March 1888*)

The concept of power, whether of a god or of a man, always includes both the ability to help and the ability to harm. Thus it is with the Arabs; thus with the Hebrews. Thus with all strong races.

It is a fateful step when one separates the power for the one from the power for the other into a dualism— In this way, morality becomes the poisoner of life—

353 (*Nov. 1887-March 1888*)

Toward a critique of the good man.— Integrity, dignity, sense of duty, justice, humanity, honesty, straightness, good conscience—are certain qualities really affirmed and approved for their own sake with these well-sounding words? or is it a case of qualities and states, in themselves of no particular value, being moved into a certain light in which they acquire value? Does the value of these qualities reside in them or in the use and advantage to which they lead (appear to lead, are expected to lead)?

Naturally, I do not mean by this an antithesis between *ego* and *alter*[91] in the judgment: the question is whether these qualities are supposed to have value on account of their consequences, either for the bearer of these qualities or for the environment, for society, for "humanity": or whether they have value in themselves—

In other words: is it utility that bids one condemn, combat, deny the opposite qualities (—untrustworthiness, falseness, perversity, lack of self-confidence, inhumanity—)? Is the essence of such qualities condemned, or only their consequences?— In other words: would it be desirable that men with these latter qualities should not exist?— In any event, that is what is believed— But here lies the error, the short-sightedness, the narrow-mindedness of nook egoism.

Otherwise expressed: would it be desirable to create conditions in which all the advantage would be with the righteous—so that the opposite natures and instincts would be discouraged and slowly die out?

This is at bottom a question of taste and of aesthetics: would it be desirable that the "most respectable," i.e., most tedious, species of man should survive? the square,[92] the virtuous, the worthies, the good people, the straight, the "oxen"?[93]

If one imagines the tremendous abundance of the "others" gone, then even the righteous no longer has a right to existence: he is no longer necessary—and here one grasps that it is only coarse utility that has brought such an *insufferable* virtue into honor.

Perhaps desirability lies on precisely the other side: to create conditions in which the "righteous man" is reduced to the modest position of a "useful tool"—as the "ideal herd animal," at best herdsman: in short, conditions in which he no longer stands among the higher orders which require other qualities.

354 (*March-June 1888*)

The "good man" as tyrant.— Man has repeated the same mis-

---

[91] The other.

[92] *Die Rechtwinkligen*—literally the right-angled—seems to be used here to connote exactly what is suggested by the American "square."

[93] See also sections 386 and 881.

take over and over again: he has made a means to life into a standard of life; instead of discovering the standard in the highest enhancement of life itself, in the problem of growth and exhaustion, he has employed the means to a quite distinct kind of life to exclude all other forms of life, in short to criticize and select life. I.e., man finally loves the means for their own sake and forgets they are means: so that they enter his consciousness as aims, as standards for aims—i.e., a certain species of man treats the conditions of its existence as conditions which ought to be imposed as a law, as "truth," "good," "perfection": it tyrannizes— It is a form of faith, of instinct, that a species of man fails to perceive its conditionality, its relativity to other species. At least, it seems to be all over for a species of man (people, races) when it becomes tolerant, allows equal rights and no longer thinks of wanting to be master—

355 (*1885-1886*)

"All good people are weak: they are good because they are not strong enough to be evil"[94]—the Latuka chieftain Comorro told Baker.

*

"The faint-hearted know no misfortune"—says a Russian proverb.

356 (*1887-1888*)

Modest, industrious, benevolent, temperate: is that how you would have men? *good men*? But to me that seems only the ideal slave, the slave of the future.

357 (*Spring-Fall 1887*)

The metamorphoses of slavery; its disguise under the cloak of religion; its transfiguration through morality.

---

[94] Cf. *Zarathustra,* II, "On Those Who Are Sublime" (*Portable Nietzsche,* p. 230): "Of all evil I deem you capable: therefore I want the good from you. Verily, I have often laughed at the weaklings who thought themselves good because they had no claws."

358 (*1887-1888*)

The ideal slave (the "good man").— He who cannot posit *himself* as a goal, not posit any goals for himself whatever, bestows honor upon *selflessness*—instinctively. Everything persuades him to this: his prudence, his experience, his vanity. And even faith is a form of selflessness.

*

Atavism: wonderful feeling to be able to obey unconditionally for once.

*

Industry, modesty, benevolence, temperance are just so many hindrances to a sovereign disposition, great inventiveness, heroic purposiveness, noble being-for-oneself.

*

It is not a matter of going ahead (—for then one is at best a herdsman, i.e., the herd's chief requirement), but of being able *to go it alone,* of being able *to be different.*

359 (*Spring-Fall 1887*)

One must reckon up *what* had been accumulated as a consequence of the highest moral idealism: how almost all other values had crystallized around the ideal. This proves that it has been desired longest and strongest—that is has not been attained: otherwise it would have disappointed (or would have been followed by a more moderate valuation).[95]

The saint as the most powerful type of man—: it is this idea that has elevated so high the value of moral perfection. One must imagine the whole of knowledge laboring to prove that the moral man is the most powerful, most godlike.— The overcoming of

---

[95] Between the two paragraphs the following words in the MS have been omitted in all editions: "The highest honor and power among men: even from the most powerful—the only genuine form of happiness—a privileged right to God, to immortality, under certain circumstances to an *unio* [mystical union?]—power over nature—the miracle worker (Parsifal)—power over God, over blessedness and damnation of souls, etc." (1911, p. 503).

the senses, the desires—everything inspired fear; the antinatural appeared as the supernatural, as something from the beyond—

360 (*1883-1888*)

Francis of Assisi: in love, popular, a poet, combats the order of rank among souls in favor of the lowliest. Denial of the hierarchy of souls—"all equal before God."

The popular ideals: the good man, the selfless man, the saint, the sage, the just man. O Marcus Aurelius!

361 (*Spring-Fall 1887*)

I have declared war on the anemic Christian ideal (together with what is closely related to it), not with the aim of destroying it but only of putting an end to its tyranny and clearing the way for new ideals, for *more robust* ideals—

The continuance of the Christian ideal is one of the most desirable things there are—even for the sake of the ideals that want to stand beside it and perhaps above it—they must have opponents, strong opponents, if they are to become *strong*.—

Thus we immoralists require the power of morality: our drive of self-preservation wants our *opponents* to retain their strength—it only wants to become *master over them*.[96]

C. Disparagement of the So-Called Evil Qualities

362 (*1885*)

Egoism and its problem! The Christian gloominess in La Rochefoucauld which extracted egoism from everything and thought he had thereby *reduced* the value of things and of virtues! To counter that, I at first sought to prove that there could not be anything other than egoism—that in men whose ego is weak and thin the power of great love also grows weak—that the greatest lovers are so from the strength of their ego—that love is

---

[96] Cf. section 287 above.

an expression of egoism, etc. In fact, the false valuation is aimed at the interests: (1) of those who are helped and aided, the herd; (2) it contains a pessimistic mistrustfulness of the basis of life; (3) it would like to deny the most splendid and best-constituted men; fear; (4) it wants to aid the subjected to their rights against their conquerors; (5) it brings with it a universal dishonesty, and precisely among the most valuable men.

363 (*Jan.-Fall 1888*)

Man is an indifferent egoist: even the cleverest thinks his habits more important than his advantage.

364 (*1884*)

Egoism! But no one has yet asked: what kind of ego? On the contrary, everyone unconsciously thinks every ego equal to every other ego. This is the consequence of the slaves' theory of *suffrage universel* and "equality."

365 (*1884*)

The actions of a higher man are indescribably complex in their motivation: any such word as "pity" says nothing whatever. The most essential thing is the feeling "Who am I? who is the other in relation to me?"— Value judgments are continually at work.

366 (*1885-1886*)

That the history of all phenomena of morality could be simplified in the way Schopenhauer believed—namely, so that pity is to be discovered as the root of all moral impulse hitherto—only a thinker denuded of all historical instinct, and one who had eluded in the strangest way even that strong schooling in history undergone by the Germans from Herder to Hegel, could have attained to this degree of absurdity and naiveté.

367 (*1885*)

My kind of "pity."— This is a feeling for which I find no name adequate: I sense it when I see precious capabilities squandered, e.g., at the sight of Luther: what force and what insipid backwoodsman problems! (at a time when in France the bold and light-hearted skepticism of a Montaigne was already possible!) Or when I see anyone halted, as a result of some stupid accident, at something less than he might have become. Or especially at the idea of the lot of mankind, as when I observe with anguish and contempt the politics of present-day Europe, which is, under all circumstances, also working at the web of the future of *all* men. Yes, what could not become of "man," if——! This is a[97] kind of "compassion" although there is really no "passion" I share.[98]

368 (*1883-1888*)

Pity a squandering of feeling, a parasite harmful to moral health,[99] "it cannot possibly be our duty to increase the evil in the world." If one does good merely out of pity, it is oneself one really does good to, and not the other. Pity does not depend upon maxims but upon affects;[100] it is pathological. The suffering of others infects us, pity is an infection.

369 (*1885-1886*)

No egoism at all exists that remains within itself and does not encroach—consequently, that "allowable," "morally indifferent" egoism of which you speak does not exist at all.

"One furthers one's ego always at the expense of others;" "Life always lives at the expense of other life"—he who does not grasp this has not taken even the first step toward honesty with himself.

370 (*Spring-Fall 1887*)

The "subject" is only a fiction: the ego of which one speaks when one censures egoism does not exist at all.

---

[97] Gratuitously changed to "my" in all editions.

[98] The play on words is better in the original: *Dies ist eine Art "Mitleid"; ob es schon keinen Leidenden giebt,* mit *dem ich da litte.* The German word for pity means literally "with-suffering" but in this case those for whom the pity is felt are *not* suffering. More's the pity!

[99] Spinoza.

[100] Kant.

371 (*1885-1886*)

The "ego"—which is *not* one with the central government of our nature!—is, indeed, only a conceptual synthesis—thus there *are* no *actions prompted by "egoism."*

372 (*1883-1888*)

As every drive lacks intelligence, the viewpoint of "utility" cannot exist for it. Every drive, in as much as it is active, sacrifices force and other drives: finally it is checked; otherwise it would destroy everything through its excessiveness. Therefore: the "unegoistic," self-sacrificing, imprudent, is nothing special—it is common to all the drives—they do not consider the advantage of the whole ego (because they do not consider at all!), they act contrary to our advantage, against the ego: and often *for* the ego—innocent in both cases!

373 (*March-June 1888*)

Origin of moral values.[101]— Egoism is of as much value as the physiological value of him who possesses it.

Every individual consists of the whole course of evolution (and not, as morality imagines, only of something that begins at birth). If he represents the ascending course of mankind, then his value is in fact extraordinary; and extreme care may be taken over the preservation and promotion of his development. (It is concern for the future promised him that gives the well-constituted individual such an extraordinary right to egoism.) If he represents the descending course, decay, chronic sickening, then he has little value: and the first demand of fairness is for him to take as little space, force, and sunshine as possible away from the well-constituted. In this case, it is the task of society to suppress egoism (—which sometimes expresses itself in absurd, morbid and rebel-

---

[101] This section was put to use by Nietzsche in *Twilight,* section 33 (*Portable Nietzsche,* p. 533 ff). Cf. also Aristotle, *Nicomachean Ethics,* 1169a: "The good man ought to be a lover of self, since he will then act nobly, and so both benefit himself and aid his fellows; but the bad man ought not to be a lover of self, since he will follow his base passions, and injure both himself and his neighbors" (tr. Rackham, Loeb Classical Library).

lious ways), whether it be a question of individuals or of whole decaying and atrophying classes of people. A doctrine and religion of "love," of *suppression* of self-affirmation, of patience, endurance, helpfulness, of cooperation in word and deed, can be of the highest value within such classes, even from the point of view of the rulers: for it suppresses feelings of rivalry, of *ressentiment,* of envy —the all too natural feelings of the underprivileged—it even deifies a life of slavery, subjection, poverty, sickness, and inferiority for them under the ideal of humility and obedience. This explains why the ruling classes (or races) and individuals have at all times upheld the cult of selflessness, the gospel of the lowly, the "God on the cross."

The preponderance of an altruistic mode of valuation is the consequence of an instinct that one is ill-constituted. The value judgment here is at bottom: "I am not worth much": a merely physiological value judgment; even more clearly: the feeling of impotence, the absence of the great affirmative feelings of power (in muscles, nerves, ganglia). This value judgment is translated into a moral or a religious judgment, according to the culture of this class (—the predominance of religious and moral judgments is always a sign of a lower culture—): it seeks to establish itself by relating to spheres in which it recognizes the concept "value" in general. The interpretation by means of which the Christian sinner believes he understands himself is an attempt to justify his lack of power and self-confidence: he would rather consider himself guilty than feel bad for no reason: it is a symptom of decay to require interpretations of this sort at all.

In other cases, the underprivileged man seeks the reason not in his "guilt" (as the Christian does), but in society: the socialist, the anarchist, the nihilist—in as much as they find their existence something of which someone must be *guilty,* they are still the closest relations of the Christian, who also believes he can better endure his sense of sickness and ill-constitutedness by finding someone whom he can make responsible for it. The instinct of revenge and *ressentiment* appears here in both cases as a means of enduring, as the instinct of self-preservation: just as is the preference for altruistic theory and practice.

Hatred of egoism, whether it be one's own (as with Christians) or another's (as with socialists), is thus revealed as a value judgment under the predominating influence of revenge; on the other hand, as an act of prudence for the self-preservation of the suffering by an enhancement of their feelings of cooperation and solidarity—

Finally, even that release of *ressentiment* in the judging, rejecting, punishing of egoism (one's own or another's) is also, as already indicated, an instinct of self-preservation on the part of the underprivileged. *In summa*: the cult of altruism is a specific form of egoism that regularly appears under certain physiological conditions.

When the socialist with a fine indignation demands "justice," "right," "equal rights," he is merely acting under the impress of his inadequate culture that cannot explain why he is suffering: on the other hand, he enjoys himself; if he felt better he would refrain from crying out: he would then find pleasure in other things. The same applies to the Christian: he condemns, disparages, curses the "world"—himself not excluded. But that is no reason for taking his clamor seriously. In both cases we are in the presence of invalids who feel better for crying out, for whom defamation is a relief.

374 (*Spring-Fall 1887; rev. Spring-Fall 1888*)

Every society has the tendency to reduce its opponents to caricatures—at least in imagination—and, as it were, to starve them. Such a caricature is, e.g., our "criminal." Within the aristocratic Roman order of values, the Jew was reduced to a caricature. Among artists, the "philistine and bourgeois" become caricatures; among the pious, the godless; among aristocrats, the man of the people. Among immoralists it is the moralist: Plato, for example, becomes a caricature in my hands.

375 (*1883-1888*)

All the drives and powers that morality praises seem to me to be essentially the same as those it defames and rejects: e.g., justice as will to power, will to truth as a tool of the will to power.

376 (*1883-1888*)

Man's growing inwardness. Inwardness grows as powerful drives that have been denied outward release by the establishment of peace and society seek compensation by turning inward in concert with the imagination. The thirst for enmity, cruelty, revenge, violence turns back, is repressed;[102] in the desire for knowledge there is avarice and conquest; in the artist there reappears the repressed[103] power to dissimulate and lie; the drives are transformed into demons whom one fights, etc.

377 (*1883-1888*)

Falsity.— Every sovereign instinct has the others for its tools, retainers, flatterers: it never lets itself be called by its *ugly* name: and it countenances no praise in which it is not also praised indirectly. All praise and blame in general crystallizes around every sovereign instinct to form a rigorous order and etiquette. This is *one* of the causes of falsity.

Every instinct that struggles for mastery but finds itself under a yoke requires for itself, as strengthening and as support for its self-esteem, all the beautiful names and recognized values: so, as a rule, it ventures forth under the name of the "master" it is combatting and from whom it wants to get free (e.g., the fleshly desires or the desires for power under the dominion of Christian values).— This is the *other* cause of falsity.

Perfect naiveté reigns in both cases: the falsity does not become conscious. It is a sign of a broken instinct when man sees the driving force and its "expression" ("the mask") as separate things—a sign of self-contradiction, and victorious far less often. Absolute innocence in bearing, word, affect, a "good conscience" in falsity, the certainty with which one grasps the greatest and most splendid words and postures—all this is necessary for victory.

In the other case: when one has extreme clearsightedness one needs the genius of the actor and tremendous training in self-control if one is to achieve victory. That is why priests are the most skillful *conscious* hypocrites; then princes, whom rank and ancestry have endowed with a kind of acting ability. Thirdly, men of society, diplomats. Fourthly, women.

Basic idea: falsity seems so profound, so omnisided, the will so clearly opposed to direct self-knowledge and the calling of

---

[102] *Tritt zurück.*

[103] *Zurückgetretene.* This note on *"Die* Verinnerlichung *des Menschen"* should be compared with section 16 of the second essay in the *Genealogy of Morals,* where the same phrase is used and discussed.

things by their right names, that it is very highly probable that truth, will to truth is really something else and only a disguise. (The need for faith is the greatest brake-shoe on truthfulness.)

378 (*1883-1888*)

"Thou shalt not lie": one demands truthfulness. But acknowledgement of the factual (refusal to let oneself be lied to) has been greatest precisely among liars: they have recognized that just this popular "truthfulness" is *not* a fact. What is said is always too much or too little: the demand that one should denude oneself with every word one says is a piece of naiveté.

One says what one thinks, one is "truthful," only under certain conditions: namely, that one is understood (*inter pares*),[104] and understood with good will (once again *inter pares*). One conceals oneself in presence of the unfamiliar: and he who wants to attain something says what he would like to have thought of him, but *not* what he thinks. ("The powerful always lie.")

379 (*Spring-Fall 1887*)

The great nihilistic counterfeiting through artful misuse of moral values:

a. Love as depersonalization; also pity.

b. Only the most depersonalized intellect ("the philosopher") knows the truth, "the true being and nature of things."

c. The genius, the great human beings, are great because they do not seek their own advantage: the value of a man increases in proportion as he denies himself.

d. Art as the work of the "pure free-willed subject"; misunderstanding of "objectivity."

e. Happiness as the end of life: virtue as means to an end.

The pessimistic condemnation of life by Schopenhauer is a moral one. Transference of herd standards into the realm of metaphysics.

The "individuum" meaningless, necessitating an origin in the "in-itself" (and an explanation of his existence as an "aberration"); parents only "accidental cause."— We are paying for the fact that science has not understood the individuum: he comprises the entirety of life hitherto in one development, and is not its *result*.

---

[104] Among equals.

380 (*Spring-Fall 1887*)

1. Systematic falsification of history; so that it may provide the proof of moral valuation:

a. decline of a people and corruption;[105]

b. rise of a people and virtue;

c. zenith of a people ("its culture") as consequence of moral elevation.

2. Systematic falsification of great human beings, the great creators, the great epochs:

one desires that faith should be the distinguishing mark of the great: but slackness, skepticism, "immorality," the right to throw off a faith, belong to greatness (Caesar, also Homer, Aristophanes, Leonardo, Goethe). One always suppresses the main thing, their "freedom of will"—

381 (*Spring-Fall 1887*)

Great lie in history: as if the corruption of the church were the cause of the Reformation! Only pretext and self-deception on the part of the instigators—strong needs were present whose brutality very much required a spiritual cloak.[106]

382 (*Spring-Fall 1887; rev. Spring-Fall 1888*)

Schopenhauer interpreted high intellectuality as liberation from the will; he did not *want* to see the freedom from moral prejudice which is part of the emancipation of the great spirit, the typical immorality of the genius; he artfully posited the only thing he held in honor, the moral value of "depersonalization," as the condition of spiritual activity, of "objective" viewing. "Truth," even in art, appears after the withdrawal of the will—

I see a fundamentally different valuation cutting across all the moral idiosyncrasies: I know nothing of such an absurd distinction between "genius" and the moral and immoral world of the will. The moral man is a lower species than the immoral, a weaker species; indeed—he is a type in regard to morality, but

---

[105] Cf. section 334 above; also 41-44 and *Twilight*, Chapter VI (*Portable Nietzsche*, p. 492 *ff*).

[106] See 150n above.

not a type in himself; a copy, a good copy at best—the measure of his value lies outside him. I assess a man by the quantum of power and abundance of his will: not by its enfeeblement and extinction; I regard a philosophy which teaches denial of the will as a teaching of defamation and slander— *I assess the power of a will by how much resistance, pain, torture it endures and knows how to turn to its advantage; I do not account the evil and painful character of existence a reproach to it, but hope rather that it will one day be more evil and painful than hitherto*—[107]

The high point of the spirit imagined by Schopenhauer was to attain to the recognition that there is no meaning in anything, in short, to *recognize* what the good man already instinctively *does*— He denies the possibility of a higher kind of intellect—he took his insight for a *non plus ultra.* Here spirituality is placed much lower than goodness; its highest value (e.g., as art) would be to urge and prepare moral conversion: absolute domination of moral values.—

Beside Schopenhauer I would characterize *Kant*: nothing Greek, absolutely antihistorical (his passage on the French Revolution) and a moral fanatic (Goethe's passage on radical evil). Saintliness was in the background in his case, too.

I need a critique of the *saint*—

Hegel's value. "Passion."—

Shopkeeper's philosophy of Mr. Spencer; complete absence of an ideal, except that of the mediocre man.

Fundamental instinctive principle of all philosophers and historians and psychologists: everything of value in man, art, history, science, religion, technology must be proved to be of *moral value, morally* conditioned, in aim, means and outcome. Everything understood in the light of the supreme value: e.g., Rousseau's question concerning civilization: "Does man become *better* through it?"—an amusing question, since the reverse is obvious and is precisely that which speaks in *favor* of civilization.

383 (*March-June 1888*)

Religious morality.— Affect, great desire, the passion for power, love, revenge, possessions—: moralists want to extinguish and uproot them, to "purify" the soul of them.

---

[107] Italics supplied. In the original only "power" and "will" are emphasized. Sections 382-88 are of exceptional interest.

The logic is: the desires often produce great misfortune—consequently they are evil, reprehensible. A man must free himself from them: otherwise he cannot be a *good* man—

This is the same logic as: "if thine eye offend thee, pluck it out." In the particular case in which that dangerous "innocent from the country," the founder of Christianity, recommended this practice to his disciples, the case of sexual excitation, the consequence is, unfortunately, not only the loss of an organ but the *emasculation* of a man's character— And the same applies to the moralist's madness that demands, instead of the restraining of the passions, their extirpation. Its conclusion is always: only the castrated man is a good man.

Instead of taking into service the great sources of strength, those impetuous torrents of the soul that are so often dangerous and overwhelming, and economizing them, this most shortsighted and pernicious mode of thought, the moral mode of thought, wants to make them dry up.[108]

384 (*1885-1886*)

Overcoming of the affects?— No, if what is implied is their weakening and extirpation. But putting them into service: which may also mean subjecting them to a protracted tyranny (not only as an individual, but as a community, race, etc.). At last they are confidently granted freedom again: they love us as good servants and go voluntarily wherever our best interests lie.

385 (*Spring-Fall 1887*)

Moral intolerance is an expression of weakness in a man: he is afraid of his own "immorality," he must deny his strongest drives because he does not yet know how to employ them. Thus the most fruitful regions of the earth remain uncultivated the longest:— the force is lacking that could here become master—

386 (*Spring-Fall 1887*)

There are very naive peoples and men who believe that continual fine weather is something desirable: even today they believe,

---

[108] A section of the utmost importance for the understanding of Nietzsche's opposition to Christianity and his contrast of Dionysus and Christ.

in *rebus moralibus,* [109] that the "good man," and nothing but the "good man," is something desirable—and that the course of human evolution is directed toward the survival of the "good man" only (and that one must bend all one's efforts in that direction—). This is in the highest degree an *uneconomic* thought and, as stated, the acme of naiveté, nothing but the expression of the pleasing effect produced by the "good man" (—he arouses no fear, he permits one to relax, he gives what one is able to take).[110]

From a superior viewpoint one desires the contrary: the ever-increasing dominion of evil, the growing emancipation of man from the narrow and fear-ridden bonds of morality, the increase of force, in order to press the mightiest natural powers—the affects—into service.

387 (*Nov. 1887-March 1888*)

The whole conception of an order of rank among the passions: as if the right and normal thing were for one to be guided by reason—with the passions as abnormal, dangerous, semi-animal, and, moreover, so far as their aim is concerned, nothing other than desires for pleasure—

Passion is degraded (1) as if it were only in unseemly cases, and not necessarily and always, the motive force; (2) in as much as it has for its object something of no great value, amusement—

The misunderstanding of passion and reason, as if the latter were an independent entity and not rather a system of relations between various passions and desires; and as if every passion did not possess its quantum of reason—

388 (*Spring-Fall 1887*)

How, under the impress of the ascetic morality of depersonali-

---

[109] Moral matters.

[110] The reading "nothing but the expression" is doubtful, as the words in the MS are somewhat illegible.

In the first edition (1901) only the first paragraph was printed (as section 225). In the MS the second paragraph does not follow the first; it appears earlier in the same notebook, preceded by the words: "The same kind of man who wishes us 'good weather' also wishes only for 'good men' and, quite generally, for good qualities—at least the ever-growing dominion of what is good."

Schlechta ignores 1911, p. 504, and also p. 486, and reprints the text of the standard editions.

See also section 881 below.

zation, it was precisely the affects of love, goodness, pity, even those of justice, magnanimity, heroism, that were necessarily misunderstood:[111]

It is richness in personality, abundance in oneself, overflowing and bestowing, instinctive good health and affirmation of oneself, that produce great sacrifice and great love: it is strong and godlike selfhood from which these affects grow, just as surely as do the desire to become master, encroachment, the inner certainty of having a right to everything. What according to common ideas are opposite dispositions are rather *one* disposition; and if one is not firm and brave within oneself, one has nothing to bestow and cannot stretch out one's hand to protect and support—

How was one able so to transform these instincts that man thought valuable that which was directed against his self? when he sacrificed his self to another self. Oh the psychological wretchedness and mendaciousness that has hitherto laid down the law in the church and in church-infected philosophy!

If man is sinful through and through, then he ought only to hate himself. Fundamentally, he would have to treat his fellow men on the same basis as he treats himself; charity needs to be justified—its justification lies in the fact that God has commanded it.— It follows from this, that all the natural instincts of man (the instinct of love, etc.) appear to be forbidden in themselves and only after they have been denied are they restored to their rights on the basis of obedience to God—Pascal, the admirable logician of Christianity, went so far! consider his relations to his sister. "*Not* to make oneself love"[112] seemed Christian to him.

389 (*1883-1888*)

Let us consider the cost of such a moral canon ("an ideal"). (Its enemies are—well? The "egoists.")

The melancholic astuteness in self-disparagement in Europe (Pascal, La Rochefoucauld)—the inner enfeeblement, discouragement, self-vexation of the non-herd animals—

the perpetual emphasizing of the qualities of mediocrity as the most valuable (modesty in rank and file, the tool-like nature)—

the bad conscience associated with all that is self-glorifying and original;

---

[111] In the MS, after the colon, doubly underlined, "Main Chapter."

[112] Or: loved.

therefore displeasure; therefore the world of the more strongly constituted made gloomy!

herd-consciousness transferred to philosophy and religion; also its timorousness.

Let us leave aside the psychological impossibility of a purely selfless action!

390 (*Nov. 1887-March 1888*)

My final proposition is: that the *actual* man represents a much higher value than the "desirable" man of any ideal hitherto; that all "*desiderata*" with reference to man have been absurd and dangerous excesses through which a single type of man tried to establish *his* conditions of preservation and growth as a law for all mankind; that every "*desideratum*" of this kind ever brought into a position of dominance has reduced the value of man, his strength, his certainty of the future; that the nook-intellectuality and poverty of spirit of man is most apparent, even today, when he *desires;* that man's ability to posit values has hitherto been too little developed for him to be just, not merely to the "desirable" values, but to the real values of man; that the ideal has hitherto been the actual force for disparaging the world and man, the poisonous vapor over reality, the great *seduction to nothingness*—

D. Critique of the Words: Improvement, Perfecting, Elevation

391 (*1885-1886*)

Standard by which the value of moral evaluation is to be determined.

The fundamental fact that has been overlooked: the contradiction between "becoming more moral" and the elevation and strengthening of the type man.

Homo natura. The "will to power."

392 (*March-June 1888*)

Moral values as illusory values compared with physiological values.

393 (*Spring-Fall 1887*)

Thought about the most universal subjects is always behind the times: the ultimate *"desiderata"* for mankind, for example, have never really been grasped as a problem by philosophers. They all naively postulate the "improvement" of man as if an intuition answered for us the question *why* we ought to "improve." To what extent is it desirable that man should become more virtuous? or cleverer? or happier? Provided we do not already know the "wherefore" of mankind, such an outlook has no meaning; and if one desires one of these things, who knows, perhaps one is precluded from desiring the others. Is an increase in virtuousness compatible with an increase in cleverness and insight? *Dubito*;[113] only too often I shall have occasion to show the reverse. Has virtuousness as a goal not hitherto been in the most rigorous sense incompatible with being happy? does it not, on the contrary, require misfortune, self-denial and self-mistreatment as a necessary means? And if the deepest insight were the goal, would one not then have to renounce the increase of happiness? and choose danger, adventure, mistrust, seduction as the road to insight?— And if one desires happiness, well, perhaps one has to become one of the "poor in spirit."

394 (*March-June 1888*)

The universal deception and cheating in the realm of so-called moral improvement.— We do not believe that a man will become another if he is not that other already; i.e., if he is not, as is often the case, a multiplicity of persons, at least the embryos of persons. In this case, one can bring a different role into the foreground and draw "the former man" back— The aspect is changed, not the essence— That someone ceases to perform certain actions is a mere *fatum brutum*[114] that permits the most various interpretations. It is not always the case that the habit of a certain act is broken, the ultimate reason for it removed. He who is a criminal through fate and facility unlearns nothing, but learns more and more: and a long abstinence even acts as a tonic to his talent—

---

[113] I doubt [it].

[114] Brute fate.

For society, to be sure, all that is of interest is precisely that someone no longer performs certain actions: to this end it removes him from those conditions in which he *can* perform certain actions; that is wiser, in any event, than to attempt the impossible, namely, to disrupt the fatality by which he is thus and thus. The church—and in this it has done nothing but succeed and inherit from the philosophy of antiquity—proceeding from a different standard and desiring to save a "soul," the "eternal destiny" of a soul, first believes in the expiatory power of punishment and then in the obliterating power of forgiveness: both are deceptions of religious prejudice—punishment does not expiate, forgiveness does not extinguish, what is done is not undone. That someone forgets something is certainly not evidence that something has ceased to exist—

A deed produces its consequences, within the man and outside the man, regardless of whether it is considered as punished, "expiated," "forgiven" and "extinguished," regardless of whether the church has in the meantime promoted the doer to a saint. The church believes in things that do not exist, in "souls;" it believes in effects that do not exist, in divine effects; it believes in states that do not exist, in sin, in redemption, in the salvation of the soul: it stays everywhere on the surface, at signs, gestures, words to which it gives an arbitrary meaning. It possesses a thoroughly thought-out method of psychological counterfeiting.

395 (*1887-1888*)

—"Illness makes men better": this famous opinion, which one encounters throughout the centuries, in the mouth of the sage as often as in the mouth and maw of the people, makes one wonder. As to whether it is valid, one would like to ask: were morality and illness originally connected, perhaps? The "improvement of man," regarded as a whole, e.g., the undeniable softening, humanizing, mellowing of the European within the last millennium—is it perhaps the result of long hidden and mysterious suffering and failure, abstinence, stunting? Has "illness" made the European "better"? Or, in other words; is our morality—our modern sensitive European morality, which may be compared with the morality of the Chinese—the expression of a physiological regression?—

For one cannot deny that every period in history in which "man" has shown himself in exceptional splendor and power at once assumed an impetuous, dangerous, and eruptive character under which humanity fared ill; and perhaps in those cases in which it seems otherwise, all that was lacking was the courage or subtlety to take psychology into the depths and to find there, too, the universal law: "the healthier, stronger, richer, more fruitful, more enterprising a man feels, the more 'immoral' he will be, too." A painful thought! in which one certainly ought not to indulge! If, however, one goes along with it for just a few moments, how astonishing the future seems then! What would then be paid for more dearly than precisely that which we are promoting with all our strength—the humanizing, the "improvement," the growing "civilization" of man? Nothing would be more costly than virtue: for one would in the end have turned the earth into a hospital: and ultimate wisdom would be "everyone as everyone else's nurse." To be sure, one would then possess that much-desired "peace on earth"! But how little "delight in each other"! How little beauty, high spirits, daring, danger! How few "works" for the sake of which life on earth is worth while! And, alas, no more "deeds" whatever! All *great* works and deeds that have remained and have not been washed away by the waters of time—were they not all in the profoundest sense immoralities?—

396 (*Jan.-Fall 1888*)

The priests—and with them the semi-priests, the philosophers—have at all times called true any teaching whose educative effect was beneficial or seemed beneficial—which "improved." In this they resemble a naive quack and miracle man of the people, who, because he has used a poison as a cure, denies it is a poison—"By their fruits shall ye know them—namely, our 'truths' ": that has been the reasoning of the priests to this day. With fateful results, they have expended their subtlety to make the "proof of power" (or "from their fruits") pre-eminent, even decisive, above all other forms of proof. "What makes good must be good; what is good cannot lie"—that is their relentless conclusion—: "what bears good fruit must be true: there is no other criterion of truth"—

But if "making better" counts as an argument, then making worse must count as a refutation. One can prove an error to be an error by testing the lives of those who espouse it: a mistake, a vice can refute— This most indecent form of opposition, from behind and below, the doglike form of opposition, has not died out either: the priests, in so far as they are psychologists, have never discovered anything more interesting than to sniff at the secrets of their adversaries—they demonstrate their Christianity by looking about the "world" for filth. Especially with the first men of the world, with the "geniuses": one will remember how Goethe has been attacked in Germany at all times (Klopstock and Herder were the first to provide a "good example" of this—kind sticks to kind).

397 (*Jan.-Fall 1888*)

One must be very immoral in order to make morals by deeds— The means of the moralist are the most terrible means that have ever been employed; he who has not the courage for immorality in deeds is fit for anything, but he is not fit to be a moralist.

Morality is a menagerie; its presupposition is that iron bars can be more profitable than freedom, even for the prisoners; its other presupposition is that there exist animal-trainers who are not afraid of terrible means—who know how to handle red-hot iron. This frightful species which takes up the fight against the wild animal is called "priest."

*

Man, imprisoned in an iron cage of errors, became a caricature of man, sick, wretched, ill-disposed toward himself, full of hatred for the impulses of life, full of mistrust of all that is beautiful and happy in life, a walking picture of misery: this artificial, arbitrary, *recent* abortion that the priests have pulled up out of their soil, the "sinner": how shall we be able, in spite of all, to *justify* this phenomenon?

*

In order to be fair to morality, we must put two zoological concepts in its place: *taming* of the beast and *breeding* of a particular species.

The priests have pretended at all times that they want to "improve"— But we others would laugh if an animal-trainer spoke of his "improved" animals. In most cases, the taming of a beast is achieved through the harming of a beast: the moral man, too, is not a better man but only a weaker one. But he is less harmful—[115]

---

[115] Cf. *Twilight*, "The 'Improvers' of Mankind" (*Portable Nietzsche*, p. 501 *ff*).

398 (*Jan.-Fall 1888*)

What I want to make clear by all the means in my power:

a. that there is no worse confusion than the confusion of breeding with taming: which is what has been done— Breeding, as I understand it, is a means of storing up the tremendous forces of mankind so that the generations can build upon the work of their forefathers—not only outwardly, but inwardly, organically growing out of them and becoming something stronger—

b. that it is extraordinarily dangerous to believe that mankind as a whole will progress and grow stronger if individuals become flabby, equal, average— Mankind is an abstraction: the goal of breeding, even in the case of a single individual, can only be the *stronger* man (—the man without breeding is weak, extravagant, unstable—).

6. Further Considerations for a Critique of Morality

399 (*1885-1886*)

These are the demands I make upon you—however ill they may sound to you: that you should undertake a critique of the moral evaluations themselves. That you should call a halt to the moral impulse, which here demands submission and not a critique, with the question: "why submission?" That you should regard this demand for a "wherefore?", for a critique of morality, as precisely your present form of morality, as the sublimest form of morality, which does honor to you and to your age. That our honesty, our will not to deceive *ourselves*, must prove itself: why *not*?— Before what tribunal? The will not to let oneself be deceived is of different origin: a caution against being overpowered, exploited—one of life's instincts of self-defense.[116]

---

[116] The last sentence, omitted from all editions, has here been restored, and the penultimate sentence revised, in acordance with the MS and 1911, p. 504.

For the contrast implicit in the last two sentences see also *The Gay Science*, Book V, section 344, which is discussed at length in my *Nietzsche*, Chapter 12, section III.

400 (*1883-1888*)

The three *assertions*:

The ignoble is the higher (protest of the "common man"); the antinatural is the higher (protest of the underprivileged); the average is the higher (protest of the herd, of the "mediocre").

Thus in the history of morality a will to power finds expression, through which now the slaves and oppressed, now the ill-constituted and those who suffer from themselves, now the mediocre attempt to make those value judgments prevail that are favorable to *them*.

To this extent, the phenomenon of morality is, from a biological standpoint, highly suspicious. Morality has developed hitherto at the expense of: the rulers and their specific instincts, the well-constituted and beautiful natures, those who are in any sense independent and privileged.

Morality is therefore an opposition movement against the efforts of nature to achieve a higher type. Its effect is: mistrust of life in general (in so far as its tendencies are considered "immoral")—hostility toward the senses (in so far as the supreme values are considered to be opposed to the supreme instincts)—degeneration and self-destruction of "higher natures," because it is precisely in them that the conflict becomes *conscious*.

401 (*March-June 1888*)

The Values That Have Been on Top Hitherto

Morality as the supreme value, in all phases of philosophy (even among the skeptics). Result: this world is good for nothing, there must be a "real world."

What really determines the supreme value here? What is morality really? The instinct of decadence; it is the exhausted and disinherited who in this way take their revenge and play the master—

Historical proof: the philosophers always decadents, always in the service of the nihilistic religions.

The instinct of decadence which appears as will to power. Introduction of its system of means: absolute immorality of means.

General insight: supreme values hitherto are a special case of the will to power; morality itself is a special case of immorality.

*

Why the Opposing Values Always Succumbed

1. How was this really possible? Question: why did life, physiological well-constitutedness everywhere succumb? Why was there no affirmative philosophy, no affirmative religion?—

The historical signs of such movements: the pagan religion. Dionysus versus the "Crucified." The Renaissance. Art.

2. The strong and the weak: the healthy and the sick; the exception and the rule. There is no doubt who is the stronger—

General aspect of history: Is man therefore an exception in the history of life?—Objection to Darwinism. The means the weak employ to keep themselves on top have become instincts, "humanity," "institutions"—

3. Proof of this dominion in our political instincts, in our social value judgments, in our arts, in our science.

*

The declining instincts have become master over the ascending instincts— The will to nothingness has become master over the will to life!

—Is this true? is there perhaps not a stronger guarantee of life in this victory of the weak and mediocre?—is it perhaps only a means in the total movement of life, a slackening of tempo? a self-defense against something even worse?

—Suppose the strong had become master in everything, and even in moral valuation: let us draw the consequences of how they would think about sickness, suffering, sacrifice! Self-contempt on the part of the weak would be the result; they would try to disappear and extinguish themselves. And would this be *desirable*?—and would we really want a world in which the influence of the weak, their subtlety, consideration, spirituality, *pliancy* was lacking?—

*

We have seen two "wills to power" in conflict (in this special case: we had a principle, that of considering right those who hitherto succumbed, and wrong those who hitherto prevailed): we have recognized the "real world" as a "false world" and morality as a form of immorality. We do *not* say: "The stronger is wrong."

We have grasped what it was that determined supreme value and why it became master over the opposing valuation—: it was stronger numerically.

Now let us purify the opposite valuation of the infection and half-measures of the degeneration characteristic of the form in which it is known to us.

Restoration of nature: moraline-free.

402 (*Jan.-Fall 1888*)

Morality a useful error; more clearly in the case of the greatest and least prejudiced of its advocates, a lie that is considered necessary.

403 (*1886-1887*)

One may admit the truth to oneself to the point where one is sufficiently elevated no longer to require the disciplinary school of [moral][116] error— When one judges existence morally, it disgusts.

One should not invent unreal persons, e.g., one should not say "nature is cruel." Precisely the insight that no such central responsible being exists is a relief!

Evolution of man. a. To gain power over nature and in addition a certain power over oneself. (Morality was needed that man might prevail in his struggle with nature and the "wild animal.")

b. If power has been attained over nature, one can employ this power in the further free development of oneself: will to power as self-elevation and strengthening.

404 (*1886-1887*)

Morality as an illusion of the species, designed to motivate the individual to sacrifice himself to the future: apparently allowing him an infinite value, so that by means of this self-conscious-

[116] Placed in brackets above because this word, although found in all previous editions, including Schlechta's, is not found in the MS.

ness he should tyrannize over and keep down other sides of his nature and find it hard to be content with himself.

Profoundest gratitude for that which morality has achieved hitherto: but now it is only a burden which may become a fatality! Morality itself, in the form of honesty, compels us to deny morality.

405 (*1885-1886*)
End[117]

To what an extent the self-destruction of morality is still a part of its own force. We Europeans have in us the blood of those who died for their faith; we have taken morality to be serious and awesome, and there is nothing that we have not in some way sacrificed to it. On the other hand: our spiritual subtlety has essentially been attained through conscience-vivisection. We do not yet know the "wither" toward which we are driven once we have detached ourselves from our old soil. But it was from this same soil that we acquired the force which now drives us forth into the distance, into adventures, thrusting us into the boundless, the untried, the undiscovered—we have no choice left, we have to be conquerors once we no longer have any country in which we are at home, in which we would want to "preserve" things. A concealed Yes drives us that is stronger than all our No's. Our strength itself will no longer endure us in the old decaying soil: we venture away, we venture *ourselves*: the world is still rich and undiscovered, and even to perish is better than to become half-hearted and poisonous. Our strength itself drives us to sea, where all suns have hitherto gone down: we *know* of a new world—

---

[117] This heading, though in the MS, has been deleted in all previous editions, including Schlechta's.

III. CRITIQUE OF PHILOSOPHY

1. General Observations

406 (*1885-1886*)

Let us get rid of a few superstitions about philosophers that have been common so far!

407 (*1884*)

Philosophers are prejudiced against appearance, change, pain, death, the corporeal, the senses, fate and bondage, the aimless.

They believe first in: absolute knowledge, (2) in knowledge for the sake of knowledge, (3) in an association between virtue and happiness, (4) in the comprehensibility of human actions. [They are][118] led by instinctive moral definitions in which former cultural conditions are reflected (more dangerous ones).

408 (*1884*)

What do philosophers lack? (a)[119] an historical sense, (b) knowledge of physiology, (c) a goal in the future— The ability to formulate a critique without any irony or moral condemnation.

409 (*1885*)

Philosophers (1) have had from the first a wonderful capacity for the *contradictio in adjecto*; (2) they have trusted in concepts as completely as they have mistrusted the senses: they have not stopped to consider that concepts and words are our inheritance from ages in which thinking was very modest and unclear.

What dawns on philosophers last of all: they must no longer accept concepts as a gift, nor merely purify and polish them, but first *make* and *create* them, present them and make them convincing. Hitherto one has generally trusted one's concepts as if

---

[118] Not in the MS. The German editors made other minor changes in this note.

[119] Although the MS has (a), (b), (c), all previous editions have 1, 2, 3.

they were a wonderful dowry from some sort of wonderland: but they are, after all, the inheritance from our most remote, most foolish as well as most intelligent ancestors. This piety toward what we find in us is perhaps part of the moral element in knowledge. What is needed above all is an absolute skepticism toward all inherited concepts (of the kind that one philosopher *perhaps* possessed—Plato, of course—for he taught the reverse).

410 (*1885-1886*)
For the Preface[120]

Deeply mistrustful of the dogmas of epistemology, I loved to look now out of this window, now out of that; I guarded against settling down with any of these dogmas, considered them harmful —and finally: is it likely that a tool is *able* to criticize its own fitness?— What I noticed was rather that no epistemological skepticism or dogmatism had ever arisen free from ulterior motives —that it acquires a value of the second rank as soon as one has considered what it was that *compelled* the adoption of this point of view.

Fundamental insight: Kant as well as Hegel and Schopenhauer—the skeptical-epochistic attitude as well as the historicizing, as well as the pessimistic—have a *moral* origin. I saw no one who had ventured a critique of moral value feelings: and I soon turned my back on the meagre attempts made to arrive at a description of the origin of these feelings (as by the English and German Darwinists).

How can Spinoza's position, his denial and rejection of moral value judgments, be explained? (It was one consequence of his theodicy!)

411 (*Spring-Fall 1887; rev. 1888*)

Morality as supreme devaluation.— *Either* our world is the work and expression (*modus*) of God: in which case it must be supremely perfect (Leibniz's conclusion)—and one never doubted that one knew what constituted perfection—in which case evil must be only apparent (Spinoza is more radical, applying this to

[120] This heading has been deleted in all previous editions. This section is discussed in my *Nietzsche,* Chapter 2, section II.

the concepts good and evil), or must proceed from God's supreme purpose (—perhaps as consequence of a particular mark of favor by God, who allows a choice between good and evil: the privilege of not being an automaton; "freedom" at the risk of making a mistake, of choosing wrongly—e.g., see Simplicius in his commentary on Epictetus).

Or our world is imperfect, evil and guilt are actual and determined and absolutely inherent in its nature; in which case it cannot be the *real* world: in which case knowledge is only the way to a denial of it, for the world is an error which can be known to be an error. This is the opinion of Schopenhauer on the basis of Kantian presuppositions. Pascal is even more desperate: he comprehended that, in that case, even knowledge must be corrupt and falsified—that *revelation* was needed even to understand that the world ought to be denied.

412 (*1883-1888*)

Because we are used to unconditional authorities we have come to need unconditional authorities:—this need is so strong that, even in a critical age such as Kant's, it showed itself superior to the need for criticism and was, in a certain sense, able to subject the entire work of critical reason and put it to its own uses.— It proved its superiority once again in the following generation, which was necessarily drawn by its historical instinct toward a relativity of all authority, by pressing into its service even the Hegelian philosophy of evolution, history re-baptized philosophy, and presenting history as the progressive self-revelation, self-surpassing of moral ideas. Since Plato, philosophy has been dominated by morality. Even in his predecessors, moral interpretations play a decisive role (with Anaximander, the perishing of all things as punishment for their emancipation from pure being; with Heraclitus, the regularity of phenomena as witness to the moral-legal character of the whole world of becoming).

413 (*1885*)

Ulterior moral motives have hitherto most obstructed the course of philosophy.

414 (*Jan.-Fall 1888*)[121]

In all ages, one has taken "beautiful feelings" for arguments, the "heaving bosom" for the bellows of divinity, convictions for a "criterion of truth," the need of an opponent for a question mark against wisdom: this falsehood, this counterfeiting, permeates the whole history of philosophy. The skeptics—respectable but rare—excepted, an instinct for intellectual integrity is nowhere evident. At last even Kant tried in all innocence to make this thinkers' corruption scientific by means of the concept "practical reason": he invented a reason expressly for those cases in which one would not need to bother about reason: namely, when the needs of the heart, when morality, when "duty" speaks.

415 (*1885-1886*)

Hegel: his popular side the doctrine of war and great men. Right is with the victorious: they represent the progress of mankind. Attempt to prove the dominion of morality by means of history.

Kant: a realm of moral values, withdrawn from us, invisible, real.

Hegel: a demonstrable development, a becoming-visible of the moral realm.

Let us not be deceived either in the Kantian or in the Hegelian manner:—we no longer *believe* in morality, as they did, and consequently we have no need to found a philosophy with the aim of justifying morality. Neither the critical nor the historicist philosophy has any charm for us in *this* respect:—so what charm has it, then?—

416 (*1885-1886*)

The significance of German philosophy (Hegel): to evolve a pantheism through which evil, error, and suffering are not felt as arguments against divinity. This grandiose project has been misused by the existing powers (state, etc.), as if it sanctioned the rationality of whoever happened to be ruling.

---

[121] Utilized in *Antichrist*, section 12 (*Portable Nietzsche*, pp. 578-79).

Schopenhauer, on the other hand, appears as a stubborn morality-man who, in order to justify his moral valuation, finally becomes a world-denier. Finally a "mystic."

I myself have attempted an *aesthetic* justification: how is the ugliness of the world possible?— I took the will to beauty, to persist in like forms, for a temporary means of preservation and recuperation: fundamentally, however, the eternally-creative appeared to me to be, as the eternal compulsion to destroy, associated with pain. The ugly is the form things assume when we view them with the will to implant a meaning, a new meaning, into what has become meaningless: the accumulated force which compels the creator to consider all that has been created hitherto as unacceptable, ill-constituted, worthy of being denied, ugly!—

417 (*1883-1888*)

My first solution: Dionysian wisdom. Joy in the destruction of the most noble and at the sight of its progressive ruin: in reality joy in what is coming and lies in the future, which triumphs over existing things, however good. Dionysian: temporary identification with the principle of life (including the voluptuousness of the martyr).

My innovations.— Further development of pessimism: intellectual pessimism; critique of morality, disintegration of the last consolation. Knowledge of the signs of decay: veils with illusion every firm action; culture isolates, is unjust and therefore strong.

1. My endeavor to oppose decay and increasing weakness of personality. I sought a new *center*.

2. Impossibility of this endeavor recognized.

3. Thereupon I advanced further down the road of disintegration—where I found new sources of strength for individuals. We have to be destroyers!—— I perceived that the state of disintegration, in which individual natures can perfect themselves as never before—is an image and isolated example of existence in general. To the paralyzing sense of general disintegration and incompleteness I opposed the *eternal recurrence*.

418 (*1883-1888*)

One seeks a picture of the world in that philosophy in which we feel freest; i.e., in which our most powerful drive feels free to function. This will also be the case with me!

419 (*1885*)

German philosophy as a whole—Leibniz, Kant, Hegel, Schopenhauer, to name the greatest—is the most fundamental form of *romanticism* and homesickness there has ever been: the longing for the best that ever existed. One is no longer at home anywhere; at last one longs back for that place in which alone one can be at home, because it is the only place in which one would want to be at home: the *Greek* world! But it is in precisely that direction that all bridges are broken—except the rainbow-bridges of concepts! And these lead everywhere, into all the homes and "fatherlands" that existed for Greek souls! To be sure, one must be very subtle, very light, very thin to step across these bridges! But what happiness there is already in this will to spirituality, to ghostliness almost! How far it takes one from "pressure and stress," from the mechanistic awkwardness of the natural sciences, from the market hubbub of "modern ideas"! One wants to go *back,* through the Church Fathers to the Greeks, from the north to the south, from the formulas to the Forms; one still relishes the exit from antiquity, Christianity, as an entrance to it, as in itself a goodly piece of the old world, as a glittering mosaic of ancient concepts and ancient value judgments. Arabesques, flourishes, rococo of scholastic abstractions—still better, that is to say subtler and thinner, than the peasant and mob reality of the European north, still a protest of higher spirituality against the peasants' war and mob rebellion that has become master of spiritual taste in northern Europe and has found its leader in the great "unspiritual man," Luther: in this respect, German philosophy is a piece of counter-Reformation, even of Renaissance, at least will to Renaissance, will to go on with the discovery of antiquity, the digging up of ancient philosophy, above all of the pre-Socratics—the most deeply buried of all Greek temples! A few centuries hence, perhaps, one will judge that all German philosophy derives its real dignity from being a gradual reclamation of the soil of antiquity, and that all claims to "originality" must sound petty and ludicrous in relation to that higher claim of the Germans to have joined anew the bond that seemed to be broken, the bond with the Greeks, the hitherto highest type of man. Today we are again getting close to all those fundamental forms of world interpretation devised by the Greek spirit through Anaximander, Heraclitus, Parmenides, Empedocles, Democritus, and Anaxagoras—we are growing more Greek by the day; at first, as is only fair, in concepts and evaluations, as Hellenizing ghosts, as it were: but one day, let us hope, also in our bodies! Herein lies (and has always lain) my hope for the German character!

420 (*1884*)

I do not wish to persuade anyone to philosophy: it is inevitable, it is perhaps also desirable, that the philosopher should be a *rare* plant. I find nothing more repugnant than didactic praise of philosophy, as one finds it in Seneca, or worse, Cicero. Philosophy has little to do with virtue. Permit me to say that the scholar and scientist,[122] too, are fundamentally different from the philosopher.— What I desire is that the genuine concept of the philosopher should not utterly perish in Germany. There are so many half-hearted creatures of all kinds in Germany who would be glad to conceal their ill-constitutedness beneath so noble a name.

421 (*1884*)

I have to set up the most difficult ideal of the philosopher. Learning is not enough! The scholar is the herd animal in the realm of knowledge—who inquires because he is ordered to and because others have done so before him.—

422 (*1885*)

Superstition about philosophers: confusion with scholars and scientists. As if values were inherent in things and all one had to do was grasp them! To what extent they study under the direction[123] of given values (their hatred of appearance, the body, etc.). Schopenhauer concerning morality (mockery of utilitarianism). At last, confusion goes so far that one regards Darwinism as philosophy: and now the scholars and scientists dominate. Even Frenchmen like Taine inquire, or think they inquire, without being already in possession of a standard of values. Prostration before "facts,"

---

[122] "Scholar and scientist": *der wissenschaftliche Mensch.*

[123] *Einflüsterung*: Peter Gast's conjecture; MS illegible.

a kind of cult. In reality, they destroy the existing evaluations.

Explanation of this misunderstanding. The man who can command rarely appears: he misinterprets himself. One positively *wants* to repudiate one's own authority and assign it to circumstances.— In Germany, the esteem of the critic belongs to the history of awakening *manhood*. Lessing, etc. (Napoleon on Goethe). As a matter of fact, this movement was again reversed by German romanticism; and the fame of German philosophy depends on that, as if the danger of skepticism had thus been removed and faith could be proved. Both tendencies culminate in Hegel: at bottom, he generalized German criticism and German romanticism—a kind of dialectical fatalism, but in honor of the spirit, in fact with the submission of the philosopher to reality. The critic prepares the way: no more!

With Schopenhauer the task of the philosopher dawns: the determination of value; still under the domination of eudaemonism. The ideal of pessimism.

423 (*March-June 1888*)

Theory and practice.[124]— Fateful distinction, as if there were an actual *drive for knowledge* that, without regard to questions of usefulness and harm, went blindly for the truth; and then, separate from this, the whole world of *practical* interests—

I tried to show, on the other hand, what instincts have been active behind all these *pure* theoreticians—how they have all, under the spell of their instincts, gone fatalistically for something that was "truth" *for them*—for them and only for them. The conflict between different systems, including that between epistemological scruples, is a conflict between quite definite instincts (forms of vitality, decline, classes, races, etc.).

The so-called drive for knowledge can be traced back to a drive to appropriate and conquer: the senses, the memory, the instincts, etc. have developed as a consequence of this drive. The quickest possible reduction of the phenomena, economy, the accumulation of the spoils of knowledge (i.e., of world appropriated and made manageable)—

Morality is such a curious science because it is in the highest degree *practical*: so that the position of pure knowledge, scientific integrity, is at once abandoned as soon as the claims of morality

---

[124] Cf. section 458 below.

must be answered. Morality says: I *need* many answers—reasons, arguments; scruples can come afterward, or not at all—.

"How should one act?"— If one considers that one is dealing with a sovereignly developed type that has "acted" for countless millennia, and in which everything has become instinct, expediency, automatism, fatality, then the urgency of this moral question must actually seem ridiculous.

"How should one act?"— Morality has always been a misunderstanding: in reality, a species fated to act in this or that fashion wanted to justify itself, by dictating its norm as the universal norm—

"How should one act?" is not a cause but an effect. Morality follows, the ideal comes at the end.

—On the other hand, the appearance of moral scruples (in other words: the becoming-conscious of the values by which one acts) betrays a certain sickliness; strong ages and peoples do not reflect on their rights, on the principles on which they act, on their instincts and reasons. Becoming-conscious is a sign that real morality, i.e., instinctive certainty in actions, is going to the devil— Every time a new world of consciousness is created, the moralists are a sign of damage, impoverishment, disorganization.— The deeply instinctive are shy of logicizing duties: among them are found Pyrrhonic opponents of dialectics and of knowability in general— A virtue is *refuted* with a "for"—

Thesis: the appearance of moralists belongs to an age in which morality is coming to an end.

Thesis: the moralist disintegrates the moral instincts, however much he may suppose himself to be their restorer.

Thesis: that which really drives the moralist is not the moral instincts but the *instincts of decadence* translated into the formulas of morality— (he regards it as corruption when the instincts become uncertain).

Thesis: the *instincts of decadence,* which, through the moralists, want to become master over the instinctive morality of strong races and ages, are

1. the instincts of the weak and underprivileged;
2. the instincts of the exceptions, the solitaries, the abandoned, of the *abortus*[125] in what is lofty and what is petty.
3. the instincts of those habituated to suffering, who need

---

[125] Abortion.

a noble interpretation of their condition and therefore must know as little as possible about physiology.

424 (*1885*)

The tartuffery of scientific manners.[126]—— One must not affect scientific manners where the time has not yet come to be scientific; but even the genuine investigator has to abandon the vanity of affecting a kind of method for which fundamentally the time has not yet come. Just as he must not "falsify" things and thoughts at which he has arrived in another way by imposing on them a false arrangement of deduction and dialectic. Thus Kant falsified in his "morality" his inner psychological tendency; a more recent example is Herbert Spencer's ethics.—

One should not conceal and corrupt the facts of how our thoughts have come to us. The profoundest and least exhausted books will probably always have something of the aphoristic and unexpected character of Pascal's *Pensées*. The driving forces and evaluations have long lain below the surface; what comes out is effect.

I fight all the tartuffery of false scientific manners:

1. in the demonstration, if it does not correspond to the genesis of thoughts;

2. in the claims to methods that are perhaps not yet possible at a certain stage of science;

3. in the claims to objectivity, to cold impersonality, where, as in the case of all valuations, we describe ourselves and our inner experiences in a couple of words. There are ludicrous forms of vanity, e.g., that of Saint-Beuve, who worried all his life that he had now and then exhibited real warmth and passion either "for" or "against," and would gladly have lied that fact out of his life.

425 (*Nov. 1887-March 1888*)

"Objectivity" in the philosopher: moral indifference toward oneself, blindness toward good or ill consequences: lack of scruples about using dangerous means; perversity and multiplicity of character considered and exploited as an advantage.

My profound indifference toward myself: I desire no advan-

---

[126] *Wissenschaftlichkeit.*

tage from my insights and do not avoid the disadvantages that accompany them.— Here I include what might be called *corruption* of the character; this perspective is beside the point: I use my character, but try neither to understand nor to change it—the personal calculus of virtue has not entered my head for a moment. It seems to me that one shuts the door on knowledge as soon as one becomes interested in one's own case—or, worse, the "salvation of one's soul"!— One must not take one's morality too seriously and not let oneself be deprived of a modest right to its opposite—

A sort of inherited wealth of morality is perhaps presupposed here: one senses that one can squander a lot of it and throw it out the window without really impoverishing oneself. Never to feel tempted to admire "beautiful souls"; always to know oneself their superior. To encounter the monsters of virtue with an inward mockery; *déniaiser la vertu*[127]—a secret pleasure.

To revolve about oneself; no desire to become "better" or in any way "other." Too interested not to throw the tentacles or nets of every morality out to things—.

426 (*March-June 1888*)

Toward a psychology of the psychologist. Psychologists as they are possible only beginning with the nineteenth century: no longer those loafers who look a mere three or four steps ahead and are almost content to burrow inside themselves. We psychologists of the future—we have little patience with introspection: we almost take it for a sign of degeneration when an instrument tries "to know itself": we are instruments of knowledge and would like to possess all the naiveté and precision of an instrument—consequently, we must not analyze ourselves, "know" ourselves. First mark of the self-preservative instinct of the great psychologist: he never seeks himself, he has no eyes for himself, no interest or curiosity in himself[128]— The great egoism of our dominating will requires that we shut our eyes to ourselves—that we must seem to be "impersonal," *"désintéressé,"* "objective"!—oh, how much we are the opposite of this! Just because we are to an eccentric degree psychologists.

---

[127] To best virtue.

[128] Cf. *Twilight,* Chapter I, section 35: "A psychologist must turn his eyes from himself to eye anything at all." (*Portable Nietzschce,* p. 471.)

We are no Pascals, we are not especially interested in the "salvation of the soul," in our own happiness, in our own virtue.—We have neither the time nor the curiosity to rotate about ourselves in that way. Considered more deeply, the case is different yet: we mistrust from the heart all navel gazing, because to us self-observation counts as a form of degeneration of the psychological genius, as a question mark against the instinct of the psychologist: just as surely as a painter's eye is degenerate if it is governed by the will to see for the sake of seeing.

2. Critique of Greek Philosophy

427 (*Nov. 1887-March 1888*)

The appearance of the Greek philosophers from Socrates onwards is a symptom of decadence; the anti-Hellenic instincts come to the top——

The "Sophist" is still completely Hellenic—including Anaxagoras, Democritus, the great Ionians—but as a transitional form. The *polis* loses its faith in the uniqueness of its culture, in its right to rule over every other *polis*— One exchanges cultures, i.e., "the gods"—one thereby loses faith in the sole prerogative of the *deus autochthonus*. Good and evil of differing origin are mingled: the boundary between good and evil is blurred— This is the "Sophist"—

The "philosopher," on the other hand, is the *reaction*: he desires the *old* virtue. He sees the grounds of decay[129] in the decay of institutions, he desires *old* institutions;—he sees the decay in the decay of authority: he seeks new authorities (travels abroad, into foreign literatures, into exotic religions—); he desires the ideal *polis* after the concept *"polis"* has had its day (approximately as the Jews held firm as a "people" after they had fallen into slavery). They are interested in all tyrants: they want to restore virtue by *force majeure*.

Gradually everything genuinely Hellenic is made responsible for the state of decay (and Plato is just as ungrateful to Pericles, Homer, tragedy, rhetoric, as the prophets were to David and Saul). The decline of Greece is understood as an objection to the

---

[129] "Of decay": uncertain reading; MS illegible.

foundations of Hellenic culture: basic error of philosophers—. Conclusion: the Greek world perishes. Cause: Homer, myth, the ancient morality, etc.

The anti-Hellenic development of the philosophers' value judgment:—the Egyptian ("life after death" as a court of law—); the Semitic (the "dignity of the sage," the "sheik");—the Pythagoreans, the subterranean cults, silence, terrorization with a beyond, mathematics; the religious valuation, a kind of traffic with the cosmos;—the priestly, ascetic, transcendental;—dialectic—surely a repellent and pedantic concept splitting already in Plato?— Decline of good taste in spiritual matters: one is already insensitive to the ugliness and noisiness of all direct dialectics.

Two decadence movements and extremes run side by side: (a) sensual, charmingly wicked decadence, loving art and show, and (b) gloomy religio-moral pathos, Stoic self-hardening, Platonic slander of the senses, preparation of the soil for Christianity.

428 (*March-June 1888*)

How far psychologists have been corrupted by the moral idiosyncrasy:—not one of the ancient philosophers had the courage for a theory of the "unfree will" (i.e., for a theory that denies morality);—no one had the courage to define the typical element in pleasure, every sort of pleasure ("happiness") as the feeling of power: for to take pleasure in power was considered immoral; —no one had the courage to conceive virtue as a consequence of immorality (of a will to power) in the service of the species (or of the race or *polis*), for the will to power was considered immorality.

In the entire evolution of morality, truth never appears: all the conceptual elements employed are fictions; all the *psychologica* accepted are falsifications; all the forms of logic dragged into this realm of lies are sophistries. What distinguishes moral philosophers themselves is a complete absence of cleanliness and intellectual self-discipline: they take "beautiful feelings" for arguments: they regard their "heaving bosom" as the bellows of divinity— Moral philosophy is the scabrous period in the history of the spirit.[130]

The first great example: in the name of morality, under the patronage or morality, an unheard-of wrong was perpetrated, in

[130] Cf. section 414 above.

fact a piece of decadence in every respect. One cannot insist too strongly upon the fact that the great Greek philosophers represent the decadence of every kind of Greek excellence and make it contagious— "Virtue" made completely abstract was the greatest seduction to make oneself abstract: i. e., to detach oneself.

It is a very remarkable moment: the Sophists verge upon the first *critique of morality,* the first *insight* into morality:—they juxtapose the multiplicity (the geographical relativity) of the moral value judgments;—they let it be known that every morality can be dialetically justified; i.e., they divine that all attempts to give reasons for morality are necessarily *sophistical*— a proposition later proved on the grand scale by the ancient philosophers, from Plato onwards (down to Kant);—they postulate the first truth that a "morality-in-itself," a "good-in-itself" do not exist, that it is a swindle to talk of "truth" in this field.

Where was intellectual integrity in those days?

The Greek culture of the Sophists had developed out of all the Greek instincts; it belongs to the culture of the Periclean age as necessarily as Plato does *not*: it has its predecessors in Heraclitus, in Democritus, in the scientific types of the old philosophy; it finds expression in, e.g., the high culture of Thucydides. And— it has ultimately shown itself to be right: every advance in epistemological and moral knowlege has reinstated the Sophists— Our contemporary way of thinking is to a great extent Heraclitean, Democritean, and Protagorean: it suffices to say it is Protagorean, because Protagoras represented a synthesis of Heraclitus and Democritus.

(Plato: a great Cagliostro—remember how Epicurus judged him;[131] how Timon, the friend of Pyrrho, judged him—— Is Plato's integrity beyond question?— But we know at least that he wanted to have *taught* as absolute truth what he himself did not regard as even conditionally true: namely, the separate existence and separate immortality of "souls.")

429 (*March-June 1888*)

The Sophists are no more than realists: they formulate the values and practices common to everyone on the level of values—

---

[131] See *Beyond Good and Evil,* section 7 (New York: Vintage, 1966); also section 434 below.

they possess the courage of all strong spirits to *know* their own immorality—

Do you suppose perchance that these little Greek free cities, which from rage and envy would have liked to devour each other, were guided by philanthropic and righteous principles? Does one reproach Thucydides for the words he put into the mouths of the Athenian ambassadors when they negotiated with the Melians on the question of destruction or submission?

Only complete Tartuffes could possibly have talked of virtue in the midst of this terrible tension—or men living apart, hermits, refugees, and emigrants from reality—people who negated in order to be able to live themselves—

The Sophists were Greeks: when Socrates and Plato took up the cause of virtue and justice, they were *Jews* or I know not what— Grote's tactics in defense of the Sophists are false: he wants to raise them to the rank of men of honor and ensigns of morality—but it was their honor not to indulge in any swindle with big words and virtues—

430 (*March-June 1888*)

The great rationality of all education in morality has always been that one tried to attain to the certainty of an instinct: so that neither good intentions nor good means had to enter consciousness as such. As the soldier exercises, so should man learn to act. In fact, this unconsciousness belongs to any kind of perfection: even the mathematician employs his combinations unconsciously—

What, then, is the significance of the reaction of Socrates, who recommended dialectics as the road to virtue and made mock when morality did not know how to justify itself logically?— As if this were not part of its value—without unconsciousness it is no good—

Positing proofs as the presupposition for personal excellence in virtue signified nothing less than the disintegration of Greek instincts. They are themselves types of disintegration, all these great "virtuous men" and word-spinners.

In praxi, this means that moral judgments are torn from their conditionality, in which they have grown and alone possess any meaning, from their Greek and Greek-political ground and soil, to be denaturalized under the pretense of sublimation. The great concepts "good" and "just" are severed from the presuppositions to which they belong and, as liberated "ideas," become objects of dialectic. One looks for truth in them, one takes them for entities or signs of entities: one *invents* a world where they are at home, where they originate—

In summa: the mischief has already reached its climax in Plato— And then one had need to invent the abstractly perfect man as well:—good, just, wise, a dialectician—in short, the scarecrow of the ancient philosopher: a plant removed from all soil; a humanity without any particular regulating instincts; a virtue that "proves" itself with reasons. The perfectly absurd "individuum" in itself! unnaturalness of the first water—

In short, the consequence of the denaturalization of moral values was the creation of a degenerate type of man—"the good man," "the happy man," "the wise man."— Socrates represents a moment of the profoundest perversity in the history of values.

431 (*1885-1886 and 1888*)

Socrates.[132]— This reversal of taste in favor of dialectics is a great question mark. What was it that really happened?— Socrates, the *roturier*[133] who accomplished it, achieved by means of it victory over a more noble taste, the taste of the nobility:— the mob achieved victory with dialectics. Before Socrates, the dialectical manner was repudiated in good society; one believed it compromised one; youth was warned against it. Why this display of reasons? Why should one demonstrate? Against others one possessed authority. One commanded: that sufficed. Among one's own, *inter pares,* one possessed tradition, *also* an authority: and, finally, one "understood one another"! One simply had no place for dialectic. Besides, one mistrusted such public presentation of one's arguments. Honest things do not display their reasons in that way. There is something indecent about showing all one's cards. What can be "demonstrated" is of little worth.—

The instinct of all party orators knows, moreover, that dialectics inspire mistrust, that they are very unconvincing. Nothing is easier to expunge than the effect of a dialectician. Dialectics can

---

[132] The last paragraph of this section comes from a different notebook. The first paragraphs were utilized—in part *verbatim*—in *Twilight,* Chapter II, sections 5-6 (*Portable Nietzsche,* pp. 475-76). For a detailed discussion of Nietzsche's highly complex attitude toward Socrates, see Kaufmann's *Nietzsche,* chapter 13.

[133] Nonaristocrat.

only be an emergency measure. One must experience an emergency, one must be obliged to *extort* one's rights: otherwise one makes no use of dialectics. That is why the Jews were dialecticians, why Reynard the Fox was one, why Socrates was one. One has a merciless weapon in one's hand. One can tyrannize with it. One compromises when one conquers. One leaves it to one's victim to prove that he is not an idiot. One makes others furious and helpless, while one remains the embodiment of cool, triumphant reasonableness oneself—one deprives one's opponent's intelligence of potency.—

The irony of the dialectician is a form of mob revenge: the ferocity of the oppressed finds an outlet in the cold knife-thrust of the syllogism—

In Plato, as a man of overexcitable sensuality and enthusiasm, the charm of the concept had grown so strong that he involuntarily honored and deified the concept as an ideal Form. Intoxication by dialectic: as the consciousness of exercising mastery over oneself by means of it——as a tool of the will to power.

432[134] (*March-June 1888*)

The problem of Socrates.— The two antitheses: the tragic disposition, the Socratic disposition—measured according to the law of life.

To what extent the Socratic disposition is a phenomenon of decadence: to what extent, however, a robust health and strength is still exhibited in the whole *habitus,* in the dialectics, efficiency, and self-discipline of the scientific man (—the health of the plebeian; his wickedness, *esprit frondeur,*[135] his cunning, his *canaille au fond*[136] are held in check by shrewdness; "ugly").

Making ugly: self-mockery, dialectical dryness, shrewdness as tyrant in opposition to a "tyrant" (instinct). Everything is exaggerated, eccentric, caricature, in Socrates, a *buffo* with the instincts of Voltaire. He discover a new form of *agon;*[137] he is the first fencing master to the leading circles of Athens; he represents

---

[134] This section and the immediately following one (433) are found together in the same notebook and were utilized in *Twilight,* Chapter II (*Portable Nietzsche,* p. 473 *ff*).

[135] Censorious spirit.

[136] Plebeian at bottom.

[137] Contest.

nothing but the highest form of shrewdness: he calls it "virtue" (—he divined it to be deliverance: he was not shrewd from choice, it was *de rigueur*[138]); to have oneself under control, so as to go into battle with reasons and not with affects (—the cunning of Spinoza—the unravelling of the errors caused by affects);—to discover that one can capture anyone in whom one produces affects, to discover that affects proceed illogically; practice in self-mockery, so as to damage the feeling of rancor at its roots.

I try to understand from what partial and idiosyncratic states the Socratic problem derives: his equalization of reason = virtue = happiness. It was with this absurdity of a doctrine of identity that he fascinated: the philosophers of antiquity never again freed themselves from this fascination—

Absolute lack of objective interest: hatred for science; the idiosyncrasy of feeling oneself as a problem. Socrates' acoustic hallucination: morbid element. When the spirit is rich and independent it most resists any preoccupation with morality. How came it that Socrates was a monomaniac in regard to morality?— In emergencies, "practical" philosophy steps at once to the fore. Morality and religion as chief interests are signs of an emergency.

433[139] (*March-June 1888*)

—Shrewdness, clarity, severity and logicality as weapons against the ferocity of the drives. These must be dangerous and threaten destruction: otherwise there would be no sense in developing shrewdness to the point of making it into a tyrant. To make a tyrant of shrewdness:—but for that the drives must be tyrants. This is the problem.— In those days it was a very timely problem. Reason became = virtue = happiness.

Solution: The Greek philosophers rest on the same fundamental facts of inner experience as Socrates: five steps from excess, from anarchy, from intemperance—all men of decadence. They need him as a physician: logic as will to power, to self-mastery, to "happiness." The ferocity and anarchy of the instincts in the case of Socrates is a symptom of decadence. The superfetation of logic and of clarity of reason included. Both are abnormalities, both belong together.

Critique. Decadence betrays itself in this preoccupation with

[138] Unavoidable.

[139] See footnote to the preceding section.

"happiness" (i.e., with "salvation of the soul," i.e., to feel one's condition as a danger). The fanaticism of its interest in "happiness" indicates the pathological nature of the hidden cause: it was a life-or-death interest. To be reasonable or perish was the alternative before which they all stood. The moralism of the Greek philosophers indicates that they felt themselves to be in danger—

434 (*March-June 1888*)

Why everything resolved itself into play-acting.— The rudimentary psychology that considered only the *conscious* motives of men (as causes), that took "consciousness" for an attribute of the soul, that sought a will (i.e., an intention) behind all action: it needed, first, only to answer "Happiness" to the question: What do men want? (one dared not say "Power": that would have been immoral);—consequently there is in all the actions of men the intention of attaining happiness. Secondly: if man does in fact not achieve happiness, why is it? Because he blunders in respect of the means.— What is unfailingly the means to happiness? Answer: virtue.— Why virtue?— Because it is supremely rational and because rationality makes it impossible to err in the choice of means: it is as *reason* that virtue is the way to happiness. Dialectic is the constant occupation of virtue, because it excludes all clouding of the intellect and all affects.

In fact, man does *not* want "happiness." Pleasure is a feeling of power: if one excludes the affects, then one excludes the states that give the highest feeling of power, consequently of pleasure. The highest rationality is a cold, clear state very far from giving that feeling of happiness that intoxication of any kind brings with it—

The philosophers of antiquity combat everything that intoxicates—that impairs the absolute coldness and neutrality of the consciousness— They were consistent with their false presupposition: that consciousness is the exalted, the supreme state, the precondition of perfection—whereas the opposite is true——

To the extent that it is willed, to the extent that it is conscious, there is no perfection in action of any kind. The philosophers of antiquity were the greatest duffers in practice because they condemned themselves to be duffers in theory— *In praxi,* everything resolved itself into play-acting;—and whoever saw through this, e.g., Pyrrho, judged as everyone did, namely that in goodness and integrity "little people" were far superior to philosophers.

All the more profound natures of antiquity were disgusted with the philosophers of virtue: they were looked upon as quarrelsome and play actors. (Judgment on Plato: that of Epicurus,[140] that of Pyrrho).

Result: little people are superior to them in their way of living, in patience, in goodness and mutual assistance:—approximately the claim made by Dostoevsky or Tolstoy for his muzhiks: they are more philosophical in practice, they meet the exigencies of life more courageously—

435 (*March-June 1888*)

Toward a critique of the philosopher.— It is a self-deception of philosophers and moralists to imagine that they escape decadence by opposing it. That is beyond their will; and, however little they acknowledge it, one later discovers that they were among the most powerful promoters of decadence.

[Let us take][141] the philosophers of Greece, e.g., Plato. He severed the instincts from the *polis,* from contest, from military efficiency, from art and beauty, from the mysteries, from belief in tradition and ancestors— He was the seducer of the nobility: he was himself seduced by the *roturier* Socrates— He negated all the presuppositions of the "noble Greek" of the old stamp, made dialectic an everyday practice, conspired with tyrants, pursued politics of the future and provided the example of the most complete severance of the instincts from the past. He is profound, passionate in everything *anti*-Hellenic—

These great philosophers represent one after the other the typical forms of decadence: the moral-religious idiosyncrasy, anarchism, nihilism (*adiaphora*),[142] cynicism, obduracy, hedonism, reaction.

---

[140] Cf. section 428 above; also *Beyond,* section 7.

[141] Placed in brackets because not in the MS although found in all editions. After "Plato" the MS continues "the man of the good. But he. . . ." The reading "the man" is uncertain as the two words were crossed out by Nietzsche and are illegible. Near the end, the following lines in the MS have been omitted in all editions: "Why does none of them dare to deny the freedom of the will? They are all preoccupied with their 'salvation of the soul'—what is truth to them!"

[142] Indifference.

The question of "happiness," of "virtue," of "salvation of the soul" is the expression of physiological contradictoriness in these types of decline: their instincts lack a center of gravity, a purpose.

436 (*1885-1886*)

To what extent dialectic and faith in reason still rest on moral prejudices. With Plato we are, as former inhabitants of an intelligible world of the good, still in possession of a heritage from that time: divine dialectic, as proceeding from the good, leads to all things good (—therefore, as it were, "backwards"—). Even Descartes had a notion of the fact that in a fundamentally Christian-moral mode of thought, which believes in a *good* God as the creator of things, only God's veracity *guarantees* to us the judgments of our senses. Apart from a religious sanction and guarantee of our senses and rationality—where should we derive a right to trust in existence! That thinking is a measure of actuality—that what cannot be thought, *is* not—is a rude *non plus ultra* of a moralistic trustfulness (in an essential truth-principle at the bottom of things), in itself a mad assumption, which experience contradicts every moment. We are altogether unable to think anything at all just as it *is*—

437 (*March-June 1888*)

The real philosophers of Greece are those before Socrates[143] (—with Socrates something changes). They are all noble persons, setting themselves apart from people and state,[144] traveled, serious to the point of somberness, with a slow glance, no strangers to state affairs and diplomacy. They anticipate all the great conceptions of things: they themselves represent these conceptions, they bring themselves into a system. Nothing gives a higher idea of the Greek spirit than this sudden fruitfulness in types, than this involuntary completeness in the erection of the great possibilities of the philosophical ideal.— I seen only one original figure in those

---

[143] This view was taken up by Karl Jaspers in his *Psychologie der Weltanschauungen* (1919) and by Martin Heidegger in *Platons Lehre von der Wahrheit* ("Plato's Doctrine of Truth," 1942).

[144] Word not clear in the MS: possibly "custom" (*Sitte*) rather than "state" (*Staat*).

that came after: a late arrival but necessarily the last—the nihilist Pyrrho:—his instinct was opposed to all that had come to the top in the meantime: the Socratics, Plato, the artist's optimism[145] of Heraclitus. (Pyrrho goes back, through Protagoras, to Democritus—).

*

Sagacious weariness: Pyrrho. To live a lowly life among the lowly. No pride. To live in the common way; to honor and believe what all believe. On guard against science and spirit, also against all that inflates—

Simple: indescribably patient, carefree, mild. *Apatheia,*[146] or rather *praótes.*[147] A Buddhist for Greece, grown up amid the tumult of the schools; a latecomer; weary; the protest of weariness against the zeal of the dialecticians; the unbelief of weariness in the importance of all things. He had seen Alexander, he had seen the Indian penitents. To such refined latecomers, everything lowly, everything poor, even everything idiotic is seductive. It has a narcotic effect: it relaxes (Pascal). On the other hand, in the midst of the crowd and confounded with everyone else, they feel a little warmth: these weary people need warmth—

To overcome contradiction; no contest; no will to distinction; to deny the Greek instincts. (Pyrrho lived with his sister who was a midwife.) To disguise wisdom so that it no longer distinguishes; to cloak it in poverty and rags; to perform the lowliest offices: to go to market and sell suckling pigs—

Sweetness; light; indifference; no virtues that require gestures: to be everyone's equal even in virtue: ultimate self-overcoming, ultimate indifference.

Pyrrho, like Epicurus, two forms of Greek decadence: related, in hatred for dialectics and for all theatrical virtues—these two together were in those days called philosophy—; deliberately holding in low esteem that which they loved; choosing common, even despised names for it; representing a state in which one is neither sick nor well, neither alive nor dead—

Epicurus more naive, idyllic, grateful; Pyrrho more traveled, experienced, nihilistic— His life was a protest against the great doctrine of identity (happiness = virtue = knowledge). One can-

---

[145] The word is illegible and this reading highly questionable.

[146] Apathy.

[147] Gentleness.

not promote the right way of life through science: wisdom does not make "wise"— The right way of life does not want happiness, turns away from happiness—

438 (*Spring 1888*)

The struggle against the "old faith" as undertaken by Epicurus was, in a strict sense, a struggle against pre-existing Christianity—a struggle against the old world grown senile and sick, already gloomy, moralized, soured by feelings of guilt.

Not the "moral corruption" of antiquity, but precisely its *moralization* is the prerequisite through which alone Christianity could become master of it. Moral fanaticism (in short: Plato) destroyed paganism, by revaluing its values and poisoning its innocence.—

We ought finally to understand that what was then destroyed was *higher* than what became master!—

Christianity has grown out of psychological decay, could only take root in decayed soil.

439 (*March-June 1888*)

Scientific manners: as training or as instinct.—In the Greek philosophers I see a decline of the instincts: otherwise they could not have blundered so far as to posit the *conscious* state as *more valuable.* Intensity of consciousness stands in inverse ratio to ease and speed of cerebral transmission. Among Greek philosophers the reverse opinion about instinct prevailed: which is always a sign of weakened instincts.

We must in fact seek perfect life where it has become least conscious (i.e., least aware of its logic, its reasons, its means and intentions, its utility). The return to the facts of *bon sens,* of the *bon homme,* of the "little people" of all kinds. The stored-up integrity and shrewdness of generations which are never conscious of their principles and are even a little afraid of principles. The demand for a virtue that reasons is not reasonable— A philosopher is compromised by such a demand.

440 (*Jan.-Fall 1888*)

When morality—that is to say subtlety, caution, bravery,

equity—has been as it were stored up through the practice of a whole succession of generations, then the total force of this accumulated virtue radiates even into that sphere where integrity is most seldom found, into the spiritual sphere. In all becoming-conscious there is expressed a discomfiture of the organism; it has to try something new, nothing is sufficiently adapted for it, there is toil, tension, strain—all this *constitutes* becoming-conscious—

Genius resides in instinct; goodness likewise. One acts perfectly only when one acts instinctively. Even from the viewpoint of morality, all conscious thinking is merely tentative, usually the reverse of morality. Scientific integrity is always ruptured when the thinker begins to reason: try the experiment of putting the wisest men on the most delicate scales by making them talk about morality—

It could be proved that all conscious thinking would also show a far lower standard of morality than the thinking of the same man when it is directed by his instincts.[148]

---

[148] According to 1911, p. 505, "This aph. [*sic.* In fact these are not "aphorisms" but mere notes] replaces aph. 243 of the old vol. XV [the first edition of *The Will to Power,* published in 1901], which represents another formulation of the same content." Here is the other version:

"When enough subtlety, bravery, caution, and moderation have been collected through the practice of a long chain of generations, then the instinctive power of such incorporated virtue radiates even into the most spiritual matters—and that phenomenon becomes visible which we call *intellectual integrity*. This is very rare: among philosophers it is lacking.

"One can take the scientific manner or, morally speaking the *intellectual integrity of a thinker,* the subtlety, bravery, caution, and moderation that have become instinct in him and transposed even into the most spiritual matters, and place them on the most delicate scales—by letting him talk about morality: then the most famous philosophers show that their scientific manner is as yet only a conscious affair, a beginning, a 'good will,' something laborious—and as soon as their instincts begin to speak, as soon as they moralize, it is all over with the discipline and subtlety of their conscience.

"The scientific manner—whether mere training and external or the final result of long discipline and moral practice: in the former case it abdicates as soon as the instincts speak (e.g., the religious instincts or those of the concept of duty); in the latter case it replaces these instincts and no longer grants them admission, feeling they represent *uncleanliness* and *seductions*—"

Although omitted in most editions, this version is printed in an appendix in both the Grossoktav edition and the Musarion edition, as #1074. Schlechta omits it. It is included here not only as a matter of principle but also for three additional reasons: (1) it is interesting to see how the editors of the various editions proceeded; (2) it is even more interesting to be able to compare two alternative drafts from Nietzsche's hand; and (3) parts of this draft compare very favorably with the one included in the text.

441 (*March-June 1888*)

The struggle against Socrates, Plato, all the Socratic schools, proceeds from the profound instinct that one does not make men better when one represents to them that virtue is demonstrable and asks for reasons—

Ultimately, it is the measly fact that the agonal instinct in all these born dialecticians compelled them to glorify their personal ability as the highest quality and to represent all other good things as conditioned by it. The anti-scientific spirit of this entire "philosophy": it is determined to be in the right.

442 (*March-June 1888*)

This is extraordinary. We find from the beginning of Greek philosophy onwards a struggle against science with the means of an epistemology or skepticism: and with what object? Always for the good of *morality*—

(Hatred for physicists and physicians.) Socrates, Aristippus, the Megarian school, the Cynics, Epicurus, Pyrrho—a general assault on knowledge for the good of morality—

(Hatred for dialectics also.) A problem remains: they approach the Sophists in order to get rid of science. On the other hand, the physicists are all so completely subjected as to take up the schema of truth,[149] of real being, into the fundamentals of their science; e.g., the atom, the four elements (juxtaposition of beings to explain multiplicity and change—). Contempt for objective interest is taught: return to the practical interest, the personal utility of all knowledge—

The struggle against science is directed against (1) its pathos (objectivity), (2) its means (i.e., against its utility), (3) its results (as childish).

It is the same struggle that is later conducted by the church in the name of piety: the church inherited the entire arsenal of antiquity for its struggle. Epistemology played in this the same role as it did in the case of Kant, in the case of the Indians— One does not want to be troubled by it: one wants one's hands free for one's "course."

What were they really defending themselves against? Against

[149] "Truth" is an uncertain reading of an illegible word.

obligation, against legality, against the compulsion to go hand in hand— I believe one calls this *freedom*—

Decadence manifests itself in this: the instinct of solidarity is so degenerate that solidarity is felt as tyranny: they want no authority, no solidarity, no lining up with the rank and file to adopt its ignobly slack pace. They hate the measured step, the tempo of science, they hate the lack of urgency, the perserverance, the indifference to himself of the man of science.

443 (*March-June 1888*)

Fundamentally, morality is hostile to science: Socrates was so already—and for this reason, that science takes things seriously that have nothing to do with "good" and "evil," consequently makes the feeling for "good" and "evil" seem less important. For morality demands that the whole man and all his forces should stand in its service: it considers it a squandering on the part of one not rich enough to squander when man concerns himself seriously with plants and stars. This is why scientific procedures rapidly declined in Greece once Socrates had introduced into science the disease of moralizing; the height attained in the disposition of a Democritus, Hippocrates, and Thucydides was not attained a second time.

444 (*March-June 1888*)

Problem of the philosopher and the man of science.— Influence of age; depressive habits (staying-at-home à la Kant; overwork; insufficient nourishment of the brain; reading). More essentially: whether a tendency toward generalities is not already a symptom of decadence; objectivity as disintegration of the will (—to be *able* to stand so distant—) This presupposes a great *adiaphora* in regard to the powerful drives: a kind of isolation, exceptional stance, resistance in regard to the normal drives.

Type: desertion of the homeland; further and further afield; increasing exoticism; the old imperatives become dumb——; certainly this continual questioning "whither?" ("happiness") is a sign of disengagement from forms of organization, of a breaking loose.

Problem: whether the man of science is more of a symptom of decadence than the philosophers:—he is not disengaged as a whole, only a part of him is absolutely dedicated to knowledge, trained to one corner and perspective—he needs *all* the virtues of a strong race and health, great severity, manliness, shrewdness. He is a symptom more of a higher multiplicity of culture than of its weariness. The scholar of decadence is a *bad* scholar. While the philosopher of decadence has counted, hitherto at least, as the typical philosopher.

445 (*Jan.-Fall 1888*)

Nothing is rarer among philosophers than *intellectual integrity*: perhaps they say the opposite, perhaps they even believe it. But a condition of their entire occupation is that only certain truths are admitted; they know that which they *have* to prove; that they are at one over these "truths" is virtually their means of recognizing one another as philosophers. There are, e.g., moral truths. But a faith in morals is not a proof of morality: there are cases—and the case of the philosopher is one—in which such a faith is simply a piece of *immorality*.

446 (*March-June 1888*)

What, then, is regressive in the philosopher?— That he teaches that *his* qualities are the necessary and sole qualities for the attainment of the "highest good" (e.g., dialectic, as with Plato). That he orders men of all kinds *gradatim*[150] up to *his* type as the highest. That he despises what is generally esteemed—that he opens up a gulf between priestly values and worldly values. That he *knows* what is true, what God is, what the goal is, what the way is—

The typical philosopher is here an absolute dogmatist;—if he has need of skepticism, it is so as to be able to speak dogmatically about his main interest.

447 (*March-June 1888*)

The philosopher in opposition to his rivals; e.g., in opposition to science: then he becomes a skeptic; then he reserves to himself a form of knowledge that he denies the man of science; then he goes hand in hand with the priest so as not[151] to arouse

[150] By degrees.

[151] "Not" is missing in the MS but was very reasonably inserted by the German editors.

the suspicion of atheism, materialism; he regards an attack on himself as an attack on morality, virtue, religion, order—he knows how to discredit his opponents as "seducers" and "underminers": then he goes hand in hand with power.

The philosopher in a struggle with other philosophers—he tries to compel them to appear as anarchists, unbelievers, opponents of authority. *In summa*: in so far as he struggles, he struggles just as a priest does, just as priesthood does.

3. Truth and Error of Philosophers

448 (*Manuscript source uncertain*)[152]

Philosophy defined by Kant as "the science of the limitations of reason"!!

449 (*Spring-Fall 1887*)

Philosophy as the art of discovering truth: according to Aristotle. Contradicted by the Epicureans, who made use of Aristotle's sensualistic theory of knowledge: they rejected the search for truth with irony; "Philosophy as an art of *living*."

450 (*Spring-Fall 1887*)

The three great naiveties:

Knowledge as a means to happiness (as if—),

as a means to virtue (as if—),

as a means to "denial of life"—to the extent that it is a means to disappointment—(as if—)

451 (*Manuscript source uncertain*)[153]

That there should be a "truth" which one could somehow approach—!

452 (*Jan.-Fall 1888*)

Error and ignorance are fateful.— The view that *truth is*

[152] Therefore omitted by Schlechta.

[153] Therefore omitted by Schlechta.

found and that ignorance and error are at an end is one of the most potent seductions there is. Supposing it is believed, then the will to examination, investigation, caution, experiment is paralyzed: it can even count as criminal, namely as *doubt* concerning truth—

"Truth" is therefore more fateful than error and ignorance, because it cuts off the forces that work toward enlightenment and knowledge.

The affect of *laziness* now takes the side of "truth"— ("thinking is distress, misery!"); as do order, rule, happiness in possessing, pride in wisdom—vanity *in summa*:—it is more comfortable to obey than to examine; it is more flattering to think "I possess the truth" than to see only darkness around one—above all: it is reassuring, it gives confidence, it alleviates life—it "improves" the character, to the extent that it lessens mistrust. "Peace of soul," "a quiet conscience": all inventions made possible only by presupposing that *truth has been found.*— "By their fruits shall ye know them"— "Truth" is truth, *for* it makes men *better*— The process goes on: everything good, all success, is placed to the credit of "truth."

This is the *proof of strength*:[154] the happiness, the contentment, the well-being of the community, as of the individual, are henceforth understood as the consequence of belief in morality— The converse: ill success is attributed to lack of faith—.

453 (*Jan.-Fall 1888*)

The causes of error lie just as much in the good will [as in the ill will[155]] of man—: in a thousand cases he conceals reality from himself, he falsifies it, so as not to suffer from his good [or ill][156] will. E.g., God as the director of human destiny: or the interpretation of his own petty destiny as if everything were contrived and sent with a view to the salvation of his soul—this lack of "philology," which to a more subtle intellect would have to count as uncleanliness and counterfeiting, is, on the average, performed under the inspiration of good will. Good will, "noble feelings," "lofty states" are in the means they employ just as much

[154] See *Antichrist*, sections 50 *ff* (*Portable Nietzsche*); also in connection with sections 453-57.

[155] Interpolated by Nietzsche, brackets mine.

[156] Interpolated by German editors, brackets mine.

counterfeiters and deceivers as the affects repudiated by morality and called egoistic: love, hate, revenge.

Errors are what mankind has had to pay for most dearly: and, on the whole, it is the errors of "good will" which have harmed it most profoundly. The illusion that makes happy is more pernicious than that which has immediate bad consequences: the latter sharpens and purifies[157] reason and makes it more mistrustful—the former lulls it to sleep.—

Beautiful feelings, sublime agitations, are, physiologically speaking, among the narcotics: their misuse has precisely the same consequences as the misuse of any other opiate—neurasthenia—

454 (*1888*)

Error is the most expensive luxury that man can permit himself; and if the error happens to be a physiological error, then it is perilous to life. What, consequently, has man hitherto paid for most dearly? For his "truths": for they have all been errors *in physiologicis*—

455 (*Jan.-Fall 1888*)

Psychological confusions:—the demand for belief—confused with the "will to truth" (e.g., in the case of Carlyle).[158] But in the same way, the demand for unbelief has been confused with the "will to truth" (—the need to get free from a belief, for a hundred reasons: to be in the right against some "believers"). What inspires the skeptic? *Hatred* of the dogmatist—or a need for rest, a weariness, as in the case of Pyrrho.

The advantages that one anticipated from truth were advantages resulting from belief in it:—in itself, that is, truth could be altogether painful, harmful, fateful—. One likewise disputed the "truth" only when one promised oneself advantages from one's victory—e.g., freedom from the ruling powers.

The methods of truth were not invented from motives of truth, but from motives of power, of wanting to be superior.

How is truth proved? By the feeling of enhanced power[159]—

[157] Reading uncertain, word illegible.

[158] Cf. *Twilight*, "Skirmishes," section 12 (*Portable Nietzsche*, p. 521).

[159] After "power" three illegible words follow in the MS: "of certainty, faith—"?

by utility—by indispensability—in short, by advantages (namely, presuppositions concerning what truth *ought* to be like for us to recognize it). But that is a prejudice: a sign that truth is not involved at all—

What, e.g., is the meaning of the "will to truth" in the case of the Goncourts?[160] in the case of the naturalists?— Critique of "objectivity."

Why know: why not rather be deceived?— What one always wanted was faith—and *not* truth— Faith is created by means antithetical to the methods of research—: they even exclude the latter—.

456 (*March-June 1888*)

A Certain degree of faith serves us today as an *objection* to what is believed—even more as a question mark against the spiritual health of the believer.

457 (*Jan-Fall 1888*)

Martyrs.— In order to combat anything founded on reverence, the attacker must be possessed of a somewhat audacious, relentless, even shameless disposition— Now if one considers that mankind has for millennia sanctified as truths only what was error, that is has even branded any critique of these as a sign of a wicked disposition, then one is bound to confess with regret that a goodly amount of *immorality* was needed to provide the initiative for aggression, in other words for *reason*—

These immoralists should be forgiven for always having posed as "martyrs to truth": the truth is that it was not the drive to truth which made them negate, but disintegration, sacrilegious skepticism, pleasure in adventure—. In other cases, it is personal rancor that drives them into the domain of problems—they combat problems in order to be in the right against particular people. But it is revenge above all that science has been able to employ—the revenge of the oppressed, those who had been pushed aside and, in fact, oppressed by the *prevailing* truth—

Truth, that is to say, the scientific method, was grasped and promoted by those who divined in it a weapon of war—an in-

---

[160] Cf. *Twilight,* "Skirmishes," section 7 (*Portable Nietzsche,* p. 517).

strument of destruction— To make their opposition honorable, they needed, moreover, an apparatus similar in kind to that used by those they were attacking:—they adopted the concept "truth" just as ostentatiously and unconditionally as their opponents—they became fanatics, at least they posed as such, because no other pose was taken seriously. What remained to be done was accomplished by persecution, passion and the insecurity of the persecuted—hatred grew and consequently the precondition for remaining scientific was diminished. Ultimately, they all wanted to be right in the same absurd fashion as their opponents— The words "conviction," "faith," the pride of martyrdom—these are the least favorable states for the advancement of knowledge. The opponents of truth at last reaccepted the entire subjective manner of deciding questions of truth, namely by poses, sacrifices, heroic resolutions—and thus prolonged the dominion of antiscientific methods. As martyrs they compromised their own deed.

458 (*March-June 1888*)[161]

Dangerous distinction between "theoretical" and "practical," e.g., in the case of Kant, but also in the case of the ancients:—they act as if pure spirituality presented them with the problems of knowledge and metaphysics;—they act as if practice must be judged by its own measure, whatever the answer of theory may be.

Against the former I direct my *psychology of philosophers*: their most alienated calculations and their "spirituality" are still only the last pallid impression of a physiological fact; the voluntary is absolutely lacking, everything is instinct, everything has been directed along certain lines from the beginning—

Against the latter I ask whether we know of any other method of acting well than always thinking well; the latter *is* an action, and the former presupposes thought. Have we a different method for judging the value of a way of life from judging the value of a theory: by induction, by comparison?—

The naive believe that we are better equipped here, that here we know what is "good"—philosophers repeat it. We conclude that a faith is here at work, nothing more—

"One must act; *consequently* rules of conduct are needed"—said even the skeptics of antiquity. The urgent need for a decision as an argument for considering something *true*!

---

[161] Cf. section 423 above.

"One must *not* act"—said their more consistent brothers, the Buddhists, and conceived a rule of conduct to liberate one from actions—

To accommodate oneself, to live as the "common man" lives, to hold right and good what *he* holds right: this is to submit to the herd instinct. One must take one's courage and severity so far as to feel such a submission as a *disgrace*. Not to live with two different standards!— Not to separate theory and practice!—

459 (*Jan.-Fall 1888*)

That nothing formerly held true is true— What was formerly despised as unholy, forbidden, contemptible, fateful—all these flowers grow today along the lovely paths of truth.

This entire old morality concerns us no more: there is not a concept in it that still deserves respect. We have outlived it—we are no longer coarse and naive enough to have to let ourselves be deceived in this fashion— In more polite words: we are too virtuous for it— And if truth in the old sense was "truth" only because the old morality affirmed it, had a right to affirm it, then it follows that we no longer have need of any former truths, either— Our criterion of truth is by no means morality: we *refute* an opinion by showing it to be dependent on morality, to be inspired by noble feelings.

460 (*March-June 1888*)

All these values are empirical and conditional. But he who believes in them, who reverences them, refuses to recognize just this characteristic of them. Philosophers believe one and all in these values, and one form their reverence took was the attempt to make *a priori* truths of them. The falsifying character of reverence—

Reverence is the supreme test of integrity: but in the entire history of philosophy there *is* no intellectual integrity—but only "love of the good"—

The absolute lack of methods of testing the value of these values; secondly: reluctance to test values, to take them as being in any way conditional.— In the case of moral values, all the antiscientific instincts came together with the object of *excluding* science—

4. Further Considerations for a Critique of Philosophy

461 (*March-June 1888*)

Why philosophers are slanderers.— The treacherous and blind hostility of philosophers towards the senses[162]—how much of mob and middle class there is in this hatred!

The common people always consider an abuse of which they feel the ill consequences as an objection to that which is abused: all insurrectionary movements aimed against principles, whether political or economic, argue thus, with the idea of representing an abuse as being necessary to, and inherent in, the principle.

It is a miserable story: man seeks a principle through which he can despise men—he invents a world so as to be able to slander and bespatter this world: in reality, he reaches every time for nothingness and construes nothingness as "God," as "truth," and in any case as judge and condemner of *this* state of being—

If one wants a proof of how profoundly and thoroughly the actually barbarous needs of man seek satisfaction, even when he is tamed and "civilized," one should take a look at the "leitmotifs" of the entire evolution of philosophy:—a sort of revenge on reality, a malicious destruction of the valuations by which men live, an unsatisfied soul that feels the tamed state as a torture and finds a voluptuous pleasure in a morbid unraveling of all the bonds that tie it to such a state.

The history of philosophy is a secret raging against the preconditions of life, against the value feelings of life, against partisanship in favor of life. Philosophers have never hesitated to affirm a world provided it contradicted this world and furnished them with a pretext for speaking ill of this world. It has been hitherto the grand school of slander; and it has imposed itself to such an extent that today our science, which proclaims itself the advocate

---

[162] At this point the German editors saw fit to omit the following lines: "It is *not* the senses that deceive. Our nose, of which, as far as I know, no philosopher has ever spoken with due respect, is as yet the most delicate scientific [*physikalisch*] instrument in existence: it is capable of registering vibrations where even the spectroscope fails."

This section, including the passage just cited, was utilized by Nietzsche in *Twilight*, Chapters III and IV.

of life, has accepted the basic slanderous position and treated this world as apparent, this chain of causes as merely phenomenal. What is it really that hates here?

I fear it is still the Circe of philosophers, morality, that has here bewitched them into having to be slanderers forever— They believed in moral "truths," they found there the supreme values—what else could they do but deny existence more firmly the more they got to know it?— For this existence is immoral— And this life depends upon immoral preconditions: and all morality *denies* life—.

Let us abolish the real world: and to be able to do this we first have to abolish the supreme value hitherto, morality— It suffices to demonstrate that even morality is immoral, in the sense in which immorality has always been condemned. If the tyranny of former values is broken in this way, if we have abolished the "real world," then a new order of values must follow of its own accord.

The apparent world and the world invented by a lie—this is the antithesis. The latter has hitherto been called the "real world," "truth," "God." This is what we have to abolish.

Logic of my conception:

1. Morality as supreme value (master over all phases of philosophy, even over the skeptics). Result: this world is good for nothing, it is not the "real world."

2. What here determines the supreme value? What is morality, really?— The instinct of decadence; it is the exhausted and disinherited who *take revenge* in this fashion. Historical proof: philosophers are always decadents—in the service of the *nihilistic* religions.

3. The instinct of decadence which appears as will to power. Proof: the absolute immorality of means throughout the entire history of morality.

General insight: the highest values hitherto are a special case of the will to power; morality itself is a special case of immorality.[163]

---

[163] The short last paragraph was taken by the editors from another more detailed section. At this point the MS had merely: "In this whole movement we have recognized merely a special case of the will to power." The first edition (1901) followed the MS.

Schlechta omits the lines deleted in all other editions; he follows the standard edition and not the manuscript in the final paragraph; and he

462 (*Spring-Fall 1887*)

Fundamental innovations: In place of "moral values," purely naturalistic values. Naturalization of morality.

In place of "sociology," a theory of the forms of domination.

In place of "society," the culture complex, as my chief interest (as a whole or in its parts).

In place of "epistemology," a perspective theory of affects (to which belongs a hierarchy of the affects; the affects transfigured; their superior order, their "spirituality").

In place of "metaphysics" and religion, the theory of eternal recurrence (this as a means of breeding and selection).

463 (*1885*)

My precursors: Schopenhauer; to what extent I deepened pessimism and by devising its extremest antithesis first really experienced it.

Then: the ideal artists, that after-product of the Napoleonic movement.

Then: the higher Europeans, predecessors of great politics.

Then: the Greeks and their origins.[164]

464 (*1885*)

I have named those who were unknowingly my workers and precursors. But where may I look with any kind of hope for my kind of philosopher himself, at the least for my need of new philosophers?[165] In that direction alone where a noble mode of thought is dominant, such as believes in slavery and in many degrees of bondage as the precondition of every higher culture; where a

---

prints the second half of the section, beginning with "The history of philosophy . . ." (along with the conclusion that does not belong to it) a couple of pages before the first half.

[164] The MS goes on: "In *The Birth of Tragedy* I gave hints concerning the relation of 'distress' and 'art'; personal education of the philosopher in solitude. The Dionysian."

Schlechta not only omits these lines, following the example of all previous editors; he also omits the second paragraph—in which, incidentally, the MS has "Napol." instead of Napoleonic."

[165] Cf. *Beyond Good and Evil,* sections 211 *f.*

creative mode of thought dominates that does not posit the happiness of repose, the "Sabbath of Sabbaths" as a goal for the world, and honors even in peace the means to new wars;[166] a mode of thought that prescribes laws for the future, that for the sake of the future is harsh and tyrannical towards itself and all things of the present; a reckless, "immoral" mode of thought, which wants to develop both the good and the bad qualities in man to their fullest extent, because it feels it has the strength to put both in their right place—in the place where each needs the other. But he who thus looks for philosophers today, what prospect has he of finding what he is looking for? Is it not likely that, even with the best Diogenes lantern, he will search about in vain all day and all night? The age possesses the *reverse* instincts; it wants, first and above all, comfort; it wants, in the second place, publicity and that great actors' hubbub, that great drum banging that appeals to its fun-fair tastes; it wants, thirdly, that everyone should fall on his face in the profoundest subjection before the greatest of all lies—it is called "equality of men"—and honor exclusively those virtues that *level and equalize*. But the rise of the philosopher, as I understand him, is therewith rendered altogether impossible, notwithstanding that it is thought in all innocence to be favorable to him. Indeed, all the world bewails today the evil situation of the philosopher in *earlier* times, hemmed in between the stake, bad conscience, and the arrogant wisdom of the Church Fathers: the truth, however, is that precisely this was a much more favorable condition for the education of a powerful, comprehensive, cunning and audaciously daring spirituality than the conditions of life at present. Today, another kind of spirit, namely the spirit of the demagogue, the spirit of the actor, perhaps also the scholarly beaver- and ant-like spirit, finds conditions favorable. But things are so much the worse even for superior artists: for are they not, almost all of them, perishing from a lack of inner discipline? They are no longer tyrannized over from without by a church's tables of absolute values or those of a court; thus they also no longer learn to develop their "inner tyrants," their will. And what is true of artists is true in a higher and more fateful sense of

---

[166] Cf. *Zarathustra,* I, "On War and Warriors" and my commentary on the parallel passage in my translation (*Portable Nietzsche,* p. 158 *ff*); also my *Nietzsche,* Chapter 12, section VII.

Many, if not most, of the ideas in this section are developed in *Zarathustra* and *Beyond Good and Evil.*

philosophers. For where are there free spirits today? Show me a free spirit today!—

465 (*Summer-Fall 1888*)

I understand by "freedom of spirit" something quite definite: being a hundred times superior[167] to philosophers and other disciples of "truth" in severity towards oneself, in cleanliness and courage, in the unconditional will to say No where it is dangerous to say No—I treat previous philosophers as contemptible libertines hiding in the cloak of the woman "truth."

---

[167] This word is not found in the MS but was very reasonably supplied by the German editors.

BOOK THREE

PRINCIPLES OF A NEW EVALUATION

I. THE WILL TO POWER AS KNOWLEDGE[1]

1. Method of Inquiry

466 (*Jan.-Fall 1888*)

It is not the victory of science that distinguishes our nineteenth century, but the victory of scientific method over science.

467 (*Spring-Fall 1887*)

History of scientific method, considered by Auguste Comte as virtually philosophy itself.

468 (*Spring-Fall 1887*)

The great methodologists: Aristotle, Bacon, Descartes, Auguste Comte.

469 (*Jan.-Fall 1888*)

The most valuable insights are arrived at last; but the most valuable insights are *methods.*

All the methods, all the presuppositions of our contemporary science were for millennia regarded with the profoundest contempt; on their account one was excluded from the society of respectable people—one was considered as an "enemy of God," as a reviler of the highest ideal, as "possessed."

---

[1] Much of the material in this part was utilized by Nietzsche in the first chapter of *Beyond Good and Evil,* published in 1886, and in *Twilight of the Idols* (completed in the early fall of 1888), especially in the chapter "The Four Great Errors" and—some of the sections on the "true" and the "apparent" world—in the chapters " 'Reason' in Philosophy" and "How the 'True World' Finally Became a Fable." But there are also many ideas and a great many formulations that were not included in any of the books Nietzsche finished—presumably in most cases because Nietzsche was not fully satisfied with his notes. *What follows, then, does not represent his final point of view; but some of his most interesting suggestions are to be found only in these sections.*

We have had the whole pathos of mankind against us—our conception of what "truth" should be, what service of truth should be, our objectivity, our method, our silent, cautious, mistrustful ways were considered perfectly contemptible—

At bottom, it has been an aesthetic taste that has hindered mankind most: it believed in the picturesque effect of truth, it demanded of the man of knowledge that he should produce a powerful effect on the imagination.

This looks as if an antithesis has been achieved, a leap made; in reality, the schooling through moral hyperbole prepared the way step by step for that milder of pathos that became incarnate in the scientific character—

The conscientiousness in small things, the self-control of the religious man were a preparatory school for the scientific character: above all, the disposition that takes problems seriously, regardless of the personal consequences—

2. The Epistemological Starting Point

470 (*1885-1886*)

Profound aversion to reposing once and for all in any one total view of the world. Fascination of the opposing point of view: refusal to be deprived of the stimulus of the enigmatic.

471 (*1885-1886*)

The presupposition that things are, at bottom, ordered so morally that human reason must be justified—is an ingenuous presupposition and a piece of naiveté, the after-effect of belief in God's veracity—God understood as the creator of things.— These concepts an inheritance from a former existence in a beyond——

472 (*1883-1888*)

Contradiction of the alleged "facts of consciousness." Observation is a thousand times more difficult, error perhaps a condition of observation in general.

473 (*1886-1887*)

The intellect cannot criticize itself, simply because it cannot be compared with other species of intellect and because its capacity to know would be revealed only in the presence of "true reality," i.e., because in order to criticize the intellect we should have to be a higher being with "absolute knowledge." This presupposes that, distinct from every perspective kind of outlook or sensual-spiritual appropriation, something exists, an "in-itself."— But the psychological derivation of the belief in things forbids us to speak of "things-in-themselves."

474 (*Nov. 1887-March 1888*)

That a sort of adequate relationship subsists between subject and object, that the object is something that if seen from within would be a subject, is a well-meant invention which, I think, has had its day. The measure of that of which we are in any way conscious is totally dependent upon the coarse utility of its becoming-conscious: how could this nook-perspective of consciousness permit us to assert anything of "subject" and "object" that touched reality!—

475 (*1885-1886*)

Critique of modern philosophy: erroneous starting point, as if there existed "facts of consciousness"—and no phenomenalism in introspection.

476 (*1884*)

"Consciousness"—to what extent the idea of an idea, the idea of will, the idea of a feeling (known to ourselves alo are totally superficial! Our inner world, too, "appearance"

477 (*Nov. 1887-March 1888*)

I maintain the phenomenality of the inner w thing of which we become conscious is a schematized, interpreted through and through—the actual process of inner "perception," the causal connection between thoughts, feelings, desires, between subject and object, are absolutely hidden from us—and are perhaps purely imaginary. The "apparent *inner* world" is governed by just the same forms and procedures as the "outer" world. We never encounter "facts": pleasure and displeasure are subsequent and derivative intellectual phenomena—

"Causality" eludes us; to suppose a direct causal link beween thoughts, as logic does—that is the consequence of the crudest and clumsiest observation. Between two thoughts all kinds of affects play their game: but their motions are too fast, therefore we fail to recognize them, we deny them—

"Thinking," as epistemologists conceive it, simply does not occur: it is a quite arbitrary fiction, arrived at by selecting one element from the process and eliminating all the rest, an artificial arrangement for the purpose of intelligibility—

The "spirit," something that thinks: where possible even "absolute, pure spirit"—this conception is a second derivative of that false introspection which believes in "thinking": first an act is imagined which simply does not occur, "thinking," and secondly a subject-substratum in which every act of thinking, and nothing else, has its origin: that is to say, both the deed and the doer are fictions.

478 (*March-June 1888*)

One must not look for phenomenalism in the wrong place: nothing is more phenomenal (or, more clearly:) nothing is so
...rld which we observe with the

... as cause to such an extent that
...rience introduced a cause into
... a cause of events—).
...hey succeed one another in our
... relation: the logician especially,
...t instances which never occur in
...he prejudice that thoughts *cause*

... philosopers still believe—that
... reactions, that the purpose of

pleasure and pain is to occasion reactions. For millennia, pleasure and the avoidance of displeasure have been flatly asserted as the *motives* for every action. Upon reflection, however, we should concede that everything would have taken the same course, according to exactly the same sequence of causes and effects, if these states "pleasure and displeasure" had been absent, and that one is simply deceiving oneself if one thinks they cause anything at all: they are epiphenomena with a quite diffferent object than to evoke reactions; they are themselves effects within the instituted process of reaction.

In summa: everything of which we become conscious is a terminal phenomenon, an end—and causes nothing; every successive phenomenon in consciousness is completely atomistic— And we have sought to understand the world through the reverse conception—as if nothing were real and effective but thinking, feeling, willing!—

479 (*Jan.-Fall 1888*)

The phenomenalism of the "inner world." Chronological inversion, so that the cause enters consciousness later than the effect.— We have learned that pain is projected to a part of the body without being situated there—we have learned that sense impressions naively supposed to be conditioned by the outer world are, on the contrary, conditioned by the inner world; that we are always unconscious of the real activity of the outer world— The fragment of outer world of which we are conscious is born after an effect from outside has impressed itself upon us, and is subsequently projected as its "cause"—

In the phenomenalism of the "inner world" we invert the chronological order of cause and effect. The fundamental fact of "inner experience" is that the cause is imagined after the effect has taken place— The same applies to the succession of thoughts: —we seek the reason for a thought before we are conscious of it; and the reason enters consciousness first, and then its consequence— Our entire dream life is the interpretation of complex feelings with a view to possible causes—and in such way that we are conscious of a condition only when the supposed causal chain associated with it has entered consciousness.

The whole of "inner experience" rests upon the fact that a

cause for an excitement of the nerve centers is sought and imagined —and that only a cause thus discovered enters consciousness: this cause in no way corresponds to the real cause—it is a groping on the basis of previous "inner experiences," i.e., of memory. But memory also maintains the habit of the old interpretations, i.e., of erroneous causality—so that the "inner experience" has to contain within it the consequences of all previous false causal fictions. Our "outer world" as we project it every moment is indissolubly tied to the old error of the ground: we interpret it by means of the schematism of "things," etc.

"Inner experience" enters our consciousness only after it has found a language the individual understands—i.e., a translation of a condition into conditions familiar to him—; "to understand" means merely: to be able to express something new in the language of something old and familiar. E.g., "I feel unwell"—such a judgment presupposes a great and late neutrality of the observer—; the simple man always says: this or that makes me feel unwell —he makes up his mind about his feeling unwell only when he has seen a reason for feeling unwell.— I call that a *lack of philology;* to be able to read off a text as a text without interposing an interpretation is the last-developed form of "inner experience"— perhaps one that is hardly possible—

480 (*March-June 1888*)

There exists neither "spirit," nor reason, nor thinking, nor consciousness, nor soul, nor will, nor truth: all are fictions that are of no use. There is no question of "subject and object," but of a particular species of animal that can prosper only through a certain relative rightness; above all, regularity of its perceptions (so that it can accumulate experience)—

Knowledge works as a tool of power. Hence it is plain that it increases with every increase of power—

The meaning of "knowledge": here, as in the case of "good" or "beautiful," the concept is to be regarded in a strict and narrow anthropocentric and biological sense. In order for a particular species to maintain itself and increase its power, its conception of reality must comprehend enough of the calculable and constant for it to base a scheme of behavior on it. The utility of preservation —not some abstract-theoretical need not to be deceived—stands as the motive behind the development of the organs of knowledge —they develop in such a way that their observations suffice for our preservation. In other words: the measure of the desire for knowledge depends upon the measure to which the will to power grows in a species: a species grasps a certain amount of reality in order to become master of it, in order to press it into service.

3. Belief in the "Ego." The Subject

481 (*1883-1888*)

Against positivism, which halts at phenomena—"There are only *facts*"—I would say: No, facts is precisely what there is not, only interpretations. We cannot establish any fact "in itself": perhaps it is folly to want to do such a thing.

"Everything is subjective," you say; but even this is interpretation. The "subject" is not something given, it is something added and invented and projected behind what there is.— Finally, is it necessary to posit an interpreter behind the interpretation? Even this is invention, hypothesis.

In so far as the word "knowledge" has any meaning, the world is knowable; but it is *interpretable* otherwise, it has no meaning behind it, but countless meanings.— "Perspectivism."

It is our needs that interpret the world; our drives and their For and Against. Every drive is a kind of lust to rule; each one has its perspective that it would like to compel all the other drives to accept as a norm.

482 (*1886-1887*)

We set up a word at the point at which our ignorance begins, at which we can see no further, e.g., the word "I," the word "do," the word "suffer":—these are perhaps the horizon of our knowledge, but not "truths."

483 (*1885*)

Through thought the ego is posited; but hitherto one believed as ordinary people do, that in "I think" there was something of immediate certainty, and that this "I" was the given *cause* of thought, from which by analogy we understood all other causal relationships. However habitual and indispensable this fiction may have become by now—that in itself proves nothing against its imaginary origin: a belief can be a condition of life and nonetheless be false.[2]

484 (*Spring-Fall 1887*)

"There is thinking: therefore there is something that thinks": this is the upshot of all Descartes' argumentation. But that means positing as "true *a priori*" our belief in the concept of substance—that when there is thought there has to be something "that thinks" is simply a formulation of our grammatical custom that adds a doer to every deed. In short, this is not merely the substantiation of a fact but a logical-metaphysical postulate— Along the lines followed by Descartes one does not come upon something absolutely certain but only upon the fact of a very strong belief.

If one reduces the proposition to "There is thinking, therefore there are thoughts," one has produced a mere tautology: and precisely that which is in question, the "reality of thought," is not touched upon—that is, in this form the "apparent reality" of thought cannot be denied. But what Descartes desired was that thought should have, not an *apparent* reality, but a reality *in itself*.

485 (*Spring-Fall 1887*)

The concept of substance is a consequence of the concept of the subject: not the reverse! If we relinquish the soul, "the subject," the precondition for "substance" in general disappears. One acquires degrees of being, one loses that which *has* being.

Critique of "reality": where does the "more or less real," the gradation of being in which we believe, lead to?—

The degree to which we feel life and power (logic and coherence of experience) gives us our measure of "being," "reality," not-appearance.

The subject: this is the term for our belief in a unity underlying all the different impulses of the highest feeling of reality: we

[2] Cf. sections 487 and 493 and *Beyond*, section 4. This section, not in Nietzsche's handwriting, was evidently dictated.

understand this belief as the *effect* of one cause—we believe so firmly in our belief that for its sake we imagine "truth," "reality," "substantiality" in general.— "The subject" is the fiction that many similar states in us are the effect of one substratum: but it is we who first created the "similarity" of these states; our adjusting them and making them similar is the fact, not their similarity (—which ought rather to be denied—).

486 (*1885-1886*)

One would have to know what *being* is, in order to decide whether this or that is real (e.g., "the facts of consciousness"); in the same way, what *certainty* is, what *knowledge* is, and the like.— But since we do not know this, a critique of the faculty of knowledge is senseless: how should a tool be able to criticize itself when it can use only itself for the critique? It cannot even define itself![3]

487 (*1883-1886*)

Must all philosophy not ultimately bring to light the preconditions upon which the process of reason depends?—our belief in the "ego" as a substance, as the sole reality from which we ascribe reality to things in general? The oldest "realism" at last comes to light: at the same time that the entire religious history of mankind is recognized as the history of the soul superstition. Here we come to a limit: our thinking itself involves this belief (with its distinction of substance, accident; deed, doer, etc.); to let it go means: being no longer able to think.

But that a belief, however necessary it may be for the preservation of a species, has nothing to do with truth, one knows from the fact that, e.g., we have to believe in time, space, and motion, without feeling compelled to grant them absolute reality.

488 (*Spring-Fall 1887*)

Psychological derivation of our belief in reason.— The concept "reality," "being," is taken from our feeling of the "subject."

"The subject": interpreted from within ourselves, so that the ego counts as a substance, as the cause of all deeds, as a doer.

---

[3] Cf. section 473.

The logical-metaphysical postulates, the belief in substance, accident, attribute, etc., derive their convincing force from our habit of regarding all our deeds as consequences of our will—so that the ego, as substance, does not vanish in the multiplicity of change.— But there is no such thing as will.—

We have no categories at all that permit us to distinguish a "world in itself" from a "world of appearance." All our categories of reason are of sensual origin: derived from the empirical world. "The soul," "the ego"—the history of these concepts shows that here, too, the oldest distinction ("breath," "life")—

If there is nothing material, there is also nothing immaterial. The concept no longer contains anything.

No subject "atoms." The sphere of a subject constantly growing or decreasing, the center of the system constantly shifting; in cases where it cannot organize the appropriate mass, it breaks into two parts. On the other hand, it can transform a weaker subject into its functionary without destroying it, and to a certain degree form a new unity with it. No "substance," rather something that in itself strives after greater strength, and that wants to "preserve" itself only indirectly (it wants to *surpass* itself—).

489 (*1886-1887*)

Everything that enters consciousness as "unity" is already tremendously complex: we always have only a semblance of unity.

The phenomenon of the body is the richer, clearer, more tangible phenomenon: to be discussed first, methodologically, without coming to any decision about its ultimate significance.

490 (*1885*)

The assumption of one single subject is perhaps unnecessary; perhaps it is just as permissible to assume a multiplicity of subjects, whose interaction and struggle is the basis of our thought and our consciousness in general? A kind of aristocracy of "cells" in which dominion resides? To be sure, an aristocracy of equals, used to ruling jointly and understanding how to command?

My hypotheses: The subject as multiplicity.

Pain intellectual and dependent upon the judgment "harmful": projected.

The effect always "unconscious": the inferred and imagined cause is projected, *follows* in time.

Pleasure is a kind of pain.

The only force that exists is of the same kind as that of the will: a commanding of other subjects, which thereupon change.

The continual transitoriness and fleetingness of the subject. "Mortal soul."

Number as perspective form.

491 (*1885-1886*)

Belief in the body is more fundamental than belief in the soul: the latter arose from unscientific reflection on [the agonies of][4] the body (something that leaves it. Belief in the truth of dreams—).

492 (*1885*)

The body and physiology the starting point: why?— We gain the correct idea of the nature of our subject-unity, namely as regents at the head of a communality (not as "souls" or "life forces"), also of the dependence of these regents upon the ruled and of an order of rank and division of labor as the conditions that make possible the whole and its parts. In the same way, how living unities continually arise and die and how the "subject" is not eternal; in the same way, that the struggle expresses itself in obeying and commanding, and that a fluctuating assessment of the limits of power is part of life. The relative ignorance in which the regent is kept concerning individual activities and even disturbances within the communality is among the conditions under which rule can be exercised. In short, we also gain a valuation of *not-knowing,* of seeing things on a broad scale, of simplification and falsification, of perspectivity. The most important thing, however, is: that we understand that the ruler and his subjects are of the same kind, all feeling, willing, thinking—and that, wherever we see or divine movement in a body, we learn to conclude that there is a subjective, invisible life appertaining to it. Movement is symbolism for the eye; it indicates that something has been felt, willed, thought.

---

[4] The words I have placed in brackets were interpolated by the German editors, on the basis of one of Nietzsche's other notes.

The danger of the direct questioning of the subject *about* the subject and of all self-reflection of the spirit lies in this, that it could be useful and important for one's activity to interpret oneself *falsely*. That is why we question the body and reject the evidence of the sharpened senses: we try, if you like, to see whether the inferior parts themselves cannot enter into communication with us.

4. Biology of the Drive to Knowledge. Perspectivism

493 (*1885*)

Truth is the kind of error without which a certain species of life could not live. The value for *life* is ultimately decisive.[5]

494 (*1885*)

It is improbable that our "knowledge" should extend further than is strictly necessary for the preservation of life. Morphology shows us how the senses and the nerves, as well as the brain, develop in proportion to the difficulty of finding nourishment.

495

If the morality of "thou shalt not lie" is rejected, the "sense for truth" will have to legitimize itself before another tribunal:—as a means of the preservation of man, as *will to power*.

Likewise our love of the beautiful: it also is our shaping will. The two senses stand side-by-side; the sense for the real is the means of acquiring the power to shape things according to our wish. The joy in shaping and reshaping—a primeval joy! We can comprehend only a world that we ourselves have made.

496 (*1884*)

Of the multifariousness of knowledge. To trace one's own relationship to many other things (or the relationship of kind)—how should that be "knowledge" of other things! The way of knowing and of knowledge is itself already part of the conditions

[5] Cf. sections 483 and 487; but also 172.

of existence: so that the conclusion that there could be no other kind of intellect (for us) than that which preserves us is precipitate: this actual condition of existence is perhaps only accidental and perhaps in no way necessary.

Our apparatus for acquiring knowledge is not *designed* for "knowledge."

497 (*1884*)

The most strongly believed a priori "truths" are for me—*provisional assumptions*; e.g., the law of causality, a very well acquired habit of belief, so much a part of us that not to believe in it would destroy the race. But are they for that reason truths? What a conclusion! As if the preservation of man were a proof of truth!

498 (*1884*)

To what extent even our intellect is a consequence of conditions of existence—: we would not have it if we did not *need* to have it, and we would not have it *as it is* if we did not need to have it *as it is,* if we could live *otherwise.*

499 (*1885*)

"Thinking" in primitive conditions (pre-organic) is the crystallization of forms, as in the case of crystal.— In *our* thought, the essential feature is fitting new material into old schemas (= Procrustes' bed), *making* equal what is new.

500 (*1885-1886*)

Sense perceptions projected "outside": "inside" and "outside"—does the *body* command here—?

The same equalizing and ordering force that rules in the idioplasma, rules also in the incorporation of the outer world: our sense perceptions are already the result of this assimiliation and equalization in regard to *all* the past in us; they do not follow directly upon the "impression"—

501 (*1886-1887*)

All thought, judgment, perception, considered as comparison, has as its precondition a *"positing* of equality," and earlier still a *"making* equal." The process of making equal is the same as the process of incorporation of appropriated material in the amoeba.

"Memory" late, in so far as here the drive to make equal seems already to have been subdued: differentiation is preserved. Remembering as a process of classification and pigeonholing: who is active?

502 (*1885*)

One must revise one's ideas about *memory*: here lies the chief temptation to assume a "soul," which, outside time, reproduces, recognizes, etc. But that which is experienced lives on "in the memory"; I cannot help it if it "comes back," the will is inactive in this case, as in the coming of any thought. Something happens of which I become conscious: now something similar comes—who called it? roused it?

503 (*1884*)

The entire apparatus of knowledge is an apparatus for abstraction and simplification—directed not at knowledge but at taking possession of things: "end" and "means" are as remote from its essential nature as are "concepts." With "end" and "means" one takes possession of the process (one invents a process that can be grasped); with "concepts," however, of the "things" that constitute the process.

504 (*1883-1888*)

Consciousness—beginning quite externally, as coordination and becoming conscious of "impressions"—at first at the furthest distance from the biological center of the individual; but a process that deepens and intensifies itself, and continually draws nearer to that center.

505 (*1885-1886*)

Our perceptions, as we understand them: i.e., the sum of all those perceptions the becoming-conscious of which was useful and essential to us and to the entire organic process—therefore not all perceptions in general (e. g., not the electric); this means: we have senses for only a selection of perceptions—those with which we have to concern ourselves in order to preserve ourselves. *Consciousness is present only to the extent that consciousness is useful.* It cannot be doubted that *all sense perceptions are permeated with*[6] *value judgments* (useful and harmful—consequently, pleasant or unpleasant). Each individual color is also for us an expression of value (although we seldom admit it, or do so only after a protracted impression of exclusively the same color; e.g., a prisoner in prison, or a lunatic). Thus insects also react differently to different colors: some like [this color, some that];[7] e.g., ants.

506 (*1884*)

First *images*—to explain how images arise in the spirit. Then *words,* applied to images. Finally *concepts,* possible only when there are words—the collecting together of many images in something nonvisible but audible (word). The tiny amount of emotion to which the "word" gives rise, as we contemplate similar images for which *one* word exists—this weak emotion is the common element, the basis of the concept. That weak sensations are regarded as alike, sensed *as being the same,* is the fundamental fact. Thus confusion of two sensations that are close neighbors, as we take note of these sensations; but *who* is taking note? Believing is the primal beginning even in every sense impression: a kind of affirmation the first intellectual activity! A "holding-true" in the beginning! Therefore it is to be explained: how "holding-true" arose! What sensation lies *behind* "true"?

507 (*Spring-Fall 1887*)

The *valuation* "I believe that this and that is so" as the *essence* of *"truth."* In valuations are expressed conditions of preservation and growth. All our organs of knowledge and our senses are developed only with regard to conditions of preservation and

---

[6] Emphasis mine, to call attention to an exceptionally interesting statement. In the original the preceding sentence *is* emphasized, but in this one only "value judgments."

[7] The words I have placed in brackets were substituted for Nietzsche's "them" by the German editors.

growth. Trust in reason and its categories, in dialectic, therefore the valuation of logic, proves only their usefulness for life, proved by experience—*not* that something is true.

That a great deal of *belief* must be present; that judgments may be ventured; that doubt concerning all essential values is *lacking*—that is the precondition of every living thing and its life. Therefore, what is needed is that something must be held to be true—*not* that something *is* true.

"The *real* and the *apparent* world"—I have traced this antithesis back to *value* relations. We have projected the conditions of *our* preservation as predicates of being in general. Because we have to be stable in our beliefs if we are to prosper, we have made the "real" world a world not of change and becoming, but one of being.

5. Origin of Reason and Logic

508 (*1883-1888*)

Originally a chaos of ideas. The ideas that were consistent with one another remained, the greater number perished—and are perishing.

509 (*1883-1888*)

The earthly kingdom of desires out of which logic grew: the herd instinct in the background. The assumption of similar cases presupposes "similar souls." For the purpose of mutual agreement and dominion.

510 (*1883-1888*)

On the *origin of logic*. The fundamental inclination to posit as equal, to *see* things as equal, is modified, held in check, by consideration of usefulness and harmfulness, by considerations of success: it adapts itself to a milder degree in which it can be satisfied without at the same time denying and endangering life. This whole process corresponds exactly to that external, mechanical process (which is its symbol) by which protoplasm makes what it appropriates equal to itself and fits it into its own forms and files.

511 (*1885-1886*)

Equality and similarity.

1. The coarser organ sees much apparent equality;

2. the spirit *wants* equality, i.e., to subsume a sense impression into an existing series: in the same way as the body *assimilates* inorganic matter.

Toward an understanding of logic:

> *the will to equality is the will to power*—the belief that something is thus and thus (the essence of *judgment*) is the consequence of a will that as much as possible *shall be* equal.

512 (*1885*)

Logic is bound to the condition: assume there are identical cases. In fact, to make possible logical thinking and inferences, this condition must first be treated fictitously as fulfilled. That is: the will to logical truth can be carried through only after a fundamental *falsification* of all events is assumed. From which it follows that a drive rules here that is capable of employing both means, firstly falsification, then the implementation of its own point of view: logic does *not* spring from will to truth.

513 (*Fall 1886*)

The inventive force that invented categories labored in the service of our needs, namely of our need for security, for quick understanding on the basis of signs and sounds, for means of abbreviation:—"substance," "subject," "object," "being," "becoming" have nothing to do with metaphysical truths.—

It is the powerful who made the names of things into law, and among the powerful it is the greatest artists in abstraction who created the categories.

514 (*March-June 1888*)

A morality, a mode of living tried and *proved* by long experience and testing, at length enters consciousness as a law, as *dominating*— And therewith the entire group of related values and states enters into it: it becomes venerable, unassailable, holy, true;

it is part of its development that its origin should be forgotten— That is a sign it has become master—

Exactly the same thing could have happened with the categories of reason: they could have prevailed, after much groping and fumbling, through their relative utility— There came a point when one collected them together, raised them to consciousness as a whole—and when one commanded them, i.e., when they had the effect of a command— From then on, they counted as a priori, as beyond experience, as irrefutable. And yet perhaps they represent nothing more than the expediency of a certain race and species —their utility alone is their "truth"—

515 (*March-June 1888*)

Not "to know" but to schematize—to impose upon chaos as much regularity and form as our practical needs require.

In the formation of reason, logic, the categories, it was *need* that was authoritative: the need, not to "know," but to subsume, to schematize, for the purpose of intelligibility and calculation— (The development of reason is adjustment, invention, with the aim of making similar, equal—the same process that every sense impression goes through!) No pre-existing "idea" was here at work, but the utilitarian fact that only when we see things coarsely and made equal do they become calculable and usable to us— Finality in reason is an effect, not a cause: life miscarries with any other kinds of reason, to which there is a continual impulse—it becomes difficult to survey—too unequal—

The categories are "truths'" only in the sense that they are conditions of life for us: as Euclidean space is a conditional[8] "truth." (Between ourselves: since no one would maintain that there is any necessity for men to exist, reason, as well as Euclidean space, is a mere idiosyncracy of a certain species of animal, and one among many—)

The subjective compulsion not to contradict here is a biological compulsion: the instinct for the utility of inferring as we do infer is part of us, we almost *are* this instinct— But what naiveté to extract from this a proof that we are therewith in possession

---

[8] MS: *bedingt* (conditioned); printed versions: *bedingende* (conditioning). The editors took their cue from Kant, not from Nietzsche's next sentence.

of a "truth in itself"!— Not being able to contradict is proof of an incapacity, not of "truth."

516 (*Spring-Fall 1887; rev. Spring-Fall 1888*)

We are unable to affirm and to deny one and the same thing: this is a subjective empirical law, not the expression of any "necessity" but only of an inability.

If, according to Aristotle, the law of contradiction is the most certain of all principles, if it is the ultimate and most basic, upon which every demonstrative proof rests, if the principle of every axiom lies in it; then one should consider all the more rigorously what *presuppositions* already lie at the bottom of it. Either it asserts something about actuality, about being, as if one already knew this from another source; that is, as if opposite attributes *could* not be ascribed to it. Or the proposition means: opposite attributes *should* not be ascribed to it. In that case, logic would be an imperative, not to know the true, but to posit and arrange a world that shall be called true by us.

In short, the question remains open: are the axioms of logic adequate to reality or are they a means and measure for us to *create* reality, the concept "reality," for ourselves?— To affirm the former one would, as already said, have to have a previous knowledge of being—which is certainly not the case. The proposition therefore contains no *criterion of truth,* but an *imperative* concerning that which *should* count as true.

Supposing there were no self-identical *"A"*, such as is presupposed by every proposition of logic (and of mathematics), and the *"A"* were already mere appearance, then logic would have a merely apparent world as its condition. In fact, we believe in this proposition under the influence of ceaseless experience which seems continually to confirm it. The "thing"— that is the real substratum of *"A"; our belief in things* is the precondition of our belief in logic. The *"A"* of logic is, like the atom, a reconstruction of the thing— If we do not grasp this, but make of logic a criterion of true being, we are on the way to positing as realities all those hypostases: substance, attribute, object, subject, action, etc.; that is, to conceiving a metaphysical world, that is, a "real world" (*—this, however, is the apparent world once more—*).

The very first acts of thought, affirmation and denial, holding true and holding not true, are, in as much as they presuppose, not only the habit of holdings things true and holding them not true, but a right to do this, already dominated by the belief that we can gain possession of knowledge, that judgments really can hit upon the truth;—in short, logic does not doubt its ability to assert something about the true-in-itself (namely, that it *cannot* have opposite attributes).

Here reigns the coarse sensualistic prejudice that sensations teach us truths about things—that I cannot say at the same time of one and the same thing that it is hard and that it is soft. (The instinctive proof "I cannot have two opposite sensations at the same time"—quite coarse and false.)

The conceptual ban on contradiction proceeds from the belief that we are *able* to form concepts, that the concept not only designates the essence of a thing but *comprehends* it— In fact, logic (like geometry and arithmetic) applies only to fictitious entities that we have created. Logic is the attempt to comprehend the actual world by means of a scheme of being posited by ourselves; more correctly, to make it formulatable and calculable for us—

517 (*Spring-Fall 1887*)

In order to think and infer it is necessary to assume beings: logic handles only formulas for what remains the same. That is why this assumption would not be proof of reality: "beings" are part of our perspective. The "ego" as a being (—not affected by becoming and development).

The fictitious world of subject, substance, "reason," etc., is needed—: there is in us a power to order, simplify, falsify, artificially distinguish. "Truth" is the will to be master over the multiplicity of sensations:—to classify phenomena into definite categories. In this we start from a belief in the "in-itself" of things (we take phenomena as *real*).

The character of the world in a state of becoming as incapable of formulation, as "false," as "self-contradictory." Knowledge and becoming exclude one another. Consequently, "knowledge" must be something else: there must first of all be a will to make knowable, a kind of becoming must itself create the deception of beings.

518 (*1885-1886*)

If our "ego" is for us the sole being, after the model of which we fashion and understand all being: very well! Then there would be very much room to doubt whether what we have here is not a perspective illusion—an apparent unity that encloses everything like a horizon. The evidence of the body reveals a tremendous multiplicity; it is allowable, for purposes of method, to employ the more easily studied, richer phenomena as evidence for the understanding of the poorer. Finally: supposing everything is becoming, then knowledge is possible only on the basis of belief in being.

519 (*1883-1888*)

If there "is only one being, the ego" and all other "being" is fashioned after its model—if, finally, belief in the "ego" stands or falls with belief in logic, i.e., the metaphysical truth of the categories of reason; if, on the other hand, the ego proves to be something in a state of becoming: then—

520 (*1885*)

Continual transition forbids us to speak of "individuals," etc; the "number" of beings is itself in flux. We would know nothing of time and motion if we did not, in a coarse fashion, believe we see what is at "rest" beside what is in motion. The same applies to cause and effect, and without the erroneous conception of "empty space" we should certainly not have acquired the conception of space. The principle of identity has behind it the "apparent fact" of things that are the same. A world in a state of becoming could not, in a strict sense, be "comprehended" or "known"; only to the extent that the "comprehending" and "knowing" intellect encounters a coarse, already-created world, fabricated out of mere appearances but become firm to the extent that this kind of appearance has preserved life—only to this extent is there anything like "knowledge"; i.e., a measuring of earlier and later errors by one another.

521 (*Spring-Fall 1887*)

On "logical semblance"— The concepts "individual" and "species" equally false and merely apparent. "Species" expresses only the fact that an abundance of similar creatures appear at the same time and that the tempo of their further growth and change is for a long time slowed down, so actual small continuations and increases are not very much noticed (—a phase of evolution in which the evolution is not visible, so an equilibrium *seems* to have been attained, making possible the false notion *that a goal has been attained*—and that evolution has a goal—).

The form counts as something enduring and therefore more valuable; but the form has merely been invented by us; and however often "the same form is attained," it does not mean that it *is* the same form—what appears is always something new, and it is only we, who are always comparing, who include the new, to the extent that it is similar to the old, in the unity of the "form." As if a *type* should be attained and, as it were, was intended by and inherent in the process of formation.

Form, species, law, idea, purpose—in all these cases the same error is made of giving a false reality to a fiction, as if events were in some way obedient to something—an artificial distinction is made in respect of events between that which acts and that toward which the act is directed (but this "which" and this "toward" are only posited in obedience to our metaphysical-logical dogmatism: they are not "facts").

One should not understand this compulsion to construct concepts, species, forms, purposes, laws ("a world of identical cases") as if they enabled us to fix the *real world;* but as a compulsion to arrange a world for ourselves in which our existence is made possible:—we thereby create a world which is calculable, simplified, comprehensible, etc., for us.

This same compulsion exists in the sense activities that support reason—by simplification, coarsening, emphasizing, and elaborating, upon which all "recognition," all ability to make oneself intelligible rests. Our needs have made our senses so precise that the "same apparent world" always reappears and has thus acquired the semblance of reality.

Our subjective compulsion to believe in logic only reveals that, long before logic itself entered our consciousness, we did nothing but introduce its postulates into events: now we discover them in events—we can no longer do otherwise—and imagine that this compulsion guarantees something connected with "truth." It is we who created the "thing," the "identical thing," subject, attribute, activity, object, substance, form, after we had long pursued the process of making identical, coarse and simple. The world seems logical to us because we have made it logical.

522 (*1886-1887*)

Ultimate solution.— We believe in reason: this, however, is the philosophy of gray *concepts.* Language depends on the most naive prejudices.

Now we read disharmonies and problems into things because we think *only* in the form of language—and thus believe in the "eternal truth" of "reason" (e.g., subject, attribute, etc.)

We cease to think when we refuse to do so under the constraint of language; we barely reach the doubt that sees this limitation as a limitation.

Rational thought is interpretation according to a scheme that we cannot throw off.

6. Consciousness

523 (*March-June 1888*)

Nothing is more erroneous than to make of psychical and physical phenomena the two faces, the two revelations of one and the same substance. Nothing is explained thereby: the concept "substance" is perfectly useless as an explanation. Consciousness in a subsidiary role, almost indifferent, superfluous, perhaps destined to vanish and give way to a perfect automatism—

When we observe only the inner phenomena we may be compared with the deaf-and-dumb, who divine through movements of the lips the words they do not hear. From the phenomena of the inner sense we conclude the existence of invisible and other phenomena that we would apprehend if our means of observation were adequate and that one calls the nerve current.

We[9] lack any sensitive organs for this inner world, so we sense

[9] Not a real sentence in the MS where this paragraph begins: "That an inner world, for which we lack . . ."

a thousandfold complexity as a unity; so we introduce causation where any reason for motion and change remains invisible to us —the sequence of thoughts and feelings is only their becoming-visible in consciousness. That this sequence has anything to do with a causal chain is completely unbelievable: consciousness has never furnished us with an example of cause and effect.

524 (*Nov. 1887-March 1888*)

The role of "consciousness."— It is essential that one should not make a mistake over the role of "consciousness": it is our relation with the "outer world" that evolved it. On the other hand, the direction or protection and care in respect of the co-ordination of the bodily functions does *not* enter our consciousness; any more than spiritual accumulation: that a higher court rules over these things cannot be doubted—a kind of directing committee on which the various chief desires make their votes and power felt. "Pleasure," "displeasure" are hints from this sphere; also the act of will; also ideas.

In summa: That which becomes conscious is involved in causal relations which are entirely withheld from us—the sequence of thoughts, feelings, ideas in consciousness does not signify that this sequence is a causal sequence; but apparently it is so, to the highest degree. Upon this *appearance* we have founded our whole idea of spirit, reason, logic, etc. (—none of these exist: they are fictitious syntheses and unities), and projected these *into* things and *behind* things!

Usually, one takes consciousness itself as the general sensorium and supreme court; nonetheless, it is only a means of communication: it is evolved through social intercourse and with a view to the interests of social intercourse— "Intercourse" here understood to include the influences of the outer world and the reactions they compel on our side; also our effect upon the outer world. It is not the directing agent, but an organ of the directing agent.

525 (*1888*)

My proposition compressed into a formula that smells of antiquity, Christianity, scholasticism, and other muskiness: in the concept "God as *spirit,*" God as perfection is *negated*—

526 (*March-June 1888*)

Where a certain unity obtains in the grouping of things, one has always posited *spirit* as the cause of this coordination: for which notion there is no ground whatever. Why should the idea of a complex fact be one of the conditions of this fact? or why should the *notion* of a complex fact have to precede it as its cause?—

We shall be on our guard against explaining purposiveness in terms of spirit: there is no ground whatever for ascribing to spirit the properties of organization and systematization. The nervous system has a much more extensive domain; the world of consciousness is added to it. Consciousness plays no role in the total process of adaptation and systematization.

527 (*1886-1887*)

Physiologists, like philosophers, believe that consciousness increases in value in proportion as it increases in clarity: the clearest consciousness, the most logical and coldest thinking, is supposed to be of the *first* rank. However—by what measure is this value determined?— In regard to release of will, the most superficial, most simplified thinking is the most useful—it could therefore—etc. (because it leaves few motives over).

Precision in action is antagonistic to far-seeing providentiality, the judgments of which are often uncertain: the latter is led by the deeper instinct.

528 (*1886-1887*)

Principal error of psychologists: they regard the indistinct idea as a lower kind of idea than the distinct: but that which removes itself from our consciousness and for that reason becomes obscure *can* on that account be perfectly clear in itself. Becoming obscure is a matter of perspective of consciousness.

529 (*March-June 1888*)

Tremendous blunders:

1. the absurd overestimation of consciousness, the transfor-

mation of it into a unity, an entity: "spirit," "soul," something that feels, thinks, wills—

2. spirit as cause, especially wherever purposiveness, system, co-ordination appear;

3. consciousness as the highest achieveable form, as the supreme kind of being, as "God";

4. will introduced wherever there are effects;

5. the "real world" as a spiritual world, as accessible through the facts of consciousness;

6. knowledge as uniquely the faculty of consciousness wherever there is knowledge at all.

Consequences:

every advance lies in an advance in becoming conscious; every regression in becoming unconscious; (—becoming unconscious was considered a falling back to the desires and senses —as becoming animal—)

one approaches reality, "real being," through dialectic; one distances oneself from it through the instincts, senses, mechanism—

to resolve man into spirit would mean to make him into God: spirit, will, goodness—all one;

all good must proceed from spirituality, must be a fact of consciousness;

any advance toward the better can only be an advance in becoming conscious.

7. Judgment. True—False

530 (*1883-1888*)

In the case of Kant, theological prejudice, his unconscious dogmatism, his moralistic perspective, were dominant, directing, commanding.

The *prōton pseudos:*[10] how is the fact of knowledge possible? is knowledge a fact at all? what is knowledge? If we do not know what knowledge is, we cannot possibly answer the question whether there is knowledge.— Very well! But if I do not already "know" whether there is knowledge, whether there can be knowledge, I cannot reasonably put the question "what is knowledge?" Kant

[10] First falsehood or original error.

believes in the fact of knowledge: what he wants is a piece of naiveté: knowledge of knowledge!

"Knowledge is judgment!" But judgment is a belief that something is thus and thus! And *not* knowledge! "All knowledge consists of synthetic judgments" of *universal* validity (the case is thus and not otherwise in every case), of *necessary* validity (the opposite of the assertion can never occur).

The legitimacy of belief in knowledge is always presupposed: just as the legitimacy of the feelings of conscience-judgments is presupposed. Here moral ontology is the dominant prejudice.

The conclusion is therefore:

1. there are assertions that we consider universally valid and necessary;

2. necessity and universal validity cannot be derived from experience;

3. consequently they must be founded, not upon experience, but upon something else, and derive from another source of knowledge!

(Kant infers (1) there are assertions which are valid only under a certain condition; (2) this condition is that they derive, not from experience, but from pure reason.)

Therefore: the question is, whence do we derive our reasons for believing in the truth of such assertions? No, how our belief is caused! But the origin of a belief, of a strong conviction, is a psychological problem: and a *very* narrow and limited experience often produces such a belief! It already presupposes that there is not *"data a posteriori"* but also *data a priori,* "preceding experience." Necessity and universal validity could never be given to us by experience: why does that mean that they are present without any experience at all?

There are no isolated judgments!

An isolated judgment is never "true," never knowledge; only in the connection and relation of many judgments is there any surety.

What distinguishes the true from the false belief? What is knowledge? He "knows" it, that is heavenly!

Necessity and universality can never be given by experience! Thus they are independent of experience, prior to all experience! That insight that occurs a priori, therefore independently of all experience, out of sheer reason, is "a *pure* form of knowledge"!

"The basic laws of logic, the law of identity and the law of contradiction, are forms of pure knowledge, because they precede all experience."— But these are not forms of knowledge at all! they are regulative articles of belief.

To establish the a priori character (the pure rationality) of the judgments of mathematics, space must be conceived as a form of pure reason.

Hume had declared: "There are no synthetic a priori judgments." Kant says: But there are! Those of mathematics! And if there are such judgments, perhaps there is also metaphysics, a knowledge of things by pure reason!

Mathematics is possible under conditions under which metaphysics is *never* possible. All human knowlege is either experience or mathematics.

A judgment is synthetic; i.e., it connects different ideas.

It is a priori; i.e., every connection is a universally valid and necessary one, which can never be given by sense perception but only through pure reason.

If there are to be synthetic a priori judgments, then reason must be in a position to make connections: connection is a form. Reason must possess the capacity of giving form.

531 (*1885-1886*)

Judgment is our oldest belief, our most habitual holding-true or holding-untrue, an assertion or denial, a certainty that something is thus and not otherwise, a belief that here we really "know"— what is it that is believed true in all judgments?

What are attributes?— We have not regarded change in us as change but as an "in itself" that is foreign to us, that we merely "perceive": and we have posited it, not as an event, but as a being, as a "quality"—and in addition invented an entity to which it adheres; i.e., we have regarded the *effect* as something that *effects,* and this we have regarded as a being. But even in this formulation, the concept "effect" is arbitrary: for those changes that take place in us, and that we firmly believe we have not ourselves caused, we merely infer to be effects, in accordance with the conclusion: "every change must have an author";—but this conclusion is already mythology: it separates that which effects from the effecting. If I say "lightning flashes," I have posited the flash once as an activity and a second time as a subject, and thus added to the event a being that is not one with the event but is rather fixed, *is,* and does not "become."— To regard an event as an "effecting," and this as being, that is the double error, or interpretation, of which we are guilty.

532 (*1885*)

Judgment—this is the belief: "This and that are so." Thus there is in every judgment the avowal of having encountered an "identical case": it therefore presupposes comparison with the aid of memory. The judgment does not produce the appearance of an identical case. Rather it believes it perceives one: it works under the presupposition that identical cases exist. Now, what is that function that must be much older and must have been at work much earlier, that makes cases identical and similar which are in themselves dissimilar? What is that second function, which on the basis of the first, etc. "Whatever arouses the same sensation is the same": but what is it that makes sensations the same, "accepts" them as the same? There could be no judgments at all if a kind of equalization were not practiced within sensations: memory is possible only with a continual emphasizing of what is already familiar, experienced.— Before judgment occurs, the process of assimilation must already have taken place; thus here, too, there is an intellectual activity that does not enter consciousness, as pain does as a consequence of a wound. Probably an inner event corresponds to each organic function; hence assimilation, rejection, growth, etc.

Essential: to start from the *body* and employ it as guide. It is the much richer phenomenon, which allows of clearer observation. Belief in the body is better established than belief in the spirit.

"No matter how strongly a thing may be believed, strength of belief is no criterion of truth." But what is truth? Perhaps a kind of belief that has become a condition of life? In that case, to be sure, strength could be a criterion; e.g., in regard to causality.

533 (*Spring-Fall 1887*)

Logical certainty, transparency, as criterion of truth ("*omne illud verum est, quod clare et distincte percipitur.*"[11]—Descartes):

---

[11] All that is true which is perceived clearly and distinctly.

with that, the mechanical hypothesis concerning the world is desired and credible.

But this is a crude confusion: like *simplex sigillum veri.*[12] How does one know that the real nature of things stands in *this* relation to our intellect?— Could it not be otherwise? that it is the hypothesis that gives the intellect the greatest feeling of power and security, that is most preferred, valued and consequently characterized as true?— The intellect posits its freest and strongest capacity and capability as criterion of the most valuable, consequently of the true—

"True": from the standpoint of feeling—: that which excites the feeling most strongly ("ego");

from the standpoint of thought—: that which gives thought the greatest feeling of strength;

from the standpoint of touch, seeing, hearing—: that which calls for the greatest resistance.

Thus it is the highest degrees of performance that awaken belief in the "truth," that is to say reality, of the object. The feeling of strength, of struggle, of resistance convinces us that there is something that is here being resisted.

534 (*1887-1888*)

The criterion of truth resides in the enhancement of the feeling of power.

535 (*1885*)[13]

"Truth": this, according to my way of thinking, does not necessarily denote the antithesis of error, but in the most fundamental cases only the posture of various errors in relation to one another. Perhaps one is older, more profound than another, even ineradicable, in so far as an organic entity of our species could not live without it; while other errors do not tyrannize over us in this way as conditions of life, but on the contrary when compared with such "tyrants" can be set aside and "refuted."

An assumption that is irrefutable—why should it for that reason be "true"? This proposition may perhaps outrage logicians,

[12] Simplicity is the seal of truth.
[13] MS not in Nietzsche's hand; evidently dictated.

who posit *their* limitations as the limitations of things: but I long ago declared war on this optimism of logicians.

536 (*Jan.-Fall 1888*)

Everything simple is merely imaginary, is not "true." But whatever is real, whatever is true, is neither one nor even reducible to one.

537 (*1885-1888*)

What is truth?—Inertia; that hypothesis which gives rise to contentment; smallest expenditure of spiritual force, etc.

538 (*1883-1888*)

First proposition. The easier mode of thought conquers the harder mode;—as dogma: *simplex sigillum veri.—Dico:*[14] to suppose that clarity proves anything about truth is perfect childishness—

Second proposition. The doctrine of being, of things, of all sorts of fixed unities is a hundred times easier than the doctrine of becoming, of development—

Third proposition. Logic was intended as facilitation; as a means of expression—not as truth— Later it acquired the effect of truth—

539 (*March-June 1888*)

Parmenides said, "one cannot think of what is not";—we are at the other extreme, and say "what can be thought of must certainly be a fiction."[15]

540 (*1885*)

There are many kinds of eyes. Even the sphinx has eyes—and consequently there are many kinds of "truths," and consequently there is no truth.

---

[14] I say.

[15] In the MS an incomplete sentence follows: "thinking has no relation [reading uncertain] to what is real, but only to. . . ."

541 (*March-June 1888*)

Inscriptions for the Door of a Modern Madhouse

"What is thought necessarily is morally necessary." Herbert Spencer.

"The ultimate test of the truth of a proposition is the inconceivability of its negation." Herbert Spencer.[16]

542 (*Nov. 1887-March 1888*)

If the character of existence should be false—which would be possible—what would truth, all our truth, be then?— An unconscionable falsification of the false? The false raised to a higher power?—

543 (*Nov. 1887-March 1888*)

In a world that is essentially false, truthfulness would be an antinatural tendency: such a tendency could have meaning only as a means to a higher power of falsehood. In order for a world of the true, of being, to be invented, the truthful man would first have to be created (including the fact that such a man believes himself "truthful").

Simple, transparent, not in contradiction with himself, durable, remaining always the same, without wrinkle, volt, concealment, form: a man of this kind conceives a world of being as "God" in his own image.

For truthfulness to be possible, the whole sphere of man must be very clean, small and, respectable; advantage in every sense must be with the truthful man.— Lies, deception, dissimulation must arouse astonishment—

544 (*1885-1887; rev. Spring-Fall 1888*)

Increase in "dissimulation" proportionate to the rising order of rank of creatures. It seems to be lacking in the inorganic world—power against power, quite crudely—cunning begins in the organic world; plants are already masters of it. The highest human beings,

[16] Quotations translated from Nietzsche's German.

such as Caesar, Napoleon (Stendhal's remark on him),[17] also the higher races (Italians), the Greeks (Odysseus); a thousandfold craftiness belongs to the essence of the enhancement of man— Problem of the actor. My Dionysus ideal— The perspective of all organic functions, all the strongest instincts of life: the force in all life that *wills* error; error as the precondition even of thought. Before there is "thought" there must have been "invention";[18] the *construction* of identical cases, of the appearance of sameness, is more primitive than the *knowledge* of sameness.

8. Against Causalism

545 (*1885*)

I believe in absolute space as the substratum of force: the latter limits and forms. Time eternal. But space and time do not exist in themselves. "Changes" are only appearances (or sense processes for us); if we posit the recurrence of these, however regular, nothing is established thereby except this simple fact, that it has always happened thus. The feeling that *post hoc* is *propter hoc* can easily be shown to be a misunderstanding; it is comprehensible. But appearances cannot be "causes"!

546 (*1885-1886*)

The interpretation of an event as either an act or the suffering of an act (—thus every act a suffering) says: every change, every

---

[17] Nietzsche copied a passage from Stendhal's *Vie de Napoléon* ("Life of Napoleon," Preface, p. *xv*) into another notebook: "*Une croyance presque instinctive chez moi c'est que tout homme puissant ment quand il parle et à plus forte raison quand il écrit*" (An almost instinctive faith with me that every powerful man lies when he speaks and the more when he writes).

[18] *Bevor "gedacht" wird, muss schon "gedichtet" worden sein.* The phrase *Das Volk der Dichter und Denker* (*gedacht* is the past participle of *denken*) means "the people of thinkers and poets," and *dichten* usually means writing poetry. But the title of Goethe's autobiographical *Dichtung und Wahrheit* means "Fiction and Truth" no less than "Poetry and Truth," and *erdichten* generally means to make up, to invent. In the present work *erdichtet* has generally been rendered as invented; but this is a good place to insist that this translation loses some essential overtones: the emphatic contrast with reality-in-itself is intended by Nietzsche, but he also means to stress the quasi-poetic function of the imagination.

becoming-other, presupposes an author and someone upon whom "change" is effected.

547 (*1885-1886*)

Psychological history of the concept "subject." The body, the thing, the "whole" construed by the eye, awaken the distinction between a deed and a doer; the doer, the cause of the deed, conceived ever more subtly, finally left behind the "subject."

548 (*1885-1886*)

Our bad habit of taking a mnemonic, an abbreviative formula, to be an entity, finally as a cause, e.g., to say of lightning "it flashes." Or the little word "I." To make a kind of perspective in seeing the cause of seeing: that was what happened in the invention of the "subject," the "I"!

549 (*1885*)

"Subject," "object," "attribute"—these distinctions are fabricated and are now imposed as a schematism upon all the apparent facts. The fundamental false observation is that I believe it is *I* who do something, suffer something, "have" something, "have" a quality.

550 (*1885-1886*)

In every judgment there resides the entire, full, profound belief in subject and attribute, or in cause and effect (that is, as the assertion that every effect is an activity and that every activity presupposes an agent); and this latter belief is only a special case of the former, so there remains as the fundamental belief the belief that there are subjects, that everything that happens is related attributively to some subject.[19]

I notice something and seek a reason for it; this means originally: I seek an intention in it, and above all someone who has intentions, a subject, a doer: every event a deed—formerly

[19] The first paragraph represents a collage from two similar versions and was put together by the German editors.

one saw intentions in all events, this is our oldest habit. Do animals also possess it? As living beings, must they not also rely on interpretations based on *themselves?*—

The question "why?" is always a question after the *causa finalis,*[20] after the "what for?" We have no "sense for the *causa efficiens*":[21] here Hume was right; habit (but not only that of the individual!) makes us expect that a certain often-observed occurrence will follow another: nothing more! That which gives the extraordinary firmness to our belief in causality is not the great habit of seeing one occurrence following another but our inability to interpret events otherwise than as events caused by intentions. It is belief in the living and thinking as the only effective force—in will, in intention—it is belief that every event is a deed, that every deed presupposes a doer, it is belief in the "subject." Is this belief in the concept of subject and attribute not a great stupidity?

Question: is intention the cause of an event? Or is that also illusion?

Is it not the event itself?

551 (*March-June 1888*)

Critique of the concept "cause."[22]— We have absolutely no experience of a cause; psychologically considered, we derive the entire concept from the subjective conviction that *we* are causes, namely, that the arm moves— But that is an error. We separate ourselves, the doers, from the deed, and we make use of this pattern everywhere—we seek a doer for every event. What is it we have done? We have misunderstood the feeling of strength, tension, resistance, a muscular feeling that is already the beginning of the act, as the cause, or we have taken the will to do this or that for a cause because the action follows upon it—cause, i.e.,——

There is no such thing as "cause"; some cases in which

---

[20] Final cause or purpose.

[21] Efficient cause.

[22] Before the beginning of this section Nietzsche later added: "I require the starting point of 'will to power' as the origin of motion. Hence motion may not be conditioned from the outside—not caused——I require beginnings and centers of motion from which the will spreads—" (1911, p. 507).

it seemed to be given us, and in which we have projected it out of ourselves in order to understand an event, have been shown to be self-deceptions. Our "understanding of an event" has consisted in our inventing a subject which was made responsible for something that happens and for how it happens. We have combined our feeling of will, our feeling of "freedom," our feeling of responsibility and our intention to perform an act, into the concept "cause": *causa efficiens* and *causa finalis* are fundamentally one.

We believed that an effect was explained when a condition was detected in which the effect was already inherent. In fact, we invent all causes after the schema of the effect: the latter is known to us— Conversely, we are not in a position to predict of any thing what it will "effect." The thing, the subject, will, intention—all inherent in the conception "cause." We search for things in order to explain why something has changed. Even the atom is this kind of super-added "thing" and "primitive subject"—

At length we grasp that things—consequently atoms, too—effect nothing: because they do not exist at all—that the concept of causality is completely useless.— A necessary sequence of states does not imply a causal relationship between them (—that would mean making their effective capacity leap from 1 to 2, to 3, to 4, to 5). There are neither causes nor effects. Linguistically we do not know how to rid ourselves of them. But that does not matter. If I think of the muscle apart from its "effects," I negate it—

In summa: an event is neither effected nor does it effect. *Causa* is a capacity to produce effects that has been super-added to the events—

Interpretation by causality a deception— A "thing" is the sum of its effects, synthetically united by a concept, an image. In fact, science has emptied the concept causality of its content and retained it as a formula of an equation, in which it has become at bottom a matter of indifference on which side cause is placed and on which side effect. It is asserted that in two complex states (constellations of force) the quanta of force remain constant.

The *calculability of an event* does not reside in the fact that a rule is adhered to, or that a necessity is obeyed, or that a law of causality has been projected by us into every event: it resides in the *recurrence of "identical cases."*

There is no such thing as a sense of causality, as Kant thinks. One is surprised, one is disturbed, one desires something familiar to hold on to— As soon as we are shown something old in the new, we are calmed. The supposed instinct for causality is only fear of the unfamiliar and the attempt to discover something familiar in it—a search, not for causes, but for the familiar.

552 (*Spring-Fall 1887*)

Against determinism and teleology.— From the fact that something ensues regularly and ensues calculably, it does not follow that it ensues *necessarily*. That a quantum of force determines and conducts itself in every particular case in one way and manner does not make it into an "unfree will." "Mechanical necessity" is not a fact: it is we who first interpreted it into events. We have interpreted the formulatable character of events as the consequence of a necessity that rules over events. But from the fact that I do a certain thing, it by no means follows that I am compelled to do it. Compulsion in things certainly cannot be demonstrated: the rule proves only that one and the same event is not another event as well. Only because we have introduced subjects, "doers," into things does it appear that all events are the consequences of compulsion exerted upon subjects—exerted by whom? again by a "doer." Cause and effect—a dangerous concept so long as one thinks of something that causes and something upon which an effect is produced.

a. Necessity is not a fact but an interpretation.

*

b. When one has grasped that the "subject" is not something that creates effects, but only a fiction, much follows.

It is only after the model of the subject that we have invented the reality of things and projected them into the medley of sensations. If we no longer believe in the effective subject, then belief also disappears in effective things, in reciprocation, cause and effect between those phenomena that we call things.

There also disappears, of course, the world of effective atoms: the assumption of which always depended on the supposition that one needed subjects.

At last, the "thing-in-itself" also disappears, because this is fundamentally the conception of a "subject-in-itself." But we have grasped that the subject is a fiction. The antithesis "thing-in-itself" and "appearance" is untenable; with that, however, the concept "appearance" also disappears.

*

c. If we give up the effective subject, we also give up the object upon which effects are produced. Duration, identity with itself, being are inherent neither in that which is called subject nor in that which is called object: they are complexes of events apparently durable in comparison with other complexes—e.g., through the difference in tempo of the event (rest—motion, firm—loose: opposites that do not exist in themselves and that actually express only variations in degree that from a certain perspective appear to be opposites. There are no opposites:[23] only from those of logic do we derive the concept of opposites—and falsely transfer it to things).

d. If we give up the concept "subject" and "object," then also the concept "substance"—and as a consequence also the various modifications of it, e.g., "matter," "spirit," and other hypothetical entities, "the eternity and immutability of matter," etc. We have got rid of *materiality*.

*

From the standpoint of morality, the world is false. But to the extent that morality itself is a part of this world, morality is false.

Will to truth is a making firm, a making true and durable, an abolition of the false character of things, a reinterpretation of it into beings. "Truth" is therefore not something there, that might be found or discovered—but something that must be created and that gives a name to a process, or rather to a will to overcome that has in itself no end—introducing truth, as a *processus in infinitum,* an active determining—not a becoming-conscious of something that is in itself firm and determined. It is a word for the "will to power."

Life is founded upon the premise of a belief in enduring and regularly recurring things; the more powerful life is, the wider must be the knowable world to which we, as it were, attrib-

[23] Cf. *Beyond,* section 2.

ute being. Logicizing, rationalizing, systematizing as expedients of life.

Man projects his drive to truth, his "goal" in a certain sense, outside himself as a world that has being, as a metaphysical world, as a "thing-in-itself," as a world already in existence. His needs as creator invent the world upon which he works, anticipate it; this anticipation (this "belief" in truth) is his support.

*

All events, all motion, all becoming, as a determination of degrees and relations of force, as a *struggle*—

*

As soon as we imagine someone who is responsible for our being thus and thus, etc. (God, nature), and therefore attribute to him the intention that we should exist and be happy or wretched, we corrupt for ourselves the *innocence of becoming*.[24] We then have someone who wants to achieve something through us and with us.

*

The "'welfare of the individual" is just as imaginary as the "welfare of the species": the former is *not* sacrificed to the latter, species viewed from a distance is just as transient as the individual. "Preservation of the species" is only a consequence of the growth of the species, i.e., the overcoming of the species on the road to a stronger type.

*

[Theses.—][25] That the apparent "purposiveness" ("that purposiveness which endlessly surpasses all the arts of man") is merely the consequence of the will to power manifest in all events; that becoming stronger involves an ordering process which looks like a sketchy purposiveness; that apparent ends are not intentional but, as soon as dominion is established over a lesser power and the latter operates as a function of the greater power, an order of rank, of

[24] *Unschuld des Werdens*—used as a title for a popular German two-volume edition of selections from Nietzsche's notes not included in *The Will to Power*.

[25] The word I have placed in brackets was supplied by the German editors.

organization is bound to produce the appearance of an order of means and ends.

Against apparent "*necessity*":

—this is only an expression for the fact that a force is not also something else.

Against apparent "*purposiveness*":

—the latter only an expression for an order of spheres of power and their interplay.

9. Thing-in-Itself and Appearance

553 (*1886-1887*)

The sore spot of Kant's critical philosophy has gradually become visible even to dull eyes: Kant no longer has a right to his distinction "appearance" and "thing-in-itself"—he had deprived himself of the right to go on distinguishing in this old familiar way, in so far as he rejected as impermissible making inferences from phenomena to a cause of phenomena—in accordance with his conception of causality and its purely intra-phenomenal validity—which conception, on the other hand, already anticipates this distinction, as if the "thing-in-itself" were not only inferred but *given*.

554 (*1885-1886*)

Causalism.[26]— It is obvious that things-in-themselves cannot be related to one another as cause and effect, nor can appearance be so related to appearance; from which it follows that in a philosophy that believes in things-in-themselves and appearances the concept "cause and effect" *cannot be applied*. Kant's mistakes—— In fact, the concept "cause and effect" derives, psychologically speaking, only from a mode of thought that believes that always and everywhere will operates upon will—that believes only in living things and fundamentally only in "*souls*" (and *not* in things). Within the mechanistic view of the world (which is logic and its application to space and time), that concept is reduced to the formulas of mathematics—with which, as one must emphasize

---

[26] Title omitted in all printed versions.

again and again, nothing is ever comprehended, but rather designated and distorted.[27]

555 (*1885-1886*)

Against the scientific prejudice.[28]— The biggest fable of all is the fable of knowledge. One would like to know what things-in-themselves are; but behold, there are no things-in-themselves! But even supposing there were an in-itself, an unconditioned thing, it would for that very reason be unknowable! Something unconditioned cannot be known; otherwise it would not be unconditioned! Coming to know, however, is always "placing oneself in a conditional relation to something"——one who seeks to know the unconditioned desires that it should not concern him, and that this same something should be of no concern to anyone. This involves a contradiction, first, between *wanting* to know and the desire that it not concern us (but why know at all, then?) and, secondly, because something that is of no concern to anyone *is* not at all, and thus cannot be known at all.—

Coming to know means "to place oneself in a conditional relation to something"; to feel oneself conditioned by something and oneself to condition it—it is therefore under all circumstances establishing, denoting, and making-conscious of conditions (not forthcoming entities, things, what is "in-itself").

556 (*1885-1886*)

A "thing-in-itself" just as perverse as a "sense-in-itself," a "meaning-in-itself." There are no "facts-in-themselves," for a sense must always be projected into them before there can be "facts."

The question "what is that?" is an imposition of meaning from some other viewpoint. "Essence," the "essential nature," is something perspective and already presupposes a multiplicity. At the bottom of it there always lies "what is that for *me*?" (for us, for all that lives, etc.)

A thing would be defined once all creatures had asked "what is that?" and had answered their question. Supposing one single

---

[27] *Bezeichnet, verzeichnet*: the last word *could* also mean "registered," but in this context certainly doesn't.

[28] Title omitted in all previous versions.

creature, with its own relationships and perspectives for all things, were missing, then the thing would not yet be "defined."

In short: the essence of a thing is only an *opinion* about the "thing." Or rather: "it is considered" is the real "it is," the sole "this is."

One may not ask: "who then interprets?" for the interpretation itself is a form of the will to power, exists (but not as a "being" but as a process, a becoming) as an affect.

The origin of "things" is wholly the work of that which imagines, thinks, wills, feels. The concept "thing" itself just as much as all its qualities.— Even "the subject" is such a created entity, a "thing" like all others: a simplification with the object of defining the force which posits, invents, thinks, as distinct from all individual positing, inventing, thinking as such. Thus a capacity as distinct from all that is individual—fundamentally, action collectively considered with respect to all anticipated actions (action and the probability of similar actions).

557 (*1885-1886*)

The properties of a thing are effects on other "things":
if one removes other "things," then a thing has no properties,
i.e., there is no thing without other things,
i.e., there is no "thing-in-itself."

558 (*Spring-Fall 1887*)

The "thing-in-itself" nonsensical. If I remove all the relationships, all the "properties," all the "activities" of a thing, the thing does not remain over; because thingness has only been invented by us owing to the requirements of logic, thus with the aim of defining, communication (to bind together the multiplicity of relationships, properties, activities).

559 (*Nov. 1887-March 1888*)

"Things that have a constitution in themselves"—a dogmatic idea with which one must break absolutely.

560 (*Spring-Fall 1887*)

That things possess a constitution in themselves quite apart from interpretation and subjectivity, is a quite idle hypothesis: it presupposes that interpretation and subjectivity are not essential, that a thing freed from all relationships would still be a thing.

Conversely, the apparent *objective* character of things: could it not be merely a difference of degree within the subjective?—that perhaps that which changes slowly presents itself to us as "objectively" enduring, being, "in-itself"—that the objective is only a false concept of a genus and an antithesis *within* the subjective?

561 (*1885-1886*)

Suppose all unity were unity only as an organization? But the "thing" in which we believe was only invented as a foundation for the various attributes. If the thing "effects," that means: we conceive all the other properties which are present and momentarily latent, as the cause of the emergence of one single property; i.e., we take the sum of its properties— "*x*"—as cause of the property "*x*": which is utterly stupid and mad!

All unity is unity only as organization and co-operation—just as a human community is a unity—as opposed to an atomistic anarchy, as a pattern of domination that *signifies* a unity but *is* not a unity.

562 (*1883-1888*)

"In the development of thought a point had to be reached at which one realized that what one called the properties of things were sensations of the feeling subject: at this point the properties ceased to belong to the thing." The "thing-in-itself" remained. The distinction between the thing-in-itself and the thing-for-us is based on the older, naive form of perception which granted energy to things; but analysis revealed that even force was only projected into them, and likewise—substance. "The thing affects a subject"? Root of the idea of substance in language, not in beings outside us! The thing-in-itself is no problem at all!

Beings will have to be thought of as sensations that are no longer based on something devoid of sensation.

In motion, no new *content* is given to sensation. That which is, cannot contain motion: therefore it is a *form* of being.

N.B. The explanation of an event can be sought firstly:
through mental images of the event that precede it (aims);

secondly: through mental images that succeed it (the mathematical-physical explanation).

One should not confuse the two. Thus: the physical explanation, which is a symbolization of the world by means of sensation and thought, can in itself never account for the origin of sensation and thought; rather physics must construe the world of feeling consistently as lacking feeling and aim—right up to the highest human being. And teleology is only a history of purposes and never physical!

563 (*1886-1887*)

Our "knowing" limits itself to establishing quantities; but we cannot help feeling these differences in quantity as qualities. Quality is a perspective truth for *us;* not an "in-itself."

Our senses have a definite quantum as a mean within which they function; i.e., we sense bigness and smallness in relation to the conditions of our existence. If we sharpened or blunted our senses tenfold, we should perish; i.e., with regard to making possible our existence we sense even relations between magnitudes as qualities.

564 (*1885-1886*)

Might all quantities not be signs of qualities? A greater power implies a different consciousness, feeling, desiring, a different perspective; growth itself is a desire to be more; the desire for an increase in quantum grows from a *quale;*[29] in a purely quantitative world everything would be dead, stiff, motionless.—The reduction of all qualities to quantities is nonsense: what appears is that the one accompanies the other, an analogy—

565 (*Fall 1886*)

Qualities are insurmountable barriers for us; we cannot help feeling that mere quantitative differences are something fundamentally distinct from quantity, namely that they are *qualities* which can no longer be reduced to one another. But everything for which the word "knowledge" makes any sense refers to the domain of reckoning, weighing, measuring, to the domain of

[29] How constituted? or of what quality?

quantity; while, on the other hand, all our sensations of value (i.e., simply our sensations) adhere precisely to qualities, i.e., to our perspective "truths" which belong to us alone and can by no means be "known"! It is obvious that every creature different from us senses different qualities and consequently lives in a different world from that in which we live. Qualities are an idiosyncrasy peculiar to man; to demand that our human interpretations and values should be universal and perhaps constitutive values is one of the hereditary madnesses of human pride.

566 (*Nov. 1887-March 1888*)

The "real world," however one has hitherto conceived it—it has always been the apparent world *once again.*[30]

567 (*March-June 1888*)

The apparent world, i.e., a world viewed according to values; ordered, selected according to values, i.e., in this case according to the viewpoint of utility in regard to the preservation and enhancement of the power of a certain species of animal.

The perspective therefore decides the character of the "appearance"! As if a world would still remain over after one deducted the perspective! By doing that one would deduct relativity!

Every center of force adopts a perspective toward the entire remainder, i.e., its own particular valuation, mode of action, and mode of resistance. The "apparent world," therefore, is reduced to a specific mode of action on the world, emanating from a center.

Now there is no other mode of action whatever; and the "world" is only a word for the totality of these actions. Reality consists precisely in this particular action and reaction of every individual part toward the whole—

No shadow of a right remains to speak here of *appearance*—

The specific mode of reacting is the only mode of reacting; we do not know how many and what kinds of other modes there are.

But there is no "other," no "true," no essential being—for this would be the expression of a world *without* action and reaction—

---

[30] This section and those immediately following should be compared with *Twilight,* Chapters III and IV (*Portable Nietzsche,* p. 479 *ff*).

The antithesis of the apparent world and the true world is reduced to the antithesis "world" and "nothing."—

568 (*March-June 1888*)

Critique of the concept "true and apparent world."— Of these, the first is a mere fiction, constructed of fictitious entities.

"Appearance" itself belongs to reality: it is a form of its being; i.e., in a world where there is no being, a certain calculable world of identical cases must first be created through appearance: a tempo at which observation and comparison are possible, etc.

Appearance is an arranged and simplified world, at which our practical instincts have been at work; it is perfectly true for *us;* that is to say, we live, we are able to live in it: proof of its truth for us—

the world, apart from our condition of living in it, the world that we have not reduced to our being, our logic and psychological prejudices, does not exist as a world "in-itself"; it is essentially a world of relationships; under certain conditions it has a differing aspect from every point; its being is essentially different from every point; it presses upon every point, every point resists it—and the sum[31] of these is in every case quite incongruent.

The measure of power determines what being possesses the other measure of power; in what form, force, constraint it acts or resists.

Our particular case is interesting enough: we have produced a conception in order to be able to live in a world, in order to perceive just enough to endure it—

569 (*Spring-Fall 1887*)

Our psychological perspective is determined by the following:

1. that communication is necessary, and that for there to be communication something has to be firm, simplified, capable of precision (above all in the [so-called][32] *identical* case). For it to be communicable, however, it must be experienced as adapted, as "recognizable." The material of the senses adapted by the understanding, reduced to rough outlines, made similar, sub-

---

[31] The reading of this word is doubtful.

[32] The word I have placed in brackets was supplied by the German editors.

sumed under related matters. Thus the fuzziness and chaos of sense impressions are, as it were, logicized;

2. the world of "phenomena" is the adapted world which we feel to be real. The "reality" lies in the continual recurrence of identical, familiar, related things in their logicized character, in the belief that here we are able to reckon and calculate;

3. the antithesis of this phenomenal world is not "the true world," but the formless unformulable world of the chaos of sensations—*another kind* of phenomenal world, a kind "unknowable" for us;

4. questions, what things "in-themselves" may be like, apart from our sense receptivity and the activity of our understanding, must be rebutted with the question: how could we know that things exist? "Thingness" was first created by us. The question is whether there could not be many other ways of creating such an apparent world—and whether this creating, logicizing, adapting, falsifying is not itself the best-guaranteed reality; in short, whether that which "posits things" is not the sole reality; and whether the "effect of the external world upon us" is not also only the result of such active subjects— The other "entities" act upon us; our adapted apparent world is an adaptation and overpowering of their actions; a kind of defensive measure. The subject alone is demonstrable; hypothesis that only subjects exist—that "object" is only a kind of effect produced by a subject upon a subject—a *modus* of *the subject.*

10. Metaphysical Need

570 (*Nov. 1887-March 1888*)

If one is a philosopher as men have always been philosophers, one cannot see what has been and becomes—one sees only what *is*. But since nothing *is*, all that was left to the philosopher as his "world" was the imaginary.

571 (*Spring-Fall 1887; rev. Spring-Fall 1888*)

To assert the existence as a whole of things of which we know nothing whatever, precisely because there is an advantage in not being able to know anything of them, was a piece of naiveté of Kant, resulting from needs, mainly moral-metaphysical.

572 (*1883-1888*)

An artist cannot endure reality, he looks away from it, back: he seriously believes that the value of a thing resides in that shadowy residue one derives from colors, form, sound, ideas; he believes that the more subtilized, attenuated, transient a thing or a man is, the more valuable he becomes; the less real, the more valuable. This is Platonism, which, however, involved yet another bold reversal: Plato measured the degree of reality by the degree of value and said: The more "Idea," the more being. He reversed the concept "reality" and said: "What you take for real is an error, and the nearer we approach the 'Idea,' the nearer we approach 'truth.' "— Is this understood? It was the greatest of rebaptisms; and because it has been adopted by Christianity we do not recognize how astonishing it is. Fundamentally, Plato, as the artist he was, preferred appearance to being! lie and invention to truth! the unreal to the actual! But he was so convinced of the value of appearance that he gave it the attributes "being," "causality" and "goodness," and "truth," in short everything men value.

The concept of value itself considered as a cause: first insight.

The ideal granted all honorific attributes: second insight.

573 (*Jan.-Fall 1888*)

The idea of the "true world" or of "God" as absolutely immaterial, spiritual, good, is an emergency measure necessary while the opposite instincts are still all-powerful—

The degree of moderation and humanity attained is exactly reflected in the humanization of the gods: the Greeks of the strongest epoch, who were not afraid of themselves but rejoiced in themselves, brought their gods close to all their own affects—.

The spiritualization of the idea of God is therefore far from being a sign of *progress*: one is heartily conscious of this when considering Goethe—in his case, the vaporization of God into virtue and spirit is felt as being on a *coarser* level—

574 (*1883-1888*)

Senselessness of all metaphysics as the derivation of the conditioned from the unconditioned.

It is in the nature of thinking that it thinks of and invents the unconditioned as an adjunct to the conditioned; just as it thought of and invented the "ego" as an adjunct to the multiplicity of its processes; it measures the world according to magnitudes posited by itself—such fundamental fictions as "the unconditional," "ends and means," "things," "substances," logical laws, numbers and forms.

There would be nothing that could be called knowledge if thought did not first re-form the world in this way into "things," into what is self-identical. Only because there is thought is there untruth.

Thought cannot be derived, any more than sensations can be; but that does not mean that its primordiality or "being-in-itself" has been proved! all that is established is that we cannot get beyond it, because we *have* nothing but thought and sensation.

575 (*1885-1886*)

"Knowledge" is a referring back: in its essence a *regressus in infinitum*. That which comes to a standstill (at a supposed *causa prima*, at something unconditioned, etc.) is laziness, weariness——

576 (*1883-1888*)

Psychology of metaphysics: the influence of timidity.

That which has been feared the most, the cause of the most powerful suffering (lust to rule, sex, etc.),[33] has been treated by men with the greatest amount of hostility and eliminated from the "true" world. Thus they have eliminated the affects one by one—posited God as the antithesis of evil, that is, placed reality in the negation of the desires and affects (i.e., in *nothingness*).

In the same way, they have hated the irrational, the arbitrary, the accidental (as the causes of immeasurable physical suffering). As a consequence, they negated this element in being-in-itself and conceived it as absolute "rationality" and "purposiveness."

In the same way, they have feared change, transitoriness: this expresses a straitened soul, full of mistrust and evil experiences (the case of Spinoza: an opposite kind of man would account change a stimulus).

A creature overloaded and *playing* with force would call

---

[33] Cf. the chapter "On the Three Evils" in *Zarathustra*, III (*Portable Nietzsche*, p. 298 *ff*).

precisely the affects, irrationality, and change good in a eudaemonistic sense, together with their consequences: danger, contrast, perishing, etc.

577 (*Spring-Fall 1887*)

Against the value of that which remains eternally the same (*vide* Spinoza's naiveté; Descartes' also), the values of the briefest and most transient, the seductive flash of gold on the belly of the serpent *vita*[34]—

578 (*Spring-Fall 1887*)

Moral values even in theory of knowledge:

trust in reason—why not mistrust?

the "true world" is supposed to be the good world—why?

appearance, change, contradiction, struggle devalued as immoral; desire for a world in which these things are missing;

the transcendental world invented, in order that a place remains for "moral freedom" (in Kant);

dialectic a way to virtue (in Plato and Socrates: evidently because Sophistry counted as the way to immorality);

time and space ideal: consequently "unity" in the essence of things; consequently no "sin," no evil, no imperfection —a justification of God;

Epicurus denied the possibility of knowledge, in order to retain moral (or hedonistic) values as the highest values. Augustine, later Pascal ("corrupted reason"), did the same for the benefit of Christian values;

Descartes' contempt for everything that changes; also that of Spinoza.

579 (*1883-1888*)

Psychology of metaphysics.— This world is apparent: consequently there is a true world;—this world is conditional: consequently there is an unconditioned world;—this world is full of contradiction: consequently there is a world free of contradiction;—this world is a world of becoming: consequently there is a world of

---

[34] Life.

being:—all false conclusions (blind trust in reason: if *A* exists, then the opposite concept *B* must also exist). It is suffering that inspires these conclusions: fundamentally they are *desires* that such a world should exist; in the same way, to imagine another, more valuable world is an expression of hatred for a world that makes one suffer: the *ressentiment* of metaphysicians against actuality is here creative.

Second series of questions: *for what* is there suffering?—and from this a conclusion is derived concerning the relation of the true world to our apparent, changing, suffering, contradictory world: (1) Suffering as a consequence of error: how is error possible? (2) Suffering as a consequence of guilt: how is guilt possible? (—experiences derived from nature or society universalized and projected to the sphere of "in-itself"). If, however, the conditioned world is causally conditioned by the unconditioned world, then freedom to err and incur guilt must also be conditioned by it: and again one asks, *what for?*— The world of appearance, becoming, contradiction, suffering, is therefore *willed: what for*?

The error in these conclusions: two opposite concepts are constructed—because one of them corresponds to a reality, the other "must" also correspond to a reality. "Whence should one derive this opposite concept if this were not so?"— Reason is thus a source of revelation concerning being-in-itself.

But the origin of these antitheses need not necessarily go back to a supernatural source of reason: it is sufficient to oppose to it the real genesis of the concepts. This derives from the practical sphere, the sphere of utility; hence the strength of the faith it inspires (one would perish if one did not reason according to this mode of reason; but this is no "proof" of what it asserts).

The preoccupation with suffering on the part of metaphysicians—is quite naive. "Eternal bliss": psychological nonsense. Brave and creative men *never* consider pleasure and pain as ultimate values—they are epiphenomena: one must *desire* both if one is to achieve anything—. That they see the problem of pleasure and pain in the foreground reveals something weary and sick in metaphysicians and religious people. Even morality is so important to them only because they see in it an essential condition for the abolition of suffering.

In the same way, their preoccupation with appearance and error: cause of suffering, superstition that happiness attends truth (confusion: happiness in "certainty," in "faith").

580 (*Spring-Fall 1887*)

To what extent the basic epistemological positions (materialism, idealism) are consequences of evaluations: the source of the supreme feelings of pleasure ("feelings of value") as decisive also for the problem of reality!

—The measure of positive knowledge is quite subsidiary or a matter of indifference: as witness the development of India.

The Buddhistic negation of reality in general (appearance = suffering) is perfectly consistent: undemonstrability, inaccessibility, lack of categories not only for a "'world-in-itself," but an insight into the erroneous procedures by means of which this whole concept is arrived at. "Absolute reality," "being-in-itself" a contradiction. In a world of becoming, "reality" is always only a simplification for practical ends, or a deception through the coarseness of organs, or a variation in the tempo of becoming.

Logical world-denial and nihilation[35] follow from the fact that we have to oppose non-being with being and that the concept "becoming" is denied. ("*Something*" becomes.)

581 (*Spring-Fall 1887*)

Being and becoming.— "Reason," evolved on a sensualistic basis, on the prejudices of the senses, i.e., in the belief in the truth of the judgments of the senses.

"Being" as universalization of the concept "life" (breathing), "having a soul," "willing, effecting," "becoming."

The antithesis is: "not to have a soul," "not to become," "not to will." Therefore: "being" is *not* the antithesis of non-being, appearance, nor even of the dead (for only something that can live can be dead).

The "soul," the "ego" posited as primeval fact, and introduced everywhere where there is any becoming.

582 (*1885-1887*)

Being—we have no idea of it apart from the idea of "living."— How can anything dead "be"?

---

[35] *Nihilisierung.*

583 (*March-June 1888*)

(A)

I observe with astonishment that science has today resigned itself to the apparent world; a real world—whatever it may be like—we certainly have no organ for knowing it.

At this point we may ask: by means of what organ of knowledge can we posit even this antithesis?—

That a world accessible to our organs is also understood to be dependent upon these organs, that we understand a world as being subjectively conditioned,[36] is not to say that an objective world is at all possible. Who compels us to think that subjectivity is real, essential?

The "in-itself" is even an absurd conception; a "constitution-in-itself" is nonsense; we possess the concept "being," "thing," only as a relational concept—

The worst thing is that with the old antithesis "apparent" and "true" the correlative value judgment "lacking in value" and "absolutely valuable" has developed.

The apparent world is not counted as a "valuable" world; appearance is supposed to constitute an objection to supreme value. Only a "true" world can be valuable in itself—

Prejudice of prejudices! Firstly, it would be possible that the true constitution of things was so hostile to the presuppositions of life, so opposed to them, that we needed appearance in order to be able to live— After all, this is the case in so many situations; e.g., in marriage.

Our empirical world would be determined by the instincts of self-preservation even as regards the limits of its knowledge: we would regard as true, good, valuable that which serves the preservation of the species—

a. We possess no categories by which we can distinguish a true from an apparent world. (There might only be an apparent world, but not *our* apparent world.)

b. Assuming the *true* world, it could still be a world less valuable for us; precisely the quantum of illusion might be of a higher rank on account of its value for our preservation. (Unless appearance as such were grounds for condemnation?)

---

[36] The reading of "understand" and "conditioned" is uncertain.

c. That a correlation exists between degrees of value and degrees of reality (so that the supreme values also possess the supreme reality) is a metaphysical postulate proceeding from the presupposition that we *know* the order of rank of values; namely, that this order of rank is a *moral* order— Only with this presupposition is truth necessarily part of the definition of all the highest values.

(B)

It is of cardinal importance that one should abolish the *true* world. It is the great inspirer of doubt and devaluator in respect of the world *we are*: it has been our most dangerous attempt yet to assassinate life.

War on all presuppositions on the basis of which one has invented a true world. Among these is the presupposition that moral values are the supreme values.

The supremacy of moral valuation would be refuted if it could be shown to be the consequence of an immoral valuation —as a special case of actual immorality—it would thus reduce itself to an appearance, and as appearance it would cease to have any right as such to condemn appearance.

(C)

The "will to truth" would then have to be investigated psychologically: it is not a moral force, but a form of the will to power. This would have to be proved by showing that it employs every *immoral* means: metaphysicians above all—.

We are today faced with testing the assertion that moral values are the supreme values. Method in investigation is attained only when all moral prejudices have been overcome:—it represents a victory over morality—

584 (*March-June 1888*)

The aberration of philosophy is that, instead of seing in logic and the categories of reason means toward the adjustment of the world for utilitarian ends (basically, toward an expedient *falsification*), one believed one possessed in them the criterion of truth and *reality*. The "criterion of truth" was in fact merely the biological utility of such a system of systematic falsification; and since a species of animals knows of nothing more important than its own preservation, one might indeed be permitted to speak here of "truth." The naiveté was to take an anthropocentric idiosyncrasy as the *measure of things*, as the rule[37] for determining "real" and "unreal": in short, to make absolute something conditioned. And behold, suddenly the world fell apart into a "true" world and an "apparent" world: and precisely the world that man's reason had devised for him to live and settle in was discredited. Instead of employing the forms as a tool for making the world manageable and calculable, the madness[38] of philosophers divined that in these categories is presented the concept of that world to which the one in which man lives does not correspond— The means were misunderstood as measures of value, even as a condemnation of their real intention—

The intention was to deceive oneself in a useful way; the means, the invention of formulas and signs by means of which one could reduce the confusing multiplicity to a purposive and manageable schema.

But alas! now a moral category was brought into play: no creature wants to deceive itself, no creature may deceive—consequently there is only a will to truth. What is "truth"?

The law of contradiction provided the schema: the true world, to which one seeks the way, cannot contradict itself, cannot change, cannot become, has no beginning and no end.

This is the greatest error that has ever been committed, the essential fatality of error on earth: one believed one possessed a criterion of reality in the forms of reason—while in fact one possessed them in order to become master of reality, in order to misunderstand reality in a shrewd manner—

And behold: now the world became false, and precisely on account of the properties that constitute its reality: change, becoming, multiplicity, opposition, contradiction, war. And then the entire fatality was there:

1. How can one get free from the false, merely apparent world? (—it was the real, the only one);

---

[37] "Rule": uncertain reading.

[38] "Madness": very doubtful conjecture; in the original, two illegible words.

2. how can one become oneself as much as possible the antithesis of the character of the apparent world? (Concept of the perfect creature as an antithesis to the real creature; more clearly, as the contradiction of life—)

The whole tendency of values was toward slander of life; one created a confusion of idealist dogmatism and knowledge in general: so that the opposing party also was always attacking *science*.

The road to science was in this way doubly blocked: once by belief in the "true" world, and again by the opponents of this belief. Natural science, psychology was (1) condemned with regard to its objects, (2) deprived of its innocence—

In the actual world, in which everything is bound to and conditioned by everything else, to condemn and think away anything means to condemn and think away everything. The expression "that should not be," "that should not have been," is farcical— If one thinks out the consequences, one would ruin the source of life if one wanted to abolish whatever was in some respect harmful or destructive. Physiology teaches us better!

—We see how morality (a) poisons the entire conception of the world, (b) cuts off the road to knowledge, to science, (c) disintegrates and undermines all actual instincts (in that it teaches that their roots are immoral).

We see at work before us a dreadful tool of decadence that props itself up by the holiest names and attitudes.

585 (*Spring-Fall 1887; rev. Spring-Fall 1888*)

Tremendous self-examination: becoming conscious of oneself, not as individuals but as mankind. Let us reflect, let us think back; let us follow the highways and byways!

(A)

Man seeks "the truth": a world that is not self-contradictory, not deceptive, does not change, a *true* world—a world in which one does not suffer; contradiction, deception, change—causes of suffering! He does not doubt that a world as it ought to be exists; he would like to seek out the road to it. (Indian critique: even the "ego" as apparent, as not real.)

Whence does man here derive the concept *reality*?— Why

is it that he derives *suffering* from change, deception, contradiction? and why not rather his happiness?—

Contempt, hatred for all that perishes, changes, varies—whence comes this valuation of that which remains constant? Obviously, the will to truth is here merely the desire for a world of the constant.

The senses deceive, reason corrects the errors; consequently, one concluded, reason is the road to the constant; the least sensual ideas must be closest to the "true world."— It is from the senses that most misfortunes come—they are deceivers, deluders, destroyers.—

Happiness can be guaranteed only by being; change and happiness exclude one another. The highest desire therefore contemplates unity with what has being. This is the formula for: the road to the highest happiness.

In summa: the world as it ought to be exists; this world, in which we live, is an error—this world of ours ought not to exist.

Belief in what has being is only a consequence: the real *primum mobile* is disbelief in becoming, mistrust of becoming, the low valuation of all that becomes—

What kind of man reflects in this way? An unproductive, suffering kind, a kind weary of life. If we imagine the opposite kind of man, he would not need to believe in what has being; more, he would despise it as dead, tedious, indifferent—

The belief that the world as it ought to be *is,* really exists, is a belief of the unproductive who do *not desire to create a world* as it ought to be. They posit it as already available, they seek ways and means of reaching it. "Will to truth"—*as the impotence of the will to create.*

<table>
<tr><td>To know that something is thus and thus:</td><td rowspan="2">Antagonism in the degree of power in different natures.</td></tr>
<tr><td>To act so that something becomes thus and thus:</td></tr>
</table>

The fiction of a world that corresponds to our desires: psychological trick and interpretation with the aim of associating everything we honor and find pleasant with this true world.

"Will to truth" at this stage is essentially an art of interpretation: which at least requires the power to interpret.

This same species of man, grown one stage poorer, no longer possessing the strength to interpret, to create fictions, produces *nihilists.* A nihilist is a man who judges of the world as it is that it ought *not* to be, and of the world as it ought to be that it does not exist.[39] According to this view, our existence (action, suffering, willing, feeling) has no meaning: the pathos of "in vain" is the nihilists' pathos—at the same time, as pathos, an inconsistency on the part of the nihilists.

Whoever is incapable of laying his will into things, lacking will and strength, at least lays some *meaning* into them, i.e., the faith that there is a will in them already.[40]

It is a measure of the degree of strength of will to what extent one can do without meaning in things, to what extent one can endure to live in a meaningless world *because one organizes a small portion of it oneself.*

The philosophical objective outlook can therefore be a sign that will and strength are small. For strength organizes what is close and closest; "men of knowledge," who desire only to ascertain what is, are those who cannot *fix* anything *as it ought to be.*

Artists, an intermediary species: they at least fix an image of that which ought to be; they are productive, to the extent that they actually alter and transform; unlike men of knowledge, who leave everything as it is.[41]

Connection between philosophers and the pessimistic religions: the same species of man (—they ascribe the highest degree of reality to the most highly valued things—).

Connection between philosophers and moral men and their evaluations (—the moral interpretation of the world as meaning: after the decline of the religious meaning—).

---

[39] This remarkable definition furnishes a splendid illustration of the inadequacy of the present systematic arrangement of *The Will to Power:* it is separated by hundreds of pages from Book I, which is supposed to contain the sections on nihilism. But ever so many of Nietzsche's sections are relevant to a great many topics, and he was plainly no system-thinker. Cf. my discussion of "Nietzsche's Method" in Chapter 2 of my *Nietzsche,* especially section II.

[40] This epigram was included with slight changes in *Twilight,* as aphorism 18 in Chapter I (*Portable Nietzsche,* p. 469).

[41] This formulation invites comparison with Ludwig Wittgenstein's admonition: "Philosophy must not in any way, however slight, interfere with the ordinary use of language; in the end, philosophy can only describe it. . . . It leaves everything as it is" (*Philosophical Investigations,* New York: Macmillan, 1953, # 124). Also with the last of Karl Marx's "Theses Against Feuerbach": "The philosophers have merely interpreted the world differently; but what matters is to change it."

Overcoming of philosophers through the destruction of the world of being: intermediary period of nihilism: before there is yet present the strength to reverse values and to deify becoming and the apparent world as the only world, and to call them good.

(B)

Nihilism as a normal phenomenon can be a symptom of increasing *strength* or of increasing *weakness*:

partly, because the strength to create, to will, has so increased that it no longer requires these total interpretations and introductions of meaning ("present tasks," the state, etc.);

partly because even the creative strength to create meaning has declined and disappointment becomes the dominant condition. The incapability of believing in a "meaning," "unbelief."

What does science mean in regard to both possibilities?

1. As a sign of strength and self-control, as being able to do without healing, comforting worlds of illusion;

2. as undermining, dissecting, disappointing, weakening.

(C)

Belief in truth, the need to have a hold on something believed true, psychological reduction apart from all previous value feelings. Fear, laziness.

The same way, *unbelief*: reduction. To what extent it acquires a new value if a true world does not exist (—thus the value feelings that hitherto have been squandered on the world of being, are again set free).

586 (*March-June 1888*)

The "True" *and the* "Apparent World"

(A)

The seductions that proceed from this concept are of three kinds:

a. an *unknown* world:—we are adventurers, inquisitive—that which is known seems to weary us (—the danger of this concept lies in its insinuation that "this" world is known to us—);

b. *another* world, where things are different; something in us calculates, our still submission, our silence, lose their value—perhaps everything will turn out well, we have not hoped in vain—the world where things are different, where we ourselves—who knows?—are different—

c. a *true* world: this is the most amazing trick and attack that has ever been perpetrated upon us; so much has become encrusted in the word "true," and involuntarily we make a present of all this to the "true world": the true world must also be a truthful world, one that does not deceive us, does not make fools of us: to believe in it is virtually to be compelled to believe in it (—out of decency, as is the case among people worthy of confidence—).

*

The concept "the unknown world" insinuates that *this* world is "known" to us (is tedious—);

the concept "another world" insinuates that the world could be otherwise—abolishes necessity and fate (useless to submit oneself—to adapt oneself—);

the concept "the true world" insinuates that this world is untruthful, deceptive, dishonest, inauthentic, inessential—and consequently also not a world adapted to our needs (—inadvisable to adapt oneself to it; better to resist it).

*

We therefore elude "this" world in three ways:

a. by our inquisitiveness—as if the more interesting part were elsewhere;

b. by our submission—as though it were not necessary to submit oneself—as if this world were not a necessity of the ultimate rank:

c. by our sympathy and respect—as if this world did not deserve them, were impure, were not honest with us—

In summa: we have revolted in three ways: we have made an "*x*" into a critique of the "known world."

(B)

First step toward sobriety: to grasp to what extent we have been seduced—for things could be exactly the reverse:

a. the *unknown* world could be a stupid and meaner form of existence—and "this" world might be rather enjoyable by comparison;

b. the *other* world, far from taking account of our desires which would find no fulfillment in it, could be among the mass of things that make *this* world possible for us: to get to know it might be a means of making us contented;

c. the true world: but who is it really who tells us that the apparent world must be of less value than the true one? Does our instinct not contradict this judgment? Does man not eternally create a fictitious world for himself because he wants a better world than reality? *Above all:* how do we arrive at the idea that our world is *not* the true world?—it could be that the other world is the "apparent" one (in fact the Greeks thought of, e.g., a *shadow kingdom,* an *apparent existence,* beside true existence). And finally: what gives us the right to posit, as it were, degrees of reality? This is something different from an unknown world—it is already a wanting to know something of the unknown— The "other," the "unknown" world—very good! But to say "true world" means "to *know* something of it"— That is the *opposite* of the assumption of an *"x"* world—

In summa: the world *"x"* could be in every sense more tedious, less human, and less worthy than this world.

It would be another thing to assert the existence of *"x"* worlds, i.e., of every possible world besides this one. But this has *never been asserted*—

(C)

Problem: why the notion of another world has always been unfavorable for, or critical of "this" world—what does this indicate?—

For a people proud of itself, whose life is ascending, always thinks of another kind of being as a lower, less valuable kind of being; it regards the strange, the unknown world as its enemy, as its opposite; it feels no inquisitiveness, it totally rejects the strange— A people would never admit that another people was the "true people."—

It is symptomatic that such a distinction should be at all possible—that one takes this world for the "apparent" one and the other world as "true."

The places of origin of the notion of "another world":
the philosopher, who invents a world of reason, where reason and the logical functions are adequate: this is the origin of the "true" world;
the religious man, who invents a "divine world": this is the origin of the "denaturalized, anti-natural" world;
the moral man, who invents a "free world": this is the origin of the "good, perfect, just, holy" world.

What the three places of origin have in common: the psychological blunder, the physiological confusions.

By what attributes is the "other world," as it actually appears in history, distinguished? By the stigmata of philosophical, religious, moral prejudice.

The "other world," as illumined by these facts, as a synonym for nonbeing, nonliving, not wanting to live—

General insight: it is the instinct of life-weariness, and not that of life, which has created the "other world."

Consequence: philosophy, religion, and morality are *symptoms of decadence.*[42]

11. Biological Value of Knowledge

587 (*1885-1886*)

It might seem as though I had evaded the question of "certainty." The opposite is true; but by inquiring after the criterion of certainty I tested the scales upon which men have weighed in general hitherto—and that the question of certainty itself is a dependent question, a question of the second rank.

588 (*1883-1886*)

The question of values is more *fundamental* than the question of certainty: the latter becomes serious only by presupposing that the value question has already been answered.

---

[42] In the MS an earlier version of *Twilight*, Chapter III, section 6, follows at this point. All of the sections dealing with the contrast of the "true" and the "apparent" world should be considered as background material for *Twilight*, Chapters III and IV (*Portable Nietzsche*, pp. 479 *ff* and 485 *ff*); but these sections contain many interesting passages that did not find their way into the book.

Being and appearance, psychologically considered, yield no "being-in-itself," no criterion of "reality," but only for grades of appearance measured by the strength of the *interest* we show in an appearance.

There is no struggle for existence between ideas and perceptions, but a struggle for dominion: the idea that is overcome is not annihilated, only driven back or subordinated. There is no annihilation in the sphere of spirit—[43]

589 (*1885-1886*)

"Ends and means" "Cause and effect" "Subject and object" "Acting and suffering" "Thing-in-itself and appearance"	as interpretations (not as facts) and to what extent perhaps *necessary* interpretations? (as required for "preservation")—all in the sense of a will to power.

590 (*1885-1886*)

Our values are interpreted *into* things.

Is there then any *meaning* in the in-itself? !

Is meaning not necessarily relative meaning and perspective?

All meaning is will to power (all relative meaning resolves itself into it).

591 (*1885*)

The desire for "solid facts"—epistemology: how much pessimism there is in it!

592 (*1883-1888*)

The antagonism between the "true world," as revealed by pessimism, and a world possible for life—here one must test the rights of truth. It is necessary to measure the meaning of all these "ideal drives" against *life* to grasp what this antagonism really is: the struggle of sickly, despairing life that cleaves to a beyond, with healthier, more stupid and mendacious, richer, less degenerate life. Therefore it is not "truth" in struggle with life but *one* kind of life

[43] *Es gibt im Geistigen keine Vernichtung* might have been written by Hegel—or by Freud.

in struggle with another.— But it wants to be the higher kind!— Here one must demonstrate the need for an order of rank—that the first problem is the *order of rank of different kinds of life.*

593 (*1885-1886*)

To transform the belief "it *is* thus and thus" into the will "it *shall become* thus and thus."

12. Science

594 (*1883-1888*)

Science—this has been hitherto a way of putting an end to the complete confusion in which things exist, by hypotheses that "explain" everything—so it has come from the intellect's dislike of chaos.— This same dislike seizes me when I consider myself: I should like to form an image of the inner world, too, by means of some schema, and thus triumph over intellectual confusion. Morality has been a simplification of this kind: it taught that men were known, familiar.— Now we have destroyed morality—we have again become completely obscure to ourselves! I know that I know nothing of myself. Physics proves to be a boon for the heart: science (as the way to knowledge) acquires a new charm after morality has been eliminated—and because it is here alone that we find consistency, we have to construct our life so as to preserve it. This yields a sort of practical reflection on the conditions of our existence as men of knowledge.

595 (*1884*)

Our presuppositions: no God: no purpose: finite force. Let us guard against thinking out and prescribing the mode of thought necessary to lesser men! !

596 (*1886-1887*)

No "moral education" of the human race: but an enforced schooling in [scientific][44] errors is needed, because "truth" dis-

[44] The word I have placed in brackets was added by the German editors.

gusts and makes one sick of life—unless man is already irrevocably launched upon his path and has taken his honest insight upon himself with a tragic pride.

597 (*1886-1887*)

The presupposition of scientific work: belief in the unity and perpetuity of scientific work, so the individual may work at any part, however small, confident that his work will not be in vain.

There is one great paralysis: to work *in vain,* to struggle in vain.——

*

The accumulative epochs, in which force and means of power are discovered that the future will one day make use of; science an intermediary station, at which the more intermediary, more multifarious, more complicated natures find their most natural discharge and satisfaction—all those who should avoid *action.*

598 (*Nov. 1887-March 1888*)

A philosopher recuperates differently and with different means: he recuperates, e.g., with nihilism. Belief that there is no truth at all, the nihilistic belief, is a great relaxation for one who, as a warrior of knowledge, is ceaselessly fighting ugly truths. For truth is ugly.[45]

599 (*1885-1886*)

The "meaninglessness of events": belief in this is the consequence of an insight into the falsity of previous interpretations, a generalization of discouragement and weakness—not a *necessary* belief.

The immodesty of man: to deny meaning where he sees none.

---

[45] Another version, written a few months later, is printed in 1911, p. 508: "For a warrior of knowledge, who is always fighting ugly truths, the belief *that there is no truth at all* is a great bath and relaxation.— Nihilism is our kind of leisure."

Cf. the chapter "On War and Warriors" in *Zarathustra,* I (*Portable Nietzsche,* p. 158 *ff*). And note the deliberate antithesis, especially of the formulation in the text, to the romantic identification of truth and beauty.

600 (*1885-1886*)

No limit to the ways in which the world can be interpreted; every interpretation a symptom of growth or of decline.

Inertia needs unity (monism); plurality of interpretations a sign of strength. Not to desire to deprive the world of its disturbing and enigmatic character!

601 (*1885-1886*)

Against peaceableness and the desire for reconciliation.[46] The attempt at monism belongs here.

602 (*1884*)

This perspective world, this world for the eye, tongue, and ear, is very false, even if compared for[47] a very much more subtle sense-apparatus. But its intelligibility, comprehensibility, practicability, and beauty begin to cease if we refine our senses; just as beauty ceases when we think about historical processes; the order of purpose is already an illusion. It suffices that the more superficially and coarsely it is conceived, the more valuable, definite, beautiful, and significant the world appears. The deeper one looks, the more our valuations disappear—meaninglessness approaches! We have *created* the world that possesses values! Knowing this, we know, too, that reverence for truth is already the consequence of an illusion—and that one should value more than truth the force that forms, simplifies, shapes, invents.

"Everything is false! Everything is permitted!"

Only with a certain obtuseness of vision, a will to simplicity, does the beautiful, the "valuable" appear: in itself, it is I know not what.

---

[46] This note helps to illuminate the chapter "On War and Warriors" in *Zarathustra.*

[47] Unless either "compared" or "for" represents a misreading of the MS, Nietzsche would seem to have slipped.

The quotation comprising the next paragraph should be compared with "Nothing is true, everything is permitted," in *Genealogy* III, section 24; see also my notes on that section.

603 (*1885*)

That the destruction of an illusion does not produce truth but only one more piece of ignorance, an extension of our "empty space," an increase of our "desert"[48]—

604[49] (*1885-1886*)

"Interpretation," the introduction of meaning—not "explanation" (in most cases a new interpretation over an old interpretation that has become incomprehensible, that is now itself only a sign). There are no facts, everything is in flux, incomprehensible, elusive; what is relatively most enduring is—our opinions.

605 (*Spring-Fall 1887*)

The ascertaining of "truth" and "untruth," the ascertaining of facts in general, is fundamentally different from creative positing, from forming, shaping, overcoming, willing, such as is of the essence of philosophy. To introduce a meaning—this task still remains to be done, assuming there is no meaning yet. Thus it is with sounds, but also with the fate of peoples: they are capable of the most different interpretations and direction toward different goals.

On a yet higher level is to *posit a goal* and mold facts according to it; that is, active interpretation and not merely conceptual translation.

606 (*1885-1886*)

Ultimately, man finds in things nothing but what he himself has imported into them: the finding is called science, the importing—art, religion, love, pride. Even if this should be a piece of childishness, one should carry on with both and be well disposed toward both—some should find; others—*we* others!—should import!

---

[48] The German editors made a complete sentence of this note by adding "We know" at the beginning.

[49] At the beginning of this note Peter Gast placed the question, printed in all editions: "What alone can knowledge be?"

607 (*Spring-Fall 1886*)

Science: its two sides:
in regard to the individual;
in regard to the cultural complex (level);
—valuations from one side or the other are mutually antagonistic.

608 (*1886-1887*)

The development of science resolves the "familiar" more and more into the unfamiliar:—it desires, however, the reverse, and proceeds from the instinct to trace the unfamiliar back to the familiar.

In summa, science is preparing a sovereign ignorance, a feeling that there is no such thing as "knowing," that it was a kind of arrogance to dream of it, more, that we no longer have the least notion that warrants our considering "knowledge" even a possibility—that "knowing" itself is a contradictory idea. We translate a primeval mythology and vanity of mankind into the hard fact: "knowledge-in-itself" is as impermissible a concept as is "thing-in-itself." Seduction by "number and logic," seduction by "laws."

"Wisdom" as the attempt to get beyond perspective valuations (i.e., beyond the "will to power"): a principle hostile to life and decadent, a symptom as among the Indians, etc., of the weakening of the power of appropriation.

609 (*1884*)

It is not enough that you understand in what ignorance man and beast live; you must also have and acquire the *will* to ignorance. You need to grasp that without this kind of ignorance life itself would be impossible, that it is a condition under which alone the living thing can preserve itself and prosper: a great, firm dome of ignorance must encompass you.

610 (*1884*)

Science—the transformation of nature into concepts for the purpose of mastering nature—belongs under the rubric "means."

But the purpose and will of man must grow in the same way, the intention in regard to the whole.

611 (*1883-1888*)

We find that the strongest and most constantly employed faculty at all stages of life is thought—even in every act of perceiving and apparent passivity! Evidently, it thus becomes most powerful and demanding, and in the long run it tyrannizes over all other forces. Finally it becomes "passion-in-itself."

612 (*Spring-Fall 1887*)

To win back for the man of knowledge the right to great affects! after self-effacement and the cult of "objectivity" have created a false order of rank in this sphere, too. Error reached its peak when Schopenhauer taught: the only way to the "true," to knowledge, lies precisely in getting free from affects, from will; the intellect liberated from will cannot but see the true, real essence of things.

The same error *in arte*:[50] as if everything were beautiful as soon as it is viewed without will.

613 (*Fall 1888*)

Competition between affects and the dominion of one of the affects over the intellect.

614 (*1884*)

To "humanize" the world, i.e., to feel ourselves more and more masters within it—

615 (*1884*)

Among a higher kind of creatures, knowledge, too, will acquire new forms that are not yet needed.

---

[50] In art. About this section, see also the Appendix, below.

616 (*1885-1886*)

That the value of the world lies in our interpretation (—that other interpretations than merely human ones are perhaps somewhere possible—); that previous interpretations have been perspective valuations by virtue of which we can survive in life, i.e., in the will to power, for the growth of power; that every elevation of man brings with it the overcoming of narrower interpretations; that every strengthening and increase of power opens up new perspectives and means believing in new horizons—this idea permeates my writings. The world with which we are concerned is false, i.e., is not a fact but a fable and approximation on the basis of a meager sum of observations; it is "in flux," as something in a state of becoming, as a falsehood always changing but never getting near the truth: for—there is no "truth."

617 (*1883-1885*)[51]

To impose upon becoming the character of being—that is the supreme will to power.

Twofold falsification, on the part of the senses and of the spirit, to preserve a world of that which is, which abides, which is equivalent, etc.

That *everything recurs*[52] is the closest *approximation of a world of becoming to a world of being:*—high point of the meditation.

From the values attributed to being proceed the condemnation of and discontent with becoming, after such a world of being had first been invented.

The metamorphoses of what has being (body, God, ideas, laws of nature, formulas, etc.)

"Beings" as appearance; reversal of values; appearance was that which conferred value—.

Knowledge-in-itself in a world of becoming is impossible; so how is knowledge possible? As error concerning oneself, as will to power, as will to deception.

---

[51] Gast entitled this section *"Recapitulation,"* and all printed versions retain this title.

[52] A reference to Nietzsche's doctrine of the eternal recurrence of the same events. Cf. sections 55 and 1,057 *ff*.

Becoming as invention, willing, self-denial, overcoming of oneself: no subject but an action, a positing, creative, no "causes and effects."

Art as the will to overcome becoming, as "eternalization," but shortsighted, depending on the perspective: repeating in miniature, as it were, the tendency of the whole.

Regarding that which all life reveals as a diminutive formula for the total tendency; hence a new definition of the concept "life" as will to power.

Instead of "cause and effect" the mutual struggle of that which becomes, often with the absorption of one's opponent; the number of becoming elements not constant.

Uselessness of old ideals for the interpretation of the totality of events, once one knows the animal origin and utility of these ideals; all, moreover, contradictory to life.

Uselessness of the mechanistic theory—it gives the impression of meaninglessness.

The entire idealism of mankind hitherto is on the point of changing suddenly into nihilism—into the belief in absolute *worth*-lessness, i.e., *meaning*lessness.

The destruction of ideals, the new desert; new arts by means of which we can endure it, we amphibians.

Presupposition: bravery, patience, no "turning back," no haste to go forward. (N.B. Zarathustra adopts a parodistic attitude toward all former values as a consequence of his abundance.)

II. THE WILL TO POWER IN NATURE[53]

1. The Mechanistic Interpretation of the World[54]

618 (*1885*)

Of all the interpretations of the world attempted hitherto, the mechanistic one seems today to stand victorious in the foreground. It evidently has a good conscience on its side; and no science believes it can achieve progress and success except with the aid of mechanistic procedures. Everyone knows these procedures: one leaves "reason" and "purpose" out of account as far as possible, one shows that, given sufficient time, anything can evolve out of anything else, and one does not conceal a malicious chuckle when "apparent intention" in the fate of a plant or an egg yolk is once again traced back to pressure and stress: in short, one pays heartfelt homage to the principle of the greatest possible stupidity, if a playful expression may be allowed concerning such serious matters. Meanwhile, a presentiment, or anxiety, is to be noted among select spirits involved in this movement, as if the theory had a hole in it that might sooner or later prove to be its final hole: I mean the shrill one through which one whistles in an extreme emergency.[55] One cannot "explain" pressure and stress themselves, one cannot get free of the *actio in distans*:[56]—one has lost the belief in being able to explain at all, and admits with a wry expression that description and not explanation is all that is possible, that the dynamic interpretation of the world, with its denial of "empty space" and its little clumps of atoms, will shortly come to dominate physicists; though an inner quality in *dynamis*——

619 (*1885*)

The victorious concept "force," by means of which our

---

[53] Much of this material has no close parallels in Nietzsche's books.

[54] For a discussion of this section see my *Nietzsche*, Chapter 9, section I.

[55] "Whistling out of the final hole" is a German expression for extreme emergencies.

[56] Action at a distance. *Dynamis*, at the end of this section, means *power*, energy, potency.

physicists have created God and the world, still needs to be completed: an inner will must be ascribed to it, which I designate as "will to power," i.e., as an insatiable desire to manifest power; or as the employment and exercise of power, as a creative drive, etc. Physicists cannot eradicate "action at a distance" from their principles; nor can they eradicate a repellent force (or an attracting one). There is nothing for it: one is obliged to understand all motion, all "appearances," all "laws," only as symptoms of an inner event and to employ man as an analogy to this end. In the case of an animal, it is possible to trace all its drives to the will to power; likewise all the functions of organic life to this one source.

620 (*1885-1886*)

Has a *force* ever been demonstrated? No, only *effects* translated into a completely foreign language. We are so used, however, to regularity in succession that its oddity no longer seems odd to us.

621 (*1885-1886*)

A force we cannot imagine is an empty word and should be allowed no rights of citizenship in science; like the so-called purely mechanistic forces of attraction and repulsion, which are intended to make it possible for us to form an image of the world, no more!

622 (*1885-1886*)

Pressure and stress, something unspeakably late, derivative, un-primeval. For they presuppose something that holds together and is *able* to exert pressure and stress! But how can it hold together?

623 (*March-June 1888*)

There is nothing unchanging in chemistry: this is only appearance, a mere school prejudice. We have *slipped in* the unchanging, my physicist friends, deriving it from metaphysics as always. To assert that diamond, graphite, and carbon are identical is to read off the facts naively from the surface. Why? Merely because no loss in substance can be shown on the scales! Very well, they have something in common; but the activity of molecules during the transformation, which we cannot see or weigh, turns one material into something different—with specifically different properties.

624 (*1883-1888*)

Against the physical *atom*.-- To comprehend the world, we have to be able to calculate it; to be able to calculate it, we have to have constant causes; because we find no such constant causes in actuality, we invent them for ourselves—the atoms. This is the origin of atomism.

The calculability of the world, the expressibility of all events in formulas—is this really "comprehension"? How much of a piece of music has been understood when that in it which is calculable and can be reduced to formulas has been reckoned up?— And "constant causes," things, substances, something "unconditioned"; *invented*—what has one achieved?

625 (*March-June 1888*)

The mechanistic concept of "motion" is already a translation of the original process into the sign language of sight and touch.

The concept "atom," the distinction between the "'seat of a driving force and the force itself," is a sign language derived from our logical-psychical world.

We cannot change our means of expression at will: it is possible to understand to what extent they are mere signs. The demand for an adequate mode of expression is senseless: it is of the essence of a language, a means of expression, to express a mere relationship—

The concept "truth" is nonsensical. The entire domain of "true-false" applies only to relations, not to an "in-itself"— There is no "essence-in-itself" (it is only relations that constitute an essence—), just as there can be no "knowledge-in-itself."

626 (*1883-1886*)

"The sensation of force cannot proceed from motion: sensation in general cannot proceed from motion."

"It is only an apparent experience that speaks in favor of this: in a substance (brain), sensations are produced by transmitted motion (stimuli). But produced? Would this prove that the sensation did not exist there at all? so that its appearance would have to be conceived as a creative act on the part of the motion? The sensationless state of this substance is only a hypothesis! it is not experienced!— Sensation is thus a *property* of substance: there are substances that have sensations."

"Do we discover from certain substances that they have *no* sensations? No, we only fail to discover *that* they have any. It is impossible to derive sensation from a substance without sensation."— Oh what overhastiness!

627 (*1885-1886*)

"Attraction" and "repulsion" in a purely mechanistic sense are complete fictions: a word. We cannot think of an attraction divorced from an *intention*.— The will to take possession of a thing or to defend oneself against it and repel it—that, we "understand": that would be an interpretation of which we could make use.

In short: the psychological necessity for a belief in causality lies in the inconceivability of an event divorced from intent; by which naturally nothing is said concerning truth or untruth (the justification of such a belief)! The belief in *causae*[57] falls with the belief in télē[58] (against Spinoza and his causalism).

628 (*1885-1886*)

It is an illusion that something is *known* when we possess a mathematical formula for an event: it is only designated, described; nothing more!

629 (*1883-1888*)

If I reduce a regular event to a formula, I have foreshortened, facilitated, etc., the description of the whole phenomenon. But I have established no "law," I have raised the question how it

[57] Efficient causes.

[58] Final causes; purposes.

happens that something here repeats itself: that the formula corresponds to a complex of initially unknown forces and discharges of force, is a supposition; it is mythology to think that forces here obey a law, so that, as a consequence of their obedience, we have the same phenomenon each time.

630 (*1885*)

I beware of speaking of chemical "laws": that savors of morality. It is far rather a question of the absolute establishment of power relationships: the stronger becomes master of the weaker, in so far as the latter cannot assert its degree of independence—here there is no mercy, no forbearance, even less a respect for "laws"!

631 (*1885-1886*)

The unalterable sequence of certain phenomena demonstrates no "law" but a power relationship between two or more forces. To say "But this relationship itself remains constant" is to say no more than "One and the same force cannot also be another force."— It is a question, not of succession, but of interpenetration, a process in which the individual successive moments are not related to one another as cause and effect—

The separation of the "deed" from the "doer," of the event from someone who produces events, of the process from a something that is not process but enduring, substance, thing, body, soul, etc.—the attempt to comprehend an event as a sort of shifting and place-changing on the part of a "being," of something constant: this ancient mythology established the belief in "cause and effect" after it had found a firm form in the functions of language and grammar.

632 (*1885-1886*)

"Regularity" in succession is only a metaphorical expression, *as if* a rule were being followed here; not a fact. In the same way "conformity with a law." We discover a formula by which to express an ever-recurring kind of result: we have therewith discovered no "law," even less a force that is the cause of the recurrence of a succession of results. That something always happens thus and thus is here interpreted as if a creature always acted thus and thus as a result of obedience to a law or a lawgiver, while it would be free to act otherwise were it not for the "law." But precisely this thus-and-not-otherwise might be inherent in the creature, which might behave thus and thus, not in response to a law, but because it is constituted thus and thus. All it would mean is: something cannot also be something else, cannot do now this and now something else, is neither free nor unfree but simply thus and thus. *The mistake lies in the fictitious insertion of a subject.*

633 (*March-June 1888*)

Two successive states, the one "cause," the other "effect": this is false. The first has nothing to effect, the second has been effected by nothing.

It is a question of a struggle between two elements of unequal power: a new arrangement of forces is achieved according to the measure of power of each of them. The second condition is something fundamentally different from the first (not its effect): the essential thing is that the factions in struggle emerge with different quanta of power.

634 (*March-June 1888*)

Critique of the mechanistic theory.— Let us here dismiss the two popular concepts "necessity" and "law": the former introduces a false constraint into the world, the latter a false freedom. "Things" do not behave regularly, according to a *rule*: there are no things (—they are fictions invented by us); they behave just as little under the constraint of necessity. There is no obedience here: for that something is as it is, as strong or as weak, is not the consequence of an obedience or a rule or a compulsion—

The degree of resistance and the degree of superior power—this is the question in every event: if, for our day-to-day calculations, we know how to express this in formulas and "laws," so much the better for us! But we have not introduced any "morality" into the world by the fiction that it is obedient—.

There is no law: every power draws its ultimate consequence at every moment. Calculability exists precisely because things are unable to be other than they are.

A quantum of power is designated by the effect it produces

and that which it resists. The adiaphorous state is missing, though it is thinkable. It is essentially a will to violate and to defend oneself against violation. Not self-preservation: every atom affects the whole of being—it is thought away if one thinks away this radiation of power-will. That is why I call it a quantum of "will to power": it expresses the characteristic that cannot be thought out of the mechanistic order without thinking away this order itself.

A translation of this world of effect into a visible world—a world for the eyes—is the conception "motion." This always carries the idea that *something* is moved—this always supposes, whether as the fiction of a little clump of atom or even as the abstraction of this, the dynamic atom, a thing that produces effects—i.e., we have not got away from the habit into which our senses and language seduce us. Subject, object, a doer added to the doing, the doing separated from that which it does: let us not forget that this is mere semeiotics and nothing real. Mechanistic theory as a theory of motion is already a translation into the sense language of man.[59]

635 (*March-June 1888*)

We need "unities" in order to be able to reckon: that does not mean we must suppose that such unities exist. We have borrowed the concept of unity from our "ego" concept—our oldest article of faith. If we did not hold ourselves to be unities, we would never have formed the concept "thing." Now, somewhat late, we are firmly convinced that our conception of the ego does not guarantee any actual unity. In order to sustain the theory of a mechanistic world, therefore, we always have to stipulate to what extent we are employing two fictions: the concept of *motion* (taken from our sense language) and the concept of the *atom* (= unity, deriving from our psychical "experience"): the mechanistic theory presupposes a sense prejudice and a psychological prejudice.

Mechanistic theory formulates consecutive appearances, and it does so semeiotically, in terms of the senses and of psychology (that all effect is motion; that where there is motion *something* is moved); it does not touch upon the causal force.

---

[59] In the MS section 635 follows immediately, without break; but the German editors divided this notebook entry into two sections.

Cf. my note 54 above.

The mechanistic world is imagined as only sight and touch imagine a world (as "moved")—so as to be calculable—thus causal unities are invented, "things" (atoms) whose effect remains constant (—transference of the false concept of subject to the concept of the atom).

The following are therefore phenomenal: the injection of the concept of number, the concept of the thing (concept of the subject), the concept of activity (separation of cause from effect), the concept of motion (sight and touch): our eye and our psychology are still part of it.

If we eliminate these additions, no things remain but only dynamic quanta, in a relation of tension to all other dynamic quanta: their essence lies in their relation to all other quanta, in their "effect" upon the same. The will to power not a being, not a becoming, but a *pathos*[60]—the most elemental fact from which a becoming and effecting first emerge—

636 (*March-June 1888*)

Physicists believe in a "true world" in their own fashion: a firm systematization of atoms in necessary motion, the same for all beings—so for them the "apparent world" is reduced to the side of universal and universally necessary being which is accessible to every being in its own way (accessible and also already adapted—made "subjective"). But they are in error. The atom they posit is inferred according to the logic of the perspectivism of consciousness—and is therefore itself a subjective fiction. This world picture that they sketch differs in no essential way from the subjective world picture: it is only construed with more extended senses, but with *our* senses nonetheless— And in any case they left something out of the constellation without knowing it: precisely this necessary perspectivism by virtue of which every center of force—and not only man—construes all the rest of the world from its own viewpoint, i.e., measures, feels, forms, according to its own force— They forgot to include this perspective-setting force in "true being" —in school language: the subject. They think this is "evolved," added later; but even the chemist needs it: it is being specific,

---

[60] Occasion, event, passion, suffering, destiny are among the meanings of this Greek word. A comparison of the sections in this part with Whitehead's philosophy of occasions and events would be fruitful.

definitely acting and reacting thus and thus, as may be the case.

Perspectivism is only a complex form of specificity. My idea is that every specific body strives to become master over all space and to extend its force (—its will to power:) and to thrust back all that resists its extension. But it continually encounters similar efforts on the part of other bodies and ends by coming to an arrangement ("union") with those of them that are sufficiently related to it: thus they then conspire together for power. And the process goes on—

637 (*1885*)

Even in the domain of the inorganic an atom of force is concerned only with its neighborhood: distant forces balance one another. Here is the kernel of the perspective view and why a living creature is "egoistic" through and through.

638 (*1885-1886*)

Supposing that the world had a certain quantum of force at its disposal, then it is obvious that every displacement of power at any point would affect the whole system—thus together with sequential causality there would be a contiguous and concurrent dependence.

639 (*Spring-Fall 1887*)

The sole way of maintaining a meaning for the concept "God" would be: God *not* as the driving force, but God as a maximal state, as an epoch—a point in the evolution of the will to power by means of which further evolution just as much as previous evolution up to him could be explained.

Regarded mechanistically, the energy of the totality of becoming remains constant; regarded economically, it rises to a high point and sinks down again in an eternal circle. This "will to power" expresses itself in the interpretation, in the manner in which force is used up; transformation of energy into life, and "life at its highest potency," thus appears as the goal. The same quantum of energy means different things at different stages of evolution.

That which constitutes growth in life is an ever more thrifty and more far-seeing economy, which achieves more and more with less and less force— As an ideal, the principle of the smallest expenditure—

That the world is not striving toward a stable condition is the only thing that has been proved. Consequently one must conceive its climactic condition in such a way that it is not a condition of equilibrium—

The absolute necessity of similar events occurring in the course of one world, as in all others, is in eternity *not* a determinism ruling events, but merely the expression of the fact that the impossible is not possible; that a certain force cannot be anything other than this certain force; that it can react to a quantum of resisting force only according to the measure of its strength;—event and necessary event is a *tautology*.

2. The Will to Power as Life

A. The Organic Process

640 (*1883-1888*)

Man thinks of himself as having been present when the organic world originated: what was there to be perceived by sight and touch when this event took place? What can be reduced to figures? What laws are revealed in the motions? Thus: man wants to arrange all events as events accessible to sight and touch, consequently as motions: he wants to find formulas so as to simplify the tremendous quantity of his experiences. Reduction of all events to the level of the man of the senses and the mathematician. It is a question of an inventory of human experiences—under the supposition that man, or rather the human eye and ability to form concepts, are the eternal witness of all things.

641 (*1883-1888*)

A multiplicity of forces, connected by a common mode of nutrition, we call "life." To this mode of nutrition, as a means of making it possible, belong all so-called feelings, ideas, thoughts; i.e., (1) a resistance to all other forces; (2) an adjustment of the same according to form and rhythm; (3) an estimate in regard to assimilation or excretion.

642 (*1885*)

The connection between the inorganic and the organic must lie in the repelling force exercised by every atom of force. "Life" would be defined as an enduring form of processes of the establishment of force, in which the different contenders grow unequally. To what extent resistance is present even in obedience; individual power is by no means surrendered. In the same way, there is in commanding an admission that the absolute power of the opponent has not been vanquished, incorporated, disintegrated. "Obedience" and "commanding" are forms of struggle.

643 (*1885-1886*)

The will to power *interprets* (—it is a question of interpretation when an organ is constructed): it defines limits, determines degrees, variations of power. Mere variations of power could not feel themselves to be such: there must be present something that wants to grow and interprets the value of whatever else wants to grow. Equal *in that*— In fact, interpretation is itself a means of becoming master of something. (The organic process constantly presupposes interpretations.)

644 (*1883-1888*)

Greater complexity, sharp differentiation, the contiguity of developed organs and functions with the disappearance of the intermediate members—if that is perfection, then there is a will to power in the organic process by virtue of which dominant, shaping, commanding forces continually extend the bounds of their power and continually simplify within these bounds: the imperative grows.

"Spirit" is only a means and tool in the service of higher life, of the enhancement of life; and as for the good, as Plato (and after him Christianity) understood it, it seems to me to be actually a life-endangering, life-calumniating, life-denying principle.

645 (*1885*)

That "heredity," as something quite unexplained, cannot be employed as an explanation but only to describe and fix a problem. The same applies to "power of adaptation." Indeed, the morphological presentation, even if it were complete, explains nothing, but only describes a tremendous fact. How an organ can be employed to achieve something is not explained. In these matters, the assumption of *causae finales* explains as little as the assumption of *causae efficientes*. The concept of *"causa"* is only a means of expression, nothing more; a means of description.

646 (*1885*)

There are analogies; e.g., a memory analogous to our memory that reveals itself in heredity and evolution and forms. An inventiveness in the application of tools to new ends analogous to our inventiveness and experimentation, etc.

That which we call our "consciousness" is innocent of any of the essential processes of our preservation and our growth; and no head is so subtle that it could construe more than a machine —to which every organic process is far superior.

647 (*1883-1888*)

Against Darwinism.[61]— The utility of an organ does not explain its origin; on the contrary! For most of the time during which a property is forming it does not preserve the individual and is of no use to him, least of all in the struggle with external circumstances and enemies.

What, after all, is "useful"? One must ask "useful in relation to what?" E.g., that which is useful for the long life of the individual might be unfavorable to its strength and splendor; that which preserves the individual might at the same time arrest and halt its evolution. On the other hand, a *deficiency*, a *degeneration*, can be of the highest utility in so far as it acts as a stimulant to other organs. In the same way, a state of need can be a condition of existence, in so far as it reduces an individual to that measure of

[61] Cf. sections 684 and 685.

expenditure which holds it together but prevents it from squandering itself.— The individual itself as a struggle between parts (for food, space, etc.): its evolution tied to the victory or predominance of individual parts, to an atrophy, a "becoming an organ" of other parts.

The influence of "external circumstances" is overestimated by Darwin to a ridiculous extent: the essential thing in the life process is precisely the tremendous shaping, form-creating force working from within which *utilizes* and *exploits* "external circumstances"— The new forms molded from within are not formed with an end in view; but in the struggle of the parts a new form is not left long without being related to a partial usefulness and then, according to its use, develops itself more and more completely.[62]

648 (*1883-1888*)

"Useful" in respect of acceleration of the tempo of evolution is a different kind of "useful" from that in respect of the greatest possible stability and durability of that which is evolved.

649 (*1883-1888*)

"Useful" in the sense of Darwinist biology means: proved advantageous in the struggle with others. But it seems to me that the feeling of increase, the feeling of becoming stronger, is itself, quite apart from any usefulness in the struggle, the real *progress*: only from this feeling does there arise the will to struggle—

650 (*1885-1886*)

Physiologists should think again before positing the "instinct of preservation" as the cardinal drive in an organic creature. A living thing wants above all to *discharge* its force: "preservation" is only a consequence of this.— Beware of *superfluous* teleological principles! The entire concept "instinct of preservation" is one of them.

---

[62] The MS continues: "If only that had been preserved which proved useful *all the time,* then above all the noxious, destructive, disintegrating capacities—the senseless, accidental, . . ."

651 (*Nov. 1887-March 1888*)

One cannot ascribe the most basic and primeval activities of protoplasm to a will to self-preservation, for it takes into itself absurdly more than would be required to preserve it; and, above all, it does not thereby "preserve itself," it falls apart— The drive that rules here has to explain precisely this absence of desire for self-preservation: "hunger" is an interpretation based on far more complicated organisms (—hunger is a specialized and later form of the drive, an expression of a division of labor in the service of a higher drive that rules over it).

652 (*March-June 1888*)

It is not possible to take hunger as the *primum mobile,*[63] any more than self-preservation. To understand hunger as a consequence of undernourishment means: hunger as the consequence of a will to power that no longer achieves mastery. It is by no means a question of replacing a loss—only later, as a result of the division of labor, after the will to power has learned to take other roads to its satisfaction, is an organism's need to appropriate *reduced* to hunger, to the need to replace what has been lost.

653 (*Spring-Fall 1887*)

The false "altruism" of biologists is ridiculous: propagation among amoebas seems to be the throwing off of ballast, a pure advantage. The excretion of useless material.

654 (*1885-1886*)

A protoplasm divides in two when its power is no longer adequate to control what it has appropriated: procreation is the consequence of an impotency.

When, from hunger, the males seek out the females and are united with them, procreation is the consequence of a hunger.

---

[63] First motive.

655 (*1885*)

The weaker presses to the stronger from a need for nourishment; it wants to get under it, if possible to become one with it. The stronger, on the contrary, drives others away; it does not want to perish in this manner; it grows and in growing it splits itself into two or more parts. The greater the impulse toward unity, the more firmly may one conclude that weakness is present; the greater the impulse towards variety, differentiation, inner decay, the more force is present.

The drive to approach—and the drive to thrust something back are the bond, in both the inorganic and the organic world. The entire distinction is a prejudice.

The will to power in every combination of forces, defending itself against the stronger, lunging at the weaker, is more correct. N.B.: Processes as "entities."[64]

656 (*Spring-Fall 1887*)

The will to power can manifest itself only against resistances; therefore it seeks that which resists it—this is the primeval tendency of the protoplasm when it extends pseudopodia and feels about. Appropriation and assimilation are above all a desire to overwhelm, a forming, shaping and reshaping, until at length that which has been overwhelmed has entirely gone over into the power domain of the aggressor and has increased the same.— If this incorporation is not successful, then the form probably falls to pieces; and the duality appears as a consequence of the will to power: in order not to let go what has been conquered, the will to power divides itself into two wills (in some cases without completely surrendering the connection between its two parts).

"Hunger" is only a narrower adaptation after the basic drive for power has won a more spiritual form.

657 (*1886-1887*)

What is "passive"?— To be hindered from moving forward: thus an act of resistance and reaction.

---

[64] Or: as "essence" (*Die Prozesse als "Wesen"*).

What is "active"?—reaching out for power.

"Nourishment"—is only derivative; the original phenomenon is: to desire to incorporate everything.

"Procreation"—only derivative; originally: where one will was not enough to organize the entire appropriated material, there came into force an opposing will which took in hand the separation; a new center of organization, after a struggle with the original will.

"Pleasure"—as a feeling of power (presupposing displeasure).

658 (*1885*)

1. The organic functions translated back to the basic will, the will to power—and understood as offshoots.

2. The will to power specializes as will to nourishment, to property, to tools, to servants (those who obey) and masters: the body as an example.— The stronger will directs the weaker. There is absolutely no other kind of causality than that of will upon will. Not explained mechanistically.

3. Thinking, feeling, willing in all living beings. What is a pleasure but: an excitation of the feeling of power by an obstacle (even more strongly by rhythmic obstacles and resistances)—so it swells up. Thus all pleasure includes pain.— If the pleasure is to be very great, the pains must be very protracted and the tension of the bow tremendous.

4. The spiritual functions. Will to shape, to assimilate, etc.

B. Man

659 (*1885*)

The evidence of the body.— Granted that the "soul" is an attractive and mysterious idea which philosophers have rightly abandoned only with reluctance—perhaps that which they have since learned to put in its place is even more attractive, even more mysterious. The human body, in which the most distant and most recent past of all organic development again becomes living and corporeal, through which and over and beyond which a tremendous inaudible stream seems to flow: the body is a more astonishing idea than the old "soul." In all ages, there has been more faith in the body, as our most personal possession, our most certain being, in short our ego, than in the spirit (or the "soul," or the subject, as school language now has it instead of soul). It has never occurred to anyone to regard his stomach as a strange or, say, a divine stomach: but to conceive his ideas as "inspired," his evaluations as "implanted by a God," his instincts as activity in a half-light—for this tendency and taste in men there are witnesses from all ages of mankind. Even now there is ample evidence among artists of a sort of wonderment and respectful suspension of judgment when they are faced with the question of the means by which they achieved their best work and from which world the creative idea came to them; when they ask this, they exhibit somethink like innocence and childlike shamefacedness; they hardly dare to say "it came from me, it was my hand that threw the dice."

Conversely, even those philosophers and religious teachers who had the most compelling ground in their logic and piety to consider their bodies a deception (and, indeed, as a deception overcome and done with) could not help acknowledging the foolish fact that the body has not gone away; of which the strangest witnesses are to be found partly in Paul, partly in the Vedanta philosophy. But what, after all, does *strength of belief* mean? It could still be a very foolish belief!— This should be reflected on:—

And after all, if belief in the body is only the result of an inference: supposing it were a false inference, as the idealists assert, is it not a question mark against the spirit itself that it should be the cause of such false inferences? Supposing multiplicity, space and time, and motion (and whatever else may be the presuppositions of a belief in what is bodily) were errors—what mistrust would this arouse against the spirit that had prompted such presuppositions? Let is suffice that, for the present, belief in the body is always a stronger belief than belief in the spirit; and whoever desires to undermine it, also undermines at the same time most thoroughly belief in the authority of the spirit!

660 (*1885-1886*)
The Body as a Political Structure.

The aristocracy in the body, the majority of the rulers (struggle between cells and tissues).

Slavery and division of labor: the higher type possible only through the subjugation of the lower, so that it becomes a function.

Pleasure and pain not opposites. The feeling of power.

"Nourishment" only a consequence of insatiable appropriation, of the will to power.

"Procreation," the crumbling that supervenes when the ruling cells are incapable of organizing that which has been appropriated.

It is the shaping force that desires an ever new supply of "material" (more "force"). The masterpiece of the construction of an organism from an egg.

"Mechanistic interpretation": desires nothing but quantities; but force is to be found in quality. Mechanistic theory can therefore only *describe* processes, not explain them.

"Purpose." One should start from the "sagacity" of plants.

Concept of "perfecting": *not* only greater complexity, but greater *power* (—does not have to be merely greater mass—).

Inference concerning the evolution of mankind: perfecting consists in the production of the most powerful individuals, who will use the great mass of people as their tools (and indeed the most intelligent and most pliable tools).

661 (*1883-1888*)

Why is all activity, even that of a sense, associated with pleasure? Because before it an obstacle, a burden existed? Or rather because all doing is an overcoming, a becoming master, and increases the feeling of power?— Pleasure in thinking.— Ultimately, it is not only the feeling of power, but the pleasure in creating and in the thing created; for all activity enters our consciousness as consciousness of a "work."

662 (*1883-1888*)

Creation—as selection and finishing of the thing selected. (This is the essential thing in every act of will.)

663 (*1885-1886*)

All events that result from intention are reducible to the intention to increase power.

664 (*1883-1888*)

When we do something there arises a feeling of force,[65] often even before the deed, occasioned by the idea of what is to be done (as at the sight of an enemy or an obstacle to which we feel ourselves equal): it is always an accompanying feeling. We instinctively think that this feeling of force is the cause of the action, that it is "the force." Our belief in causality is belief in force and its effect; a transference from our experience; and we identify force and the feeling of force.— Force, however, never moves things; the force we feel "does not set the muscles in motion." "We have no idea, no experience, of such a process."— "Just as we have no experience of force as the cause of motion, so we have no experience of the *necessity* of any motion." Force is supposed to be that which compels! "We experience only that one thing follows upon another.— We have no experience of either compulsion or arbitrariness in the following of one thing upon another." Causality is created only by thinking compulsion into the process. A certain "comprehension" is the consequence, i.e., we have made the process more human, "more familiar": the familiar is the familiar habit of human compulsion associated with the feeling of force.

665 (*1883-1888*)

I have the intention of raising my arm: supposing I know as little of the physiology of the human body and the mechanical laws of its motion as the man in the street, what could really be more vague, pale, uncertain than this intention, when compared with what follows upon it? And suppose I am the most astute of mechanics and specially instructed in the formulas applicable here, I should not be able to raise my arm one whit the better or the worse. Our "knowledge" and our "deed" lie in this case coldly apart, as if in two different domains.—

On the other hand: Napoleon executed a plan of campaign —what does that mean? Here everything pertaining to the execution of the plan is *known,* because everything has to be transmitted by command; but here, too, subordinates are presupposed

[65] *Kraftgefühl* could also be translated: feeling of strength.

who interpret and apply the general plan to the needs of the moment, measure of force, etc.

666 (*1883-1888*)

From time immemorial we have ascribed the value of an action, a character, an existence, to the *intention*, the *purpose* for the sake of which one has acted or lived: this age-old idiosyncrasy finally takes a dangerous turn—provided, that is, that the absence of intention and purpose in events comes more and more to the forefront of consciousness. Thus there seems to be in preparation a universal disvaluation: "Nothing has any meaning"—this melancholy sentence means "All meaning lies in intention, and if intention is altogether lacking, then meaning is altogether lacking, too." In accordance with this valuation, one was constrained to transfer the value of life to a "life after death," or to the progressive development of ideas or of mankind or of the people or beyond mankind; but with that one had arrived at a *progressus in infinitum* of purposes: one was at last constrained to make a place for oneself in the "world process" (perhaps with the dysdaemonistic[66] perspective that it was a process into nothingness).

In this regard, "purpose" requires a more vigorous critique: one must understand that an action is never caused by a purpose; that purpose and means are interpretations whereby certain points in an event are emphasized and selected at the expense of other points, which, indeed, form the majority; that every single time something is done with a purpose in view, something fundamentally different and other occurs; that every purposive action is like the supposed purposiveness of the heat the sun gives off: the enormously greater part is squandered; a part hardly worth considering serves a "purpose," has "meaning"; that a "purpose" and its "means" provide an indescribably imprecise description, which can, indeed, issue commands as a prescription, as a "will," but which presupposes a system of obedient and trained tools, which in place of indefinite entities posit nothing but fixed magnitudes (i.e., we imagine a system of shrewder but narrower intellects that posit purposes and means, in order to be able to ascribe to our only

---

[66] Nietzsche's coinage, after "eu-daemon," "eu-daemonism," which means "good spirit," "an ethic of happiness." "Dys-" is the antonym of "eu-" and means "ill" or "bad." Hence: evil-spirited or unhappy.

known "purpose" the role of the "cause of an action," to which procedure we really have no right: it would mean solving a problem by placing the solution in a world inaccessible to our observation—).

Finally: why could "a purpose" not be an epiphenomenon in the series of changes in the activating forces that bring about the purposive action—a pale image sketched in consciousness beforehand that serves to orient us concerning events, even as a symptom of events, *not* as their cause?— But with this we have criticized the will itself: is it not an illusion to take for a cause that which rises to consciousness as an act of will? Are not all phenomena of consciousness merely terminal phenomena, final links in a chain, but apparently conditioning one another in their succession on one level of consciousness? This could be an illusion—

667 (*1883-1888*)

Science does *not* ask what drives us to this will: it rather denies that will is exercised, and holds that something quite different occurs—in short, that the belief in "will" and "purpose" is an illusion. It does not inquire after the *motives* of an action, as if these had been present in consciousness before the action; but it first breaks up the action into a group of mechanistic phenomena and seeks the previous history of this mechanistic motion—but it does not seek it in feeling, sensation, thinking. It can never take the explanation from this quarter: sensation is precisely the material that is to be explained.— Its problem is: to explain the world *without* taking sensations as causes; for that would mean: considering sensations as the cause of sensations. Its task is certainly not accomplished.

Therefore: either no will—the hypothesis of science—or free will. The latter assumption the dominant feeling from which we cannot get loose, even if the scientific hypothesis were proved true.

The popular belief in cause and effect is founded on the presupposition that free will is the cause of every effect: it is only from this that we derive the feeling of causality. Thus there is also in it the feeling that every cause is *not* an effect but always only a cause—if the will is the cause. "Our acts of will are not necessary"— this idea is contained in the concept "will." What is necessary is the effect following upon the cause—that is what we feel. That our willing, too, is in every case a compulsion is a hypothesis.

668 (*Nov. 1887-March 1888*)

"Willing" is not "desiring," striving, demanding: it is distinguished from these by the affect of commanding.

There is no such thing as "willing," but only a willing *something*: one must not remove the aim from the total condition—as epistemologists do. "Willing" as they understand it is as little a reality as "thinking": it is a pure fiction.

It is part of willing that something is commanded (—which naturally does not mean that the will is "effected").

That state of tension by virtue of which a force seeks to discharge itself—is not an example of "willing."

669 (*Nov. 1887-March 1888*)

"Displeasure" and "pleasure" are the most stupid means imaginable of expressing judgments: which naturally does not mean that the judgments made audible in this manner must be stupid. The abandonment of all substantiation and logicality, a Yes or No in the reduction to a passionate desire to have or a rejection, an imperative abbreviation whose utility is unmistakable: this is pleasure and displeasure. It originates in the central sphere of the intellect; its presupposition is an infinitely speeded-up perception, ordering, subsumption, calculating, inferring: pleasure and displeasure are always terminal phenomena, not "causes."

The decision about what arouses pleasure and what arouses displeasure depends upon the degree of power: something that in relation to a small quantum of power appears dangerous and seems to require the speediest defense, can evoke, given the consciousness of greater power, a voluptuous excitation and a feeling of pleasure.

All feelings of pleasure and displeasure presuppose a calculation of utility and harmfulness to the whole; in other words, a sphere where an end (a state) is desired and means for it are selected. Pleasure and displeasure are never "basic facts."

Feelings of pleasure and displeasure are reactions of the will (affects), in which the intellectual center fixes the value of certain changes which have occurred in relation to the value of the whole; at the same time the introduction of counteractions.

670 (*1883-1888*)

The belief in "affects."— Affects are a construction of the intellect, an invention of causes that do not exist. All general bodily feelings that we do not understand are interpreted intellectually; i.e., a reason is sought in persons, experiences, etc., for why one feels this way or that. Thus something disadvantageous, dangerous, or strange is posited as the cause of our ill humor; in fact, it is added on to ill humor, in order to render our condition comprehensible. Frequent rushes of blood to the brain accompanied by a choking sensation are *interpreted* as "anger": persons and things that rouse us to anger are means of relieving our physiological condition.— Subsequently, after long habituation, certain incidents are so regularly associated with certain general feelings that the sight of certain incidents arouses the corresponding feeling and in particular brings with it this congestion of blood, production of semen, etc., through closeness of association. We then say that "the affect is aroused."

Judgments already inhere in "pleasure" and "displeasure"; stimuli are differentiated according to whether or not they further the feeling of power.

The belief in willing. To posit a belief as the cause of a mechanistic motion is to believe in miracles. The consistency of science demands that, once we have made the world thinkable by means of little images, we should also make the affects, desires, will, etc., thinkable, i.e., deny them and treat them as errors of the intellect.

671 (*1883-1888*)

Freedom of will or no freedom of will?— There is no such thing as "will"; it is only a simplifying conception of understanding, as is "matter."

All actions must first be made possible mechanically before they are willed. Or: the "purpose" *usually* comes into the mind only after everything has been prepared for its execution. The end is an "inner" "stimulus"—no more.

672 (*1883-1888*)

The most recent history of an action relates to this action: but further back lies a prehistory which covers a wider field: the individual action is at the same time a part of a much more extensive, *later* fact. The briefer and the more extended processes are not separated—

673 (*1883-1888*)

Theory of chance. The soul a selective and self-nourishing entity, perpetually extremely shrewd and creative (this creative force is usually overlooked! is conceived only as "passive").

To recognize the active force, the creative force in the chance event:—chance itself is only the clash of creative impulses.

674 (*Nov. 1887-March 1888*)

In the tremendous multiplicity of events within an organism, the part which becomes conscious to us is a mere means: and the little bit of "virtue," "selflessness," and similar fictions are refuted radically by the total balance of events. We should study our organism in all its immorality—

The animal functions are, as a matter of principle, a million times more important than all our beautiful moods and heights of consciousness: the latter are a surplus, except when they have to serve as tools of those animal functions. The entire *conscious* life, the spirit along with the soul, the heart, goodness, and virtue—in whose service do they labor? In the service of the greatest possible perfection of the means (means of nourishment, means of enhancement) of the basic animal functions: above all, the enhancement of life.

What one used to call "body" and "flesh" is of such unspeakably greater importance: the remainder is a small accessory. The task of spinning on the chain of life, and in such a way that the thread grows ever more powerful—that is the task.

But consider how heart, soul, virtue, spirit practically conspire together to subvert this systematic task—as if *they* were the end in view!— The degeneration of life is conditioned essentially by the extraordinary proneness to error of consciousness: it is held in check by instinct the least of all and therefore blunders the longest and the most thoroughly.

To measure whether existence has value according to the pleasant or unpleasant feelings aroused in this consciousness: can one think of a madder extravagance of vanity? For it is only a means—and pleasant or unpleasant feelings are also only means!

What is the objective measure of value? Solely the quantum of enhanced and organized power.[67]

675 (*Nov. 1887-March 1888*)

[The value of devaluing.— What I demand is][68] that one should take the doer back into the deed after having conceptually removed the doer and thus emptied the deed; that one should take doing *something,* the "aim," the "intention," the "purpose," back into the deed after having artificially removed all this and thus emptied the deed.

All "purposes," "aims," "meaning" are only modes of expression and metamorphoses of one will that is inherent in all events: the will to power. To have purposes, aims, intentions, *willing* in general, is the same thing as willing to be stronger, willing to grow—and, in addition, willing the means to this.

The most universal and basic instinct in all doing and willing has for precisely this reason remained the least known and most hidden, because *in praxi* we always follow its commandments, because we *are* this commandment—

All valuations are only consequences and narrow perspectives in the service of this one will: valuation itself is only this will to power.

A critique of being from the point of view of any one of these values is something absurd and erroneous. Even supposing that a process of decline begins in this way, this process still stands in the service of this will.

To appraise being itself! But this appraisal itself is still this being!—and if we say no, we still do what we *are*.

One must comprehend the absurdity of this posture of judging

[67] In the MS the text continues: "according to what happens in all events, a will for more . . ."

[68] The words I have placed in brackets were added by Peter Gast.

existence, and then try to understand what is really involved in it. It is symptomatic.

676 (*1883-1888*)
On the Origin of Our Evaluations

We can analyze our body spatially, and then we gain precisely the same image of it as we have of the stellar system, and the distinction between the organic and inorganic is no longer noticeable. Formerly, one explained the motions of the stars as effects produced by entities conscious of a purpose. One no longer needs this explanation, and in regard to bodily motions and changes, too, one has long since abandoned the belief in an explanation by means of a consciousness that determines purposes. By far the greater number of motions have nothing whatever to do with consciousness; nor with sensation. Sensations and thoughts are something extremely insignificant and rare in relation to the countless number of events that occur every moment.

On the other hand, we perceive that a purposiveness rules over the smallest events that is beyond our understanding: planning, selectivity, co-ordination, reparation, etc. In short, we discover an activity that would have to be ascribed to a far higher and more comprehensive intellect than we know of. We learn to think less highly of all that is conscious; we unlearn responsibility for ourselves, since we as conscious, purposive creatures, are only the smallest part of us. Of the numerous influences operating at every moment, e.g., air, electricity, we sense almost nothing: there could well be forces that, although we never sense them, continually influence us. Pleasure and pain are very rare and scarce appearances compared with the countless stimuli that a cell or organ exercises upon another cell or organ.

We are in the phase of modesty of consciousness. Ultimately, we understand the conscious ego itself only as a tool in the service of a higher, comprehensive intellect; and then we are able to ask whether all conscious willing, all conscious purposes, all evaluations are not perhaps only means through which something essentially different from what appears in consciousness is to be achieved. We think: it is a question of our pleasure and displeasure——but pleasure and displeasure could be means through which we have to achieve something that lies outside our consciousness.—— It must be shown to what extent everything conscious remains on the surface; how an action and the image of an action differ, how little one knows of what precedes an action; how fantastic are our feelings of "freedom of will," "cause and effect"; how thoughts and images are, like words, only signs of thoughts; the inexplicability of every action; the superficiality of all praise and blame; how essential fiction and conceits are in which we dwell consciously; how all our words refer to fictions (our affects, too), and how the bond between man and man depends on the transmission and elaboration of these fictions; while fundamentally the real bond (through procreation) goes its unknown way. Does this belief in common fictions really *change* men? Or is the entire realm of ideas and evaluations itself only an expression of unknown changes? *Are* there really will, purposes, thoughts, values? Is the whole of conscious life perhaps only a reflected image? And even when evaluation seems to determine the nature of a man, fundamentally something quite different is happening! In short: supposing that purposiveness in the work of nature could be explained without the assumption of an ego that posits purposes: could *our* positing of purposes, our willing, etc., not perhaps be also only a language of signs for something altogether different, namely something that does not will and is unconscious? Only the faintest reflection of that natural expediency in the organic but not different from it?

Put briefly: perhaps the entire evolution of the spirit is a question of the body; it is the history of the development of a higher body that emerges into our sensibility. The organic is rising to yet higher levels. Our lust for knowledge of nature is a means through which the body desires to perfect itself. Or rather: hundreds of thousands of experiments are made to change the nourishment, the mode of living and of dwelling of the body; consciousness and evaluations in the body, all kinds of pleasure and displeasure, are signs of these changes and experiments. In the long run, it is not a question of man at all: he is to be overcome.

677 (*1883-1888*)

To What Extent Interpretations of the World are Symptoms of a Ruling Drive

The *artistic* view of the world: to sit down to contemplate life. But any analysis of the aesthetic outlook is lacking: its reduction to cruelty, a feeling of security, playing the judge and standing outside, etc. One must examine the artist himself, and his psychology (critique of the drive to play as a release of force, a pleasure in change, in impressing one's soul on something foreign, the absolute egoism of the artist, etc.) What drives he sublimates.

The *scientific* view of the world: critique of the psychological need for science. The desire to make comprehensible; the desire to make practical, useful, exploitable—to what extent anti-aesthetic. Only value, what can be counted and calculated. How an average type of man seeks to gain the upper hand in this way. Dreadful when *history* is appropriated in this way—the realm of the superior, of those who judge. What drives they sublimate!

The *religious* view of the world: critique of the religious man. He is *not* necessarily the moral man, but the man of powerful exaltations and deep depressions who interprets the former with gratitude or suspicion and does not derive them from himself (—not the latter either). Essentially the man who feels himself "unfree," who sublimates his moods, his instincts of subjection.

The *moral* view of the world: The feelings of a social order of rank are projected into the universe: irremovability, law, classification and co-ordination, because they are valued the highest, are also sought in the highest places—above the universe or behind the universe.

What is common to all: the ruling drives want to be viewed also as the highest courts of value in general, indeed as creative and ruling powers. It is clear that these drives either oppose or subject each other (join together synthetically or alternate in dominating). Their profound antagonism is so great, however, that where they *all* seek satisfaction, a man of profound mediocrity must result.

678 (*1883-1888*)

Whether the origin of our apparent "knowledge" is not to be sought solely in older evaluations which have become so much part of us that they belong to our basic constitution? So that what really happens is only that newer needs grapple with the results of the oldest needs?

The world seen, felt, interpreted as thus and thus so that organic life may preserve itself in this perspective of interpretation. Man is not only a single individual but one particular line of the total living organic world. That *he* endures proves that a species of interpretation (even though accretions are still being added) has also endured, that the system of interpretation has not changed. "Adaptation."

Our "dissatisfaction," our "ideal," etc., is perhaps the consequence of this incorporated piece of interpretation, of our perspective point of view; perhaps organic life will in the end perish through it—even as the division of labor in organisms is accompanied by a withering and weakening of the parts, and finally leads to the death of the whole. The destruction of organic life, even in its highest form, must follow the same pattern as the destruction of the individual.

679 (*1883-1888*)

Individuation, judged from the standpoint of the theory of descent, demonstrates a continual falling apart of one into two, and also the continual passing away of individuals who carry forward the evolution: by far the greater number die out every time ("the body").

The basic phenomenon: countless individuals sacrificed for the sake of a few, to make them possible.— One must not let oneself be deceived; it is just the same with peoples and races: they constitute the "body" for the production of isolated valuable individuals, who carry on the great process.

680 (*1883-1888*)

Against the theory that the isolated individual has in view the advantage of the species, of his posterity, at the cost of his own advantage: that is only an appearance.

The tremendous importance the individual accords to the sexual instinct is not a result of its importance for the species, but arises because procreation is the real achievement of the individual and consequently his highest interest, his highest expression of power (not judged from the consciousness but from the center of the whole individuation).

681 (*1883-1888*)

Basic errors of biologists hitherto: it is not a question of the species but of more powerful individuals. (The many are only a means).

Life is not the adaptation of inner circumstances to outer ones, but will to power, which, working from within, incorporates and subdues more and more of that which is "outside."

These biologists carry forward moral evaluations (—the "higher value of altruism," hostility against the lust to dominate, against war, against what is not useful, against orders of rank and class).

682 (*Spring-Fall 1887*)

In natural science, the moral depreciation of the ego goes hand in hand with an overestimation of the species. But the species is something just as illusory as the ego: one had made a false distinction. The ego is a hundred times more than merely a unit in the chain of members; it is this chain itself, entirely; and the species is a mere abstraction from the multiplicity of these chains and their partial similarity. That the individual is sacrificed to the species, as has so often been asserted, is certainly not a fact; rather only an example of false interpretation.

683 (*March-June 1888*)

Formula for the superstitious belief in "progress," by a famous physiologist of the cerebral activities:

"*L'animal ne fait jamais de progrès comme espèce. L'homme seul fait de progrès comme espèce.*"[68]

684 (*March-June 1888*)

Anti-Darwin. The domestication of man: what definite value can it have? or has domestication in general any definite value?—There are grounds for denying the latter.

The school of Darwin certainly makes a great effort to convince us of the reverse: it wants to show that the effect of domestication can become profound, even fundamental. In the meantime, we stick to our old opinion: up to now, domestication has produced only quite superficial effects—when it has not produced degenera-

[68] "Animals never progress as a species. Only man progresses as a species."

tion. And everything that eludes the hand and discipline of man returns almost at once to its natural state. The type remains constant: one cannot "'*dénaturer la nature*.'"

One counts on the struggle for existence, the death of the weaker creatures and the survival of the most robust and gifted; consequently one imagines a continual growth in perfection. We have convinced ourselves, conversely, that in the struggle for existence chance serves the weak as well as the strong; that cunning often prevails over strength; that the fruitfulness of the species stands in a notable relation to its chances of destruction—

One credits natural selection at the same time with the power of slow and endless metamorphosis; one wants to believe that every advantage is inherited and grows stronger and stronger with succeeding generations (whereas heredity is so capricious that—); one observes the fortunate adaptation of certain creatures to very special conditions of life, and one explains that these adaptations result from the influence of the milieu.

But one nowhere finds any example *of unconscious selection* (absolutely not). The most disparate individuals unite with one another, the extremes are submerged in the mass. Everything competes to preserve its type; creatures with exterior markings to protect them from danger do not lose them when they encounter conditions in which they live without danger— When they live in places in which their dress ceases to hide them they do not by any means adapt to the new milieu.

One has so exaggerated the selection of the most beautiful that it greatly exceeds the drive to beauty in our own race! In fact, the most beautiful mate with utterly disinherited creatures, and the biggest with the smallest. We almost always see males and females take advantage of any chance encounter, exhibiting no selectivity whatsoever.— Modification through food and climate —but in reality a matter of complete indifference.

There are no *transitional forms*.—

Different species derived from one. Experience says that one type becomes master again.[69]

One asserts the increasing evolution of creatures. All grounds

---

[69] This paragraph is omitted in all editions, including Schlechta's, but printed in the back of 1911, p. 508 *f*, with the explanation: "What is missing in the text could be deciphered in full only recently, and is uncertain on account of its difficulty."

are lacking. Every type has its limits; beyond these there is no evolution. Up to this point, absolute regularity.

Primitive creatures are said to be the ancestors of those now existing. But a look at the fauna and flora of the Tertiary merely permits us to think of an as yet unexplored country that harbors types that do not exist elsewhere, while those existing elsewhere are missing.[70]

*

My general view.— First proposition: man as a species is not progressing. Higher types are indeed attained, but they do not last. The level of the species is *not* raised.

Second proposition: man as a species does not represent any progress compared with any other animal. The whole animal and vegetable kingdom does not evolve from the lower to the higher—but all at the same time, in utter disorder, over and against each other. The richest and most complex forms— for the expression "higher type" means no more than this—perish more easily: only the lowest preserve an apparent indestructibility. The former are achieved only rarely and maintain their superiority with difficulty; the latter are favored by a compromising fruitfulness.

Among men, too, the higher types, the lucky strokes of evolution, perish most easily as fortunes change. They are exposed to every kind of decadence: they are extreme, and that almost means decadents.

The brief spell of beauty, of genius, of Caesar, is *sui generis*: such things are not inherited. The *type* is hereditary; a type is nothing extreme, no "lucky stroke"—

This is not due to any special fatality or malevolence of nature, but simply to the concept "higher type": the higher type represents an incomparably greater complexity—a greater sum of co-ordinated elements: so its disintegration is also incomparably more likely. The "genius" is the sublimest machine there is—consequently the most fragile.

Third proposition: the domestication (the "culture") of man does not go deep— Where it does go deep it at once becomes degeneration (type: the Christian). The "savage" (or, in moral

[70] The immediately preceding note applies to this paragraph, too. The criticisms of Darwin should be compared with sections 647 and 685.

terms, the evil man) is a return to nature—and in a certain sense his recovery, his *cure* from "culture"—

685 (*March-June 1888*)

Anti-Darwin.— What surprises me most when I survey the broad destinies of man is that I always see before me the opposite of that which Darwin and his school see or *want* to see today: selection in favor of the stronger, better-constituted, and the progress of the species. Precisely the opposite is palpable: the elimination of the lucky strokes, the uselessness of the more highly developed types, the inevitable dominion of the average, even the *sub-average* types. If we are not shown why man should be an exception among creatures, I incline to the prejudice that the school of Darwin has been deluded everywhere.

That will to power in which I recognize the ultimate ground and character of all change provides us with the reason why selection is not in favor of the exceptions and lucky strokes: the strongest and most fortunate are weak when opposed by organized herd instincts, by the timidity of the weak, by the vast majority. My general view of the world of values shows that it is not the lucky strokes, the select types, that have the upper hand in the supreme values that are today placed over mankind; rather it is the decadent types—perhaps there is nothing in the world more interesting than this *unwelcome* spectacle—

Strange though it may sound, one always has to defend[71] the strong against the weak; the fortunate against the unfortunate; the healthy against those degenerating and afflicted with hereditary taints. If one translates reality into a morality, this morality is: the mediocre are worth more than the exceptions; the decadent forms more than the mediocre; the will to nothingness has the upper hand over the will to life—and the overall aim is, in Christian, Buddhist, Schopenhauerian terms: "better *not* to be than to be."

I rebel against the translation of reality into a morality: therefore I abhor Christianity with a deadly hatred, because it created sublime words and gestures to throw over a horrible reality the cloak of justice, virtue, and divinity—

---

[71] The printed text has "prove" (*beweisen*); but the word is illegible, and this is a mere conjecture (1911, p. 509) and makes little sense.

I see all philosophers, I see science kneeling before a reality that is the reverse of the struggle for existence as taught by Darwin's school—that is to say, I see on top and surviving everywhere those who compromise life and the value of life.— The error of the school of Darwin becomes a problem to me: how can one be so blind as to see so badly at *this* point?

That *species* represent any progress is the most unreasonable assertion in the world: so far they represent one level. That the higher organisms have evolved from the lower has not been demonstrated in a single case. I see how the lower preponderate through their numbers, their shrewdness, their cunning—I do not see how an accidental variation gives an advantage, at least not for so long a period; why an accidental change should grow so strong would be something else needing explanation.

I find the "cruelty of nature," of which so much is said, in another place: she is cruel towards her children of fortune, she spares and protects and loves *les humbles,* just as—[72]

In summa: growth in the *power* of a species is perhaps guaranteed less by a preponderance of its children of fortune, of strong members, than by a preponderance of average and lower types— The latter possess great fruitfulness and duration; with the former comes an increase in danger, rapid wastage, speedy reduction in numbers.

686 (*1884*)

Man hitherto—as it were, an embryo of the man of the future;—all the form-giving forces directed toward the latter are present in the former; and because they are tremendous, the more a present-day individual determines the future, the more he will suffer. This is the profoundest conception of suffering: the form-giving forces are in painful collision.— The isolation of the individual ought not to deceive us: something flows on *underneath* individuals. That the individual feels himself isolated is itself the most powerful goad in the process towards the most distant goals: his search for *his* happiness is the means that holds together and moderates the form-giving forces, so they do not destroy themselves.

---

[72] "Just as" is omitted in all editions.

687 (*Spring-Fall 1887*)

Superabundant force in *spirituality*, setting *itself* new goals; by no means merely commanding and leading on behalf of the lower world or the preservation of the organism, the "individual."

We are *more* than the individuals: we are the whole chain as well, with the tasks of all the futures of that chain.

3. Theory of the Will to Power and of Values

688 (*March-June 1888*)

Unitary conception of psychology.— We are accustomed to consider the development of an immense abundance of forms compatible with an origin in unity.

[My theory would be:—][73] that the will to power is the primitive form of affect, that all other affects are only developments of it;

that it is notably enlightening to posit *power* in place of individual "happiness" (after which every living thing is supposed to be striving): "there is a striving for power, for an increase of power";—pleasure is only a symptom of the feeling of power attained, a consciousness of a difference (—there is no striving for pleasure: but pleasure supervenes when that which is being striven for is attained: pleasure is an accompaniment, pleasure is not the motive—);

that all driving force is will to power, that there is no other physical, dynamic or psychic force except this.

In our science, where the concept of cause and effect is redued to the relationship of equivalence, with the object of proving that the same quantum of force is present on both sides, the driving force is lacking: we observe only results, and we consider them equivalent in content and force[74]—

[73] The words I have placed in brackets were added by the German editors but are uncritically reproduced in all editions, including Schlechta's.

These ideas, as well as many of those developed in the following sections, down through 715, are discussed in Chapter 9, "Power versus Pleasure," of my *Nietzsche*.

[74] The immediately following words in the MS are omitted in all editions: "We spare ourselves the question of the *simplification* of a change. . . ."

It is simply a matter of experience that change never ceases: we have not the slightest inherent reason for assuming that one change must follow upon another. On the contrary: a condition once achieved would seem to be obliged to preserve itself if there were not in it a capacity for desiring not to preserve itself— Spinoza's law of "self-preservation" ought really to put a stop to change: but this law is false, the opposite is true. It can be shown most clearly that every living thing does everything it can not to preserve itself but to become *more*—

689 (*March-June 1888*)

Critique of the concept: cause.[75]— From a psychological point of view the concept "cause" is our feeling of power resulting from the so-called act of will—our concept "effect" the superstition that this feeling of power is the motive power itself—

A condition that accompanies an event and is itself an effect of the event is projected as the "sufficient reason" for the event;— the relation of tensions in our feeling of power (pleasure as the feeling of power), of a resistance overcome—are they illusions?—

If we translate the concept "cause" back to the only sphere known to us, from which we have derived it, we cannot imagine any change that does not involve a will to power. We do not know how to explain a change except as the encroachment of one power upon another power.

Mechanics shows us only the results, and then only in images (motion is a figure of speech). Gravity itself has no mechanistic cause, since it itself is the ground of mechanistic results.

The will to accumulate force is special to the phenomena of life, to nourishment, procreation, inheritance—to society, state, custom, authority. Should we not be permitted to assume this will as a motive cause in chemistry, too?—and in the cosmic order?

Not merely conservation of energy, but maximal economy in use, so the only reality is the will to grow stronger of every center of force—not self-preservation, but the will to appropriate, dominate, increase, grow stronger.

The possibility of science should be *proved* by a principle

---

[75] I have restored the title found in the MS. In the printed texts a title devised by Peter Gast has been substituted: "Will to power and causalism."

of causality?[76] "From like causes like effects"— "A permanent law governing things"—"An invariable order"?— Because something is calculable, does that mean it is necessary?

If something happens thus and not otherwise, that does not imply a "principle," "law," "order," [but the operation of][77] quanta of force the essence of which consists in exercising power against other quanta of force.

Can we assume a striving for power divorced from a sensation of pleasure and displeasure, i.e., divorced from the feeling of enhanced or diminished power? Is mechanism only a sign language for the *internal* factual world of struggling and conquering quanta of will? All the presuppositions of mechanistic theory —matter, atom, gravity, pressure and stress—are not "facts-in-themselves" but interpretations with the aid of psychical fictions.

Life, as the form of being most familiar to us, is specifically a will to the accumulation of force; all the processes of life depend on this: nothing wants to preserve itself, everything is to be added and accumulated.

Life as a special case (hypothesis based upon it applied to the total character of being—) strives after a *maximal feeling of power;* essentially a striving for more power; striving is nothing other than striving for power; the basic and innermost thing is still this will. (Mechanics is merely the semeiotics of the results.)

690 (*Nov. 1887-March 1888*)

One cannot discover the cause of there being any evolution at all by studying evolution; one should not wish to think of it as "becoming," even less as having become— The "will to power" cannot have become.

691 (*1885-1886*)

What has been the relation of the total organic process to

[76] At this point the following marginal comment is found in the MS: "Over the belief in cause and effect one always forgets the main thing: the event itself. One has posited an agent, one has hypothesized the event again." The reading is uncertain.

[77] The words I have placed in brackets are found in all editions but not in the MS.

the rest of nature?— That is where its fundamental will stands revealed.

692 (*March-June 1888*)

Is "will to power" a *kind* of "will" or identical with the concept "will"? Is it the same thing as desiring? or *commanding*? Is it that "will" of which Schopenhauer said it was the "in-itself of things"?

My proposition is: that the will of psychology hitherto is an unjustified generalization, that this will *does not exist at all*, that instead of grasping the idea of the development of one definite will into many forms, one has eliminated the character of the will by subtracting from it its content, its "whither?"—this is in the highest degree the case with *Schopenhauer*: what he calls "will" is a mere empty word. It is even less a question of a "will to live"; for life is merely a special case of the will to power; —it is quite arbitrary to assert that everything strives to enter into *this* form of the will to power.

693 (*March-June 1888*)

If the innermost essence of being is will to power, if pleasure is every increase of power, displeasure every feeling of not being able to resist or dominate; may we not then posit pleasure and displeasure as cardinal facts? Is will possible without these two oscillations of Yes and No?— But *who* feels pleasure?— But *who* wants power?— Absurd question, if the essence itself is power-will and consequently feelings of pleasure and displeasure! Nonetheless: opposites, obstacles are needed; therefore, relatively, encroaching units—

694 (*Nov. 1887-March 1888*)

The measure of failure and fatality must grow with the resistance a force seeks to master; and as a force can expend itself only on what resists it, there is necessarily an *ingredient of displeasure* in every action. But this displeasure acts as a lure of life and strengthens the will to power!

695 (*March-June 1888*)

If pleasure and displeasure relate to the feeling of power, then life must represent a growth in power, so that the difference caused by this growth must enter consciousness— If one level of power were maintained, pleasure would have only lowerings of this level by which to set its standards, only states of displeasure—not states of pleasure— The will to grow is of the essence of pleasure: that power increases, that the difference enters consciousness.

From a certain point onwards, in decadence, the opposite difference enters consciousness, the decrease: the memory of former moments of strength depresses present feelings of pleasure —comparison now *weakens* pleasure.

696 (*Nov. 1887-March 1888*)

It is *not* the satisfaction of the will that causes pleasure (I want to fight this superficial theory—the absurd psychological counterfeiting of the nearest things—), but rather the will's forward thrust and again and again becoming master over that which stands in its way. The feeling of pleasure lies precisely in the dissatisfaction of the will, in the fact that the will is never satisfied unless it has opponents and resistance.— "The happy man": a herd ideal.

697 (*Nov. 1887-March 1888*)

The normal dissatisfaction of our drives, e.g., hunger, the sexual drive, the drive to motion, contains in it absolutely nothing depressing; it works rather as an agitation of the feeling of life, as every rhythm of small, painful stimuli strengthens it, (whatever pessimists may say). This dissatisfaction, instead of making one disgusted with life, is the great stimulus to life.

(One could perhaps describe pleasure in general as a rhythm of little unpleasurable stimuli.)

698 (*Summer-Fall 1883*)

Kant said: "I subscribe entirely to these sentences of Count

Verri (*Sull' indole del piacere e del dolore;* 1781): *Il solo principio motore dell' uomo è il dolore. Il dolore precede ogni piacere. Il piacere non è un essere positivo.*"[78]

699 (*March-June 1888*)

Pain is something different from pleasure—I mean it is *not* its opposite.

If the essence of "pleasure" has been correctly described as a feeling of more power (hence as a feeling of difference, presupposing a comparison), this does not yet furnish a definition of the essence of "displeasure." The false opposites in which the people, and *consequently* language, believes, have always been dangerous hindrances to the advance of truth. There are even cases in which a kind of pleasure is conditioned by a certain *rhythmic sequence* of little unpleasurable stimuli: in this way a very rapid increase of the feeling of power, the feeling of pleasure, is achieved. This is the case, e.g., in tickling, also the sexual tickling in the act of coitus: here we see displeasure at work as an ingredient of pleasure. It seems, a little hindrance that is overcome and immediately followed by another little hindrance that is again overcome—this game of resistance and victory arouses most strongly that general feeling of superabundant, excessive power that constitutes the essence of pleasure.

The opposite, an increase in the sensation of pain through the introduction of little pleasurable stimuli, is lacking; for pleasure and pain are not opposites.

Pain is an *intellectual* occurrence in which a definite judgment is expressed—the judgment *"harmful,"* in which a long experience is summarized. There is no pain as such. It is not being wounded that hurts; but the experience of the bad consequences being wounded can have for the whole organism expresses itself in that profound shock that is called displeasure; (in the case of harmful influences with which former men were unacquainted, e.g., those of new combinations of poisonous chemicals, pain bears no witness—and we are lost).

The really specific thing in pain is always the protracted shock, the lingering vibrations of a terrifying *choc* in the cerebral center of the nervous system:— one does not really suffer from

---

[78] *On the Nature of Pleasure and Pain:* The only moving principle of man is pain. Pain precedes every pleasure. Pleasure is not a positive state.

the cause of pain (any sort of injury, for example), but from the protracted disturbance of equilibrium that occurs as a result of the *choc*. Pain is a sickness of the cerebral nerve centers—pleasure is certainly not a sickness.

That pain is the cause of reflex actions has appearance and even the prejudice of philosophers in its favor; but, if one observes it closely, in cases of sudden pain the reflex comes noticeably earlier than the sensation of pain. It would go ill with me if, when I stumbled, I had to wait for the fact to ring the bell of consciousness and for instructions how to act to be telegraphed back. What I notice with the greatest possible clarity is rather that the reflex of my foot follows first to prevent my falling, and then, at a measurable distance in time, the sudden sensation of a kind of painful wave in the front part of my head. Thus one does *not* react to the pain. Pain is subsequently projected to the wounded place—but the nature of this local pain is nonetheless not an expression of the kind of the local injury; it is a mere place-sign corresponding to the force and pitch of the injury the nerve centers have received. That as a result of this *choc* the muscular strength of the organism is measurably lowered does not warrant our seeking the *essence* of pain in a diminution of the feeling of power.

To repeat it again, one does *not* react to pain; displeasure is not a "cause" of action. Pain itself is a reaction, the reflex is another and *earlier* reaction—both originate in different places—

700 (*1883-1888*)

Intellectual nature of pain: it does not indicate what has been damaged at the moment, but the value of the damage in relation to the individual as a whole.

Whether there are pains from which "the species" and *not* the individual suffers—?

701 (*Nov. 1887-March 1883*)

"The sum of displeasure outweighs the sum of pleasure; consequently it would be better if the world did not exist"— "The world is something that rationally should not exist because it causes the feeling subject more displeasure than pleasure"—chatter of this sort calls itself pessimism today!

Pleasure and displeasure are accidentals, not causes; they are value judgments of the second rank, derived from a ruling value—"useful," "harmful," speaking in the form of feelings, and consequently absolutely sketchy and dependent. For with every "useful," "harmful," one still has to ask in a hundred different ways: "for what?"

I despise this *pessimism of sensibility*: it is itself a sign of deeply impoverished life.[79]

702 (*March-June 1888*)

Man does *not* seek pleasure and does not avoid displeasure: one will realize which famous prejudice I am contradicting. Pleasure and displeasure are mere consequences, mere epiphenomena—what man wants, what every smallest part of a living organism wants, is an increase of power. Pleasure or displeasure follow from the striving after that; driven by that will it seeks resistance, it needs something that opposes it— Displeasure, as an obstacle to its will to power, is therefore a normal fact, the normal ingredient of every organic event; man does not avoid it, he is rather in continual need of it; every victory, every feeling of pleasure, every event, presupposes a resistance overcome.

Let us take the simplest case, that of primitive nourishment: the protoplasm extends it pseudopodia in search of something that resists it—not from hunger but from will to power.[80] Thereupon it attempts to overcome, appropriate, assimilate what it encounters: what one calls "nourishment" is merely a derivative phenomenon, an application of the original will to become *stronger*.

Displeasure thus does not merely not have to result in a diminution of our feeling of power, but in the average case it actually stimulates this feeling of power—the obstacle is the stimulus of this will to power.

703 (*March-June 1888*)

One has confused displeasure with one *kind* of displeasure,

---

[79] The MS continues: "I shall never permit such a meager [——] as Hartmann to speak of his 'philosophical pessimism.'" Printed in 1911, p. 509, with the noun omitted. Eduard von Hartmann (1842-1906) tried to synthesize Schopenhauer and Hegel. His books include *Philosophie des Unbewussten* (*Philosophy of the Unconscious*), 1869; 12th ed., 1923.

[80] The words that immediately follow in the MS have been omitted in all editions: "Duality as the consequence of too weak a unity."

with exhaustion; the latter does indeed represent a profound diminution and reduction of the will to power, a measurable loss of force. That is to say: there exists (a) displeasure as a means of stimulating the increase of power, and (b) displeasure following an overexpenditure of power; in the first case a stimulus, in the second the result of an excessive stimulation— Inability to resist is characteristic of the latter kind of displeasure: a challenge to that which resists belongs to the former— The only pleasure still felt in the condition of exhaustion is falling asleep; victory is the pleasure in the other case—

The great confusion on the part of psychologists consisted in not distinguishing beween these two kinds of pleasure—that of falling asleep and that of victory. The exhausted want rest, relaxation, peace, calm—the happiness of the nihilistic religions and philosophies; the rich and living want victory, opponents overcome, the overflow of the feeling of power across wider domains than hitherto. All healthy functions of the organism have this need—and the whole organism[81] is such a complex of systems struggling for an increase of the feeling of power——

704 (*Nov. 1887-March 1888*)

How does it happen that the basic articles of faith in psychology are one and all the most arrant misrepresentations and counterfeits? "Man strives after happiness," e.g.—how much of that is true? In order to understand what "life" is, what kind of striving and tension life is, the formula must apply as well to trees and plants as to animals. "What does a plant strive after?"—but here we have already invented a false unity which does not exist: the fact of a millionfold growth with individual and semi-individual initiatives is concealed and denied if we begin by positing a crude unity "plant." That the very smallest "individuals" cannot be understood in the sense of a "metaphysical individuality" and atom, that their spere of power is continually changing—that is the first thing that becomes obvious; but does each of them strive after happiness when it changes in this way?—

But all expansion, incorporation, growth means striving against something that resists; motion is essentially tied up with

[81] The words that immediately follow in the MS have been omitted in all editions: "up to the age of puberty."

states of displeasure; that which is here the driving force must in any event desire something else if it desires displeasure in this way and continually looks for it.— For what do the trees in a jungle fight each other? For "happiness"?— *For power!*—

Man, become master over the forces of nature, master over his own savagery and licentiousness (the desires have learned to obey and be useful)—man, in comparison with a pre-man—represents a tremendous quantum of *power—not* an increase in "happiness"! How can one claim that he has *striven* for happiness?—

705 (*1883-1888*)[82]

As I say this I see above me, glittering under the stars, the tremendous rat's tail of errors that has hitherto counted as the highest inspiration of humanity: "All happiness is a consequence of virtue, all virtue is a consequence of free will!"

Let us reverse the values: all fitness the result of fortunate organization, all freedom the result of fitness (—freedom here understood as facility in self-direction. Every artist will understand me).

706 (*Spring-Fall 1887*)

"The value of life."— Life is a unique case; one must justify all existence and not only life—the justifying principle[83] is one that explains life, too.

Life is only a *means* to something; it is the expression of forms of the growth of power.

707 (*Spring-Fall 1887; rev. Spring-Fall 1888*)

The *"conscious* world" cannot serve as a starting point for values: need for an *"objective"* positing of values.

In relation to the vastness and multiplicity of collaboration and mutual opposition encountered in the life of every organism,

---

[82] In the MS this section follows immediately upon the text of *Twilight*, "The Four Great Errors," section 2.

[83] "The last three lines are crossed out in the MS": 1911, p. 510. Unless "three" is a misprint (for two), the deletion would begin at the point indicated.

the *conscious* world of feelings, intentions, and valuations is a small section. We have no right whatever to posit this piece of consciousness as the aim and wherefore of this total phenomenon of life: becoming conscious is obviously only one more means toward the unfolding and extension of the power of life. Therefore it is a piece of naiveté to posit pleasure or spirituality or morality or any other particular of the sphere of consciousness as the highest value —and perhaps even to justify "the world" by means of this.

This is my *basic objection* to all philosophic-moralistic cosmo- and theodicies, to all *wherefores* and *highest values* in philosophy and theology hitherto. One kind of means has been misunderstood as an end; conversely, life and the enhancement of its power has been debased to a means.

If we wished to postulate a goal adequate to life, it could not coincide with any category of conscious life; it would rather have to explain all of them as a means to itself—

The "denial of life" as an aim of life, an aim of evolution! Existence as a great stupidity! Such a lunatic interpretation is only the product of measuring life by aspects of consciousness (pleasure and displeasure, good and evil). Here the means are made to stand against the end—the "unholy," absurd, above all unpleasant means—: how can an end that employs such means be worth anything! But the mistake is that, instead of looking for a purpose that explains the *necessity* of such means, we presuppose in advance a goal that actually *excludes* such means; i.e., we take a desideratum in respect of certain means (namely pleasant, rational, and virtuous ones) as a norm, on the basis of which we posit what general purpose would be desirable—

The fundamental mistake is simply that, instead of understanding consciousness as a tool and particular aspect of the total life, we posit it as the standard and the condition of life that is of supreme value: it is the erroneous perspective of *a parte ad totum*[84] —which is why all philosophers are instinctively trying to imagine a total consciousness, a consciousness involved in all life and will, in all that occurs, a "spirit," "God." But one has to tell them that precisely this turns life into a monstrosity; that a "God" and total sensorium would altogether be something on account of which life would have to be condemned— Precisely that we have *eliminated* the total consciousness that posited ends and means, is our great

[84] From a part to the whole.

relief—with that we are no longer *compelled* to be pessimists—*Our* greatest *reproach* against existence was the *existence of God*—

708 (*Nov. 1887-March 1888*)

[*On the value of "becoming."*—][85] If the motion of the world aimed at a final state, that state would have been reached. The sole fundamental fact, however, is that it does not aim at a final state; and every philosophy and scientific hypothesis (e.g., mechanistic theory) which necessitates such a final state is *refuted* by this fundamental fact.

I seek a conception of the world that takes this fact into account. Becoming must be explained without recourse to final intentions; becoming must appear justified at every moment (or incapable of being evaluated; which amounts to the same thing); the present must absolutely not be justified by reference to a future, nor the past by reference to the present. "Necessity" not in the shape of an overreaching, dominating total force, or that of a prime mover; even less as a necessary condition for something valuable. To this end it is necessary to deny a total consciousness of becoming, a "God," to avoid bringing all events under the aegis of a being who feels and knows but does not *will*: "God" is useless if he does not want anything, and moreover this means positing a summation of displeasure and unlogic which would debase the total value of "becoming." Fortunately such a summarizing power is missing (—a suffering and all-seeing God, a "total sensorium" and "cosmic spirit"[86] would be the greatest objection to being).

More strictly: one must admit nothing that has being—because then becoming would lose its value and actually appear meaningless and superfluous.

Consequently one must ask how the illusion of being could have arisen (was bound to arise);

likewise: how all value judgments that rest on the hypothesis that there are beings are disvalued.

But here one realizes that this hypothesis of beings is the source of all world-defamation (—the "better world," the "true world," the "world beyond," the "thing-in-itself.")

---

[85] This title was inserted by Peter Gast.

[86] "*Allgeist.*"

1. Becoming does not aim at a *final state,* does not flow into "being."

2. Becoming is not a merely *apparent state;* perhaps the world of beings is mere appearance.

3. Becoming is of equivalent value every moment; the sum of its values always remains the same; in other words, it has no value at all, for anything against which to measure it, and in relation to which the word "value" would have meaning, is lacking. *The total value of the world cannot be evaluated;* consequently philosophical pessimism belongs among comical things.

709 (*Spring-Fall 1887*)

That we do not make our "*desiderata*" judges of being!

That we do not also set up terminal forms of evolution (e.g., spirit) as another "in-itself" behind evolution!

710 (*March-June 1888*)

Our knowledge has become scientific to the extent that it is able to employ number and measure. The attempt should be made to see whether a scientific order of values could be constructed simply on a numerical and mensural scale of force— All other "values" are prejudices, naiveties, misunderstandings.— They are everywhere *reducible* to this numerical and mensural scale of force. The ascent on this scale represents every rise in value; the descent on this scale represents diminution in value.

Here one has appearance and prejudice against one. (For moral values are only apparent values compared with physiological values.)

711 (*Nov. 1887-March 1888*)

Where the point of view of "value" is inadmissible:—

That in the "process of the totality" the labor of man is of no account, because a total process (considered as a system—) does not exist at all;

that there is no "totality"; that no evaluation of human existence, of human aims, can be made in regard to something that does not exist;

that "necessity," "causality," "purposiveness," are useful *unrealities;*[87]

that *not* "increase in consciousness" is the aim, but enhancement of power—and in this enhancement the utility of consciousness is included; the same applies to pleasure and displeasure;

that one does not take the means as the supreme measure of value (therefore not states of consciousness, such as pleasure and pain, if becoming conscious itself is only a means—);

that the world is not an organism at all, but chaos; that the evolution of "spirituality" is only a means towards the relative duration of the organization;

that all "desirability" has no meaning in relation to the total character of being.

712 (*Spring-Fall 1887*)

"God" as the moment of culmination: existence an eternal deifying and un-deifying. But in that not a high point of value, but a high point of power.

Absolute exclusion of mechanism and matter: both are only expressions of lower stages, the most despiritualized form of affect (of "will to power").[88]

Retreat from the high-point in becoming (the highest spiritualization of power on the most slavish ground) to be represented as a consequence of this highest force, which, turning against itself when it no longer has anything left to organize, expends its force on disorganization—

a. The ever-increasing conquest of societies and subjection of them by a smaller but more powerful number;

b. the ever-increasing conquest of the priviliged and stronger

---

[87] *Nützliche "Scheinbarkeiten."*

[88] The words that immediately follow in the MS have been omitted in all editions:

"The world made stupid, as an aim, as a consequence of the will to power which makes the elements as independent of each other as possible. Beauty as a sign of the habituation and pampering [*Gewöhnung und Verwöhnung*] of the victorious; what is ugly as the expression of many defeats (within the organism). No heredity! The chain as a *whole* changing—"

On the margin of the same page:

" 'Beautiful' has a delightful effect on the feeling of pleasure; one need only think of the transfiguring power of 'love.' Might not the transfigured and perfect, conversely, mildly excite sensuality, so life has the effect of a pleasant feeling?—"

and the consequent rise of democracy, and ultimately anarchy of the elements.

713 (*March-June 1888*)

Value is the highest quantum of power that a man is able to incorporate—a man: not mankind! Mankind is even a means sooner than an end. It is a question of the type: mankind is merely the experimental material, the tremendous surplus of failures: a field of ruins.[89]

714 (*Manuscript source uncertain*)

Value words are banners raised where a *new bliss* has been found—a new *feeling*.

715 (*Nov. 1887-March 1888*)

The standpoint of "value" is the standpoint of conditions of preservation and enhancement for complex forms of relative life-duration within the flux of becoming.

There are no durable ultimate units, no atoms, no monads: here, too, "beings" are only introduced by us (from perspective grounds of practicality and utility).

"Forms of domination"; the sphere of that which is dominated continually growing or periodically increasing and decreasing according to the favorability or unfavorability of circumstances (nourishment—).

"Value" is essentially the standpoint for the increase or decrease of these dominating centers ("multiplicities" in any case; but "units" are nowhere present in the nature of becoming).[90]

Linguistic means of expression are useless for expressing "becoming"; it accords with our inevitable need to preserve ourselves to posit a crude world of stability, of "things," etc. We may venture to speak of atoms and monads in a relative sense; and

[89] The image of the field of ruins is also found in the early "meditation" on *Schopenhauer as Educator* (1874), section 6. For detailed discussion see my *Nietzsche*, Chapter 5, section III.

[90] The words that immediately follow in the MS are omitted in all editions: "—a quantum of power, a becoming, in so far as none of it has the character of 'being'—in so far—"

it is certain that the smallest world is the most durable— There is no will: there are treaty drafts of will[91] that are constantly increasing or losing their power.

---

[91] *Willens-Punktationen:* meaning unclear; perhaps the point is that the will is not a single entity but more like a constantly shifting federation or alliance of drives.

III. THE WILL TO POWER AS SOCIETY AND INDIVIDUAL

1. Society and State

716 (*March-June 1888*)

Basic principle: only individuals feel themselves responsible. Multiplicities are invented in order to do things for which the individual lacks the courage. It is for just this reason that all communalities and societies are a hundred times more upright and instructive about the nature of man than is the individual, who is too weak to have the courage for his own desires—

The whole of "altruism" reveals itself as the prudence of the private man: societies are not "altruistic" towards one another— The commandment to love one's neighbor has never yet been extended to include one's actual neighbor. That relationship is still governed by the words of Manu: "We must consider all countries that have common borders with us, and their allies, too, as our enemies. For the same reason, we must count all *their* neighbors as being well-disposed toward us."

The study of society is so invaluable because man as society is much more naive than man as a "unit." "Society" has never regarded virtue as anything but a means to strength, power, and order.

How simple and dignified is Manu when he says: "Virtue could scarcely endure by its own strength. Fundamentally it is only the fear of punishment that keeps men within bounds and leaves everyone in peaceful possession of his own."[92]

717 (*Nov. 1887-March 1888*)

The state organized immorality—*internally*: as police, penal law, classes, commerce, family; *externally*: as will to power, to war, to conquest, to revenge.

How does it happen that the state will do a host of things that the individual would never countenance?— Through division of responsibility, of command, and of execution. Through the interposition of the virtues of obedience, duty, patriotism, and

---

[92] The two quotations—in the second and in the last paragraphs—were inserted by Peter Gast.

loyalty. Through upholding pride, severity, strength, hatred, revenge—in short, all typical characteristics that contradict the herd type.

718 (*Nov. 1887-March 1888*)

None of you has the courage to kill a man, or even to whip him, or even to—but the tremendous machine of the state overpowers the individual, so he repudiates responsibility for what he does (obedience, oath, etc.)

—Everything a man does in the service of the state is contrary to his nature.

—in the same way, everything he learns with a view to future state service is contrary to his nature.

This is achieved through division of labor (so that no one any longer possesses the full responsibility):

the lawgiver—and he who enacts the law;

the teacher of discipline—and those who have grown hard and severe under discipline.

719 (*Spring-Fall 1887*)

A division of labor among the affects within society: so individuals and classes produce an incomplete, but for that reason more useful kind of soul. To what extent certain affects have remained almost rudimentary in every type within society (with a view to developing another affect more strongly).

Justification of morality:

economic (the intention to exploit individual strength to the greatest possible extent to prevent the squandering of everything exceptional);

aesthetic (the formation of firm types, together with pleasure in one's own type);

political (the art of enduring the tremendous tension between differing degrees of power);

physiological (as a pretended high evaluation in favor of the underprivileged or mediocre—for the preservation of the weak).

720 (*1886-1887*)

The most fearful and fundamental desire in man, his drive

for power—this drive is called "freedom"— must be held in check the longest. This is why ethics, with its unconscious instinct for education and breeding, has hitherto aimed at holding the desire for power in check: it disparages the tyrannical individual and with its glorification of social welfare and patriotism emphasizes the power-instinct of the herd.

721 (*Spring-Fall 1887*)

Inability to acquire power: its hypocrisy and shrewdness: as obedience (subordination, pride in duty, morality—); as submission, devotion, love (idealization, deification of him who commands as compensation and indirect self-transfiguration); as fatalism, resignation; as "objectivity"; as self-tyranny (Stoicism, asceticism, "emancipation from the self," "sanctification"); as criticism, pessimism, indignation, torment; as "beautiful soul," "virtue," "self-deification," "detachment," "unspotted by the world," etc. (—the insight into an inability to acquire power disguised as *dédain*). In all this there is expressed the need to exercise some sort of power nonetheless, or to create for oneself the temporary appearance of power—as intoxication.

Men who want power for the sake of the happiness power provides: political parties.

Other men who want power even accompanied by obvious disadvantages and sacrifices in happiness and well-being: the ambitious.

Other men who want power merely because it would otherwise fall into other hands upon which they do not want to be dependent.

722 (*1886-1887*)

Critique of "justice" and "equality before the law": what is really supposed to be *abolished* through this? Tension, enmity, hatred.— But it is an error to suppose that "happiness" will be increased in this way: Corsicans, e.g., enjoy more happiness than Continentals.

723 (*Nov. 1887-March 1888*)

Reciprocity, the hidden intention to claim reward: one of the most insidious forms of the diminution of the value of man. It brings with it that "equality" which depreciates the distancing gulf as immoral—

724 (*Spring-Fall 1887*)

What "useful" means is entirely dependent upon the *intention,* the wherefore? The intention, the "goal," is again entirely dependent on the degree of power. Therefore utilitarianism is not a foundation but only a theory of consequences, and absolutely cannot be made obligatory for everyone.

725 (*Summer-Fall 1883*)

Formerly one had the theory of the state as a calculating utility: now one has the practice as well!— The age of kings is past because the peoples are no longer worthy of them: they do not *want* to see the symbol of their ideal in kings, but a means for their profit.— That is the whole truth!

726 (*Spring-Fall 1887*)

Attempt on my part to grasp the absolute rationality of social judgment and evaluation (naturally without the desire to deduce moral conclusions).

the degree of psychological falsity and opacity needed to sanctify the affects essential for preservation and enhancement of power (in order to create a good conscience for them).

the degree of stupidity needed to maintain the possibility of common rules and valuations (in addition education, supervision of the elements of culture, training).

the degree of inquisition, mistrust, and intolerance needed to deal with the exceptions as criminals and to suppress them—to give them a bad conscience, so they suffer their exceptionalness as a disease.

727 (*Spring-Fall 1887*)

Morality essentially a shield, a means of defense; to this extent a sign of the immature (armored, stoical).

The mature man has, above all, weapons: he attacks.

Instruments of war transformed into instruments of peace (from scales and armor, feathers and hair).

728 (*March-June 1888*)

It is part of the concept of the living that it must grow—that it must extend its power and consequently incorporate alien forces. Intoxicated by moral narcotics, one speaks of the right of the individual to *defend* himself; in the same sense one might also speak of his right to attack: for both—and the second even more than the first—are necessities for every living thing:—aggressive and defensive egoism are not matters of choice, to say nothing of "free will," but the fatality of life itself.

In this case it is all the same whether one has in view an individual or a living body, an aspiring "society." The right to punish (or the self-defense of society) is at bottom called a "right" owing to a misuse of the word. A right is acquired through treaties—but self-protection and self-defense do not rest on the basis of a treaty. At least a people might just as well designate as a right its need to conquer, its lust for power, whether by means of arms or by trade, commerce and colonization—the right to growth, perhaps. A society that definitely and *instinctively* gives up war and conquest is in decline: it is ripe for democracy and the rule of shopkeepers— In most cases, to be sure, assurances of peace are merely narcotics.

729 (*Nov. 1887-March 1888*)

The maintenance of the military state is the last means of all of acquiring or maintaining the great tradition with regard to the supreme type of man, the strong type. And all concepts that perpetuate enmity and difference in rank between states (e.g., nationalism, protective tariffs) may appear sanctioned in this light.

730 (*1885-1886*)

That something longer-lasting than an individual should endure, that a *work* should endure which has perhaps been created by an individual: to that end, every possible kind of limitation, one-sidedness, etc., must be imposed upon the individual.

By what means? Love, reverence, gratitude toward the person who created the work helps; or that our forefathers fought for it; or that my descendants will be guaranteed only if I guarantee this work (e.g., the *polis*). Morality is essentially the means of ensuring the duration of something beyond individuals, or rather through an enslavement of the individual. It is obvious that the perspective from below will produce quite different expressions from that from above.

A complex of power: how is it maintained? By the fact that many generations sacrifice themselves for it; i.e.,—[93]

731 (*Spring-Fall 1887*)

The continuum: "marriage, property, language, tradition, tribe, family, people, state" are continuums of lower and higher orders. Their economy resides in the preponderance of the advantages of uninterrupted work and of multiplicity over the disadvantages: the higher cost of exchange between parts or of making them last. (Multiplication of the effective parts, which, however, often remain unemployed; thus a higher cost of acquisition and a not inconsiderable cost in maintenance.) The advantage resides in the fact that interruptions are avoided and losses that would arise from them are saved. Nothing is more costly than a beginning.

"The greater the advantages for existence, the greater the cost of maintenance and production (food and propagation); the greater, too, the danger and probability of perishing before the high point is reached."

732 (*Summer-Fall 1888*)

Marriage in the bourgeois sense of the word—I mean, in the most respectable sense of the word "marriage"—is not a matter of love, any more than it is a question of money; no institution can be founded on love. It is a question of society's granting permission to two people to gratify their sexual desires with one another, under certain conditions, to be sure, but conditions that keep the interests of society in view. It is obvious that a certain attraction between the parties and very much good will—will to patience, compatibility, care for one another—will be among the presuppositions of such a contract; but one should not misuse the

---

[93] In all previous editions the section ends: ". . . for it."

word love to describe this! For two lovers in the complete and strong sense of the word sexual gratification is not essential and is really no more than a symbol: for one party, as already said, a symbol of unconditional submission, for the other a symbol of assent to this, a sign of taking possession.

In marriage in the aristocratic, old aristocratic sense of the word it was a question of the breeding of a race (is there still an aristocracy today? *Quaeritur*[94])— thus of the maintenance of a fixed, definite type of ruling man: man and woman were sacrificed to this point of view. It is obvious that love was not the first consideration here; on the contrary! and not even that measure of mutual good will that is a condition of the good bourgeois marriage. What was decisive was the interest of a family, and beyond that—the class. We would shiver a little at the coldness, severity, and calculating clarity of such a noble concept of marriage as has ruled in every healthy aristocracy, in ancient Athens as in the eighteenth century, we warm-blooded animals with sensitive hearts, we "moderns"! Precisely this is why love as a passion—in the great meaning of the word—was *invented* for the aristocratic world and in it, where constraint and privation were greatest[95]—

733 (*1888*)

On the future of marriage:—an additional tax (on inheritance), also additional war service for bachelors from a certain age onwards and increasing (within the community);

advantages of all kinds for fathers who bring many boys into the world: possibly a plural vote;

a medical certificate preceding every marriage and endorsed by the communal authorities, several definite questions must be answered by the couple and by doctors ("family history"—);

as an antidote to prostitution (or as its ennoblement): marriages for a period, legalized (for years, for months), with guarantees for the children;

every marriage warranted and sanctioned by a certain number of trusted men of the community, as a matter of concern to the community.[96]

---

[94] One asks.

[95] This section and the next should be compared with *Twilight*, "Skirmishes," section 39 (*Portable Nietzsche*, pp. 543-44).

[96] See the preceding footnote.

734 (*Summer-Fall 1888*)

Also a commandment of the love of man.— There are cases in which a child would be a crime: in the case of chronic invalids and neurasthenics of the third degree. What should one do in such cases?— One might at least try encouraging them to chastity, perhaps with the aid of *Parsifal* music: Parsifal himself, this typical idiot, had only too many reasons not to propagate himself. The trouble is that a certain inability to "control" oneself (—*not* to react to stimuli, even to very slight sexual stimuli) is one of the most regular consequences of general exhaustion. One would be mistaken, for example, to think of a Leopardi as chaste. The priest, the moralist play a hopeless game in such cases; it would make more sense to go to a pharmacy. After all, society has a *duty* here: few more pressing and fundamental demands can be made upon it. Society, as the great trustee of life, is responsible to life itself for every miscarried life—it also has to pay for such lives: consequently it ought to prevent them. In numerous cases, society ought to prevent procreation: to this end, it may hold in readiness, without regard to descent, rank, or spirit, the most rigorous means of constraint, deprivation of freedom, in certain circumstances castration.—

The Biblical prohibition "thou shalt not kill!" is a piece of naiveté compared with the seriousness of the prohibition of life to decadents: "thou shalt not procreate!"— Life itself recognizes no solidarity, no "equal rights," between the healthy and the degenerate parts of an organism: one must excise the latter—or the whole will perish.— Sympathy for decadents, equal rights for the ill-constituted—that would be the profoundest immorality, that would be antinature itself as morality![97]

735 (*1887; rev. 1888*)

There are delicate and sickly inclined natures, so-called idealists, who cannot achieve anything better than a crime, *cru, vert*:[98] it is the great justification of their little, pale existences, a

---

[97] This section was originally meant to be included in *Twilight*, under the title *"My categorical imperative."* The printer's proof, corrected by Nietzsche, is preserved along with the MS. But then Nietzsche withdrew this section.

[98] Raw, green.

payment for a protracted cowardice and mendaciousness, a moment at least of strength: afterwards they perish of it.[99]

736 (*Spring-Fall 1887*)

In our civilized world, we learn to know almost only the wretched criminal, crushed by the curse and the contempt of society, mistrustful of himself, often belittling and slandering his deed, a miscarried type of criminal; and we resist the idea that all great human beings have been criminals (only in the grand and not in a miserable style), that crime belongs to greatness (—for that is the experience of those who have tried the reins and of all who have *descended* deepest into great souls—). To be "free as a bird" from tradition, the conscience of duty—every great human being knows this danger. But he also desires it: he desires a great goal and therefore also the means to it.[100]

737 (*March-June 1888*)

Ages in which one leads men with *reward* and *punishment* have a low, still primitive kind of man in view: it is as if they were children—

Within our late culture, fatality and degeneration are something that completely abolishes all meaning of reward and punishment— This real determination of action through reward and punishment presupposes young, strong, forceful races. In old races, the impulses are so irresistible that a mere idea is quite powerless;—to be unable to offer resistance where a stimulus is given, but to *have* to respond to it: this extreme susceptibility of decadents renders such systems of punishment and improvement perfectly meaningless.

*

The concept "improvement" rests on the presupposition of a normal and strong man, whose individual action must in some

---

[99] Possibly a comment on Dostoevsky's *Crime and Punishment*. See also the next footnote and section 740 below.

[100] Cf. *Twilight*, "Skirmishes," section 45, which deals at greater length with *"The criminal and what is related to him"* and says: "The testimony of Dostoevsky is relevant . . .—Dostoevsky, the only psychologist, incidentally, from whom I had something to learn . . ." (*Portable Nietzsche*, pp. 549-51). Cf. also section 740 below. See also the Appendix, below.

way be balanced in order not to lose him [to the community],[101] in order not to have him as an enemy.

738 (*Spring-Fall 1887*)

Effect of a *prohibition.*— Every power that forbids, that knows how to arouse fear in those to whom something is forbidden, creates a "bad conscience" (that is, the desire for something combined with the consciousness of danger in satisfying it, with the necessity for secrecy, for underhandedness, for caution). Every prohibition worsens the character of those who do not submit to it willingly, but only because they are compelled.

739 (*March-June 1888*)

"Reward and punishment."— They stand together, they fall together. Today one does not want to be rewarded, one will not acknowledge the right of anyone to punish— One has put oneself on a war footing: one desires something, one meets with opposition, one can perhaps gain what one wants most reasonably if one gets along—if one draws up a contract.

A modern society, in which every individual has drawn up his "contract"—the criminal breaks a contract— That would be a clear concept. But then one could not tolerate within a society anarchists and those who oppose the form of that society or principle—

740 (*Spring-Fall 1887*)

Crime belongs to the concept "revolt against the social order." One does not "punish" a rebel; one *suppresses* him. A rebel can be a miserable and contemptible man; but there is nothing contemptible in a revolt as such—and to be a rebel in view of contemporary society does not in itself lower the value of a man. There are even cases in which one might have to honor a rebel, because he finds something in our society against which war ought to be waged—he awakens us from our slumber.

If a criminal perpetrates an individual act against an individual this does not demonstrate that his whole instinct is not

---

[101] The words I have placed in brackets were added by the German editors.

in a state of war with the whole order: his deed as a mere symptom.

One should reduce the concept "punishment" to the concept: suppression of a revolt, security measures against the suppressed (total or partial imprisonment). But one should not express contempt through punishment: a criminal is in any case a man who risks his life, his honor, his freedom—a man of courage. Neither should one take punishment to be a penance; or as a payment, as if an exchange relationship existed between guilt and punishment—punishment does not purify, *for* crime does not sully.

One should not deprive the criminal of the possibility of making his peace with society; provided he does not belong to the race of criminals. In that case one should make war on him even before he has committed any hostile act (first operation as soon as one has him in one's power: his castration).

One should not hold against the criminal his bad manners or the low level of his intelligence. Nothing is more common than that he should misunderstand himself (for often his rebellious instinct, the rancor of the *déclassé*, has not reached consciousness, *faute le lecture*),[102] that he should slander and dishonor his deed under the influence of fear and failure—quite apart from those cases in which, psychologically speaking, the criminal surrenders to an uncomprehended drive and by some subsidiary action ascribes a false motive to his deed (perhaps by a robbery when what he wanted was blood).[103]

One should beware of assessing the value of a man according to a single deed. Napoleon warned against this. For our *haut-relief* deeds are quite especially insignificant. If men like us have no crime, e.g., murder, on our conscience—why is it? Because a few opportune circumstances were lacking. And if we did it, what would that indicate about our value? In a way one would despise us if one thought we had not the strength to kill a man under certain circumstances. In almost all crimes some qualities also find expression which ought not to be lacking in a man. It was not without justification that Dostoevsky said of the inmates of his Siberian prisons that they formed the strongest and most valuable

[102] For lack of reading.

[103] Cf. *Zarathustra* I, "On the Pale Criminal" (*Portable Nietzsche*, p. 149 *ff*), and *Crime and Punishment*; but when Nietzsche wrote *Zarathustra*, he had not even heard of Dostoevsky. For the details concerning his reading of Dostoevsky, see my notes on *Genealogy*, essay III, sections 15 and 24.

part of the Russian people.[104] If with us the criminal is an ill-nourished and stunted plant, this is to the dishonor of our social relationships; in the age of the Renaissance the criminal throve and acquired for himself his own kind of virtue—virtue in the Renaissance style, to be sure, *virtù,* moraline-free virtue.

One can enhance only those men whom one does not treat with contempt; moral contempt causes greater indignity and harm than any crime.

741 (*1883-1888*)

The derogatory element first entered into punishment when certain penalties became associated with contemptible men (e.g., slaves). Those punished most were contemptible men, and at length punishment came to contain something derogatory.

742 (*March-June 1888*)

In ancient penal law a *religious* concept was at work: that of the expiatory power of punishment. Punishment purifies: in the modern world it sullies. Punishment is a payment: one is really *rid* of that for which one was *willing* to suffer so much. Provided there is a belief in this power of punishment, there follows a profound sense of relief which is really very close to a new health, a restoration. One has not only made one's peace with society again, one has also regained one's self-respect and feels—"pure."

Today punishment isolates even more than the crime; the fatality behind a crime has grown so great that it has grown incurable. One emerges from punishment as an *enemy* of society. From then on, it has one more enemy.

Jus talionis[105] can be dictated by the spirit of retribution (i.e., by a kind of moderation of the instinct for revenge); but with Manu, e.g., it is the need to possess an equivalent in order to *expiate,* in order to be "free" again in a religious sense.

743 (*1885-1886*)

My rather radical question mark set against all modern penal

---

[104] Cf. *Twilight,* "Skirmishes," section 45 (*Portable Nietzsche,* pp. 549-51), and section 736 above.

[105] The law of talion.

codes is this: if the punishment should hurt in proportion to the magnitude of the crime—and fundamentally that is what all of you want!—you would have to measure the susceptibility to pain of every criminal. Does that not mean: a previously determined punishment for a crime, a penal code, ought not to exist at all? But considering that one would scarcely be able to determine a criminal's degrees of pleasure and displeasure, wouldn't one have to do without punishment in practice? What a loss! Isn't it? Consequently——

744 (*1883-1888*)

Ah, the philosophy of right! A science that, like all moral science, has not even reached the cradle yet!

One still misunderstands, e.g., even among jurists who think themselves enlightened, the oldest and most valuable significance of punishment—one does not know it at all; and as long as jurisprudence does not put itself on a new footing, namely on that of comparative history and anthropology, it will persist in the useless struggle between fundamentally false abstractions that today pass for "philosophy of right" and that are all based on contemporary man. This contemporary man, however, is so intricate, also in his legal evaluations, that he permits the most varied interpretations.

745 (*1883-1888*)

An old Chinese said he had heard that when empires were doomed they had many laws.

746 (*Spring-Fall 1887*)

Schopenhauer wanted rascals to be castrated and silly geese to be shut up in convents: from what point of view would this be desirable? The rascal has this advantage over many other men, that he is not mediocre; and the fool has this advantage over us, that he does not suffer at the sight of mediocrity.

It would be more desirable that the gulf should be made wider; so rascality and folly should increase. In this way human nature would be expanded— But, after all, this is dictated by necessity; it does not depend on whether we desire it or not. Folly, rascality increase: that is part of "progress."

747 (*Spring-Fall 1887; rev. Spring-Fall 1888*)

In contemporary society a great deal of consideration, of tact and forbearance, of good-natured respect for the rights of others, even for the claims of others, is quite widespread; even more, a certain benevolent instinctive estimation of human value in general, which finds expression in trustfulness and credit of all kinds. Respect for man—and not merely for virtuous men—is perhaps what divides us most sharply from a Christian evaluation. It seems to us ironic to a degree when we still hear morals preached; a man lowers himself in our eyes and becomes comical if he preaches morals.

This moral liberality is one of the best signs of our age. When we discover cases in which it is noticeably lacking, this strikes us as a kind of sickness (the case of Carlyle in England, the case of Ibsen in Norway, the case of Schopenhauerian[?][106] pessimism[?] throughout Europe[?]). If anything can reconcile us to our age, it is the great amount of immorality it permits itself without thinking any the worse of itself. On the contrary! What constitutes the superiority of culture over unculture? of the Renaissance over the Middle Ages, for example?— One thing alone; the great amount of *admitted* immorality. From this it follows of necessity what all the heights of human evolution must represent to the eye of the moral fanatic: the *non plus ultra* of corruption (—consider Savonarola's judgment of Florence, Plato's judgment of Periclean Athens, Luther's[?] judgment[?] of Rome, Rousseau's judgment of Voltaire's society, the German judgment *contra* Goethe).

748 (*Nov. 1887-March 1888*)

A little fresh air! This absurd condition of Europe shall not go on much longer! Is there any idea at all behind this bovine nationalism? What value can there be now, when everything points to wider and more common interests, in encouraging this boorish self-conceit? And this in a state of affairs in which spiritual dependency and disnationalization meet the eye and in which the value and meaning of contemporary culture lie in mutual blending and fertilization!— And the "new *Reich*" again founded on

[106] The five words followed by question marks in brackets represent uncertain but extremely plausible readings.

the most threadbare and despised ideas: equal rights and universal suffrage.

The struggle for advantage within a state of affairs that is no good; this culture of big cities, newspapers, feverishness and "pointlessness"—!

The economic unification of Europe is coming of necessity—and also, as a reaction, a peace party—

A party of peace, without sentimentality, that forbids itself and its children to wage war; forbids recourse to the courts; that provokes struggle, contradiction, persecution against itself: a party of the oppressed, at least for a time; soon the big party. Opposed to feelings of revenge and resentment.

A war party, equally principled and severe toward itself, proceeding in the opposite direction—

749[107] (*Spring-Fall 1887; rev. Spring-Fall 1888*)

The princes of Europe should consider carefully whether they can do without our support. We immoralists—we are today the only power that needs no allies in order to conquer: thus we are by far the strongest of the strong. We do not even need to tell lies: what other power can dispense with that? A powerful seduction fights on our behalf, the most powerful perhaps that there has ever been—the seduction of truth—"Truth"? Who has forced this word on me? But I repudiate it; but I disdain this proud word: no, we do not need even this; we shall conquer and come to power even without truth. The spell that fights on our behalf, the eye of Venus that charms and blinds even our opponents, is *the magic of the extreme,* the seduction that everything extreme exercises: we immoralists—we are the most extreme.

750 (*1884*)

The rotted ruling classes have ruined the image of the ruler. The "state" as a court of law is a piece of cowardice, because the great human being is lacking to provide a standard of measurement. Finally, the sense of insecurity grows so great that men cower in the dust before *any* forceful will that commands. N.B.

---

[107] In the MS this section is crossed out.

Scorn for the kings with the virtues of petty virtuous people.[108]

751 (*March-June 1888*)

"The will to power" is so hated in democratic ages that their entire psychology seems directed toward belittling and defaming it. The type of the great ambitious man who thirsts after honor is supposed to be Napoleon! And Caesar! And Alexander!— As if these were not precisely the great *despisers* of honor!

And Helvétius demonstrates to us that men strive after power so as to possess the enjoyments available to the powerful: he understands this striving for power as will to enjoyment! as hedonism!

752 (*1884*)

According to whether a people feels "right, vision, the gift of leadership, etc., belong to the few" or "to the many"—there will be an oligarchic or a democratic government.

Monarchy represents the belief in one man who is utterly superior, a leader, savior, demigod.

Aristocracy represents the belief in an elite humanity and higher caste.

Democracy represents the disbelief in great human beings and an elite society: "Everyone is equal to everyone else." "At bottom we are one and all self-seeking cattle and mob."

753 (*1885*)

I am opposed to 1. socialism, because it dreams quite naively of "the good, true, and beautiful" and of "equal rights" (—anarchism also desires the same ideal, but in a more brutal fashion);

2. parliamentary government and the press, because these are the means by which the herd animal becomes master.

754 (*1884*)

The arming of the people—is ultimately the arming of the mob.

---

[108] The last sentence, beginning with NB, has been omitted in all editions.

755 (*1884*)

How ludicrous I find the socialists, with their nonsensical optimism concerning the "good man," who is waiting to appear from behind the scenes if only one would abolish the old "order" and set all the "natural drives" free.

And the party opposed to them is just as ludicrous, because it does not admit the element of violence in the law, the severity and egoism in every kind of authority. " 'I and my kind' want to rule and survive; whoever degenerates will be expelled or destroyed"—this is the basic feeling behind every ancient legislation.

The idea of a higher kind of man is hated more than monarchs. Anti-aristocratic: that assumes hatred of monarchy only as a mask—

756 (*1885-1886*)

How treacherous all parties are!—they bring to light something about their leaders which the latter have perhaps always taken great care to hide under a bushel.

757 (*1884*)

Modern socialism wants to create the secular counterpart to Jesuitism: *everyone* a perfect instrument. But the purpose, the wherefore? has not yet been ascertained.

758 (*Summer-Fall 1883*)

Slavery today: a piece of barbarism! Where are those *for whom* they work? One must not always expect the contemporaneity of the two complementary castes.

Utility and pleasure are *slave theories* of life: the "blessing of work" is the self-glorification of slaves.— Incapacity for *otium.*[109]

759 (*Nov. 1887-March 1888*)

One has no right to existence or to work, to say nothing of

[109] Leisure.

a right to "happiness": the individual human being is in precisely the same case as the lowest worm.

760 (*Fall 1888*)

We must think of the masses as unsentimentally as we think of nature: they preserve the species.

761 (*1885-1886*)

To look upon the distress of the masses with an ironic melancholy: they want something *we* are capable of—ah!

762 (*1885*)

European democracy represents a release of forces only to a very small degree. It is above all a release of laziness, of weariness, of *weakness*.

763 (*Spring-Fall 1887*)

From the future of the worker.[110]— Workers should learn to feel like soldiers. An honorarium, an income, but no pay!

No relation between payment and achievement! But the individual, each according to his kind, should be so placed that he can achieve the highest that lies in his power.

764 (*1882*)

The workers shall live one day as the bourgeois do now—but *above* them, distinguished by their freedom from wants, the *higher caste*: that is to say, poorer and simpler, but in possession of power.

For *lower* men the reverse valuation obtains; it is a question of implanting "virtues" in them. Absolute commands; terrible means of compulsion; to tear them away from the easy life. The others may *obey*; and their vanity demands that they appear to be dependent, not on great men, but on *"principles."*

---

[110] This title was supplied by the German editors, who found it in a list Nietzsche had made of his notes.

765 (*Jan.-Fall 1888*)
"Redemption from all guilt"

One speaks of the "profound injustice" of the social pact; as if the fact that this man is born in favorable circumstances, that in unfavorable ones, were in itself an injustice; or even that it is unjust that this man should be born with these qualities, that man with those. Among the most honest of these opponents of society it is asserted: "we ourselves, with all our bad, sick, criminal qualities, which we admit to, are only the inescapable *consequences* of a long suppression of the weak by the strong"; they make the ruling classes responsible for their characters. And they threaten, they rage, they curse; they become virtuous from indignation—they do not want to have become bad men, *canaille,* for nothing.

This pose, an invention of the last few decades, is also called pessimism, as I hear; the pessimism of indignation. Here the claim is made to judge history, to divest it of its fatality, to discover responsibility behind it, guilty men in it. For this is the rub: one needs guilty men. The underprivileged, the decadents of all kinds are in revolt on account of themselves and need victims so as not to quench their thirst for destruction by destroying themselves (—which would perhaps be reasonable). To this end, they need an appearance of justice, i.e., a theory through which they can shift the responsibility for their existence, for their being thus and thus, on to some sort of scapegoat. This scapegoat can be God—in Russia there is no lack of such atheists from *ressentiment*—or the social order, or education and training, or the Jews, or the nobility, or those who have turned out well in any way. "It is a crime to be born in favorable circumstances; for thus one has disinherited the others, pushed them aside, condemned them to vice, even to *work*— How can *I* help it that I am wretched! But somebody must be responsible, *otherwise it would be unberable*!"

In short, the pessimism of indignation invents responsibility in order to create a *pleasant* feeling for itself—revenge—"Sweeter than honey" old Homer called it.—

*

That such a theory is no longer rightly understood, that is to say despised, is a consequence of the bit of *Christianity* that we all still have in our blood; so we are tolerant toward things merely because they smell somewhat Christian from a distance— The socialists appeal to the Christian instincts, that is their most subtle piece of shrewdness.

Christianity has accustomed us to the superstitious concept of the "soul," the "immortal soul," soul-monads that really are at home somewhere else and have only by chance fallen, as it were into this or that condition, into the "earthly" and become "flesh"; but their essence is not held to be affected, to say nothing of being conditioned, by all this. Social, family, historical circumstances are for the soul only incidental, perhaps embarrassments; in any event, it is not produced by them. With this idea, the individual is made transcendent; as a result, he can attribute a senseless importance to himself.

In fact, it was Christianity that first invited the individual to play the judge of everything and everyone; megalomania almost became a duty: one has to enforce *eternal* rights against everything temporal and conditioned! What of the state! What of society! What of historical laws! What of physiology! What speaks here is something beyond becoming, something unchanging throughout history, something immortal, something divine: a *soul*!

Another Christian concept, no less crazy, has passed even more deeply into the tissue of modernity: the concept of the "equality of souls before God." This concept furnishes the prototype of all theories of equal rights: mankind was first taught to stammer the proposition of equality in a religious context, and only later was it made into morality: no wonder that man ended by taking it seriously, taking it practically!—that is to say, politically, democratically, socialistically, in the spirit of the pessimism of indignation.

*

Wherever responsibilities have been sought it was the *instinct of revenge* that sought. This instinct of revenge has so mastered mankind in the course of millennia that the whole of metaphysics, psychology, conception of history, but above all morality, is impregnated with it. As far as man has thought, he has introduced the bacillus of revenge into things. He has made even God ill with it, he has *deprived existence* in general *of its innocence*; namely, by tracing back every state of being thus and thus to a will, an intention, a responsible act. The entire doctrine of the will, this most fateful *falsification* in psychology hitherto, was essentially invented for the sake of punishment. It was the social *utility* of punishment that guaranteed this concept its dignity, its power, its truth. The originators of this psychology—the psychology of will—are to be sought in the classes that administered the penal law, above all among the priests at the head of the oldest communality: they wanted to create for themselves a right to take revenge—they wanted to create a right for *God* to take revenge. To this end, man was conceived of as "free"; to this end, every action had to be conceived of as willed, the origin of every action as conscious. But these sentences refute the old psychology.[111]

Today, when Europe seems to have entered upon the opposite course, when we halcyonians especially are trying with all our might to withdraw, banish, and extinguish the concepts of guilt and punishment from the world, when our most serious endeavor is to purify psychology, morality, history, nature, social institutions and sanctions, and even God of this filth—whom must we recognize as our most natural antagonists? Precisely those apostles of revenge and *ressentiment,* those pessimists from indignation *par excellence,* who make it their mission to sanctify their filth under the name of "indignation."

We others, who desire to restore innocence to becoming, would like to be the missionaries of a cleaner idea: that no one has given man his qualities, neither God, nor society, nor his parents and ancestors, nor he himself—that no one is to *blame* for him.

There is no being that could be held responsible for the fact that anyone exists at all, that anyone is thus and thus, that anyone was born in certain circumstances, in a certain environment.— It is a tremendous restorative that such a being is lacking.

We are *not* the result of an eternal intention, a will, a wish: we are *not* the product of an attempt to achieve an "ideal of perfection" or an "ideal of happiness" or an "ideal of virtue"—any more than we are a blunder on the part of God that must frighten even him (an idea with which, as is well known, the Old Testament begins). There is no place, no purpose, no meaning, on which we can shift the responsibility for our being, for our being thus and thus. Above all: no one could do it; one cannot judge, measure, compare the whole, to say nothing of denying it! Why not?— For

---

[111] Uncertain reading.

five reasons, all accessible even to modest intellects; for example, *because nothing exists besides the whole*—

And, to say it again, this is a tremendous restorative; this constitutes the innocence of all existence.[112]

2. The Individual

766 (*1886-1887*)

Basic error: to place the goal in the herd and not in single individuals! The herd is a means, no more! But now one is attempting to understand the herd as an individual and to ascribe to it a higher rank than to the individual—profound misunderstanding! ! ! Also to characterize that which makes herdlike, sympathy, as the more valuable side of our nature!

767 (*1883-1888*)

The individual is something quite new which creates new things, something absolute; all his acts are entirely his own.

Ultimately, the individual derives the values of his acts from himself; because he has to interpret in a quite individual way even the words he has inherited. His interpretation of a formula at least is personal, even if he does not create a formula: as an interpreter he is still creative.

768 (*1882*)

The "ego" subdues and kills: it operates like an organic cell: it is a robber and violent. It wants to regenerate itself—pregnancy. It wants to give birth to its god and see all mankind at his feet.

769 (*Fall 1888*)

Every living thing reaches out as far from itself with its force

[112] The suggestion in 1911, p. 511, that the last sentences should be compared with VIII, 149, which is *Twilight*, "Skirmishes," section 38 (*Portable Nietzsche*, pp. 541-43), seems unhelpful. But section 765 *was* utilized in *Twilight*, "The Four Great Errors," sections 7-8 (*Portable Nietzsche*, pp. 499-501).

as it can, and overwhelms what is weaker: thus it takes pleasure in itself. The increasing "humanizing" of this tendency consists in this, that there is an ever subtler sense of how hard it is really to incorporate another: while a crude injury done him certainly demonstrates our power over him, it at the same time estranges his will from us even more—and thus makes him less easy to subjugate.

770 (*Jan.-Fall 1888*)

The degreee of resistance that must be continually overcome in order to remain on top is the measure of freedom, whether for individuals or for societies—freedom understood, that is, as positive power, as will to power. According to this concept, the highest form of individual freedom, of sovereignty, would in all probability emerge not five steps from its opposite,[113] where the danger of slavery hangs over existence like a hundred swords of Damocles. Look at history from this viewpoint: the ages in which the "individual" achieves such ripe perfection, i.e., *freedom,* and the classic type of the *sovereign man* is attained—oh no! they have never been humane ages!

One must have no choice: either on top—or underneath, like a worm, mocked, annihilated, trodden upon. One must oppose tyrants to become a tyrant, i.e., *free.* It is no small advantage to live under a hundred swords of Damocles: that way one learns to dance, one attains "freedom of movement."

771 (*1883-1888*)

Man, more than any animal, originally altruistic: hence his slow development (child) and lofty culture; hence, too, his extraordinary, ultimate kind of egoism.— Beasts of prey are much more individual.

772 (*Spring-Fall 1880*)

[*Critique of "selfishness."*—][114] The involuntary naiveté

---

[113] Cf. *Twilight,* section 38 (*Portable Nietzsche,* pp. 541-43). See footnote 112 above, but even here the correct reference would be VIII, 150.

[114] The title was added by Peter Gast.

of La Rochefoucauld, who thought he was saying something bold, free and paradoxical—in those days "truth" in psychological matters was something that aroused astonishment— Example: *"les grandes âmes ne sont pas celles qui ont moins de passions et plus de vertus que les âmes communes, mais seulement celles qui ont de plus grands desseins."*[115]— To be sure, John Stuart Mill (who calls Chamfort the nobler and more philosophical La Rouchefoucauld of the eighteenth century—) sees in him only an astute observer of all that in the human breast that derives from "habitual selfishness," and adds: "a noble spirit will be unable to convince himself of the need to impose upon himself a constant contemplation of commonness and baseness, unless it were to show over what corrupting influences a lofty mind and nobility of character are able to triumph."

773 (*Nov. 1887-March 1888*)
Morphology of self-esteem

First viewpoint: to what extent feelings of sympathy and community are the lower, preparatory stage at a time when personal self-esteem and individual initiative in evaluation are not yet possible.

Second viewpoint: to what extent the height of collective self-esteem, pride in the distinction of the clan, the feeling of inequality, the aversion to mediation, equality of rights, reconciliation, is a school for individual self-reliance; that is, in so far as it compels the individual to represent the pride of the whole: he has to speak and act with extreme respect for himself in so far as he represents the community in his own person. Also when the individual feels like the instrument and mouthpiece of the deity.

Third viewpoint: to what extent these forms of depersonalization in fact give the person a tremendous importance, in so far as higher powers employ him; religious awe before oneself the condition of the prophet and poet.

Fourth viewpoint: to what extent responsibility for the whole trains the individual to, and permits him, a broad view, a stern and terrible hand, a circumspection and coolness, a grandeur of bear-

---

[115] Great souls are not those with fewer passions and more virtues than common souls, but only those with greater designs.—The Mill quotation has been retranslated from Nietzsche's German.

ing and gesture, which he would not permit himself on his own behalf.

In summa: collective self-esteem is the great preparatory school for personal sovereignty. The noble class is that which inherits this training.

774 (*1883-1888*)

The *disguised* forms of the will to power:

1. Desire for freedom, independence, also for equilibrium, peace, co-ordination. Also the hermit, "spiritual freedom." In the lowest form: will to exist at all, "the drive to self-preservation."

2. Enrollment, so as to satisfy the will to power in a larger whole: submission, making oneself indispensable and useful to those in power; love, as a secret path to the heart of the more powerful—so as to dominate him.

3. The sense of duty, conscience, the imaginary consolation of outranking those who actually possess power; the recognition of an order of rank that permits judgment even of the more powerful; self-condemnation; the invention of new tables of value (Jews: classical example).

775 (*Spring-Fall 1887*)

Praise and gratitude as will to power.[116]— Praise and gratitude on the occasions of harvest, good weather, victory, marriage, peace:—all these festivals require a subject upon which the feeling can be discharged. One desires that all good things that happen to one should have been *done* to one: one desires a *doer*. The same applies to works of art: one is not satisfied with them alone: one praises the doer.

What, then is praise? A sort of restoration of balance in respect of benefits received, a giving in return, a demonstration of *our* power—for those who praise affirm, judge, evaluate, pass sentence: they claim the right of being *able* to affirm, of being *able* to dispense honors. A heightened feeling of happiness and life is also a heightened feeling of power: it is from this that man

[116] The title is not found at this place in the MS, but is taken from a list of aphorisms. The idea was stated in 1878 in Nietzsche's *Human, All too Human*, section 44, which is cited and discussed in my *Nietzsche*, Chapter 6, section 1.

praises (—from this that he invents and seeks a doer, a "subject"—). Gratitude as virtuous revenge: most strenuously demanded and practiced where equality and pride must both be upheld, where revenge is practiced best.

776 (*Spring-Fall 1887*)
On the "Machiavellianism" of Power

The will to power appears

a. among the oppressed, among slaves of all kinds, as will to *"freedom"*: merely getting free seems to be the goal (religio-morally: "responsible to one's own conscience alone"; "evangelical freedom," etc.);

b. among a stronger kind of man, getting ready for power, as will to overpower; if it is at first unsuccessful, then it limits itself to the will to *"justice,"* i.e., to the *same measure of rights* as the ruling type possesses;

c. among the strongest, richest, most independent, most courageous, as *"love* of mankind," of "the people," of the gospel, of truth, God; as sympathy; "self-sacrifice," etc.; as overpowering, bearing away with oneself, taking into one's service, as instinctive self-involvement with a great quantum of power to which one is able to give direction: the hero, the prophet, the Caesar, the savior, the shepherd; (—sexual love, too, belongs here: it desires to overpower, to take possession, and it *appears* as self-surrender. Fundamentally it is only love of one's "instrument," of one's "steed"—the conviction that this or that belongs to one because one is in a position to use it).

"Freedom," "justice," and *"love"!!!*

777 (*Nov. 1887-March 1888*)

Love.— Look into it; women's love and sympathy—is there anything more egoistic?—And if they sacrifice themselves, their honor, their reputation, to whom do they sacrifice themselves? To the man? Or is it not rather to an unbridled urge?— These desires are just as selfish even if they please others and implant gratitude—

To what extent this sort of hyperfetation of one valuation can sanctify everything else!!

778 (*March-June 1888*)

"Senses," "passions."— Fear of the senses, of the desires, of the passions, when it goes so far as to counsel us against them, is already a symptom of weakness: extreme measures always indicate abnormal conditions. What is lacking, or crumbling, here is the strength to restrain an impulse: if one's instinct is to have to succumb, i.e., to *have* to react, then one does well to avoid the opportunities ("seductions") for it.

A "stimulation of the senses" is a seduction only for those whose system is too easily moved and influenced: in the opposite case, that of a system of great slowness and severity, strong stimuli are needed to set the functions going.

Excess is a reproach only against those who have no right to it; and almost all the passions have been brought into ill repute on account of those who were not sufficiently strong to employ them—.

One must understand that the same objections can be made to the passions as are made to sickness: nonetheless—we cannot do without sickness, and even less without the passions. We *need* the abnormal, we give life a tremendous *choc* by these great sicknesses.

In detail, the following must be distinguished:

1. the dominating passion, which even brings with it the supremest form of health; here the co-ordination of the inner systems and their operation in the service of one end is best achieved—but this is almost the definition of health!

2. the antagonism of the passions; two, three, a multiplicity of "souls in one breast":[117] very unhealthy, inner ruin, disintegration, betraying and increasing and inner conflict and anarchism —unless one passion at last becomes master. Return to health—

3. juxtaposition without antagonism or collaboration: often periodic, and then, as soon as an order has been established, also healthy. The most interesting men, the chameleons, belong here; they are not in contradiction with themselves, they are happy and secure, but they do not develop—their differing states lie juxtaposed, even if they are separated sevenfold. They change, they do not *become*.

---

[117] Allusion to Goethe's *Faust,* line 1112.

779 (*Spring-Fall 1887*)

The *quantity* of the aim in its effect on the perspective of evaluation: the great criminal and the small one. The quantity of the aim that is wanted is also decisive for him who wills—whether he respects himself or feels dejected and miserable.—

Then the degree of spirituality in the means in its effect on the perspective of evaluation. How different the *philosophical* innovator, experimenter and man of violence appears from the robber, barbarian and adventurer!— Appearance of "disinterestedness."

Finally, noble manners, bearing, courage, self-confidence—how they alter the valuation of that which is attained in this way!

*

Perspective of evaluation:

Influence of the quantity (great, small) of the aim.
Influence of the spirituality of the means.
Influence of manners during the act.
Influence of success or failure.
Influence of the opposing forces and their value.
Influence of that which is permitted and forbidden.

780 (*Nov. 1887-March 1888*)

The artifices for making possible actions, measures, affects that, from an individual standpoint, are no longer "allowable"—nor "in good taste":

that art "makes them tasteful to us" that allows us to enter such "estranged" worlds.

historians show in what way they are right and reasonable; travels; exoticism; psychology; penal codes; madhouse; criminals; sociology;

"impersonality" (so that, as media of a collective, we permit ourselves these affects and actions—council of judges, jury, citizen, soldier, cabinet minister, prince, association, "critic"—) gives us the feeling we are making a sacrifice—

781 (*Spring-Fall 1887*)

Preoccupation with itself and its "eternal salvation" is not the expression of a rich and self-confident type; for that type does not give a damn about its salvation—it has no such interest in happiness of any kind; it is force, deed, desire—it imposes itself upon things, it lays violent hands on things. Christianity is a romantic hypochondria of those whose legs are shaky.

Wherever the hedonistic perspective comes into the foreground one may infer suffering and a type that represents a failure.

782 (*Nov. 1887-March 1888*)

The "growing autonomy of the individual": these Parisian philosophers such as Fouillée speak of this; they ought to take a look at the *race moutonnière*[118] to which they belong! Open your eyes, you sociologists of the future! The individual has grown strong under *opposite* conditions; what you describe is the most extreme weakening and impoverishment of mankind; you even desire it and employ to that end the whole mendacious apparatus of the old ideal! you are so constituted that you actually regard your herd-animal needs as an ideal!

A complete lack of psychological integrity!

783 (*1885*)

The modern European is characterized by two apparently opposite traits: individualism and the demand for equal rights; that I have at last come to understand. For the individual is an extremely vulnerable piece of vanity: conscious of how easily it suffers, this vanity demands that every other shall count as its equal, that it should be only *inter pares*. In this way a social race is characterized in which talents and powers do not diverge very much. The pride that desires solitude and few admirers is quite beyond comprehension; a really "great" success is possible only through the masses, indeed one hardly grasps the fact any more

[118] Race of sheep. Alfred Fouillée (1838-1912) wrote books on Plato (1869) and Socrates (1874), a history of philosophy (1875), a critique of contemporary moral systems (1883), a work on democracy (1884), and, in addition to many other books, "*Nietzsche et l'immoralisme*" (Nietzsche and Immoralism, 1903).

that a success with the masses is always really a *petty* success: because *pulchrum est paucorum hominum.*[119]

All moralities know nothing of an "order of rank" among men; teachers of law nothing of a communal conscience. The principle of the individual rejects *very great* human beings and demands, among men approximately equal, the subtlest eye and the speediest recognition of a talent; and because everyone has some kind of talent in such late and civilized cultures—and therefore can expect to receive back his share of honor—there is more flattering of modest merits today than ever before: it gives the age a veneer of *boundless fairness.* Its unfairness consists in a boundless rage, *not* against tyrants and public flatterers even in the arts, but against *noble* men, who despise the praise of the many. The demand for equal rights (i.e., to be allowed to sit in judgment on everything and everyone) is *anti-aristocratic.*

Equally strange to the age is the vanished individual, the absorption in a great type, the desire not to be a personality—which constituted the distinction and ambition of many lofty men in earlier days (the greatest poets among them); or "to be a city" as in Greece; Jesuitism, Prussian officer corps and bureaucracy; or to be a pupil and continuator of great masters—for which nonsocial conditions and a lack of *petty vanity* are needed.

784 (*Spring-Fall 1887; rev. Spring-Fall 1888*)

Individualism is a modest and still unconscious form of the "will to power"; here it seems sufficient to the individual to get free from an overpowering domination by society (whether that of the state or of the church). He does not oppose them as a person but only as an individual; he represents all individuals against the totality. That means: he instinctively posits himself as equal to all other individuals; what he gains in this struggle he gains for himself not as a person but as a representative of individuals against the totality.

Socialism is merely a means of agitation employed by individualism: it grasps that, to attain anything, one must organize oneself to a collective action, to a "power." But what it desires is not a social order as the goal of the individual but a social order as a means for making possible many individuals: this is the instinct of socialists about which they frequently deceive themselves (—apart

[119] Beauty belongs to the few.

from the fact that, in order to prevail, they frequently *have* to deceive themselves). The preaching of altruistic morality in the service of individual egoism: one of the most common lies of the nineteenth century.

Anarchism, too, is merely a means of agitation employed by socialism; by means of it, socialism arouses fear, by means of fear it begins to fascinate and to terrorize: above all—it draws the courageous, the daring to its side, even in the most spiritual matters.

All this notwithstanding: individualism is the *most modest* stage of the will to power.

*

Once one has achieved a certain degree of independence, one wants more: people arrange themselves according to their degree of force: the individual no longer simply supposes himself the equal of others, he seeks his equals—he distinguishes himself from others. Individualism is followed by the formation of groups and organs; related tendencies join together and become active as a power; between these centers of power friction, war, recognition of one another's forces, reciprocation, approaches, regulation of an exchange of services. Finally, an order of rank.

N.B.:[120]

1. Individuals liberate themselves;
2. they enter into struggle with one another, they come to an agreement over "equality of rights" (—"justice" as an aim—);
3. once this is achieved, the actual inequalities of force produce an enhanced effect (because peace rules on the whole and many small quanta of force now constitute differences that formerly did not count). Now individuals organize themselves in groups; the groups struggle for privileges and predominance. Strife breaks out again in a milder form.

One desires *freedom* so long as one does not possess power. Once one does possess it, one desires to overpower; if one cannot do that (if one is still too weak to do so), one desires *"justice,"* i.e., *equal power.*

785 (*Spring-Fall 1887*)

Correction of the concept "egoism."— When one has grasped to what extent the concept "individual" is an error because every

[120] Changed to "Recapitulation" by the German editors.

single creature constitutes the entire process in its entire course (not merely as "inherited," but the process itself—), then the single creature acquires a tremendously great significance. Instinct speaks quite correctly here. Where this instinct weakens—where the individual seeks a value for himself only in the service of others, one can be certain that exhaustion and degeneration are present. An altruistic disposition, genuine and without tartuffery, is an instinct for creating at least a secondary value for oneself in the service of other egoisms. Usually, however, altruism is only apparent; a detour to the preservation of one's own feeling of vitality and value.

786 (*Spring-Fall 1887*)
History of Moralization and Dismoralization

First proposition: There are no moral actions whatsoever: they are completely imaginary. Not only are they *indemonstrable* (which Kant, e.g., admitted, and Christianity as well)—they are *altogether impossible*. Through a psychological misunderstanding, one has invented an *antithesis* to the motivating forces, and believes one has described another kind of force; one has imagined a *primum mobile* that does not exist at all. According to the valuation that evolved the antithesis "moral" and "immoral" in general, one has to say: *there are only immoral intentions and actions.*

Second proposition: This entire distinction "moral" and "immoral" proceeds from the idea that moral as well as immoral actions are acts arising from free spontaneity—in short, that such a spontaneity exists, or in other words: that moral judgments in general relate only to one species of intentions and actions, those that are *free*. But this whole species of intentions and actions is purely imaginary; the world to which alone the moral standard can be applied does not exist at all:—*there are neither moral nor immoral actions.*

*

The psychological error out of which the antithetical concepts "moral" and "immoral" arose is: "selfless," "unegoistic," "self-denying"—all unreal, imaginary.

False dogmatism regarding the "ego": it is taken in an atomistic sense, in a false antithesis to the "non-ego"; at the same time, pried out of becoming, as something that is a being. The false substantialization of the ego: (in the faith in individual immortality) this is made into an article of faith, especially under the influence of religio-moral training. After this artificial separation of the ego, and the declaration that it exists in and for itself, one confronted a value antithesis that seemed irrefutable: the single ego and the tremendous non-ego. It seemed evident that the value of the single ego could lie only in relating itself to the tremendous "non-ego"—being subject to it and existing for its sake.— Here the herd instincts were decisive: nothing is so contrary to this instinct as the sovereignty of the individual. But if the ego is conceived as something in and for itself, then its value must lie in self-negation.

Thus: 1. the false autonomy of the "individual," as atom;

2. the herd valuation, which abhors the desire to remain an atom and regards it as hostile;

3. as a result: the individual overcome by moving his goal;

4. now there seemed to be actions that were self-negating: one wove a whole sphere of fantastic antitheses about them;

5. one asked: in what actions does man affirm himself most strongly? Around these (sexuality, avarice, lust to rule, cruelty, etc.) prohibition, hatred, and contempt were heaped: one *believed* there were unselfish drives, one condemned all the selfish ones, one demanded the unselfish;

6. as a result: what had one done? One had placed a prohibition upon all the strongest, most natural, indeed the only real drives —henceforth, in order to find an action praiseworthy, one had to deny the presence in it of such drives;—tremendous falsification *in psychologicis*. Even any kind of "self-satisfaction" had first to be made possible by misunderstanding and construing oneself *sub specie boni*. Conversely: that species that derived its advantage from depriving man of his self-satisfaction (the representatives of the herd instinct; e.g., the priests and philosophers) became subtle and psychologically astute, so as to demonstrate how nonetheless selfishness ruled everywhere. Christian conclusion: "*Everything* is sin; even our virtues. Absolute reprehensibility of man. The unselfish action is not possible." Original sin. In short: once man had made of his instincts an antithesis to a purely imaginary world of the good, he ended by despising himself as incapable of performing actions that were "good."

N.B. Christianity thus demonstrates an advance in the sharpening of psychological insight: La Rochefoucauld and Pascal. It grasped the essential equivalence of human actions and their equivalence of value in essentials (—all immoral).

*

Now one *seriously* set about the task of forming men in whom selfishness was dead:—priests, saints. And if one doubted the possibility of becoming "perfect," one did not doubt that one knew what is perfect.

The psychology of the saint, the priest, the "good man" naturally had to be purely phantasmagorical. One had declared the *real* motives of actions *bad*: in order still to be able to act at all, to prescribe actions, one had to describe as possible and as it were sanctify actions that are utterly impossible. With the falseness of one's former slanders, one now honored and idealized.

Rage against the instincts of life as "holy," as venerable. Absolute chastity, absolute obedience, absolute poverty: the *priestly* ideal. Alms, pity, sacrifice,[121] denial of beauty, of reason, of sensuality, a morose eye cast on all strong qualities one possessed: the *lay* ideal.

*

One advances: the slandered instincts, too, try to create a right for themselves (e.g., Luther's Reformation: coarsest form of moral mendaciousness under the guise of "evangelical freedom") —one rebaptized them with holy names;

the slandered instincts try to prove themselves necessary for the existence of the virtuous instincts; one must *vivre, pour vivre pour autrui*:[122] egoism as means to an end;

one goes further, one tries to grant both the egoistic and the altruistic impulses a right to exist: equal rights for the one as for the other (from the standpoint of utility);

one goes further, one seeks a higher utility in a preference of the egoistic viewpoint over the altruistic: more useful in relation to the happiness of the majority or the progress of mankind, etc. Thus: a preponderance of the rights of egoism, but under the perspective of extreme altruism ("collective utility for mankind");

one tries to reconcile the altruistic mode of action with naturalness, one seeks altruism in the foundations of life; one seeks egoism

[121] Followed by an undeciphered word.

[122] Live to live for others.

and altruism as equally founded in the essence of life and nature;

one dreams of a disappearance of the antithesis in some future, when, owing to continual adaptation, egoism will at the same time be altruism;

finally, one grasps that altruistic actions are only a species of egoistic actions—and that the degree to which one loves, spends oneself, proves the degree of individual power and personality. In short, *that when one makes men more evil, one makes them better*—and that one cannot be one without being the other—At this point the curtain rises on the dreadful *forgery of the psychology of man hitherto.*

*

Consequences: there are *only* immoral intentions and actions; —the so-called moral ones must be shown to be immoral.[123] The derivation of all affects from the one will to power: the same essence. The concept of life:—in the apparent antithesis (of "good" and "evil") degrees of power in instinct express themselves, temporary orders of rank under which certain instincts are held in check or taken into service.— Justification of morality: economical, etc.

*

Against the second propostion. Determinism: attempt to rescue the moral world by transporting it—into the unknown. Determinism is only a *modus* of permitting ourselves to juggle our evaluations away once they have no place in a mechanistically conceived world. One must therefore attack determinism and undermine it: and also dispute our right to a distinction between a world in itself and a phenomenal world.

787 (*1883-1888*)

The absolute necessity of a total liberation from ends: otherwise we should not be permitted to try to sacrifice ourselves and let ourselves go. Only the innocence of becoming gives us the *greatest courage* and the *greatest freedom!*

---

[123] The following words are omitted in all editions: "This is the task of the *tractatus politicus.*

788 (*1883-1888*)

To restore a good conscience to the evil man—has this been my unconscious endeavor? I mean, to the evil man in so far as he is the *strong* man? (Dostoevsky's judgment on the criminals in prison should be cited here.)

789 (*1885-1886*)

Our new "freedom."— What a feeling of freedom there is in feeling as we freed spirits do, that we are not harnessed to any system of "purposes"! Likewise, that the concepts "reward" and "punishment" do not reside in the essence of things! Likewise, that the good and the evil action cannot be called good and evil in themselves, but only in the perspective of what tends to preserve certain types of human communities! Likewise, that our assessments of pleasure and pain have no cosmic, let alone a metaphysical, significance! (—that pessimism, the pessimism of Herr von Hartmann, who claims to put the pleasure and displeasure of existence itself on the scales, with his arbitrary incarceration in the pre-Copernican prison and field of vision, would be something retarded and regressive unless it is merely a bad joke of a Berliner.)

790 (*Nov. 1887-March 1888*)

Once one is clear about the "why?" of one's life, one can let its How? take care of itself. It is itself a sign of disbelief in a Why, in purpose and meaning, a sign of a *lack of will*, if the value of pleasure and displeasure step into the foreground and hedonistic-pessimistic theories get a hearing; and renunciation, resignation, virtue, and "objectivity" *may* at least be a sign that what matters most is beginning to be defective.

791 (*1885*)

Up to now there has not yet been any German culture. It is no objection to this statement that there have been great hermits in Germany (e.g., Goethe); for these had their own culture. But like mighty, defiant, solitary rocks, they were surrounded by the rest of what was German as by their antithesis—a soft, marshy, insecure ground upon which every step from other countries made an "impression" and created a "form": German culture was a thing without character, an almost limitless compliance.

792 (*1885*)

Germany, rich in clever and well-informed scholars, has lacked great souls, mighty spirits, to such an extent and for so long that it seems to have forgotten what a *great* soul, a *mighty* spirit, is; and today mediocre and quite ill-constituted men place themselves in the market square almost with a good conscience and without any embarrassment and praise themselves as great men and reformers, as, e.g., Eugen Dühring does—indeed a clever and well-informed scholar, but one who nevertheless betrays with almost every word he says that he harbors a petty soul and is tormented by narrow, envious feelings; also that what drives him is not a mighty, overflowing, benevolent, spendthrift spirit—but ambition! But to lust after honors in this age is even more unworthy of a philosopher than it was in any previous age: today, when the mob rules, when the mob bestows the honors!

793 (*Nov. 1887-March 1888*)

My "future":—a rigorous polytechnic education. Military service; so that, on an average, every man of the higher classes would be an officer, whatever else he might be.

IV. THE WILL TO POWER AS ART

794 (*March-June 1888*)

Our religion, morality, and philosophy are decadence forms of man.

The *countermovement: art.*

795 (*1885-1886*)[124]

The *artist*-philosopher. Higher concept of art. Whether a man can place himself so far distant from other men that he can form them? (—Preliminary exercises: (1) he who forms himself, the hermit; (2) the artist hitherto, as a perfecter on a small scale, working on material.)

796 (*1885-1886*)

The work of art where it appears without an artist, e.g., as body, as organization (Prussian officer corps, Jesuit order). To what extent the artist is only a preliminary stage.

The world as a work of art that gives birth to itself——

797 (*1885-1886*)

The phenomenon "artist" is still the most transparent:—to see through it to the basic instincts of power, nature, etc.! Also those of religion and morality!

"Play," the useless—as the ideal of him who is overfull of strength, as "childlike." The "childlikeness" of God, *pais paizon.*[125]

798 (*March-June 1888*)

Apollinian—Dionysian.[126]— There are two conditions in

---

[124] 1911, p. 511: "Contemporaneous with the beginning of work on *Beyond Good and Evil,* and initially planned as the continuation of the preface.

"Line 1: After 'The artist-philosopher' the MS goes on: '(hitherto mentioned scientific procedure, attitude to religion and politics).'

"In the margin, this comment on the whole aphorism: 'here belongs the *sequence of rank* of the higher men, which must be described.' "

[125] A child playing.

[126] With this and the following sections compare *Twilight,* "Skirmishes," sections 8-11 (*Portable Nietzsche,* pp. 518-21).

which art appears in man like a force of nature and disposes of him whether he will or no: as the compulsion to have visions and as a compulsion to an orgiastic state. Both conditions are rehearsed in ordinary life, too, but weaker: in dream and in intoxication.

But the same antithesis obtains between dream and intoxication: both release artistic powers in us, but different ones: the dream those of vision, association, poetry; intoxication those of gesture, passion, song, dance.

799 (*March-June 1888*)

In the Dionysian intoxication there is sexuality and voluptuousness: they are not lacking in the Apollinian. There must also be a difference in tempo in the two conditions— The extreme calm in certain sensations of intoxication (more strictly: the retardation of the feelings of time and space) likes to be reflected in a vision of the calmest gestures and types of soul. The classical style is essentially a representation of this calm, simplification, abbreviation, concentration—*the highest feeling of power* is concentrated in the classical type. To react slowly; a great consciousness; no feeling of struggle.

800 (*March-June 1888*)

The feeling of intoxication, in fact corresponding to an increase in strength; strongest in the mating season: new organs, new accomplishments, colors, forms; "becoming more beautiful" is a consequence of *enhanced* strength.[127] Becoming more beautiful as the expression of a *victorious* will, of increased co-ordination, of a harmonizing of all the strong desires, of an infallibly perpendicular stress. Logical and geometrical simplification is a consequence of enhancement of strength: conversely the apprehension of such a simplification again enhances the feeling of strength— High point of the development: the grand style.

Ugliness signifies the decadence of a type, contradiction and lack of co-ordination among the inner desires—signifies a decline in organizing strength, in "will," to speak psychologically.

The condition of pleasure called intoxication is precisely an

---

[127] The following words in the MS are omitted in all editions: "Becoming more beautiful as a necessary consequence of the enhancement of strength."

exalted feeling of *power*— The sensations of space and time are altered: tremendous distances are surveyed and, as it were, for the first time apprehended; the extension of vision over greater masses and expanses; the refinement of the organs for the apprehension of much that is extremely small and fleeting; *divination,* the power of understanding with only the least assistance, at the slightest suggestion: "intelligent" *sensuality*—; strength as a feeling of dominion in the muscles, as suppleness and pleasure in movement, as dance, as levity and *presto;* strength as pleasure in the proof of strength, as bravado, adventure, fearlessness, indifference to life or death— All these climactic moments of life mutually stimulate one another; the world of images and ideas of the one suffices as a suggestion for the others:—in this way, states finally merge into one another though they might perhaps have good reason to remain apart. For example: the feeling of religious intoxication and sexual excitation (—two profound feelings, co-ordinated to an almost amazing degree. What pleases all pious women, old or young? Answer: a saint with beautiful legs, still young, still an idiot). Cruelty in tragedy and sympathy (—also normally co-ordinated—) Spring, dance, music:—all competitions between the sexes—and even that Faustian "infinity in the breast."

Artists, if they are any good, are (physically as well) strong, full of surplus energy, powerful animals, sensual; without a certain overheating of the sexual system a Raphael is unthinkable— Making music is another way of making children; chastity is merely the economy of an artist—and in any event, even with artists fruitfulness ceases when potency ceases— Artists should see nothing as it is, but fuller, simpler, stronger: to that end, their lives must contain a kind of youth and spring, a kind of habitual intoxication.

801 (*Spring-Fall 1887; rev. Spring-Fall 1888*)

The states in which we infuse a transfiguration and fullness into things and poetize about them until they reflect back our fullness and joy in life: sexuality; intoxication; feasting; spring; victory over an enemy, mockery; bravado; cruelty; the ecstacy of religious feeling. *Three* elements principally: *sexuality, intoxication, cruelty*—all belonging to the oldest *festal joys* of mankind, all also preponderate in the early "artist."

Conversely, when we encounter things that display this transfiguration and fullness, the animal responds with an excitation of those spheres in which all those pleasurable states are situated—and a blending of these very delicate nuances of animal well-being and desires constitutes the *aesthetic state*. The latter appears only in natures capable of that bestowing and overflowing fullness of bodily vigor; it is this that is always the *primum mobile*. The sober, the weary, the exhausted, the dried-up (e.g., scholars) can receive absolutely nothing from art, because they do not possess the primary artistic force, the pressure of abundance: whoever cannot give, also receives nothing.

"Perfection": in these states (in the case of sexual love especially) there is naively revealed what the deepest instinct recognizes as higher, more desirable, more valuable in general, the upward movement of its type; also toward what status it really aspires. Perfection: that is the extraordinary expansion of its feeling of power, riches, necessary overflowing of all limits.

802 (*Spring-Fall 1887*)

Art reminds us of states of animal vigor; it is on the one hand an excess and overflow of blooming physicality into the world of images and desires; on the other, an excitation of the animal functions through the images and desires of intensified life;—an enhancement of the feeling of life, a stimulant to it.

How can even ugliness possess this power? In so far as it still communicates something of the artist's victorious energy which has become master of this ugliness and awfulness; or in so far as it mildly excites in us the pleasure of cruelty (under certain conditions even a desire to harm *ourselves*, self-violation—and thus the feeling of power over ourselves).

803 (*1883-1888*)

"Beauty" is for the artist something outside all orders of rank, because in beauty opposites are tamed; the highest sign of power, namely power over opposites; moreover, without tension:—that violence is no longer needed; that everything follows, obeys, so easily and so pleasantly—that is what delights the artist's will to power.

804 (*Spring-Fall 1887*)

Origin of the beautiful and ugly.[128]—Biological value of the *beautiful* and the *ugly.*— That which is instinctively *repugnant* to us, aesthetically, is proved by mankind's longest experience to be harmful, dangerous, worthy of suspicion: the suddenly vocal aesthetic instinct (e.g., in disgust) contains a *judgment*. To this extent the beautiful stands within the general category of the biological values of what is useful, beneficent, life-enhancing—but in such a way that a host of stimuli that are only distantly associated with, and remind us only faintly of, useful things and states give us the feeling of the beautiful, i.e., of the increase of the feeling of power (—not merely things, therefore, but also the sensations that accompany such things, or symbols of them).

Thus the beautiful and the ugly are recognized as *relative* to our most fundamental values of preservation. It is senseless to want to posit anything as beautiful or ugly apart from this. *The* beautiful exists just as little as does *the* good, or *the* true. In every case it is a question of the conditions of preservation of a certain type of man: thus the *herd man* will experience the value feeling of the beautiful in the presence of different things than will the *exceptional* or over-man.

It is the perspective of the foreground, which concerns itself only with immediate consequences, from which the value of the beautiful (also of the good, also of the true) arises.

All instinctive judgments are shortsighted in regard to the chain of consequences: they advise what is to be done immediately. The understanding is essentially a brake upon immediate reactions on the basis of instinctive judgments: it retards, it considers, it looks further along the chain of consequences.

Judgments concerning beauty and ugliness are shortsighted (—they are always opposed by the understanding—) but persuasive in the highest degree; they appeal to our instincts where they decide most quickly and pronounce their Yes and No before the understanding can speak.

The most habitual affirmations of beauty excite and stimulate each other; once the aesthetic drive is at work, a whole host of other perfections, originating elsewhere, crystallize around "the

[128] Title omitted in all editions, which substitute the following phrase.

particular instance of beauty." It is not possible to remain objective, or to suspend the interpretive, additive, interpolating, poetizing power (—the latter is the forging of the chain of affirmations of beauty). The sight of a "beautiful woman"—

Thus 1. the judgment of beauty is shortsighted, it sees only the immediate consequences;

2. it lavishes upon the object that inspires it a magic conditioned by the association of various beauty judgments—that are quite alien to the nature of that object. To experience a thing as beautiful means: to experience it necessarily wrongly—(which, incidentally, is why marriage for love is, from the point of view of society, the most unreasonable kind of marriage).

805 (*1883-1888*)

On the genesis of art.— That making perfect, seeing as perfect, which characterizes the cerebral system bursting with sexual energy (evening with the beloved, the smallest chance occurrences transfigured, life a succession of sublime things, "the misfortune of the unfortunate lover worth more than anything else"): on the other hand, everything perfect and beautiful works as an unconscious reminder of that enamored condition and its way of seeing—every perfection, all the beauty of things, revives through contiguity[128a] this aphrodisiac bliss. (Physiologically: the creative instinct of the artist and the distribution of semen in his blood—) The demand for art and beauty is an indirect demand for the ecstasies of sexuality communicated to the brain. The world become perfect, through "love"—

806 (*1883-1888*)

Sensuality in its disguises: (1) as idealism ("Plato"), peculiar to youth, creating the same kind of concave image that the beloved in particuar assumes, imposing an encrustation, magnification, transfiguration, infinity upon everything—; (2) in the religion of love: "a handsome young man, a beautiful woman," somehow divine, a bridegroom, a bride of the soul—; (3) in *art,* as the "embellishing" power: as man sees woman and, as it were, makes her a present of everything excellent, so the sensuality of the artist puts into one object everything else that he honors and

[128a] Nietzsche uses the English term, as in *Genealogy* III, section 4.

esteems—in this way he *perfects* an object ("idealizes" it). Woman, conscious of man's feelings concerning women, assists his efforts at idealization by adorning herself, walking beautifully, dancing, expressing delicate thoughts: in the same way, she practices modesty, reserve, distance—realizing instinctively that in this way the idealizing capacity of the man will grow. (—Given the tremendous subtlety of woman's instinct, modesty remains by no means conscious hypocrisy: she divines that it is precisely an actual naive modesty that most seduces a man and impels him to overestimate her. Therefore woman is naive—from the subtlety of her instinct, which advises her of the utility of innocence. A deliberate *closing of one's eyes to oneself*— Wherever dissembling produces a stronger effect when it is unconscious, it *becomes* unconscious.)

807 (*Summer-Fall 1888*)

What a tremendous amount can be accomplished by that intoxication which is called "love" but which is yet something other than love!— But everyone has his own knowledge of this. The muscular strength of a girl *increases* as soon as a man comes into her vicinity; there are instruments to measure this. When the sexes are in yet closer contact, as, e.g., at dances and other social events, this strength is augmented to such a degree that real feats of strength are possible: in the end one scarcely believes one's own eyes—or one's watch. In such cases, to be sure, we must reckon with the fact that dancing in itself, like every other swift movement, brings with it a kind of intoxication of the whole vascular, nervous, and muscular system. So one has to reckon with the combined effects of a twofold intoxication.— And how wise it is at times to be a little tipsy!

There are realities that one may never admit to oneself; after all, one is a woman; after all, one has a woman's *pudeurs*— Those young creatures dancing over there are obviously beyond all reality: they are dancing with nothing but palpable ideals; what is more, they even see ideals sitting around them: the mothers!— Opportunity to quote *Faust*— They look incomparably better when they are a little tipsy like that, these pretty creatures—oh, how well they know that, too. They actually become amiable *because* they know it.

Finally, they are also inspired by their finery; their finery is their *third* intoxication: they believe in their tailors as they believe in their God—and who would dissuade them from this faith? This faith makes blessed! And self-admiration is healthy! Self-admiration protects against colds. Has a pretty woman who knew herself to be well dressed ever caught cold? Never! I am even assuming that she was barely dressed.[129]

808 (*March-June 1888*)

Do you desire the most astonishing proof of how far the transfiguring power of intoxication can go?— "Love" is this proof: that which is called love in all the languages and silences of the world. In this case, intoxication has done with reality to such a degree that in the consciousness of the lover the cause of it is extinguished and something else seems to have taken its place—a vibration and glittering of all the magic mirrors of Circe—

Here it makes no difference whether one is man or animal; even less whether one has spirit, goodness, integrity. If one is subtle, one is fooled subtly; if one is coarse, one is fooled coarsely; but love, and even the love of God, the saintly love of "redeemed souls," remains the same in its roots: a fever that has good reason to transfigure itself, an intoxication that does well to lie about itself— And in any case, one lies well when one loves, about oneself and to oneself: one seems to oneself transfigured, stronger, richer, more perfect, one *is* more perfect— Here we discover *art* as an organic function: we discover it in the most angelic instinct, "love"; we discover it as the greatest stimulus of life—art thus sublimely expedient even when it lies—

But we should do wrong if we stopped with its power to lie: it does more than merely imagine; it even transposes values. And it is not only that it transposes the *feeling* of values: the lover *is* more valuable, is stronger. In animals this condition produces new weapons, pigments, colors, and forms; above all, new movements, new rhythms, new love calls and seductions. It is no different with man. His whole economy is richer than before,

[129] Cf. *Twilight*, "Maxims and Arrows," aphorism 25: "Contentment protects even against colds. Has a woman who knew herself to be well dressed ever caught cold? I am assuming that she was barely dressed." (*Portable Nietzsche*, p. 470.)

more powerful, more *complete* than in those who do not love. The lover becomes a squanderer: he is rich enough for it. Now he dares, becomes an adventurer, becomes an ass in magnanimity and innocence; he believes in God again, he believes in virtue, because he believes in love; and on the other hand, this happy idiot grows wings and new capabilities, and even the door of art is opened to him. If we subtracted all traces of this intestinal fever from lyricism in sound and word, what would be left of lyrical poetry and music?— *L'art pour l'art* perhaps: the virtuoso croaking of shivering frogs, despairing in their swamp— All the rest was created by love—

809 (*March-June 1888*)

All art exercises the power of suggestion over the muscles and senses, which in the artistic temperament are originally active: it always speaks only to artists—it speaks to this kind of a subtle flexibility of the body. The concept "layman" is an error. The deaf man is not a species of the man with good hearing.

All art works tonically, increases strength, inflames desire (i.e., the feeling of strength), excites all the more subtle recollections of intoxication—there is a special memory that penetrates such states: a distant and transitory world of sensations here comes back.

The ugly, i.e., the contradiction to art, that which is excluded from art, its No—every time decline, impoverishment of life, impotence, disintegration, degeneration are suggested even faintly, the aesthetic man reacts with his No. The effect of the ugly is depressing: it is the expression of a depression. It takes away strength, it impoverishes, it weighs down—

The ugly suggests ugly things; one can use one's states of health to test how variously an indisposition increases the capacity for imagining ugly things. The selection of things, interests, and questions changes. A state closely related to the ugly is encountered in logic, too: heaviness, dimness. Mechanically speaking, equilibrium is lacking: the ugly limps, the ugly stumbles: antithesis to the divine frivolity of the dancer.

The aesthetic state possesses a superabundance of means of communication, together with an extreme receptivity for stimuli and signs. It constitutes the high point of communication and transmission between living creatures—it is the source of languages. This is where languages originate: the languages of tone as well as the languages of gestures and glances. The more complete phenomenon is always the beginning: our faculties are subtilized out of more complete faculties. But even today one still hears with one's muscles, one even reads with one's muscles.

Every mature art has a host of conventions as its basis—in so far as it is a language. Convention is the condition of great art, *not* an obstacle—

Every enhancement of life enhances man's power of communication, as well as his power of understanding. Empathy with the souls of others is originally nothing moral, but a physiological susceptibility to suggestion: "sympathy," or what is called "altruism," is merely a product of that psychomotor rapport which is reckoned a part of spirituality (*induction psycho-motrice,* Charles Féré thinks). One never communicates thoughts: one communicates movements, mimic signs, which we then trace back to thoughts.

810 (*Spring-Fall 1887*)

Compared with music all communication by words is shameless; words dilute and brutalize; words depersonalize; words make the uncommon common.

811 (*March-June 1888*)

It is exceptional states that condition the artist—all of them profoundly related to and interlaced with morbid phenomena—so it seems impossible to be an artist and not to be sick.

Physiological states that are in the artist as it were molded into a "personality" and that characterize men in general to some degree:

1. *intoxication:* the feeling of enhanced power; the inner need to make of things a reflex of one's own fullness and perfection;

2. the *extreme sharpness* of certain senses, so they understand a quite different sign language—and create one—the condition that seems to be a part of many nervous disorders—; extreme mobility that turns into an extreme urge to communicate; the desire to speak on the part of everything that knows how to make signs—; a need to get rid of oneself, as it were, through signs

and gestures; ability to speak of oneself through a hundred speech media—an *explosive* condition. One must first think of this condition as a compulsion and urge to get rid of the exuberance of inner tension through muscular activity and movements of all kinds; then as an involuntary co-ordination between this movement and the processes within (images, thoughts, desires)—as a kind of automatism of the whole muscular system impelled by strong stimuli from within—; inability to prevent reaction; the system of inhibitions suspended, as it were. Every inner movement (feeling, thought, affect) is accompanied by vascular changes and consequently by changes in color, temperature, and secretion. The suggestive power of music, its "*suggestion mentale*";—

3. the *compulsion to imitate*: an extreme irritability through which a given example becomes contagious—a state is divined on the basis of signs and immediately enacted— An image, rising up within, immediately turns into a movement of the limbs—a certain suspension of the will—(Schopenhauer!!!) A kind of deafness and blindness towards the external world—the realm of admitted stimuli is sharply defined.

This is what distinguishes the artist from laymen (those susceptible to art): the latter reach the high point of their susceptibility when they receive; the former as they give—so that an antagonism between these two gifts is not only natural but desirable. The perspectives of these two states are opposite: to demand of the artist that he should practice the perspective of the audience (of the critic—) means to demand that he should impoverish himself and his creative power— It is the same here as with the difference between the sexes: one ought not to demand of the artist, who gives, that he should become a woman—that he should receive.

Our aesthetics hitherto has been a woman's aesthetics to the extent that only the receivers of art have formulated their experience of "what is beautiful?" In all philosophy hitherto the artist is lacking—

This, as the foregoing indicates, is a necessary mistake; for the artist who began to understand himself would misunderstand himself: he ought not to look back, he ought not to look at all, he ought to give.—

It is to the honor of an artist if he is unable to be a critic—otherwise he is half and half, he is "modern."

812 (*March-June 1888*)

I set down here a list of psychological states as signs of a full and flourishing life that one is accustomed today to condemn as morbid. For by now we have learned better than to speak of healthy and sick as of an antithesis: it is a question of degrees. My claim in this matter is that what is today called "healthy" represents a lower level than that which under favorable circumstances *would be* healthy—that we are relatively sick—

The artist belongs to a still stronger race. What would be harmful and morbid in us, in him is nature—— But one objects to us that it is precisely the impoverishment of the machine that makes possible extravagant powers of understanding of every kind of suggestion: witness our hysterical females.

An excess of sap and force can bring with it symptoms of partial constraint, of sense hallucinations, susceptibility to suggestion, just as well as can impoverishment of life: the stimulus is differently conditioned, the effect remains the same— But the after-effect is not the same; the extreme exhaustion of all morbid natures after their nervous eccentricities has nothing in common with the states of the artist, who does not have to atone for his good periods— He is rich enough for them: he is able to squander without becoming poor.

As one may today consider "genius" as a form of neurosis, so perhaps also the artistic power of suggestion—and indeed our *artists* are painfully like hysterical females!!! But that is an objection to "today," not to "artists."

Inartistic states: those of objectivity, mirroring, suspended will—(*Schopenhauer's* scandalous misunderstanding when he took art for a bridge to the denial of life)— Inartistic states: among those who become impoverished, withdraw, grow pale, under whose eyes life suffers:—the Christian.

813 (*1888*)

The *modern* artist, in his physiology next-of-kin to the hysteric, is also distinguished by this morbidity as a character. The hysteric is false—he lies from love of lying, he is admirable in every art of dissimulation—unless his morbid vanity plays a trick on him. This vanity is like a continual fever that requires narcotics and does not shrink from any self-deception, any farce, that promises momentary relief. (Incapacity for pride and the continual need for revenge for a deeply ingrained self-contempt—this is almost the definition of this kind of vanity.)

The absurd irritability of his system, which turns all experiences into crises and introduces the "dramatic" into the smallest accidents of life, robs him of all calculability: he is no longer a person, at most a rendezvous of persons and now this one, now that one shoots forward with shameless assurance. Precisely for this reason, he is great as an actor: all these poor will-less people whom doctors study so closely astonish one with their virtuosity in mimicry, transfiguration, assumption of almost any *desired* character.

814 (*Spring-Fall 1887; rev. Spring-Fall 1888*)

Artists are *not* men of great passion, whatever they may like to tell us and themselves. And this for two reasons: they lack any sense of shame before themselves (they observe themselves *while they live*; they spy on themselves, they are too inquisitive) and they also lack any sense of shame before great passion (they exploit it as artists). Secondly, however, their vampire, their talent, grudges them as a rule that squandering of force which one calls passion.— If one has a talent, one is also its victim: one lives under the vampirism of one's talent.

One does not get over a passion by representing it: rather, it is over *when* one is able to represent it. (Goethe teaches otherwise; but here it seems that he wanted to misunderstand himself—from *delicatezza*.[130])

815 (*Summer-Fall 1888*)

The rationale of life.— A relative chastity, a prudent caution on principle regarding erotic matters, even in thought, can belong to the grand rationale of life even in richly endowed and complete natures. This principle applies especially to artists, it is part of their best wisdom of life. Completely non-suspect voices have lent sup-

---

[130] Delicacy of feeling, tact—consideration for the women who had inspired him.

port to this opinion: I name Stendhal and Th. Gautier, also Flaubert. The artist is perhaps necessarily a sensual man, generally excitable, susceptible in every sense to stimuli, meeting the very suggestion of a stimulus halfway even from afar. This notwithstanding, he is on the average, under the pressure of his task, of his will to mastery, actually moderate, often even chaste. His dominant instinct demands this of him: it does not permit him to expend himself in any casual way. The force that one expends in artistic conception is the same as that expended in the sexual act: there is only one kind of force. An artist betrays himself if he succumbs *here*, if he squanders himself *here*: it betrays a lack of instinct, of will in general; it can be a sign of decadence—in any case, it devalues his art to an incalculable degree.[131]

816 (*March-June 1888*)

Compared with the *artist*, the appearance of the *scientific* man is actually a sign of a certain damming-up and lowering of the level of life (—but also of strengthening, severity, hardness, will power).

To what extent falsity, indifference to truth and utility may be signs of youth, of "childishness," in an artist— Their habitual manner, their unreasonableness, their ignorance about themselves, their indifference to "eternal values," their seriousness in "play"—their lack of dignity; buffoon and god side by side; saint and *canaille*— Imitation as an instinct, commanding.— Artists of ascending life—artists of declining life: do they not belong to all phases?— Yes![132]

817 (*Spring-Fall 1887; rev. Spring-Fall 1888*)

Would any link at all be missing in the chain of art and science if woman, if the works of women were missing? Admitting exceptions—they prove the rule—woman attains perfection in everything that is not a work: in letters, in memoirs, even in the most delicate handiwork, in short in everything that is not a

---

[131] 1911, p. 512: "A second part of this aphorism, dealing with Richard Wagner, has been omitted." This part will be found, in the facsimile pages, and in translation in the Appendix.

[132] Cf. section 339 above.

métier—precisely because in these things she perfects herself, because she here obeys the only artistic impulse she has—she wants to *please*—

But what has woman to do with the passionate indifference of the true artist, who assigns more importance to a sound, a breath, a heyday![133] than to himself? who strains with every finger to reach his innermost secrets? who accords no value to anything that cannot become form (—that cannot surrender itself, make itself public—). Art as it is practiced by the artist—do you not grasp what it is: an attempt to assassinate all *pudeurs*?[134]

Only in this century has woman ventured to turn to literature (—*vers la canaille plumière écrivassière*,[135] in the words of old Mirabeau): she dabbles in writing, she dabbles in art, she is losing her instincts. But *why*? if one may ask.

818 (*Nov. 1887-March 1888*)

One is an artist at the cost of regarding that which all non-artists call "form" as content, as "the matter itself." To be sure, then one belongs in a topsy-turvy world: for henceforth content becomes something merely formal—our life included.

819 (*1883-1888*)

A sense for and a delight in *nuances* (—the real mark of modernity), in that which is *not* general, runs counter to the drive that delights and excels in grasping the *typical*: like the Greek taste of the best period. There is an overpowering of the fullness of life in it; *measure* becomes master; at bottom there is that *calm* of the strong soul that moves slowly and feels repugnance toward what is too lively. The general rule, the law, is *honored* and *emphasized*: the exception, conversely, is set aside, the nuance obliterated. The firm, powerful, solid, the life that reposes broad and majestic and conceals its strength—that is what "*pleases*"; i.e., that corresponds to what one thinks of oneself.

---

[133] *Hopsasa:* Perhaps an allusion to Papageno in *The Magic Flute*.

[134] Cf. *Twilight*, "Maxims and Arrows," aphorism 16 (*Portable Nietzsche*, p. 468).

[135] Toward the scribbling rabble. Cf. also *Twilight*, "Skirmishes," section 27 (*Portable Nietzsche*, p. 531).

820 (*1885*)

In the main, I agree more with the artists than with any philosopher hitherto: they have not lost the scent of life, they have loved the things of "this world"—they have loved their senses. To strive for "desensualization": that seems to me a misunderstanding or an illness or a cure, where it is not merely hypocrisy or self-deception. I desire for myself and for all who live, *may* live, without being tormented by a puritanical conscience, an ever-greater spiritualization and multiplication of the senses; indeed, we should be grateful to the senses for their subtlety, plenitude, and power and offer them in return the best we have in the way of spirit. What are priestly and metaphysical calumnies against the senses to us! We no longer need these calumnies: it is a sign that one has turned out well when, like Goethe, one clings with ever-greater pleasure and warmth to the "things of this world":—for in this way he holds firmly to the great conception of man, that man becomes the transfigurer of existence when he learns to transfigure himself.[136]

821 (*March-June 1888*)

Pessimism in art?— The artist gradually comes to love for their own sake the means that reveal a condition of intoxication: extreme subtlety and splendor of color, definiteness of line, nuances of tone: the *distinct* where otherwise, under normal conditions, distinctness is lacking. All distinct things, all nuances, to the extent that they recall these extreme enhancements of strength that intoxication produces, awaken this feeling of intoxication by association: the effect of works of art is to *excite the state that creates art*—intoxication.

What is essential in art remains its perfection of existence, its production of perfection and plenitude; art is essentially *affirmation, blessing, deification of existence*— What does a *pessimistic art* signify? Is it not a *contradictio*?— Yes.— Schopenhauer is *wrong* when he says that certain works of art serve pessimism. Tragedy does *not* teach "resignation"— To represent terrible and questionable things is in itself an instinct for power and magnifi-

---

[136] MS not in Nietzsche's handwriting—evidently dictated by him—but then revised by his hand.

cence in an artist: he does not fear them— There is no such thing as pessimistic art— Art affirms. Job affirms.— But Zola? But the Goncourts?— The things they display are ugly: but *that* they display them comes from their *pleasure in the ugly*— It's no good! If you think otherwise, you're deceiving yourselves.— How liberating is Dostoevsky!

822 (*1888*)

If my readers are sufficiently initiated into the idea that "the good man" represents, in the total drama of life, a form of *exhaustion*, they will respect the consistency of Christianity in conceiving the good man as ugly. Christianity was right in this.

For a philosopher to say, "the good and the beautiful are one," is infamy; if he goes on to add, "also the true," one ought to thrash him. Truth is ugly.

We possess *art* lest we *perish of the truth.*

823 (*Spring-Fall 1887*)

The moralization of the arts.— Art as freedom from moral narrowness and corner-perspectives; or as mockery of them. Flight into nature, where its beauty is coupled with frightfulness. Conception of the great human being.

—Fragile, useless luxury souls, troubled even by a breath, "beautiful souls."

—To awaken deceased ideals in all their merciless severity and brutaliy, as the most magnificent monsters they are.

—A joyful delight in the psychological insight into the sinuosity and unconscious play-acting of all moralized artists.

—The falsity of art—to bring to light its immorality.

—To bring to light "basic idealizing powers" (sensuality, intoxication, superabundant animality).

824 (*Spring-Fall 1887; rev. 1888*)[137]

Modern counterfeiting in the arts: regarded as *necessary*, namely as corresponding to the most characteristic needs of the modern soul.

One plugs the gaps of talent, even more the gaps in education, tradition, schooling.

---

[137] Utilized in *The Case of Wagner*.

First: one seeks for oneself a less artistic public, which loves unconditionally (—and soon kneels down before the *person*). The superstition of our century, the superstitious belief in the "genius," helps.

Second: one harangues the obscure instincts of the dissatisfied, ambitious, self-disguised spirits in a democratic age: importance of *poses*.

Third: one transfers the procedures of one art to the other arts, confounds the objectives of art with those of knowledge or the church or racial interests (nationalism) or philosophy—one pulls all the stops at once and awakens the dark suspicion that one may be a god.

Fourth: one flatters women, sufferers, the indignant, one makes narcotics and opiates dominant in art, too. One tickles the cultured, readers of poets and ancient stories.

825 (*Spring-Fall 1887*)

The division into "public hall" and "private chamber"; in the former one *has* to be a charlatan today, in the latter one is *determined* to be a virtuoso and nothing more! The specific "genius" of our century spans this division, is great in both: the great charlatanry of Victor Hugo and Richard Wagner, but coupled with so much genuine virtuosity that they satisfied even the most refined artistic connoisseurs. Hence their lack of greatness: their perspective was continually changing, now directed to the coarsest demands, now to the most refined.

826 (*Spring-Fall 1887*)

False "intensification": 1. in romanticism: this constant *Espressivo* is no sign of strength but of a feeling of deficiency;

2. picturesque music, so-called dramatic music, is above all *easier* (as is the brutal colportage and the enumeration of *faits* and *traits*[138] in the naturalistic novel);

3. "passion" a matter of nerves and wearied souls; like the delight in high mountains, deserts, storms, orgies, and horrors—in the bulky and massive (e.g., on the part of historians); *there actually exists a cult of orgies of feeling* (—how does it happen

[138] Facts and traits.

that strong ages have an opposite need in art—a need for a realm beyond passion?)

4. preference for exciting material (erotica or socialistica or pathologica): all signs that show for whom one is working today: for the overworked and absent-minded or enfeebled.

One has to tyrannize in order to produce any effect at all.[139]

827 (*Spring-Fall 1887*)

Modern art as an art of tyrannizing—— A coarse and strongly defined logic of delineation; motifs simplified to the point of formulas; the formula tyrannizes. Within the delineations a wild multiplicity, an overwhelming mass, before which the senses become confused; brutality in color, material, desires. Examples: Zola, Wagner; in a more spiritual order, Taine. Thus: *logic*, *mass* and *brutality*.

828 (*1883-1888*)

In regard to painters: *tous ces modernes sont des poètes qui ont voulu être peintres. L'un a cherché des drames dans l'histoire, l'autre des scènes de moeurs, celui-ci traduit des religions, celui-là une philosophie.*[140] One imitates Raphael, another the early Italian masters; landscape artists employ trees and clouds to make odes and elegies. No one is simply a painter; all are archaeologists, psychologists, theatrical producers of this or that recollection or theory. They enjoy our erudition, our philosophy. Like us, they are full and overfull of general ideas. They like a form, not for the sake of what it is, but for the sake of what it expresses. They are sons of a scholarly, tormented, and reflective generation—a thousand miles removed from the old masters, who did not read and only thought of feasting their eyes.

829 (*1888*)

Fundamentally, even Wagner's music is still literature, no less than the whole of French romanticism: the charm of exoticism

---

[139] Clearly, this section is largely about Wagner, but not only about him; see the next section.

[140] All these moderns are poets who have wished to be painters. One has looked for dramas in history, another for scenes of manners; this one transposes religions, that one a philosphy.

(strange times, customs, passions), exercised on sentimental stay-at-homes. The delight of entering the vastly distant foreign prehistoric land, accessible only through books, and of finding the whole horizon painted with new colors and possibilities—

The intuition of yet more distant, unexplored worlds; disdain for the boulevards— For nationalism, let us not deceive ourselves, is merely another form of exoticism—

Romantic musicians relate what exotic books have made of them: one would like to experience exotic things, passions after the Florentine and Venetian taste: in the end one contents oneself with seeking them in pictures— The essential thing is the type of new desire, the wish to imitate and to experience the lives of others, disguise, dissimulation of the soul— Romantic art is only a makeshift substitute for a defective "reality."

The attempt to *do* new things: revolution, Napoleon. Napoleon, the passion of new possibilities of the soul, an expansion of the soul.

Weariness of will; all the greater excesses in the desire to feel, imagine, and dream new things—consequence of the excesses one has experienced: hunger for excessive feelings— Foreign literatures offered the strongest spices.

830 (*Nov. 1887-March 1888*)

Winckelmann's and Goethe's Greeks, Victor Hugo's orientals, Wagner's Edda characters, Walter Scott's Englishmen of the thirteenth century—some day the whole comedy will be exposed! it was all historically false beyond measure, *but*—modern.[141]

831 (*Spring-Fall 1887*)

Toward a characterization of national genius in relation to what is foreign and borrowed:—

The *English* genius coarsens and makes natural everything it takes up;

the *French* makes thin, simplifies, logicizes, adorns;

the *German* confuses, compromises, confounds and moralizes;

the *Italian* has made by far the freest and subtlest use of what it has borrowed, and introduced a hundred times more into

[141] 1911, p. 512: "Last line, another reading: 'modern, true.' "

it than it took out of it: as the richest genius which had the most to bestow.

832 (*Spring-Fall 1887*)

The Jews approached genius in the sphere of art with Heinrich Heine and Offenbach, this most gifted and high-spirited satyr, who as a musician clung to the great tradition and who is for those who have more than mere ears a real liberation from the sentimental and at bottom *degenerate* musicians of German romanticism.

833 (*Spring-Fall 1887*)

Offenbach: French music with the spirit of Voltaire, free, high-spirited, with a little sardonic grin, but bright, clever almost to the point of banality (—he does not use make-up—) and without the *mignardise*[142] of morbid or blond-Viennese sensuality.

834 (*1884*)

If one understands by artistic genius the greatest freedom under the law, divine frivolity, facility in the hardest things, then Offenbach has even more right to the name "genius" than Wagner. Wagner is heavy and ponderous: nothing is more foreign to him than moments of the most high-spirited perfection, such as this buffoon Offenbach achieves five or six times in almost every one of his buffooneries.[143] But perhaps one might understand something else by the word genius.[144]—

835 (*1885-1886*)

For the chapter "*Music.*"[145]—German and French and Italian

---

[142] Affectation.

[143] For Nietzsche's praise of the buffoon (*Hanswurst*) in his last books, see my *Nietzsche*, Chapter 13, section III.

[144] 1911, p. 512: These lines were "taken from a note about Richard Wagner." This note is included in the facsimile pages and in translation in the Appendix.

[145] In the MS: "A chapter 'Music'!—The doctrine of 'intoxication' (enumeration, e.g., worship of *petits faits*)." Also according to 1911, p. 512, this section was originally intended for *Beyond Good and Evil;* but cf. also *The Case of Wagner.*

music. (Our lowest periods politically the most fruitful. The Slavs?)— The cultural-historical ballet: has overcome opera.— Actors' music and musicians' music.— An error that what Wagner created was a form:—it was formlessness. The possibility of a dramatic construction has still to be discovered.— Rhythm. "Expression" at any cost.— In praise of *Carmen*.— In praise of Heinrich Schütz (and the "Liszt Society"—)— Whorish instrumentation.— In praise of Mendelssohn: an element of Goethe in him and nowhere else! (just as another element of Goethe came to perfection in Rahel;[146] a third in Heinrich Heine.)[147]

836 (*Spring-Fall 1887*)

Descriptive music; leave it to reality to be effective— All these kinds of art are easier, more imitable; the poorly gifted employ them. Appeal to the instincts; art with the power of suggestion.

837 (*Spring-Fall 1887*)

On our *modern music*.— The decay of melody is the same as the decay of the "idea," of dialectic, of freedom of the most spiritual activity—a piece of clumsiness and constipation that is developing to new heights of daring and even to principles;—finally, one has only the principles of one's talents, one's narrowmindedness of a talent.

"Dramatic music" nonsense! It is simply bad music— "Feeling," "passion" as surrogates when one no longer knows how to achieve an exalted spirituality and the happiness that attends it (e.g., that of Voltaire). Technically, "feeling" and "passion" are easier—they presuppose much poorer artists. Recourse to drama betrays that an artist is more a master of false means than of genuine means. We have dramatic painting, dramatic lyrics, etc.

838 (*1888*)

We lack in music an aesthetic that would impose laws on musicians and give them a conscience; we lack, as a consequence,

---

[146] Rahel von Varnhagen (1771-1833): her salon was a great cultural center in Berlin.

[147] Mendelssohn, Rahel, and Heine—and Offenbach (see sections 832-34) were of Jewish descent, while Wagner was a rabid anti-Semite.

a genuine conflict over "principles"—for as musicians we laugh at Herbart's velleities in this realm as much as we do at Schopenhauer's. In fact, this results in a great difficulty: we no longer know on what basis to found the concepts "model," "mastery," "perfection"—we grope blindly in the realm of values with the instinct of old love and admiration; we come close to believing "what is good is what pleases *us*"—

It awakens my mistrust when Beethoven is everywhere quite innocently described as a "classicist": I would strictly maintain that in the other arts one understands by a classicist an artist of the opposite type of Beethoven's. But when even the complete and obvious *disintegration of style* in Wagner, his so-called dramatic style, is taught and honored as "exemplary," as "mastery," as "progress," my impatience reaches its height. The dramatic style in music, as Wagner understands it, is the renunciation of style in general, on the presupposition that something else is a hundred times more important than music, namely the drama. Wagner can paint, he employs music for something other than music, he emphasizes poses, he is a poet; finally, he appealed to "beautiful feelings" and "heaving bosoms" like all artists of the theater—and with all this he won over the women and even those in need of culture: but what is music to women and those in need of culture! They have no conscience for art; they do not suffer when all the principal and most indispensable virtues of an art are trampled under foot and mocked for the benefit of secondary objectives (as *ancilla*[148] *dramaturgica*). What is the point of extending the means of expression if that which expresses, art itself, has lost the law of its being! The picturesque pomp and power of tones, the symbolism of sound, rhythm, colors of harmony and disharmony, the suggestive significance of music, the whole sensuality of music which Wagner has brought into dominance—all this Wagner recognized in music, drew out of it, developed. Victor Hugo did something similar to language; but already today the French are asking themselves whether, in Hugo's case, it was not a corruption of language—whether, with the increase of sensuality in language, reason, spirituality, the profound obedience to law in language have not been depressed? That the poets in France have become sculptors, that the musicians in Germany have become actors and culture-mongers—are these not signs of decadence?

[148] Handmaid.

839 (*Spring-Fall 1887; rev. Spring-Fall 1888*)

Today we have a musical pessimism, even among the nonmusical. Who has not met him, who has not cursed him—the wretched youth who tortures his piano into cries of despair, who single-handed heaves forward the mud of the gloomiest gray-brown harmonies? This identifies one as a pessimist— But whether this also identifies one as a musician? I cannot be made to think so. The Wagnerian *pur sang*[149] is unmusical; he succumbs to the elemental powers of music somewhat as a woman succumbs to the will of her hypnotist—and in order to be able to do this, he must not be made suspicious by a severe and subtle conscience *in rebus musicis et musicantibus.*[150] I said "somewhat as"—: but perhaps we have more than a metaphor here. Consider the means for producing effects that Wagner prefers to use (—and had for the most part to invent for himself): they are strangely similar to those with which a hypnotist achieves his effect (—his choice of tempo and tonal color for his orchestra; the repellent avoidance of logic and squareness in his rhythm; the lingering, soothing, mysterious, hysterical quality of his "endless melody").— And is the condition to which the *Lohengrin* prelude, for example, reduces its hearers, especially women, essentially different from a somnambulistic trance?—

I heard an Italian woman who had just listened to the prelude in question say, with those entranced eyes that Wagneriennes know how to affect: *"come si* dorme *con questa musica!"*[151]

840 (*March-June 1888*)

Religion in music.— How much unadmitted and even uncomprehended satisfaction of all religious needs is still to be found in Wagnerian music! How much prayer, virtue, unction, "virginity," "redemption" speak through it!— That music may dispense with words and concepts—oh what advantage she derives from that fact, this cunning saint, who leads and *seduces back* to all that was for-

---

[149] Of pure blood.

[150] In matters of music and musicians.

[151] How one *sleeps* with this music!

"Squareness" in the preceding paragraph: *Quadratur.*

All of these notes on Wagner should be compared with *The Case of Wagner.*

merly believed!— Our intellectual conscience has no need to feel ashamed—it remains outside—when some ancient instinct or other drinks with trembling lips from forbidden cups— This is shrewd, healthy and, in so far as it betrays shame at the satisfaction of the religious instinct, even a good sign— Underhand Christianity: type of the music of "Wagner's final period."

841 (*March-June 1888*)[152]

I distinguish between courage in the face of people, courage in the face of things, and courage in the face of paper. The latter was, e.g., the courage of David Strauss. I distinguish further between courage before witnesses and courage without witnesses: the courage of a Christian, of a believer in God in general, can never be courage without witnesses—this fact alone degrades it. I distinguish, finally, courage rooted in temperament and courage rooted in fear of fear: a particular instance of the latter type is moral courage. There should also be added courage from despair.

Wagner possessed this kind of courage. His situtaion regarding music was, at bottom, desperate. He lacked the two things needed to make a *good* musician: nature and culture, a predisposition toward music and training and schooling in music. He possessed courage: he made a principle of what he lacked—he *invented* a style of music for himself. "Dramatic music," as invented by him, is the music he was capable of making—Wagner's limitations define this concept.

And he was misunderstood!— *Was* he misunderstood?— Five-sixths of modern artists are in this position. Wagner is their savior; five-sixths is in any case the "lowest estimate." In every instance in which nature has shown herself inexorable and in which on the other hand culture has remained accidental, tentative, dilettante, the artist turns instinctively—what am I saying?— enthusiastically to Wagner: "half did he drag him, half he sank," as the poet says.[153]

842 (*March-June 1888*)

"Music"—and the grand style.— The greatness of an artist

---

[152] 1911, p. 512: "From a larger draft used in *The Case of Wagner.*"

[153] Goethe, "Der Fischer," penultimate line: *halb zog sie ihn, halb sank er hin.* Nietzsche changes *sie* to *er.*

cannot be measured by the "beautiful feelings" he arouses: leave that idea to females. But according to the degree to which he approaches the grand style, to which he is capable of the grand style. This style has this in common with great passion, that it disdains to please; that it forgets to persuade; that it commands; that it *wills*— To become master of the chaos one is; to compel one's chaos to become form: to become logical, simple, unambiguous, mathematics, *law*—that is the grand ambition here.— It repels; such men of force are no longer loved—a desert spreads around them, a silence, a fear as in the presence of some great sacrilege— All the arts know such aspirants to the grand style: why are they lacking in music? No musician has yet built as that architect did who created the Palazzo Pitti— Here lies a problem. Does music perhaps belong to that culture in which the domain of men of force of all kinds has ceased? Does the concept grand style ultimately stand in contradiction to the soul of music—to the "woman" in our music?—

I here touch upon a cardinal question: where does our entire music belong? The ages of classical taste knew nothing to compare with it: it began to blossom when the Renaissance world had attained its evening, when "freedom" had departed from morals and even from men:—is it part of its character to be counter-Renaissance? Is it the sister of the Baroque style, since it is in any case its contemporary? Is music, modern music, not already decadence?—

Once before I pointed to this question: whether our music is not a piece of counter-Renaissance in art? whether it is not next-of-kin to the Baroque style? whether it has not grown up in contradiction to all classical taste, so that all ambitions to become classical are forbidden to it by its nature?

The answer to this first-rank question of values would not remain in doubt if the proper inferences had been drawn from the fact that music achieved its greatest ripeness and fullness as romanticism—once again as a movement of reaction against classicism.

Mozart—a delicate and amorous soul, but entirely eighteenth century, even when he is serious.— Beethoven the first great romantic, in the sense of the *French* conception of romanticism, as Wagner is the last great romantic—both instinctive opponents of classical taste, of severe style—to say nothing of "grand" style.

843 (*March-June 1888*)

Romanticism: an ambiguous question, like everything modern.
The aesthetic states twofold.
The full and bestowing as opposed to the seeking, desiring.

844 (*1885-1886*)

A romantic is an artist whose great dissatisfaction with himself makes him creative—who looks away, looks back from himself and from his world.

845 (*1885-1886*)

Is art a consequence of *dissatisfaction with reality*? Or an expression of *gratitude for happiness enjoyed*? In the former case, *romanticism;* in the latter, aureole and dithyramb (in short, art of apotheosis): Raphael, too, belongs here; he merely had the falsity to deify what looked like the Christian interpretation of the world. He was grateful for existence where it was *not* specifically Christian.

The *moral* interpretation makes the world unbearable. Christianity was the attempt to "overcome" the world by it; i.e., to negate it. *In praxi*, such a murderous attempt of insanity—an insane self-elevation of man above the world—resulted in making man gloomy, small, and impoverished: only the most mediocre and harmless type of man, the herd type, profited by it, was advanced by it, if you like.

Homer as an *artist of apotheosis*; Rubens also. Music has not yet had one.

The idealization of the man of *great sacrilege* (a sense of his *greatness*) is Greek;[154] depreciation, slandering, contempt for the sinner is Judeo-Christian.

846 (*1885-1886*)

What is romanticism?— In regard to all aesthetic values, I now employ this fundamental distinction: I ask in each individual case "has hunger or superabundance become creative here?" At

[154] Cf. Prometheus and *The Birth of Tragedy*, section 9.

first sight, another distinction might seem more plausible—it is far more obvious—namely the distinction whether the desire for rigidity, eternity, "*being*" has been the cause of creation, or rather the desire for destruction, for change, for *becoming*. But both kinds of desire prove, when examined more closely, to be ambiguous and interpretable according to the scheme mentioned above, which, I think, is to be preferred.

The desire for destruction, change, becoming *can* be the expression of an overfull power pregnant with the future (my term for this, as is known, is the word "Dionysian"); but it can also be the hatred of the ill-constituted, disinherited, underprivileged, which destroys, *has* to destroy, because what exists, indeed existence itself, all being itself, enrages and provokes it.

"Eternalization," on the other hand, *can* proceed from gratitude and love—an art of this origin will always be an art of apotheosis, dithyrambic perhaps with Rubens, blissful with Hafiz, bright and gracious with Goethe, and shedding a Homeric aureole over all things—but it can also be that tyrannic will of a great sufferer who would like to forge what is most personal, individual, and narrow—most idiosyncratic—in his suffering, into a binding *law* and compulsion, taking revenge on all things, as it were, by impressing, forcing, and branding into them his image, the image of his torture. The latter is romantic pessimism in its most expressive form, whether as Schopenhauerian philosophy of will or as Wagnerian music.[155]

847 (*Spring-Fall 1887*)

Whether behind the antithesis classic and romantic there does not lie hidden the antithesis active and reactive?—

848 (*Spring-Fall 1887*)

To be classical, one must possess *all* the strong, seemingly contradictory gifts and desires—but in such a way that they go together beneath one yoke; arrive at the *right* time to bring to its climax and high point a *genus* of literature or art or politics (not

---

[155] This section was used in Book V of *The Gay Science* (1887), section 370, which was later included also in *Nietzsche contra Wagner* under the heading "We Antipodes" (*Portable Nietzsche*, pp. 669-71).

after this has already happened—); reflect a total state (of a people or a culture) in one's deepest and innermost soul, at a time when it still exists and has not yet been overpainted with imitations of foreign things (or when it is still dependent—); and one must not be a reactive but a *concluding* and forward-leading spirit, saying Yes in all cases, even with one's hatred.

"Is the highest personal value *not* part of it?"— To consider perhaps whether moral prejudices are not playing their game here and whether great *moral* loftiness is not perhaps in itself a *contradiction* of the *classical*?[156]— Whether the moral monsters must not necessarily be *romantics*, in word and deed?— Precisely such a preponderance of one virtue over the others (as in the case of a moral monster) is hostile to the classical power of equilibrium: supposing one possessed this loftiness and was nonetheless classical, then we could confidently infer that one also possessed immorality of the same level: possibly the case of Shakespeare (assuming it was really Lord Bacon).[157]

849 (*Nov. 1887-March 1888*)

Future things.— Against the romanticism of great "passion."— To grasp that a quantum of coldness, lucidity, hardness is part of all "classical" taste: logic above all, happiness in spirituality, "three unities," concentration, hatred for feeling, heart, *esprit*, hatred for the manifold, uncertain, rambling, for intimations, as well as for the brief, pointed, pretty, good-natured. One should not play with artistic formulas: one should remodel life so that afterward it *has* to formulate itself.

It is an amusing comedy at which we have only now learned to laugh, which we only now *see*: that the contemporaries of Herder, Winckelmann, Goethe, and Hegel claimed to have *rediscovered the classical ideal*—and at the same time Shakespeare!— And the same generation had meanly repudiated the French classical school! as if the essential things could not have been learned here as well as there!— But one desired "nature," "naturalness": oh stupidity! One believed that classicism was a kind of naturalness!

---

[156] At this point all editions omit the words: "To '*mediterraneanize*' music—that is *my* slogan."

[157] Cf. *Ecce Homo,* "Why I am so clever," section 4.

To think through, without prejudice or indulgence, in what soil a classical taste can grow. Hardening, simplification, strengthening, making man more evil: these belong together. Logical-psychological simplification. Contempt for detail, complexity, the uncertain.

The romantics in Germany do *not* protest against classicism, but against reason, enlightenment, taste, the eighteenth century.

The sensibility of romantic-Wagnerian music: antithesis of *classical sensibility*.

The will to unity (because unity tyrannizes—namely over the listener, spectator); but inability to tyrannize over oneself concerning the main thing—namely in regard to the work itself (omitting, shortening, clarifying, simplifying). Overwhelming through masses (Wagner, Victor Hugo, Zola, Taine).

850 (*Spring-Fall 1887*)

The nihilism of artists.— Nature cruel in her cheerfulness; cynical in her sunrises. We are enemies of sentimental emotions. We flee to where nature moves our senses and our imagination; where we have nothing to love, where we are not reminded of the moral semblances and delicacies of this northerly nature—and the same is the case in the arts. We prefer that which no longer reminds us of "good and evil." Our moralistic susceptibility to stimuli and pain is, as it were, redeemed by a terrible and happy nature, in the fatalism of the senses and forces. Life without goodness.

The benefit consists in the contemplation of nature's magnificent *indifference* to good and evil.

No justice in history, no goodness in nature: that is why the pessimist, if he is an artist, goes *in historicis*[158] to those places where the absence of justice itself is revealed with splendid naiveté, where *perfection* comes into view—and also in nature, to those places where her evil and indifferent character is not disguised, where she exhibits the character of *perfection*— The nihilistic artist betrays himself in willing and preferring *cynical history, cynical nature*.

---

[158] In historical matters.

Nietzsche's repeated emphasis on the magnificent indifference of nature invites comparison with the conclusion of Camus' *The Stranger;* indeed this whole section—and not only *this* section—may have left its mark on Camus. Note also Nietzsche's frequent use of the word "absurd."

851 (*Jan.-Fall 1888*)

What is tragic?— On repeated occasions I have laid my finger on Aristotle's great misunderstanding in believing the tragic affects to be two *depressive* affects, terror and pity. If he were right, tragedy would be an art dangerous to life: one would have to warn against it as notorious and a public danger. Art, in other cases the great stimulant of life, an intoxication with life, a will to life, would here, in the service of a declining movement and as it were the handmaid of pessimism, become *harmful to health* (—for that one is "purged" of these affects through their arousal, as Aristotle seems to believe, is simply not true). Something that habitually arouses terror or pity disorganizes, weakens, discourages—and supposing Schopenhauer were right that one should learn resignation from tragedy (i.e., a gentle renunciation of happiness, hope, will to life), then this would be an art in which art denies itself. Tragedy would then signify a process of disintegration: the instinct for life destroying itself through the instinct for art. Christianity, nihilism, tragic art, physiological decadence—these would go hand in hand, come into predominance at the same time, assist one another forward—*downward*— Tragedy would be a symptom of decline.

One can refute this theory in the most cold-blooded way: namely, by measuring the effects of a tragic emotion with a dynamometer. And one would discover as a result what ultimately only the absolute mendaciousness of a systematizer could misunderstand—that tragedy is a *tonic*. If Schopenhauer did not *want* to grasp this, if he posited a general depression as the tragic condition, if he suggested to the Greeks (—who to his annoyance did not "resign themselves"—) that they had not attained the highest view of the world—that is *parti pris*, logic of a system, counterfeit of a systematizer: one of those dreadful counterfeits that ruined Schopenhauer's whole psychology, step by step (—arbitrarily and violently, he misunderstood genius, art itself, morality, pagan religion, beauty, knowledge, and more or less everything).

852 (*Spring-Fall 1887; rev. Spring-Fall 1888*)

The tragic artist.[159]— It is a question of *strength* (of an

[159] This title does not appear in this place in the MS, but was taken by the German editors from one of Nietzsche's lists of his sections.

individual or of a people), *whether* and *where* the judgment "beautiful" is applied. The feeling of plenitude, of *dammed-up strength* (which permits one to meet with courage and good-humor much that makes the weakling *shudder*)—the feeling of *power* applies the judgment "beautiful" even to things and conditions that the instinct of impotence could only find *hateful* and "ugly." The nose for what we could still barely deal with if it confronted us in the flesh—as danger, problem, temptation—this determines even our aesthetic Yes. ("That is beautiful" is an *affirmation.*)

From this it appears that, broadly speaking, a *preference for questionable and terrifying things* is a symptom of *strength*; while a taste for the *pretty and dainty* belongs to the weak and delicate. *Pleasure* in tragedy characterizes *strong* ages and natures: their *non plus ultra* is perhaps the *divina commedia.* It is the *heroic* spirits who say Yes to themselves in tragic cruelty: they are hard enough to experience suffering as a *pleasure.*

Supposing, on the other hand, that the weak desire to enjoy an art that is not meant for them; what would they do to make tragedy palatable for themselves? They would interpret *their own value feelings* into it; e.g., the "triumph of the moral world-order" or the doctrine of the "worthlessness of existence" or the invitation to "resignation" (—or half-medicinal, half-moral discharges of affects à la Aristotle).[160] Finally: the *art of the terrifying,* in so far as it excites the nerves, can be esteemed by the weak and exhausted as a stimulus: that, for example, is the reason Wagnerian art is esteemed today. It is a sign of one's *feeling of power and well-being* how far one can acknowledge the terrifying and questionable character of things; and *whether* one needs some sort of "solution" at the end.

This type of *artists' pessimism* is precisely the *opposite of that religio-moral pessimism* that suffers from the "corruption" of man and the riddle of existence—and by all means craves a solution, or at least a hope for a solution. The suffering, desperate, self-mistrustful, in a word the sick, have at all times had need of entrancing *visions* to endure life (*this* is the origin of the concept "blessedness"). A related case: the artists of decadence, who fundamentally have a *nihilistic* attitude toward life, take *refuge* in the *beauty of form*—in those *select* things in which nature has become perfect, in which she is indifferently *great* and *beautiful*—

[160] Cf. Aristotle's conception of catharsis, *Poetics,* 1449 b *ff.*, which is also criticized in section 851.

(—"Love of beauty" can therefore be something other than the *ability* to *see* the beautiful, *create* the beautiful; it can be an expression of the very *inability* to do so.)

Those imposing artists who let a *harmony* sound forth from every conflict are those who bestow upon things their own power and self-redemption: they express their innermost experience in the symbolism of every work of art they produce—their creativity is gratitude for their existence.

The *profundity of the tragic artist* lies in this, that his aesthetic instinct surveys the more remote consequences, that he does not halt shortsightedly at what is closest at hand, that he affirms the *large-scale economy* which justifies the *terrifying*, the *evil*, the *questionable*—and more than merely justifies them.

853
Art in the "Birth of Tragedy"[161]

(1)

The conception of the work that one encounters in the background of this book is singularly gloomy and unpleasant: no type of pessimism known hitherto seems to have attained to this degree of malevolence. The antithesis of a real and an apparent world is lacking here: there is only *one* world, and this is false, cruel, contradictory, seductive, without meaning— A world thus constituted is the real world. *We have need of lies* in order to conquer this reality, this "truth," that is, in order to *live*— That lies are necessary in order to live is itself part of the terrifying and questionable character of existence.

Metaphysics, morality, religion, science—in this book these things merit consideration only as various forms of lies: with their help one can have *faith* in life. "Life *ought* to inspire confidence": the task thus imposed is tremendous. To solve it, man must be a liar by nature, he must be above all an *artist*. And he *is* one: metaphysics, religion, morality, science—all of them only products

---

[161] Title supplied by Peter Gast. According to 1911, p. 512, this is a fragmentary draft for a preface for the new edition of *The Birth of Tragedy*, and probably dates from the fall of 1886. But the list at the end of the Musarion edition dates this section "November 1887-March 1888," basing itself solely on the notebook in which these pages were filed. The internal evidence for a date earlier than the preface actually published in 1886 seems very strong, as that preface is vastly superior in form and content to the section above.

of his will to art, to lie, to flight from "truth," to *negation* of "truth." This ability itself, thanks to which he violates reality by means of lies, this artistic ability of man *par excellence*—he has it in common with everything that is. He himself is after all a piece of reality, truth, nature: how should he not also be a piece of *genius in lying!*

That the character of existence is to be misunderstood—profoundest and supreme secret motive behind all that is virtue, science, piety, artistry. Never to see many things, to see many things falsely, to imagine many things: oh how shrewd one still is in circumstances in which one is furthest from thinking oneself shrewd! Love, enthusiasm, "God"— So many subtleties of ultimate self-deception, so many seductions to life, so much faith in life! In those moments in which man was deceived, in which he duped himself, in which he believes in life: oh how enraptured he feels! What delight! What a feeling of power! How much artists' triumph in the feeling of power!— Man has once again become master of "*material*"—master of truth!— And whenever man rejoices, he is always the same in his rejoicing: he rejoices as an artist, he enjoys himself as power, he enjoys the lie as his form of power.—

(II)

Art and nothing but art! It is the great means of making life possible, the great seduction to life, the great stimulant of life.

Art as the only superior counterforce to all will to denial of life, as that which is anti-Christian, anti-Buddhist, antinihilist *par excellence*.

Art as the *redemption of the man of knowledge*—of those who see the terrifying and questionable character of existence, who want to see it, the men of tragic knowledge.

Art as the *redemption of the man of action*—of those who not only see the terrifying and questionable character of existence but live it, want to live it, the tragic-warlike man, the hero.

Art as the *redemption of the sufferer*—as the way to states in which suffering is willed, transfigured, deified, where suffering is a form of great delight.

(III)

One will see that in this book pessimism, or to speak more

clearly, nihilism, counts as "truth." But truth does not count as the supreme value, even less as the supreme power. The will to appearance, to illusion, to deception, to becoming and change (to objectified deception) here counts as more profound, primeval, "metaphysical" than the will to truth, to reality, to mere appearance:—the last is itself merely a form of the will to illusion. In the same way, pleasure counts as being more primeval than pain: pain only as conditioned, as a consequence of the will to pleasure (of the will to become, grow, shape, i.e., *to create*: in creation, however, destruction is included). A highest state of affirmation of existence is conceived from which the highest degree of pain cannot be excluded: the *tragic-Dionysian* state.

(IV)

In this way, this book is even anti-pessimistic: that is, in the sense that it teaches something that is stronger than pessimism, "more divine" than truth: *art*. Nobody, it seems, would more seriously propose a radical negation of life, a really *active* negation even more than merely *saying* No to life, than the author of this book. Except that he knows—he has experience of it, perhaps he has experience of nothing else!—that art is *worth more* than truth.

Already in the preface, in which Richard Wagner is invited as to a dialogue, this confession of faith, this artists' gospel, appears: "art as the real task of life, art as life's *metaphysical* activity—"[162]

---

[162] The quotation is not exact.

BOOK FOUR

DISCIPLINE AND BREEDING*

---

* *Zucht und Züchtung*: See my note on section 980 below; also sections 398, 462, 862, 1053; *Beyond*, sections 225 and 262; and the last three pages of Chapter 10 of my *Nietzsche*.

Very few of Nietzsche's notes deal with "breeding," and the contents of Book IV therefore bear little relation to this title. The same consideration appiies to the second part of Book IV: "Dionysus."

Nietzsche's sister might have chosen a later draft instead of this one, of March 17, 1887, which put down *Zucht und Züchtung* as the title of Book IV (this draft consists only of the four book titles, and does not include any subdivisions). But most of the other drafts, being more detailed, would have posed even greater problems.

I. ORDER OF RANK

1. The Doctrine of Order of Rank

854 (*1884*)

In the age of *suffrage universel,* i.e., when everyone may sit in judgment on everyone and everything, I feel impelled to re-establish *order of rank.*

855 (*Spring-Fall 1887*)

What determines rank, sets off rank, is only quanta of power, and nothing else.

856 (*1885-1886*)

The will to power.— How those men would have to be constituted who took upon themselves this revaluation. Order of rank as order of power: war and danger the presupposition for a rank to retain the conditions of its existence. The grandiose prototype: man in nature—the weakest, shrewdest creature making himself master, subjugating the stupider forces.

857 (*Jan.-Fall 1888*)

I distinguish between a type of ascending life and another type of decay, disintegration, weakness. Is it credible that the question of the relative rank of these two types still needs to be posed?

858 (*Nov. 1887-March 1888*)

What determines your rank is the quantum of power you are: the rest is cowardice.

859 (*1883-1888*)

Advantage of detachment from one's age.— In a state of detachment from both movements, individualistic and collectivistic morality—for even the former does not recognize order of rank and would grant one the same freedom as all. My ideas do not revolve around the degree of freedom that is granted to the one or to the other or to all, but around the degree of *power* that the one or the other should exercise over others or over all, and to what extent a sacrifice of freedom, even enslavement, provides the basis for the emergence of a *higher type*. Put in the crudest form: *how could one sacrifice the development of mankind* to help a higher species than man to come into existence?—

860 (*1884*)

Of rank. The terrible consequence of "equality"—finally, everyone believes he has a right to every problem. All order of rank has vanished.

861 (*1884*)

A declaration of war on the masses by *higher men* is needed! Everywhere the mediocre are combining in order to make themselves master! Everything that makes soft and effeminate, that serves the ends of the "people" or the "feminine," works in favor of *suffrage universel,* i.e., the dominion of *inferior* men. But we should take reprisal and bring this whole affair (which in Europe commenced with Christianity) to light and to the bar of judgment.

862 (*1884*)

A doctrine is needed powerful enough to work as a breeding agent: strengthening the strong, paralyzing and destructive for the world-weary.[1]

---

[1] Cf. section 1053 below and 462 above.

The annihilation of the decaying races. Decay of Europe.— The annihilation of slavish evaluations.— Dominion over the earth as a means of producing a higher type.— The annihilation of the tartuffery called "morality" (Christianity as a hysterical kind of honesty in this: Augustine, Bunyan).— The annihilation of *suffrage universel;* i.e., the system through which the lowest natures prescribe themselves as laws for the higher.— The annihilation of mediocrity and its acceptance. (The onesided, individuals—peoples; to strive for fullness of nature through the pairing of opposites: race mixture to this end).— The new courage—no *a priori* truths (such truths were sought by those accustomed to faith!), but a *free* subordination to a ruling idea that has its time: e.g., time as a property of space, etc.

2. The Strong and the Weak

863 (*Jan.-Fall 1888*)

The concept "stronger and weaker man" reduces itself to the idea that in the first case a great deal of force is inherited—he is a summation—in the second, as yet little—(—inadequate inheritance, splintering of that which is inherited). Weakness can be an inaugural phenomenon: "as yet little"; or a terminal phenomenon: "no more."

The starting point is where great force is, where force is to be discharged. The mass, as the sum of the weak, reacts slowly; defends itself against much for which it is too weak—of which it can make no use; does not create, does not advance.

This in opposition to the theory that denies the strong individual and believes "the mass does it." It is the same difference as between two separated generations: four or five generations may lie between the active agent and the mass—a chronological difference.

The values of the weak prevail because the strong have taken them over as devices of leadership.

864 (*March-June 1888*)

Why the weak conquer. In summa: the sick and weak have more sympathy, are "more humane"—: the sick and weak have more spirit, are more changeable, various, entertaining—more malicious: it was the sick who invented malice. (A morbid precociousness is often found in the rickety, scrofulous and tubercular—.) *Esprit*: quality of late races: Jews, Frenchmen, Chinese. (The anti-Semites do not forgive the Jews for possessing "spirit"—and money. Anti-Semites—another name for the "underprivileged.")

The sick and weak have had fascination on their side: they are more interesting than the healthy: the fool and the saint—the two most interesting kinds of man—closely related to them, the "genius." The great "adventurers and criminals" and all men, especially the most healthy, are sick at certain periods in their lives: —the great emotions, the passions of power, love, revenge, are accompanied by profound disturbances. And as for decadence, it is represented in almost every sense by every man who does not die too soon:—thus he also knows from experience the instincts that belong to it:—almost every man is decadent for half his life.

Finally: woman! One-half of mankind is weak, typically sick, changeable, inconstant—woman needs strength in order to cleave to it; she needs a religion of weakness that glorifies being weak, loving, and being humble as divine: or better, she makes the strong weak—she rules when she succeeds in overcoming the strong. Woman has always conspired with the types of decadence, the priests, against the "powerful," the "strong," the men—. Woman brings the children to the cult of piety, pity, love:—the mother represents altruism convincingly.

Finally: increasing civilization, which necessarily brings with it an increase in the morbid elements, in the neurotic-psychiatric and criminal. An intermediary species arises: the artist, restrained from *crime* by weakness of will and social timidity, and not yet ripe for the *madhouse,* but reaching out inquisitively toward both spheres with his antennae: this specific culture plant, the modern artist, painter, musician, above all novelist, who describes his mode of life with the very inappropriate word "naturalism"— Lunatics, criminals, and "naturalists" are increasing: sign of a growing culture rushing on precipitately—i.e., the refuse, the waste, gain importance—the decline keeps pace.

Finally: the social hodgepodge, consequence of the Revolution, the establishment of equal rights, of the superstition of "equal men." The bearers of the instincts of decline (of *ressentiment,* discontent, the drive to destroy, anarchism, and nihilism), including the slave instincts, the instincts of cowardice, cunning, and *canaille* in those orders that have long been kept down, mingle with the blood of all classes: two, three generations later the race is no longer recognizable—everything has become mob. From this there results a collective instinct against selection, against privilege of all kinds, that is so powerful and self-assured, hard, and cruel in its operation, that the privileged themselves actually soon succumb to it: whoever still wants to retain power flatters the mob, works with the mob, *must* have the mob on its side—the "geniuses" above all: they become heralds of those feelings with which one moves the masses—the note of sympathy, even reverence, for all that has lived a life of suffering, lowliness, contempt, persecution, sounds above all other notes (types: Victor Hugo and Richard Wagner).— The rise of the mob signifies once again the ascendancy of the *old* values.

Such an extreme movement in respect of tempo and means as our civilization represents, shifts men's center of gravity: *those* men who matter most, who have, as it were, the task of compensating for the vast danger of such a morbid movement;—they will become procrastinators *par excellence,* slow to adopt, reluctant to let go, and relatively enduring in the midst of this tremendous change and mixture of elements. In such circumstances, the center of gravity necessarily shifts to the mediocre: against the dominion of the mob and of the eccentric (both are usually united), mediocrity consolidates itself as the guarantee and bearer of the future. Thus emerges a new opponent for exceptional men—or a new seduction. Provided they do not accommodate themselves to the mob and try to flatter the instincts of the "disinherited," they will have to be "mediocre" and "solid." They know: *mediocritas* is also *aurea*[2]—indeed, it alone disposes of money and *gold* (—of all that glitters—) —And once more the old virtue, and the entire dated world of the ideal in general, gains a body of gifted advocates.— Result:

---

[2] Mediocrity is also gold.

mediocrity acquires spirit, wit, genius—it becomes entertaining, it seduces.[3]

*

Result.— A high culture can stand only upon a broad base, upon a strong and healthy consolidated mediocrity. Science—and even art—work in its service and are served by it. Science could not wish for a better situation: it belongs as such to a mediocre kind of man—it is out of place among the exceptional—it has nothing aristocratic, and even less anything anarchistic, in its instinct.

The power of the middle is, further, upheld by trade, above all trade in money: the instinct of great financiers goes against everything extreme—that is why the Jews are at present the most *conserving* power in our intensely threatened and insecure Europe. They can have no use for revolution, socialism, or militarism: if they desire and employ power, even over the revolutionary party, this is only a consequence of the aforesaid and not a contradiction. They need occasionally to arouse fear of other extreme tendencies—by demonstrating *how* much power they have in their hands. But their instinct itself is unswervingly conservative—and "mediocre"—Wherever there is power, they know how to be powerful; but the employment of their power is always in one direction. The honorable term for *mediocre* is, of course, the word *"liberal."*

*

Reflection.— It is absurd to assume that this whole victory of values is antibiological: one must try to explain it in terms of an interest life has in preserving the type "man" even through this method of the dominance of the weak and underprivileged—: otherwise, man would cease to exist?—Problem———

The *enhancement* of the type fatal for the *preservation* of the species? Why?

History shows: the strong races decimate one another: through war, thirst for power, adventurousness; the strong affects: wastefulness—(strength is no longer hoarded, spiritual disturbance arises through excessive tension); their existence is costly; in brief—they

[3] In the MS the following words are written in the margin before the next paragraph: "The crafts, trade, agriculture, science, a large part of the arts—all this can rest only on a broad base, on a strongly and healthily consolidated mediocrity." These notes were used in *The Antichrist,* section 57 (*Portable Nietzsche,* p. 646).

ruin one another; periods of profound exhaustion and torpor supervene: all great ages are *paid for*— The strong are subsequently weaker, more devoid of will, more absurd than the weak average.

They are races that squander. "Duration" as such has no value: one might well prefer a shorter but more valuable existence for the species.— It would remain to be proved that, even so, a richer yield of value would be gained than in the case of the shorter existence; i.e., that man as summation of strength acquires a much greater quantum of mastery over things if life is as it is— We stand before a problem of economics———

865 (*Spring-Fall 1887*)

An attitude that calls itself "idealism" and that will not allow mediocrity to be mediocre, or woman to be woman!— No uniformity! Let us be clear how dearly a virtue is bought; and that virtue is not something of average desirability, but a noble madness, a beautiful exception, with the privilege of strong feelings—

866 (*Spring-Fall 1887; rev. Spring-Fall 1888*)

The need to show that as the consumption of man and mankind becomes more and more economical and the "machinery" of interests and services is integrated ever more intricately, a countermovement is inevitable. I designate this as the secretion of a luxury surplus of mankind: it aims to bring to light a stronger species, a higher type that arises and preserves itself under different conditions from those of the average man. My concept, my metaphor for this type is, as one knows, the word "overman."

On that first road which can now be completely surveyed, arise adaptation, leveling, higher Chinadom, modesty in the instincts, satisfaction in the dwarfing of mankind—a kind of *stationary level of mankind*. Once we possess that common economic management of the earth that will soon be inevitable, mankind will be able to find its best meaning as a machine in the service of this economy— as a tremendous clockwork, composed of ever smaller, ever more subtly "adapted" gears; as an ever-growing superfluity of all dominating and commanding elements; as a whole of tremendous force, whose individual factors represent *minimal forces, minimal values*.

In opposition to this dwarfing and adaptation of man to a

specialized utility, a reverse movement is needed—the production of a synthetic, summarizing, justifying man for whose existence this transformation of mankind into a machine is a precondition, as a base on which he can invent his *higher form of being*.

He needs the opposition of the masses, of the "leveled," a feeling of distance from them! he stands on them, he lives off them. This higher form of aristocracy is that of the future.— Morally speaking, this overall machinery, this solidarity of all gears, represents a maximum in the exploitation of man; but it presupposes those on whose account this exploitation has meaning. Otherwise it would really be nothing but an overall diminution, a value diminution of the type man—a regressive phenomenon in the grand style.

It is clear, what I combat is economic optimism: as if increasing expenditure of everybody must necessarily involve the increasing welfare of everybody. The opposite seems to me to be the case: *expenditure of everybody amounts to a collective loss*: man is *diminished*—so one no longer knows what *aim* this tremendous process has served. An aim? a new aim?—*that* is what humanity needs.

867 (*Spring-Fall 1887*)

Insight into the increase of overall power: to calculate to what extent even the decline of individuals, of classes, of ages, of peoples is included in this growth.

Shifting of the center of gravity of a culture. The cost of every great growth: who bears it! *Why it must now be tremendous.*

868 (*Nov. 1887-March 1888*)

Overall view of the future European: the most intelligent slave animals, very indutsrious, fundamentally very modest, inquisitive to excess, multifarious, pampered, weak of will—a cosmopolitan chaos of affects and intelligence. How could a stronger species raise itself out of him? A species with *classical* taste? Classical taste: this means will to simplification, strengthening, to visible happiness, to the terrible, the courage of psychological nakedness (—simplification is a consequence of the will to strengthening; allowing happiness to become visible, also nakedness, a consequence of the will to be terrible—). To fight upward out of that chaos to this form—requires a compulsion: one must be faced with the choice of perishing or prevailing. A dominating race can grow up only out of terrible and violent beginnings. Problem: where are the *barbarians* of the twentieth century? Obviously, they will come into view and consolidate themselves only after tremendous socialist crises—they will be the elements capable of the greatest severity toward themselves and able to gurantee the most enduring will.

869 (*1885-1886*)

The most powerful and most dangerous passions of man, of which he can most easily perish, have been outlawed so completely that the most powerful men themselves have become impossible or have had to feel evil—"harmful and forbidden." This loss is considerable, but hitherto it has been unavoidable: now that a host of counterforces has been reared by the temporary suppression of those passions (of lust for power, pleasure in change and deception), it is again possible to unloose them: they will no longer possess their old savagery. We permit ourselves a tame barbarism: just look at our artists and statesmen.

870 (*1884*)

The root of all evil: that the slavish morality of meekness, chastity, selflessness, absolute obedience, has triumphed—ruling natures were thus condemned (1) to hypocrisy, (1) to torments of conscience—creative natures felt like rebels against God, uncertain and inhibited by eternal values.

The barbarians showed that the ability for restraint was not at home among them: they feared and slandered the passions and drives of nature:—also the view of the ruling Caesars and classes. On the other hand, the suspicion arose that all moderation was weakness, or a sign of growing old and weary (—thus La Rochefoucauld suspected that "virtue" was a pretty word among those who could no longer take any pleasure in vice). Moderation itself was represented as a matter of severity, self-conquest, asceticism, as a fight with the devil, etc. The natural delight of aesthetic natures in measure, the enjoyment of the beauty of measure, was overlooked or denied, because one desired an anti-eudaemonistic morality.

The faith in the pleasure of moderation—that pleasure of the rider on a fiery steed!—has been lacking hitherto.— The mediocrity of weaker natures has been confused with the moderation of the strong!

In summa: the best things have been slandered because the weak or the immoderate swine have cast a bad light on them—and the best men have remained hidden—and have often misunderstood themselves.

871 (*Nov. 1887-March 1888*)

The vicious and unbridled: their depressive influence on the value of the desires. It was the dreadful barbarism of custom that, especially in the Middle Ages, compelled the creation of a veritable "league of virtue"—together with an equally dreadful exaggeration of that which constitutes the value of man. Struggling "civilization" (taming) needs every kind of irons and torture to maintain itself against terribleness and beast-of-prey natures.

Here a confusion is quite natural, although its influence has been fatal: that which men of power and will are able to demand of themselves also provides a measure of that which they may permit themselves. Such natures are the antithesis of the vicious and unbridled: although they may on occasion do things that would convict a lesser man of vice and immoderation.

Here the concept of the "equal value of men before God" is extraordinarily harmful; one forbade actions and attitudes that were in themselves among the prerogatives of the strongly constituted—as if they were in themselves unworthy of men. One brought the entire tendency of the strong into disrepute when one erected the protective measures of the weakest (those who were weakest also when confronting themselves) as a norm of value.

Confusion went so far that one branded the very virtuosi of life (whose autonomy offered the sharpest antithesis to the vicious and unbridled) with the most opprobrious names. Even now one believes one must disapprove of a Cesare Borgia; that is simply laughable. The church has excommunicated German emperors on account of their vices: as if a monk or priest had any right to join in a discussion about what a Frederick II may demand of himself. A Don Juan is sent to hell: that is very naive. Has it been noticed that in heaven all interesting men are missing?— Just a hint to the girls as to where they can best find their salvation.— If one reflects with some consistency, and moreover with a deepened insight into what a "great man" is, no doubt remains that the church sends all "great men" to hell—it fights *against* all "greatness of man."

872 (*1884*)

The rights a man arrogates to himself are related to the duties he imposes upon himself, to the tasks to which he feels equal. The great majority of men have no right to existence, but are a misfortune to higher men.[4]

873 (*1884*)

Misunderstanding of egoism—on the part of *common* natures who know nothing whatever of the pleasure of conquest and the insatiability of great love, nor of the overflowing feeling of strength that desires to overpower, to compel to itself, to lay to its heart—the drive of the artist in relation to his material. Often it is merely the penchant for activity that is looking for a field of action.

In ordinary "egoism" it is precisely the "non-ego," the profoundly average creature, the species man, who desires to preserve himself: if *this* is perceived by rarer, subtler, and less average men, it enrages them. For they judge: "we are nobler! Our preservation is more important than that of those cattle!"

874 (*1884*)

The degeneration of the rulers and the ruling classes has been the cause of the greastest mischief in history! Without the Roman Caesars and Roman society, the insanity of Christianity would never have come to power.

---

[4] The words that immediately follow in the MS have been omitted in all editions: "I do not yet grant the failures [*den Missrathenen*] the right. There are also peoples that are failures [*missrathene Völker*]." While these words in a note not intended for publication (first printed in 1911, p. 512) sound ominous, it is clear from Nietzsche's books that he is not thinking of the Jews, the Poles, the Russians, or any other peoples whom the Nazis later decimated.

When lesser men begin to doubt whether higher men exist, then the danger is great! And one ends by discovering that there is *virtue* also among the lowly and subjugated, the poor in spirit, and that *before God* men are equal—which has so far been the *non plus ultra* of nonsense on earth! For ultimately, the higher men measured themselves according to the standard of virtue of slaves —found they were "proud," etc., found all their higher qualities reprehensible.

When Nero and Caracalla sat up there, the paradox arose: "the lowest man is worth more than that man up there!" And the way was prepared for an image of God that was as remote as possible from the image of the most powerful—the god on the cross!

875 (*1884*)

The higher man and the herd man. When great men are lacking, one makes demigods or whole gods out of the great men of the past: the outbreak of religion demonstrates that man no longer delights man (—"no, nor woman neither," with Hamlet). Or: one brings many men together into one heap as a parliament and hopes they will be equally tyrannical.

"Tyrannization" is the quality of great men: they make lesser men stupid.

876 (*1888*)

The best example of the degree to which a plebeian agitator of the mob is incapable of comprehending the concept "higher nature" is provided by Buckle. The view he combats so passionately—that "great men," individuals, princes, statesmen, geniuses, generals are the levers and causes of all great movements—is instinctively misunderstood by him, as if it meant that what is essential and valuable in such "higher men" were their capacity for setting masses in motion: in short, their effect.

But the "higher nature" of the great man lies in being different, in incommunicability, in distance of rank, not in an effect of any kind—even if he made the whole globe tremble.[5]

[5] The misunderstanding attacked here is widespread among those who have attempted popular expositions of Nietzsche. Again and again, the view

877 (*Spring-Fall 1887; rev. Spring-Fall 1888*)

The Revolution made Napoleon possible: that is its justification. For the sake of a similar prize one would have to desire the anarchical collapse of our entire civilization. Napoleon made nationalism possible: that is its excuse.[6]

The value of a man (apart from his morality or immorality, naturally; for with these concepts the value of a man is not even touched) does not reside in his utility; for it would continue to exist even if there were no one to whom he could be of any use. And why could not precisely that man who produced the most disastrous effects be the pinnacle of the whole species of man: so high, so superior that everything would perish from envy of him?

878 (*Spring-Fall 1887*)

To appraise the value of a man according to how useful he is to men, or how much he costs, or what harm he does them—that is as much—or as little—as to appraise a work of art according to the effects it produces. But in this way, the value of a man in comparison with other men is not even touched upon. "Moral evaluation," in so far as it is a social evaluation, measures men exclusively according to the effects they produce. A man with a taste of his own, enclosed and concealed by his solitude, incommunicable, reserved—an unfathomed man, thus a man of a higher, at any rate a different species: how should you be able to evaluate him, since you cannot know him, cannot compare him?

Moral valuation has resulted in the greatest obtuseness of judgment: the value of a man in himself is underrated, almost overlooked, almost denied. Remnant of naive teleology: the value of man only in relation to men.

---

he castigates has been attributed to him. In this connection, the sections that immediately follow are also of great interest; especially 877-81 and 885-88, as well as 983-84.

[6] But see also section 1,026 below for Nietzsche's criticism of Napoleon, and compare the end of the penultimate section (# 16) of the first essay in the *Genealogy:* ". . . Napoleon, this synthesis of the *inhuman* and *superhuman*." For a detailed discussion of Nietzsche's attitude toward Napoleon, with documentation, see Kaufmann's *Nietzsche,* Chapter 11, end of section I.

879 (*Spring-Fall 1887*)

Preoccupation with morality places a spirit in a low order of rank: he lacks the instinct for privilege, the *a parte*, the feeling of freedom of creative natures, of the "children of God" (or of the devil—). And it is all one whether he preaches current morality or uses his ideal for a critique of current morality: he belongs to the herd—even if it be as the herd's supreme requirement, its "shepherd."

880 (*Spring-Fall 1887*)

Replacement of morality by the will to our goal, and consequently to the means to it.

881 (*Spring-Fall 1887; rev. Spring-Fall 1888*)

Order of rank:— What is mediocre in the typical man? That he does not understand the necessity for the reverse side of things: that he combats evils as if one could dispense with them; that he will not take the one with the other—that he wants to erase and extinguish the typical character of a thing, a condition, an age, a person, approving of only one part of their qualities and wishing to abolish the others. The "desirability" of the mediocre is what we others combat: the ideal conceived as something in which nothing harmful, evil, dangerous, questionable, destructive would remain. Our insight is the opposite of this: that with every growth of man, his other side must grow too; that the highest man, if such a concept be allowed, would be the man who represented the antithetical character of existence most strongly, as its glory and sole justification— Commonplace men can represent only a tiny nook and corner of this natural character: they perish when the multiplicity of elements and the tension of opposites, i.e., the preconditions for greatness in man, increases. That man must grow better *and* more evil is my formula for this inevitability—

Most men represent pieces and fragments of man: one has to add them up for a complete man to appear. Whole ages, whole peoples are in this sense somewhat fragmentary; it is perhaps part of the economy of human evolution that man should evolve piece by piece. But that should not make one forget for a moment that the real issue is the production of the synthetic man; that lower men, the tremendous majority, are merely preludes and rehearsals out of whose medley the whole man appears here and there, the milestone man who indicates how far humanity has advanced so far. It does *not* advance in a single straight line; often a type once achieved is lost again (—with all the tensions of the past three hundred years, for example, we have not yet reattained the man of the Renaissance, and the man of the Renaissance, in turn, is inferior to the man of antiquity).[7]

882 (*Nov. 1887-March 1888*)

One recognizes the superiority of the Greek man and the Renaissance man—but one would like to have them without the causes and conditions that made them possible.

883 (*Spring-Fall 1887*)

"Purification of taste" can only be the result of a strengthening of the type. Our society of today only *represents* culture; the cultured man is lacking. The great synthetic man is lacking, in whom the various forces are unhesitatingly harnessed for the attainment of one goal. What we possess is the multifarious man, perhaps the most interesting chaos there has ever been, but not the chaos *before* the creation of a world, but that after—Goethe as the most beautiful expression of the type (—absolutely not an Olympian!).[7a]

884 (*Spring-Fall 1887*)

Handel, Leibniz, Goethe, Bismarck—characteristic of the *strong* German type. Existing blithely among antitheses, full of that supple strength that guards against convictions and doctrines

---

[7] The words that immediately follow in the MS have been omitted in all editions: "One must have a standard: I distinguish the grand style; I distinguish activity and reactivity; I distinguish the excessive, the squandering from the *suffering* who are passionate [*die Leidend-Leidenschaftlichen*] (—the idealists)."

See also section 386 above, and *Zarathustra* IV, "On the Higher Man," section 5 (*Portable Nietzsche,* p. 400), as well as III, "The Convalescent," section 2 (*ibid.,* p. 330 *f*).

[7a] See the Appendix, below.

by employing one against the other and reserving freedom for itself.

885 (*Nov. 1887-March 1888*)

I have grasped this much: if one had made the rise of great and rare men dependent upon the approval of the many (assuming that the latter knew what qualities belonged to greatness and also at whose expense all greatness evolves)—well, there would never have been a single significant man!—

That the course of things makes its way independently of the approval of the great majority: that is why a few astonishing things have insinuated themselves on the earth.

886 (*Spring-Fall 1887*)

The order of rank of human values.—

a. One should not evaluate a man according to individual works. *Epidermal actions.* Nothing is rarer than a personal action. A class, a rank, a race, an environment, an accident—anything is more likely to be expressed in a work or act than is a "personality" [*eine "Person"*].

b. One should not assume in any case that many men are "personalities." And then some are *several* personalities, most are *none.* Wherever the average qualities preponderate, on which the preservation of a type depends, being a personality would be a waste, a luxury, it would be senseless to demand a "personality." They are bearers, tools of transmission.

c. The "personality," a relatively *isolated* fact; considering the far greater importance of continuation and averageness, almost something *antinatural.* For the production of a personality one needs early isolation, a compulsion to an existence of defense and combat, something like an incarceration, a greater power of self-definition; and above all a much lower impressionability than that of the average man, whose humanity is contagious.

First question concerning order of rank: how solitary or how gregarious one is. (In the latter case, one's value resides in the qualities that secure the survival of one's herd, one's type; in the former, in that which distinguishes, isolates, defends one, and makes one's solitariness possible.)

Consequence: one should not evaluate the solitary type from

the viewpoint of the gregarious, nor the gregarious from the viewpoint of the solitary.

Viewed from a height, both are necessary; their antagonism is also necessary—and nothing should be banished more thoroughly than the "desirability" that some third thing might evolve out of the two ("virtue" as hermaphroditism). That is as little "desirable" as the approximation and reconciliation of the sexes. To evolve further that which is typical, to make the gulf wider and wider——

Concept of degeneration in both cases: when the herd starts to acquire the qualities of the solitary, and the latter the qualities of the herd—in short, when they approximate each other. This concept of degeneration has nothing to do with moral evaluation.

887 (*Spring-Fall 1887*)

Where one must seek the stronger natures.— The ruin and degeneration of the solitary species is much greater and more terrible; they have the instincts of the herd, the tradition of values, against them; their instruments of defense, their protective instincts, are from the beginning not sufficiently strong or certain —chance must be very favorable to them if they are to prosper (—they prosper most often in the lowest and socially most abandoned elements; if one looks for personality, that is where one finds it much more certainly than in the middle classes!).

The strata and class struggle that aims at "equality of rights" —once it is more or less over, the war against the solitary personality will begin. (In a certain sense, *the latter can maintain and develop himself most easily in a democratic society*: namely, when the coarser means of defense are no longer necessary and habits of order, honesty, justice, and trust are part of the usual conditions.)

The strongest must be bound most firmly, watched, laid in chains, and guarded—if the instinct of the herd has its way. For them a regime of self-control, ascetic detachment, or "duty" in exhausting work in which one completely loses oneself.

888 (*Spring-Fall 1887; rev. Spring-Fall 1888*)

I attempt an *economic* justification of virtue.— The task is to make man as useful as possible and to approximate him, as far as possible, to an infallible machine: to this end he must be equipped with the virtues of the machine (—he must learn to experience the states in which he works in a mechanically useful way as the supremely valuable states; hence it is necessary to spoil the other states for him as much as possible, as highly dangerous and disreputable).

The first stumbling block is the boredom, the monotony, that all mechanical activity brings with it. To learn to endure this—and not only endure it—to learn to see boredom enveloped in a higher charm: this has hitherto been the task of all higher schooling. To learn something that is of no concern to us, and to find one's "duty" precisely in this "objective" activity; to learn to value pleasure and duty as altogether separate things—that is the invaluable task and achievement of higher schooling. This is why the philologist has hitherto been the educator *as such*: because his activity provides the model of sublime monotony in action; under his banner the young man learns to "grind": first prerequisite for future efficiency in the fulfillment of mechanical duties (as civil servant, husband, office slave, newspaper reader, and soldier). Such an existence perhaps requires a philosophical justification and transfiguration more than any other: agreeable feelings in general must be relegated to a lower rank by some sort of infallible court of appeal; "duty in itself," perhaps even the pathos of reverence in regard to everything disagreeable—and this demand speaking imperatively from beyond any question of utility, amusement, purpose— The mechanical form of existence as the highest, most venerable form of existence, worshiping itself (—type: Kant as a fanatic of the formal concept "thou shalt").[8]

889 (*Spring-Fall 1887; rev. Spring-Fall 1888*)

The economic valuation of ideals hitherto—i.e., selection of certain affects and states, selected and reared at the expense of others. The lawgiver (or the instinct of society) selects a number of states and affects through whose operation a regularity in performance is guaranteed (namely, a mechanical performance as a consequence of the regular requirements of those affects and states).

Supposing that these states and affects contain painful in-

[8] Cf. *Twilight*, "Skirmishes," section 29 (*Portable Nietzsche*, p. 532), where these ideas receive the definitive formulation.

gredients, then a means must be found to overcome these painful ingredients through a value-idea designed to make displeasure seem valuable and therefore pleasurable in a higher sense. Reduced to a formula: *"How can something disagreeable become agreeable?"* For example, when our obedience, our submission to the law, attain honor through the strength, power, self-overcoming they entail.[9] As do our consideration for the community, the neighbor, the fatherland, our "humanization," our "altruism," "heroism."

That one should like to do disagreeable things—that is the object of ideals.

890 (*Spring-Fall 1887*)

The dwarfing of man must for a long time count as the only goal; because a broad foundation has first to be created so that a stronger species of man can stand upon it. (To what extent every strengthened species of man hitherto has stood upon a level of the lower———)

891 (*Spring-Fall 1887*)

Absurd and contemptible form of idealism that would *not* have mediocrity *mediocre* and, instead of feeling a sense of triumph at a state of exceptionalness, becomes *indignant* over cowardice, falsity, pettiness, and wretchedness. *One should not desire these things to be different*! and should make the gulf *wider*!— One should *compel* the higher kind of man to *sever* himself from the others through the sacrifices he has to make to his state of being.

Chief viewpoint: establish *distances*, but *create no antitheses*. Dissolve the *intermediate forms* and reduce their influence: chief means of preserving distances.

892 (*Jan.-Fall 1888*)

How should one wish to spoil mediocrity for the mediocre! As one will see, I do the opposite: every step away from it—so I teach—leads to *immorality*.[10]

---

[9] From this point on the "text" is "uncertain," according to 1911, p. 512.

[10] Cf. *The Antichrist*, section 57 (*Portable Nietzsche*, p. 643 *ff*).

893 (*Spring-Fall 1887*)

Hatred for mediocrity is unworthy of a philosopher: it is almost a question mark against his "*right* to philosophy." Precisely because he is an exception he has to take the rule under his protection, he has to keep the mediocre in good heart.

894 (*Spring-Fall 1887*)

What *I* fight against: that an exceptional type should make war on the rule—instead of grasping that the continued existence of the rule is the precondition for the value of the exception. For example, the ladies who, instead of feeling their abnormal thirst for scholarship as a distinction, want to disrupt the status of woman in general.

895 (*Spring-Fall 1887*)

The increase of force despite the temporary decline of the individual:

to establish a new level:

a method of assembling forces for the preservation of small achievements, in opposition to uneconomic waste;

destructive nature temporarily subdued as an instrument for this future economy;

preservation of the weak, because a tremendous number of petty tasks have to be performed;

preservation of an attitude of mind that makes existence still possible for the weak and suffering;

to implant solidarity as an instinct against the instinct of fear and servility;

struggle against accident, also against the accident of "great men."

896 (*Spring-Fall 1887*)

Struggle against men justified on economic grounds. They are dangerous, accidents, exceptions, tempests, strong enough to call in question things slowly built and established. Explosives should not merely be detonated harmlessly; where possible detonation should be prevented: fundamental instinct of all civilized society.

897 (*Jan.-Fall 1888*)

Whover reflects upon the way in which the type man can be raised to his greatest spendor and power will grasp first of all that he must place himself outside morality; for morality has been essentially directed to the opposite end: to obstruct or destroy that spendid evolution wherever it has been going on. For such an evolution does indeed consume so great a quantity of men in its service that a reverse movement is only too natural: the weaker, more delicate, intermediate existences need to take sides *against* that gloriousness of life and strength; and to that end they have to acquire a new valuation of themselves by virtue of which they can condemn life in this highest plenitude, and where possible destroy it. A tendency hostile to life is therefore characteristic of morality, in so far as it wants to overpower the types of life.

898 (*Spring-Fall 1887*)

The strong of the future.— That which partly necessity, partly chance has achieved here and there, the conditions for the production of a stronger type, we are now able to comprehend and consciously *will*: we are able to create the conditions under which such an elevation is possible.

Until now, "education" has had in view the needs of society: not the possible needs of the future, but the needs of the society of the day. One desired to produce "tools" for it. Assuming the wealth of force were greater, one could imagine forces being subtracted, not to serve the needs of society but some future need.

Such a task would have to be posed the more it was grasped to what extent the contemporary form of society was being so powerfully transformed that at some future time it would be unable to exist for its own sake alone, but only as a tool in the hands of a stronger race.

The increasing dwarfing of man is precisely the driving force that brings to mind the breeding of a stronger race—a race that would be excessive precisely where the dwarfed species was weak and growing weaker (in will, responsibility, self-assurance, ability to posit goals for oneself).

The means would be those history teaches: isolation through interests in preservation that are the reverse of those which are average today; habituation to reverse evaluations; distance as a pathos; a free conscience in those things that today are most undervalued and prohibited.

The homogenizing of European man is the great process that cannot be obstructed: one should even hasten it. The necessity to create a gulf, distance, order of rank, is given *eo ipso*—*not* the necessity to retard this process.

As soon as it is established, this homogenizing species requires a justification: it lies in serving a higher sovereign species that stands upon the former and can raise itself to its task only by doing this. Not merely a master race whose sole task is to rule, but a race with its own sphere of life, with an excess of strength for beauty, bravery, culture, manners to the highest peak of the spirit; an affirming race that may grant itself every great luxury—strong enough to have no need of the tyranny of the virtue-imperative, rich enough to have no need of thrift and pedantry, beyond good and evil; a hothouse for strange and choice plants.

899 (*1885*)

Our psychologists, whose glance lingers involuntarily on symptoms of decadence alone, again and again induce us to mistrust the spirit. One always sees only those effects of the spirit that make men weak, delicate, and morbid; but now there are coming

new barbarians { cynics / experimenters / conquerors } union of spiritual superiority with well-being and an excess of strength.[11]

900 (*1885*)

I point to something new: certainly for such a democratic type there exists the danger of the barbarian, but one has looked

[11] For some discussion see Kaufmann's *Nietzsche,* Chapter 12, beginning of section IV.

for it only in the depths. There exists also another type of barbarian, who comes from the heights: a species of conquering and ruling natures in search of material to mold. Prometheus was this kind of barbarian.

901 (*Spring-Fall 1887*)[12]

Main consideration: not to see the task of the higher species in leading the lower (as, e.g., Comte does), but the lower as a base upon which higher species performs its *own* tasks—upon which alone it can stand.

The conditions under which a strong and noble species maintains itself (regarding spiritual discipline) are the reverse of those which govern the "industrial masses," the shopkeepers à la Spencer.

That which is available only to the strongest and most fruitful natures and makes their existence possible—leisure, adventure, disbelief, even dissipation—would, if it were available to mediocre natures, necessarily destroy them—and actually does. This is where industriousness, rule, moderation, firm "conviction" have their place—in short, the "herd virtues": under them this intermediate type of man grows perfect.

902 (*Manuscript source uncertain*)

On the sovereign types.— The "shepherd" as opposed to the "master" (—the former a *means* of preserving the herd; the latter the *end* for which the herd exists).

903 (*Spring-Fall 1887*)

Temporary preponderance of the social value-feelings comprehensible and useful: it is a question of creating a foundation upon which a stronger species will ultimately be possible.— Standard of strength: to be able to live under the reverse evaluations and to will them again eternally. State and society as foundation: world-economic point of view, education as breeding.[13]

---

[12] "In the MS, underlined, 'For the third esay.' Refers to the planned continuation of the *Genealogy*, which was supposed to comprise three further essays" (1911, p. 512).

[13] This section has been excerpted from a plan printed in 1911, p. 422.

904 (*Nov. 1887-March 1888*)

Insight that "free spirits" lack: the identical discipline that makes a strong nature even stronger and capable of great undertakings, shatters and withers the mediocre:—doubt—*la largeur de coeur*[14]—experiment—independence.

905 (*1885-1886*)

The hammer. How would men have to be constituted whose evaluations would be the reverse?— Men who possess *all* the qualities of the modern soul, but are strong enough to transform them into pure health?— The means they employ in their task.

906 (*1883-1888*)

The strong man, mighty in the instincts of a powerful health, digests his deeds in just the same way as he digests his meals; he can cope even with heavy food: in the main, however, he is led by a faultless and severe instinct into doing nothing that disagrees with him, just as he eats nothing he does not enjoy.

907 (*1884*)

If only we *could* foresee the most favorable conditions under which creatures of the highest value arise! It is a thousand times too complicated and the probability of failure very great: so it is not inspiring to look for them!— Skepticism.— On the other hand: we can increase courage, insight, hardness, independence, and the feeling of responsibility; we can make the scales more delicate and hope for the assistance of favorable accidents.

908 (*1884*)

Before we can think of acting, a tremendous amount of work has to be done. In the main, however, a shrewd exploitation of the given situation is, no doubt, our best, most advisable course of action. The actual *creation* of such conditions as are created

[14] Largeness of heart.

by chance presupposes iron men who have never yet lived. The immediate task is to make the personal ideal prevail and become real!

He who has grasped the nature of man, the origin of man's highest, shudders at man and flees from all action: consequence of inherited valuations! !

That the nature of man is evil, is my consolation: it guarantees *strength!*

909 (*Jan.-Fall 1888*)

The typical forms of self-formation. Or: the eight principal questions.

1. Whether one wants to be more multifarious or simpler?
2. Whether one wants to become happier or more indifferent to happiness and unhappiness?
3. Whether one wants to become more contented with oneself or more exacting and inexorable?
4. Whether one wants to become softer, more yielding, more human, or more "inhuman"?
5. Whether one wants to become more prudent or more ruthless?
6. Whether one wants to reach a goal or to avoid all goals (as, e.g., the philosopher does who smells a boundary, a nook, a prison, a stupidity in every goal)?
7. Whether one wants to become more respected or more feared? Or more despised?
8. Whether one wants to become tyrant or seducer or shepherd or herd animal?

910 (*Spring-Fall 1887*)

Type of my disciples.— To those human beings who are of any concern to me I wish suffering, desolation, sickness, ill-treatment, indignities—I wish that they should not remain unfamiliar with profound self-contempt, the torture of self-mistrust, the wretchedness of the vanquished: I have no pity for them, because I wish them the only thing that can prove today whether one is worth anything or not—that one endures.[15]

[15] This very remarkable note continues in Nietzsche's MS: "I have not yet got to know any idealist, but many liars——" (1911, p. 513).

911 (*1885-1886*)

The happiness and self-contentment of the Lazzaroni[16] or the "bliss" of "beautiful souls" or the consumptive love of Herrnhuteristic[17] pietists prove nothing regarding order of rank among men. As a great educator, one would have to scourge such a race of "blessed people" mercilessly into unhappiness. The danger of dwarfing, of relaxation is present at once:—against Spinozistic or Epicurean happiness and against all relaxation in contemplative states. But if virtue is the means to such a happiness, very well, *then one has to become master over virtue, too.*

912 (*March-June 1888*)

I absolutely cannot see how one can later make up for having failed to go to a *good school* at the proper time. Such a man does not know himself; he walks through life without having learned to walk; his flabby muscles reveal themselves with every step. Sometimes life is so merciful as to offer this hard schooling once more later: sickness for years perhaps, that demands the most extreme strength of will and self-sufficiency; or a sudden calamity, affecting also one's wife and child, that compels one to a form of activity that restores energy to the slack fibers and toughness to the will to live. The most desirable thing is still under all circumstances a hard discipline *at the proper time,* i.e., at that age at which it still makes one proud to see that much is demanded of one. For this is what distinguishes the hard school as a good school from all others: that much is demanded; and sternly demanded; that the good, even the exceptional, is demanded as the norm; that praise is rare, that indulgence is nonexistent; that blame is apportioned sharply, objectively, without regard for talent or antecedents.

One needs such a school from every point of view: that

---

[16] "*Lazzarone,* a name now often applied generally to beggars, is an Italian term, particularly used of the poorest class of Neapolitans, who, without any fixed abode, live by odd jobs and fishing, but chiefly by begging" (*Encyclopaedia Britannica,* 11th ed., article on "Lazar").

[17] *Herrnhuterischen:* "Herrnhut, a town . . . in . . . Saxony . . . is chiefly known as the principal seat of the Moravian or Bohemian brotherhood, the members of which are called Herrnhuter" (*ibid.,* article on "Herrnhut").

applies to the most physical as well as to the most spiritual matters; it would be fatal to desire to draw a distinction here! The same discipline makes both the good soldier and the good scholar; and looked at more closely, there is no good scholar who does not have the instincts of a good soldier in his makeup. To be able to command and also proudly to obey; to stand in the ranks, but also capable at any time of leading; to prefer danger to comfort; not to weigh the permitted and the forbidden on a shopkeeper's scales; to be a foe more of the petty, sly, parasitic, than of the evil.— What does one *learn* in a hard school? Obeying and commanding.

913 (*1885-1886*)

To disavow merit: but to do that which is above all praise, indeed above all understanding.

914 (*1885-1886*)

New form of morality: common vows over what one intends to do and leave undone, emphatic renunciation of many things. Tests to see if one is ripe for it.[18]

915 (*Spring-Fall 1887*)

I also want to make asceticism natural again: in place of the aim of denial, the aim of strengthening; a gymnastics of the will; abstinence and periods of fasting of all kinds, in the most spiritual realm, too; a casuistry of deeds in regard to the opinions we have regarding our strengths; an experiment with adventures and arbitrary dangers. (*Dîners chez Magny*: nothing but spiritual gourmets with indigestion.[19])— One should even devise tests for one's strength in being able to keep one's word.

916 (*1884; rev. Spring-Fall 1888*)

What has been ruined by the church's misuse of it:

---

[18] In the MS this section is marked: "For the chapter 'Our Virtues.'" According to 1911, p. 513, this section was originally intended for *Beyond Good and Evil.*

[19] See section 82 above.

1. *asceticism:* one has hardly the courage so far to display its natural utility, its indispensability in the service of the education of the will. Our absurd pedagogic world, before which the "useful civil servant" hovers as a model, thinks it can get by with "instruction," with brain drill; it has not the slightest idea that something else is needed *first*—education of will power; one devises tests for everything except for the main thing: whether one can will, whether one may promise; the young man finishes school without a single question, without any curiosity even, concerning this supreme value-problem of his nature;

2. *fasting:* in every sense—even as a means of preserving the delicacy of one's ability to enjoy all good things (e.g., occasionally to stop reading, listening to music, being pleasant; one must have fast days for one's virtues, too);

3. the *"monastery":* temporary isolation, accompanied by strict refusal, e.g., of letters; a kind of most profound self-reflection and self-recovery that desires to avoid, not "temptations," but "duties": an escape from the daily round; a detachment from the tyranny of stimuli and influences that condemns us to spend our strength in nothing but reactions and does not permit their accumulation to the point of *spontaneous activity* (one should observe our scholars from close up: they think only *reactively;* i.e., they have to read before they can think);

4. *feasts*: One has to be very coarse in order not to feel the presence of Christians and Christian values as an oppression beneath which all genuine festive feelings go to the devil. Feasts include: pride, exuberance, wantonness; mockery of everything serious and Philistine; a divine affirmation of oneself out of animal plenitude and perfection—one and all states which the Christian cannot honestly welcome. The feast is paganism *par excellence;*

5. *courage confronted with one's own nature: dressing up in "moral" costumes.*— That one has no need of moral formulas in order to welcome an affect; standard: how far we can affirm what is nature in us—how much or how little we need to have recourse to morality;

6. *death.*— One must convert the stupid physiological fact into a moral necessity. So to live that one can also *will at the right time to die!*[19a]

[19a] Cf. *Zarathustra* I, "On Free Death," and *Twilight*, "Skirmishes," section 36 (*Portable Nietzsche*, pp. 183 *ff* and 536 *f*). The idea of the non-

917 (*Nov. 1887-March 1888*)

To feel stronger—or in other words, joy—always presupposes a comparison (but not necessarily with others, but with oneself in the midst of a state of growth and without one's first *knowing* in how far one is making comparisons—).

Artificial strengthening: whether by stimulating chemicals or by stimulating errors ("delusions"):

e.g., the feeling of *security* such as a Christian possesses; he feels strong in being able to trust, to be patient and composed: he owes this artificial strength to the illusion of being protected by a god;

e.g., the feeling of *superiority*: as when the caliph of Morocco is allowed to see only globes upon which his three united kingdoms occupy four-fifths of the surface;

e.g., the feeling of *uniqueness*: as when the European imagines that the march of culture takes place in Europe, and when he seems to himself to be a kind of abridged world process; or when the Christian makes all existence in general revolve around the "salvation of man."

—It is a question of where one feels the pressure, the constraint: according to where this is, a different feeling of being stronger will be produced. A philosopher, e.g., feels in the midst of the coolest, most transmontane abstraction acrobatics like a fish in water, while colors and tones oppress him; to say nothing of the dim desires—that which others call "the ideal."

918 (*Jan.-Fall 1888*)

One would make a fit little boy stare if one asked him: "Would you like to become virtuous?"— but he will open his eyes wide if asked: "Would you like to become stronger than your friends?"—

*

How does one become stronger?— By coming to decisions

---

ecclesiastical monastery was developed by Hermann Hesse in his Nobel Prize winning novel, *Das Glasperlenspiel* (*The Bead Game*, also translated as *Magister Ludi*).

slowly; and by clinging tenaciously to what one has decided. Everything else follows.

The sudden and the changeable: the two species of weakness. Not to mistake oneself for one of them; to feel the distance—before it is too late!

Beware of the good-natured! Association with them makes one languid. All associations are good that make one practice the weapons of defense and offense that reside in one's instincts. All one's inventiveness toward testing one's strength of will— To see the distinguishing feature in this, and not in knowledge, astuteness, wit.

One must learn in time to command—just as much as to obey. One must learn modesty, *tact* in modesty: that is, to confer distinction and to honor by being modest; the same with trust—to confer distinction, to honor.

*

For what does one have to atone most? For one's modesty; for having failed to listen to one's most personal requirements; for having mistaken oneself; for having underestimated oneself; for having lost a good ear for one's instincts: this lack of reverence for oneself revenges itself through every kind of deprivation: health, friendship, well-being, pride, cheerfulness, freedom, firmness, courage. One never afterward forgives oneself for this lack of genuine egoism: one takes it for an objection, for a doubt about a real ego.

919 (*March-June 1888*)

I wish men would begin by *respecting* themselves: everything else follows from that. To be sure, as soon as one does this one is finished for others: for this is what they forgive last: "What? A man who respects himself?"—

This is something different from the blind drive to *love* oneself: nothing is more common, in the love of the sexes as well as of that duality which is called "I," than contempt for what one loves:—fatalism in love.

920 (*Spring-Fall 1887*)

"I want this or that"; "I wish that this or that were thus"; "I know that this or that is thus"—the degrees of strength: the man of will, the man of desire, the man of faith.

921 (*Nov. 1887-March 1888*)

The means by which a stronger species maintains itself.

To grant oneself the right to exceptional actions; as an experiment in self-overcoming and freedom.

To venture into states in which it is not permitted *not* to be a barbarian.

To create control and certainty in regard to one's strength of will through asceticism of every kind.

Not to communicate oneself; silence; bewaring of charm.[20]

To learn obedience in such a way that it provides a test of one's self-support. Casuistry of honor taken to the greatest extreme of subtlety.

Never to conclude "what is right for one is fair for another"—but conversely!

To treat requital, the permission to give back, as a privilege and a rare distinction.

To have no ambition to emulate the virtues of others.

922 (*Spring-Fall 1887*)

What means one has to employ with rude peoples, and that "barbarous" means are not arbitrary and capricious, becomes palpable in practice as soon as one is placed, with all one's European pampering, in the necessity of keeping control over barbarians, in the Congo or elsewhere.

923 (*Jan.-Fall 1888*)

The warlike and the peaceful.— Are you a man with the instincts of a warrior in your system? If so, a second question arises: are you by instinct a warrior of attack or a warrior of defense? The remainder of mankind, all that is not warlike by instinct, wants peace, wants concord, wants "freedom," wants "equal rights": these are only different names and stages of the same thing. To go where one has no need to defend oneself—

---

[20] "Charm" (*Anmut*) represents a doubtful reading.

such men become dissatisfied with themselves if they are obliged to offer resistance: [they want to][21] create conditions in which there is no longer war of any kind. If the worst comes to the worst, to submit, obey, acquiesce: anything is better than waging war—thus, e.g., does a Christian's instinct counsel him. In the case of the born warrior, there is something like armament in his character, in his choice of states, in the development of every quality: in the first type, it is the "weapon" that is developed best, in the latter the armor.

The unarmed, the unarmored: what expedients and virtues they need in order to endure—to triumph.

924 (*Spring-Fall 1887*)

What will become of the man who no longer has any reasons for defending himself or for attacking? What affects does he have left if he has lost those in which lie his weapons of defense and attack?

925 (*Summer-Fall 1888*)

Marginal note on a *niaiserie anglaise*.[22]— "Do not unto others what you would not have them do unto you." That counts as wisdom; that counts as prudence; that counts as the basis of morality—as the "golden rule." John Stuart Mill believes in it (and what Englishman does not?) But this rule does not brook the slightest attack. The calculation, "do nothing that ought not to be done to you," prohibits actions on account of their harmful consequences: the concealed premise is that an action will always be requited. But what if someone holding the *Principe*[23] in his hand were to say: "It is precisely such actions that one *must* perform, to prevent others from performing them first—to deprive others of the chance to perform them on *us*"?

On the other hand: let us consider a Corsican whose honor demands a vendetta. He does not want a bullet in his body either; but this prospect, the probability of getting shot, does not deter

[21] The words I have placed in brackets were supplied by the original German editors and retained in all editions, including Schlechta's.

[22] English folly.

[23] Machiavelli's book, *The Prince*.

him from vindicating his honor— And in all decent actions, are we not deliberately indifferent to the prospect of what may happen to us? To avoid an action that might have harmful consequences for us—that would mean a ban on decent actions in general.

Nonetheless, the rule is valuable because it betrays a type of man: it is the instinct of the herd that finds its formula in this rule—one is equal, one takes oneself for equal: as I to you, thus you to me.— Here there is a real belief in an equivalence of actions that in all actual circumstances simply does not exist. Not every action *can* be returned: between actual "individuals" there are no equal actions, consequently no "requital"— When I do something, I am very far from thinking that anyone else can do much the same: it belongs to *me*— One cannot pay me back, it will always be "another" action that is perpetrated against me.—

926 (*Nov. 1887-March 1888*)

Against John Stuart Mill.— I abhor his vulgarity, which says: "What is right for one is fair for another"; "what you would not, etc., do not unto others"; which wants to establish all human intercourse on the basis of mutual services, so that every action appears as a kind of payment for something done to us. The presupposition here is ignoble in the lowest sense: here an equivalence of value between my actions and yours is presupposed; here the most personal value of an action is simply annulled (that which cannot be balanced or paid in any way—).

"Reciprocity" is a piece of gross vulgarity; precisely that something I do may not and could not be done by another, that no balance is possible (—except in the most select sphere of "my equals," *inter pares*—), that in a deeper sense one never gives back, because one is something unique and does only unique things—this fundamental conviction contains the cause of aristocratic segregation from the masses, because the masses believe in "equality" and *consequently* in equivalence and "reciprocity."

927 (*Spring-Fall 1887*)

The parochial narrowness of moral valuation with its "useful" and "harmful" has its own good reasons; it is the necessary perspective of society, which is able to survey only the close and closest in regard to consequences.

The state and the politician already have need of a more supra-moral attitude, because they have to reckon with a much greater complexity of effects.

A world economy would also be possible with such distant perspectives that all its individual demands might seem unjust and arbitrary at the moment.

928 (*Nov. 1887-March 1888*)

"Should one follow one's feelings?"—That one should put one's life in danger, yielding to a generous feeling and under the impulse of a moment, that is of little value and does not even characterize one. Everyone is equally capable of that—and in this resolution, a criminal, a bandit, and a Corsican certainly excel decent people.

A higher stage is: to overcome even this pressure within us and to perform a heroic act not on impulse—but coldly, *raisonnable,* without being overwhelmed by stormy feelings of pleasure— The same applies to compassion: it must first be habitually sifted by reason; otherwise it is just as dangerous as any other affect.

Blind indulgence of an affect, totally regardless of whether it be a generous and compassionate or a hostile affect, is the cause of the greatest evils.

Greatness of character does not consist in not possessing these affects—on the contrary, one possesses them to the highest degree—but in having them under control. And even that without any pleasure in this restraint, but merely because—

929 (*Jan.-Fall 1888*)

"To give one's life for a cause"—a great effect. But there are many things for which one would give one's life: the affects one and all desire to be gratified. Whether it be compassion or anger or revenge—that one stakes one's life on it does not make any value difference. How many have sacrified their lives for pretty girls—and, worse, even their health! If one has the temperament, one instinctively chooses what is dangerous; e.g., adventures in speculation if one is a philosopher; or in immorality if one is virtuous. One kind of man will risk nothing, another wants risks. Are we others despisers of life? On the contrary, we seek life raised to a higher power, life lived in danger—[24] But that, to repeat it, does not mean we want to be more virtuous than others. Pascal, e.g., wanted to risk nothing[25] and remained a Christian: perhaps that was virtuous.— One always makes sacrifices.

930 (*Nov. 1887-March 1888*)

How much advantage man sacrifices, how little "self-interested" he is! All his affects and passions demand their rights—and how remote from the prudent utility of self-interest is an affect!

One does *not* desire "happiness"; one must be English to be able to believe that man always seeks his advantage.[26] Our desires want to violate things with a protracted passion—their accumulated strength seeks resistance.

931 (*Spring-Fall 1887*)

The affects are one and all useful, some directly, others indirectly; in regard to utility it is quite impossible to fix any scale of values—even though in economic terms the forces of nature are one and all good, i.e., useful, and also the source of so much terrible and irrevocable fatality. The most one could say is that the most powerful affects are the most valuable, in as much as there are no greater sources of strength.

---

[24] Cf. section 283 of *The Gay Science* (*Portable Nietzsche,* p. 97): ". . . the secret of the greatest fruitfulness and the greatest enjoyment of life is: to *live dangerously!* Build your cities under Vesuvius! . . ."

[25] An allusion to Pascal's famous wager that God exists (*Pensées,* available in many editions and translations; in the bilingual edition by H. F. Stewart, with an English translation on facing pages, and notes and an introduction, Routledge and Kegan Paul, London 1950, pp. 116-21). For a critical analysis, see my *Critique of Religion and Philosophy,* section 49.

Cf. also Jean-Marie Guyau, *Esquisse d'une morale sans obligation ni sanction* (F. Alcan, Paris 1885), p. 212: *"Il y avait donc dans le pari de Pascal un élément qu'il n'a pas mis en lumière. Il n'a guère vu que la crainte du risque, il n'a pas vu le plaisir du risque."* (There is in the wager of Pascal an element he did not make clear. He saw only the fear of risk, he did not see the pleasure of risk.)

[26] Cf. *Twilight,* "Maxims and Arrows," aphorism 12 (*Portable Nietzsche,* p. 468): "If we have our own *why* of life, we shall get along with almost any *how.* Man does *not* strive for pleasure; only the Englishman does."

932 (*Spring-Fall 1887*)

Well-meaning, helpful, good-natured attitudes of mind have not come to be honored on account of their usefulness, but because they are states of richer souls that are capable of bestowing and have their value in the feeling of the plenitude of life. Observe the eyes of benefactors: what one sees is the antithesis of self-denial, of hatred for the *moi,* of "Pascalism."

933 (*Spring-Fall 1887*)

In Summa: domination of the passions, *not* their weakening or extirpation!— The greater the dominating power of a will, the more freedom may the passions be allowed.

The "great man" is great owing to the free play and scope of his desires and to the yet greater power that knows how to press these magnificent monsters into service.

The "good man" is at every stage of civilization the harmless and the useful combined: a kind of mean; the expression of the general consciousness of the kind of man whom one has no reason to fear but whom one must nonetheless not despise.

Education: essentially the means of ruining the exceptions for the good of the rule.[27] Higher education:[28] essentially the means of directing taste *against* the exceptions for the good of the mediocre.

Only when a culture has an excess of powers at its disposal can it also constitute a hothouse for the luxury cultivation of the exception, the experiment, of danger, of the nuance:—this is the tendency of every aristocratic culture.

934 (*Spring-Fall 1887*)

Nothing but questions of strength: how far to prevail against the conditions that preserve society and against its prejudices?—how far to unchain one's terrible qualities through which most people perish?—how far to oppose truth and reflect on its most

[27] After "rule," the MS has the following words, omitted in all editions: "At least for that long time," "a deviation, seduction, sicklying over," and "That is hard, but considered economically perfectly reasonable."

[28] *Bildung.* "Education" in the preceding line: *Erziehung.*

questionable sides?—how far to oppose suffering, self-contempt, pity, sickness, vice, with the query as to whether one cannot become master of them? (—what does not destroy us makes us stronger[29]—)—finally: how far to acknowledge in one's mind the rule, the commonplace, the petty, good, upright, the average nature, without letting oneself be vulgarized by them?— Hardest test of character: not to let oneself be ruined through seduction by the good. The good as luxury, as subtlety,[30] as vice.

3. The Noble Man[31]

935 (*Fall 1888*)

Type: True graciousness, nobility, greatness of soul proceed from abundance; do not give in order to receive—do not try to exalt themselves by being gracious;—prodigality as the type of true graciousness, abundance of personality as its presupposition.

936 (*Nov. 1887-March 1888*)

Aristocracy. Herd-animal ideals—now culminating as the highest value standard of "society": attempt to give them a cosmic, even a metaphysical value.— Against them I defend aristocracy.

A society that preserves a regard and *delicatesse* for freedom must feel itself to be an exception and must confront a power from which it distinguishes itself, toward which it is hostile, and on which it looks down.

The more I relinquish my rights and level myself down, the more I come under the dominion of the average and finally of the majority. The presupposition inherent in an aristocratic society for preserving a high degree of freedom among its members is the extreme tension that arises from the presence of an antagonistic drive in all its members: the will to dominate—

If you would do away with firm opposition and differences

---

[29] Used in *Twilight,* "Maxims and Arrows," aphorism 8 (*Portable Nietzsche,* p. 467): "What does not destroy me, makes me stronger."

[30] "Subtlety": uncertain reading.

[31] The notes assembled under this heading should be compared with *Beyond Good and Evil,* last chapter, "What is Noble?"

in rank, you will also abolish all strong love, lofty attitudes, and the feeling of individuality.

*

Toward a true psychology of the society based on freedom and equality— What *diminishes?*

The will to self-responsibility, sign of the decline of autonomy; efficiency in defense and attack, also in the most spiritual things: the power of commanding; the sense of reverence, subservience, ability to keep silent; great passion, the great task, tragedy, cheerfulness.

937 (*Spring-Fall 1887*)

Augustin Thierry read in 1814 what De Montlosier had said in his work *De la monarchie française*: he answered with a cry of indignation and commenced his work. That emigrant had said: *Race d'affranchis, race d'esclaves arrachés de nos mains, peuple tributaire, peuple nouveau, licence vous fut octroyée d'être libres, et non pas à nous d'être nobles; pour nous tout est de* droit, *pour vous tout est de* grâce, *nous ne sommes point de votre communauté; nous sommes un tout par nous-mêmes.*[32]

938 (*1884*)

How the aristocratic world increasingly bleeds itself and makes itself weaker! Because of the nobility of its instincts it throws away its privileges and because of the refinement of its hyper-culture it takes an interest in the people, the weak, the poor, the poetry of the petty, etc.

939 (*1885-1886*)

There is a noble and dangerous carelessness that permits a profound inference and insight: the carelessness of the self-assured and overrich soul that has never troubled about friends but knows only hospitality, and practices, and knows how to practice,

---

[32] "Tribe of freedmen, tribes of slaves torn from our hands, tributary people, new people, license has been granted to you to be free, but not to us to be noble; for us everything is a right, for you everything is a matter of grace; we are not part of your community; we are entire by ourselves."

only hospitality—heart and home open to anyone who cares to enter, whether beggar or cripple or king. This is genuine geniality: whoever has that, has a hundred "friends" but in all probability not a single friend.

940 (*1884*)

The teaching *mēden agan*[33] applies to men of overflowing strength—not to the mediocre. The *enkrateia*[34] and *askēsis*[35] is only a stage toward the heights: the "golden nature" is higher.

"Thou shalt"—unconditional obedience in Stoics, in the Christian and Arab orders, in the philosophy of Kant (it is immaterial whether to a superior or to a concept).

Higher than "thou shalt" is "I will" (the heroes); higher than "I will" stands: "I am" (the gods of the Greeks).

The barbarian gods express nothing of the pleasure of restraint—are neither simple nor frivolous nor moderate.

941 (*Summer-Fall 1883*)

The meaning of our gardens and palaces (and to this extent also the meaning of all desire for riches) is: to remove disorder and vulgarity from sight and to build a home for nobility of soul.

The majority, to be sure, believe they will acquire higher natures when those beautiful, peaceful objects have operated upon them: hence the rush to go to Italy and on travels, etc.; all reading and visits to theatres. They want to have themselves formed—that is the meaning of their cultural activity! But the strong, the mighty want to form and no longer to have anything foreign about them!

Thus men also plunge into wild nature, not to find themselves but to lose and forget themselves in it. "To be outside oneself" as the desire of all the weak and the self-discontented.

942 (*1885*)

There is only nobility of birth, only nobility of blood. (I am

---

[33] Nothing in excess.

[34] Temperance.

[35] Originally, exercise. In the present context, the meaning would seem to be halfway between exercise and asceticism.

not speaking here of the little word "*von*" or of the Almanach de Gotha:[36] parenthesis for asses.) When one speaks of "aristocrats of the spirit," reasons are usually not lacking for concealing something; as is well known, it is a favorite term among ambitious Jews. For spirit alone does not make noble; rather, there must be something to ennoble the spirit.— What then is required? Blood.[37]

943 (*1885*)

What is *noble*?[38]

—Care for the most external things, in so far as this care forms a boundary, keeps distant, guards against confusion.

—Apparent frivolity in word, dress, bearing, through which a stoic severity and self-constraint protects itself against all immodest inquisitiveness.

—Slowness of gesture, and of glance. There are not too many valuable things: and these come and wish to come of themselves to the valuable man. We do not easily admire.

—Endurance of poverty and want, also of sickness.

—Avoidance of petty honors and mistrust of all who praise readily: for whoever praises believes he understands what he praises: but to understand—Balzac, that typical man of ambition, has revealed it—*comprendre c'est égaler*.[39]

—Our doubt as to the communicability of the heart goes deep; solitude not as chosen but as given.

—The conviction that one has duties only to one's equals, toward the others one acts as one thinks best: that justice can

---

[36] "The *Almanach de Gotha,* which has existed since 1763, published since 1871 both in French and German, gives a particular account of all the royal and princely families of Europe . . ." (*Encyclopaedia Britannica,* 11th ed., vol. I, p. 712). The word *von* is the mark of nobility in this sense, and when Friedrich Schiller, for example, was elevated to the nobility his name became Friedrich von Schiller.

[37] When Heinrich Härtle quoted this note in *Nietzsche und der Nationalsozialismus* (Eher, Zentralverlag der NSDAP, Munich 1937), p. 55, he omitted the "parenthesis for asses," without indicating that anything had been omitted. This was entirely typical of the Nazis' use of Nietzsche. For a discussion of this note, see my *Nietzsche,* Chapter 10, near the end.

[38] Cf. the last chapter of *Beyond Good and Evil,* which bears the same title. According to 1911, p. 513, this section was originally intended for use in the preface to (the second edition of) *Mixed Opinions and Aphorisms,* the second volume of *Human, All-Too-Human.*

[39] To comprehend is to equalize.

be hoped for (unfortunately not counted on) only *inter pares*.[40]

—An ironic response to the "talented," the belief in a nobility by birth in moral matters too.

—Always to experience oneself as one who bestows honors, while there are not many fit to honor one.

—Always disguised: the higher the type, the more a man requires an incognito. If God existed, he would, merely on grounds of decency, be obliged to show himself to the world only as a man.

—The ability for *otium*,[41] the unconditional conviction that although a craft in any sense does not dishonor, it certainly takes away nobility. No "industriousness" in the bourgeois sense, however well we may know how to honor and reward it, or like those insatiably cackling artists who act like hens, cackle and lay eggs and cackle again.

—We protect artists and poets and those who are masters in anything; but as natures that *are* of a higher kind than these, who have only the ability to do something, merely "productive men," we do not confound ourselves with them.

—Pleasure in forms; taking under protection everything formal, the conviction that politeness is one of the greatest virtues; mistrust for letting oneself go in any way, including all freedom of press and thought, because under them the spirit grows comfortable and doltish and relaxes its limbs.

—Delight in women, as in a perhaps smaller but more delicate and ethereal kind of creature. What joy to encounter creatures who have only dancing, foolishness, and finery in their heads! They have been the delight of every very tense and profound male soul whose life was weighed down with great responsibilities.

—Pleasure in princes and priests, because they preserve the belief in differences in human values even in the valuation of the past, at least symbolically and on the whole even actually.

—Ability to keep silent: but not a word about that in the presence of listeners.

—Endurance of protracted enmities: lack of easy reconcilability.

---

[40] Among equals. But see *The Antichrist*, which is later: "When the exceptional human being treats the mediocre more tenderly than himself and his peers, this is not mere courtesy of the heart—it is simply his *duty*" (section 57; *Portable Nietzsche*, p. 647).

[41] Leisure.

—Disgust for the demagogic, for the "enlightenment," for "being cozy,"[42] for plebeian familiarity.

—The collection of precious things, the needs of a high and fastidious soul; to desire to possess nothing in common. One's own books, one's own landscapes.

—We rebel against experiences, good and bad, and are slow to generalize. The individual case: how ironic we feel toward the individual case if it has the bad taste to pose as the rule!

—We love the naive and naive people, but as spectators and higher natures; we find Faust just as naive as his Gretchen.

—We esteem the good very little, as herd animals: we know that in the worst, most malignant, hardest men a priceless golden drop of goodness is often concealed, that outweighs all mere benevolence of milk souls.

—We consider that a man of our kind is not refuted by his vices, nor by his follies. We know that we are hard to recognize, and that we have every reason to give ourselves foregrounds.

944 (*Jan.-Fall 1888*)

What is noble?— That one constantly has to play a part. That one seeks situations in which one has constant need of poses. That one leaves happiness to the great majority: happiness as peace of soul, virtue, comfort, Anglo-angelic shopkeeperdom à la Spencer. That one instinctively seeks heavy responsibilities. That one knows how to make enemies everywhere, if the worst comes to the worst even of oneself. That one constantly contradicts the great majority not through words but through deeds.

945 (*1886-1887*)

Virtue (e.g., in the form of truthfulness) as *our* noble and dangerous luxury; we must not refuse the disadvantages it brings with it.

946 (*Spring-Fall 1887*)

To desire no praise: one does what profits one, or what gives one pleasure, or what one *must*.

---

[42] *Gemütlichkeit.*

947 (*Jan.-Fall 1888*)

What is chastity in a man? That his sexual taste has remained noble; that in *eroticis* he likes neither the brutal nor the morbid nor the prudent.

948 (*Nov. 1887-March 1888*)

The "concept of honor": resting on the faith in "good society," in chivalrous basic traits, in the obligation continually to maintain poise. Essential: that one does not think one's life important; that one insists unconditionally on good manners on the part of everyone with whom one comes in contact (at least, when they do not belong to "*us*"); that one is neither familar, nor genial, nor merry, nor modest, except *inter pares;* that one *always maintains poise.*

949 (*Nov. 1887-March 1888*)

That one stakes one's life, one's health, one's honor, is the consequence of high spirits and an overflowing, prodigal will: not from love of man but because every great danger challenges our curiosity about the degree of our strength and our courage.

950 (*1884-1886*)

"Eagles dive straight to the point."— Not the least sign of nobility of soul is the magnificent and proud stupidity with which it *attacks*—"straight to the point."

951 (*Spring-Fall 1887*)

War on the effeminate conception of "nobility"!—a quantum more of brutality cannot be dispensed with, any more than closeness to crime. Even "self-satisfaction" is *not* part of it; one should be adventurous, experimental, destructive also toward oneself—no beautiful-soul twaddle—. I want to make room for a more robust ideal.

952 (*1884-1886*)

"Paradise lies in the shadow of swords"—also a symbol and

motto by which souls of noble and warlike origin betray themselves and divine each other.

953 (*1886-1887*)

The two paths.— [There comes][43] a point in time when man has strength in excess at his disposal: science aims at establishing this slavery of nature.

Then man acquires leisure: to cultivate himself into something new, higher. New aristocracy. Then a host of virtues are superseded that had been conditions of existence.— Qualities no longer needed are lost. We no longer need virtues: consequently we lose them (—as we do the morality of "one thing is needful," of salvation of soul, and of immortality: they were means of making possible for man a tremendous self-constraint through the affect of a tremendous fear: : :).

The various kinds of indigence through whose discipline man is formed: indigence teaches work, thought, self-constraint.

*

Physiological purification and strengthening. The new aristocracy has need of an opposite against which it struggles: preservation must be a dreadfully urgent matter.

The two futures of mankind: (1) consistent growth of mediocrity; (2) conscious distinction, self-shaping.

A doctrine that creates a gulf: it preserves the highest and the lowest kind (it destroys the mean).

Aristocrats so far, spiritual and temporal, prove nothing *against* necessity for a new aristocracy.

4. The Masters of the Earth

954 (*1885-1886*)

A question constantly keeps coming back to us, a seductive and wicked question perhaps: may it be whispered into the ears

---

[43] The words I have placed in brackets were supplied by the original German editors and retained in all editions.

of those who have a right to such questionable questions, the strongest souls of today, whose best control is over themselves: is it not time, now that the type "herd animal" is being evolved more and more in Europe, to make the experiment of a fundamental, artificial and conscious *breeding* of the opposite type and its virtues? And would it not be a kind of goal, redemption, and justification for the democratic movement itself if someone arrived who could make use of it—by finally producing beside its new and sublime development of slavery (—that is what European democracy must become ultimately) a higher kind of dominating and Caesarian spirits who would stand upon it, maintain themselves by it, and elevate themselves through it? To new, hitherto impossible prospects, to their own prospects? To their own tasks?

955 (*1885*)

To view the contemporary European makes me very hopeful: an audacious ruling race is developing on the basis of an extremely intelligent herd mass. It will not be long before the movement for the cultivation of the latter will no longer have the foreground all to itself.

956 (*1885*)

The same conditions that hasten the evolution of the herd animal also hasten the evolution of the leader animal.

957 (*1885*)

Inexorably, hesitantly, terrible as fate, the great task and question is approaching: how shall the earth as a whole be governed? And to what end shall "man" as a whole—and no longer as a people, a race—be raised and trained?

Law-giving moralities are the principal means of fashioning man according to the pleasure of a creative and profound will, provided that such an artist's will of the first rank has the power in its hands and can make its creative will prevail through long periods of time, in the form of laws, religions, and customs. Such men of great creativity, the really great men according to my understanding, will be sought in vain today and probably for a long time to come: they are lacking; until, after much disappointment, one must begin to comprehend *why* they are lacking and that nothing stands more malignantly in the way of their rise and evolution, today and for a long time to come, than what in Europe today is called simply "morality"—as if there were no other morality and could be no other—the aforementioned herd-animal morality which is striving with all its power[44] for a universal green-pasture happiness on earth, namely for security, absence of danger, comfort, the easy life, and ultimately, "if all goes well," hopes to do away with any kind of shepherd or bellwhether. The two doctrines it preaches most often are: "equal rights" and "sympathy with all that suffers"—and it takes suffering itself to be something that must absolutely be abolished. That such "ideas" as these are still modern gives one a bad opinion of modernity.

Whoever has thought profoundly about where and how the plant man has hitherto grown most vigorously must conclude that this has happened under the *reverse* conditions: that the dangerousness of his situation must grow to tremendous proportions, that his power of invention and dissembling must struggle up beneath protracted oppression and compulsion, that his will to live must be enhanced to an unconditional will to power and to overpower, and that danger, severity, violence, danger in the street as well as in the heart, inequality of rights, concealment, stoicism, the art of experiment, devilry of all kinds, in short the opposite of all the herd thinks desirable, are necessary for the elevation of the type man. A morality with such reverse intentions, which desires to train men for the heights, not for comfort and mediocrity, a morality with the intention of training a ruling caste—the future *masters of the earth*—must, if it is to be taught, appear in association with the prevailing moral laws, in the guise of their terms and forms. That for this, however, many transitional means of deception must be devised, and that, because the lifetime of a single man signifies virtually nothing in relation to the accomplishment of such protracted tasks and aims, the very first thing to be done is the rearing of a new kind of man, in whom the duration of the necessary will and the necessary instinct will be guaranteed through many generations—a new master type and caste—all this

---

[44] According to 1911, p. 513, an illegible word has been omitted at this point—and this note was evidently dictated (it is in another hand) and then revised in Nietzsche's hand.

is as obvious as is the protracted and not easily expressible etcetera of this idea.

To prepare a *reversal of values* for a certain strong kind of man of the highest spirituality and strength of will and to this end slowly and cautiously to unfetter a host of instincts now kept in check and calumniated—whoever reflects on this becomes one of us, the free spirits—to be sure, a different kind of "free spirit" from those before us; for the latter wanted approximately the opposite of what we do. To us, it seems to me, belong above all the pessimists of Europe, the poets and thinkers of an enraged idealism, in so far as their discontent with all existence involved them at least by logical necessity in a discontent with present-day man; also certain insatiably ambitious artists who unhesitatingly and unconditionally fight for the special rights of higher men and against the "herd animal" and who, by means of the seductions of art, lull to sleep all herd instincts and herd cautiousness in choice spirits; thirdly and finally all those critics and historians who courageously carry forward the happily-begun discovery of the world of antiquity—it is the work of the *new* Columbus, the German spirit (for we still stand at the beginning of this conquest). For in the world of antiquity there reigned a different, more lordly morality than today; and the man of antiquity, raised in this morality, was a stronger and deeper man than the man of today—he alone has hitherto been "the man that has turned out well." But the seductive power that antiquity exercises on such well-turned-out, i.e., strong and enterprising, souls is the most subtle and effective of all anti-democratic and anti-Christian influences even today, as at the time of the Renaissance.

958 (*1884*)

I write for a species of man that does not yet exist: for the "masters of the earth."

Religions, as consolations and relaxations, dangerous: man believes he has a right to take his ease.

In Plato's *Theages* it is written: "Each one of us would like to be master over all men, if possible, and best of all God." This attitude must exist again.[44a]

[44a] This dialogue is now usually attributed to "an imitator of Plato"; e.g., by W. D. Ross in *The Oxford Classical Dictionary* (Clarendon Press,

Englishmen, Americans, and Russians——

959 (*1885-1886*)[45]

The jungle-growth "man" always appears where the struggle for power has been waged the longest. *Great* men.

The Romans—jungle animals.

960 (*1885-1886*)

From now on there will be more favorable preconditions for more comprehensive forms of dominion, whose like has never yet existed. And even this is not the most important thing; the possibility has been established for the production of international racial unions whose task will be to rear a master race, the future "masters of the earth";—a new, tremendous aristocracy, based on the severest self-legislation, in which the will of philosophical men of power and artist-tyrants will be made to endure for millenia—a higher kind of man who, thanks to their superiority in will, knowledge, riches, and influence, employ democratic Europe as their most pliant and supple instrument for getting hold of the destinies of the earth, so as to work as artists upon "man" himself. Enough: the time is coming when politics will have a different meaning.

5. The Great Human Being[46]

961 (*1885*)

To see at which points in history great human beings arise. The significance of protracted despotic moralities: they tense the bow, if they do not break it.

Oxford 1949), p. 891. But see the chapter on "Theages" in Paul Friedländer, *Plato,* vol. II (2nd rev. ed., Walter de Gruyter, Berlin 1957), especially pp. 141 *f* and 301 *f*. There is a similar passage in Plato's *Theaetetus* 176.

[45] These are two entirely separate notes, placed together under a single number by the German editors.

[46] *Der grosse Mensch*. In the following notes *Mensch* has been translated, more often than not, as "man"; but it should be noted that Nietzsche is not speaking of *der grosse Mann*.

962 (*1885*)

A great man—a man whom nature has constructed and invented in the grand style—what is he?

First: there is a long logic in all of his activity, hard to survey because of its length, and consequently misleading; he has the ability to extend his will across great stretches of his life and to despise and reject everything petty about him, including even the fairest, "divinest" things in the world.

Secondly: he is colder, harder, less hesitating, and without fear of "opinion"; he lacks the virtues that accompany respect and "respectability," and altogether everything that is part of the "virtue of the herd." If he cannot lead, he goes alone; then it can happen that he may snarl at some things he meets on his way.

Third: he wants no "sympathetic" heart, but servants, tools; in his intercourse with men he is always intent on *making* something out of them. He knows he is incommunicable: he finds it tasteless to be familiar; and when one thinks he is, he usually is not. When not speaking to himself, he wears a mask. He rather lies than tells the truth: it requires more spirit and *will.*[47] There is a solitude within him that is inaccessible to praise or blame, his own justice that is beyond appeal.

963 (*Spring-Fall 1887*)

The great man is necessarily a skeptic[48] (which is not to say that he has to appear to be one), provided that greatness consists in this: to *will* something great and the means to it. Freedom from any kind of conviction is part of the strengh of his will. Thus it accords with that "englightened despotism" exercised by every great passion. Such a passion takes the intellect into its service; it has the courage even for unholy means; it removes scruples; it permits itself convictions, it even *needs* them, but it does not submit to them. The need for faith, for anything unconditional

---

[47] The theme of the mask and the need for masks is more fully developed in *Beyond Good and Evil*. For the many relevant passages see the index to my translation (New York: Vintage Books, 1966).

[48] This note was put to use in *The Antichrist,* section 54 (*Portable Nietzsche,* pp. 638-39).

in Yes and No, is a proof of weakness; all weakness is weakness of will. The man of faith, the believer, is necessarily a small type of man. Hence "freedom of spirit," i.e., unbelief as an instinct [is a precondition of greatness.][49]

964 (*1884*)

The great man feels his *power* over a people, his temporary coincidence with a people or a millenium; this enlargement in his experience of himself as *causa* and *voluntas* is misunderstood as "altruism"; it drives him to seek means of communication: all great men are inventive in such means. They want to embed themselves in great communities; they want to give a single form to the multifarious and disordered; chaos stimulates them.

Misunderstanding of love. There is a slavish love that submits and gives itself; that idealizes, and deceives itself—there is a divine love that despises and loves, and reshapes and elevates the beloved.

To gain that tremendous energy of greatness in order to shape the man of the future through breeding and, on the other hand, the annihilation of millions of failures, and not to perish of the suffering one creates, though nothing like it has ever existed!—

965 (*1884*)

The revolution, confusion, and distress of peoples is, in my view, inferior to the distress of great individuals during their development. One must not let oneself be deceived: the many distresses of all the small constitute a sum only in the feelings of powerful human beings.— To think of oneself in moments of great danger, to derive advantage from the disadvantage of many: this can be, in the case of a very high degree of deviation, a sign of a *great* character who manages to master his compassionate and just impulses.

966 (*1884*)

In contrast to the animals, man has cultivated an abundance

[49] The words I have placed in brackets were added by the German editors.

of *contrary* drives and impulses within himself: thanks to this synthesis, he is master of the earth.— Moralities are the expression of locally limited orders of rank in his multifarious world of drives, so man should not perish through their contradictions. Thus a drive as master, its opposite weakened, refined, as the impulse that provides the stimulus for the activity of the chief drive.

The highest man would have the greatest multiplicity of drives, in the relatively greatest strength that can be endured. Indeed, where the plant "man" shows himself strongest one finds instincts that conflict powerfully (e.g., in Shakespeare), but are controlled.

967 (*1885*)

Whether one does not have the right to account all great men *evil?* This cannot be shown in a pure state in all individual cases. Often they have been capable of masterly dissimulation and assumed the outward forms and gestures of great virtues. Often they honored virtue seriously and with a passionate hardness against themselves, but out of cruelty: seen from a distance, this is deceptive. Many misunderstood themselves; not infrequently a great task calls forth great qualities, e.g., justice. The essential point is: the greatest perhaps also possess great virtues, but in that case also their opposites. I believe that it is precisely through the presence of opposites and the feelings they occasion that the great man, *the bow with the great tension,* develops.

968 (*1886-1887*)

In great men, the specific qualities of life—injustice, falsehood, exploitation—are at their greatest. But in so far as they have had an *overwhelming* effect, their essence has been most misunderstood and interpreted as goodness. Type: Carlyle as interpreter.[50]

---

[50] Cutting remarks about Carlyle are also found in *The Gay Science,* section 97 ("Garrulity from inner satisfaction with noise and confused feelings; e.g., in Carlyle"); in *Beyond Good and Evil,* section 252; in *Twilight,* "Skirmishes," sections 1 and 12 (he is also mentioned in section 44); in *The Antichrist,* section 54; and in sections 27, 312, 343, 455, 747 above.

969 (*Spring-Fall 1887*)

In general, every thing is *worth as much as one has paid for it*. This does not hold, to be sure, if one takes the individual in isolation; the great capabilities of the individual are utterly out of proportion to what he himself has done, sacrificed, and suffered for them. But if one considers his family history, one discovers the history of a tremendous storing up and capital accumulation of strength through all kinds of renunciation, struggle, work, and prevailing. It is because the great man has *cost* so much, and *not* because he appears as a miracle and gift of heaven and "chance," that he has become great: "heredity" a false concept. One's forebears have paid the price for what one is.

970 (*1883-1888*)

Danger in modesty.— To adapt ourselves too early to the tasks, societies, everyday life and everyday work, in which chance has placed us, at a time when neither our strength nor our goal has yet entered our consciousness with the force of law; the all-too-early certainty of conscience, comfortableness, sociability thus achieved, this premature resignation that insinuates itself into our feelings as a release from inner and outer unrest, pampers and holds one back in the most dangerous fashion. To learn to feel respect after the fashion of "those like us," as if we ourselves had no measure in us and no right to determine values; the effort to evaluate as others do, *against* the inner voice of our taste, which is also a form of conscience, becomes a terrible, subtle constraint: if there is not finally an explosion, with a sudden bursting asunder of all the bonds of love and morality, then such a spirit becomes withered, petty, effeminate, and factual.

The opposite is bad enough, but better nonetheless: to suffer from one's environment, from its praise as well as from its blame, wounded by it and festering inwardly without betraying the fact; to defend oneself with involuntary mistrust against its love, to learn silence, perhaps concealing it behind speech,[51] to create for oneself nooks and undiscoverable solitudes for moments of relief,

[51] See the footnote on section 962 above. This section should be compared with section 918 above.

of tears, of sublime consolation—until one is finally strong enough to say, "what do I have to do with *you?*" and to go one's *own* way.

971 (*Nov. 1887-March 1888*)

Men who are destinies, who by bearing themselves bear destinies, the whole species of *heroic* bearers of burdens: oh how they would like to rest from themselves for once! how they thirst for strong hearts and necks, so as to be free from what oppresses them, at least for a few hours! And how vainly they thirst!— They wait; they look at everything that passes: no one approaches them with as much as a thousandth part of their suffering[52] and passion,[53] no one divines *in what way* they are waiting—At length, at length they learn their first piece of worldly prudence—not to wait any more; and soon another one: to be genial, to be modest, from now on to endure everyone, to endure everything—in short, to endure even a little more than they have endured so far.

6. The Highest Man as Legislator of the Future

972[54] (*1884*)

Legislators of the future.— After having tried in vain for a long time to attach a definite concept to the word "philosopher"—for I found many contradictory characteristics—I recognized at last that there are two distinct kinds of philosopher:

1. those who want to ascertain a complex fact of evaluations (logical or moral);
2. those who are *legislators* of such evaluations.

The former try to master the world of the present or the past by concentrating and abridging the multiplicity of events through signs: their aim is to make previous events surveyable,

---

[52] *Leiden.*

[53] *Leidenschaft.*

[54] According to 1911, p. 513, this section was composed by the editor from two drafts, but Schlechta, too, follows all previous editions in printing it as a single note. Roughly the first half of this material was put to use in *Beyond Good and Evil,* section 211.

comprehensible, graspable, and usable—they assist the task of man to employ all past things for the benefit of his future.

The latter, however, are *commanders;* they say: "Thus it shall be!" They alone determine the "whither" and the "wherefore," what is useful and what constitutes utility for men; they dispose of the preparatory work of scientific men, and all knowledge is for them only a means for creation. This second kind of philosopher rarely prospers; and their situation and danger is indeed fearful. How often they have deliberately blindfolded themselves simply so as not to have to behold the narrow ledge that separates them from a plunge into the abyss; e.g., Plato, when he convinced himself that the "good" as *he* desired it was not the good of Plato but the "good in itself," the eternal treasure that some man, named Plato, had chanced to discover on his way! This same will to blindness dominates the founders of religions in a much coarser form: their "thou shalt" must not by any means sound in their ears like "I will"— they dare to fulfill their task only as the command of a god; only as an "inspiration" is their value legislation a *bearable* burden under which their conscience is not crushed.

As soon as these two means of comfort, that of Plato and that of Mohammed, have fallen away and no thinker can relieve his conscience with the hypothesis of a "god" or "eternal values," the claim of the legislator of new values rises to a new fearfulness never yet attained. From then on, those elect on whom the suspicion of having such a duty begins to dawn, try to see if they cannot, "at the right moment," elude it, as their greatest danger, through some kind of detour; for example, by convincing themselves that the task has already been accomplished, or cannot be accomplished, or that their shoulders are not strong enough for such burdens, or that they are already overburdened with other, more immediate tasks, or that even this new, distant duty is a seduction and temptation, drawing them away from all other duties, a sickness, a kind of madness. Many may indeed succeed in eluding it: history is full of the traces of men who have eluded this task, and of their bad consciences. Usually, however, there came to these men of fate that redeeming hour, that autumnal hour of ripeness, in which they *had* to do what they did not even "want" to do—and the deed of which they had hitherto been most afraid fell easily and unsought from the tree, as an involuntary deed, almost as a gift.—

973 (*1885*)

The human horizon.— One can conceive philosophers as those who make the most extreme efforts to *test* how far man could *elevate* himself— Plato especially: how *far* his strength will reach. But they do it as individuals; perhaps the instinct of the Caesars, of founders of states, etc., was greater, as they pondered how far man might be driven in his evolution and under "favorable conditions." But they had an insufficient understanding of the nature of favorable circumstances. Great question: where has the plant "man" hitherto grown up most magnificently? For this question the study of comparative history is necessary.

974 (*Fall 1888*)

A fact, a work is eloquent in a *new* way for every age and every new type of man. History always enunciates *new truths.*

975 (*1885-1886*)

To remain objective, hard, firm, severe in carrying through an idea—artists succeed best in this; but when one needs men for this (as teachers, statesmen, etc., do), then the repose and coldness and hardness soon vanish. With natures like Caesar and Napoleon, one gets some notion of "disinterested" work on their marble, whatever the cost in men. On this road lies the future of the highest men: to bear the *greatest responsibility* and *not* collapse under it.— Hitherto, the delusions of inspiration were almost always needed in order not to lose one's *faith in one's right and one's hand.*

976 (*1884*)

Why the philosopher rarely turns out well. His requirements include qualities that usually destroy a man:

1. a tremendous multiplicity of qualities; he must be a brief abstract of man, of all man's higher and lower desires: danger from antitheses, also from disgust at himself;
2. he must be inquisitive in the most various directions: danger of going to pieces;

3. he must be just and fair in the highest sense, but profound in love, hate (and injustice), too;
4. he must be not only a spectator, but also a legislator: judge and judged (to the extent that he is a brief abstract of the world);
5. extremely multifarious, yet firm and hard. Supple.

977 (*1885*)

The really *royal* calling of the philosopher (as expressed by Alcuin the Anglo-Saxon): *prava corrigere, et recta corroborare, et sancta sublimare.*[55]

978 (*1885*)

The new philosopher can arise only in conjunction with a ruling caste, as its highest spiritualization. Great politics, rule over the earth, are at hand; complete *lack* of the *principles* that are needed.

979 (*1885*)

Fundamental thought: the new values must first be created—we shall not be *spared* this task! For us the philosopher must be a legislator. New types. (How the highest types hitherto [e.g., Greeks] were reared: to will this type of "chance" consciously.)

980[56] (*1885*)

Assuming one thinks of a philosopher as a great educator, powerful enough to draw up to his lonely height a long chain of generations, then one must also grant him the uncanny privileges of the great educator. An educator never says what he himself thinks, but always only what he thinks of a thing in relation to the requirements of those he educates. He must not be detected in this dissimulation; it is part of his mastery that one believes in his honesty. He must be capable of employing every means of discipline:[57] some he can drive toward the heights only

[55] To correct what is wrong, and strengthen the right, and raise what is holy.

[56] Not in Nietzsche's hand; dictated.

with the whips of scorn; others, who are sluggish, irresolute, cowardly, vain, perhaps only with exaggerated praise. Such an educator is beyond good and evil; but no one must know it.

981 (*Spring-Fall 1887*)

Not to make men "better," *not* to preach morality to them in any form, as if "morality in itself," or any ideal kind of man, were given; but to *create conditions* that *require stronger men* who for their part need, and consequently will *have,* a morality (more clearly: a physical-spiritual discipline) *that makes them strong!*

Not to allow oneself to be misled by blue eyes or heaving bosoms: *greatness of soul*[58] *has nothing romantic about it.* And unfortunately nothing at all amiable.

982 (*1884*)

One must learn from war: (1) to associate death with the interests for which one fights—that makes *us* venerable; (2) one must learn to sacrifice *many* and to take one's cause seriously enough not to spare men; (3) rigid discipline, and to permit oneself force and cunning in war.

983 (*1884*)

Education in those rulers' virtues that master even one's benevolence and pity: the great cultivator's virtues ("forgiving one's enemies" is child's play by comparison), the affect of the creator must be elevated—no longer to work on marble!— The exceptional situation and powerful position of those beings (compared with any prince hitherto): the Roman Caesar with Christ's soul.[59]

---

[57] *Zucht und Züchtigung.* Nietzsche often uses *Zucht und Züchtung,* suggesting the double sense of "breeding" and the importance of discipline (*Zucht*) for cultivation (*Züchtung*). *Züchtigung* means discipline in the sense of punishment or chastisement.

[58] For "greatness of soul" cf. Kaufmann's *Nietzsche,* Chapter 12, section VI, and, above all, Aristotle's description of *megalopsychia,* cited there.

[59] For discussions of "the Roman Caesar with Christ's soul," see Karl Jaspers, *Nietzsche und das Christentum* (Hameln, Verlag der Bücherstube Fritz Seifert, n.d. [1938]; reprinted by R. Piper, Munich); *Nietzsche and*

984 (*1884*)

Greatness of soul is inseparable from greatness of spirit.[60] For it involves *independence;* but in the absence of spiritual greatness, independence ought not to be allowed, it causes mischief, even through its desire to do good and practice "justice." Small spirits must *obey*—hence cannot possess *greatness.*

985 (*1885*)

The higher philosophical man, who has solitude not because he wishes to be alone but because he *is* something that finds no equals: what dangers and new sufferings have been reserved for him precisely today, when one has unlearned belief in order of rank and consequently does not know how to honor and understand this solitude! Formerly the sage almost sanctified himself in the mind of the crowd by going apart in this way—today the hermit sees himself surrounded as if by a cloud of gloomy doubts and suspicions. And not merely on the part of the envious and

---

Christianity, translated by E. B. Ashton (Chicago, Henry Regnery, 1961), the end of the section on "Self-Identification with the Opponent"; and Kaufmann, "Jaspers' Relation to Nietzsche," in *From Shakespeare to Existentialism* (Garden City: Doubleday Anchor Books, 1960, p. 300). In a nutshell: for Jaspers this phrase represents one of "the most amazing attempts to bring together again into a higher unity what [Nietzsche] has first separated and opposed to each other . . . Nietzsche imagines—without any power of vision and unrealizably—the synthesis of the ultimate opposition." For me the same phrase represents "the very heart of Nietzsche's vision of the overman. Being capable of both sympathy and hardness, of loving and ruling, not using claws though having them . . ."

[60] *Seelengrösse nicht zu trennen von geistiger Grösse.* This is one of the occasional passages in which it is tempting to translate *Geist* and *geistig* as intellect and intellectual; for these would come closer to Nietzsche's meaning here. It is important to realize that when Nietzsche uses these terms he generally means neither spirit alone nor intellect alone but also mind, wit, and *esprit.* But if we used spirit in one passage, wit in another, intellect in a third, and mind elsewhere, something of considerable importance would be lost. It seems better to ask the reader to kep in mind what *Geist* means, and that "spirit" always stands for *Geist.*

This whole matter, of course, transcends philological niceties; what is at stake is one of the most crucial points of Nietzsche's philosophy: he was not an irrationalist. And all the men he most admired were, without exception, great intellects—but not merely great intellects. Cf. sections 876 *ff* above.

wretched: he must sense misunderstanding, neglect, and superficiality even in all benevolence shown him. He knows that crafty cunning of narrow-minded pity that feels itself good and holy when it tries to "save" him from himself, perhaps by means of more comfortable situations or more orderly, more reliable company—indeed, he will have to admire the unconscious instinct of destruction with which all the spiritually mediocre go to work against him, with a perfect faith in their right to do so!

It is necessary for these men of incomprehensible loneliness to wrap themselves vigorously and boldly in the cloak of external, spatial solitude, too: that is part of their prudence. Even cunning and disguise are needed today if such a man is to preserve himself, to keep himself aloft, in the midst of the dangerous, downdragging currents of the age. Every attempt to endure *in* the present, to endure the present, every approach to the men and aims of today, he will have to atone as if it were his own special sin; and he may marvel at the concealed wisdom of his nature that, after every such attempt, at once draws him back to himself by means of sickness and bad accidents.

986 (*1885*)

"—*Maledetto colui*
che contrista un spirto immortal!"[61]

MANZONI (*Conte di Carmagnola,* ACT II).

987 (*1884*)[62]

The most difficult and highest form of man will succeed most rarely: thus the history of philosophy reveals a superabundance of failures, of accidents, and an extremely slow advance; whole millennia intervene and overwhelm what had been achieved; the continuity is broken again and again. It is an appalling history—the history of the highest man, the *sage*.—

---

[61] Cursed whoever saddens an immortal spirit.

[62] In the MS preceded by the words: "*For the introduction.*" 1911, p. 513, it is pointed out that this note belongs to the same period as drafts for *Beyond Good and Evil;* but that in itself does not establish that the introduction for that book was meant: Nietzsche was contemplating more than one project.

What is most harmed is precisely the memory of the great, for the semi-failures and the failures misunderstand them and vanquish them by means of "successes." Every time "an influence" shows itself, a mob crowds upon the scene; the chatter of the petty and the poor in spirit is a terrible torment for the ears of those who remember with a shudder *that the destiny of humanity depends upon the attainment of its highest type.*

From my childhood I have pondered the conditions for the existence of the sage, and I will not conceal my joyous conviction that he is again becoming *possible* in Europe—perhaps only for a short time.

988 (*1885*)

We new philosophers, however, not only do we start by describing the actual order of rank and differences in the value of men, we also desire precisely the opposite of an assimilation, an equalization:[63] we teach estrangement in every sense, we open up gulfs such as have never existed before, we desire that man should become more evil than he has ever been before. In the meantime, we are still strangers to and from one another. We have many reasons to be hermits and to put on masks—we shall therefore be poor at looking for those like us. We shall live alone and probably suffer the torments of all seven solitudes. But if we should come across one another, one may wager that we mistake or mutually deceive one another.

989 (*Spring-Fall 1887*)

Les philosophes ne sont pas faits pour s'aimer. Les aigles ne volent point en compagnie. Il faut laisser cela aux perdrix, aux étourneaux. . . . Planer au-dessus et avoir des griffes, voilà le lot des grands génies.[64]

GALIANI.

[63] Nietzsche originally began this note: "The new philosophers. . . ." Then he changed this to read: "We new philosophers. . . ." And he carried this through to the point indicated. Beyond that point, the editors changed the text to maintain consistency. The note was written in pencil and bears all the earmarks of haste (1911, p. 514).

[64] Philosophers are not made to love one another. Eagles do not fly in company. One must leave that to partridges and starlings . . . Soaring on high and having talons, that is the lot of great geniuses.

990 (*1885*)

I forgot to say that such philosophers are cheerful and that they like to sit in the abyss below a perfectly clear sky: they need different means from other men for enduring life; for they suffer differently (namely, as much from the profundity of their contempt for man as from their love for man).— The most suffering animal on earth invented for itself—laughter.

991 (*1885-1886*)

On the misunderstanding of "cheerfulness." Temporary relief from a protracted tension; the high spirits, the saturnalia of a spirit that is dedicating and preparing itself for protracted and terrible decisions. The "fool" in the form of "science."

992 (*March-June 1888*)

New order of rank of spirits: the tragic natures no longer to the fore.

993 (*1885*)

It is a comfort to me to know that above the steam and filth of human lowlands there is a *higher, brighter humanity,* very small in number (for everything outstanding is by its nature rare): one belongs to it, not because one is more talented or more virtuous or more heroic or more loving than the men below, but—because one is colder, brighter, more far-seeing, more solitary; because one endures, prefers, demands solitude as happiness, as privilege, indeed as a condition of existence; because one lives among clouds and lightning as among one's own kind, but equally among rays of sunlight, drops of dew, flakes of snow, and everything that necessarily comes from the heights and, when it moves, moves eternally only in the direction from above to below. Aspirations *toward* the heights are not ours.— Heroes, martyrs, geniuses and enthusiasts are not still, patient, subtle, cold, slow enough for us.

994 (*Spring-Fall 1887*)

Absolute conviction: that value feelings above and below are different; that countless experiences are lacking in those below; that between below and above misunderstanding is *necessary*.

995 (*1884*)

How do men attain great strength and a great task? All the virtues and efficiency of body and soul are acquired laboriously and little by little, through much industry, self-constraint, limitation, through much obstinate, faithful repetition of the same labors, the same renunciations; but there are men who are the heirs and masters of this slowly-acquired manifold treasure of virtue and efficiency—because, through fortunate and reasonable marriages, and also through fortunate accidents, the acquired and stored-up energies of many generations have not been squandered and dispersed but linked together by a firm ring and by will. In the end there appears a man, a monster of energy, who demands a monster of a task. For it is our energy that disposes of us; and the wretched spiritual game of goals and intentions and motives is only a foreground—even though weak eyes may take them for the matter itself.

996 (*1885-1886*)

The sublime man has the highest value, even if he is terribly delicate and fragile, because an abundance of very difficult and rare things has been bred and preserved together through many generations.

997 (*1884*)

I teach: that there are higher and lower men, and that a single individual can under certain circumstances justify the existence of whole millennia—that is, a full, rich, great, whole human being in relation to countless incomplete fragmentary men.

998 (*1884*)

The highest men live beyond the rulers, freed from all bonds; and in the rulers they have their instruments.

999 (*1884*)

Order of rank: He who *determines* values and directs the will of millenia by giving direction to the highest natures is the *highest* man.

1000 (*1884*)

I believe I have *guessed* some of the things in the soul of the highest man; perhaps anyone who unriddles him must perish; but whoever has seen him must help to make him *possible.*

Fundamental thought: we must consider the future as decisive for all our evaluations—and not seek the laws of our actions *behind* us!

1001 (*1884*)

Not "mankind" but *overman* is the goal!

1002 (*Spring-Fall 1887*)

Come l'uom s'eterna—[65]

INF. XV 85

---

[65] How man makes himself eternal.—Dante.

II. DIONYSUS

1003 (*Jan-Fall 1888*)

To him that has turned out well, who does my heart good, carved from wood that is hard, gentle, and fragrant—in whom even the nose takes pleasure—this book is dedicated.

He enjoys the taste of what is wholesome for him;

his pleasure in anything ceases when the bounds of the wholesome are crossed;

he divines the remedies for partial injuries; he has illnesses as great stimulants of his life;

he knows how to exploit ill chances;

he grows stronger through the accidents that threaten to destroy him;

he instinctively gathers from all that he sees, hears, experiences, what advances his main concern—he follows a principle of selection—he allows much to fall through;

he reacts with the slowness bred by a long caution and a deliberate pride—he tests a stimulus for its origin and its intentions, he does not submit;

he is always in his *own* company, whether he deals with books, men, or landscapes;

he honors by choosing, by admitting, by trusting.

1004 (*Nov. 1887-March 1888*)

To attain a height and bird's eye view, so one grasps how everything actually happens as it ought to happen; how every kind of "imperfection" and the suffering to which it gives rise are part of the highest desirability.

1005 (*Spring-Fall 1887*)

Around 1876 I was terrified to see all I had desired hitherto *compromised,* as I grasped which way Wagner was going now; and I was bound very closely to him by all the bonds of a profound identity of needs, by gratitude, by his irreplaceability and the absolute privation I saw before me.

At the same time I seemed to myself irrevocably incarcerated in my philology and teaching—in an accident and makeshift of my life: I no longer knew how to extricate myself, and was weary, spent, used up.

At the same time I grasped that my instinct went into the opposite direction from Schopenhauer's: toward a *justification of life,* even at its most terrible, ambiguous, and mendacious; for this I had the formula *"Dionysian."*

Against the theory that an "in-itself of things" must necessarily be good, blessed, true, and one, Schopenhauer's interpretation of the "in-itself" as will was an essential step; but he did not understand how to *deify* this will: he remained entangled in the moral-Christian ideal. Schopenhauer was still so much subject to the dominion of Christian values that, as soon as the thing-in-itself was no longer "God" for him, he had to see it as bad, stupid, and absolutely reprehensible. He failed to grasp that there can be an infinite variety of ways of being different, even of being god.[66]

1006 (*Spring-Fall 1887*)

Moral values have hitherto been the highest values: would anybody call this in question?— If we remove these values from this position, we alter *all* values: the principle of their order of rank hitherto is thus overthrown.

1007 (*Spring-Fall 1887*)

To revalue values—what would that mean? All the spontaneous—new, future, stronger—movements must be there; but they still appear under false names and valuations and have not yet become conscious of themselves.

A courageous becoming-conscious and affirmation of what has been achieved—a liberation from the slovenly routine of old valuations that dishonor us in the best and strongest things we have achieved.

1008 (*Spring-Fall 1887*)

Every doctrine for which all accumulated energies and ex-

---

[66] The words that immediately follow in the MS are omitted in all editions: "A curse on that bigoted freedom: 'good and evil.' "

plosives are not yet ready at hand, is superfluous. A revaluation of values is achieved only when there is a tension of new needs, of men with new needs, who suffer from the old values without attaining this consciousness.

1009 (*Spring-Fall 1887*)

Points of view for *my* values: whether out of abundance or out of want?[67]—whether one looks on or lends a hand—or looks away and walks off?[68]—whether out of stored-up energy, "spontaneously," or merely stimulated *reactively,* and provoked? whether *simple,* out of a paucity of elements, *or* out of overwhelming mastery over many, so they are pressed into service when they are needed? —whether one is a *problem* or a *solution*?—whether *perfect* with a small task or *imperfect* with an extraordinary goal? whether one is *genuine* or merely an *actor,* whether one is genuine as an actor or merely a copy of an actor, whether one is a "representative" or that which is represented?[69] whether a "personality" or merely a rendezvous of personalities—whether *sick* from sickness or excessive health? whether one goes on ahead as a shepherd or as an "exception" (third species: as a fugitive)?[70] whether one needs *dignity,* or to be a "buffoon"? whether one seeks resistance or avoids it? whether one is imperfect through being "too early" or "too late"? whether by nature one says Yes or No or is a peacock's tail of many colors? whether one is sufficiently proud not to be ashamed even of one's vanity? whether one is still capable of a bite of conscience? (—this species is becoming rare: formerly the conscience had too much to chew: now it seems to have lost its teeth)?[71] whether one is still capable of a "duty"? (—there are those who would lose their whole joy in living if their duty were taken from them—especially the womanly, the born subjects.)

---

[67] Cf. *The Gay Science,* section 370 (published in 1887): ". . . Regarding all aesthetic values, I now avail myself of this main distinction: I ask in every single case, 'Is it hunger or overabundance that has here become creative?'. . ." Cf. also section 59 above.

[68] Cf. *Twilight,* in *Portable Nietzsche,* "Maxims and Arrows," aphorism 40 (p. 472).

[69] Cf. *ibid.,* aphorism 38 (page 472).

[70] Cf. *ibid.,* aphorism 37 (page 472).

[71] Cf. *ibid.,* aphorism 29 (page 470).

1010 (*1883-1888*)

Suppose our usual conception of the world were a misunderstanding: could a form of perfection be conceived within which even such misunderstandings would receive their sanction?

Conception of a new perfection: that which does not correspond to our logic, our "beautiful," our "good," our "true," could be perfect in a higher sense than even our ideal.

1011 (*Manuscript source uncertain*)

Our great renunciation: not to deify the unknown; we are just beginning to know little. False and wasted endeavors.

Our "new world": we have to realize to what degree we are the *creators* of our value feelings—and thus capable of projecting "meaning" into history.

This faith in truth attains its ultimate conclusion in us—you know what it is: that if there is anything that is to be worshipped it is *appearance* that must be worshipped, that the lie—and *not* the truth—is divine!

1012 (*1883-1888*)

Whoever pushes rationality forward also restores new strength to the opposite power, mysticism and folly of all kinds.

To distinguish in *every movement* (1) that it is *in part* exhaustion from a preceding movement (satiety from it, the malice of weakness toward it, sickness); (2) that it is *in part* newly-awakened, long slumbering, accumulated energy—joyous, exuberant, violent: health.

1013 (*1885-1886*)

Health and sickliness: one should be careful! The standard remains the efflorescence of the body, the agility, courage, and cheerfulness of the spirit—but also, of course, how much of the sickly it can take and overcome—how much it can make healthy. That of which more delicate men would perish belongs to the stimulants of *great* health.

1014 (*1885*)

It is only a question of strength: to have all the morbid traits of the century, but to balance them through a superabundant, recuperative strength. The strong man.

1015 (*Spring-Fall 1887; rev. Spring-Fall 1888*)

On the strength of the nineteenth century.— We are more medieval than the eighteenth century; not *merely* more curious about or easily stimulated by the strange and rare. We have revolted against the Revolution— We have emancipated ourselves from fear of reason, the ghost that haunted the eighteenth century: we again dare to be absurd, childish, lyrical—in one word: "we are musicians." We are as little afraid of the ridiculous as of the absurd. The devil finds that the tolerance of God works in his favor: even more, he is interesting as one who has been misunderstood and slandered from of old—we rescue the honor of the devil.

We no longer separate the great from the terrible. We include together the good things, in their complexity, and the worst things: we have overcome the absurd "desirability" of former days (which desired increase of the good without increase of the evil). Cowardice before the ideal of the Renaissance has receded—we even dare to aspire to its *mores*. Intolerance toward the priest and the church has come to an end at the same time; "it is immoral to believe in God"—but precisely this seems to us the best justification of such faith.

We have granted all these things their rights. We are not afraid of the *reverse side* of "good things" (—we *seek* them: we are brave and curious enough); e.g., of Hellenism, of morality, of reason, of good taste (we compute the losses one sustains with all such precious things: one almost makes oneself poor with such a precious thing—). Just as little do we conceal from ourselves the reverse side of *bad* things.

1016 (*March-June 1888*)

What does us honor.— If anything does us honor, it is this: we have transferred seriousness: we regard as important the lowly things that have at all times been despised and left aside—on the other hand, we let "beautiful feelings" go cheap.

Is there a more dangerous aberration than contempt for the body? As if it did not condemn all spirituality to become sickly —to the *vapeurs* of "idealism"!

Whatever Christians and idealists have devised has neither rhyme nor reason: we are more radical. We have discovered the "smallest world" as that which is decisive everywhere.[72]

The way our streets are paved, good air in our room,[73] food —we grasp their value; we have taken all the necessities of existence seriously and despise all "beautiful-soulism" as a kind of "levity and frivolity."— What was formerly most despised has been brought to the front.

1017 (*Spring-Fall 1887*)

In place of the "natural man" of Rousseau, the nineteenth century has discovered a *truer image of* "man"—it has had the *courage* to do so.— On the whole, the Christian concept "man" has thus been reinstated. What one has *not* had the courage for is to call *this* "man in himself" good and to see in him the guarantee of the future. Neither has one dared to grasp that an increase in the terribleness of man is an accompaniment of every increase in culture; in this, one is still subject to the Christian ideal and takes *its* side against paganism, also against the Renaissance concept of *virtù*. But the key to culture is not to be found in this way: and *in praxi* one retains the falsification of history in favor of the "good man" (as if he alone constituted the progress of man) and the socialist ideal (i.e., the residue of Christianity and of Rousseau in the de-Christianized world).

The struggle against the eighteenth century: its supreme overcoming by Goethe and Napoleon. Schopenhauer, too, struggles against it; but he involutarily steps back into the seventeenth century—he is a modern Pascal, with Pascalian value judgments *without* Christianity. Schopenhauer was not strong enough for a new Yes.

Napoleon: insight that the higher and the terrible man neces-

---

[72] At this point the MS has the words: "we are dangerously in the" The theme of this section is developed at length in *Ecce Homo*.

[73] At this point the MS has the words: "the soil [*Boden:* the word is illegible, and 1911, p. 514, also gives *Quellen*, i.e., wells] not poisoned."

sarily belong together. The "man" reinstated; the woman again accorded her due tribute of contempt and fear. "Totality" as health and highest activity; the straight line, the grand style in action rediscovered; the most powerful instinct, that of life itself, the lust to rule, affirmed.

1018 (*1887*)[74]

(*Revue des deux mondes,* Feb. 15, 1887. Taine on Napoleon): "Suddenly the *faculté maîtresse*[75] unfolds: the artist enclosed in the politician emerges *de sa gaine;*[76] he creates *dans l'idéal et l'impossible.*[77] He is once more recognized for what he is: the posthumous brother of Dante and Michelangelo: and in truth, in view of the firm contours of his vision, the intensity, coherence, and inner logic of his dream, the profundity of his meditation, the superhuman grandeur of his conception, he is like them *et leur égal: son génie a la même taille et la même structure; il est un des trois esprits souverains de la renaissance italienne.*"[78]

Nota bene—Dante, Michelangelo, Napoleon.

1019 (*Spring-Fall 1887; rev. Spring-Fall 1888*)

On the pessimism of strength.— In the inner psychic economy of the primitive man, fear of evil predominates. What is evil? Three things: chance, the uncertain, the sudden. How does primitive man fight against evil?— He conceives it as reason, as power, even as a person. In this way he establishes the possibility of entering into a kind of treaty with it and in general to exercise influence over it in advance—to forestall it.

—Another expedient is to assert that its malice and harmfulness is merely appearance: one interprets the consequences of chance, of the uncertain and sudden as well meant, as meaningful.

---

[74] The Musarion edition, vol. XIX, p. 431, actually gives the date as follows: "1018: 86-87." As usual, it bases its information on 1911, where we are told on p. 494 that 1018 comes from "N XLII, 77"—and on p. 480, that the MS identified as "N XLII" belongs to the period 1886/87. The editors did not notice that the contents of the note rules out 1886.

[75] Mistress talent, or ruling talent: no wonder Nietzsche left this and some of the following phrases in the original French.

[76] From her vagina.

[77] In the ideal and the impossible.

[78] And their equal: his genius has the same cut and the same structure; he is one of the three sovereign spirits of the Italian Renaissance.

—A third means: one interprets the bad above all as "deserved": one justifies evil as punishment.

—*In summa one submits to it:* the whole religio-moral interpretation is only a form of submission to evil.— The faith that a good meaning lies in evil means to abandon the struggle against it.

Now the whole history of culture represents a diminution of this fear of chance, the uncertain, the sudden. For culture means learning to calculate, to think causally, to forestall, to believe in necessity. With the increase of culture, man can do without that *primitive* form of submission to ills (called religion or morality), that "justification of evil." Now he makes war on "ills"—he abolishes them. Indeed, a state is possible in which the sense of security and belief in law and calculability enter consciousness in the form of satiety and disgust—while the delight in chance, the uncertain and sudden becomes titillating.

Let us dwell a moment on this symptom of highest culture—I call it the pessimism of strength. Man no longer needs a "justification of ills"; "justification" is precisely what he abhors: he enjoys ills *pur, cru;* he finds senseless ills the most interesting. If he formerly had need of a god, he now takes delight in a world disorder without God, a world of chance, to whose essence belong the terrible, the ambiguous, the seductive.

In such a state it is precisely the *good* that needs "justifying," i.e., it must be founded in evil and danger or involve some great stupidity: then it still pleases. Animality no longer arouses horror; *esprit* and happy exuberance[79] in favor of the animal in man is in such ages the most triumphant form of spirituality. Man is now strong enough to be ashamed of any faith in God: he may again play the *advocatus diaboli.* If he *in praxi* advocates the preservation of virtue, he does it for reasons that recognize in virtue a subtlety, a cunning, a form of lust for gain and power.

This pessimism of strength also ends in a *theodicy,* i.e., in an absolute affirmation of the world—but for the very reasons that formerly led one to deny it—and in this fashion to a conception of this world as the actually-achieved highest possible ideal.

1020 (*Nov. 1887-March 1888*)

The chief kinds of pessimism:

---

[79] *Ein geistreicher und glücklicher Übermut.*

the pessimism of sensibility (excessive irritability with a preponderance of unpleasurable feelings);
the pessimism of "unfree will" (in other words: a lack of strength in resisting stimuli);
the pessimism of doubt (a distaste for everything firm, for all grasping and touching).

The psychological states proper to these can all be observed in the madhouse, even if in a somewhat exaggerated form. Also "nihilism" (the penetrating feeling of—"nothingness").

But where does the moral pessimism of Pascal belong? the metaphysical pessimism of the Vedanta philosophy? the social pessimism of the anarchists (or of Shelley)? the pessimism of sympathy (like that of Leo Tolstoy, Alfred de Vigny)?

Are all these not likewise phenomena of decay and sickness?—To give excessive weight to moral values or to fictions of the "beyond" or to social distress or to suffering in general: every such exaggeration of a narrow viewpoint is in itself already a sign of sickness. Likewise the preponderance of No over Yes!

What must not be confused with all this: pleasure in saying No and doing No out of a tremendous strength and tension derived from saying Yes—peculiar to all rich and powerful men and ages. A luxury, as it were; also a form of bravery that opposes the terrible; a sympathetic feeling for the terrible and questionable because one is, among other things, terrible and questionable: the *Dionysian* in will, spirit, taste.

1021 (*Manuscript source uncertain*)
My Five "No's"

1. My struggle against the *feeling of guilt* and the projection of the concept of *punishment* into the physical and metaphysical world; also into psychology and the interpretation of history. Insight into the *moralization* of all previous philosophies and valuations.

2. My recognition and identification of the traditional ideal, the Christian, even where the dogmatic form of Christianity has been abandoned. *The dangerousness of the Christian ideal* lies in its value feelings, in that which can do without conceptual expression: my struggle against *latent Christianity* (e.g., in music, in socialism).

3. My struggle against the eighteenth century of Rousseau,

against his "nature," his "good man," his belief in the dominion of feeling—against the softening, weakening, moralization of man: an ideal born of *hatred for aristocratic culture; in praxi,* the dominion of the feelings of unbridled *ressentiment,* devised as a banner for the struggle (—the morality of guilt feelings of the Christian, the morality of *ressentiment* a posture of the mob).

4. My struggle against *romanticism,* in which Christian ideals and the ideals of Rousseau unite, but compounded with a nostalgia for the old days of priestly-aristocratic culture, for *virtù,* for the "strong human being"—something extremely hybrid; a false and impersonated strong humanity that values extreme states in general and sees in them a symptom of strength ("cult of passion"; an imitation of the most expressive forms, *furore espressivo,* not out of plenitude but out of a lack).— (What in the nineteenth century is born of a relative plenitude, with gusto: cheerful music, etc.; among poets, e.g., Stifter and Gottfried Keller are signs of greater strength, inner well-being, than——. Grand technique and inventiveness, the natural sciences, history (?)[80]: products of relative strength, self-confidence of the nineteenth century.)

5. My struggle against the *predominance of the herd instincts* now that science makes common cause with them; against the inward hatred with which every kind of order of rank and distance are treated.

1022 (*Spring 1887-March 1888*)

From the pressure of plenitude, from the tension of forces that continually increase in us and do not yet know how to discharge themselves, there arises a condition like that preceding a storm: the nature we constitute becomes dark. This, too, is "pessimism"—

A doctrine that puts an end to such a condition by *commanding* something or other—a revaluation of values by virtue of which the accumulated forces are shown a way, a whither, so they explode into lightning flashes and deeds—certainly does not need to be a doctrine of happiness: by releasing force that had been compressed and dammed to the point of torment it *brings happiness.*

1023 (*March-June 1888*)

Pleasure appears where there is the feeling of power.

---

[80] Nietzsche's question mark.

Happiness: in the triumphant consciousness of power and victory.

Progress: the strengthening of the type, the ability for great willing; everything else is misunderstanding, danger.

1024 (*Spring-Fall 1887*)

A period when the old masquerade and moral decking-up of the affects arouses antipathy: naked nature; where the decisiveness of quanta of power is simply admitted (as determining rank); where the grand style appears again as the consequence of grand passion.

1025 (*Spring-Fall 1887*)

To press everything terrible into *service,* one by one, step by step, experimentally: this is what the task of culture demands; but until it is *strong enough* for this, it must oppose, moderate, veil, even curse all this.

Everywhere that a culture *posits evil,* it gives expression to a relationship of *fear,* thus a *weakness.*

Thesis: everything good is the evil of former days made serviceable. *Standard*: the greater and more terrible the passions are that an age, a people, an individual can permit themselves, because they are capable of employing them as *means, the higher stands their culture;*[81] the more mediocre, the weaker, the more submissive and cowardly a man is, the more he will posit as *evil*: it is with him that the realm of evil is most comprehensive. The basest man will see the realm of evil (i.e., of that which is forbidden and hostile to him) everywhere.

1026 (*Summer-Fall 1883*)

Not "happiness follows virtue"—but the more powerful man first designates his happy state as virtue.

Evil actions belong to the powerful and virtuous: bad, base ones to the subjected.

---

[81] At this point the MS has the phrase: "(the realm of evil becomes ever *smaller*—)" There seems to be no good reason for omitting this, but though the words are printed in the notes of 1911, p. 514, all editions, including Schlechta's, leave them out.

The most powerful man, the creator, would have to be the most evil, in as much as he carries his ideal against the ideals of other men and remakes them in his own image. Evil here means: hard, painful, enforced.

Such men as Napoleon must come again and again and confirm the belief in the autocracy of the individual: but he himself was corrupted by the means he *had to* employ and lost *noblesse* of character. If he had had to prevail among a different kind of man he could have employed other means; and it would thus not seem to be a necessity for a *Caesar* to become bad.

1027 (*Spring-Fall 1887*)

Man is beast and superbeast;[82] the higher man is inhuman and superhuman: these belong together. With every increase of greatness and height in man, there is also an increase in depth and terribleness: one ought not to desire the one without the other—or rather: the more radically one desires the one, the more radically one achieves precisely the other.

1028 (*Spring-Fall 1887*)

Terribleness is part of greatness: let us not deceive ourselves.

1029 (*1884-1886*)

I have presented such terrible images to knowledge that any "Epicurean delight" is out of the question. Only Dionysian joy is sufficient: *I have been the first to discover the tragic.*[83] The Greeks, thanks to their moralistic superficiality, misunderstood it. Even

---

[82] *Untier und Übertier*. Cf. the note to section 877 above, for a passage in which Nietzsche calls Napoleon "this synthesis of the *inhuman* and *superhuman*"—*Unmensch und Übermensch*. *Übertier* is strictly analagous to *Übermensch*, overman, and is a coinage. *Untier* is an established German word and means monster, beast.

[83] This may sound so mad that few if any readers will understand what Nietzsche means. Plato's and Aristotle's approaches to tragedy were moralistic, and they failed to understand tragedy; so did Schopenhauer and, in various ways, others who wrote about it. Nietzsche's suggestion, first offered in *The Birth of Tragedy*, at the very end of section 7, is that tragedy is born of an insight into the utter terror and absurdity of existence and of a despair so profound that only the sublime beauty of the great tragedies can engender a "Dionysian joy . . . sufficient" to save man.

resignation is *not* a lesson of tragedy, but a misunderstanding of it! Yearning for nothingness is a *denial* of tragic wisdom, its opposite!

1030 (*1883-1888*)

A full and powerful soul not only copes with painful, even terrible losses, deprivations, robberies, insults; it emerges from such hells with a greater fullness and powerfulness; and, most essential of all, with a new increase in the blissfulness of love. I believe that he who has divined something of the most basic conditions for this growth in love will understand what Dante meant when he wrote over the gate of his Inferno: "I, too, was created by eternal love."[84]

1031 (*Spring-Fall 1887*)

To explore the whole sphere of the modern soul, to have sat in its every nook—my ambition, my torture, and my happiness.

Really to *overcome* pessimism—a Goethean eye full of love and good will as the result.

1032 (*1883-1885*)[85]

The first question is by no means whether we are content with ourselves, but whether we are content with anything at all.[86] If we affirm one single moment, we thus affirm not only ourselves but all existence.[87] For nothing is self-sufficient, neither in us ourselves nor in things; and if our soul has trembled with happiness and sounded like a harp string just once, all eternity was needed

[84] It is doubtful that this section really helps us to "understand what Dante meant," or that it is very well considered; after all, it is a mere note and was not embodied in a book. But the point seems to be that there is an ultimate connection between the most terrible suffering and the best love.

[85] "Above the beginning, the MS has the incomplete sentence: 'Once one has comprehended, not only in how far every one of our actions is necessary but also how they mutually entail each other and how every nuance of feeling——'" (1911, p. 514).

[86] Cf. *The Gay Science*, section 290, toward the end (*Portable Nietzsche*, p. 99).

[87] Cf. *Zarathustra*, IV, "The Drunken Song," section 10 (*Portable Nietzsche*, p. 435).

to produce this one event—and in this single moment of affirmation all eternity was called good, redeemed, justified, and affirmed.

1033 (*March-June 1888*)

The affirmative affects: pride, joy, health, love of the sexes, enmity and war, reverence, beautiful gestures and manners,[88] strong will, the discipline of high spirituality, will to power, gratitude toward earth and life—everything that is rich and desires to bestow and that replenishes and gilds and immortalizes and deifies life—the whole force of *transfiguring* virtues, everything that declares good and affirms in word and deed—

1034 (*1888*)

We few or many who again dare to live in a dismoralized world, we pagans in faith: we are probably also the first to grasp what a pagan faith is:—to have to imagine higher creatures than man, but beyond good and evil; to have to consider all being higher as also being immoral. We believe in Olympus—and *not* in the "Crucified."

1035 (*Spring-Fall 1887; rev. Spring-Fall 1888*)

Latter-day man has employed his power of idealization in regard to a god chiefly to make the god more and more moral. What does that signify?—Nothing good, a diminution of the strength of man.

For in itself the opposite would be possible; and there are indications of this. God conceived as an emancipation from morality, taking into himself the whole fullness of life's antitheses and, in a divine torment, redeeming and justifying them: God as the beyond and above of the wretched loafers' morality of "good and evil."

1036 (*1885-1886*)

A humanitarian God cannot be *demonstrated* from the world we know: today you can be compelled to admit this much. But

[88] After "manners" the MS has another word that is illegible.

what conclusions do you draw?[89] "He cannot be demonstrated to *us*": epistemological skepticism. You are all *afraid* of the conclusion: "from the world we know, a very different god would be demonstrable, one who at any rate is *not* humanitarian"—and, in short, you hold fast to your God and devise for him a world we do *not* know.

1037 (*Spring-Fall 1887*)

Let us remove supreme goodness from the concept of God: it is unworthy of a god. Let us also remove supreme wisdom: it is the vanity of philosophers that is to be blamed for this mad notion of God as a monster of wisdom: he had to be as like them as possible. No! God the *supreme power*—that suffices! Everything follows from it, "the world" follows from it!

1038 (*March-Fall 1888*)[90]

—And how many new gods are still possible! As for myself, in whom the religious, that is to say god-forming, instinct occasionally becomes active at impossible times—how differently, how variously the divine has revealed itself to me each time!

So many strange things have passed before me in those timeless moments that fall into one's life as if from the moon, when one no longer has any idea how old one is or how young one will yet be—I should not doubt that there are many kinds of gods— There are some one cannot imagine without a certain halcyon and frivolous quality in their make-up— Perhaps light feet are even an integral part of the concept "god"— Is it necessary to elaborate that a god prefers to stay beyond everything bourgeois and rational? and, between ourselves, also beyond good and evil? His prospect is *free*—in Goethe's words.[91]— And to call upon

[89] Originally Nietzsche had written: "(1) Either he cannot be demonstrated to us: epistemological skepticism (2) he must be absolutely other and unknowable." When crossing out the words that do not appear in the text above, he forgot to delete "Either."

[90] According to 1911, p. 514, this note "was intended for *The Antichrist* and was supposed to constitute section 20 and conclude the segment 16-19, which in this preliminary version bears the title 'On the history of the concept of God.' "

[91] Allusion to the last scene of *Faust,* line 11,989. The quotation in the next sentence is from "On Reading and Writing" in Part I of *Zarathustra* (*Portable Nietzsche,* p. 153).

the inestimable authority of Zarathustra in this instance: Zarathustra goes so far as to confess: "I would believe only in a God who could *dance*"—

To repeat: how many new gods are still possible!— Zarathustra himself, to be sure, is merely an old atheist: he believes neither in old nor in new gods. Zarathustra says he *would;* but Zarathrusta *will* not— Do not misunderstand him.

The type of God after the type of creative spirits, of "great men."

1039 (*March-June 1888*)

And how many new *ideals* are, at bottom, still possible!— Here is a little ideal I stumble upon once every five weeks on a wild and lonely walk, in an azure moment of sinful happiness. To spend one's life amid delicate and absurd things; a stranger to reality; half an artist, half a bird and metaphysician; with no care for reality, except now and then to acknowledge it in the manner of a good dancer with the tips of one's toes; always tickled by some sunray of happiness; exuberant and encouraged even by misery—for misery *preserves* the happy man; fixing a little humorous tail even to the holiest things: this, as is obvious, is the ideal of a heavy, hundredweight spirit—a *spirit of gravity.*

1040 (*Summer-Fall 1888*)

From the soul's school of war.[92] (Dedicated to the brave, the cheerful, the temperate.)

I should not like to undervalue the amiable virtues; but greatness of soul is not compatible with them. Even in the arts, the grand style excludes the pleasing.

*

In times of painful tension and vulnerability, choose war: it hardens, it produces muscles.

*

The deeply wounded have Olympian laughter; one has only what one needs to have.

---

[92] Cf. *Twilight,* "Maxims and Arrows," the title of aphorism 8 (*Portable Nietzsche,* p. 467).

*

It has been ten years already: not a sound reaches me any longer—a land without rain. One must have a great deal of humanity left not to die of thirst in the drought.

1041 (*1888*)

My new path to a "Yes".— Philosophy, as I have hitherto understood and lived it, is a voluntary quest for even the most detested and notorious[93] sides of existence. From the long experience I gained from such a wandering through ice and wilderness, I learned to view differently all that had hitherto philosophized: the *hidden* history of philosophy, the psychology of its great names, came to light for me. "How much truth can a spirit *endure,* how much truth does a spirit *dare*?"—this became for me the real standard of value.[94] Error is *cowardice*—every achievement of knowledge is a consequence of courage, of severity toward oneself, of cleanliness toward oneself— Such an experimental philosophy as I live anticipates experimentally even the possibilities of the most fundamental nihilism; but this does not mean that it must halt at a negation, a No, a will to negation. It wants rather to cross over to the opposite of this—to a Dionysian affirmation of the world as it is, without subtraction, exception, or selection—it wants the eternal circulation:—the same things, the same logic and illogic of entanglements. The highest state a philosopher can attain: to stand in a Dionysian relationship to existence—my formula for this is *amor fati.*[95]

It is part of this state to perceive not merely the necessity of those sides of existence hitherto denied, but their desirability; and not their desirability merely in relation to the sides hitherto affirmed (perhaps as their complement or precondition), but for

---

[93] The reading of these two words "detested" and "notorious" is uncertain.

[94] Cf. *Beyond Good and Evil,* section 39, and above all section 3 of the Preface to *Ecce Homo,* where "error is cowardice" is also used.

[95] Love of fate. Nietzsche introduced this term in *The Gay Science,* section 276: "*Amor fati*: let this be my love from now on." He used it twice in *Ecce Homo,* in "Why I am so clever," section 10, and "The Case of Wagner," section 4; and also near the beginning of the Epilogue to *Nietzsche contra Wagner.*

their own sake, as the more powerful, more fruitful, *truer* sides of existence, in which its will finds clearer expression.

It is also part of this state to depreciate that side of existence which alone has been affirmed hitherto; to perceive the origin of this valuation and how little a Dionysian value standard for existence is obliged to it: I pulled up and perceived what it really was that here affirmed (on one hand, the instinct of the suffering; on the other the instinct of the herd; and thirdly, the instinct of the majority against the exceptions—).

Thus I guessed to what extent a stronger type of man would necessarily have to conceive the elevation and enhancement of man as taking place in another direction: higher beings, beyond good and evil, beyond those values which cannot deny their origin in the sphere of suffering, the herd, and the majority—I sought in history the beginnings of this construction of reverse ideals (the concepts "pagan," "classical," "noble" newly discovered and expounded—).

1042 (*1885-1886*)

To demonstrate to what extent the Greek religion was higher than the Judaeo-Christian. The latter conquered because the Greek religion had become degenerate (had retrogressed).

1043 (*1884*)

It is nothing to be wondered at that a couple of millenia are needed to re-establish contact—a couple of millennia mean little!

1044 (*1885-1886*)

There is a need for those who will sanctify all activities, not only eating and drinking—and not merely in remembrance of them and to become one with them, but this world must be transfigured ever anew and in new ways.

1045 (*1886-1887*)

The most spiritual men feel the stimulus and charm of sensuous things in a way that other men—those with "fleshly hearts"—cannot possibly imagine and ought not to imagine: they are sensualists in the best faith, because they accord the senses a more fundamental value than to that fine sieve, that thinning and reducing machine, or whatever we may call what in the language of the people is named "spirit." The strength and power of the senses—this is the essential thing in a well-constituted and complete man: the splendid "animal" must be given first—what could any "humanization" matter otherwise!

1046 (*1884*)

1. We want to hold fast to our senses and to our faith in them—and think their consequences through to the end! The nonsensuality of philosophy hitherto as the greatest nonsensicality of man.

2. The existing world, upon which all earthly living things have worked so that it appears as it does (durable and changing *slowly*), we want to go on building—and not criticize it away as false!

3. Our valuations are a part of this building; they emphasize and underline. Of what significance is it if entire religions say: "all is bad and false and evil"! This condemnation of the entire process can only be a judgment of the ill-constituted!

4. To be sure, the ill-constituted can be the greatest sufferers and the most subtle? The contented could be of little value?

5. One must understand the artistic basic phenomenon that is called "life"—the building spirit that builds under the most unfavorable conditions: in the slowest manner—— A demonstration of all its combinations must first be produced afresh: it preserves itself.

1047 (*Nov. 1887-March 1888*)

Sexuality, the lust to rule, pleasure in appearance and deception, great and joyful gratitude for life and its typical states—these are of the essence of the pagan cults and have a good conscience on their side.— Unnaturalness (already in Greek antiquity) fights against the pagan, as morality, as dialectic.

1048 (*1885-1886*)

An anti-metaphysical view of the world—yes, but an artistic one.

1049 (*1885-1886*)

Apollo's deception: the *eternity* of beautiful form; the aristocratic legislation, "*thus shall it be for ever!*"

Dionysus: sensuality and cruelty. Transitoriness could be interpreted as enjoyment of productive and destructive force, as *continual creation.*

1050 (*March-June 1888*)

The word "*Dionysian*" means: an urge to unity, a reaching out beyond personality, the everyday, society, reality, across the abyss of transitoriness: a passionate-painful overflowing into darker, fuller, more floating states; an ecstatic affirmation of the total character of life as that which remains the same, just as powerful, just as blissful, through all change; the great pantheistic sharing of joy and sorrow that sanctifies and calls good even the most terrible and questionable qualities of life; the eternal will to procreation, to fruitfulness, to recurrence; the feeling of the necessary unity of creation and destruction.

The world "*Apollinian*" means: the urge to perfect self-sufficiency, to the typical "individual," to all that simplifies, distinguishes, makes strong, clear, unambiguous, typical: freedom under the law.

The further development of art is as necessarily tied to the antagonism between these two natural artistic powers as the further development of man is to that between the sexes. Plenitude of power and moderation, the highest form of self-affirmation in a cool, noble, severe beauty: the Apollinianism of the Hellenic will.

This antithesis of the Dionysian and the Apollinian within the Greek soul is one of the great riddles to which I felt myself drawn when considering the nature of the Greeks. Fundamentally I was concerned with nothing except to guess why precisely Greek Apollinianism had to grow out of a Dionysian subsoil;

why the Dionysian Greek needed to become Apollinian; that is, to break his will to the terrible, multifarious, uncertain, frightful, upon a will to measure, to simplicity, to submission to rule and concept. The immoderate, disorderly Asiatic lies at his roots: the bravery of the Greek consists in his struggle with his Asiaticism; beauty is not given to him, as little as is logic or the naturalness of customs—it is conquered, willed, won by struggle—it is his *victory*.[96]

1051 (*1885*)

The highest and most illustrious human joys, in which existence celebrates its own transfiguration, come, as is reasonable, only to the rarest and best-constituted men; and even to these only when they themselves and their ancestors have lived long, preparatory lives directed to this goal, and not even in the knowledge of this goal. Then an overflowing wealth of the most multifarious forces and the most dextrous power of "free willing" and lordly command dwell amicably together in one man; the spirit is then as much at home in the senses as the senses are at home in the spirit; and whatever takes place in the spirit must enkindle a subtle extraordinary happiness and play in the senses. And also the other way around! Consider this reverse process in the case of Hafiz; even Goethe, however much more faintly, gives us an idea of this occurrence. It is probable that with such perfect and well-constituted men the most sensual functions are finally transfigured by a symbol-intoxication of the highest spirituality: they experience a kind of deification of the body in themselves and are as distant as possible from the ascetic philosophy of the proposition "God is a spirit"—and this shows clearly that

---

[96] Nietzsche first introduced the contrast of the Dionysian and Apollinian in *The Birth of Tragedy*, his first book. In his later works there are relatively few references to the Apollinian, and the Dionysian comes to be contrasted more and more with the Christian, as in section 1,052 below. The spirit of these two juxtapositions is not at all the same, and the conception of the Dionysian changes accordingly. In the former contrast, neither element is given preference: note, e.g., the penultimate paragraph of section 1,050. In the later contrast, Nietzsche uses Dionysus as the symbol of his own world view.

These reflections on *The Birth of Tragedy*—apparently in connection with the section on that book in *Ecce Homo*—help our understanding of Nietzsche's first work.

the ascetic is the "ill-constituted man," who calls good only a something-in-itself, and indeed a something that judges and condemns—and also calls it "God."

From that height of joy where man feels himself to be altogether a deified form and a self-justification of nature, down to the joy of healthy peasants and healthy half-human animals, this whole, long, tremendous light and color scale of happiness, the Greeks, not without the grateful shudder of him who is initiated into a mystery, not without much caution and pious silence, called by the divine name: *Dionysus*.— What do any latter-day men, the children of a fragmentary, multifarious, sick, strange age, know of the *range* of Greek happiness; what *could* they know of it! Whence would the slaves of "modern ideas" derive a right to Dionysian festivals!

When the Greek body and the Greek soul "bloomed," and not in conditions of morbid exaltation and madness, there arose that mysterious symbol of the highest world-affirmation and transfiguration of existence that has yet been attained on earth. Here we have a standard by which everything that has grown up since is found too short, too poor, too narrow. One only needs to pronounce the word "Dionysus" in the presence of the best latter-day names and things, in the presence of Goethe perhaps, or Beethoven, or Shakespeare, or Raphael—at once we feel that our best things and moments have been *judged*. Dionysus is a *judge!*— Have I been understood?

There can be no doubt that the Greeks sought to interpret the ultimate mysteries "of the destiny of the soul" and everything they knew concerning education and purification, above all concerning the immovable order of rank and inequality of value between man and man, on the basis of their Dionysian experiences: here is the great depth, the great silence, in all matters Greek—*one does not know the Greeks* as long as this hidden subterranean entrance lies blocked. Importunate scholar's eyes will never see anything in these things, however much scholarship still has to be employed in this excavation. Even the noble zeal of such friends of antiquity as Goethe and Winckelmann here has something unpermitted, even immodest about it.

To wait and to prepare oneself; to await the emergence of new sources; to prepare oneself in solitude for strange faces and voices; to wash one's soul ever cleaner from the marketplace dust and noise of this age; to *overcome* everything Christian through something supra-Christian, and not merely to put it aside—for the Christian doctrine was the counterdoctrine to the Dionysian; to rediscover the South in one and to spread out above one a bright, glittering, mysterious southern sky; to reconquer southern health and hidden powerfulness of soul; step by step to become more comprehensive, more supranational, more European, more Near Eastern, finally more *Greek*—for the Greek was the first great union and synthesis of everything Near Eastern, and on that account the *inception* of the European soul, the discovery of *our "new world"*: whover lives under such imperatives, who knows what he may not encounter one day? Perhaps—a *new day*!

1052 (*March-June 1888*)

The two types: Dionysus and the Crucified.[97]— To determine: whether the typical *religious* man [is][98] a form of decadence (the great innovators are one and all morbid and epileptic); but are we not here omitting one type of religious man, the *pagan*? Is the pagan cult not a form of thanksgiving and affirmation of life? Must its highest representative not be an apology for and deification of life? The type of a well-constituted and ecstatically overflowing spirit! The type of a spirit[99] that takes into itself and *redeems* the contradictions and questionable aspects of existence!

It is here I set the *Dionysus* of the Greeks: the religious affirmation of life, life whole and not denied or in part; (typical —that the sexual act arouses profundity, mystery,[100] reverence).

Dionysus versus the "Crucified": there you have the anti-

---

[97] The last section of *Ecce Homo* reads, in full: "—Have I been understood?— *Dionysus versus the Crucified* . . ."

[98] The word "is" was supplied by the German editors.

[99] In the MS *Typus,* which the German editors very sensibly changed to *Geist.* This does not mean that the MS reads: "The type of a type"; the whole clause that follows "spirit" appears in the German original between *Typus* and *Typus,* which makes the slip readily understandable.

[100] The reading of "mystery" is uncertain; but see section 148 above. The same idea is found in *The Birth of Tragedy,* at the beginning of section 8, and above all in section 4 of the last chapter of *Twilight* (*Portable Nietzsche,* p. 561 *f*). But Aristophanes and some Greek vase paintings suggest a somewhat different perspective.

thesis. It is *not* a difference in regard to their martyrdom—it is a difference in the meaning of it. Life itself, its eternal fruitfulness and recurrence, creates torment, destruction, the will to annihilation. In the other case, suffering—the "Crucified as the innocent one"—counts as an objection to this life, as a formula for its condemnation.— One will see that the problem is that of the meaning of suffering: whether a Christian meaning or a tragic meaning. In the former case, it is supposed to be the path to a holy existence; in the latter case, being is counted as *holy enough* to justify even a monstrous amount of suffering. The tragic man affirms even the harshest suffering: he is sufficiently strong, rich, and capable of deifying to do so. The Christian denies even the happiest lot on earth: he is sufficiently weak, poor, disinherited to suffer from life in whatever form he meets it. The god on the cross is a curse on[101] life, a signpost to seek redemption from life; Dionysus cut to pieces is a *promise* of life: it will be eternally reborn and return again from destruction.[102]

---

[101] In the MS the definite article, needed in German before "life," is missing, but it was added by the German editors and appears in all editions.

In sum: this section is in many ways typical of the whole book. It was written in extreme haste, and it would be an understatement to say that it was not polished for publication; but for all that it is remarkable—as a document that aids our understanding of Nietzsche, as a prose passage, and for the ideas it expresses.

Schlechta's edition, as usual, does not follow the MS but the standard editions, ignoring the information furnished in 1911 (p. 514 in this case).

[102] According to 1911, p. 514, this note is followed in the MS by a draft for *Beyond Good and Evil,* section 56.

III. THE ETERNAL RECURRENCE

1053 (*1884*)

My philosophy brings the triumphant idea of which all other modes of thought will ultimately perish. It is the great cultivating idea: the races that cannot bear it stand condemned; those who find it the greatest benefit are chosen to rule.

1054 (*1885-1886*)

The *greatest* of struggles: for this a new weapon is needed.

The hammer: to provoke a fearful decision, to confront Europe with the consequences: whether its will "wills" destruction.

Prevention of reduction to mediocrity. Rather destruction!

1055 (*1885*)

A pessimistic teaching and way of thinking, an ecstatic nihilism, can under certain conditions be indispensable precisely to the philosopher—as a mighty pressure and hammer with which he breaks and removes degenerate and decaying races to make way for a new order of life, or to implant into that which is degenerate and desires to die a longing for the end.

1056 (*1884*)

It want to teach the idea that gives many the right to erase themselves—the great *cultivating* idea.

1057 (*1883-1888*)

The eternal recurrence. A prophecy.[103]

1. Presentation of the doctrine and its *theoretical* presuppositions and consequences.
2. Proof of the doctrine.
3. Probable consequences of its being *believed* (it makes everything *break open*).
   a) Means of enduring it;

---

[103] In the MS: "A Book of Prophecy." According to 1911, p. 514, this section represents the plan for a book, *The Eternal Recurrence*.

b) Means of disposing of it.

4. Its place in history as a *mid-point.*

Period of greatest danger.

Foundation of an oligarchy *above* peoples and their interests: education to a universally human politics.

Counterpart of Jesuitism.

1058 (*1883-1888*)

The two greatest philosophical points of view (devised by Germans):

a) that of *becoming,* of *development.*

b) that according to the *value of existence* (but the wretched form of German pessimism must first be overcome!)—both brought together my me in a *decisive* way.

Everything becomes and recurs eternally— escape is impossible!— Supposing we *could* judge value, what follows? The idea of recurrence as a *selective* principle, in the service of strength (and barbarism!!).

Ripeness of man for this idea.

1059 (*1884*)

1. The idea [of the eternal recurrence]:[104] the presuppositions that would have to be true if it were true. Its consequences.

2. As the *hardest* idea: its probable effect if it were not prevented, i.e., if all values were not revalued.

3. Means of *enduring it*: the revaluation of all values. No longer joy in certainty but in uncertainty; no longer "cause and effect" but the continually creative; no longer will to preservation but to power; no longer the humble expression, "everything is *merely* subjective," but "it is also *our* work!— Let us be proud of it!"

1060 (*1884*)

To *endure* the idea of the recurrence one needs: freedom from morality; new means against the fact of *pain* (pain con-

[104] The words I have placed in brackets were supplied by the German editors.

ceived as a tool, as the father of pleasure; there is no cumulative consciousness of displeasure); the enjoyment of all kinds of uncertainty, experimentalism, as a counterweight to this extreme fatalism; abolition of the concept of necessity; abolition of the "will"; abolition of "knowledge-in-itself."

Greatest elevation of the consciousness of strength in man, as he creates the overman.

1061 (*1887-1888*)

The two most extreme modes of thought—the mechanistic and the Platonic—are reconciled in the *eternal recurrence*: both as ideals.

1062 (*1885*)

If the world had a goal, it must have been reached. If there were for it some unintended final state, this also must have been reached. If it were in any way capable of a pausing and becoming fixed, of "being," if in the whole course of its becoming it possessed even for a moment this capability of "being," then all becoming would long since have come to an end, along with all thinking, all "spirit." The fact of "spirit" as a form of becoming proves that the world has no goal, no final state, and is incapable of being.

The old habit, however, of associating a goal with every event and a guiding, creative God with the world, is so powerful that it requires an effort for a thinker not to fall into thinking of the very aimlessness of the world as intended. This notion—that the world intentionally avoids a goal and even knows artifices for keeping itself from entering into a circular course—must occur to all those who would like to force on the world the ability for *eternal novelty,* i.e., on a finite, definite, unchangeable force of constant size, such as the world is, the miraculous power of infinite novelty in its forms and states. The world, even if it is no longer a god, is still supposed to be capable of the divine power of creation, the power of infinite transformations; it is supposed to consciously prevent itself from returning to any of its old forms; it is supposed to possess not only the intention but the *means* of avoiding any repetition; to that end, it is supposed to control every one of its movements at every moment so as to escape goals, final states, repetitions—and whatever else may follow from such an unforgiveably insane way of thinking and desiring. It is still the old religious way of thinking and desiring, a kind of longing to believe that *in some way* the world is after all like the old beloved, infinite, boundlessly creative God—that in some way "the old God still lives"—that longing of Spinoza which was expressed in the words *"deus sive natura"*[105] (he even felt *"natura sive deus"*).

What, then, is the law and belief with which the decisive change, the recently attained preponderance of the scientific spirit over the religious, God-inventing spirit, is most clearly formulated? Is it not: the world, as force, may not be thought of as unlimited, for it *cannot* be so thought of; we forbid ourselves the concept of an infinite force as incompatible with the concept "force." Thus —the world also lacks the capacity for eternal novelty.

1063 (*1886-1887*)

The law of the conservation of energy demands *eternal recurrence.*

1064 (*1885*)

That a state of equilibrium is never reached proves that it is not possible. But in an indefinite space it would have to have been reached. Likewise in a spherical space. The *shape* of space must be the cause of eternal movement, and ultimately of all "imperfection."

That "force" and "rest," "remaining the same," contradict one another. The measure of force (as magnitude) as fixed, but its essence in flux.[106]

"Timelessness" to be rejected. At any precise moment of a force, the absolute conditionality of a new distribution of all its forces is given: it cannot stand still. "Change" belongs to the essence, therefore also temporality: with this, however, the necessity of change has only been posited once more conceptually.

1065 (*Nov. 1887-March 1888*)

A certain emperor always bore in mind the transitoriness of

---

[105] God or nature.

[106] The MS continues: "in tension, compelling."

all things so as not to take them too seriously and to live at peace among them. To me, on the contrary, everything seems far too valuable to be so fleeting: I seek an eternity for everything: ought one to pour the most precious salves and wines into the sea?— My consolation is that everything that has been is eternal: the sea will cast it up again.

1066 (*March-June 1888*)

The new world-conception.— The world exists; it is not something that becomes, not something that passes away. Or rather: it becomes, it passes away, but it has never begun to become and never ceased from passing away—it maintains itself in both.— It lives on itself: its excrements are its food.

We need not worry for a moment about the hypothesis of a *created* world. The concept "create" is today completely indefinable,[107] unrealizable; merely a word, a rudimentary survival from the ages of superstition; one can explain nothing with a mere word. The last attempt to conceive a world that had a beginning has lately been made several times with the aid of logical procedures—generally, as one may divine, with an ulterior theological motive.

Lately one has sought several times to find a contradiction in the concept "temporal infinity of the world in the past" (*regressus in infinitum*): one has even found it, although at the cost of confusing the head with the tail. Nothing can prevent me from reckoning backward from this moment and saying "I shall never reach the end"; just as I can reckon forward from the same moment into the infinite. Only if I made the mistake—I shall guard against it—of equating this correct concept of a *regressus in infinitum* with an utterly unrealizable concept of a finite *progressus* up to this present, only if I suppose that the direction (forward or backward) is logically a matter of indifference, would I take the head—this moment—for the tail: I shall leave that to you, my dear Herr Dühring!—

I have come across this idea in earlier thinkers: every time it was determined by other ulterior considerations (—mostly theological, in favor of the *creator spiritus*). If the world could in any way become rigid, dry, dead, *nothing*, or if it could reach a

---

[107] This word is illegible.

state of equilibrium, or if it had any kind of goal that involved duration, immutability, the once-and-for-all (in short, speaking metaphysically: if becoming *could* resolve itself into being or into nothingness), then this state must have been reached. But it has not been reached: from which it follows—

This is the sole certainty we have in our hands to serve as a corrective to a great host of world hypotheses possible in themseves. If, e.g., the mechanistic theory cannot avoid the consequence, drawn for it by William Thomson,[108] of leading to a final state, then the mechanistic theory stands refuted.

If the world may be thought of as a certain definite quantity of force and as a certain definite number of centers of force—and every other representation remains indefinite and therefore useless —it follows that, in the great dice game of existence, it must pass through a calculable number of combinations. In infinite time, every possible combination would at some time or another be realized; more: it would be realized an infinite number of times. And since between every combination and its next recurrence all other possible combinations would have to take place, and each of these combinations conditions the entire sequence of combinations in the same series, a circular movement of absolutely identical series is thus demonstrated: the world as a circular movement that has already repeated itself infinitely often and plays its game *in infinitum.*

This conception is not simply a mechanistic conception; for if it were that, it would not condition an infinite recurrence of identical cases, but a final state. *Because* the world has not reached this, mechanistic theory must be considered an imperfect and merely provisional hypothesis.

1067[109] (*1885*)

And do you know what "the world" is to me? Shall I show

---

[108] First Baron Kelvin (1824-1907), British physicist and mathematician who introduced the Kelvin or Absolute Scale of temperature.

For Nietzsche's argument see also section 55 above, as well as my *Nietzsche,* Chapter 11, section II, and my article on Nietzsche in the *Encyclopedia of Philosophy,* ed. Paul Edwards, New York, 1967.

[109] Most of this section was written by Nietzsche over an earlier version that he had crossed out. The earlier version is printed in the first edition of 1901 as # 385, and again in 1911, p. 515.

it to you in my mirror? This world: a monster of energy, without beginning, without end; a firm, iron magnitude of force that does not grow bigger or smaller, that does not expend itself but only transforms itself; as a whole, of unalterable size, a household without expenses or losses, but likewise without increase or income; enclosed by "nothingness" as by a boundary; not something blurry or wasted, not something endlessly extended, but set in a definite space as a definite force, and not a space that might be "empty" here or there, but rather as force throughout, as a play of forces and waves of forces, at the same time one and many, increasing here and at the same time decreasing there; a sea of forces flowing and rushing together, eternally changing, eternally flooding back, with tremendous years of recurrence, with an ebb and a flood of its forms; out of the simplest forms striving toward the most complex, out of the stillest, most rigid, coldest forms toward the hottest, most turbulent, most self-contradictory, and then again returning home to the simple out of this abundance, out of the play of contradictions back to the joy of concord, still affirming itself in this uniformity of its courses and its years, blessing itself as that which must return eternally, as a becoming that knows no satiety, no disgust, no weariness: this, my *Dionysian* world of the eternally self-creating, the eternally self-destroying, this mystery world of the twofold voluptuous delight, my "beyond good and evil," without goal, unless the joy of the circle is itself a goal; without will, unless a ring feels good will toward itself—do you want a *name* for this world? A *solution* for all its riddles? A *light* for you, too, you best-concealed, strongest, most intrepid, most midnightly men?— *This world is the will to power—and nothing besides!* And you yourselves are also this will to power—and nothing besides!

APPENDIX

Commentary on the FACSIMILES

In the Bibliography of my *Nietzsche* (Princeton, N. J., Princeton University Press, 1950), which was omitted in the paperback edition (New York, Meridian Books, 1956), I stated:

> "Any work on Nietzsche might seem merely provisional, pending the publication of all hitherto suppressed words and sentences. Such an inference, however, would be unwarranted. The principles which guided Gast and Frau Förster-Nietzsche in making omissions are very plain—from their published Nietzsche interpretations, from the explanations which accompany some of the omissions (WM [*Der Wille zur Macht*]), from the context, and from the nature of those censored passages which have been published from time to time; e.g., by Hofmiller and Podach. Some unkind comments on Frau Förster-Nietzsche, Richard Wagner, anti-Semitism, the German *Reich*, and Christianity were suppressed; but there is no reason whatever for believing that the hitherto withheld material includes anything of significance that would have corroborated Frau Förster-Nietzsche's version of her brother's thought. It is therefore quite unlikely that future editions of Nietzsche's works will necesitate any radical revision of an interpretation which does justice to the material so far published" (p. 385).

In spite of the attention Karl Schlechta's edition of Nietzsche's works received in the popular press, and notwithstanding uninformed and misleading reviews of Podach's last two works in some leading American philosophical periodicals, nothing that has been brought to light from Nietzsche's manuscripts from 1950 until 1966 is of any philosophical importance. I have dealt in detail with this matter in an article on "Nietzsche in the Light of His Suppressed Manuscripts," in *Journal of the History of Philosophy*, October 1964 (II.2), pp. 205-225, which will be included in a forthcoming third revised edition of my *Nietzsche*. There is no need for covering the same ground here. But I present the selections from Nietzsche's notebooks that have become known as *The Will to Power*, without feeling apologetic about not having spent years studying the manuscripts in Weimar. Let others do that; let philological cleanliness flourish! But I doubt that the results will be philosophically rewarding. For all my interest in Nietzsche, I still believe as firmly as ever that the books he finished are his legacy, and that his notebooks are of secondary interest—as I explained in section I of the second chapter of my *Nietzsche*. Far from feeling any keen desire to know everything he ever jotted down, I feel more nearly like an intruder when I scrutinize a manuscript page, trying to decipher some note that was never intended to be read by anyone else, much less to be published.

To do a decent job on notes that have long been in print is one thing—many of them are extremely interesting, but the way in which they have been published so far is open to many objections. I am offering a translation with notes that are intended to clarify both the nature of this material and hundreds of particular points. But going out of one's way to dredge up a few more personal remarks that have not been published so far is not a job that appeals to me. Nietzsche's view of Wagner, Germans, anti-Semites, and Christians are on record in his books; *The Will to Power* contains much similar material, and so do the notes not incorporated in *The Will to Power* but included in the Grossoktav edition and the Musarion edition of his works. There is no need to spice this volume with a few allegedly sensational revelations, *alla tedesca* (to use a phrase from *Ecce Homo*, second chapter, first section), in the manner that has become popular in Germany.

Nevertheless, I am including in this volume (preceding the text) several facsimile pages. In *The Will to Power* there was some indication that in a few places something had been omitted, or that a section consisted of an excerpt from a longer note. In these cases I requested photostats of the manuscript pages from the *Goethe-Schiller Archiv* in Weimar, in East Germany, where the manuscripts that were formerly in the *Nietzsche Archiv* are now housed. After some correspondence, Professor Hahn, the Director, graciously sent me eight photostats, with permission to publish them—but this permission does not cover reproduction elsewhere.

These are not typical pages, nor pages picked at random: Each was requested because there was evidence that the previously printed texts were inadequate. These pages contain some material that has never been published before, either in German or in English; they also show the German editors at their arbitrary worst and—perhaps most important—they give the reader some idea of the appearance of the manuscripts. Those able to read some German may discover to their surprise how little they can decipher of these pages, and how difficult it is in places to decide in what order these notes should be printed. By way of contrast, Nietzsche's letters and finished manuscripts are often quite beautiful and, in general, not particularly difficult to read.

In keeping with what I have said, I shall not transcribe or translate these pages in full. Instead I shall offer a detailed but brief analysis of each page.

The Roman numerals below refer to the reproduced facsimile pages in the present volume. The alphabetic letters in parentheses do not appear on the facsimile pages but are given below to facilitate dicussion of lines within the facsimile pages.

Analysis of Facsimile Pages I-III

The first three pages are consecutive ones (46-48) from a notebook identified in the archives as W II, 1, Nr. 157. Approximate date: Spring-Fall, 1887.

I: The first seven lines (a) were published as the beginning of section 124 and are translated in the first seven lines of our edition.

The following six lines (b), assigned a different number by Nietzsche himself, have not been published to date.

The last eight lines (c), again set off by a different number by Nietzsche himself, constitute section 736, entire.

II: The first line ("The problem of civilization spirit everything") was not published.

A horizontal line across the page clearly divides what follows into two separate notes, of which the second has a title of its own. Yet Nietzsche assigned the number 80 to both—the same number he placed over the first seven lines on the preceding page, which were published as the beginning of section 124.

The German editors published lines 2-5 (d) as the continuation and conclusion of section 124 (the final paragraph in the present volume). Lines 6-10 (e), which comprise a separate paragraph in Nietzsche's MS, were omitted in the editions of 1906 and 1911, and in all subsequent editions. However this omission is not indicated in the editorial apparatus, 1911, p. 500. In the first edition of 1901, on the other hand, section 36 contains everything to which Nietzsche had assigned the number 80: the first seven lines on the preceding page, followed by all of the material on this page, excepting only the first line (which Nietzsche apparently did not mean to include), and the final sentence of the second paragraph, of which it was duly said in the editorial apparatus (p. 531): "A short sentence has been omitted here." A translation of the material not included in section 124 will be found in my note on that section.

The material below the horizontal line (f) was published as section 117. In 1911, p. 500, it is duly noted that the editors added five words at the end of this section (to clarify the meaning); but Schlechta follows the printed text, as usual, and not the MS.

III: The first eight lines (g), set off from what follows by a horizontal line across the page, were printed as section 883 (1901, section 439).

The next seven lines (h), not published in the edition of 1901, were published as section 612; and the immediately following two lines (i), though set off by another horizontal line and crossed out along with the last four lines on the page, were also published—as the conclusion of section 612.

The final four lines (j) were printed by Nietzsche himself, as the beginning of section 24 of "Skirmishes," in *Twilight of the Idols* (*Portable Nietzsche*, p. 529).

The editorial notes at the end of 1911 offer no comments on either section 883 or section 612.

A note on Schlechta's handling of this material:

In vol. III, Schlechta prints some of this material on pp. 531 *f*, in the following sequence: (a) and (d) as one note; (c); (f)—deviating from the MS as noted above; (h) and (i) as one note; and finally (g).

In sum: the way the notes on these three pages have been published is a mess; but as long as we keep in mind that we are dealing with mere notes, the arrangement is hardly very important, and even Nietzsche scholars did not lose much by the "suppression" of (b) and (e). For that matter, (e) was actually published in 1901, with the exception of one very dispensable sentence; and all of this material is included in my note on section 124.

Discovery: (b), published here for the first time, contains one remarkable aphorism, entitled "On the *Genealogy* of *Christianity* —It requires more courage and strength of character to turn back than to go on. *To turn back without* [?] *cowardice is more difficult than to go on with* [?] *cowardice*."

Facsimile Pages IV and V

These are consecutive pages (15-16) from a notebook identified in the archives as W II, 2, Nr. 158. Approximate date: Spring-Fall, 1887.

IV: The first seven lines (k), which form a unit and were assigned number 279 by Nietzsche, have not been published until now.

The rest of the material (l) on that page, which was assigned number 280 by Nietzsche, was printed as section 172, along with its continuation on the next page,

V: but a little less than two lines (m), beginning at the end of line 7 and ending with the second word of line 9, were deleted in print; and in 1911, p. 502, it is duly noted that "one sentence has been omitted here." It is not stated that a few words, added by Nietzsche in the lower right-hand corner, were also omitted, perhaps because they could not be deciphered with any assurance. The same comments apply to the corresponding section (119) in the edition of 1901.

(k) and (m) contain a few words that are extremely hard to decipher, but the over-all meaning is clear enough, and these "suppressed" passages add nothing of interest to what Nietzsche said in *The Antichrist*. In the following translations ". . ." indicates that I cannot read the writing with any certainty.

(k): *Salvation is of the Jews*—the founder of Christianity said (John 4.22) And one has *believed* this! ! !

If one admits to oneself the first impression or merely instinct [?]: . . . bad taste, bigots' sentimentality, nothing but repulsive symbols in the foreground; and the . . . air of the nook and conventicle:—one does *not* sympathize.—

Pilate, . . .

(m): In the whole history of the spirit there is no more brazen kind of lie, no more premeditated . . .

Facsimile Pages VI and VII

In the note on section 815 (1911, p. 512) we read: "A second part of this aphorism, dealing with Richard Wagner, has been omitted." Schlechta, who follows the printed versions without indicating any omission, as is his general practice, lends this section special emphasis by placing it at the end of his edition, leaving the last half of the page on which it ends blank, and then printing section 256, which comprises only two lines, on the facing page, centered.

VI is from Mp XVI, 3, Nr. 232, p. 17 (inside). Approximate date: Summer-Fall 1888. This is no mere note but a carefully written page with a great many corrections. What is crossed out is made illegible—this procedure was characteristic of Nietzsche—and the corrections are written very clearly, though the writing is very small because this material had to be squeezed between lines. Because of its smallness, some of it is not easy to read, especially in facsimile; but all of it can be deciphered with practical certainty.

The first nine and a half lines were printed as section 815 (section 367 in the edition of 1901); what follows has never been published so far. A complete translation follows, after a description of facsimile page VII.

VII is identified by the archives as W II, 4, Nr. 160, p. 19, and appears to be a draft for the second part of VI, with which it agrees literally in large part.

Translation of the Suppressed Second Part of Section 815

I take the most disagreeable case, the case of Wagner.— Wagner, under the spell of his incredibly pathological sexuality, which was the curse of his life, knew only too well what an artist forfeits when he loses his freedom, his *respect* for himself. He is condemned to be an actor. His very art becomes for him a constant attempt to escape, a means of self-oblivion, of self-narcosis—it eventually changes and determines the character of his art. Such an "unfree" man requires a hashish world, strange, heavy, enveloping vapors, every kind of exoticism and symbolism of the ideal, merely in order to be rid for once of his own reality—he requires Wagnerian music.— A certain catholicity of the ideal above all is almost sufficient proof in the case of an artist of self-contempt, of "morass": the case of Baudelaire in France, the case of Edgar Allan Poe in America, the case of Wagner in Germany.— Need I still add that Wagner also owes his *success* to his sensuality? that his music attracts the lowest instincts to him, to Wagner? that this holy conceptual vapor of the ideal, of three-eighths Catholicism, is one more art of seduction? (it permits one to expose oneself to the magic, ignorant, innocent, Christian—) Who would risk the word, the *proper* word, for the *ardeurs* of the *Tristan* music? I put on gloves when I read the score of *Tristan*.— Wagnerianism, which keeps spreading, is a relatively light epidemic of sensuality that "does not realize this"; against Wagnerian music every caution seems appropriate to me.

COMMENTS ON THE DRAFT (PAGE VII)

Compared with VI, which I have translated, the draft offers nothing of great interest. In the final version *respect* (*Achtung*: the word is emphasized by Nietzsche and therefore easy to locate, also in my translation) has been written above another word that has been crossed out: with the help of the draft, we can tell that the word Nietzsche crossed out was "reverence" (*Ehrfurcht*). Indeed, in the draft Nietzsche crossed out *Achtung* to substitute *Ehrfurcht*. In the end, he returned to "respect." There would be no point here to a more detailed comparison.

Facsimile Page VIII

Identified by the Archive as W II, 7, Nr. 163, p. 136. Approximate date: 1884. Lines 8-12 were printed as section 834 (section 61 in the edition of 1901). In the edition of 1911, but not in that of 1901, we find the comment (p. 512): "Taken from a note about Richard Wagner."

The last seven lines on this page were evidently put down at a later time; they comprise a separate note, and they are singularly difficult to decipher.

A partial translation of the note from which section 834 was excerpted follows: ". . ." indicates that I cannot decipher the writing with any certainty.

TRANSLATION

The impact of Wagner's art is deep; it is above all heavy, immensely heavy: why is this? The depth and above all heavy, immensely heavy impact of Wagner's art does not really belong to the music of Wagner: it is Wagner's general pathos with which his art overpowers; it is the tremendous persuasive power of his edifice, it is his holding his[1] breath, of his extreme feeling that refuses to let go, it is the frightening *length of his pathos* by virtue of which he triumphs and always will triumph.—Whether with such a pathos one is a "genius"? Or even *could* be one?—[At this point, section 834 follows, ending with a dash. Then the note proceeds:] Another question . . .: whether Wagner, precisely because he had such pathos, is German? is a German? Or does . . .

COMMENT

These are clearly hasty jottings that do not add up to an aphorism. If anyone wants to know what the later Nietzsche "really" thought of Wagner, he should begin by reading *The Case of Wagner* and *Nietzsche contra Wagner*. Next, he should look up the passages on Wagner in Nietzsche's other late works. Only then should one turn to Nietzsche's posthumously published notes and correspondence. Whoever has done all this, is not likely to feel any anxiety or indignation because he knows that there are still a few jottings in Nietzsche's notebooks that have not yet been published.

There are many topics with which Nietzsche never dealt as fully in his books as he did with Wagner, or with Christianity, or with the Germans: for example, but by no means only, some philosophical problems. And

---

[1] *Atemanhalten: anhalten* (holding) is the conjecture of Professor Michael Curschmann of the German Department at Princeton University, who also helped me by deciphering a few other words that had stumped me.

the editors had no reason to suppress interesting notes on the theory of knowledge, or on determinism, or on aesthetics. It is *this* material that makes *The Will to Power* important.

The palpable intent of the philosopher's sister to present *The Will to Power* as the systematic work that Nietzsche did not live to finish, was absurd. But the semi-systematic arrangement that allows us to read, one after another, a lot of notes that deal with related topics, jotted down over a period of time, may have the very opposite effect of that intended by her—at least when the material is presented in the manner attempted in the present volume. So far from finding any final system, we look into a vast studio, full of sketches, drafts, abandoned attempts, and unfinished dreams. And in the end we should be less tempted than ever to mistake a random quotation for an ultimate position. This is not to say that Nietzsche never arrived at any conclusions. He did, but to know what they were one has to read his books.

INDEX

The German editors' arrangement of Nietzsche's notes is far from ideal, and their table of contents is apt to give the false impression that those interested in morality, for example, need to turn only to sections 253-405. *Any* systematic arrangement of these notes would leave much to be desired; but the Index should help to give readers a more adequate idea of the contents of this volume.

Most of the work on this Index was done by Andrew Neal Sears in June, 1966, the month he graduated from Princeton University with high honors in philosophy. He made use of the work already done by Stephen R. Watson, and of a name index started some years ago by Stephen Brown, now M.D. It is a pleasure to express my gratitude to all three of them, and also to Princeton's excellent program of undergraduate research assistantships.

I supervised the work and at various stages made hundreds of additions.

Figures refer to sections, not to pages. **E** refers to the Editor's Introduction; **EC** to the editor's comments "On the Editions of *The Will to Power*"; **N** to Nietzsche's Preface; **n** to the editor's notes. For references to Nietzsche's works see Nietzsche.

Academy, 101
action, 45, 71, 139, 155, 210, 234**n**, 235, 279, 293, 294, 458, 516, 521, 556, 567, 569, 585, 589, 597, 617, 657, 661, 672, 673, 676, 737, 847, 881**n**, 908, 916, 925, 926, 928, 941, 944; man of, 853
Adam, 224
adiaphora, 444
aesthetic(s), 353, 416; state, 341, 801; taste, 469
affect, 56, 98, 132, 135, 139, 155, 196, 204, 254, 266, 279, 284, 315, 368, 383, 384, 386, 388, 432, 434, 453, 462, 477, 556, 573, 576, 613, 669, 670, 676, 688, 712, 719, 726, 780, 786, 811, 851, 864, 868, 889, 916, 924, 928-31, 953, 1024, 1033. *See also* passions
afterlife, 141, 167, 187, 189, 196, 247, 351
Alcuin the Anglo-Saxon, 977
Alexander the Great, 437, 751
Alfieri, Vittorio, 97
Allgeist, 708**n**
Almanach de Gotha, 942
altruism, 8, 30, 44, 52, 53, 62, 95, 120, 246, 253, 269, 275, 283, 286, 296, 297, 373, 653, 674, 681, 716, 771, 784-86, 809, 864, 889, 964
ambition, 751, 792, 942
American(s), 233**n**, 958
Amiel, Henri Frédéric, 270
amor fati, 1041
anarchism, 1, 42, 50, 59, 69, 79, 82, 125, 127, 235, 329, 373, 433, 435, 447, 753, 778, 784, 864, 877, 1020
Anaxagoras, 419, 427

Anaximander, 412, 419
ancestors, 137
animality, 529, 1019, 1045
anti-Semites, 89, 89**n**, 203**n**, 347, 835**n**, 864
Apollinian, 798, 799, 1049, 1050, 1050**n**
Apollo, 1049
appearance(s), 15, 17, 113, 303, 328, 407, 476, 516, 520, 521, 524, 545, 549, 552-69, 572, 578-81, 583, 585, 588, 589, 617, 619, 623, 680, 699, 708, 710, 711, 779, 853, 1011, 1019, 1047; logical, 521
Arab(s), 90, 191, 195, 204, 352, 940; Arabic, 170
Aristippus, 442
aristocracy, 53, 95, 100, 134, 182, 215, 317, 374, 431**n**2, 752, 755, 783, 864, 866, 926, 933, 936, 938, 942, 953, 960, 1021, 1049
Aristophanes, 380, 1052**n**
Aristotle, 373**n**, 449, 468, 516, 851, 852, 852**n**, 981**n**, 1029**n**; *Poetics*, 852**n**
art, artist(ic), 1, 27, 29, 30, 41, 50, 69, 78, 81, 82, 84, 97, 116, 120, 172, 209, 213, 215, 236, 274, 294, 296, 298, 374, 376, 379, 382, 401, 426, 427, 463, 463**n**, 464, 572, 585, 606, 612**n**, 617, 659, 677, 705, 775, 780, 794-853, 795**n**, 864, 864**n**, 869, 870, 873, 877, 943, 957, 960, 975, 1009**n**, 1018, 1039, 1040, 1046, 1048
Aryan, 141-43, 145, 145**n**
ascetic, 47, 1051; asceticism, 915, 916, 921, 940**n**
Asia, 91, 143; Asiatic, 1050
atavism, 358
atheist, 132, 151
Athens, 148, 197, 432, 747; Athenian, 429
atoms, 442, 488, 516, 551, 552, 624, 625, 634, 635, 636, 642, 689, 704, 715, 786
Augustine, St., 101, 214, 578, 862
Austrians, 104

Babylon, 143
Bacon of Verulam, 249, 468, 848
Balzac, Honoré, 943
barbarian(ism), 461, 684, 868, 870, 871, 899, 900, 921, 922, 940, 1058
Baroque, 842
Baudelaire, Charles, 94, Appendix
Bäumler, Alfred, E1, E3
beast of prey, 95, 98, 99, 127, 137, 238, 287, 397, 871, 959, 1027, 1027**n**
beauty, 1, 95, 120, 127, 221, 250, 266, 283, 298, 340, 395, 400, 416, 598**n**, 480, 495, 712**n**, 783**n**, 800, 800**n**, 803-5, 811, 822, 823, 852, 898, 1010, 1049, 1050
becoming, 4, 12, 51, 253, 277, 293, 412, 507, 513, 517-20, 438, 552, 556, 576, 578-81, 584, 585, 616, 617, 639, 708, 712, 715, 715**n**, 765, 786, 787, 846, 853, 1058, 1062, 1064, 1066, 1067
Beecher-Stowe, Harriet, 94
Beethoven, Ludwig van, 105, 106, 838, 842, 1051
being, 12, 15, 51, 68, 412, 485, 486, 488, 507, 513, 516-19, 529, 531, 538, 543, 552, 556, 562, 567, 568, 570, 572, 574, 576, 579-83, 585, 586, 588, 617, 631, 634-36, 659, 675, 689, 693, 708, 709, 711, 715, 715**n**, 737, 765, 786, 846, 1052, 1062, 1066
belief, 14, 15, 44, 69**n**, 266, 455, 456, 483, 484, 487, 491, 497, 506, 507, 511, 516, 518, 530-33, 550, 556, 585, 604, 659, 670, 962
Bernard, Claude, 47
Besinnung, 133**n**
Beyle, Henri, 105, 132, 544, 544**n**, 815
beyond good and evil, 55, 132, 259, 898, 980, 1005**n**, 1034, 1038, 1041, 1067
Bible, 134**n**, 171, 241, 242, 734. *See also* Old Testament; New Testament
Biedermann, 471
Bismarck, Otto von, 87, 128, 884
Bizet, Georges, *Carmen*, 835
Björnson, Björnstjerne, 86**n**
blame, *see* praise/blame
body, 30**n**, 48, 52, 113, 117, 118, 120, 126, 127, 148, 214, 226, 227, 229, 233, 255, 314, 334, 359, 377, 392, 400, 407-9, 419, 423, 453,

458, 461, 461**n**, 489, 491, 492, 500, 505, 507, 518, 521, 524, 529, 532, 547, 550, 563, 569, 581, 583-85, 659, 660, 674, 676, 679, 765, 820, 1013, 1016, 1045, 1046, 1051
Borgia, Cesare, 871
bourgeois, 94, 247, 943
Brahma, 145
Brahmins, 116**n**, 237
Brahms, Johannes, 105
Brandes, Georg, 86**n**
breeding, 397, 398, 462, 854-1067, 980**n**
Brosses, Président de, 103
Buckle, Henry Thomas, 876
Buddha, 31, 55, 154, 204, 239; Buddhism, Buddhistic, 1, 19, 23, 55, 64, 69**n**, 82, 145, 151, 155, 159, 167, 179, 196, 204, 220, 240, 342, 580, 685, 853; Buddhists, 154, 191, 204, 437, 458; European, 55, 132
Bunyan, John, 862
Byron, Lord, 62, 100, 103

Caesar, Julius, 380, 544, 684, 751, 776, 975, 1026
Caesar with Christ's soul, 983, 983**n**
Cagliostro, Alessandro, 428
Caliph of Morocco, 917
Camus, Albert, E2, 235**n**, 850**n**
Caracalla, 874
Carlyle, Thomas, 27, 343, 455, 747, 968, 968**n**
Carlylism, 312
castration, 204, 248, 351, 383
catharsis, 851, 852
causalism, 69, 244, 288, 327, 347, 523, 524, 545-52, 550**n**, 554, 635, 689**n**, 1019
causality, 55, 477, 478, 483, 497, 532, 553, 572, 575, 579, 627, 638, 645, 658, 664, 689, 711
cause, 1, 17, 27, 31, 70, 95, 135, 461, 484, 488, 497, 529, 545, 547, 624, 627**n**, 632, 645, 666, 667, 669, 670, 689, 690, 699, 701; and effect, 41**n**, 44, 135, 136, 141, 229, 334, 479, 520, 526, 531, 550, 554, 561, 562, 569, 589, 617, 620, 631, 633, 634, 667, 676, 688, 689, 689**n**, 1059; will as, 478
certainty, 587, 588
Chamfort, Sébastien Roch Nicolas, 772
chance, 673, 685
chandala(s), 50, 116, 116**n**, 139, 145, 184, 237
change, *see* becoming
Charlemagne, 101
chastity, 947
Chateaubriand, 103
cheerfulness, 990, 991, 1040
Chinese, China, 90, 127, 129, 191, 216, 274, 395, 745, 864; Chinadom, 866
choc, 699, 778
Christianity, Christian(s), 1, 4, 17, 18**n**, 30, 30**n**, 31, 44, 51, 62, 69**n**, 80, 83, 87-91, 94, 101, 102, 116, 130, 134-36, 143, 145, 145**n**, 147-52, 154-56, 158-252, 175**n**, 253, 258, 268, 312, 334, 339, 340, 342, 349, 351, 361, 362, 373, 377, 383, 383**n**, 388, 396, 419, 427, 436, 438, 525, 572, 578, 644, 684, 685, 747, 765, 781, 786, 812, 822, 840, 841, 845, 851, 853, 861, 862, 916, 917, 923, 929, 940, 957, 1005, 1016, 1017, 1021, 1042, 1050**n**, 1051, 1052, Appendix; pagan-Christian, 147. *See also* church
church, 30, 158-160, 165**n**, 167-69, 172, 175, 177, 181, 191, 199, 209, 213, 224, 233, 242, 247, 351, 381, 388, 394, 784, 824, 871, 916, 1015; Church Fathers, 464
Cicero, 420
Cimarosa, Domenico, *Matrimonio Segreto,* 105
Circe, 808; Circe of philosophers, 461
civilization, 121, 122, 382, 395, 461, 864, 871, 896
classical; style, 186, 196, 341, 799, 838, 842, 847-49, 1041; taste, 175, 868
Columbus, Christopher, 957
commanders, *see* legislators
communication, 569, 809-811
communist, 51
Comorro, 355
compassion, *see* pity
Comte, August, 95, 127, 340, 467, 468, 901
concepts, 409, 419, 427, 430, 488,

concepts (*cont'd.*)
506, 516, 521, 522, 579, 583, 605
Confucius, 129
Congo, 922
conscience, 141, 233, 234, 250, 265, 270, 282, 283, 294, 295, 389, 405, 452, 464, 869, 898, 970, 972, 1009
conscious(ness), 68, 72, 218, 289, 400, 423, 434, 439, 440, 472, 474-80, 486, 489, 490, 502, 504, 505, 523-29, 564, 585, 636, 674, 676, 707, 708, 711, 765, 799, 1007
contempt for what one loves, 919
Continentals, 722. *See also* Europe(ans)
control, 383, 384, 928, 933
Copernicus, Nicholas, 1; Copernican, 789
Corsican(s), 90, 204, 722, 925, 928
counterfeit(ing), 338, 379, 394, 414, 453, 696, 704, 824, 851
Counter-Reformation, 419
Counter-Renaissance, 842
courage, 25, 25**n**, 33, 318, 458, 465, 841, 852, 862, 898, 907, 916, 918, 928, 929, 949, 1013, 1017, 1041
cowardice, error is, 1041
criminal, 41, 42, 50, 54**n**, 116, 130, 135, 162, 233, 235, 285, 292, 374, 736**n**, 739, 740, 765, 788, 845, 864, 928, 951
Crucified, the, versus Dionysus, 401, 1034, 1052
culture, 121, 122, 151, 199, 200, 250, 373, 380, 417, 427, 462, 464, 684, 841, 864, 883, 898, 933, 1017, 1019, 1025
custom, 283, 283**n**, 437**n**, 871, 957, 984**n**

Damocles, 770
Dancourt, Florent Carton, Sieur d'Ancourt, 120
danger(ous), 276-78, 280, 304, 383, 387, 393, 395, 425, 465, 576, 856, 864, 881, 896, 912, 915, 929, 929**n**, 933, 939, 945, 949, 957, 972, 976, 985, 1019, 1057
Dante, Alighieri, 1018, 1030, 1030**n**; *Divina Commedia,* 852
Darwin, Charles, 130, 134**n**, 647, 684, 685; Darwinism, 69, 243, 253, 401, 422, 649; Darwinists, English and German, 410
David (King), 427
death, 224, 231, 247, 407, 581, 582, 916, 982
decadence, 13, 38-45, 49, 53, 54, 56, 62, 68, 85, 88, 90, 119, 122, 153, 171, 173, 174, 180, 225, 233, 236, 239, 268, 282, 339, 401, 423, 427, 428, 432, 433, 435, 437, 442, 444, 461, 584, 586, 684, 685, 695, 734, 765, 794, 800, 815, 838, 842, 851, 852, 864, 899, 1052
Delacroix, Ferdinand Victor Eugène, 103, 105
democracy, 69**n**, 86**n**, 125, 128-30, 132, 215, 253, 712, 725, 728, 751-53, 762, 765, 783, 824, 854, 887, 900, 954, 957, 960
Democritus, 419, 427, 428, 437, 443
Descartes, Renè, 95, 436, 468, 484, 533, 577, 578
desires, *see* passion(s)
determinism, 95, 141, 288, 552, 786
dialectic, 430-32, 434-37, 441, 442, 446, 507, 529, 578, 1047
Diaspora, 175
dichten, 544**n**
Diogenes, 464
Dionysus, Dionysian, 167, 196, 383**n**, 401, 417, 463**n**, 544, 798, 799, 800, 846, 853, 1003-1052, especially, 1049-1052, 1050**n**, 1052**n**
disciples, 910
discipline, 854-1067, 980**n**
domestication, 121, 123, 128, 156, 236-38, 281, 397, 398, 461, 684, 871, 957
Dostoevsky, Fyodor Mikhailovich, 82, 233, 434, 735**n**, 736**n**, 740, 788, 821; *Crime and Punishment,* 735**n**, 740**n**
drives, *see* passion(s)
Dühring, Eugen, 130, 792, 1066

Edda, 830
education, 888, 912, 916, 933, 980
ego, 30, 252, 296, 353, 362, 363, 364, 369, 370, 371, 372, 373, 481-92,

517, 518, 519, 533, 574, 581, 585, 635, 659, 676, 682, 768, 785, 786, 918
egoism, 8, 30, 62, 167, 216, 253, 283, 296, 353, 362-64, 368-73, 389, 426, 453, 677, 728, 755, 771, 777, 784-86, 873, 918; mass, 246
Egypt(ians), 143, 202, 427
Eichendorff, Joseph von, 106
Eliot, George, 18**n**
Empedocles, 419
ends and/or means, 12, 36, 74, 142, 155, 260, 272, 298, 354, 503, 552, 574, 576, 584, 589, 610, 666, 669, 671, 674, 675, 681, 707-9, 711, 766, 778, 784, 786, 787
England, 747; English, 18**n**, 30, 31, 101, 130, 410, 830, 831, 925**n**, 930; Englishman, 925, 930**n**, 958
enlightenment, 91, 96, 943
environment, 49, 69, 95, 353, 647, 765, 886, 970
Epictetus, 411
Epicurus, 196, 428, 434, 437, 438, 442, 578, 911; "garden of," 225; Epicureanism, 225, 1029; Epicureans, 449
epistemology, 95, 101, 253, 407, 409, 410, 417, 423, 425, 426, 437, 442, 444, 447, 449, 450, 452, 455, 457, 458, 462, 466-617, 668, 1035. *See also* knowledge
equality, 30, 52, 53, 80, 86, 129, 215, 246, 278, 278**n**, 280, 283, 285, 315, 339, 354, 364, 373, 398, 464, 500, 501, 510-512, 515, 532, 723, 725, 748, 752, 753, 765, 773, 775, 783, 784, 860, 864, 871, 874, 887, 898, 923, 925, 926, 936, 957, 988, 1051
erdichten, 544**n**
error(s), 1, 266, 397, 402, 403, 411, 416, 448-60, 472, 493, 520, 521, 535, 544, 579, 612, 705, 784; is cowardice, 1041
Eschenbach, Wolfram von, 322
Eskimos, 181
eternal recurrence, **E**1, 55, 417, 462, 617, 617**n**, 1041, 1050, 1053-1067; *Eternal Recurrence, The,* 1057**n**
ethics, *see* morality
eudaemonism, *see* happiness
Europe(an)(s), **N**2, **N**3, 1-134, 143, 191, 240-42, 258, 273, 274, 276, 367, 389, 395, 405, 419, 463, 732, 747-49, 762, 765, 783, 861, 862, 868, 898, 918, 922, 954, 955, 957, 960, 1051, 1054; nihilism, **N**2, **N**3, 1-134, 69**n**
evaluations, *see* valuations
evil, 4, 47, 98, 123, 141, 155, 244, 248, 259, 265, 270, 277, 283, 284, 288, 290, 291, 298, 315, 331, 334, 338, 342, 345, 351, 354, 355, 355**n**, 362-390, 411, 416, 427, 443, 576, 578, 684, 707, 786, 788, 850, 869, 870, 881, 908, 912, 928, 988, 1015, 1019, 1025, 1026, 1035, 1046
evolution, 12, 373, 386, 391-98, 403, 412, 521, 538, 647, 666, 684, 685, 688, 690, 707, 709, 711, 747, 881, 897, 956, 957
exception(al)s, 27, 215, 235, 252, 274, 280, 283, 316, 317, 345, 401, 423, 726, 804, 829, 864, 893, 894, 896, 933, 943**n**, 983, 1009, 1041,
exhaustion, 48-50, 54, 54**n**, 71, 84, 229-31, 240, 354, 401, 812, 822, 864, 887, 1012; the exhausted, 461
explanation, 171
extreme, seduction of, 749

fact, 70, 120, 472, 475, 477, 481, 486, 521, 526, 549, 556, 604, 605
faith, 253, 354, 358, 377, 380, 452, 455, 455**n**, 456-58, 579, 635, 786, 853, 963, 975, 1015, 1034
familiar, 664
family, 59; family theory, 137. *See also* marriage
fasting, 916
fatalism, 850; joyous, 95
Faust, *see* Goethe; Faustian, 800
feast, 916
Féré, Charles, 809
Ferney, Squire of, 100, 100**n**. *See also* Voltaire
Feuerbach, Ludwig, 585**n**
Flaubert, Gustave, 82**n**, 105, 815
Florence, 747; Florentine taste, 829
Fontane, Theodor, 103
force, 13, 70, 69**n**, 109, 260, 266,

force (*cont'd.*)
310, 386, 417, 490, 537, 545, 550-52, 562, 567, 568, 576, 619-21, 626, 629, 631, 632, 636, 638, 639, 641, 642, 644, 647, 650, 660, 664, 665, 668, 673, 677, 686, 687-89, 703, 704, 719, 750, 762, 769, 779, 781, 784, 786, 798, 803, 812, 815, 842, 850, 852, 863, 883, 895, 931, 1022, 1062, 1064, 1066, 1067
form, 521, 530, 568, 572, 574, 584
Förster-Nietzsche, Elisabeth, **EC**, E1, **E**3, Appendix
Fouillée, Alfred, 782, 782**n**
France, French, **E**, 49, 87, 92, 94, 98, 101, 105, 106, 367, 422, 829, 831, 838, 842, 849, 864; music, 101, 833, 835; Revolution, 60, 90, 94, 101, 184, 382, 864, 877
Francis of Assisi, St., 221, 360
Frederick the Great, King, 280**n**, 380
Frederick II, Emperor, 871
Frederick III, 124**n**
freedom, 2, 8, 8**n**, 14, 17, 62, 79, 84, 86, 93, 124, 137, 209, 224, 235, 283, 288, 289, 313, 340, 380, 397, 411, 418, 428, 435**n**, 442, 455, 464, 551, 552, 578, 579, 705, 720, 728, 736, 765, 770, 774, 776, 784, 786, 787, 789, 811, 823, 834, 842, 859, 883, 918, 921, 923, 936, 937**n**, 957, 1005**n**, 1038, 1050
Freud, Sigmund, 336**n**, 588**n**
Friedländer, Paul, 958**n**
Fromentin, Eugène, 78

Galiani, Abbé Ferdinand, 91, 127, 133, 989
Gast, Peter, **EC**, 29**n**, 91**n**, 133**n**, 422**n**, 604**n**, 619**n**, 675**n**, 689**n**, 708**n**, 716**n**, 772**n**, 853**n**
Gautier, Théophile, 82**n**, 103, 815
Gavarni, 82**n**
Geist, 984**n**
genius, 27, 70, 94, 95, 215, 297, 379, 382, 396, 440, 684, 812, 823, 831, 853, 864, 876, 989, 994; artistic, 834
German(s), Germany, **E**, 45**n**, 49, 89-93, 91**n**, 95, 101, 104-8, 108**n**, 125, 156, 175, 191, 366, 396, 410, 416, 419, 420, 422, 747, 791, 792, 831, 832, 835, 838, 849, 871, 883, 957, 1058; *Reich*, **E**, 349**n**; *Reichsdeutscher*, 349; spirit, 89, 90, 107, 792; "un-German," 95
Gewöhnung und Verwöhnung, 712**n**
Gide, André, **E**2, 116**n**, 134a/**n**
Gluck, Christoph Willibald, 105
goal, 909. *See also* purpose
God, 1, 4, 7, 12, 17, 18, 18**n**, 54, 55, 69**n**, 91, 97, 100, 114, 116, 134a, 135-37, 137**n**, 139-41, 151, 160, 167, 170, 172, 176, 181, 182, 185, 190, 200-2, 204, 210-12, 217**n**, 224, 225, 228, 244, 245, 246, 251-53, 270, 275, 281, 283, 290, 291**n**, 296, 298, 304, 313, 320, 331, 336, 339, 343, 347, 348, 351, 359**n**, 360, 373, 388, 411, 436, 446, 453, 461, 469, 471, 525, 529, 543, 552, 573, 576, 578, 595, 617, 619, 639, 659, 707, 708, 712, 765, 768, 776, 797, 808, 841, 853, 870, 874, 929**n**, 943, 958, 1005, 1015, 1019, 1035, 1036, 1036**n**, 1037, 1038, 1062; kingdom of, 161, 204, 339; God is dead, 69**n**
Goethe, Johann Wolfgang von, 95, 101, 104, 105, 113**n**, 118, 132, 175, 175**n**, 340, 341, 380, 382, 396, 422, 544**n**, 573, 747, 778**n**, 791, 814, 814**n**, 820, 830, 835, 841**n**, 846, 849, 883, 884, 1017, 1031, 1038, 1051; *Der Fischer*, 841**n**; *Faust*, 113**n**, 778**n**, 800, 807, 943, 1038**n**; Gretchen, 943
Goncourts, Les Frères (Edmond and Jules), 82**n**, 455, 821
good, 1, 30, 47, 54**n**, 75, 95, 123, 139, 141, 155, 202-204, 218, 233, 244, 254, 259, 265, 269, 270, 284, 290, 297, 298, 304, 320, 338, 340, 347, 351-62, 355**n**, 368, 386n2, 388, 396, 411, 417, 425, 427, 428, 430, 434, 435**n**, 436, 440, 443, 458, 460, 464, 480, 529, 572, 573, 576, 578, 583, 585, 644, 707, 786, 789, 822, 850, 934, 943, 968, 972, 985, 1010, 1015, 1019, 1025, 1032, 1033, 1035, 1037, 1050, 1051
gratitude, 351, 730, 775, 777, 852, 1047
Great Mother, 196

greatness, see man, great; greatness of character, 928; of soul, 935, 981, 981**n**, 984, 984**n**, 1040
Greek(s), Greece, 92, 94, 95, 102, 175, 195, 202, 225, 261, 382, 419, 427-47, 463, 544, 573, 586, 783, 819, 845, 851, 882, 940, 979, 1029, 1047, 1050-52; Hellenism, 1015; philosophy, 94, 101, 169, 202, 261, 419, 427-47, 851 (*see also* philosophy—ancient); religion, 1042
Grimm, Jacob and Wilhelm, 106
Grossoktav edition, **E**3, **EC**
Grote, George, 429
guilt, 182, 204, 224, 229, 235, 243, 280, 290, 296, 373, 411, 438, 579, 765, 1021. *See also* sin; original sin
Guyau, Jean-Marie, 340, 929**n**

Hafiz (pseudo. for Shams ud-din Mohammed), 846, 1051
Hamlet, 875
hammer, 69**n**, 132, 905, 1054, 1055
Handel, George Frederic, 884
Hanswurst, 834**n**,
happiness, 12, 20, 32, 60, 94, 95, 135, 141, 159, 176, 185, 195, 196, 204, 209, 215, 222, 224, 243, 261, 288, 296, 310, 334, 359**n**, 379, 393, 407, 422, 426, 428, 430, 432-35, 437, 444, 450, 452, 453, 464, 579, 585, 666**n**, 686, 704, 721, 759, 765, 775, 781, 837, 845, 849, 851, 868, 870, 909, 911, 930, 944, 957, 993, 1022, 1023, 1032, 1039, 1051
Härtle, Heinrich, 942**n**
Hartmann, Eduard von, 91**n**, 701**n**, 789
Haydn, Franz Joseph, 105
Hebrews, 170, 352. *See also* Jews
hedonism, 35, 155, 240, 435, 578, 751, 781, 790
Hegel, G. W. F., **E**1, 1, 95, 96, 366, 382, 410, 415, 416, 419, 422, 588**n**, 701**n**, 849; Hegelian, 253, 412
Heidegger, Martin, 57**n**, 437**n**
Heine, Heinrich, 106, 832, 835, 835**n**
Helvétius, Claude Adrien, 751
Heraclitus, 412, 419, 428, 437
Herbart, 838
herd, 20, 27, 53,60, 132, 134, 176, 203, 237, 252, 265, 274-87, 317, 358, 362, 389, 400, 696, 717, 720, 752-54, 760, 761, 766, 782, 783, 792, 845, 886, 887, 901, 955, 962; fold, 156; herd animal, 125, 128, 129, 215, 335, 353, 421, 782, 909, 943, 954, 956, 957; herd consciousness, 389; herd ideal, 696, 782, 936; herd instinct, 132, 215, 216, 315, 349, 458, 509, 685, 786, 925, 957, 1021, 1041; herd man, 804; herd standard, 379; herd virtues, 60, 203, 279; mob, 100
Herder, Johann Gottfried, 366, 396, 849
heredity, 969
hermit, 795
Herrnhuter, 911**n**
Hesse, Hermann, 916**n**
higher type, 615, 684, 685. *See also* man, higher
Hilton, James, 335**n**
Hindus, 191
Hippocrates, 443
Hitler, Adolf, **E**1
Hoffmann, Ernst Theodor Amadeus, 106
Hollingdale, R. J., **E**3
Homer, 137, 234**n**, 380, 427, 765, 845, 846
honor, 752, 792, 949
Horace, 302**n**
Horneffer, August, **EC**
Horneffer, Ernst, **EC**
hospitality, 939
Hugo, Victor, 62, 103, 825, 830, 838, 849, 864
Hume, David, 92, 101, 530, 550
hunger, 59, 209, 652, 654, 656, 697, 702, 846

Ibsen, Henrik, **E**3, 86, 86**n**, 747
ideal(ism), 16, 17, 21, 28, 37, 51, 56, 69**n**, 80, 86, 86**n**, 95, 111, 117, 137, 204, 217-52, 253, 298, 304, 306, 311, 330-405, 423, 463, 578, 580, 617, 678, 765, 782, 786, 864, 865, 889, 891, 917, 951, 957, 1016, 1021, 1039; ideal drives, 592; idealist, 317, 584, 659, 735, 881**n**, 910**n**; idealization, 299
ideas, 430, 476, 508, 515, 521, 524,

ideas (*cont'd.*)
525, 572, 588, 641, 659, 676, 800
identity, 521, 530, 532, 544, 552, 568, 569, 574; principle of, 520
idiot, 154, 266, 431, 437, 734, 800, 808
images, 506, 551, 562
immoderate swine, 870
immoralist, 116, 132, 235, 304, 457, 749
imperatives, 271, 275, 283, 286, 299, 516, 734**n**, 898. *See also* ought
India, Indians, 31, 92, 175, 274, 437, 442, 580, 585, 608; Indian culture, 63; Indian ideal, 221
indignation, 765
individual(ism), 20**n**, 33, 60, 68, 69**n**, 86**n**, 93, 97, 130, 131, 161, 221, 243, 246, 253, 269, 275, 284, 319, 373, 379, 398, 404, 417, 520, 521, 552, 567, 585, 607, 647, 660, 678-82, 684, 686, 687, 700, 704, 716-93 (*esp.* 783-85), 852, 876, 895, 936, 943, 1026, 1050; individualistic morality, 287
indulgence, blind, 928
inertia, 279, 285, 537
infinite, 1062
Ingres, Jean Auguste Dominique, 105
innocence of becoming, 552, 765, 787
instinct(s), *see* passion(s)
intellect, 473, 498, 533
intermediaries, 75, 76, 77, 140, 891, 897, 901
interpretation, 1, 5, 12, 27, 32, 47, 48, 55, 69, 69**n**, 70, 114, 116, 141, 147, 196, 210, 228, 229, 253, 254, 258, 270, 279, 292, 373, 394, 423, 453, 477, 479, 481, 488, 492, 522, 531, 546, 550-552, 556, 560, 565, 585, 585**n**3, 589, 590, 604, 605, 616, 617, 639, 643, 675, 677, 678, 682, 689, 744, 767, 804, 846, 1017, 1021, 1051. *See also* perspectivism
intoxication, 29, 48, 55, 95, 434, 798-801, 807-9, 811, 821, 823, 835**n**1, 851, 1051
introspection, *see* inwardness
"invented," 544**n**
inwardness, 376, 426, 477, 492, 585
Ionians, 427
Isis, 196
isolation, *see* solitude
Israel, 182, 347
Italy, 75, 941; Italians, 544, 828, 831, 839; music, 101, 835

Jaspers, Karl, 437**n**, 983**n**
Jesuitism, 757, 783, 1057; Jesuit Order, 796
Jesus, 94, 154, 160, 162, 163, 163**n**, 166-71, 176, 177, 182, 184, 188, 191, 193, 195, 196, 198, 205, 207, 213, 218, 219, 221, 224, 284, 347, 383, 383**n**, 401, 983, 983**n**, 1052; The Crucified, 1034, 1052; Founder of Christianity, 198, 383; "God on the Cross," 240, 373
Jew(s), 49, 78, 116, 143, 145**n**, 146, 155, 160, 173-75, 175**n**, 177, 180, 182-86, 190, 197-99, 202, 204, 296, 299, 374, 427, 429, 431, 765, 774, 832, 835**n**, 864, 872**n**, 942; Hebrews, 170, 352; Judaism, 160, 169, 173, 181, 182, 196, 204, 214, 221, 298, 845, 1042. *See also* Semite(s)
Job, 821
Juan, Don, 871. *See also* Mozart
judgment(s), 24, 511, 530-544, 699, 701, 804
justice, 30, 59, 62, 69**n**, 80, 86, 100, 124, 207, 215, 244, 255, 259, 284, 340, 352, 373, 375, 388, 429, 430, 685, 722, 748, 750, 765, 776, 784, 850, 881, 943, 962, 967, 984; retributive, 347

Kafka, Franz, **E**2
Kant, Immanuel, 17, 92, 95, 101, 127, 254, 271, 303, 331, 368**n**, 382, 410, 412, 414, 415, 419, 424, 428, 442, 444, 448, 458, 515**n**, 530, 551, 553, 554, 571, 578, 698, 786, 888, 940; Kantian, 251, 253, 411
Keller, Gottfried, 1021
Kierkegaard, Søren, 86**n**
Klopstock, Friedrich Gottlieb, 396
knowledge, 4, 244, 298, 335, 346, 359, 376, 411, 423, 425, 437, 450, 466-617, 665, 676, 678, 710, 824,

853; knowledge-in-itself, 1060. *See also* epistemology
Kraftgefühl, 664**n**

labor, division of, 123, 492, 718, 719
Lamartine, Alphonse Marie Louis de, 102
language, 79, 80, 285, 409, 482, 484, 506, 522, 551, 562, 585**n**3, 625, 631, 634, 659, 676, 689, 699, 715, 731, 767, 808-811, 838, 840, 1066
l'art pour l'art, 808
La Rochefoucauld, Francois Duc de, 94, 362, 389, 772, 786, 870
Latuka, 355
law, 68, 135, 204, 279, 354, 514, 521, 629-32, 634, 677, 819, 838, 842, 846, 889, 957, 1019, 1062. *See also* penal law; legislator
Lazzarone, 911**n**
legislator (lawgiver), 718, 889, 972-1002
Leibniz, Gottfried Wilhelm von, 101, 411, 419, 884
Leonardo da Vinci, 380
Leopardi, Giacamo, 91
Lesage, Alain René, 120
Lessing, Gotthold Ephraim, 422
levelling, 464, 866, 936, 985, 987
Levy, Oscar, **E**3
lie(s), 5, 15, 32, 69**n**, 79, 116, 120, 134, 141, 142, 150, 150**n**, 172, 199**n**, 200, 202, 204, 211, 279, 306, 328, 343, 376-78, 380, 381, 394, 396, 401, 428, 461, 464, 495, 544**n**, 572, 584, 853, 962, 1011; liars, 910**n**
life, 33, 40, 44, 47, 53, 55, 116, 125, 141, 170, 181, 194, 201, 224, 243, 244, 246, 251, 254, 258, 266, 296, 298, 303, 333, 339, 341, 343, 351, 352, 354, 362, 369, 379, 399-401, 417, 439, 450, 453, 461, 485, 488, 493, 507, 510, 515, 532, 535, 544, 552, 577**n**, 581-84, 592, 608, 617, 640-87, 689, 692, 695, 701, 704, 706, 707, 712**n**, 734, 786, 790, 802, 805, 808, 812, 815, 818-20, 850-53, 864, 897, 968, 1017, 1046, 1050, 1052
Liszt Society, 835
Locke, John, 101
logic(al), 10-12, 17, 24, 30, 55, 90, 245, 275, 347, 428, 430, 433, 439, 461, 477, 484, 485, 488, 507, 508-522, 524, 527, 530, 533, 538, 552, 554, 558, 568, 569, 574, 580, 584, 608, 659, 669, 800, 809, 827, 839, 842, 849, 962, 1010, 1041, 1050; logicians, 535; logicizing, 423
Lortzing, Gustav Albert, 106**n**
Louis XIV, 94
love, 12, 30, 69**n**, 79, 86**n**, 105, 120, 124, 134a, 135, 155, 169, 172, 175, 176, 187, 202, 246, 255, 279, 293, 296, 312, 335, 350, 351, 362, 373, 379, 383, 388, 453, 606, 712**n**, 716, 721, 730, 732, 774, 776, 777, 786, 801, 804-8, 821, 846, 850, 852, 853, 864, 873, 911, 919, 936, 964, 976, 1030, 1030**n**, 1031, 1033
Ludovici, Anthony M., **E**3
Luther, Martin, 192, 211, 347, 367, 419, 747, 786

Machiavelli, Niccolo, 211; Machiavellianism, 304, 776; *Principe,* 925
Magny, dîners chez, 82, 915
man, 27, 39, 68, 78, 83, 90, 97, 123, 124, 130, 134, 134a, 136, 142, 144, 176, 204, 205, 225, 229, 252, 301, 303, 304, 335, 338, 339, 351, 354, 363, 367, 382, 383, 388, 390, 393, 395, 397, 398, 401, 443, 453, 461, 464, 529, 543, 565, 572, 585, 586, 594, 606, 608-10, 616, 619, 636, 640, 659-687, 683**n**, 702, 704, 711, 713, 716-93, 795, 798, 804, 806, 809, 820, 845, 853, 856, 866, 871 873, 881, 888, 890, 897, 908, 957, 960, 961-71, 961**n**, 1017, 1035, 1058; good man, 54, 59, 62, 100, 141, 163**n**, 204, 270, 319, 351-62, 382, 383, 386, 386**n**, 430, 755, 786, 933, 1017, 1021; great man, 379, 380, 415, 772**n**, 871, 876, 885, 895, 896, 933, 957, 959, 961-71, 1038; higher man, 226, 227, 400, 544, 552, 755, 795**n**, 859, 861, 875, 877, 878, 881, 891, 957, 972-1002, 1017, 1041; man of knowledge, 612; "natural man," 1017; noble man, 935-53, 937**n**; synthetic man, 881, 883, 996, 997, 1009, 1027**n**, 1051

manners, bad, 175; good, 948
Manu, 116**n**, 142, 143, 145, 716, 742
Manzoni, Alessandro, 986
Marcus Aurelius, 360
Mark, the evangelist, 164
marriage, 30, 62, 120, 132, 245, 316, 317, 583, 731-34, 775, 804, 888, 995
martyr, 457
Marx, Karl, 585**n**
mask, 132, 377, 962, 962**n**, 944, 985, 988
master(s), 55, 69**n**, 98, 154, 184, 209, 216, 275, 300, 354, 361, 377, 385, 388, 401, 423, 438, 480, 514, 517, 584, 630, 636, 643, 652, 658, 661, 696, 704, 753, 783, 802, 819, 842, 853, 861, 874, 902, 934, 943, 965, 966; master race, 145, 216, 898, 960; mastery, 377
mathematics, 516, 530, 554, 562
matter, 552
Matthew, the evangelist, 164
mean, 280, 870, 933, 940, 953
meaning, 585, 590, 599, 605
means, *see* ends
mechanism, mechanics, mechanistic, 69, 101, 141, 419, 510, 529, 533, 552, 554, 617, 618-39, 658, 660, 667, 670, 689, 708, 712, 786, 809, 888, 889, 1061, 1066
mediocrity, 316, 317, 345, 382, 389, 400, 401, 881, 891-93, 901, 903, 933, 943**n**, 953, 957, 1025, 1054
Megarian school, 442
Melians, 429
memory, 501, 502, 532
Mendelssohn, Felix, 105, 835, 835**n**
metaphysics, 12, 17, 18, 30, 275, 458, 462, 484, 488, 513, 530, 574, 575, 579, 583, 765, 853, 1048; metaphysical need, 27, 570-87
Meyer, Michael, 86**n**
Michelangelo, 1018
Michelet, Jules, 343
Middle Ages, 747, 871
Mill, John Stuart, 30, 340, 772, 925, 926
Mirabeau, Victor de Riquetti, Marquis de, 817
miracles, 190, 196, 198, 225, 229, 342, 670, 967
Mitchell, Silas Weir, 233, 233**n**
Mithras, 167, 196
Mittel, 139**n**
modernity, 74, 75. *See also* European nihilism, 1-134
modesty, danger in, 918, 970
Mohammed, 145, 973; Mohammedanism, 143, 145
monads, *see* atoms
monarchy, 752, 755
monastery, *see* solitude
Montaigne, Michel Eyquem de, 367
Montlosier, François Dominique de Reynaud, Comte de, 937
morality, 1, 3, 4, 5, 6, 11, 18-20, 30, 41, 41**n**, 43, 44, 47, 52, 55, 56, 60, 62, 68, 69, 69**n**, 79, 82, 83, 86, 91, 94, 95, 98, 119, 120, 126, 132, 134, 139, 141, 144, 146, 151, 153 155 199, 200, 202-4, 206, 215, 227, 248, 251, 253-405, 332**n**, 153, 155, 199, 200, 202-4, 206, 215, 227, 248, 251, 253-405, 332**n**, 407, 410, 411, 413, 415, 423, 425, 428, 495, 514, 552, 578, 579, 583-86, 594, 677, 707, 719-21, 726-28, 730, 734, 740, 744, 747, 749, 765, 783, 784, 786, 794, 797, 809, 823, 842, 845, 848, 850, 852, 853, 859, 862, 879, 880, 897, 914, 916, 925, 927, 943, 957, 961, 966, 970, 981, 1005, 1006, 1015, 1019-21, 1024, 1029, 1029**n**, 1034, 1047; individualistic, 287, 859; moral-metaphysical needs, *see* metaphysical need
motion, movement, 492, 520, 523, 551**n**, 552, 562
Mozart, Wolfgang Amadeus, 105, 842; *Don Giovanni,* 105, 105**n**, 871; *The Magic Flute,* 817**n**
Musarion edition, **EC**, **E**3, **E**4, 440**n**, 853**n**, 1018**n**
music, 29, 51, 59, 101, 105, 106, 119, 810, 811, 826, 835, 835**n**, 838-41, 839**n**, 845, 848**n**, 849, 1021; descriptive, 835; French, 101, 833, 835; grand style, 842; modern, 837; Viennese, 833

Napoleon I, 27, 41, 104, 128, 129, 380, 422, 544, 665, 740, 751, 829, 877, 877**n**, 975, 1017, 1018, 1026,

1027**n**; Napoleonic movement, 463, 463**n**
nationalism, 748
naturalist, 455
nature, 13, 30, 37, 41**n**, 47, 52, 55, 62, 66, 69**n**, 79, 83, 97, 99, 100, 117, 120, 123, 124, 135, 147, 150, 183, 202-4, 214, 215, 226, 228, 243, 245, 246, 283, 292, 295, 297-99, 332**n**, 340, 341, 343, 347, 351, 359, 388, 400, 401, 403, 462, 552, 579, 586, 684, 685, 704, 734, 760, 765, 786, 812, 823, 841, 849, 850, 856, 862, 864, 870, 916, 931, 941, 953, 1021, 1024, 1047, 1050, 1051
Nazi(s), **E**1, 872**n**, 942**n**
necessity, 516, 530, 541, 551, 552, 664, 707, 824, 1060
Nero, 874
neurosis, nervous disorders, 59, 85, 100, 180, 221, 232, 233, 811, 812, 845, 864; hysteric, 813
Newman, Ernest, **E**1
newspapers, 132, 888
New Testament, 130, 142, 145, 175, 186, 187, 199, 201, 206, 208, 210
Nietzsche Archive, **EC**
Nietzsche, Friedrich, *The Antichrist,* **E**3, 54**n**, 134a/**n**, 145**n**, 154**n**, 158**n**, 180**n**, 199**n**, 212**n**, 244**n**, 317**n**, 414**n**, 452**n**, 864**n**, 892**n**, 943**n**, 963**n**, 968**n**, 1038**n**; *Beyond Good and Evil,* **E**3 86**n**, 115**n**, 428**n**, 434**n**, 464**n**, Bk. III Pt. I **n**, 483**n**, 552**n**, 795**n**, 835**n**, 914**n**, 935**n**, 943**n**, 962**n**, 968**n**, 972**n**, 987**n**, 1041**n**, 1052**n**; *The Birth of Tragedy,* **E**3, 91, 463**n**, 845**n**, 853, 853**n**, 1029**n**, 1050**n**; *The Case of Wagner,* **E**3, 108**n**, 824**n**, 835**n**, 841**n**; *The Dawn,* 48**n**, 253**n**, 265**n**; *Ecce Homo,* **E**3, 86**n**, 334**n**, 848**n**, 1041**n**, 1050**n**, 1052**n**; *The Gay Science,* 59**n**, 265**n**, 399**n**, 846**n**, 929**n**, 968**n**, 1009**n**, 1032**n**; *Genealogy of Morals,* **E**3, 233**n**, 265**n**, 877**n**, 901**n**; *Human, All too Human,* 943**n**; *Nietzsche Contra Wagner,* **E**3, 846**n**; *Thus Spoke Zarathustra,* **E**3, 44**n**, 57**n**, 115**n**, 355**n**, 464**n**, 598**n**, 601**n**, 617, 704**n**, 1032**n**, 1038; *Twilight of the Idols,* **E**2, **E**3, 12**n**, 18**n**, 25**n**, 41**n**, 45**n**, 53**n**, 69**n**, 80**n**, 95**n**, 108**n**, 116**n**, 134a/**n**, 141**n**, 145**n**, 234**n**, 237**n**, 304**n**, 329**n**, 332**n**, 334**n**, 373**n**, 380**n**, 397**n**, 426**n**, 431**n**, 432**n**, 455**n**, 461**n**, Bk. III Pt. I **n**, 566**n**, 585**n**, 586**n**, 705**n**, 732**n**, 734**n**, 736**n**, 740**n**, 765**n**, 770**n**, 798**n**, 807**n**, 817**n**, 888**n**, 930**n**, 934**n**, 968**n**, 1009**n**, 1040**n**
Nihilisierung, 580
nihilism, nihilistic, **N**2-**N**4, 1-134, 2**n**, 69**n**, 220, 247, 373, 379, 435, 437, 580, 585, 585**n**, 586, 597, 598, 598**n**, 617, 685, 850-53, 864, 1020, 1041, 1055; nihilistic religion, 152-54, 156, 401, 461, 703
Norway, 747
Novalis (pseud. for Hardenberg, Friedrich von), 44**n**
nützliche "Scheinbarkeiten," 711**n**

obedience, 216, 346
object, 516, 521, 533, 549, 552, 569, 589
objectivity, 424-26, 442, 444, 455, 469, 560, 585, 790
Odysseus, 544
Offenbach, Jacques, 832-34, 835**n**
Old Testament, 145, 765
Olympian, 883; Olympic, 1, 1040; Olympus, 1034
opinion, *see* belief
opposites, 552
organic, 31, 398, 505, 532, 544, 640-58, 676, 691, 702, 728, 768, 808; organic life, 619, 678; organic world, 544; organism, 41, 47, 440, 535, 550, 687, 699, 703, 707, 711, 712**n**, 734, 769, 800; pre-organic, 499
Orient, 214
Osiris, 167
ought, 269, 332-34, 346, 853, 888, 940, 972; "thou shalt," 275. *See also* imperatives
Overbeck, Franz, 86**n**
overcoming, 1, 333, 384, 437, 552, 585, 661, 677, 699, 770, 786, 819, 845, 921, 1013, 1031, 1051, 1058

overman, 804, 866, 983**n**, 1001, 1027**n**, 1060. *See also* man
oxen, 342, 353

pain, 35, 43, 47, 64, 260, 270, 296, 389, 407, 477-79, 490, 505, 524, 532, 579, 658, 660, 669, 670, 676, 689, 693-95, 697, 698**n**, 699-704, 707, 708, 711, 743, 789, 790, 850, 853
pantheism, 1, 55
Papageno, 817**n**. *See also* Mozart
paralysis, 597
parasites, 77
Paris commune, 125
Parmenides, 419, 539
Pascal, Blaise, 51, 83, 101, 227, 240, 246, 252, 270, 276, 347, 388, 389, 411, 424, 426, 437, 578, 786, 929, 929**n**, 1017, 1020; Pascalism, 240, 312, 932
passion(s), 13, 26, 30, 46, 47, 50, 62, 79, 95, 100, 120, 135, 175, 215, 221, 228, 248, 253, 255, 266, 296, 315, 317, 367, 372, 376, 377, 382, 383, 387, 388, 401, 414, 423, 424, 433, 439, 440, 440**n**, 458, 464, 481, 509, 512, 515, 529, 544, 568, 576, 583, 584, 635**n**, 697, 715**n**, 772**n**, 778, 785, 786, 800, 806, 814, 826, 837, 849, 869, 870, 930, 933, 936, 963, 966, 971, 1021, 1025, 1050
patriotism, 717, 720
Paul, St., 155, 165, 167, 169, 171, 173, 175, 177, 190, 204, 205, 214, 347, 659
peaceful, 464, 923
penal law, 316, 464, 716, 722, 745, 755, 765, 783, 1050. *See also* law; justice
perceptions, 505, 588
perfection, 2, 17, 68, 69**n**, 148, 155, 203, 224, 226, 243, 289, 290, 304, 331, 341, 354, 391-98, 417, 430, 434, 439, 440, 525, 578, 584, 644, 660, 674, 684, 712**n**, 765, 786, 795, 801, 805, 806, 808, 811, 817, 821, 838, 850, 852, 1010, 1051
Pericles, 427, 428, 747; Periclean age, 428
Perry, Ralph Barton, 336**n**
Persian, 130
person(ality), 334, 388, 417, 425, 813, 886, 935, 1009
perspectivism, 259, 272, 293, 339, 481, 490, 493-507, 518, 548, 552, 564, 565, 567-69, 602, 616, 636, 637, 678, 730, 781, 786, 789. *See also* interpretation
pessimism, 9-11, 26, 31-34, 37, 38, 42, 51, 62, 69, 69**n**, 77, 80, 82, 91, 91**n**, 100, 102, 112, 116, 132, 134, 184, 195, 231, 258, 276, 297, 312, 362, 379, 410, 417, 422, 463, 585, 591, 592, 697, 701, 701**n**, 707, 708, 721, 747, 765, 789, 790, 821, 839, 850-53, 957, 1019, 1020, 1022, 1031, 1055, 1058; romantic, 846
Peter, St., 165**n**, 166
Petronius, 147, 187
Pharisees, 206
phenomena(lism), 475, 477-79, 481, 517, 523, 532, 552, 553, 569
philosopher, **N**3, 17, 20**n**, 27, 36, 39, 127, 140, 141, 269, 283, 302, 345, 346, 379, 382, 393, 396, 401, 406-65, 440**n**, 461**n**, 463**n**, 478, 570, 585, 585**n**, 586, 597, 598, 659, 669, 685, 779, 792, 795**n**, 820, 822, 893, 909, 917, 929, 960, 972-1002, 1037, 1041, 1055; artist-philosopher, 795; Aryan philosophers, 141; Parisian, 782; solitary, 45
philosophy, 1, 41, 47, 55, 69**n**, 74, 78, 154, 172, 202, 253, 261, 263, 283, 333, 382, 388, 389, 401, 406-65, 467, 476, 487, 522, 584-86, 585**n**, 605, 707, 708, 786, 794, 811, 824, 828**n**, 987, 1021, 1041, 1046; ancient, 349, 419; German, 416, 419, 422; modern, 475; nihilistic, 703; of right, 744; Vedanta, 659. *See also* Greek
Pitti, Palazzo, 842
pity, 27, 73, 79**n**, 94, 216, 279, 284, 365-68, 367**n**, 388, 586, 734, 765, 773, 776, 777, 800, 809, 850, 864, 928, 929, 957, 962, 964, 965, 1020
Plato, 141-43, 195, 202, 253, 304, 374, 409, 412, 427-30, 434, 435, 435**n**, 436-38, 441, 446, 572, 578, 644, 747, 806, 958, 972, 973,

1029**n**; Platonic, 1061; Platonism, 101, 214, 572
pleasure, 29, 35, 36, 43, 47, 60, 64, 120, 148, 176, 221, 240, 255, 260, 294, 296, 318, 319, 387, 428, 434, 457, 477, 478, 490, 505, 524, 579, 580, 657, 658, 661, 669, 670, 674, 676, 677, 688, 689, 693, 695-97, 698**n**, 699, 701-4, 707, 711, 712**n**, 719, 743, 751, 758, 789, 790, 800-2, 819, 821, 838, 845, 852, 853, 873, 889, 917, 928, 929**n**, 930**n**, 946, 1003, 1023, 1059, 1060, 1067
Plutarch, 217
Podach, Erich, **E1**, **2n**, **124n**, Appendix
Poles, 872**n**
Poe, E. A., Appendix
pope, 216; papacy, 129
pose, 138, 304, 377, 434, 457, 824, 838, 944, 957, 967, 1009, 1047; actor, 464; dissimulation, 544
positivism, 1, 120, 481
praise/blame, 126, 284, 676, 775, 912, 913, 943, 946, 962
preservation, 4, 45, 55, 68, 109, 169, 175, 179, 185, 202, 204, 246, 253, 258, 259, 260, 266, 284, 285, 315, 361, 373, 390, 416, 426, 480, 487, 488, 493-97, 505, 507, 515, 520, 552, 567, 568, 579, 583, 584, 647**n**, 650-52, 684, 688, 689, 715, 774, 789, 803, 864, 873, 886, 895, 898, 921, 934, 943, 953, 1059
priest, 51, 62, 89, 116, 116**n**, 119, 138-43, 145, 148, 157, 159, 167, 172, 182, 184, 196, 204, 208, 213, 248, 282, 283, 315, 317, 341, 347, 377, 396, 397, 427, 447, 786, 820, 864, 871, 943, 1015, 1021
procreation, 653-55, 657, 660, 676, 680, 689, 731, 734, 768, 1050, 1052
Procrustes' bed, 499
progress, 41, 44, 54**n**, 62, 80, 90, 112, 113, 115, 117, 123, 125, 129, 134, 243, 573, 649, 666, 683, 683**n**, 684, 685, 746, 838, 1017, 1023
Prometheus, 845**n**, 900
Protagoras, 428, 437
Protestantism, 87-90, 93, 105, 192, 211, 241, 381, 786
providence, 243
prudence, 141, 181, 240, 281, 318, 343, 349, 358, 586, 716, 815, 909, 925, 947, 971, 985
Prussian officer corps, 783, 796
psychology, 12, 47, 69, 69**n**, 86**n**, 101, 107, 135, 136, 175, 179, 180, 227, 233, 271, 296, 389, 394, 395, 426, 426**n**, 428, 434, 455, 528, 547, 551, 568, 569, 576, 579, 583, 584, 688, 692, 696, 703, 704, 736**n**, 740, 751, 765, 780, 782, 786, 812, 823, 849, 851, 899, 936, 1021
punishment, 1, 124, 141, 146, 164-66, 196, 204, 213, 224, 227, 290, 296, 313, 394, 716, 728, 737-44, 765, 780, 789, 980**n**, 1019, 1021
purpose, 12, 20, 26, 30, 35, 36, 55, 84, 141, 521, 526, 529, 552, 562, 576, 584, 666, 675, 676, 707, 708, 724, 765, 779, 789, 864, 995, 1062, 1067
Pyrrho, 428, 434, 437, 442, 455
Pythagoreans, 427

quality, 563, 564, 564**n**, 565
quantity, 563-65

race, 49, 54; race mixture, 862
rank, order of, 37, 51, 55, 69**n**, 116, 139, 143, 169, 207, 209, 228, 280, 284, 287, 360, 387, 492, 544, 552, 583, 592, 612, 681, 755, 764, 766, 774, 783, 784, 786, 795**n**, 803, 854-1002, 1006, 1021, 1024, 1051
Ranke, Leopold von, 128
Raphael, 800, 828, 845, 1051
reality, 7, 12, 13, 17, 80, 95, 183, 243, 298, 332**n**, 335, 390, 453, 461, 473, 474, 480, 485-88, 516, 517, 521, 529, 533, 536, 539, 539**n**, 552, 567-69, 572, 576, 579, 580, 583-86, 588, 685, 807, 808, 829, 836, 845, 853; in-itself, 544**n**
reason, 387, 414, 432-34, 436, 442, 453, 457, 471, 480, 487, 488, 507-22, 524, 569, 578, 579, 581, 584, 585
rebel, 740, 829, 870
rechtwinklig, 353

reciprocity, 925, 926
Reformation, 90, 381, 786
Regnard, Jean-François, 120
religion, religious, 18, 31, 41, 44, 47, 48, 63, 64, 137**n**, 135-252, 253, 261, 288, 297, 298, 347, 357, 373, 382, 383, 389, 394, 401, 427, 432, 435, 436, 447, 462, 487, 579, 585, 586, 606, 677, 742, 765, 773, 786, 794, 795**n**, 797, 800, 801, 828**n**, 840, 852, 853, 875, 957, 958, 972, 1019, 1038, 1046, 1052, 1062; of love, 806; pagan, 851
remorse, 234, 234**n**, 235. *See also* conscience
Renaissance, 75, 93, 98, 100, 129, 131, 317, 327, 401, 419, 740, 747, 842, 957, 1015, 1017, 1018**n**; man, 881, 882
Renan, Joseph Ernest, 82**n**, 128
repression, 376
resistance, 47, 185, 382, 533, 551, 567, 568, 656, 658, 661, 664, 689, 693, 694, 696, 699, 702-4, 737, 770, 930, 953, 957, 1009
responsibility, 17, 20, 221, 243, 246, 551, 676, 716, 717, 765, 773, 776, 898, 907, 936, 944, 975
ressentiment, 167, 172, 174, 179, 204, 351, 373, 579, 765, 864, 1021
revaluation of ancient values, 438
revenge, 93, 154, 155, 221, 255, 284, 347, 351, 373, 376, 383, 401, 453, 457, 461, 748, 765, 775, 813, 846, 864
reward, 66, 165, 169, 737-39, 789
Reynard the Fox, 208, 431
right (adj.), 280, 373, 387, 921, 977**n**
right(s), 120, 169, 279, 315, 362, 388, 423, 728, 734, 739, 744, 747, 748, 752, 753, 759, 765, 773, 776, 783, 874, 937**n**, 957, 975
Rilke, Rainer Maria, 44**n**
Romans, Rome, 103, 153, 195, 202, 233, 374, 874, 959; Empire, 175, 204, 261; Rome, 105, 747
romanticism, 1, 27, 55, 59, 69, 78, 79, 81, 82, 92, 95, 100, 105, 106, 116, 119, 215, 253, 419, 422, 598**n**, 842-49, 981, 1021; French, 829; German, 832
Romulus, 103, 103**n**
Ross, W. D., 958**n**
Rousseau, Jean Jacques, 62, 92, 94, 95, 98-101, 106, 117, 120, 123, 340, 347, 382, 747, 1017, 1021
Rubens, Peter Paul, 845, 846
rücksichtslose Rechtschaffenheit, 306**n**
Russia, Russian(s), 180, 740, 765, 872**n**, 958; pessimism, 82

Sabbath, 464
saint, **1**, 69**n**, 78, 190, 351-362, 382, 394, 786, 800, 864
Sainte-Beuve, Charles-Augustin de, 82**n**, 424
salvation, 30**n**, 83, 116, 135, 141, 167, 170, 172, 187, 198, 203, 210, 214, 217, 222, 224, 227-29, 232, 233, 242, 248, 261, 270, 290, 299, 339, 351, 394, 425, 426, 433, 435, 435**n**, 453, 781, 852, 918, 953
Sand, George, 62, 103
Sartre, Jean-Paul, 234**n**
Satan, 86**n**
Saul (King), 427
Savonarola, 747
scapegoat, 765
Schérer, E. H. A., 82**n**
Schiller, Friedrich, 106, 106**n**, 343; Thekla, 106, 106**n**
Schlechta, Karl, **E**1, **E**3, **EC**, 2**n**, 124**n**, 149**n**, 156**n**, 163**n**, 172**n**, 217**n**, 304**n**, 386**n**, 403**n**, 405**n**, 440**n**, 448**n**, 451**n**, 461**n**, 463**n**, 684**n**, 688**n**, 923**n**, 972**n**, 1025**n**, 1052**n**, Appendix
scholar, 420-22, 444, 464, 801, 912
scholasticism, 525
school, 911
Schopenhauer, Arthur, 17, 54, 82-85, 91, 92, 94-96, 174, 270, 276, 366, 379, 382, 410, 411, 416, 419, 422, 463, 612, 685, 692, 701**n**, 746, 747, 811, 812, 821, 838, 851, 1005, 1017, 1029**n**; Schopenhauer as Educator, 713**n**; Schopenhauerian, 846
Schumann, Robert, 106
Schütz, Heinrich, 835
science, scientific, 1, 50, 52, 53, 62, 68, 69**n**, 71, 78, 79, 95, 172, 315, 379, 382, 401, 419, 424, 432, 437, 439, 440, 440**n**, 442-44, 447, 457,

460, 461, 466, 467, 551, 554, 583-85, 594-617, 618, 621, 667, 677, 682, 688, 689, 710, 816, 817, 853, 864, 864**n**, 953, 1021, 1062
Scott, Walter, 78, 830
selection, 246, 864, 1003
self, 594, 659
self-esteem, 773; self-respect vs. self-love, 919
selfishness, 772, 777, 786
Semite(s), Semitic, 143, 145, 175, 195, 195**n**, 427. *See also* anti-Semites; Jews
Seneca, 420
sense impressions, 479, 500, 504, 505, 511, 515-17, 532, 552, 562, 569, 574
sense, inner, 478, 523
sex, 62, 86**n**, 148, 255, 275, 312, 383, 576, 680, 697, 699, 732, 776, 777, 786, 799-801, 805, 811, 815, 947, 1047, 1052; Wagner's sexuality, Appendix
Shakespeare, William, 103, 848, 849, 966, 1051
Shelley, Percy Bysshe, 1020
shepherd, 353, 358, 902, 909, 957, 1009
sickness, 29, 39, 42, 43, 45, 47, 48, 50, 52, 54**n**, 94, 100, 109, 125, 135, 152, 173, 180, 182, 187, 215, 224, 226, 227, 233, 236, 246-48, 259, 273, 282, 351, 373, 394, 397, 401, 423, 438, 579, 778, 811, 812, 852, 864, 910, 912, 933**n**, 934, 985, 1009, 1012, 1013, 1016, 1020, 1046, 1051
Simplicius, 411
sin, 160, 168-70, 181, 182, 187, 192, 196, 207, 212, 224, 229, 248, 283, 292, 296, 339, 342, 351, 388, 394, 397, 578, 765, 786; original, 347, 786
Sitte and *Sittlichkeit,* 265**n**, 283**n**
skepticism, 1, 33, 42, 43, 55, 101, 195, 266, 266**n**, 283, 380, 401, 409, 410, 414, 422, 442, 446, 447, 455, 457, 458, 461, 907, 963, 1035
slave(ry), 69, 80, 94, 116, 134, 196, 210, 215, 269, 280, 280**n**, 312, 356, 357, 364, 400, 427, 464, 471, 660, 758, 770, 776, 859, 862, 864, 868, 869, 874, 954, 962, 1051
Slavs, 835
sobriety, *see* prudence
socialism, socialist(s), 1, 10, 30, 40, 51, 125, 132, 209, 253, 339, 340, 373, 753, 755, 757, 765, 784, 864, 1017; Socialist Workers' Party, 89**n**
society, 20**n**, 27, 33, 40, 50, 52, 53, 54**n**, 55, 90, 100, 100**n**, 119, 123, 207, 235, 271, 284, 353, 373, 374, 376, 394, 462, 507, 579, 689, 712, 716-93, 883, 889, 896, 898, 903, 927, 934, 936
Socrates, 274, 427, 429-33, 435, 437, 441-43, 578
soldier and scholar, 912
solitude, 358, 417, 423, 444, 463**n**, 916, 962, 970, 985, 988, 993, 1051
Sophist, 427-29, 442, 578
soul, 12, 27, 30**n**, 67, 117, 141, 175, 226, 227, 229, 233, 248, 283, 394, 480, 485, 487, 488, 491, 492, 502, 509, 529, 554, 581, 659, 765, 799, 806, 823, 824, 829, 981**n**, 984, 1016
space, 487, 520, 530, 545, 554, 578, 1064, 1067; Euclidean, 515
Spain, 75, 103, 103**n**
species, 27, 54, 246, 354, 404, 480, 521, 552, 679-82, 684, 685, 700, 760, 786, 789, 859
Spencer, Herbert, 53, 53**n**, 382, 424, 541, 901, 944
Spengler, Oswald, 339**n**
Spinoza, Baruch, 55, 95, 340, 341, 368**n**, 410, 411, 432, 576-78, 627, 688, 911, 1062; Spinozism, 1
spirit, 2**n**, 22, 23, 31, 48, 50, 55, 60, 62, 76, 77, 79, 89, 94, 102, 125, 128, 154, 187, 195, 204, 235, 253, 279, 284, 299, 351, 382, 390, 393, 428, 432, 458, 464, 477, 480, 492, 511, 524-26, 529, 532, 537, 552, 573, 644, 659, 666**n**, 674, 676, 687, 707, 709, 711, 774, 779, 784, 789, 808, 809, 820, 837, 848, 849, 879, 898, 899, 915, 942, 962, 984, 984**n**, 1013, 1045, 1046, 1051, 1052, 1052**n**3, 1062; "absolute pure spirit," 477
"square," 107**n**, 353**n**
state, 60, 69**n**, 75, 95, 167, 169, 204, 207, 209, 211, 221, 280**n**, 281,

state (*cont'd.*)
282, 315, 416, 437**n**, 585, 689, 716-65, 903, 921, 927; community, 204
Stendhal, *see* Beyle
Stewart, H. F., 929**n**
Stifter, Adalbert, 1021
Stöcker, Adolf, 89**n**, 203**n**
Stoic(al), 60, 62, 195, 195**n**, 268, 342, 427, 721, 940, 943, 957
Strauss, David Friedrich, 841
Strindberg, August, 86**n**
strong, the, 15, 23, 24, 26, 37, 43, 45, 47, 48, 55, 56, 68, 69**n**, 97, 98, 109, 110, 113, 116, 119, 120, 123, 132, 134, 135, 154, 205, 222, 233, 248, 252, 270, 274, 284, 296, 318, 345, 351, 352, 362, 373, 382, 388-91, 395, 398, 400, 401, 405, 417, 423, 429, 464, 552, 573, 585, 600, 616, 630, 634, 655, 658, 660, 675, 684, 685, 689, 703, 712, 729, 737, 749, 765, 776, 778, 781, 782, 786, 788, 800, 800**n**, 812, 819, 821, 852, 862, 863-934, 934**n**, 940, 954, 957, 963**n**, 969, 981, 995, 1003, 1014, 1019-21, 1035, 1041, 1052, 1060, 1067
subject, 480, 481, 485, 488, 490, 492, 513, 516, 517, 521, 522, 547-52, 556, 569, 589
sublimation, 677
substance, 484, 485, 487, 488, 513, 516, 517, 521, 523, 552, 562, 574, 624, 626, 631
Sudras, 116, 116**n**
suffering, 2, 27, 35, 44, 55, 60, 75, 94, 112, 119, 119**n**, 135, 181, 195, 204, 217, 222, 224, 229, 246, 266, 274, 290, 341, 342, 367**n**, 373, 382, 395, 401, 416, 423, 576, 579, 580, 585, 589, 635**n**, 686, 781, 812, 824, 846, 852, 853, 864, 910, 934, 957, 964, 971, 990, 1004, 1020, 1030**n**, 1041, 1046, 1052
suffrage, universal, 364, 854, 861, 862
superman, *see* overman
superstition, 238, 406, 422, 487, 579, 683, 689
Swedenborg, Emanuel, 92
sympathy, *see* pity

Tacitus, 175
Tahiti, 204
Taine, Hippolyte Adolphe, 82**n**, 422, 827, 849, 1018
talent, 814, 824, 837
talion, 742**n**
taming, *see* domestication
Tartuffe, 20, 191, 312, 315, 424, 429, 862
teleology, 552, 562
Teresa, St., 216
terrible, 850, 853, 1017, 1020, 1025, 1027, 1028, 1030, 1050; terrifying, 852
Tertullian, 107**n**
Thekla (Schiller heroine), 106, 106**n**
Thierry, Augustin, 340, 937
thing-in-itself, 3, 13, 17, 244, 379, 428, 473, 517, 552-69, 583, 589, 590, 608, 692, 708, 818, 1005, 1051, 1060
things, 516, 521, 533, 535, 538, 547, 551, 552, 554, 571, 574, 578, 583
thinking, 477, 478, 480, 484, 487, 492, 499, 517, 529, 539, 539**n**, 541, 550, 556, 574
Thomson, William, 1066
thought(s), 478, 483, 484, 490, 501, 502, 516, 522, 524, 544, 554, 562, 574
Thucydides, 428, 429, 443
Tieck, Ludwig, 106
time, 487, 502, 520, 545, 554, 578
Timon, 428
toleration, 279
Tolstoy, Leo Nikolaevich, 82, 434, 1020
tradition, 65
tragedy, tragic, 29, 102, 204, 427, 596, 800, 821, 851-53, 936, 1029, 1029**n**, 1052
truth, 1, 3, 5, 12, 13, 15, 30, 51, 69, 69**n**, 79, 80, 83, 86, 95, 120, 139, 141, 142, 159, 166, 171, 172, 187, 202, 244, 251, 272, 277-79, 285, 298, 304, 346, 354, 375, 377-79, 382, 396, 401, 404, 414, 423, 428, 430, 435**n**, 445, 449, 451-53, 455, 457-59, 461, 465, 469, 480, 482, 484, 485, 487, 493, 495, 507, 512, 514-17, 521, 522, 530-44, 533**n**1 and2, 552, 563, 565, 568, 572, 574,

579, 581, 583-85, 592, 596-98, 598**n**, 603, 605, 616, 625, 749, 772, 776, 804, 816, 822, 853, 934, 945, 962, 974, 1010, 1011, 1041; a priori 460, 497, 862; Christian, 159; truthfulness, 277, 278, 378
Turgenev, Ivan S., 82**n**

ugliness, 21, 31, 95, 283, 298, 432, 712**n**, 800, 802, 804, 809, 821, 822, 852
Uhland, Ludwig, 106
unconscious, 74
unity, 489, 492, 518, 523, 526, 529, 538, 547, 561, 578, 585
Unschuld des Werdens, 552**n**
utilitarianism, 62, 253, 261, 291, 339, 422, 724
utility, 12, 20, 94, 141, 203, 204, 216, 266, 271, 276, 280, 299, 315, 318, 348, 353, 372, 423, 439, 442, 455, 474, 480, 492, 493, 505, 507, 510, 513-15, 521, 567, 579, 580, 584, 647, 647**n**, 648, 649, 669, 677, 715, 724, 725, 731, 732, 758, 765, 786, 804, 806, 816, 866, 877, 878, 888, 903, 916, 925, 927, 930-32, 972

Valhalla, 156
valuations, 235, 505, 507, 602, 607, 608, 616, 641, 659, 666, 678, 681, 701, 726, 744, 764, 767, 773, 775, 777, 779, 786, 852, 856
value(s), **N**4, 1-464, 30**n**, 69**n**, 533, 565, 567, 572, 577-80, 583-85, 588, 590, 643, 666, 669, 674-77, 681, 684, 685, 688-715, 723, 740, 747, 748, 765, 785, 790, 804, 806, 808, 838, 842, 846, 848, 853-1067; physiological, 710
Varnhagen, Rahel, 835, 835**n**
Vedanta, 141, 659, 1020
Venetian, 100, 102; taste, 829
Venus, 322, 749
Ver-Ichlichung, Ver-Aenderung, 296**n**
Vernet, Horace, 105
Verri, Count, 698
verzeichnet, 554**n**
Vesuvius, 929**n**
Viennese music, 833
Vigny, Alfred de, 1020
virtue, 30, 50, 53, 54, 95, 100, 100**n**, 120, 172, 175, 176, 185, 197, 203-5, 210, 216, 243, 244, 246, 249**n**, 255, 284, 288, 304-29, 334, 351, 353, 379, 395, 425, 428-30, 432-35, 437, 439, 447, 450, 464, 573, 578, 674, 685, 705, 716, 717, 721, 740, 764, 765, 772**n**, 790, 808, 853, 864, 865, 870, 874, 886, 888, 889, 911, 916, 918, 923, 929, 943-45, 953, 954, 962, 967, 983, 1019, 1026, 1033, 1040; herd virtues, 60, 203, 279
Voltaire, Francois Marie Arouet de, 91, 92, 99, 100, 123, 217**n**, 432, 747, 833, 837

Wagner, Richard, 1, 44**n**, 85, 87, 92, 103, 105-7, 118**n**, 815**n**, 825, 826**n**, 827, 829, 830, 834, 834**n**, 835, 835**n**, 838-42, 849, 852, 853, 864, 1005; *The Flying Dutchman,* 106; *Lohengrin,* 238; *Nibelungen,* 1, 78; *Parsifal,* 87, 118**n**, 359**n**, 734; *Tannhäuser,* 322; *Tristan und Isolde,* 44**n**; Wagnerian, 322, 846
See also Appendix
Wallace, Alfred Russel, 130
war, 53, 69**n**, 125-27, 130, 133, 133**n**, 156, 185, 204, 207, 209, 221, 335, 351, 415, 457, 464, 584, 598**n**, 601**n**, 717, 728, 733, 739, 748, 784, 801, 853, 856, 864, 952, 982, 1033, 1040; warlike, 923
weak, the, 23, 37, 44-48, 54, 56, 80, 100, 125, 130, 153-55, 195, 222, 246, 248, 296, 304, 335, 345, 351, 354, 373, 382, 397, 398, 401, 423, 585, 600, 630, 634, 655, 658, 660, 684, 685, 703, 719, 762, 765, 769, 778, 782, 852, 862, 863-934, 938, 941, 963, 1012, 1025
Weiss, Otto, **EC**
welfare, 720, 866
Whitehead, Alfred North, 635**n**
will, 20, 29, 35, 44, 46, 65, 74, 79, 84, 95, 116, 128, 136, 260, 288, 289, 382, 399, 426, 434, 444, 478,

480, 488, 490, 492, 495, 505, 524, 529, 550, 551, 551**n**, 554, 556, 579, 581, 585, 593, 612, 658, 662, 666-68, 671, 692, 696, 707, 708, 715, 715**n**, 750, 765, 769, 779, 790, 800, 811, 812, 829, 842, 898, 915, 916, 921, 949, 957, 960, 962, 1060, 1067; will to power, *passim*

Willens-Punktationen, 715**n**

Winckelmann, Johann Joachim, 830, 849, 1051

wissenschaftlicher Mensch, 420**n**; *Wissenschaftlichkeit,* 424**n**

Wittgenstein, Ludwig, 585**n**

woman, 91, 94, 95, 119, 145, 182, 196, 268, 377, 732, 777, 806, 807, 811, 817, 824, 838, 839, 842, 864, 865, 894, 934, 1009

world, 1, 12, 15, 30**n**, 32, 34, 37, 51, 72, 116, 141, 201, 202, 210, 244, 253, 260, 295, 333, 341, 390, 401, 411, 416, 418, 423, 461, 470, 478, 481, 495, 517, 520, 521, 533, 543, 552, 554, 562, 567-70, 574, 583-85, 600-2, 677, 678, 701, 707, 708, 712**n**, 715, 786, 796, 845, 853, 976, 1010, 1019, 1036, 1037, 1041, 1044, 1045, 1048, 1051, 1062, 1066, 1067; another world, 51, 116, 185, 196, 230, 253, 254, 298, 313, 461, 578, 586, 1036; apparent world, 15, 69**n**, 170, 461, Bk. III Pt. I **n**, 488, 507, 516, 521, 566-69, 579, 583, 584, 586, 586**n**, 589, 636, 786, 853 (*see also* appearance); inner world, 475-79, 500, 523; outer world, 477, 479, 500, 524, 569; true (real) world, 7, 12, 15, 37, 69, 170, 401, 411, 461, Bk. III Pt. I **n**, 473, 488, 507, 516, 521, 529, 566-69, 573, 576, 578-80, 583-86, 586**n**, 592, 636, 708, 786, 853; unknown world, 7, 586, 708

Würzbach, Friedrich, E3

Zarathustra, 1038

Zeno, the founder of Stoicism, 195**n**

Zola, Emile, 821, 827, 849

Zucht, Züchtung, Züchtigung, 980**n**

zurückgetreten, 376**n**

FRIEDRICH NIETZSCHE was born in 1844 in Röcken (Saxony), Germany. He studied classical philology at the universities of Bonn and Leipzig, and in 1869 was appointed to the chair of classical philology at the University of Basel, Switzerland. Ill health led him to resign his professorship ten years later. His works include *The Birth of Tragedy, Thus Spoke Zarathustra, Beyond Good and Evil, On the Genealogy of Morals, The Case of Wagner, Twilight of the Idols, The Antichrist, Nietzsche contra Wagner*, and *Ecce Homo*. He died in 1900. *The Will to Power*, a selection from his notebooks, was published posthumously.

WALTER KAUFMANN was born in Freiburg, Germany, in 1921, came to the United States in 1939, and studied at Williams College and Harvard University. In 1947 he joined the faculty of Princeton University, where he is now Professor of Philosophy. He has held many visiting professorships, including Fulbright grants at Heidelberg and Jerusalem. His books include *Critique of Religion and Philosophy, From Shakespeare to Existentialism, The Faith of a Heretic, Cain and Other Poems, Hegel*, and *Tragedy and Philosophy*, as well as verse translations of Goethe's *Faust* and *Twenty German Poets*. The third edition, revised, of Professor Kaufmann's critical study *Nietzsche: Philosopher, Psychologist, Antichrist* is available in Vintage Books (V-436). He has translated all of the books by Nietzsche listed in the biographical note about Nietzsche above. The following appear in Vintage Books: *Beyond Good and Evil* (V-337); *The Will to Power* (V-437); and, in one volume, *The Birth of Tragedy* and *The Case of Wagner* (V-369); *On the Genealogy of Morals* and *Ecce Homo* (V-401).

R. J. HOLLINGDALE is an English writer, best known for his book *Nietzsche: The Man and His Philosophy*.